Tolley's
Pension Cases

by

Alastair Meeks

Pinsent Curtis Biddle

™ Tolley
LexisNexis™

Members of the LexisNexis Group worldwide

United Kingdom	Butterworths Tolley, a Division of Reed Elsevier (UK) Ltd, 2 Addiscombe Road, CROYDON CR9 5AF
Argentina	Abeledo Perrot, Jurisprudencia Argentina and Depalma, BUENOS AIRES
Australia	Butterworths, a Division of Reed International Books Australia Pty Ltd, CHATSWOOD, New South Wales
Austria	ARD Betriebsdienst and Verlag Orac, VIENNA
Canada	Butterworths Canada Ltd, MARKHAM, Ontario
Chile	Publitecsa and Conosur Ltda, SANTIAGO DE CHILE
Czech Republic	Orac sro, PRAGUE
France	Editions du Juris-Classeur SA, PARIS
Hong Kong	Butterworths Asia (Hong Kong), HONG KONG
Hungary	Hvg Orac, BUDAPEST
India	Butterworths India, NEW DELHI
Ireland	Butterworths (Ireland) Ltd, DUBLIN
Italy	Giuffrè, MILAN
Malaysia	Malayan Law Journal Sdn Bhd, KUALA LUMPUR
New Zealand	Butterworths of New Zealand, WELLINGTON
Poland	Wydawnictwa Prawnicze PWN, WARSAW
Singapore	Butterworths Asia, SINGAPORE
South Africa	Butterworths Publishers (Pty) Ltd, DURBAN
Switzerland	Stämpfli Verlag AG, BERNE
USA	LexisNexis, DAYTON, Ohio

© Reed Elsevier (UK) Ltd 2001

A CIP Catalogue record for this book is available from the British Library.

ISBN 0 7545 1273 8

Typeset by Letterpart Limited, Reigate, Surrey
Printed by The Cromwell Press, Trowbridge, Wiltshire

Visit Butterworths LexisNexis *direct* at www.butterworths.com

Preface

When Butterworths Tolley first asked me to put together a pension case book, in my naive arrogance, I assumed that it would be possible not only to gather together every pension case in one volume, but also to gather all sufficiently relevant non-pension cases so as to give the pension practitioner a single reference book of the relevant case law. That, it soon became apparent, was beyond my powers. Such a handbook would require giant hands or microdot print. I was, therefore, forced to scale down my ambitions.

This case book gathers together all pension cases of possible continuing relevance that I have identified, up until 31 July 2001. My definition of a pension case is where a case involved a pension scheme *and* the point of law under consideration in some way concerned the operation of that pension scheme. For example, I have not included any cases where pension scheme trustees are being sued under the terms of a lease, unless the decision in some way turned on their status as pension scheme trustees. The cases are collected by subject matter, and assembled in alphabetical order within subject categories. I have only included non-pension cases where to have omitted the case would have been to deprive the reader of a judicial insight of compelling relevance to pension practitioners. What this means is that many highly relevant cases, particularly in the area of trust law, have, unfortunately, been put to one side. These must be dealt with by other case books.

By way of compensation, I have gone into the pension cases in some depth. Even a casual reference to the index will rapidly show that cases appear repeatedly. I have tried to extract and isolate judicial observations on points of relevance, no matter how casual those observations may be. I have not attempted to identify whether the point forms an integral part of the judgment or is nothing more than a judicial expression of opinion. In most cases, however, this should be reasonably clear.

This book shows a pathologist's view of pensions. There are no cases on normal retirement, few on the operation of the preservation requirements, and none on anti-franking. However, there are many cases on the payment of lump sum death benefits, whether a member was entitled to an incapacity pension, on whether a refund of surplus was validly taken by the employer and on the interpretation of ambiguous scheme rules. The centre of gravity in a pension scheme is far removed from that which the reader might assume from looking at the points under consideration in the cases which are summarised in this book.

This book is, moreover, Anglocentric. The case law of many jurisdictions is, however, of persuasive authority in English courts. Northern Irish law is similar to English law. Scots law, while very different in its origins, is often governed by similar or identical statutory considerations. Australian, Canadian, Irish, New Zealand and South African law are all based on the same foundations as English law. While the structure in each jurisdiction has been built upon in different ways, their courts often face similar pensions problems to those faced in England and Wales. Their case law is of great value in such instances, and I have therefore included it wherever it is of possible relevance. I have, however, included almost no case law from the United States. While it is also a common law jurisdiction, the American codification of pension law into statute makes its decisions a very dangerous guide to the proper approach to English pension law. I have in general included American pension cases only where they have been judicially considered in an English court or where for other reasons they might be of direct relevance to English pension practitioners. I have made an exception in cases relating to the investment of pension schemes, simply because at present there is little case law from the other jurisdictions relating to investment duties, and no obvious reason why the common law jurisdictions should automatically take a different approach.

I have no doubt that I have made omissions which to some will appear baffling. I also have no doubt that I have made some errors in abbreviating what inevitably are much more complicated cases than short case notes would suggest. In my defence, I adopt the words of Laddie J in *ITN v Ward [1997] OPLR 147*: 'It must be borne in mind that any precis of long and complicated documents will lose some of the detail (unless the discarded matter is mere surplusage). To that extent any precis can be said to be inaccurate'. This book should be the starting point for research on a problem, not the finishing post.

ALASTAIR MEEKS
PINSENT CURTIS BIDDLE   October 2001

Acknowledgements

It is, of course, for others to judge the quality of this book, but there are some people without whom this book would not have been as good (or would have been even worse). All mistakes are my own.

First in the list of these people must be Julia Carver, who has diligently assisted me throughout, and who has reliably, promptly and stoically provided me with even the most obscure transcripts. Of innumerable cases, the majority of which were excluded for being insufficiently relevant, she was defeated by fewer than five. Without her efforts, this book would have taken more than twice as long to complete and would have been less than half as good.

My firm, Pinsent Curtis Biddle, has been supportive of this project from start to finish at every level. Irene Thorne and Matthew de Ferrars supplied me with recent cases that might otherwise have eluded me. Several of my colleagues took the time to read extracts and gave me their constructive criticism. Susan Andrews, Sarah Boon, Nicola Bumpus and Matthew de Ferrars in particular gave me valuable assistance on this.

Many other individuals have also helped me. Eden Law assisted my researches on one key point, and I was given valuable practical guidance by Richard Jones and Robert Peden. Brian Shiels and Sarah Boon deserve special thanks for patiently enduring at close range the angst of writing a book.

Of course, my task would have been much harder if the two series of law reports were not well-established. Over the years Colin Sherwood, editor of the Occupational Pensions Law Reports, has supplied me with many of the transcripts which are digested in this case book and he has kept me informed of the existence of many more cases. His work and assistance are the foundations for much of this book.

Robin Ellison needs special mention. I have already referred to his book Private Occupational Pension Schemes, which gathers together some of the early pension cases. He was also the founder of the Pensions Law Reports and now has responsibility for the case law on Perspective. More than any other single individual, his efforts have resulted in the gathering together of the primary sources and the making of them readily available to practitioners. Perhaps because of his energy in so many areas of pensions, his contribution in this field often goes unremarked. It should not.

Finally, I must acknowledge the special debt I owe to two people in particular. The foundations of trust law were taught to me with enthusiasm and precision by Carl Emery at Durham University. On qualification, I worked with Hugh Arthur who with equal enthusiasm and precision educated me in the detail of pensions law. I hope that one day I shall be able and knowledgeable enough to communicate with such inspiration as they both did with me.

Sources

There are two series of law reports for pension cases, the Pensions Law Reports and the Occupational Pensions Law Reports. Each has different virtues. (I should declare an interest: I am one of the assistant editors of the Occupational Pensions Law Reports series). The Pensions Law Reports tend to be more international in outlook and in the past have been faster in producing the case reports, while the Occupational Pensions Law Reports have more detailed analysis in commentary. The Occupational Pensions Law Reports also report every appeal from a Pensions Ombudsman decision.

The online service Perspective has the Pension Benefits Law Reports, a case law service which contains some cases which are unreported elsewhere. The Pension Benefits Law Reports case references can in theory be cited in court, but given that it is an online service it is unlikely in practice that a court would currently look upon such citations with favour. However, many practitioners will find this the most convenient place to find these cases, and I have therefore used citations of their cases where those cases are otherwise unavailable. I have, however, also given the date each such case was decided so that those who require a version which can be cited in court can track it via LEXIS. I have not used Pension Benefits Law Reports case references where other case references are available.

Most of the other series of law reports referred to will be familiar to lawyers, but some cases are particularly difficult to locate. Robin Ellison's Private Occupational Pension Schemes contains five early pension cases which are otherwise hard to find: *Re ABC Television*, *Evans v London Co-operative*, *Worthington v Unilever*, *Re George Newnes Group Pension Fund* and *Lucas v Telegraph Construction*. The Reports of War Pensions Appeals are contained in a looseleaf binder. Solicitors can obtain this from the Law Society Library, but the librarians must be given some notice since the volume is stored in the Law Society President's house. The effort is worthwhile if one is considering a problem of causation: the volume contains over a thousand pages of short case reports, the great majority of which were heard by Denning J as he then was and are written in his unique style. Because the war pensions cases are so specialist, I have included only three. However, some of the cases in this series might have been of assistance to the courts in the recent succession of police and fire authority cases concerning incapacity pensions.

Contents

Contents

Contents

Introduction – the Role of the Pension Scheme

When the courts hear a case about a pension scheme, they are being asked to solve a specific problem or conflict between the parties. However, in order to do so, they must necessarily have a view on the status and role of pension schemes more generally. Those views will inevitably lie behind the court's decision in cases where a point of principle is at stake. Ordinarily, the courts are wary about laying down broadly-based decisions, but occasionally they do so. Because pension schemes fulfil many different roles in society, when the courts have expressed a view on the place of pension schemes in society, they have done so in widely differing terms. The quotations below set out the range of contexts in which pension schemes have been considered. They should not be seen as inconsistent, but rather as complementary.

Worringham v Lloyds (Court of Appeal) [1980] I CMLR 293 at 302 (per Lord Denning)

'Many big firms nowadays have occupational pension schemes. Actuaries, accountants and lawyers are all called in. They are complicated beyond belief. Viewed simply, the scheme is to get employers and workers to contribute sums every week, every month or every year to a trust fund . . . The contributions are paid to the trustees of the fund. In the course of time these pension funds grow to a great size. The trustees invest them in land, shares or pictures: and they use the income to distribute the benefits. Parliament has passed statutes to regulate them . . . But fundamentally it is a scheme agreed between the employers, the workers (through their union) and the trustees of the fund. The financial resources of the fund are derived from contributions from employers and workers. They are not subsidised by the State.

Such schemes are to be distinguished from the State scheme for retirement pensions. That is part of a national scheme which provides benefits of all kinds for all sorts of people . . . These benefits are payable out of the National Insurance Fund. This fund is made up in part by contributions by employers and workers, but it is subsidised to a considerable extent by moneys provided by Parliament.'

British Telecom Pension Schemes trustees v Clarke (Court of Appeal) [2000] OPLR 53, [2000] PLR 157 at para I

'Occupational pension schemes are of enormous social and economic importance to national life. Pension funds, held by responsible trustees and segregated from the assets of the employer, provide employees and pensioners with a measure of protection against the risks of the employer's insolvency and the erosion of pensions by inflation. The importance of occupational pension schemes has been marked by tax exemptions and reliefs first introduced in 1921, which have the general effect of allowing deduction of employers' and employees' contributions to exempt approved schemes, and of exempting income and gains accruing to the trustees of exempt approved schemes of income tax and capital gains tax respectively.'

Barber v GRE (European Court of Justice) [1990] ECR I-1889, [1990] IRLR 240, [1991] I WLR 72, [1990] PLR 95 at paras 80–82

'First . . . the schemes in question are the result either of an agreement between workers and employers or of a unilateral decision taken by the employer. They are wholly financed by the employer or by both the employer and the workers without any contribution being made by the public authorities in any circumstances. Accordingly, such schemes form part of the consideration offered to workers by the employer.

Secondly, such schemes are not compulsorily applicable to general categories of workers. On the contrary, they apply only to workers employed by certain undertakings, with the result that affiliation to those schemes derives of necessity from the employment relationship with a given employer. Furthermore, even if the schemes in question are established in conformity with national legislation and consequently satisfy the conditions laid down by it for recognition as contracted-out schemes, they are governed by their own rules.

Thirdly, it must be pointed out that, even if the contributions paid to those schemes and the benefits which they provide are in part a substitute for those of the general statutory scheme, that fact cannot preclude the application of *Article 119* . . .

It must therefore be concluded that, unlike the benefits awarded by national statutory social security schemes, a pension paid under a contracted-out scheme constitutes consideration paid by the employer to the worker in respect of his employment and consequently falls within the scope of *Article 119* of the *Treaty [of Rome]*'

Parry v Cleaver (House of Lords) [1970] AC 1 at 16 (per Lord Reid)

'It is generally recognised that pensionable employment is more valuable to a man than the mere amount of his weekly wage. It is more valuable because by reason of the terms of his employment money is being regularly set aside to swell his ultimate pension rights whether on retirement or disablement. His earnings are greater than his weekly wage. (Where the wage is £20 with total contributions to the pension fund of £4 per week) his employer is willing to pay £24 per week to obtain his services, and it seems to me that he ought to be regarded as having earned that sum per week. The products of the sums paid into the pension fund are in fact delayed remuneration for his current work. That is why pensions are regarded as earned income.'

Air Jamaica v Charlton (Privy Council) [1999] 1 WLR 1399, [1999] OPLR 11, [1999] PLR 247 at paras 25–27, 28, 35

'The benefits were funded in part by contributions and in part by the income of the investments held in the fund. The interposition of a trust fund between the Company and the members meant that payment of the benefits to members was the responsibility of the trustees, not the Company. The machinery employed was that of a trust, not a contract.

That is not to say that the trust is like a traditional family trust under which a settlor voluntarily settles property for the benefit of the object of his bounty. The employee members of an occupational pension scheme are not voluntary settlors. As has been repeatedly observed, their rights are derived from their contracts of employment as well as from the trust instrument. Their pensions are earned by their services under their contracts of employment as well as by their contributions. They are often not inappropriately described as deferred pay. This does not mean, however, that they have contractual rights to their pensions. It means only that, in construing the trust instrument, regard must be had to the nature of an occupational pension and the employment relationship that forms its genesis.'

'each employee becomes a member of the pension scheme by virtue of his employment, but . . . his entitlement to a pension arises under the trusts of the scheme.

Their lordships should add for completeness that, while the members' entitlements arise under the trusts of the pension plan, the Company's obligation to deduct contributions from members and to pay them to the trustees together with its own matching contributions, is contractual. The Company undertook this obligation by its covenant with the trustees in the trust deed. The obligation was, however, subject to the power of the Company unilaterally to discontinue the plan . . .'

'. . . the essential feature of a defined benefits pension scheme is that the benefits payable in respect of each member are fixed at the outset at an amount which is capable of being funded by the contributions payable in respect of the member without recourse to the contributions of any other member . . . The trust fund is only a security for the payment of benefits, and a defined benefits scheme can be regarded for this purpose as a form of mutual insurance.'

Barclays Bank v Kapur (House of Lords) [1991] PLR 45

'A man works not only for his current wage but also for his pension and to require him to work on less favourable terms as to pension is as much a continuing act [of race discrimination] as to require him to work for lower current wages.'

Kerr v British Leyland (Staff) Trustees Limited (Court of Appeal, unreported) at page 8 of transcript

'The beneficiaries here are not volunteers. Their rights derive from contractual and commercial origins. They have purchased their rights as part of their employment. Consistently with that, the power of the trustee to decline acceptance of the claim cannot be simply an uncontrolled discretion. It seems to me that the duty of this trustee was to give properly informed consideration to the application.'

LRT v Hatt (High Court) [1993] OPLR 225, [1993] PLR 227 at para 114

'Another important general consideration is that it is now well established that the rights of members of occupational pension schemes to the benefits under the Rules of the scheme are not to be equated to those of beneficiaries under trusts of a traditional nature arising under settlements, wills or intestacies where, save as regards marriage settlements, the beneficiaries are volunteers who have given no consideration. In occupational pension schemes the members are not volunteers in that sense, they have entered upon their employment part of the terms of which have included the availability to them of the scheme . . . Membership was always available to those qualified to join as a term of their employment and they contributed very significant sums towards the cost of their benefits. They were not volunteers: whether they were originally conscripts is not in my view significant.'

Edge v Pensions Ombudsman (Court of Appeal) [2000] 3 WLR 79, [1999] PLR 215 at para 34

In a defined benefits scheme, 'the task of the trustees is to maintain a balance between assets and liabilities . . .; so that, so far as the future can be foreseen, they will be in a position to provide pensions and other benefits in accordance with rules throughout the life of the scheme. That task is to be performed by setting appropriate levels for employers' and members' contributions. If that task could be performed with perfect foresight there would be no surpluses and no deficits. But, because the task has to be performed in the real world, surpluses and deficits are bound to arise from time to time and prudent trustees will aim to ensure that the likelihood of surplus outweighs the risk of deficit. Nevertheless, it is no part of the trustees' function, in a fund of this nature, to set levels for contributions which will generate surpluses beyond those properly required as a reserve against contingencies.'

Jones v Patel (Court of Appeal, unreported, 24 May 2001) at para 37 of transcript

'Pension schemes provide benefits which are regarded in some contexts as "pay" or as a form of deferred pay for services rendered in the past, but the pension schemes which govern the rights are not themselves unexecuted contracts for personal services.'

Re Baden's Deed Trusts, McPhail v Doulton (House of Lords) [1971] AC 424 at 452A (per Lord Wilberforce)

'I prefer not to suppose that the great masters of equity, if faced with the modern trust for employees, would have failed to adapt their creation to its practical and commercial character.'

Part 1 – Interpreting the Scheme's Provisions

1 – Introduction

The interpretation of the provisions of a pension scheme is perhaps the single most common problem faced by pension scheme practitioners. In some ways, this part could comprise upwards of half of the book, since problems in many areas are decided on principles of interpretation. Certainly, most of the cases in the parts on amendment, winding–up and surplus were decided on this basis.

Over the years, therefore, the courts have had to consider the principles of interpretation on many occasions, and fairly concrete principles can be drawn. The classic review of the principles was given in *Mettoy Pension Trustees v Evans [1991] 2 All ER 513*, where Warner J stated that the Court's approach to the construction of documents relating to a pension scheme should be practical and purposive, rather than detached and literal. This dictum has been quoted on many occasions since. Of course, the degree of practicality and purposiveness in fact adopted has depended to a considerable extent on the individual judge. The courts have, however, always been aware of the commercial origin of pension schemes. They have also become willing to accept that it is hard to maintain a pension scheme in a form which is entirely self-consistent.

Some problems of interpretation arise repeatedly. The impact of previous editions of the scheme documentation on the meaning of scheme rules, and the importance of earlier schemes, is a common problem faced by the advisers of older schemes. The courts are torn between the natural desire to use all tools available to them, and the prudent wish to protect the membership from being subject to trust terms of which they had no knowledge. These opposing wishes have yet to resolve themselves completely. In some cases, such as *Harwood-Smart v Caws [2000] PLR 101*, it will be essential to look to historical matters. In others, such as *Spooner v British Telecommunications [2000] PLR 65*, the courts will continue to resist making a difficult exercise still more difficult.

The decision in *Spooner v British Telecommunications* recognises the same point that arose in the decision in *Bestrustees v Stuart* (unreported) and *Capital Cranfield v Sagar* (unreported). Scheme members are not party to the decisions of the trustees and the company, and the formalities included in the trust deed and rules are there largely to protect them. If those formalities are waived by the courts, the members have no way of finding out in practice what are their rights. The interpretation of a trust is not the same as the interpretation of a contract, where those affected will have complete knowledge of the full course of dealings between the parties.

Frequently the terms of a pension scheme do not reflect the reality of the pension scheme's practice. In those circumstances, does an estoppel arise such that the pension scheme's practice is deemed to be written into the rules? Estoppel is a rule of law that results in a finding of fact, and was neatly summarised by Lord Denning in *Amalgamated Investment v Texas Bank [1982] 1 QB 84*. Lawyers often tend to categorise estoppels by type, but the case law of the last twenty years has adopted the wider approach of Lord Denning: to establish any type of estoppel, the Court will ask itself whether it is unfair or unjust to allow the parties to go back on a common assumption. This is more difficult to establish than one might expect, and for exactly the same reason as has just been given as to why the courts are reluctant to waive formalities or to look at earlier editions of the rules. Members should be able to identify their benefit entitlements with certainty. The courts have therefore been more willing to find estoppels which work against parties who have actively participated in the events leading up to the alleged estoppel than against the mass of the scheme membership.

A mistake may have been made in the drafting of the trust documentation. Can the employer or the trustees have the mistake rectified? Once again, the courts have been slow to intervene to change the terms of a pension scheme. The first rectification of pension scheme documentation took place in December 2000 in *AMP (UK) Plc v Barker [2001] PLR 77*.

Neuberger J in *Bestrustees v Stuart* accurately expressed the tensions facing the court in these problems of interpretation, and explained why the courts cannot always take the broadbrush approach. Knox J in *LRT v Hatt [1993] OPLR 225* addressed the same problem when he said that the Court would be legitimately averse to the frustration of *bona fide* transactions by technical points which passed unperceived by all concerned at the time of the transaction in question. This observation has been much quoted by lawyers. His qualification to this (that there were limits to the extent to which rules of law, whether or not properly described as technicalities or even merest technicalities, could be circumvented) is not usually quoted. However, the qualification is an integral part of the observation.

Pension scheme constitutions sometimes give a power to a party to interpret the rules, or specific rules. In practice, the courts closely monitor such powers, as the case law suggests. Where the point is a point of law, the courts will always intervene if necessary.

1.1 – General principles

Aitken v Christy Hunt (High Court) [1991] PLR 1 at paras 35–36

Implied terms

Principles

If the Court is to imply a term into the trust deed and rules of a pension scheme, it will only do so if:

- it is correct to do so as a matter of construction;
- it is required to give business efficacy to the relevant provision; or
- the officious bystander test is satisfied (that is, if an officious bystander had asked a question at the time of execution, the answer to that question would have been obvious).

When one is seeking to imply a restriction into the power of amendment, it is not possible to imply a restriction which concerns only provisions which were not in the trust deed and rules from the outset, and which therefore could not have been under consideration at the time when the power of amendment was drawn up.

Barclays Bank v Holmes (High Court) [2000] PLR 339 at paras 99–103, 106–111

Ownership of surplus – public policy

Principles

A surplus was not beneficially owned by any of the employees or pensioners. An employer was not obliged to provide a pension scheme, and it was in the public interest that employers should be encouraged to provide pension schemes, and indeed relatively generous pension schemes. The dictum of Walker J in *National Grid Co plc v Laws [1997] OPLR 207* was considered.

[1.1.3]

Bestrustees v Stuart (High Court, unreported, 10 April 2001)

Principles of interpretation – protection of beneficiaries

Principles

A pension scheme was likely to continue for a substantial period of time, and those most affected by changes and entitled to protection would be people who were comparatively poor, would not have easy access to expert legal advice, and who would not know what had been going on in relation to the management of the scheme. In those circumstances, protection of the beneficiaries required the Court to be very careful before it permitted a departure from the plain wording and plain requirements of the trust deed for written documentation. In this sort of case, the Court often found itself treading the somewhat blurred line between requiring the terms of a particular deed to be complied with, and not being too pedantic and exacting in its requirements.

[1.1.4]

British Coal Corporation v British Coal Staff Superannuation Scheme Trustees (High Court) [1995] I All ER 912, [1994] ICR 537, [1994] OPLR 51, [1993] PLR 303 at para 63

Special nature of pension trusts

Principles

It is dangerous to import concepts which have been developed in the field of private trusts created by the bounty of a settlor or testator, and apply them uncritically in the field of pension funds. In the field of private trusts the Court is concerned to ascertain the extent of the rights conferred on the beneficiaries of the trust, and the extent of the powers so conferred; whether on trustees or on an individual, as the donee of the power. In such cases the beneficiaries are volunteers. A pension trust by contrast is constituted in order to provide benefits for employees who in most cases will have contributed to the pension fund, and who, whether they have contributed or not, will have served the employer in the expectation that discretions as to the application of any surplus in the fund will be honestly and fairly exercised, with proper regard being paid to their contributions and service.

[1.1.5]

Capital Cranfield v Sagar (High Court, unreported, 19 February 2001)

Principles of interpretation – protection of beneficiaries – implied terms

Principles

When a requirement to give notice in writing is in a document which is intended to confer benefits on third parties (particularly when those third parties are beneficiaries under a trust) and those third parties are neither to send nor receive the notice, the Court should be very careful before holding that the notice need not be in writing. The Court should bear in mind that very important third party rights, namely pensions for employees, no doubt mostly of modest means, would be liable to be affected by a notice such as that contemplated. Someone in the position of a beneficiary should be able to know for certain that a notice had been given.

There was some argument on a point whether a conclusion was reached as a matter of construction or through the medium of an implied term. It did not matter. Both were routes of construction arriving at the same conclusion.

[1.1.6]

Re Courage Group's Pension Schemes, Ryan v Imperial Brewing (High Court) [1987] 1 All ER 528, [1987] 1 WLR 495

Principles of interpretation – special nature of pension trusts

Principle

There are no special rules of construction applicable to a pension scheme. Nevertheless, a scheme's provisions ought wherever possible to be construed to give reasonable and practical effect to the scheme, bearing in mind it has to be operated against a constantly changing commercial background.

Cowan v Charlesworth (High Court) [1989] PLR 79 paras 15 and 31

Principles of interpretation – purpose of the scheme

Principles

In a document as technical and detailed as a modern pension trust deed, the meanings given to crucial defined expressions often differ widely from the meanings that those expressions would bear in ordinary usage. However, the expression *contributing service* was nonetheless a pointer to the meaning of *service* in a particular trust deed, where the point at issue was whether *service* for which no contributions were paid fell within the ambit of the deed's definition of *service*.

In general, it was the purpose of a pension scheme to provide benefits as an addition to earnings which accrue and are paid in employment. It would be inconsistent with that general purpose for a scheme to be construed as providing benefits for those who refused to perform services under their contracts of employment, and who accordingly were not entitled to any earnings.

[1.1.8]

Doyle v Manchester Evening News (High Court) [1989] PLR 47, para 66

Principles of interpretation – special nature of pension trusts

Principle

When considering a power given to the employer in a pension scheme to certify earnings, authorities on private trusts were not helpful. The principal employer was not a settlor. The scheme was set up by agreement, and looking at the scheme as a whole, the power of certification was not a beneficial power reserved to the employer, but a power conferred upon it to facilitate the running of the scheme in the interests of the members.

[1.1.9]

Equitable Life v Hyman (House of Lords) [2000] PLR 249 at paras 30, 35–42

Implied terms – purpose of the power

Principles

An implied term may be derived from the language of a document read in its particular factual setting. Additionally, no legal discretion may be used for purposes contrary to those of the instrument by which it was conferred. In this case, a mutual life assurance company had issued some policies with a guaranteed annuity rate and some without such a guarantee. The terms of the power in the company's articles of association permitting the directors to award differing discretionary bonuses could not be exercised so as to deprive the guarantees of any substantial value. The reasonable reader would not understand adverse discrimination unless it had been clearly specified in the policy. The insurer therefore could not use a general power in its articles of association to distribute surplus on final bonus so as to ensure that all policyholders received the same ultimate return from the policy, when current rates fell below the guaranteed annuity rate.

[1.1.10]

Gas & Fuel Corporation of Victoria v Fitzmaurice (Supreme Court of Victoria, Australia) [1991] PLR 137

Principles of interpretation – special nature of pension trusts

Principle

It was a relevant feature of the pension scheme construction process that the Gas & Fuel Corporation of Victoria was not conferring a bounty, and that the members were not volunteers but paid their way. It followed that any construction of the power of amendment, that involved an interpretation admitting interference with the benefits given in respect of future service, was one to be approached with caution.

[1.1.11]

Harris v Shuttleworth (Court of Appeal) [1995] OPLR 79 at 89A-B, [1994] PLR 47 at para 53, [1994] ICR 991

Principles of interpretation – special nature of pension trusts

Principle

In construing pension scheme rules, it is important to bear in mind:

(a) an employee's right to a benefit under a contributory pension scheme;
(b) that pensions are regarded as earned income; and
(c) that the members have given valuable consideration for their entitlement.

[1.1.12]

Hillsdown v Pensions Ombudsman (High Court) [1997] 1 All ER 862, [1996] OPLR 291 at 309B, [1996] PLR 427 at para 62

Principles of interpretation – implied terms

Principle

As a matter of construction, implications may be made restricting general provisions in a document such as pension fund rules. This can only be done within defined limits, such as where it is shown that the implication is necessary to give business efficacy to the document in question.

[1.1.13]

International Power v Healy (House of Lords) [2001] PLR 121 at paras 55, 57

Principles of interpretation

Principles

Arguments of the *expressio unius* variety are often perilous, especially when applied to a patchwork document like a pension scheme. The fact that a specific provision is made in one place may throw very little light on whether general words in another place include the power to do something similar.

The practical consequences of a particular construction are of more importance than linguistic points of construction.

[1.1.14]

LRT v Hatt (High Court) [1993] OPLR 225 at 254C, [1993] PLR 227 at para 112

Principles of interpretation

Principle

The Court would be legitimately averse to the frustration of *bona fide* transactions by technical points, which passed unperceived by all concerned at the time of the transaction in question. However, there are limits to the extent to which rules of law, whether or not properly described as technicalities or even merest technicalities, can be circumvented.

[1.1.15]

Mettoy Pension Trustees v Evans (High Court) [1991] 2 All ER 513, [1990] 1 WLR 1587, 1610, [1990] PLR 9

Principles of interpretation

Principles

The Court's approach to the construction of documents relating to a pension scheme should be practical and purposive, rather than detached and literal. While there are no special rules of construction applicable to a pension scheme, nevertheless its provisions should be construed to give reasonable and practical effect to the scheme, especially where some of the documents which were intended to have legal effect were couched in very general terms.

[1.1.16]

Re Philips New Zealand (High Court, New Zealand) [1997] 1 NZLR 93

Principles of interpretation

Principle

The Court will not willingly construe a deed so as to stultify the ability of trustees, having proper consents, to amend a deed so as to bring it into line with changing conditions.

[1.1.17]

Stevens & others v Bell & others (High Court) [2001] All ER 193, [2001] PLR 99 at paras 47, 48 and 60

Principles of interpretation

Principle

The Court is guided more usefully by the context of a clause and the scheme as a whole, rather than by particular meanings culled from dictionaries of any date.

A legitimate reading is to be preferred where it is more flexible than alternatives, and more likely to produce sensible results. While the Court should not expect to find in an old scheme the sort of well-designed flexibility and consistency born of years of experience in drafting pension schemes, it is not a reason for not seeking a more, rather than a less practical, and sensible reading of the clauses, so long as it is based on a proper reading of the clause and the deed as a whole.

While there were some similarities between the provisions of the scheme in this case and those of the scheme in the *National Grid* case, the Court held that there were also important differences. The decision on construction in the *National Grid* case could not be a guide to the correct conclusion in this case, though the Court noted and considered the matters in each *National Grid* judgment. The decision must depend on the words used in the particular scheme before the Court, and the facts otherwise relevant to that scheme.

[1.1.18]

Thrells v Lomas (High Court) [1993] 1 WLR 456, [1993] 2 All ER 546, [1992] OPLR 21, [1992] PLR 233

Principles of interpretation

Facts and Decision

While the Court was sympathetic to a submission that a discretion to increase benefits on a winding-up applied to all the benefits to be secured, the Court was unable to read this discretion as having a wider application than the final category of benefits to be secured, this category being the part of the scheme winding-up rule to which the relevant proviso incorporating this discretion was attached. The Court was familiar with mistakes being made in the layout of documents, whereby a proviso intended to qualify more than one precedent provision was typed or printed in such a way that it read as a qualification of only the last of those provisions. As printed in this case, however, the proviso ran directly on, in mid-line and with a lower-case 'p' for the introductory word 'provided' from the preceding words. The Court could see no justification for ignoring that textual indication.

[1.1.19]

Venables v Hornby (High Court, unreported, 14 June 2001)

Principles of interpretation

Facts and Decision

Mr Venables was the managing director of a company, working 50 hours a week. He decided to step down as managing director at age 53 since he had high blood pressure, mild diabetes and was seriously overweight, but remained as an unpaid non-executive director, giving advice on occasion. His pension scheme paid him his pension, but the Inland Revenue sought to charge him tax under *s 600* of the *Income and Corporation Taxes Act 1988* on the ground that it was not a payment expressly authorised from the pension scheme. The pension allowed for a pension before age 60 only if the member retired in normal health. The Court held that if it had been necessary, it would have accepted the reference to normal health could be ignored, on the basis that something must have gone wrong with the language: *Investors Compensation Scheme v West Bromwich Building Society [1998] 1 WLR 896* was applied.

[1.1.20]

Wilson v Law Debenture (High Court) [1995] 2 All ER 337, [1995] OPLR 103, [1994] PLR 141

Principles of interpretation – special nature of pension trusts

Principles

The Court must have regard to the fact that the trusts that a pension scheme trust deed creates, and the powers it confers, are for the purposes of a pension scheme in which the members have bought their interests, as opposed to being pure volunteers. Nevertheless, the Court must also give effect to settled principles of trust law in determining the effect of the trust deed on its true construction. Of course a pension scheme is different from a private trust in that, in particular, the members of a pension scheme have purchased their interests, but the question is, what is the nature of the interest which they have purchased? That depends on the application to the relevant trust instrument of well-established principles of trust law.

1.2 – Interpreting whether entitlement to benefit is triggered

[1.2.1]

Bradley v London Fire and Civil Defence Authority [1995] OPLR 95, [1994] PLR 283, [1995] IRLR 46

Causation

Facts and Decision

A firefighter was involved in a road traffic accident, as a result of which he became worried about his ability to continue in the fire service. This worry developed to the extent that he was assessed by the fire authority's medical adviser as being incapacitated on account of a depressive illness and chronic neck pain, and that this incapacity was likely to be permanent. The Court held that if he were suffering from an incapacitating injury (which included disease) received in the execution of his duties, he would be entitled to an incapacity pension. What had to be identified was the injury or disease in question, and whether or not there was a causal connection between that injury or disease and the employment. Whether the disease was received in the execution of his duties was a question of aetiology. Since in this case the medical evidence was that the infirmity was caused by the stresses of the work, the firefighter was entitled to his incapacity pension.

[1.2.2]

Commissioner of Police v Stunt (Court of Appeal, unreported, 23 February 2001)

Interpretation – causation

Facts and Decision

Mr Stunt was a police officer who was investigated under the Police Discipline Code. He retired on the grounds of depression caused, in the doctor's opinion, as a result of his reaction to the internal proceedings brought against him, but the doctor stated that the condition was not the result of any injury received in the execution of Mr Stunt's duty. Following Mr Stunt's retirement, the disciplinary proceedings were dropped. He claimed an injury pension under a provision in the *Police Pensions Regulations 1987 (SI 1987 No 256)* on the basis that his condition amounted to an injury received without his own default in the execution of his duty. The Court held that the test of causation was not to be applied in a legalistic way, and fell to be applied by medical rather than legal experts: *Bradley v London Fire and Civil Defence Authority [1995] OPLR 95* was followed. It was sufficient for there to be a causal connection with service as a police officer. It was not necessary to establish that circumstances at work were the sole cause of the injury, but the work circumstances must have a causative role.

The Court also held that duty was not to be given a narrow meaning. The duties of a police officer included the duty to submit to the complaints procedure. It was irrelevant that his role in it might be passive. Officers whose depressive illnesses develop from the accumulated stresses of their work qualify for an award under this provision. However, if the stresses had not been suffered at work, the pension would not be payable: the case of *R v Kellam, ex parte South Wales Police Authority [2000] ICR 632* was held to have taken these principles to the limits. Injury resulting from subjection to complaints proceedings was not to be regarded as received in the execution of duty. Rather, it was properly to be characterised as resulting from the officer's status as a constable. Mr Stunt was therefore not entitled to the injury pension: the Court's dicta in *R v Merseyside Police Authority ex parte Yates* (unreported, 19 February 1999) were disapproved.

[1.2.3]

Garvin v Police Authority for City of London (Divisional Court) [1944] 1 KB 358, [1944] 1 All ER 378

Interpretation – causation

Facts and Decision

Mr Garvin was a police officer who during the war worked twelve hours a day with irregular meals and constant wettings. He developed tuberculosis and retired, claiming a pension under the *Police Pensions Act 1921* on the basis that he was incapacitated by an injury suffered by him in the execution of his duty. The quarter sessions upheld his appeal, and the Police Authority appealed from this decision. The Court held that tuberculosis was an injury for the purposes of the relevant statutory provision. The words 'in the execution of his duty' were to receive a benevolent interpretation. There must be some degree of causal relation between the injury and the duty, but there was sufficient evidence in this case for the Tribunal to conclude that there was such evidence. Mr Garvin was, therefore, entitled to his pension.

[1.2.4]

Minister of Pensions v Chennell [1947] KB 250

Causation

Facts and Decision

An unexploded bomb was picked up by boys and carried through the street, where it exploded, injuring a girl. A claim was brought for a pension on the ground that it was a war injury 'caused by' the discharge of the bomb by the enemy. The Court held that it must not be confused by analogies with cases of breach of contract or of negligence. In pension cases, foreseeability was irrelevant. Where the discharge of the missile was the immediate or precipitating cause of the injury, it was a 'war injury' notwithstanding that there was some other antecedent or concurrent cause also operating. Where there was a cause intervening between the discharge of the missile and the injury, it was still a 'war injury' unless the discharge of the missile was so remote as not to be a cause at all. Even if the intervening cause was the negligence or wrongful act of the injured person or a third party, the injury may still be a 'war injury'. When, however, an intervening or extraneous cause was so powerful that the dropping of the bomb ceased to be a cause at all, but was only part of the circumstances in or on which the cause operated, the injury was not a 'war injury'. In this case, the boys' interference was not so powerful an intervening cause as to supersede the dropping of the bomb, and so the injury was a 'war injury'.

[1.2.5]

Police Authority for Huddersfield v Watson (Divisional Court) [1947] 1 KB 842

Interpretation – causation

Facts and Decision

Mr Watson, a police constable, was called upon to resign on account of ill-health. He was suffering from a duodenal ulcer which he claimed was the result of his conditions in the police service. The quarter sessions allowed his claim to a pension under the *Police Pensions Act 1921*, on the basis that he was incapacitated for the performance of his duty by an injury received in the execution of his duty without his own default. Following *Garvin v Police Authority for City of London [1944] 1 All ER 378,* the Court held that a police officer suffering from a bodily condition, including a duodenal ulcer, directly and causally connected with his service as a police officer, has received an injury in the execution of his duty. The decision in *Garvin v Police Authority for City of London* was not based on the concept that for an illness to qualify as an injury, there needed to be some infective agent. Mr Watson was, therefore, entitled to his pension.

[1.2.6]

Povey & Stephens v Secretary of State for the Environment (Court of Appeal) [1992] PLR 59

Causation

Facts and Decision

The Trades Union Congress organised a day of support for the strike action by National Health Service workers, by means of a token withdrawal of labour. NALGO did not instruct its members to withdraw their labour but advised them to do so for one day, 23 June 1982, and many local authority NALGO members did so. They then sought to exercise a right under the local government superannuation scheme to retain the day lost as reckonable service by the payment of an additional sum of money over the normal rate of contribution. The Secretary of State concluded that since the absence from duty was not in consequence of a trade dispute, they had no right to do this. The Court held that this decision was founded on a mistaken view that absence due to an entirely voluntary act could not be in consequence of a trade dispute. *Minister for Pensions v Chennell [1947] KB 250* was applied: foreseeability was of no relevance and the issue was causation alone. On the facts, one cause of the absence from duty was the existence of the trade dispute. The NALGO members stayed away from work to show support for one side in the trade dispute. They therefore had the right to retain the day lost as reckonable service by payment of an additional sum of money.

[1.2.7]

R v Court ex parte Derbyshire (Divisional Court, unreported, 11 October 1994)

Interpretation – causation

Facts and Decision

Ms Court retired from the police force and claimed an injury pension under a provision in the *Police Pensions Regulations 1987 (SI 1987 No 256)*, on the basis that her psychiatric condition amounted to an injury received without her own default in the execution of her duty. She had previously brought a claim against the constabulary on the grounds of sexual discrimination and sexual harassment, which were compromised with an apology to her and a payment of £2,000. The doctor assigned to assess her, Dr Wells, certified that the condition was not a result of any injury received in the execution of duty as a member of the police force. Ms Court appealed, and on review, medical referee, Dr Bronks, certified that the psychiatric condition was largely if not entirely the result of events which occurred in the course of her work as a police officer. The Court held that injury was not restricted to physical injury. Ms Court's stress was intimately connected with her public duty. It was impossible to say that no reasonable medical referee could have arrived at the conclusion that the injury was received in the execution of her duty.

[1.2.8]

R v Dr J Caldbeck Meenan ex parte Clerk to Cleveland Police Authority (High Court, unreported, 22 July 1994)

Causation

Facts and Decision

Mr Weston was a police constable who retired on 12 May 1991 claiming an injury pension under a provision in the *Police Pensions Regulations 1987 (SI 1987 No 256)*, on the basis that he had received an injury without his own default in the execution of his duty. Mr Weston suffered from depressive illness. The Court held that it was not a court of appeal from the decision of the doctor. What the Court was allowed to do, and had to do, was to see whether there was any legal flaw in the decision, and to test whether the right legal principle and the right principle as to causation had been applied. In this instance, the doctor had concluded that in Mr Weston's case the compensations of camaraderie, good personnel management and support from a hierarchical structure, combined with a sense of job satisfaction, were not sufficient to counterbalance the sense of stress to which he felt exposed and as a consequence the symptoms arose: therefore, the disablement which occurred was the result of an injury received in the execution of his duty. That conclusion was flawless. Mr Weston was, therefore, entitled to the injury pension.

[1.2.9]

R v Fagin ex parte Mountstephen (High Court, unreported, 26 April 1996)

Interpretation

Facts and Decision

Mr Mountstephen retired from the police force on the grounds of ill-health. He suffered from a dissociative state, with characteristic fugue and amnesia, for six weeks and was unable to work afterwards. A doctor certified that he was permanently disabled by reason of psychiatric illness, and that the condition was not the result of any injury received in the execution of his duty as a member of the police force. A further medical report for the Secretary of State concluded that Mr Mountstephen's work circumstances had a contributory but not a determining role in his subsequent disablement. Mr Mountstephen claimed an injury pension under a provision in the *Police Pensions Regulations 1987 (SI 1987 No 256)*, on the basis that his condition amounted to an injury received without his own default in the execution of his duty. The Court held that it would be a misuse of language not to call what Mr Mountstephen had suffered an illness in its own right. No one had suggested any other triggering mechanism than the events and stresses at work, and so it was an injury he received while on duty. It had been accepted that the injury caused or contributed to his personal disablement. Mr Mountstephen was, therefore, entitled to an injury pension, and the doctor's certificate was quashed.

[1.2.10]

R v Kellam, ex parte South Wales Police Authority (High Court) [2000] ICR 632

Interpretation – causation

Facts and Decision

Mr Milton was a police officer with the South Wales Police Authority. He left the service, having gone on sick leave for some time. He had been the subject of hostility within the police force, his wife having brought a successful complaint of sex discrimination and he also having endured disciplinary investigations, though no action was taken against him. He claimed an injury pension under a provision in the *Police Pensions Regulations 1987 (SI 1987 No 256)*, on the basis that his condition amounted to an injury received without his own default in the execution of his duty, suffering from anxiety and stress. The Police Authority's medical officer recommended that he be retired on the grounds of anxiety and stress, and issued a certificate of permanent disablement. However, he also certified that the ill-health was not the result of any injury received in the execution of his duty as a police officer. Mr Milton appealed, and Dr Kellam concluded that Mr Milton's disablement was as a result of an injury, a disease of the mind, substantially contributed to by mental injuries received in the execution of his duties, and that his appeal should therefore succeed. The Police Authority argued that there had to be a direct causal connection between the injury and the police officer's duty, and that it was not enough for there to be a causal connection simply with his being a police officer. The Court held that the test of causation was not to be applied in a legalistic way. It fell to be applied by medical rather than legal experts: *Bradley v London Fire and Civil Defence Authority [1995] OPLR 95* was followed. The reference to a direct causal link in *Garvin v Police Authority for City of London [1944] 1 KB 358* did not mean that fine distinctions might be drawn between direct and indirect causes of the injury. The causal connection must be with the person's service as a police officer, not simply with his or her being a police officer: that is inherent in the reference to duty. However, duty is not to be given a narrow meaning; it relates not only to operational police duties, but to all aspects of the officer's work. It was sufficient for there to be a substantial causal connection with service as a police officer. Dr Kellam had formulated the issue correctly and applied the correct legal test. Mr Milton was, therefore, entitled to his pension.

Richards v Minister for Pensions (High Court) [1946] Reports of War Pensions Appeals 155

Causation

Facts and Decision

Mr Richards suffered an injury in February 1940 while in the army during the war, and left the army the following month. In 1942, he claimed for a war pension on the ground that he had a disability (a hernia) that was sustained by reason of the accident. The Court held that the condition was attributable to his service, and therefore his pension was payable at a higher rate. Even if he had an inherent weakness predisposing him to rupture, that weakness was not the cause of the rupture. It was only the condition from which the cause, the accident during his service, came to operate.

[1.2.12]

W v Minister for Pensions (High Court) [1946] 2 KB 501

Causation

Facts and Decision

A soldier joined the army, and was invalided out because of his chronic anxiety state caused by his wife's repeated infidelity. He claimed a war pension on the ground that his condition was attributable to his war service. The Court held that the question of causation was not to be treated in a metaphysical sense but according to common sense standards. The separation of husband and wife was caused by war service, but only provided the conditions in which the cause of the soldier's chronic anxiety state, his wife's conduct, operated.

1.3 – Status of statutory schemes and schemes established under a statutory power

[1.3.1]

Hutchings v Islington (Court of Appeal) [1998] PLR 239

Statutory scheme – nature of pension rights

Facts and Decision

Mr Hutchings was a member of the Local Government Superannuation Scheme. He claimed that his pension had been miscalculated, since the salary used for the purpose of calculation did not include money set aside from his wages to pay for his tied property and additional holiday pay. On the facts, the Court held that he was not entitled to have additional holiday pay treated as pensionable, but the money set aside to pay for the tied property was pensionable. Although the pension rights which Mr Hutchings was entitled to under the scheme were statutory rights, they were private law rights which he enjoyed by virtue of his contract of employment. Accordingly, he could bring his claim through the County Court since it was an action founded on contract for the purposes of *s 15(1)* of the *County Courts Act 1984*.

[1.3.2]

LRT v Hatt (High Court) [1993] OPLR 225 at 263C–264G, [1993] PLR 227 at paras 151–154

Scheme established under statute – nature of pension rights

Principles

There is a well–established presumption that a private Act does not remove private property rights. It may of course be that the inevitable consequence of the provisions of the Act is that private rights are taken away, in which case effect has to be given to the Act. The Court would, therefore, imply into the statutory process of amalgamation of pension schemes a term that the performance of the employer's and trustees' duties under the interim trust deed was to be carried out so far as practicable, in a way so as not to take away established private rights of members of the two amalgamating schemes. The process overall is one of a change from two precisely defined sets of pension scheme rights and duties to a single precisely defined set of rights and duties. The Court would be vigilant to see that the duties to have regard to the pre-existing rights of the members would be properly observed, and would not take away established property rights unless that action is a proper incident of the process of amalgamation. In this case, the combination of a mandatory minimum employer contribution together with the employer's inability unilaterally to determine the schemes, elevated members' rights on these points to the status of private rights of sufficient weight for them to be protected from removal on amalgamation.

1.4 – Effect of contracting out of the state scheme

[1.4.1]

Barber v GRE (European Court of Justice) [1990] ECR I–1889, [1990] IRLR 240, [1991] I WLR 72, [1990] PLR 95

Contracting-out – equal treatment

Facts and Decision

The Court held that contracting out of a state pension scheme does not affect the treatment of the scheme benefits as pay for the purposes of European law. Occupational schemes may provide greater benefits than those provided by the statutory scheme, and as such they are caught by the provisions of *Article 119* (now *Article 141*) of the *Treaty of Rome*.

[1.4.2]

Coloroll Pension Trustees v Russell (European Court of Justice) [1995] All ER (EC) 23, [1994] ECR I–4389, [1994] IRLR 586, [1994] OPLR 179 at 220B–221A, [1994] PLR 211 at paras 62–70

Contracting-out – equal treatment

Principle

The Court held that the scope of the principles laid down in the *Barber* judgment are not limited to contracted-out occupational schemes, and that those principles also concern non-contracted-out occupational schemes.

[1.4.3]

Marsh & Maclennan v Pensions Ombudsman (High Court) [2001] PLR 51

Contracting-out — equal treatment

Principle

The Court held that guaranteed minimum pensions were in the nature of calculation factors, rather than pensions themselves or discrete elements of a scheme pension. A scheme pension should not be regarded as comprising two elements, made up of a guaranteed minimum pension and any amount in excess of this.

[1.4.4]

Mettoy Pension Trustees v Evans (High Court) [1991] 2 All ER 513, [1990] 1 WLR 1587 at 1610h, [1990] PLR 9

Contracting-out — interpretation

Principle

Pension scheme documents have to be construed in the light of the requirements of the Commissioners of the Inland Revenue from time to time for their approval of a scheme, and also of the statutory requirements from time to time in force for the issue of contracting-out certificates.

[1.4.5]

Szrabjer v United Kingdom (European Commission of Human Rights) [1998] PLR 281 at paras 35–39

Contracting-out — human rights

Principle

The Commission held that employers, while able to opt out of the State earnings related pension scheme (SERPS) for their employees, had to provide a guaranteed minimum pension with at least as good a return to pensioners as under SERPS. Under State regulations governing occupational pension schemes it was permissible to suspend a pension on imprisonment, but also permissible to award such a pension to a dependant of the prisoner (a possibility not available under SERPS).

However, the fact that such schemes in such certain circumstances may have offered more advantageous conditions with regard to suspension and returns to pensioners, cannot constitute discrimination by the Government against prisoners. The payments into occupational schemes by employees and employers would have varied between different occupational schemes, and thus there can be no direct comparison with either the levels or the terms of pension returns under SERPS, and occupational pension schemes.

[1.4.6]

Warrener v Walden Engineering (Employment Appeal Tribunal) [1993] IRLR 420, [1993] ICR 967, [1993] OPLR 277, [1993] PLR 295 at paras 21 and 22

Contracting-out – transfers of undertakings

Facts and Decision

Contracted-out contributory occupational pension schemes are, the Tribunal held, 'supplementary schemes outside the statutory social security schemes of member states' for the purposes of *Article 3* of *Directive 77/187/EC*, the 'Acquired Rights Directive'. They are, therefore, outside the effect of this *Directive*.

1.5 – Effect of contracting out of a statutory obligation

[1.5.1]

Guardians of the Poor of Salford Union v Dewhurst (House of Lords) [1926] AC 619

Contracting out of a statutory obligation

Facts and Decision

Mr Dewhurst was an officer of the Salford Union. In 1918 the Salford Union awarded a temporary war bonus to its workers, on the basis that it should be free from pension deductions and therefore not included in the calculation of pension under the *Poor Law Officers' Superannuation Act 1896*. Mr Dewhurst retired and claimed a pension which included an element referable to the war bonus. The Court held that the Salford Union could not validly enter into an agreement with one of its officers that he would receive less than the amount provided for him by statute. The whole scale and framework of the *Act* was made upon the footing that it was a comprehensive scheme, and accordingly the Court did not accept the argument that a right to contract out of this scheme should be implied in.

[1.5.2]

Hamar v French (Court of Appeal) [1997] OPLR 105, [1998] PLR 321 at paras 47–70

Contracting out of a statutory obligation

Principle

The Court held that *s 95* of the *Pension Schemes Act 1993* is a hybrid scheme. Some of its provisions clearly cannot be waived. Those which restrict the use to which a transfer value can be applied, for example, are imposed as a matter of policy. Other requirements, however, are purely formal. The requirement that the application be made in writing, for example, is clearly imposed for the benefit of the trustees; it might be unwise of them to waive the requirement, but it would be absurd to hold that they could not do so if they chose. Where a transfer request purports to exercise the statutory right to take a cash equivalent, trustees are not bound to treat the application as valid, but they can choose to do so if they wish (subject to having the necessary powers under the trust deed and *s 15* of the *Trustee Act 1925*).

1.6 – Effect of non-execution of document

[1.6.1]

Davis v Richards & Wallington Industries Ltd (High Court) [1991] 2 All ER 563, [1990] 1 WLR 1511, [1990] PLR 141 at paras 108–111

Non-execution

Principle

Equity looks on that as done which ought to be done. Beneficiaries, therefore, who have given value can enforce an obligation to complete the constitution of an incompletely constituted trust, and so the obligation to execute a definitive deed can be enforced by the employees. Accordingly, the failure to do so does not detract from the efficacy of the rules.

[1.6.2]

Harwood-Smart v Caws (High Court) [2000] PLR 101

Non-execution

Principle

The Court held that where an interim trust deed contained a requirement which was not replicated in a definitive deed, the members could compel its inclusion; *Davis v Richards & Wallington Industries Ltd [1991] 2 All ER 563* was followed.

1.7 – Value of earlier documentation

[1.7.1]

Harris v Shuttleworth (Court of Appeal) [1995] OPLR 79 at 89E-F, [1994] PLR 47 at para 53, [1994] ICR 991

Earlier documentation – interpretation

Principle

Where trust deeds were expressly said to be supplemental to earlier deeds, provisions of an earlier edition of the rules were clearly a relevant consideration to be taken into account in interpreting the present rules. This was, however, only an aid to construction if the normal meaning of the present rules was not clear.

[1.7.2]

Harwood-Smart v Caws (High Court) [2000] PLR 101 at paras 5, 43

Earlier documentation – interpretation – amendments

Principle

Delving into the 'archaeology' of a pension scheme was both legitimate and necessary having regard to the nature of the argument in this case, which concerned the validity of the winding-up rule after successive amendments. Where an interim trust deed contained a requirement that was not replicated in a definitive deed, the members could compel its inclusion: *Davis v Richards & Wallington Industries Ltd [1991] 2 All ER 563* was followed.

Lloyds Bank Pension Trust Corporation Limited v Lloyds Bank PLC (High Court) [1996] OPLR 181 at 186H–187D, [1996] PLR 263 at paras 25–27

Earlier documentation – interpretation

Principle

The Court had serious reservations as to whether it could be legitimate to seek to resolve any ambiguity in pension scheme rules, by referring to earlier deeds and rules which the later rules claim to have amended and replaced. The suggestion that the meaning of an ostensibly comprehensive set of rules could be divined by looking at a deed executed almost 60 years earlier was unattractive, not least because many of the current members will have joined the scheme on the basis that their rights were governed exhaustively by the current rules.

[1.7.4]

National Grid Co plc v Laws (High Court) [1997] OPLR 207, [1997] PLR 174 at paras 69–73

Earlier documentation – interpretation – amendments

Facts and Decision

In a case where the scope of a pension scheme's power of amendment, and the validity of a particular amendment are in issue, the Court held that examination of the history of the matter is plainly permissible and indeed indispensable. In other cases one should stick to the current text as a rule, while bearing in mind that the text of any long-established pension scheme is likely to be a patchwork. There is a serious policy issue here: it is often hard enough for trustees and their advisers to interpret a pension scheme as it stands, without also having to delve into the 'archaeology' of the scheme. Nevertheless, where a pension scheme has evolved by successive amendments, provisions which have been superseded did at one time stand as part of the scheme, and a comparison of the old with the new may sometimes help to explain the purpose and meaning of new provisions. But the Court should be slow to look at superseded provisions as an aid to construction, both because of the inconvenience involved and because of the uncertainty (apart from exceptional cases) of deriving any useful assistance from the exercise.

[1.7.5]

Spooner v British Telecommunications (High Court) [2000] PLR 65 at paras 72–77

Earlier documentation – interpretation

Principle

A pension scheme is not to be regarded as on all fours with a commercial contract. A commercial contract represents by its very nature the culmination of a process of negotiation. By contrast, a new member joining a pension scheme must take the scheme as he or she finds it. A new member cannot, by definition, have any relevant intention in relation to its meaning or effect: the most he or she can have is an understanding of its meaning or effect. It cannot be right that in order to understand what the scheme means, a new member is obliged to undertake a process of historical research, the requisite materials for which may well not be readily available to the member. If that is the position so far as new members are concerned, it follows that existing members cannot be in any different position. That is not to say that a pension scheme may not by its own terms, when properly construed, require that recourse be had to sources outside the scheme as part of the process of determining its true meaning and effect. To that extent, but no further, the historical approach is justified; not as a matter of the matrix of fact, but rather because the provision itself on its true construction directs such an approach.

[1.7.6]

Stevens & others v Bell & others (High Court) [2001] All ER 193, [2001] PLR 99 at paras 20 and 55

Earlier documentation – interpretation

Principle

The Court held that the past history of a trust deed's provisions has a limited legitimate role on some questions of construction of the trust deed as it currently stands.

Where a power had been replaced by another power with different wording, the new power was to be read on its own in the context of the deed as a whole. It was not to be read in the context of the different wording of a different provision with more limited effect, no longer part of the scheme, which applied in different circumstances. This was not a point on which the history of the scheme was a legitimate aid to construction because of the different wording.

1.8 – Value of predecessor scheme provisions

[1.8.1]

Davis v Richards & Wallington Industries Ltd (High Court) [1991] 2 All ER 563, [1990] 1 WLR 1511 at 1529, [1990] PLR 141

Predecessor scheme – interpretation

Principle

The Court held that the rules of a predecessor scheme may, in appropriate circumstances, form part of the matrix that it is legitimate to consider when construing the terms of the interim trust deed of a successor scheme.

[1.8.2]

National Grid Co plc v Laws (High Court) [1997] OPLR 207, [1997] PLR 174 at para 74

Predecessor scheme – interpretation

Principle

There is no absolute bar to the Court looking at the provisions of earlier pension schemes, but the Court's scepticism about the usefulness of doing so, and its reluctance to do so, should be intensified. *Davis v Richards & Wallington Industries Ltd [1991] 2 All ER 563* required the Court to construe an interim deed, and so the circumstances of that case should be considered as special.

[1.8.3]

National Grid Co plc and others v Laws, Mayes and others (Court of Appeal) [1999] OPLR 95, [1999] PLR 37 at para 12

Predecessor scheme – interpretation

Principle

Although the Court of Appeal was asked by the parties to look at an earlier pension scheme, the Court drew no assistance from it in this case.

[1.8.4]

Spooner v British Telecommunications (High Court) [2000] PLR 65 at paras 72–77

Predecessor scheme – interpretation

See [1.7.5].

1.9 – Value of successor scheme provisions

[1.9.1]

Spooner v British Telecommunications (High Court) [2000] PLR 65 at para 106

Successor scheme – interpretation

Principles

The true construction of a pension scheme's former rules cannot be affected, let alone determined, by reference to the new rules. The true construction of the former rules must be ascertained by reading them in the context in which they appeared. By the same token, the understanding of the employers as to the true construction of the former rules is irrelevant.

1.10 – Status of beneficiaries

[1.10.1]

Imperial Group Pension Trust v Imperial Tobacco Ltd (High Court) [1991] 1 WLR 589, [1991] ICR 524, [1991] IRLR 66, [1991] 2 All ER 597, [1990] PLR 263

Interpretation – role of beneficiaries

Principles

Pension benefits are part of the consideration which an employee receives in return for the rendering of services. In this case, membership of the employer's pension scheme was a requirement of employment. In contributory schemes, the employee is bound to pay his or her contributions. Beneficiaries of the scheme, the members, far from being volunteers have given valuable consideration. The company employer is not conferring a bounty. The scheme is established against the background of such employment and falls to be interpreted against that background.

[1.10.2]

Mettoy Pension Trustees v Evans (High Court) [1991] 2 All ER 513, [1990] 1 WLR 1587 at 1611, [1990] PLR 9 at para 127

Interpretation – role of beneficiaries

Principle

It is a special factor in construing pension schemes that the beneficiaries are not volunteers. Their rights have contractual and commercial origins, deriving from the contracts of employment of the members. The benefits provided under the scheme have been earned by the service of the members under those contracts and, where the scheme is contributory, *pro tanto* by their contributions.

1.11 – Estoppel

[1.11.1]

Amalgamated Investment v Texas Bank (Court of Appeal) [1982] 1 QB 84

Estoppel by convention

Principle

When the parties to a transaction proceed on the basis of an underlying assumption – either of fact or of law (whether due to misrepresentation or mistake makes no difference) on which they have conducted the dealings between them – neither of them will be allowed to go back on that assumption when it would be unfair or unjust to allow them to do so.

[1.11.2]

Bairstow v Queens Moat Houses (High Court, unreported, 23 July 1999)

Estoppel by convention

Facts and Decision

The directors of a company allowed the company and the insurer of its pension scheme to act upon the basis of an agreed assumption as to the way in which bonus was to be treated for pension purposes. The Court held that it would be unconscionable for the directors to seek to go back on the assumptions upon which they knew that the insurer acted, and they were therefore estopped from doing so: *ITN v Ward [1997] OPLR 147* and *Icarus v Driscoll [1990] PLR 1* were applied.

[1.11.3]

Derby v Scottish Equitable (Court of Appeal) [2001] PLR 163

Estoppel – overpayment of benefits

Facts and Decision

Mr Derby came to draw his personal pension. Scottish Equitable miscalculated his pension entitlement, and when Mr Derby queried this, Scottish Equitable confirmed their erroneous calculations. Mr Derby, therefore, took a tax-free cash lump sum, and used the rest to take out an annuity with Norwich Union. Scottish Equitable had overpaid Mr Derby by £172,000. He spent most of the lump sum on reducing his mortgage, and the remaining £9,600 he used to improve his lifestyle, though modestly and not irreversibly. Eventually, Scottish Equitable realised their mistake and asked for their money back. Norwich Union agreed that it would unwind the pension policy which it had granted. The Court held that the concept of estoppel was not appropriate for dealing with the problem: it would clearly be inequitable to allow Mr Derby to make a profit by pleading estoppel, since the sums sought to be recovered were so large as to bear no relation to any detriment which he could possibly have suffered: *Avon County Council v Howlett [1983] 1 WLR 605* was distinguished. The Court of Appeal was tentatively drawn to a submission that, since the decision in *Lipkin Gorman v Karpnale [1991] 2 AC 548*, the defence of change of position pre-empts and disables the defence of estoppel. On this analysis, it was not unconscionable for a party to go back on the underlying assumption, except to the extent that the other party had changed its position. The argument was novel, but the Court could not see how it could be refuted.

[1.11.4]

Hamar v French (Court of Appeal) [1997] OPLR 105, [1998] PLR 321 at para 75

Estoppel by convention – transfer request – Pensions Ombudsman

Facts and Decision

The Court held that where trustees did not challenge before the Pensions Ombudsman the validity of a letter requesting a statutory right to a cash equivalent, it became accepted as a fact which was not in dispute. It could not, therefore, be challenged in the Court, where appeals could only be brought on points of law. The principle in play was not estoppel by convention, but the analogy was close.

Harris v Simpson (Alberta Court of Queen's Bench, 2 October 1984) 56 AR 201

Estoppel – wrongful dismissal – retirement

Facts and Decision

Mr Harris was wrongfully dismissed by his employer. He was then entitled to pension benefits, but if he had taken early retirement, the pension would have been substantially higher than if he had left on termination. The Court held that the employer was not permitted to profit from its wrongful act (it did not matter that the employer did not have a direct interest in the scheme), and was accordingly estopped from denying Mr Harris the option of electing early retirement under the scheme. The scheme booklet had stated that the termination benefit was to be paid 'if you terminate employment with' the employer, but the scheme rules provided that the benefit arose if a member's employment with the employer was terminated for any reason. The booklet did not state whether it had contractual effect, and purported to be a summary of the main features of the scheme. The booklet was effective to bind the employer on one of two bases. It was either a representation forming the basis of an estoppel or it was a term of the contract of employment.

Hood Sailmakers v Axford (High Court) [1996] 4 All ER 830, [1997] 1 WLR 625, [1997] 1 BCLC 72, [1996] OPLR 141

Estoppel – directors' resolution – Pensions Ombudsman

Facts and Decision

A company passed a resolution in writing, while one of the directors was abroad, amending its pension scheme benefit structure. The absent director did not participate in, and at the time was not aware of, the resolution. Five years later, the company sought to argue that the resolution had not been properly passed. On appeal from the Pensions Ombudsman, the Court found that as a matter of law, the resolution had not been properly passed. However, there was sufficient evidence for the Ombudsman properly to find that the company and the absent director were both estopped from denying the validity of the amendments, and the Court would not interfere with that finding.

[1.11.7]

Icarus v Driscoll (High Court) [1990] PLR 1

Estoppel by convention – scheme booklet

Facts and Decision

A contributory occupational pension scheme was set up in 1973, providing 1/80th of final salary for each year of service for staff members, and 1/60th of final salary for each year of service for special directors. In 1976, other employees were allowed to join on the basis that they would receive 1/270th of final salary for each year of service, but that they did not contribute. In 1978, when it was decided that the scheme would not contract out of SERPS, staff members' benefits were reduced to 1/270ths of final salary as well, but in compensation the scheme was made non-contributory for them. In 1979, revised booklets were issued, but the amendments within them were never documented under the scheme rules. In 1985, the employer went into liquidation. The Court held that parties to the scheme were estopped from contending that the scheme provided for any rate of benefits other than 1/270ths of final salary. All parties had accepted and worked on this basis. *Amalgamated Investment v Texas Bank [1982] 1 QB 84* was applied.

[1.11.8]

Irish Pensions Trust v First National Bank of Chicago (Irish High Court, 15 February 1989) 37 PBLR 9

Estoppel by convention – scheme booklet

Facts and Decision

A ten-page memorandum had been circulated to staff by an employer, which included the statement that if its pension scheme should be terminated, the money in the scheme must be used to provide benefits to scheme participants. The memorandum also included a statement that this summary described the highlights of the programme, and that each scheme described was subject to the terms and condition of the formal documentation which governed the obligations and benefits provided. The Court observed that any reasonable person would realise that this was a complex subject. If one wanted to consider matters of detail and the precise rights of parties, one had to refer to the underlying documentation and perhaps get legal assistance in relation to it. The memorandum, therefore, had not been shown to operate as an estoppel against the employer.

ITN v Ward (High Court) [1997] OPLR 147, [1997] PLR 131

Estoppel by convention – scheme booklet

Facts and Decision

The pension increases rule of the Independent Television News Limited Pension Scheme was amended in 1979 to provide for increases at 4% per annum compound, or such other rate as the trustees should from time to time determine. Both before and after the introduction of the rule, members were told that pensions in payment increased at 4% a year compound. In the early 1990s, inflation fell below 4%, and the trustees decided to award increases at a rate below 4%. The Court held that when deciding whether booklets and announcements form the basis of an estoppel by convention, one must look at all the relevant circumstances in a practical and common-sense way. It is not necessary to have evidence of what every member of the scheme thought before an estoppel by convention can be invoked. The test was whether it would be unjust, unfair or unconscionable for the trustees or the employer to resile from the wording of the scheme booklets; *Amalgamated Investment v Texas Bank [1982] 1 QB 84* was applied. Booklets are usually deliberately phrased in general terms in an attempt to make them more readily intelligible to those members who read them. Any precis will lose some of the detail. It was important to take account of any statements that booklets were expressly stated to be summary and incomplete, and that amendments or additions to the scheme could be made at any time. There was held to be no estoppel by convention in this case.

Comment

Members normally learn of their pension scheme benefits not from the terms of the pension scheme's constitution, but from the literature issued by the scheme. Inevitably, this literature will simplify the terms. Outright mistakes in the scheme literature are not inevitable, but are still fairly common. Members will then wish to establish which takes priority, the scheme literature or the scheme constitution. Except in the most unusual circumstances, the courts have put their trust in the pension scheme constitution. This case succinctly explains why.

The scheme literature normally is not, and normally does not purport to be, the legal framework under which the pension scheme is to be administered. Mistakes in the literature cannot give a free-standing right to the benefits mistakenly described in their own right. The only way in which the scheme literature could form part of the basis on which members could claim rights which were inconsistent with the terms of the pension scheme constitution was if it formed the basis of an estoppel. For this to succeed the members needed to show that it would be unjust, unfair or unconscionable for the trustees and the employer to invoke the terms of the scheme constitution. Taking into account that the scheme booklet in this case noted that the scheme rules were paramount and that amendments could be made at any time, it was not reasonable for the members to rely upon a statement in the booklet about pension increases without consulting the scheme rules.

It should be noted that in this case, there was no past history of the employer and trustees acting inconsistently with the scheme rules, since the rules and the scheme literature were both consistent with practice. The Court did not need to consider the extent to which scheme practice enhances the members' case. This could, though, be relevant in other circumstances. It should also be noted that the inefficacy of announcements and booklets to change the scheme constitution applies equally to the employers, as both *Lansing Linde v Alber [2000] OPLR 1* and *Bestrustees v Stuart* (unreported) attest. Only in the most extreme cases, such as *Icarus v Driscoll [1990] PLR 1*, will the courts relent.

[1.11.10]

Jones v Williams (High Court) [1989] PLR 17

Estoppel by convention – principal employer

Facts and Decision

An employer had assumed the responsibilities as principal employer of a pension scheme from another employer, but without a legal transfer taking place. The Court held that an estoppel by convention could not arise as to the identity of the principal employer, when considering to whom a scheme surplus should be distributed. The parties' understanding would not carry, as a necessary implication, the entitlement of the assumed principal employer to an interest by way of resulting trust, in relation to property originally contributed by the actual principal employer.

[1.11.11]

Lansing Linde v Alber (High Court) [2000] OPLR I at 39H–41C, 43B–44H, [2000] PLR 15

Estoppel by convention – scheme booklet

Facts and Decision

The Court held that where a new edition of a pension scheme booklet, inviting people to join a scheme, stated a normal retirement date which was not reflected in the terms of the scheme rules, and the booklet stated that the scheme rules governed the scheme, it was correct to say that the offer to join the scheme was on the terms of the scheme rules. No estoppel by convention arose. The transmission of the amended booklet had no impact on the member's normal retirement date. It was thus not unconscionable for a member to assert his or her true normal retirement date, nor to hold the company and the trustees to the legal position.

[1.11.12]

NHS Pensions Agency v Pensions Ombudsman (High Court) [1996] OPLR 119

Estoppel – calculation of benefits

Facts and Decision

A member had been given incorrect information about his pension entitlement, resulting in him believing that his pension entitlement was substantially greater than in fact it was. The Pensions Ombudsman held that he could not order that the pension entitlement be calculated in accordance with the incorrect information given; *Westminster v Haywood [1996] 2 All ER 467* was followed.

[1.11.13]

Robertson v Readman (Court of Session, Scotland) [1993] OPLR 139

Estoppel by convention – draft rules

Facts and Decision

The trustees of a pension scheme in winding-up applied to the Court for guidance as to how to apply the surplus in the scheme. The scheme had been established in 1961, and a definitive deed and rules were executed in 1962. These provided for all surplus to be returned to the employer. Draft rules were prepared in 1980 reflecting various changes to the rules since that date. These draft rules provided for surplus to be used in augmenting members' benefits, before refunding any balance to the employer. The employer was wound up and a liquidator appointed in 1982. The Court rejected the argument that the trustees had relied upon the draft rules as if they had been executed. The question was whether the actions were such as to justify the inference that, although the new documents had not been executed, the previous documents were nevertheless varied by them to the effect that they became part of the contract between the employer and the trustees, as to how the scheme was to be administered. On the facts, that inference was not justified. No actions to be relied upon could be attributed unambiguously to the preparation of the draft rules, as opposed to editions of the scheme booklet. The surplus was, therefore, to be refunded to the employer in its entirety.

[1.11.14]

Seifert v Pensions Ombudsman (Court of Appeal) [1997] OPLR 395, [1999] PLR 29

Estoppel – election of benefits

Facts and Decision

Directors of an employer, who were also trustees of its pension scheme, had given an employee misleading information in their communications about pensions. The Court held that this was a legal wrong on their part, and that but for that misleading information, the employee would have elected to receive an immediate early-retirement pension. Since the scheme subsequently went into winding-up in deficit, the employee's pension entitlement was ranked lower in the order of priorities than it otherwise would have been, and his pension was substantially reduced.

The trustees were, therefore, precluded from relying on the fact that the member had not elected to receive an immediate pension in calculating his entitlement.

[1.11.15]

Westminster v Haywood (High Court) [1996] 2 All ER 467, [1996] OPLR 95 at 107A-F, [1996] PLR 161 at paras 54–57

Estoppel – calculation of benefits – ultra vires

Principle

Estoppel cannot be used to achieve a result which Westminster Council could not have lawfully undertaken to achieve because it was not authorised to do so.

1.12 – Use of the Inland Revenue's Practice Notes as a guide to construction

[1.12.1]

Air Jamaica v Charlton (Privy Council) [1999] 1 WLR 1399, [1999] OPLR 11, [1999] PLR 247 at para 54

Interpretation – Revenue practice

Principle

The fact that pension schemes need the approval of the Inland Revenue to secure fiscal advantages is not a proper ground on which to reject the operation of a resulting trust in relation to the scheme assets, in a way which would contravene the Revenue's requirements. The Revenue in this case had had an opportunity to examine the pension plan and to withhold approval, and it had failed to do so. There was no call to distort principle in order to meet its requirements. The resulting trust took place by operation of general law, outside the scope of the relevant tax legislation and outside the scheme itself.

[1.12.2]

Barclays Bank v Holmes (High Court) [2000] PLR 339 at paras 81–84

Interpretation – Inland Revenue practice

Facts and Decision

Where a pension scheme deed was drafted with a view to obtaining Revenue approval, the Court held that it must be construed having regard to material published by the Inland Revenue at the date of the deed; the dictum of Lord Hoffman in *Investors Compensation Scheme v West Bromwich Building Society [1998] 1 WLR 896 at 912–3* was applied. Where a scheme trust deed was drawn up expressly with the intention of obtaining Inland

Revenue approval, one can and should have regard to the material published by the Inland Revenue as to what it requires or recommends of a pension scheme before it can be approved. *Harris v Shuttleworth* was distinguished, and *Mettoy v Evans* was considered. In a case where the trust deed clearly provides for something inconsistent with the requirements of the Revenue, Revenue material could not be invoked to rewrite the deed, but that certainly does not mean that it cannot be taken into account when construing the trust deed.

[1.12.3]

Davis v Richards & Wallington Industries Ltd (High Court) [1991] 2 All ER 563, [1990] I WLR 1511, [1990] PLR 141 at para 147

Interpretation – Inland Revenue practice

Facts and Decision

The Court held that a resulting trust in favour of the employees in a pension scheme was excluded, since the employees had received the benefits for which they had contracted, and a resulting trust would have breached the statutory and Inland Revenue requirements under which the scheme was established. The relevant legislative requirements prevent imputing a resulting trust.

[1.12.4]

Harris v Shuttleworth (Court of Appeal) [1995] OPLR 79 at 89G, [1994] PLR 47 at para 54, [1994] ICR 991

Interpretation – Inland Revenue practice

Principle

It was doubtful whether the Inland Revenue Practice Notes are admissible as an aid to construction, but even if admissible, in this case no great assistance would be derived from them.

[1.12.5]

International Power v Healy (House of Lords) [2001] PLR 121 at paras 18–26

Interpretation – tax legislation

Principle

The most relevant background to the interpretation of a pension scheme provision prohibiting refunds to the employer is the fiscal origin of the clause. Schemes enjoyed great fiscal privileges under the tax legislation. In these circumstances, it was hardly surprising that capital payments out of the fund were anathema to the Inland Revenue. This tax and regulatory background suggests that the wording of the relevant clause of the pension scheme was carefully chosen to exclude the release of debts owed by the employer.

[1.12.6]

Mettoy Pension Trustees v Evans (High Court) [1991] 2 All ER 513, [1990] I WLR 1587 at 1610h, [1990] PLR 9 at para 127

Interpretation – Inland Revenue practice

See [1.4.4].

[1.12.7]

Norman v Pensions Ombudsman (High Court) [1997] OPLR 85 at 91C-E

Interpretation – Inland Revenue practice

Principle

The Court, it was held, should have regard to the Inland Revenue conditions for approval of a pension scheme in assessing the interpretation of a forfeiture rule. However, although part of the background of the scheme, they did not take this question of construction very far.

[1.12.8]

Venables v Hornby (High Court, unreported, 14 June 2001) at para 25 of transcript

Interpretation – Inland Revenue practice

Principle

Among the relevant surrounding circumstances for the purpose of interpreting pension scheme rules was the then prevailing Inland Revenue practice: the dictum in *Mettoy Pension Trustees v Evans [1991] 2 All ER 513* was followed. It was therefore regrettable in this case that no evidence was available of the practice as known to pension practitioners at the time in question.

1.13 – Use of the statutory framework as a guide to construction

Davis v Richards & Wallington Industries Ltd (High Court)
[1991] 2 All ER 563, [1990] 1 WLR 1511, [1990] PLR 141 at
para 12

Interpretation – use of statute

Principle

In construing the nature of the rights and obligations both of employees and of employers under an approved pension scheme, it is important to keep in mind the statutory framework in the context of which the scheme was established.

Lesser v Lawrence, Dennison v Krasner (Court of Appeal)
[2000] PLR 213 at paras 38, 42

Interpretation – use of statute

Facts and Decision

The Court held that the insurance policy under consideration in this case was plainly intended to satisfy the requirements for approval under _s 226_ of the _Income and Corporation Taxes Act 1970_, so that in the case of ambiguity (if any) it would be appropriate to construe the policy in a sense which gave effect to that intention. It was appropriate to have the statutory provisions in mind when construing the terms of insurance policies. However, the key question was whether the policies themselves on their true construction and having regard to the general law had the effect, on the bankruptcy of the policyholder, of vesting the rights and benefits thereunder in the trustee in bankruptcy.

Venables v Hornby (High Court, unreported, 14 June 2001) at para 25 of transcript

Interpretation – use of statute

Principle

Since a pension trust deed and rules were drafted against the background of the then prevailing legislation and the need to obtain Inland Revenue approval, they must be construed against the background of that legislation.

1.14 – Use of common practice as an aid to construction

[1.14.1]

LRT v Hatt (High Court) [1993] OPLR 225 at 254D, [1993] PLR 227 at para 113

Interpretation – industry practice

Principle

The settled practice of experienced pension scheme practitioners may well constitute a valuable guide to what the law is and how its provisions should be construed, just as the settled practice of conveyancers has long been recognised and given effect by courts dealing with conveyancing matters. That is not to say, however, that pension scheme practitioners operate in a form of Alsatia, or have the power to override the provisions of statute law or equity.

[1.14.2]

Mettoy Pension Trustees v Evans (High Court) [1991] 2 All ER 513, [1990] 1 WLR 1587 at 1611, [1990] PLR 9 at para 127

Interpretation – industry practice

Principle

The relevant background facts or surrounding circumstances for interpreting a pension scheme's provisions include common practice from time to time in the field of pension schemes generally, as evinced in particular by the evidence of the actuaries and by textbooks written by practitioners in the field.

Venables v Hornby (Special Tax Commissioner) [2001] PLR 17 at paras 34–36

Interpretation – industry practice

Facts and Decision

The Commissioner held that whether pensions practitioners generally thought that certain types of transition would amount to retirement, or whether the Pension Schemes Office did or did not think so, had very little bearing on the question actually under appeal, which was whether an individual had retired in the particular circumstances under examination.

1.15 – Referral to non-judicial authority for interpretation

[1.15.1]

Doyle v Manchester Evening News (High Court) [1989] PLR 47 at paras 66, 67

Interpretation by employer

Facts and Decision

A power given to the employer to certify salary conclusively was not, the Court held, a beneficial power, but a power conferred on it to facilitate the running of the pension scheme in the interests of the members. The employer could not change the definition of salary by its certificate, because even if it considered that it was acting in the interests of the scheme as a whole, and not purely from selfish motives, it was not within the ambit of the power of certification.

[1.15.2]

Harris v Shuttleworth (Court of Appeal) [1995] OPLR 79 at 86H–87A, [1994] PLR 47 at para 36, [1994] ICR 991

Interpretation by trustees

Facts and Decision

Despite a rule empowering trustees conclusively to determine all matters, questions and disputes touching or in connection with the fund's affairs, it was held that the Court had control over the trustees' decisions. Trustees must ask themselves the correct questions. They must direct themselves correctly in law; in particular they must adopt a correct construction of the pension fund rules. They must not arrive at a perverse decision, i.e. a decision to which no reasonable body of trustees could arrive, and they must take into account all relevant but no irrelevant factors. Only if the trustees fail on one of these grounds can the Court intervene.

[1.15.3]

Harris v Simpson (Alberta Court of Queen's Bench, 2 October 1984) 56 AR 201

Interpretation by trustees

Facts and Decision

The trustees of a pension scheme were given a discretion to revalue the investments referable to the members' entitlements. All questions of interpretation or the carrying-out of the scheme were stated under the articles to be final and binding. The audited financial statements were also stated under the articles to be final and binding on all parties. The Court held that given the audited financial statements were a limit on the trustees' discretion, the trustees, while free to estimate the scheme earnings during the year, were nonetheless bound to adjust those estimates in the light of the audited financial statements at the end of that year.

[1.15.4]

HM Treasury v Lane (Court of Appeal) [1993] OPLR 155

Interpretation by employer

Facts and Decision

A pension scheme contained a provision stating that any question under the scheme shall be determined by the Treasury, whose decision on it shall be final. The Court held, however, that where the answer to a question concerning the scheme rules involved the construction and interpretation of words and phrases in the context in which they were found, the Court had a role to play in the interpretation of the scheme.

[1.15.5]

Mihlenstedt v Barclays Bank (Court of Appeal) [1989] PLR 91, [1989] Ch 91, [1989] IRLR 522

Interpretation by employer

Principle

The law of contract was sufficiently broad to allow the enforcement of an obligation to consult, or to declare that an employer's opinion on assessing incapacity had been formed dishonestly, or on an erroneous basis. It was an implied term of the employment contract that the employer would discharge its functions in good faith. In this case, this meant that the Bank would properly consider the member's claim. The Bank had asked itself the right questions, and it had formed an opinion which it could tenably hold. Accordingly, it had fulfilled that duty.

[1.15.6]

Teachers Pension Agency v Hill (High Court) [1998] OPLR 167

Interpretation by employer

Facts and Decision

Mrs Hill was employed on a succession of fixed term contracts as a teacher, and was a member of the Teachers' Superannuation Scheme, a statutory scheme. She was made redundant by her employers and her last fixed term contract was not renewed. Under the relevant regulation, Mrs Hill was entitled to a preferential redundancy pension if her employer had notified the Secretary of State in writing that her employment was terminated by reason of her redundancy, or in the interests of the efficient discharge of the employer's functions. Mrs Hill's employers wrote confirming that she was retiring on premature grounds and that her employment in pensionable service had been terminated before the contract of employment expired by reason of redundancy. The administrator then refused to pay the pension because her employment was not terminated by reason of her redundancy. The Court held that it was not enough that the employment had come to an end because a fixed term contract had run its natural course. On a literal interpretation the regulation required only written notification. It would be surprising if the administrator, as a body with responsibility for disbursing public funds, was required to make payments which it believed were based on an erroneous view of the law or on a fundamental error of fact. The administrator was obliged by the regulations to form its own view as to whether other criteria were met, and it was difficult to see why an exception should have been made here. There was no provision for the member to appeal if the employer's notification was intended to be conclusive. If the Pensions Ombudsman got involved, it was difficult to believe that the administrator could shelter behind a notification which it believed to be wrong. While judicial review would be available, it would be unduly cumbersome. The administrator was, therefore, entitled to look behind the notification from the employer if it considered that it was based on an error of law.

Re Tuck's Settlement Trusts (High Court) [1976] 2 WLR 345

Interpretation by third party

Facts and Decision

A settlor of a private trust reserved the question as to whether any given individual had been brought up in and never departed from the Jewish faith to the Chief Rabbi in London of either the Portuguese or Anglo-German community, whose decision was stated to be conclusive. The settlor plainly considered these matters to be questions of fact. The Court held that the reference for resolution of doubts on these matters was not an unlawful ouster of the Court's jurisdiction to decide the question: *Re Raven [1915] 1 Ch 673* and *Re Wynn's Will Trusts [1952] 1 All ER 341* were distinguished. Jewish blood was a question merely of degree. Questions of degree were questions which had been submitted for determination to an authority which the settlor thought appropriate, and the Court would not differ from his view. The opinion of one or other of the chief rabbis would, therefore, be conclusive on such issues.

This judgment was approved by the Court of Appeal on different grounds, with Lord Denning expressly approving the High Court's ground of decision. See *Re Tuck's Settlement Trusts [1978] 1 All ER 1047, [1978] 2 WLR 411, [1978] Ch 49.*

[1.15.8]

Wilson v Metro Goldwyn Mayer (Supreme Court of New South Wales) [1980] 18 NSWLR 730

Interpretation by employer

Facts and Decision

The employer and trustees of a pension scheme had power to amend the scheme by deed in any respect which would, in the opinion of the employer, not prejudice any benefits secured by contributions made on behalf of any member prior to the date of amendment. The Court held that the employer was obliged to form its opinion as to whether the benefits were prejudiced on the basis of a correct understanding of the question to be considered, and so an opinion formed on an erroneous construction of the power of amendment could not constitute a relevant opinion for its purposes.

1.16 – Weight to be put on announcements and booklets, and interpretation of those documents

[1.16.1]

Re Alfred Herbert Ltd Pension and Life Assurance Scheme Trusts, Alfred Herbert v Hancocks (High Court) [1960] 1 WLR 271

Effect of informal literature – interpretation of informal literature

Facts and Decision

The terms of a pension scheme were not, the Court held, to be found exclusively in the terms issued on the certificate of membership. The certificate was merely evidence of the fact that the employee had become a member of the scheme. It was quite natural that it should have endorsed on the back of it some of the main provisions of the scheme. In this case when the chairman and governing director sent out the scheme booklet setting out the rules, he asked the employees to study it and fill in their forms of application after reading it. Since there was no contradiction between the certificate and the rules, there was no reason whatsoever for saying that the power of amendment, which was not on the certificate of membership, was not part of the scheme. Had there been a contradiction, very different considerations would have arisen.

[1.16.2]

Bestrustees v Stuart (High Court, unreported, 10 April 2001)

Interpretation of informal literature

Principle

It is important to bear in mind that a pension scheme announcement was sent to the members of the scheme, some of whom were receiving pensions, and most of whom were deferred members of the scheme. They were individuals who were not legally qualified, and it was through their eyes that the document should be read.

[1.16.3]

Dorrell v May & Baker (High Court) [1991] PLR 31 at paras 47–60

Effect of informal literature – interpretation of informal literature

Facts and Decision

A pension scheme booklet directed that the rights and obligations of members were set out in the trust deed and rules, and that these were legal documents using terms which the average reader would find difficult to understand. It also emphasised that the booklet was for information purposes only, and must not be taken as in any way interpreting or modifying the trust deed and rules of the scheme. Rather, it gave instructions as to how they could be inspected. The rules therefore were, the Court held, the right documents to consult in cases of dispute.

[1.16.4]

ITN v Ward (High Court) [1997] OPLR 147, [1997] PLR 131 at paras 22–23, 32

Effect of informal literature – interpretation of informal literature

Principle

Where deciding whether pension scheme booklets and announcements form the basis of an estoppel by convention, one must look at all the relevant circumstances. The question of whether those documents are misleading, and whether in particular they give rise to or are evidence of an underlying common assumption between the parties, and whether members could reasonably have relied upon them as setting out accurately how the scheme would operate, can only be assessed by looking at them as a whole and having regard to their function. The booklet is merely the employer's or trustee's attempt to summarise the meaning and effect of the scheme and its rules. Such booklets are usually deliberately phrased in general terms in an attempt to make them more readily intelligible to those members who read them. Any precis will lose some of the detail. It was important to take account of any statements that booklets were expressly stated to be summary and incomplete, and that amendments or additions to the scheme could be made at any time.

[1.16.5]

Lansing Linde v Alber (High Court) [2000] OPLR 1 at 39H–41C, 43B–44H, [2000] PLR 15

Effect of informal literature

Facts and Decision

The Court held that where a new edition of a pension scheme booklet, inviting employees to join a pension scheme, had stated a normal retirement date which was not reflected in the terms of the scheme rules, and the booklet stated that the scheme rules governed the scheme, it was correct to say that the offer to join the scheme was on the terms of the scheme rules.

In the case, the key question was the normal retirement date that operated. The scheme rules were sex-discriminatory, but the booklet purported to equalise benefits at age 65. The only female member had not focussed on the issue of her normal retirement date, and had not acted consciously in the belief that her normal retirement date was as stated in the booklet. The Court held that the booklet's statement of normal retirement date was simply wrong, and the company and the trustees had no good reason for believing the booklet to be correct. The booklet told the member that her rights were governed by the scheme rules and that (in effect) she could not rely on the booklet. No estoppel by convention arose. The transmission of the amended booklet had no impact on the member's normal retirement date. It was thus not unconscionable for the member to assert her true normal retirement date, nor to hold the company and the trustees to the legal position.

1.17 – Rectifying mistakes in scheme documentation

[1.17.1]

AMP (UK) Plc v Barker (High Court) [2001] PLR 77

Rectification – mistake

Facts and Decision

The trustees of a pension scheme resolved to improve benefits on incapacity, and this was duly documented with the consent of the principal employer by a rule change. It had been overlooked that benefits on employees leaving service were linked to benefits provided on incapacity, with the effect that the amendment dramatically improved leaving service benefits. The principal employer applied to Court:

(a)   for the rules to be rectified; or

(b)   to have the amendments set aside on the basis that the principal employer's consent was vitiated by mistake; or alternatively

(c)   for an order setting aside the amendments on the basis that the trustees' resolution was vitiated by a failure to take into account material considerations which would or might have affected their decision.

The Court held that the reality of the matter was that the trustees had not realised that they were increasing early leaver benefits at a cost of millions. If they had appreciated it, they would have appreciated the absurd nature of what was being done and would have required an assurance that the principal employer would meet the cost (which would never have been given). The trustees could not enter into an amendment unless their wishes happened to coincide with those of the principal employer. Consequently their intentions must converge, but they do not need to agree *inter se*. The resolution could not be rectified to reflect the intentions of the trustees when that was not also the intention of the principal employer, for otherwise the resolution could take a form to which the employer had not consented, and the consent of the employer was an essential part of the machinery of amendment. There was cogent evidence in this case of a continuing common intention to affect only incapacity benefits. Rectification was possible even if the parties had quite deliberately used the wording in the instrument; *Re Butlin's Settlement [1976] Ch 251* was followed. The members were not in the position of bona fide purchasers for value without notice: it was true that they had given consideration for their pension rights, but they had given no additional consideration for the rights which the rule changes mistakenly conferred on them. Accordingly the Court granted rectification as asked. The Court would also have set aside the principal employer's consent to the amendment for mistake if it had been necessary.

Comment

Rectifying trusts of any type is very difficult to achieve. This case is notable for the degree of flexibility which the Court showed. The previous attempt at rectification of a pension scheme which had reached court, *Lansing Linde v Alber [2000] OPLR 1*, had failed completely. In that case, the Court had not accepted the evidence of the trustees and the employer as to what their common intention was, and therefore refused to grant the rectification.

In this case, the Court found the evidence much more convincing. This was perhaps unsurprising, given the obvious anomaly which the amendment had created, while no obvious anomaly was under consideration in *Lansing Linde v Alber*. What was more surprising was that the Court swept past all the technical difficulties of rectification. It had no difficulty in finding that the trustees could obtain rectification even when they intended to agree to the precise words used. While the Court was following authority, the principle feels suspect. After all, in this case the trustees had every intention of changing incapacity benefits in exactly the way carried out. What was really being complained of was not the change made, but the fact that the trustees and the employer did not make the necessary changes to ensure that other benefits remained unaltered.

The other grounds for the Court's decision seem more reliable. The review of the trustees' decision-making process and the setting aside of their decision in accordance with the rule in *Re Hastings-Bass [1974] 2 All ER 193* is an entirely orthodox application of that principle. The proposed setting aside of the rule change on the basis that the employer had acted under a mistake in giving its consent is new law, but is logical. This principle will, however, not be applied lightly: members should be able to rely with some assurance on the benefits which they have apparently been promised.

[1.17.2]

Lansing Linde v Alber (High Court) [2000] OPLR 1, [2000] PLR 15

Rectification

Facts and Decision

A company and its pension scheme's trustees altered the scheme rules by deed to comply with the requirements of *Article 141* of the *Treaty of Rome*. They did this by increasing the female members' normal retirement date to 65 in line with that of men, but also by giving men and women the right between age 60 and 65 to take an immediate pension unreduced by reason of the fact that it was being taken early. The employer maintained that the intention in this case was that the member would require the consent of the employer and the trustees, and applied for rectification. The Court did not rectify the scheme rules. On the facts, the Court concluded that the company and the trustees did not have such an intention at the time the deed was being considered and executed. For deferred members, no intention had been formed at all, but when the deed was executed, the only shared intention was to sign the deed blindly. An outward expression of trustees' and employer's accord was necessary before the Court would rectify a trust.

1.18 – Calculation of scheme offsets

[1.18.1]

Department of Health v Pensions Ombudsman and Moss (Court of Appeal) [1998] OPLR 179

Calculation of offset

Principle

Dr Moss was employed by the NHS and was a member of the NHS Pension Scheme, a statutory scheme. He took retirement at age 60 on an immediate pension. When he reached age 65, his pension was reduced under a provision in the scheme regulations. The scheme calculated the deduction by notionally reducing his pension at age 60 and applied retrospectively the pension increases awarded in the intervening years to the reduced pension. Dr Moss argued that the deduction as calculated should have been made from his pension at age 65. On considering the interaction of the scheme regulation and *s 59(5)* of the *Social Security Pensions Act 1975*, the Court held that the scheme's approach was correct. While a recalculation was required, it was for the future, not for the past, and it did not deprive the pensioner of anything to which he had already become entitled.

1.19 – Operation of underpin

[1.19.1]

Spooner v British Telecommunications (High Court) [2000] PLR 65

Historical protection of benefits – voluntary redundancy

Facts and Decision

The trustees of the BT pension scheme applied to Court for guidance on the correct interpretation of the scheme rules on various points. Its constitution stated that it would provide like superannuation benefits to the Principal Civil Service Pension Scheme, from which it had originated, for employees in service on 1 December 1971. That scheme provided a mixture of pension benefits, and benefits for compensation of loss of office. However, the BT pension scheme had not offered its employees some of these benefits for compensation for loss of office. On a proper construction, the Court held that 'like superannuation benefits' included benefits for compensation for loss of office. The Civil Service Scheme offered special benefits on redundancy for employees in mobile grades (being managerial employees with a mobility obligation in their contract of employment). This was a like superannuation benefit, and although there were no directly comparable employees, relevant members who were employed at a managerial level qualified for this benefit. It was available not only to those who were made compulsorily redundant, but also to those who took voluntary redundancy. Those who had taken voluntary redundancy could not be stopped by the employer from claiming the additional benefit from the BT pension scheme trustees, and those who had elected to change to a different class of membership in ignorance of the fact that they were giving up this benefit were entitled to rescind that election.

1.20 – Adding new sections to the pension scheme

[1.20.1]

Barclays Bank v Holmes (High Court) [2000] PLR 339 at paras 53, 54–55, 59–61

New sections – funding

Facts and Decision

In the absence of a specific provision permitting such a course, the Court held that the trustees of one scheme could not use any of the assets in that scheme for the benefit of another scheme. That the trustees of the two schemes are identical and that the purposes of the two trusts are similar in no way alters that conclusion. There was no intrinsic reason as a matter of general law why an employer cannot set up a pension scheme with a final salary section and a money purchase section: whether or not it had in fact done so was a matter of construction. *Section 149* of the *Pensions Act 1995* supported this view. *Hughes Aircraft v Jacobson [1999] 28 PBLR 20* was considered. It is unclear, the Court also observed, whether there was a presumption that where a hybrid scheme was set up under a single document, there were intended to be two trust funds. If there was such a presumption, it was not a particularly strong one, since the overall purpose of the two types of scheme was the same.

[1.20.2]

Hughes Aircraft v Jacobson (United States Supreme Court, 25 January 1999) 105 F3d 1288 and 128 F3d 1305, reversed, [1999] 28 PBLR 20

New sections – funding

Facts and Decision

An employer operated a contributory defined benefit pension scheme from 1955. By 1986, the scheme was heavily in surplus. The employer suspended its own contributions, introduced a generous early retirement programme and closed the existing basis of membership to new employees. The employer then set up a non-contributory section for new members, offering less generous benefits. Some of the long-standing members objected on the grounds that the employer was improperly using surplus. The Court held that there was no disclosable cause of action. The amendments did not affect the rights of pre-existing members and the employer did not use surplus for its own benefit. The members had no interest in surplus. It was essential to understand the difference between a defined contributions scheme and a defined benefits scheme. A defined contribution scheme was one where employees and employers could contribute to the scheme and the employer's contribution was fixed, and the employee received whatever level of benefits the amount contributed on his or her behalf would provide. Under such schemes by definition there could never be an insufficiency of funds to cover promised benefits, since each beneficiary was entitled to whatever assets are dedicated to his or her individual account. A defined benefit scheme consisted of a general pool of assets rather than individual dedicated accounts. Such a scheme as its name implied was one where the employee upon retirement was entitled to a fixed periodic payment. The asset pool could be funded by employer or employee contributions, or a combination of both. But the employer typically bore the entire investment risk and – short of the consequences of scheme termination – must cover any underfunding as the result of a shortfall that may occur from the scheme's investments. Conversely, if the defined benefits scheme was overfunded, the employer could reduce or suspend its contributions. The structure of a defined benefit scheme reflected the risk borne by the employer. Given the employer's obligation to make up any shortfall, no scheme member had a claim to any particular asset that composed a part of the scheme's general asset pool. Nothing in United States statute suggested that an amendment creating a new benefit structure also created a second scheme. Therefore the employer could not have violated the United States statutory vesting requirements or anti-inurement provisions, by using assets from the surplus attributable to the employees' contributions to fund the non-contributory structure.

[1.20.3]

Kemble v Hicks (No. 2) (High Court) [1999] OPLR 1 at 5G–7H

New sections – funding

Facts and Decision

An employer established a money purchase section in its final salary scheme. The money purchase section was documented by booklet and no amending deed was ever executed. The booklet provided that the employer would contribute at the rate of 8% of each member's basic annual salary, and these contributions together with the member's own contribution of 4% of basic annual salary would be allocated to the member's investment account. All employer contributions were paid from the surplus in the final salary section. The Court held that where a money purchase scheme was established under the same trust as a final salary scheme, it may be correct to regard them as part of the same overall scheme. However, within this overall scheme, the establishment of a money purchase scheme involved the setting up of what was a scheme quite separate from the final salary scheme, and to which different considerations applied. It was, therefore, improper for the employer contributions to be met from this surplus.

Part 2 – Powers and Duties

2 – Introduction

Most textbooks divide the classification of powers, duties and discretions by reference to types of powers. Accordingly, the sections on trustee powers, trustee duties, and employer powers and duties are usually found in entirely separate chapters. The powers vested in actuaries, if considered at all, are found under a different chapter again. In terms of legal theory, that separation is correct. In practice, those designing pension schemes think less about the different types of powers than about the identity of the people controlling them. I have therefore gathered together these categories under one heading. Of course, these themes are developed in many other parts of this book, since general principles on the exercise of powers and duties fall for specific application in relation to, for example, powers of amendment and powers to wind up a scheme.

The courts have had to adapt to new problems in relation to pension scheme duties. The typical private trust has a limited number of beneficiaries, all of whom are well known to the trustees. The typical pension scheme has a large number of beneficiaries, few of whom are well known to any of the trustees. Where trustees are exercising discretionary powers, the categories of potential beneficiaries may be different in kind from those in a private trust.

Curiously, however, some of the provisions which have been the subject of repeated litigation are those powers which are most akin to provisions in a private trust: the power to determine who receives the lump sum death benefit and the power or duty to determine whether someone qualifies for an ill-health pension. Considerations relating to these powers are reviewed in Part 5 on pension benefits.

The courts have in general not accepted that trustees are subject to more stringent duties in relation to the exercise of their powers merely because the beneficiaries have secured their rights for value. The courts have recognised on occasion that the fact that the beneficiaries are not volunteers is relevant to the process of interpreting scheme documentation, but with the possible exception of *Kerr v British Leyland (Staff) Trustees Limited* (unreported), this approach has not been carried over into the exercise of trustee powers. *Edge v Pensions Ombudsman* and *Wilson v Law Debenture [1995] 2 All ER 337* illustrate the courts' reluctance to impose further restrictions on the exercise of trustee powers and duties.

The courts have, however, developed certain trust law principles out of all recognition in a pensions context. One of the maxims of equity was that equity is equality. That may well continue to subsist in the context of a private trust, but the courts have taken their cue from *Re Baden [1969] 1 All ER 1016* (not a pension case) in determining that the trustees of a large discretionary trust need not have any qualms about preferring some beneficiaries over others, as illustrated by both *Edge v Pensions Ombudsman* and *Elliott v Pensions Ombudsman [1998] OPLR 21*. On the other hand, the mere fact that a scheme is a defined benefits scheme in surplus does not exempt the trustees from trust duties, as the critical remarks in *McDonald v Horn* testify.

As well as straining existing categorisations of powers and duties, many members of pension schemes want obligations imposed on trustees and employers that are not normally imposed on trustees and settlors of a private trust. So far, by and large, the courts have held out against this. No new duties to communicate information to members have been imposed by the courts on trustees or employers. Indeed, in some circumstances, as envisaged in *NGN Staff Pension Plan Trustees v Simmons [1994] OPLR 1*, the trustees may be under a duty actively not to communicate relevant information. The problem has been partially addressed by Parliament through extensive disclosure obligations on trustees imposed by statute.

The overwhelming trend is one of continuation of traditional trust law principles, applied in a new context. A good example of this is what is usually referred to as the rule in *Hastings-Bass*. *Re Hastings-Bass [1974] 2 All ER 193* was a case concerning the exercise of trustee duties in a traditional private trust. The Court formulated a test which set out the basis on which the courts would intervene with the exercise of a trustee discretion. This test has been enthusiastically applied and extended by the courts in pensions cases as diverse as *Mettoy Pension Trustees v Evans [1991] 2 All ER 513*, *Fisons v Stannard [1991] PLR 227* and *AMP (UK) PLC v Barker [2001] PLR 77*.

Perhaps the most interesting development of the law on powers and duties is the way in which the employer's implied obligation of good faith has been imported into its obligations in relation to the pension scheme. This obligation, which was first developed by the courts as recently as 1980, now permeates every aspect of the employer's relationship with the pension scheme. In a lecture to the Association of Pension Lawyers in 2000, Lord Millett suggested that the employer's implied obligation of good faith was an unnecessary concept in the context of a pension scheme, since it added nothing to the general trust law rule against frauds on powers. However, since then the House of Lords has looked at the concept in *International Power v Healy [2001] PLR 121*, and it now seems unlikely that Lord Millett's attractive suggestion will be adopted by the courts. It was in any case a slightly surprising submission, given that Lord Millett had himself already taken part in *Air Jamaica v Charlton [1999] 1 WLR 1399*, where the doctrine was applied with apparent approval by the Privy Council.

One interesting problem which the courts have yet to consider is the duty of a scheme actuary, where he or she has been given a power or a duty under the trust deed and rules. It is entirely possible that the duties under the trust deed and rules may be in some way objectionable to the actuary. The actuary almost certainly did not execute the trust deed and rules under which the power was introduced. If the actuary were to refuse to carry out the obligation, or were only willing to carry it out on terms which were unacceptable to the trustees, could the actuary be obliged to perform the duty? The manner in which the terms of the trust and the terms of the actuary's retainer were to be resolved could be a very difficult problem.

2.1 – Trustees' powers, duties and discretions

General

[2.1.1]

AMP (UK) Plc v Barker (High Court) [2001] PLR 77

Trustees' powers – relevant considerations

Facts and Decision

The trustees of a pension scheme resolved to improve benefits on incapacity, and this was duly documented with the consent of the principal employer by a rule change. It had been overlooked that benefits on employees leaving service were linked to benefits provided on incapacity, with the effect that the amendment dramatically improved leaving service benefits. The principal employer applied to Court:

(a) for the rules to be rectified; or
(b) to have the amendments set aside on the basis that the principal employer's consent was vitiated by mistake; or alternatively
(c) for an order setting aside the amendments on the basis that the trustees' resolution was vitiated by a failure to take into account material considerations which would or might have affected their decision.

The Court held that the reality of the matter was that the trustees had not realised that they were increasing early leaver benefits at a cost of millions. If they had appreciated it, they would have appreciated the absurd nature of what was being done and would have required an assurance that the principal employer would meet the cost (which would never have been given). If it had been necessary, the Court would have set aside the amendments on the basis that the trustees' resolution was vitiated by a failure to take into account material considerations which would or might have affected their decision, because the trustees would not have passed the resolution if they had taken the relevant matters into account. *Re Hastings-Bass [1974] 2 All ER 193* was applied.

[2.1.3]

Re Baden's Deed Trusts, McPhail v Doulton (House of Lords) [1971] AC 424 at 449

Trustees' powers – categorisation of powers – trustees' duties

Principles

A trustee of an employees' benefit fund, whether given a power or a trust power, is still a trustee, and he would surely consider in either case that he has a fiduciary duty: he is most likely to have been selected as a suitable person to administer it from his knowledge and experience, and would consider he has a responsibility to do so according to its purpose. It would be a complete mis-description of his position to say that, if what he has is a power unaccompanied by an imperative trust to distribute, he cannot be controlled by the Court unless he exercised it capriciously, or outside the field permitted by the trust. Any trustee would surely make it his duty to know what is the permissible area of selection and then consider responsibly, in individual cases, whether a contemplated beneficiary was within the power and whether, in relation to other possible claimants, a particular grant was appropriate.

> 'As a matter of reason, to hold that a principle of equal division applies to trusts such as the present is certainly paradoxical. Equal division is surely the last thing the settlor ever intended: equal division among all may, probably would, produce a result beneficial to none. Why suppose that the court would lend itself to a whimsical execution? . . . Equal division may be sensible and has been decreed, in the case of family trusts, for a limited class; here there is life in the maxim "equity is equality," but the cases provide numerous examples where this has not been so, and a different type of execution has been ordered, appropriate to the circumstances.'

[2.1.4]

Bartlett v Barclays Trust Co Ltd (No 1) (High Court) [1980] Ch 515 at 534

Trustees' duties – professional trustees

Principle

A higher duty of care is plainly due from someone like a trust corporation which carries on a specialised business of trust management than an ordinary trustee. Just as under the law of contract, a professional person possessed of a particular skill is liable for breach of contract if he or she neglects to use the skill and experience which he or she possesses, so a professional corporate trustee is liable for breach of trust if loss is caused to the trust fund because it neglects to exercise the special skill and care which it professes to have.

[2.1.5]

Bestrustees v Stuart (High Court, unreported, 10 April 2001)

Trustees' powers – partly invalid exercise of power – relevant considerations

Facts and Decision

The Court held that where trustees had exercised a power retrospectively which was only capable of being effective from the date at which it was exercised, the Court could salvage the exercise of the power for the future if there was a boundary between that part of the exercise which was valid and that part which was invalid. The correct approach to determining this question was not one of language but one of concept, and the two components of this single exercise were easily separable one from the other.

The Court must also consider whether there was anything in the exercise of the power which led it to believe that, had the trustees been told that they were not entitled to exercise the power retrospectively, they would not have exercised the power at all, or in the way in which they did. *Re Hastings-Bass [1974] 2 All ER 193, Mettoy Pension Trustees v Evans [1991] 2 All ER 513* and *AMP (UK) Plc v Barker [2001] PLR 77* were considered.

[2.1.6]

Buckley v Hudson Forge (High Court) [1999] OPLR 249 at 268A-G, [1999] PLR 151 at paras 98–102

Trustees' powers – relevant considerations – consultation of employer

Facts and Decision

The Court held that where a pension trustee had taken the interests of the wrong employer into consideration when exercising a discretion whether to augment benefits, on the facts the trustee would have reached a different decision had he taken the right interests into consideration. *Re Hastings-Bass [1974] 2 All ER 193* and *Mettoy Pension Trustees v Evans*

[1991] 2 All ER 513 were applied, with the modification that the Court will also interfere if the trustee has taken into account considerations which he or she ought not to have taken into account.

In a pensions context, given the matrix of contract, and in particular of employment, it may not be strictly necessary for a trustee to consult an employer on the exercise of a power to increase benefits, but it was certainly natural.

[2.1.7]

Buttle v Saunders (High Court) [1950] 2 All ER 193

Trustees' duties – relevant considerations

Facts and Decision

Trustees have an overriding duty, the Court held, to obtain the best price which they could on the sale of a property for beneficiaries. It would, however, be an unfortunate simplification of the problem if one were to take the view that the mere production of an increased offer at any stage, however late in the negotiations for sale, should throw on the trustees a duty to accept the higher offer and resile from the existing offer. Trustees have such a discretion in the matter as will allow them to act with proper prudence. Trustees may pray in aid the common-sense rule underlying the old proverb: 'A bird in the hand is worth two in the bush', and in appropriate cases could disregard speculative higher offers. Each case must turn on its own facts.

[2.1.8]

Cowan v Scargill (High Court) [1984] 2 All ER 750 at 760, [1985] Ch 270 at 286–7, [1990] PLR 169

Trustees' duties

Principle

The duty of trustees is to exercise their powers in the best interests of the present and future beneficiaries of the trust, holding the scales impartially between different classes of beneficiaries. This duty of the trustees towards their beneficiaries is paramount.

[2.1.9]

Crowe Engineering v Lynch (Ireland, High Court, 24 July 1991) 36 PBLR 9

Trustees' powers – nature of member's interest

Principle

When considering the exercise of a trustee power to distribute benefits on the death of a member, it was not the case that because pension scheme money represented deferred earnings of the deceased, it was his or her right to direct the trustees and that they were obliged in equity to follow. All the Court was concerned with were enforceable rights, whether expressed as legal or equitable rights. The deceased did not have an enforceable right to direct where the payment of the monies should go. The discretion of the trustees was exactly that, a discretion.

[2.1.10]

Edge v Pensions Ombudsman (Court of Appeal) [2000] 3 WLR 79, [1999] OPLR 179, [1999] PLR 215

Trustees' powers – trustees' duties – relevant considerations

Facts and Decision

The trustees of a pension scheme in surplus, which needed to be eliminated in order to avoid tax liability, agreed with the employer that the surplus would be used to reduce employer contributions and improve benefits for active members only. Some pensioners complained to the Pensions Ombudsman.

The Court held that, properly understood, the duty for trustees to act impartially is no more than the ordinary duty which the law imposes on a person who is entrusted with the exercise of a discretionary power: that he or she exercises the power for the purpose for which it is given, giving proper consideration to the matters which are relevant and excluding from consideration matters which are irrelevant. If pension fund trustees do that, they cannot be criticised if they reach a decision which appears to prefer the claims of one interest over others. The preference will be the result of a proper exercise of the discretionary power. The principles under consideration in a private pension scheme were analogous to those in the different context of public law cases (though the extent to which the analogy could be taken was not under consideration): *Harris v Shuttleworth*

[1995] OPLR 79, Wild v Smith [1996] OPLR 129 and *Associated Provincial Picture Houses v Wednesbury Corporation [1948] 1 KB 223* were considered.

The Court also held that appropriate inferences may be drawn from any failure of the trustees to give an explanation when that explanation is called for, and the explanation may be examined critically. Furthermore, when negotiating with the employers, trustees are not obliged to put forward proposals that they do not think are fair to the employers. In this case, the trustees were in no real position to bargain with the employers, and they were entitled to conclude that 'half a loaf was better than no bread', and put forward a proposal which the employers would be likely to find attractive.

[2.1.11]

Elliott v Pensions Ombudsman (High Court) [1998] OPLR 21 at 33A

Trustees' powers – preferring the interests of some classes of beneficiary

Principle

It is not correct to state that a trustee's actions in preferring certain classes of beneficiary over others is a breach of trust. In many a trust, a trustee has a discretion as to the distribution between different classes of beneficiary, the exercise of which in favour of one class will inevitably involve a preference of that class over others.

[2.1.12]

Fisons v Stannard (Court of Appeal) [1991] PLR 227 at paras 35–39, 65, [1992] IRLR 27 at 31

Trustees' powers – relevant considerations

Principle

When exercising a power to transfer out pension scheme beneficiaries, the Court held that both the transferring members and the remaining members had contributed to the scheme and a duty was owed by the trustees to both alike. In order to give properly informed consideration to the duty, the trustees should have considered the current value of the scheme and its implications. If they had done so, it might have materially affected their decision. Their determination was, therefore, flawed and the transfer amount required recalculation. In *Re Hastings-Bass [1975] Ch 25, 41*, however, it was beyond doubt that the trustees would have acted in the same way on the point at issue in that case. (See also [2.1.30]).

In the judgment of Staughton LJ: 'In a matter as important as this where a very substantial sum was to be transferred from one fund to another, I think it right to insist on a correct procedure in the decision making process.'

[2.1.13]

Froese v Montreal Trust (British Columbia Appeal Court) [1996] 76 BCAC 81

Custodian trustee – trustees' duties – duty of care

Facts and Decision

Montreal Trust was the custodian trustee and administrator of Johnson Terminals' pension scheme. The employer stopped paying contributions in 1986, but the custodian trustee took no action, neither informing the members nor taking the point up with the employer. The custodian trustee had accepted its responsibilities in an agreement with the employer and declaration of trust, which included exonerations for the custodian trustee. The employer became insolvent and the scheme was seriously underfunded as a result of the non-payment of employer contributions. The custodian trustee also reduced some pensioners' entitlement under the winding-up order of priorities, including those of Mr Froese, on the basis that they had not been properly commenced. Mr Froese sued the custodian trustee for breach of trust. The Court held that the custodian trustee owed a common law duty of care in tort to the beneficiaries, and the beneficiaries were not bound by the exoneration clauses. The duty of care, however, was not unlimited, arising only within the scope of the trustee's engagement. The custodian trustee had no duty to volunteer information to the beneficiaries. However, there was more involved in this case than volunteering information. The custodian trustee's duty of care required it to make enquiries of the employer and possibly of the actuary, which would have permitted the custodian trustee to make a prudent decision about what should be done to protect the beneficiaries. It failed to do this and was therefore in breach of its duty. Mr Froese's pension was properly put into payment, and it was therefore wrongfully reduced. The custodian trustee as administrator owed a duty of care to the beneficiaries to ensure that the scheme was properly wound up. While the custodian trustee could not be expected to check every calculation, the casual approach taken to this matter did not conform with its duty of care as an administrator.

[2.1.14]

Harris v Shuttleworth (Court of Appeal) [1995] OPLR 79 at 86–87, [1994] PLR 47, [1994] ICR 991 at 999

Trustees' duties – reviewability

Principle

Pension scheme trustees must ask themselves the correct questions. They must direct themselves correctly in law; in particular they must adopt a correct construction of the pension fund rules. They must not arrive at a perverse decision, i.e. a decision to which no reasonable body of trustees could arrive, and they must take into account all relevant but no irrelevant factors. Only if the trustees fail on one of these grounds can the Court intervene.

[2.1.15]

Re Hastings-Bass (Court of Appeal) [1975] Ch 25, 41

Trustees' powers – relevant considerations

Principle

Where a trustee is given a discretion as to some matter under which he acts in good faith:

> 'the court should not interfere with his action, notwithstanding that it does not have the full effect which he intended, unless (1) what he has achieved is unauthorised by the power conferred upon him, or (2) it is clear that he would not have acted as he did (a) had he not taken into account considerations which he should not have taken into account or (b) had he not failed to take into account considerations which he ought to have taken into account.'

[2.1.16]

Hillsdown v Pensions Ombudsman (High Court) [1997] 1 All ER 862, [1996] OPLR 291 at 309B-D, 309H–310A, 311D-F, 311G–312E, [1996] PLR 427 at paras 62, 65, 71–76

Trustees' powers – purpose of the power – collateral purpose

Principle

Powers in a pension scheme may not be exercised for a purpose or with an intention beyond the scope of, or not justified by, the instrument creating the power. This principle is commonly known as that of frauds on the power: *Vatcher v Paull [1915] AC 372* at *378* was followed.

A payment may be the purpose behind the exercise of a power, even if the payment can be described as the price for securing a desired benefit. The person who pays a price for an article out of a fund under his or her control has inevitably, as part of his or her purpose, both the acquisition of the article and the payment of its price. No doubt his or her motive is to secure the article. But motive and purpose are not the same and it is the latter which counts.

An exercise of a transfer power in such circumstances could be an improper use of the power for a collateral purpose. Such a finding would not be in conflict with the decision in *Re Vauxhall Motor Pension Fund [1989] PLR 31*. It was true that the inclusion of a specific limitation on a transfer power supported the proposition that it would be wrong to read other limitations in. However, it did not touch the question of whether the power was used for a collateral purpose. A trustee could act honestly but nevertheless intrinsically in breach of trust and in a manner damaging to the interests of the members.

[2.1.17]

HR v JAPT (High Court, interlocutory) [1997] OPLR 123 at 133H–134A, [1997] PLR 99 at para 45

Corporate trustees – duties of directors

Facts and Decision

Directors of trustee companies, the Court held, ordinarily stand in a fiduciary duty only to the company itself: *Bath v Standard Land Co [1911] 1 Ch 618* was followed. While exceptional facts can be envisaged, in which the implication of a direct fiduciary relationship between a beneficiary of a pension scheme and the directors of company acting as trustee of that scheme was justified, such an implication could not be drawn from directors of a trustee company acting as such directors might be expected to act (alleged carelessness apart).

[2.1.18]

Jones v AMP (High Court, New Zealand) [1995] PLR 53 at paras 73–74

Trustees' duties – professional trustees

Principle

A trustee whose business is as a trustee company is not under a higher duty of care than any other trustee.

[2.1.19]

Law Debenture v Malley (High Court) [1999] OPLR 167 at 174E

Trustees' powers – reviewability

Principle

When the Pensions Ombudsman is to overturn a decision which under the rules of a pension scheme is a final decision, he must apply the reasonableness test set out in *Associated Provincial Picture Houses v Wednesbury Corporation [1948] 1 KB 223*, and find perversity.

[2.1.20]

Learoyd v Whiteley (House of Lords) [1887] 12 App Cas 727 (per Lord Halsbury)

Trustees' duties

Principle

A trustee must use ordinary care and caution, and although it is impossible to lay down an absolute rule, there are some limits beyond which it is manifest no trustee is authorized in going. It is quite clear that a trustee is entitled to rely upon skilled persons in matters in which he or she cannot be expected to be experienced. He or she may perhaps rely upon a lawyer on some matters of law, and in this case he or she would be entitled to rely on a valuer upon a pure question of valuation. But unless one examines with reference to what question the skilled person gives advice, it is possible to confuse the reliance which may be properly placed upon the skill of a skilled person with the judgment which the trustee himself or herself is bound to form on the subject of the performance of his or her trust. It is not true to say that one is entitled to consider the special qualities or degree of intelligence of the particular trustee. Persons who accept that office must be supposed to accept it with the responsibility at all events for the possession of ordinary care and prudence.

[2.1.21]

Manning v Drexel Burnham Lambert (High Court) [1995] I WLR 32, [1994] OPLR 71, [1994] PLR 75

Trustees' duties – conflicts of interest – nature of pension trust

Principle

There is no material way in which the general rules of equity relating to trustees' duties when a conflict of duty and interest arises can be said to apply to trustees and fiduciaries generally, but never apply to pension trustees. A broad argument that pension trusts are radically different had previously been rejected in *Cowan v Scargill [1984] 2 All ER 750.*

[2.1.22]

McDonald v Horn (Court of Appeal) [1994] OPLR 281, [1994] PLR 155

Trustees' duties

Principle

It was unacceptable if pension scheme trustees took the view that provided the fund was in surplus, the way in which it was invested and administered was none of the members' business. The whole fund is a trust fund, whatever may be the beneficial interests on a winding-up, and the members are entitled to openness in the way it is run.

[2.1.23]

Mettoy Pension Trustees v Evans (High Court) [1991] 2 All ER 513, [1990] 1 WLR 1587, [1990] PLR 9 (paras 160, 189–198, 200)

Trustees' powers – classification of powers – relevant considerations

Principle

The Court held that the classification of trustee powers set out in *Re D'Angibau [1879] 15 Ch D 228* at *232–233* may well be of antiquarian interest only, and gave no assistance in this case. A more pertinent classification divides fiduciary discretions into four categories.

- Category 1 comprises any power given to a person to determine the destination of trust property, without that person being under any obligation to exercise the power or to preserve it.
- Category 2 comprises any power conferred on the trustees of the property, or on any other person as a trustee of the power itself.
- Category 3 comprises any discretion which is really a duty to form a judgment as to the existence or otherwise of particular circumstances giving rise to particular consequences.
- Category 4 comprises discretionary trusts, that is to say cases where someone, usually but not necessarily the trustees, is under a duty to select from among a class of beneficiaries those who are to receive income or capital of the trust property.

The rule in *Hastings-Bass* (see [2.1.15]) is indeed a principle of law, and may be stated in its positive converse, that the courts will interfere with the exercise of a trustee's discretion if it is clear that the trustee would not have acted as it did had it not failed to take into account considerations which it ought to have taken into account. However, the courts do not have a flexible jurisdiction to reform trust documents on the ground of lack of knowledge or lack of understanding on the part of their makers. The rule in *Hastings-Bass* is not necessarily an all-or-nothing argument: there may be cases where the Court is satisfied that the trustees would have acted in the same way but with, for instance, the omission of a particular provision in a deed. The Court may declare only that provision void. The remedy to be adopted will depend on the circumstances of each case. The question as to whether the trustee failed in its duty to take into account all relevant considerations is one which should be judged on a balance of probabilities.

[2.1.24]

National Trustees Co. of Australasia Ltd v General Finance Co. of Australasia Ltd (Privy Council) [1905] AC 373 at 375–6

Trustees' duties – breaches of trust

Principle

When Counsel in argument cited Lindley MR in *Perrins v Bellamy [1899] 1 Ch 797*, quoting Selwyn LJ as saying 'The main duty of a trustee is to commit *judicious* breaches of trust', Lord Lindley intervened to state that 'The words "main duty" are a mistake. They ought to be "great use".'

[2.1.25]

NBC Pension Trustees v Harrod (High Court) [1999] OPLR 113, [2000] PLR 183

Trustees' duties

Facts and Decision

The National Bus Company pension scheme was wound up, and all assets and liabilities were distributed. Subsequently, a member successfully challenged the employers' actions in the run-up to the winding-up process, with the result that the employers agreed to pay further sums to the trustees for distribution to the beneficiaries of the scheme. While this process was ongoing, the trustees asked for guidance as to the extent to which they were obliged to comply with the obligations set out by the *Pensions Act 1995*. The Court held that the scheme was no longer an occupational pension scheme for the purposes of the *Pension Schemes Act 1993*, and so the *Pensions Act 1995* obligations did not apply to it.

[2.1.26]

Nestle v National Westminster Bank (Court of Appeal) [1992] OPLR 85

Trustees' duties – breaches of trust

Facts and Decision

National Westminster Bank was the trustee of a private trust from 1922 to 1986, during which time the trust increased in value from £50,000 to £269,000. If the trust had matched the returns on shares in that period, it would have increased to £2.6 million, while to match the increase in cost of living in that period it would have needed to increase to £1 million. The beneficiary who inherited in 1986 sued the Bank for breach of trust. The Court held that the trustee had misunderstood the extent of the investment power, and failed to conduct a regular and periodic review of the investments. This was not by itself sufficient to find a breach of trust. It was for the beneficiary to prove on a balance of probabilities that there was, or must have been, a loss, and that a prudent trustee knowing the scope of the trustee's investment power and conducting regular reviews would so have invested the trust funds as to make it worth more than it was worth when the beneficiary inherited it. The beneficiary in this case had not done this.

[2.1.27]

Re Pilkington Bros Ltd Workmen's Pension Fund (High Court) [1953] 2 All ER 816, [1953] 1 WLR 1084

Corporate trustees

Facts and Decision

The Pilkington pension scheme was registered as a friendly society under the *Friendly Societies Act 1896*. It proposed an amendment to its scheme rules permitting the replacement of the existing individual trustees with a corporate trustee, but the Registrar of Friendly Societies refused to register the amendment. While the provisions relating to the role of trustees under the *Act* related exclusively to individual trustees, the Court held that there was nothing in the *Act* which excluded the rule that a 'person' included a corporate body, and therefore the proposed amendment was not contrary to the *Act*.

[2.1.28]

South West Trains v Wightman (High Court) [1997] OPLR 249 at 260D–261B, 270F–271D, [1998] PLR 113 at paras 47–53, 103–109

Trustees' powers – effect on trustees of agreement between employer and trustees

Facts and Decision

When assessing whether proposed changes in specified pension rights are less favourable than the existing pension rights for the purposes of a statutory instrument, the Court held that it was proper to look outside the terms of the pension scheme and examine the actual cash effect of the proposed changes. The legislature was more likely to be concerned to protect practical rights 'sounding in money' as opposed to more hypothetical legal or conceptual rights. Clear words would be required before the Court would conclude otherwise.

Where the employer and the employees had reached a binding agreement on pensions issues, under which the employer could prevent the employees from claiming pension at a higher rate than that agreed, the Court held that the trustee may well be able to refuse to pay pensions at such a higher rate, whether or not the employer intervened. Any claim against the trustee for pension at the higher rate may well be an abuse of the process of the Court. The trustee may well be able to argue that there was no basis upon which a member could demand a higher pension than that which was contractually agreed with the employer. Since the trustee would be obliged to look at the contract of employment to identify the member's pay for the purposes of calculating his or her pension, the trustee may well effectively be bound to follow a term of the contract of employment which deems to set the rate of pensionable pay at a different rate from the rate that would be obtained by following the scheme rules.

[2.1.29]

Speight v Gaunt (Court of Appeal) [1883] 9 App Cas 1

Trustees' duties

Principle

Trustees are not to be held liable if they honestly, and without knowing anything that makes it exceptionally risky in the case under consideration, pursue the course that the ordinary prudent man of business would pursue.

Stannard v Fisons (High Court) [1990] PLR 201 at paras 183–184

Trustees' powers – relevant considerations

Principle

The rule in *Hastings-Bass* (see [2.1.15]) had applied in cases with common features:

- the trustees had a discretion which they were free to exercise or not as they thought fit;
- they had acted within the scope of that discretion;
- they had failed to take into account through ignorance the full effect of what they had decided to do, with a result that their action had a different effect from that which was intended; and
- the question was whether what they had done should therefore be set aside to some extent, with the answer depending on whether they would have exercised their discretion in the same way had they been fully informed of the effect of their decision.

Where none of these features were present, the rule is not applicable. Whether all of these features were necessary was not decided. (See also [2.1.12]).

[2.1.31]

Taylor v Lucas Pension Trust (High Court) [1994] OPLR 29, [1994] PLR 9

Trustees' duties

Principle

In a pension scheme where the employer is not a residual beneficiary, the employer nevertheless has an interest in surplus to the extent that it could be used to relieve it of its obligation to contribute. It was proper for trustees to bear such an interest in mind.

[2.1.32]

Turner v Turner (High Court) [1984] I Ch 100

Trustees' duties

Facts and Decision

Where trustees of a private trust had paid out money, not appreciating that they had a discretionary power to exercise which they had not considered, the payment out was set aside.

[2.1.33]

Re William Makin (High Court) [1993] OPLR 171, [1992] PLR 177

Trustees' powers – conflict of interest

Facts and Decision

William Makin & Sons Limited went into receivership in 1984 and liquidation in 1985. Its pension scheme had a substantial surplus deriving wholly from overfunding by the company, and went into winding-up on the company ceasing to carry on business. The employer was the trustee, and the trust deed gave the trustees a discretion to use any surplus on a winding-up to increase benefits to members. Any part of the surplus not so used was to be refunded to the employer. The Court held that if the power had become exercisable while the company was a going concern, the company could have exercised the power despite its conflict of interest. What the company could not have done would have been to have decided not to exercise the power or to refrain from exercising the power, with the consequence that the surplus or part of it would become payable to the company.

[2.1.34]

Worthington v Unilever (High Court, unreported, 17 June 1974)

Trustees' powers – relevant considerations

Principle

Mr Worthington was dismissed from employment. He had a history of ill-health, but this was not the formal ground of his dismissal. The trustees had a discretion to commute pensions where in the exceptional circumstances of the serious ill-health of the member, the provision of a retirement pension would not constitute a reasonable benefit. The trustees declined to exercise this discretion. The Court observed that the scheme was approved for the purposes of the Inland Revenue. In exercising their discretion, the trustees would need to take into account not only Mr Worthington's level of incapacity, but also the broad picture of whether or not it would be for his benefit and the benefit of his wife and family, if any, that he should receive a capital payment at once and lose the deferred annuity, and risk having no financial resources in his old age. They would also have to consider the position of the scheme as a whole. The Inland Revenue would not accept Mr Worthington's circumstances as appropriate for such a commutation of pension. If the approval of the Inland Revenue were to be withdrawn, the tax benefits enjoyed by all the members would be jeopardised. Mr Worthington would not be allowed to substitute his own discretion for that of the trustees.

[2.1.35]

Wrightson v Fletcher Challenge Nominees (High Court of New Zealand) [1999] PLR 317 at paras 99–102

Trustees' powers – reviewability – relevant considerations

Principle

The Court's role in reviewing a trustee's decision is limited. The Court is not a court of appeal from the trustee's decision. The Court will set aside the trustee's decision only where the trustee has:

(a)   acted in bad faith or with improper motive;
(b)   failed to exercise the discretion by considering the wrong question or misinterpreting the trust deed;
(c)   considered irrelevant considerations;
(d)   failed to consider relevant considerations; or
(e)   reached a decision that is perverse or capricious.

The standard of review does not alter because reasons are given by the trustee for its actions. Reasons simply make it easier, as an evidential matter, for the plaintiff to challenge the decision on the basis of relevant or irrelevant consideration. The duty concerning such relevant or irrelevant considerations extends to an appreciation of the significant facts and their relevance to the problem at hand. Failure to advert to, and correctly appreciate, a given fact or consideration will not provide a ground for intervention if the trustee's decision would have been the same in any event. The ground that the decision was perverse or capricious may have much in common with 'unreasonableness' in an administrative law context. (See also [2.1.36]).

[2.1.36]

Wrightson v Fletcher Challenge Nominees (Privy Council) [2000] All ER 89

Trustees' powers – reviewability – relevant considerations

Facts and Decision

The Privy Council held that while some of the matters that the trustee in this case had considered might appear to be irrelevant to the exercise of its discretion, most of them had been raised by the participating company whose interest was being considered, and the trustee could not be criticised for responding to them. (See also [2.1.35]).

Communications with members

[2.1.37]

Buckley v Hudson Forge (High Court) [1999] OPLR 249 at 270G–271D, [1999] PLR 151 at paras 113–116

Communication – contract

Facts and Decision

Where a letter to a pension scheme member incorrectly states the level of pension increases, but refers to regular increases in accordance with the scheme rules, the Court held that if the member takes action on the strength of the letter, that letter does not have the effect of a contract which overrides the rules.

[2.1.38]

Froese v Montreal Trust (British Columbia Appeal Court) [1996] 76 BCAC 81

Communication – duty of care

Facts and Decision

Montreal Trust was the custodian trustee and administrator of Johnson Terminals' pension scheme. The employer stopped paying contributions in 1986, but the custodian trustee took no action, neither informing the members nor taking the point up with the employer. The custodian trustee had accepted its responsibilities in an agreement with the employer and declaration of trust, which included exonerations for the custodian trustee. The employer became insolvent and the scheme was seriously underfunded as a result of the non-payment of employer contributions. Mr Froese sued the custodian trustee for breach of trust. The Court held that the custodian trustee owed a common law duty of care in tort to the beneficiaries, and the beneficiaries were not bound by the exoneration clauses. The duty of care, however, was not unlimited, arising only within the scope of the trustee's engagement. The custodian trustee had no duty to volunteer information to the beneficiaries. However, there was more involved in this case than volunteering information. The custodian trustee's duty of care required it to make enquiries of the employer and possibly of the actuary, which would have permitted the custodian trustee to make a prudent decision about what should be done to protect the beneficiaries. It failed to do this and was, therefore, in breach of its duty.

[2.1.39]

Hamar v Pensions Ombudsman (High Court) [1996] OPLR 55 at 64C–65E, [1995] PLR 1 at paras 45–47

Communication – trustees' duties

Principle

Trustees have an obligation to give information to a beneficiary of the existence of the trust, and by showing him or her documents, to give information. Trustees have no duty to go further and to give explanations. Still less are trustees obliged to give information as to how a particular beneficiary may obtain his or her portion in a particular trust fund or may exercise his or her statutory rights, particularly where they form the view that it was not in the interests of the remaining beneficiaries that he or she should be able to obtain the money in question. It is up to the beneficiary to seek advice and follow the correct statutory procedure. Trustees are not obliged to point the beneficiary in the right direction or to tell him or her of his or her errors, even assuming that they are aware that those errors existed.

[2.1.40]

NGN Staff Pension Plan Trustees v Simmons (High Court) [1994] OPLR 1

Communication – trustees' duties

Facts and Decision

When the Advocate-General gave his opinion in the *Coloroll* case, it was apparent that if it was followed by the European Court of Justice it would be to the advantage of male members in a pension scheme with unequalised actuarial factors to bring claims against the trustees as soon as possible. The NGN Staff Pension Plan trustees were trustees of such a plan, but it was in winding-up. They applied to Court to ask what they should do. The Court held that it was not for the trustees to initiate proceedings of any sort so as to improve the lot of one class of beneficiaries at the expense of another, unless there was an express power for the purpose, or the proceedings could be justified as being in the interests of the trust as a whole. Neither was the case here. The trustees' obligation was to apply the law of the European Community as declared by the European Court of Justice, including any temporal limitation it saw fit to impose. It was no part of the trustees' duty to advise one class of their beneficiaries in connection with a proposed change or clarification of the law that might have some effect on that particular class of beneficiary's interest, let alone where the consequence would be to damage the other class of beneficiary. There was no question of the trustees pointing out implications which might involve advice. There might be some benefit in sending a circular, but it would need to include a sentence to the effect that the trustees advised the members to take legal advice. This would merely give rise to additional costs to the trust fund and was therefore not an expense which the trustees could justify. However, there was no obvious reason why the company could not issue such a communication.

[2.1.41]

NHS Pensions v Beechinor (High Court) [1997] OPLR 99, [1997] PLR 95

Communication – administrators' duties

Facts and Decision

Mrs Beechinor was given the opportunity in 1978 to transfer from her existing pension scheme to a new scheme (both of which were statutory schemes). She sought guidance from the administrators on five questions. The administrators replied to her questions, but warned that they could not advise her as to which course of action to pursue. They also provided a sample projection of benefits and accurately summarised the calculation of benefits under both schemes. She decided to transfer, and as a result her pension was considerably lower than it would otherwise have been. The Court held that there was no general duty of care on the administrators to advise or warn the member or to provide a full explanation of the advantages and disadvantages, and even if such a duty had been assumed in this case, it had been fully discharged.

[2.1.42]

Outram v Academy Plastics (Court of Appeal) [2000] PLR 283 at paras 18–25 and 31

Communication – trustees' duties

Principle

A trustee did not owe a duty to a pension scheme member, as a potential applicant for renewed membership, to advise him or her whether or not to apply to rejoin: *Hawkesley v May [1956] QB 304, Hamar v Pensions Ombudsman [1996] OPLR 55, NHS Pensions v Beechinor [1997] OPLR 99* and *BCCI v Price Waterhouse (No. 2) [1998] PNLR 564* were applied.

[2.1.43]

Re Unisys Corp Retiree Medical Benefit 'ERISA' Litigation 57 F3d 1255 (United States Courts of Appeal, 3rd Cir, 24 November 1997) 57 F. 3d 1255, 19 EBC 1556

Communication – fiduciary's duties

Facts and Decision

Senior executives of Unisys repeatedly told employees and pensioners over many years that their medical benefits could not be terminated after the employees had retired. It was an important consideration for employees when deciding whether to retire. In fact, there was a clause in the relevant agreement and in the summary plan booklet reserving the company's right to withdraw cover at any time. Unisys sought to withdraw medical cover from pensioners. The Court held that the employees and pensioners had no contractual right to continued cover. However, the employer owed a duty as a fiduciary to its employees not to misinform employees through material misrepresentations and incomplete, inconsistent or contradictory disclosures, which had been breached in this case. *Bixler v Central Pa. Teamsters Health and Welfare Fund (12 F. 3d 1292)*, *Fischer v Phila. Elec. Co. 994 F. 2d 130*, *Curcio v John Hancock Mutual Life Insurance Co. 33 F. 3d 226*, *Smith v Hartford Ins. Group 6 F. 3d 131*, *Massachusetts Mutual Life Ins. Co. v Russell 473 US 134* at *142–45*, *Stahl v Tony's Bldg Materials Inc 875 F. 2d 1404*, *Allen v Atlantic Richfield Retirement Plan 480 F. Supp 848*, *Schlomchik v Retirement Plan of Amalgamated Ins. Fund 502 F. Supp 240* and *Schiffer v Equitable Assurance Sec. of the US 838 F. 2d 78* were all considered.

[2.1.44]

Westminster v Haywood (High Court) [1996] 2 All ER 467, [1996] OPLR 95 at 108C-D, [1996] PLR 161, para 63

Communication – administrators' duties

Principle

The Pensions Ombudsman could properly conclude that it was maladministration for a local authority not to warn a pension scheme member that it had doubts as to the validity of the severance and compensation scheme it was operating, and so gave him misleading or at least incomplete advice.

[2.1.45]

Wirral BC v Evans (Court of Appeal) [2000] All ER (D) 1728

Communication – administrators' duties

Facts and Decision

Mr Evans joined the Local Government Superannuation Scheme, a statutory scheme, after having spent 19 years employed by British Telecom and having been a member of its pension scheme. The local government scheme administrators supplied him with literature on the scheme. He enquired about the possibility of transferring his entitlement, and was sent a letter which referred to 9 years' reckonable service and 9 years' qualifying service, without defining either term, but also gave figures illustrating the level of pension and lump sum he would receive. He believed that he was going to be credited with 18 years' additional service in the local government scheme, when in fact the two definitions were used in different circumstances. It was disputed whether Mr Evans had had his understanding confirmed over the telephone by an employee of the administrators. Mr Evans took the transfer, then discovered his mistake. He then complained to the Pensions Ombudsman, who upheld his complaint on the basis that the administrators had a general duty to advise members. The Court held that administrators have no general duty to advise present or intending members of the scheme: *Outram v Academy Plastics [2000] PLR 283* was followed. The Ombudsman's determination was therefore set aside, and the matter was remitted to him to establish what took place in the telephone conversation between Mr Evans and the administrators.

Administration duties

[2.1.46]

Armstrong v East-West Airlines (Supreme Court of New South Wales) [1995] OPLR 239

Administration – trustees' duties

Principle

East-West Airlines employed pilots, with whom it was also in a trade dispute. As part of that trade dispute, 130 pilots resigned from employment and claimed their pension entitlement. The payment of these pension benefits was delayed by three months for various overlapping reasons. The Court held that delegation of pension scheme matters to personnel unfamiliar with the terms of the trust, resulting in errors and delay, was a breach of trust. Delay in commencing work on the calculation of pension scheme benefits, resulting in delay in the payment of benefits, was also a breach of trust. However, delay caused by an unexpectedly high workload was not a matter for which the trustee ought to be criticised. The trustee should pay interest for the time lost by that delay for which the trustee was open to criticism.

[2.1.47]

Wirral BC v Evans (Court of Appeal) [2000] All ER (D) 1728

Administration – administrators' duties

Principle

Administrators have no general duty to advise present or intending members of the scheme: *Outram v Academy Plastics [2000] LPR 283* was followed.

Delegation

[2.1.48]

Jones v AMP (High Court, New Zealand) [1995] PLR 53 at paras 59–60

Delegation

Principle

Investment in a managed fund, the Court held, did not mean that the power of investment had been delegated.

[2.1.49]

Libby v Kennedy (High Court) [1998] OPLR 213 at 217H–218E, 218F, 218G–219A, 219B-C, [1999] PLR 143, at paras 22–27, 28, 30–31, 32–33

Delegation – ratification

Facts and Decision

The Court held that where trustees minuted that 'where there were no difficulties in establishing the rightful beneficiary [for a death in service lump sum benefit], payment might be made with the consent of one employee trustee and one member trustee', this really meant that two trustees could act when it was a fairly plain case, and was an effective delegation of the power. Even if later on it turned out that the case was more complicated, this did not mean that these trustees did not have the relevant authority. Nor was there a problem if the trustees did not consider whether the case might or might not be difficult, if it was highly improbable that the case was one which would cause them any difficulty. If a trustee signed and returned a form sent with a recommendation by the pensions manager, without entering any comment in the decision box, it could only be construed as agreement with the recommendation. The form must be construed as a matter of law and against the factual matrix by which it was sent, signed and returned. Even if the decision had not been validly delegated, when trustees noted the decision at the following meeting, on the facts the trustees knew exactly what had been done and why it had been done, and they therefore effectively ratified the decision.

Mistakes in form

[2.1.50]

Municipal Mutual Insurance v Harrop (High Court) [1998] OPLR 199 at 207C-E, 207F–209B, [1998] PLR 149, paras 39–40, 41–47

Company law – ratification

Facts and Decision

If directors purported to act in accordance with the decisions of their majority without a Board meeting, the Court held, their acts were not those of the Board or of the company. So, when all the directors give informal assent apart from those who choose to abstain on the grounds of personal interest (such directors in fact being permitted to vote on the matter), the actions are not validly those of the company or the Board. The essence of the principle that the directors can act informally is unanimity.

The resolution in this case that the chairman be authorised to sign the minutes of a meeting recording that the directors had informally approved a resolution, was implied ratification of the resolution when the resolution had in fact been approved defectively: *In re Portuguese Consolidated Copper Mines (1890) 45 Ch D 16* was followed.

Duty to form an opinion

[2.1.51]

Telstra v Flegeltaub (Supreme Court of Victoria, Court of Appeal) [2001] PLR 7

Trustees' duties

Facts and Decision

Ms Flegeltaub left employment, claiming a pension on the ground of total and permanent invalidity. Under the terms of the scheme's invalidity clause, the trustee could withhold such a pension if the condition was attributable, to a material extent, to deliberate action or inaction by any person for the purpose of causing a benefit to become or to continue to be payable from the scheme, including without limitation what the trustee considered to be an unreasonable refusal to submit to treatment. Her claim was rejected by a committee of the trustee and by the trustee's Board of directors. The Court held that the trustee was under a fiduciary obligation to form an opinion as to whether Ms Flegeltaub qualified for an invalidity pension. One cannot ordinarily decide a question of fact in good faith and give it real and genuine consideration without conducting some investigation, and in some cases this will entail making an inquiry of a person who is willing to provide information and is in the best position to do so. It is not a matter of natural justice but *bona fide* inquiry and genuine decision-making. Accordingly, Ms Flegeltaub should be given the opportunity to correct what she believed to be misinformation in the trustee's possession, or information wrongly interpreted by it, and to place material before it to allay its concerns.

Interest of trustees in decision

[2.1.52]

British Coal Corporation v British Coal Staff Superannuation Scheme Trustees (High Court) [1995] 1 All ER 912, [1994] ICR 537, [1994] OPLR 51, [1993] PLR 303 at paras 60–62

Conflicts of interest

Principle

The decision in *Re William Makin [1993] OPLR 171* was reviewed by the Court. In that case a scheme was in winding–up, the employer was the trustee and the power to distribute surplus was a fiduciary power in the full sense: the Court had noted that if a scheme of arrangements was prepared by directors of the employer, who were also beneficiaries under the pension scheme, those directors would have to accept that they themselves would have to be excluded. It had since been commented that it was outrageous that representative members who put themselves forward to help should by doing so forfeit their benefits. It would be equally outrageous, the Court held, if a person who had power to distribute assets amongst a class which included himself should be able to apply the fund or any part of it for his or her own benefit. This does not rest on any technical rule of trust law; common sense dictates that no one can be expected to weigh fairly his or her own merits against the merits of others.

[2.1.53]

Re Brooke Bond & Co Ltd's Trust Deed (High Court) [1963] Ch 357, [1963] 1 All ER 454, [1963] 1 WLR 320

Conflicts of interest – custodian trustee

Facts and Decision

The Brooke Bond pension scheme wished to invest in an insurance policy effected with Welfare Insurance, a subsidiary of Brooke Bond. Welfare Insurance was also the custodian trustee of the scheme. The Court held that the duty to account for profits applied as much to custodian trustees as to ordinary trustees. However, the Court authorised the managing trustees to enter into the insurance policy on terms that Welfare Insurance was not liable to account to the trust for any premiums or other monies or profits received or obtained by them in respect of the policy, but subject to the condition that the terms of the policy should previously have been approved by an independent actuary nominated by the managing trustees.

[2.1.54]

Buckley v Hudson Forge (High Court) [1999] OPLR 249 at 267C–267H, [1999] PLR 151 at paras 96–102

Conflicts of interest

Facts and Decision

A receiver of a company which was a trustee could not, the Court held, validly or effectually exercise a discretion, where the duties owed in the exercise of such a discretion conflicted with the duties owed to the debenture holder. *Polly Peck International v Henry [1998] OPLR 323* and *Denny v Yeldon [1995] 3 All ER 624* were distinguished on the grounds that in each case the person in the position of conflict was an administrator under the *Insolvency Act 1986*, and therefore an officer of the Court. *Simpson Curtis Pension Trustees v Readson [1994] OPLR 231* was also distinguished, on the ground that the case concerned a power to appoint a new trustee. The trustee was, therefore, obliged either to apply to the Court or to appoint a separate trustee.

In addition, the Court observed that where an employer had appointed itself as trustee, it had put itself in the potential position of conflict. When conflicts in fact arose, the employer could only avoid the conflict either by applying to the Court or by appointing an independent trustee: *Manning v Drexel Burnham Lambert [1995] 1 WLR 32* and *Edge v Pensions Ombudsman [1998] 2 All ER 547* were distinguished.

[2.1.55]

Edge v Pensions Ombudsman (High Court) [1998] 2 All ER 547, [1998] OPLR 51 at 71B–73B, [1997] PLR 15 at paras 117–133

Conflicts of interest – burden of proof on challenge to trustees

Principle

The notion that when a pension scheme's discretionary power of amendment was exercised so as to increase an existing benefit or add a new benefit, the member trustees must be excluded from benefit was, the

Court held, quite simply ridiculous. The rules providing for member trustees could not be taken to have intended so absurd a result. Why should equity intervene? Rules of equity were devised in order to produce fair and sensible results. If the constitution of a pension scheme required there to be employee member trustees, and vested in those trustees (with or without colleagues who are not employees) discretionary powers the proper exercise of which may confer, or augment, pension benefits on employees, the employee member trustees will not be accountable for those benefits: *Sargeant v National Westminster Bank plc (1990) 61 P&CR 518* was applied, and *Manning v Drexel Burnham Lambert [1995] 1 WLR 32* was considered.

[2.1.56]

Edge v Pensions Ombudsman (Court of Appeal) [2000] 3 WLR 79, [1999] OPLR 179 at 199E–200F, [1999] PLR 215 at paras 60–62

Conflicts of interest – burden of proof on challenge to trustees

Facts and Decision

Where pension scheme rules specify the composition of the trustees, the Court held, it must have been obvious at the time that the scheme was established that the trustees would need from time to time to take decisions which required them to arrive at a balance between competing interests. It must be accepted that the scheme was established on the basis that the elaborate provisions regulating the composition of the trustees as a body were intended to provide a body of trustees which could be relied upon to consider all interests fairly and properly. Those who sought to challenge a decision of that body bore the ordinary burden of proof of establishing that the decision had been reached improperly: *Hillsdown v Pensions Ombudsman [1997[1 All ER 862* was distinguished. Appropriate inferences may be drawn from any failure of the trustees to give an explanation when that explanation is called for, and the explanation itself may be examined critically.

[2.1.57]

Hillsdown v Pensions Ombudsman (High Court) [1997] I All ER 862, [1996] OPLR 291 at 319D–320G, [1996] PLR 427 at paras 106–111

Conflicts of interest – burden of proof on challenge to trustees

Principle

The rule against self-dealing is not so hard and fast as to require a negotiation between pension fund trustees and the employer to be set aside automatically, and without investigation, if one or more of the trustees are directors of the employer. Unless there is express provision in the relevant trust deed permitting a trustee to act in negotiations with the employer notwithstanding that the trustee is a director or employee of the company, the fact that negotiations have been conducted by such persons puts upon those who say that the transaction should be upheld the onus of proving that it was indeed reasonable and proper. That involves an investigation of the facts.

[2.1.58]

Jones v AMP (High Court, New Zealand) [1995] PLR 53 at paras 88–92

Conflicts of interest

Principle

There is no absolute principle which would either exclude the general principle that a trustee cannot profit from its management of a trust, or mean that it is invariably applied wherever a subsidiary acting as a trustee benefits its parent company. What is pertinent is the underlying rationale for the prohibition. This fundamental principle is designed to ensure that the trustee's loyalty to serve the interests of the trust is not distracted by a personal interest which conflicts with those more general interests. Whether there has been a breach of this principle is a question of fact and degree, and for that purpose the facts must be closely scrutinised.

[2.1.59]

Manning v Drexel Burnham Lambert (High Court) [1995] I WLR 32, [1994] OPLR 71, [1994] PLR 75

Conflicts of interest

Principle

A pension scheme went into winding-up without having equalised benefits. The various classes of beneficiaries reached a compromise over the use of surplus under the trustees' discretionary powers, and sought the Court's approval. All of the trustees were members whose benefits would be augmented under the compromise. If the trustees surrendered their discretion to the Court rather than seek its approval for the compromise, the basis for general agreement might well be lost with the inevitable associated costs, delays and difficulties. If the trustees agreed to be replaced by professional trustees, the same practical objections would arise. The Court held that it would not require the trustees to forego the augmentations. The Court had jurisdiction to give directions, where a proposal in respect of which directions was sought had been put forward by trustees who were in a position of conflict. In this case, there was no reason to think that there had been any attempt by any trustee to take advantage of his or her position improperly or unfairly, and the directions were granted.

[2.1.60]

Polly Peck International v Henry (High Court) [1998] OPLR 323 at 329G-H, [1999] PLR 135 at para 41

Conflicts of interest – trustees' duties

Facts and Decision

An administrator of an insolvent company applied to have the insolvent company replaced as trustee of the pension scheme. The insolvent company was by far the largest creditor of a scheme member, and the administrator argued that it was subject to a conflict of interest in dealing with the claims of the member and his trustee in bankruptcy in respect of his pension scheme entitlement. The Court held that unless the legal position was clear, in which case the trustee would be bound to act according to law, the question of entitlement would be referred to the Court by whoever was the trustee. Since the Court would decide the issue, there was no real conflict. Even if some future conflict could be identified, that would not be a sufficient reason to appoint a substitute trustee at this stage, since the costs of the scheme would inevitably increase.

[2.1.61]

Re William Makin (High Court) [1993] OPLR 171, [1992] PLR 177

Conflicts of interest

Facts and Decision

William Makin & Sons Limited went into receivership in 1984 and liquidation in 1985. Its pension scheme had a substantial surplus deriving wholly from overfunding by the company, and went into winding-up on the company ceasing to carry on business. The employer was the trustee, and the trust deed gave the trustees a discretion to use any surplus on a winding-up to increase benefits to members. In the interest of avoiding delay, the Court assumed the responsibility of exercising this power. Representative beneficiaries were obliged to prepare a scheme for distributing the surplus, and they were obliged to accept that they were excluded from any benefit under this scheme of arrangements.

Timing of exercise of trustee discretion

[2.1.62]

Fisons v Stannard (Court of Appeal) [1991] PLR 227, [1992] IRLR 27

Trustees' duties – timing

Facts and Decision

Fisons agreed to sell part of its business to Norsk Hydro in April 1982. Its pension fund trustee, having considered the transfer basis at that time, eventually made a transfer on the total reserve basis in March 1983. The trustee reached this decision by 31 December 1982, on a basis put forward by the employers in April 1982. In the meantime, the value of the fund had increased very substantially. The trustee should have given consideration to the current value of the trust fund and its implications. It might materially have affected its decision, since the past service reserve basis which had previously been rejected as impracticable might then have been practicable. If the trustee had been told the current value of the fund at the date of the decision and its implications, there were no doubt other matters which it would also have had to consider, such as how far a rise in stock market values could be regarded as a satisfactory basis for action.

Removal of trustees

[2.1.63]

Cowan v Scargill (High Court) [1984] 2 All ER 750, [1985] Ch 270, [1990] PLR 169 at para 72

Trustees' duties – Court discretion

Principle

The Court considered the exercise of its inherent jurisdiction to remove trustees if a trustee continued to refuse to sign accounts.

[2.1.64]

McDonald v Horn (High Court) [1993] OPLR 183, [1994] PLR 33 at paras 49, 50

Court discretion

Principle

The Court held that, in the context of a pension fund, it is unjust that the administration of funds to which members have contributed, and which require the continual exercise of discretions as to, for example, the grant of discretionary benefits, should be controlled by persons in whose fairness and probity the beneficiaries no longer have confidence. Delay of relevant court proceedings was also a relevant consideration in deciding whether to remove such a trustee.

Payment of trustees

[2.1.65]

Re Duke of Norfolk Settlement Trust (Court of Appeal) [1982] 1 Ch 61, [1981] 3 WLR 345, [1981] 3 All ER 220

Trustees' remuneration

Principle

The Court has an inherent jurisdiction to authorise payment of remuneration to trustees. There is an inherent jurisdiction on the appointment of a trustee to direct that he or she be remunerated. The Court also has the inherent jurisdiction to increase the remuneration already allowed by the trust instrument. The basis in relation to the trustee's remuneration is the good administration of trusts. If the Court concludes that it would be in the interests of the beneficiaries to increase the remuneration, having regard to the nature of the trust, the experience and skill of a particular trustee and the amounts which the trustee seeks to charge (when compared with what other trustees might require to be paid for their services), and all the other circumstances of the case, then the Court may properly do so.

[2.1.66]

Foster v Spencer (High Court) [1996] 1 All ER 672

Trustees' remuneration

Facts and Decision

In a case where the services rendered by trustees of a cricket club were totally outside their contemplation when appointed, and the obligations they undertook made great demands on their expertise and time, the Court exercised its inherent jurisdiction to authorise the payment of remuneration for them despite the absence of a charging clause: *Re Duke of Norfolk's Settlement Trusts [1982] Ch 61* was followed. However, the Court would not authorise an application for future remuneration where the remaining tasks did not call for any special expertise on the part of the trustees.

[2.1.67]

Manning v Drexel Burnham Lambert (High Court) [1995] 1 WLR 32, [1994] OPLR 71, [1994] PLR 75

Trustees' remuneration

Facts and Decision

The Court authorised payment to a trustee who had put himself and his personal knowledge at the disposal of the trustees' advisers in a way well beyond that which could reasonably be expected of him as a trustee, thereby saving the trustees and those advisers from incurring considerably higher costs.

[2.1.68]

Polly Peck International v Henry (High Court) [1998] OPLR 323 at 328B-F, [1999] PLR 135 at paras 29–32

Trustees' remuneration

Facts and Decision

The Court did not authorise the remuneration of an insolvent employer as trustee. The administrator possessed all the necessary powers to act as trustee and was entitled to be paid for its services as administrator. No further payments would be necessary to secure the proper administration of the schemes or the interests of their members. It would be quite wrong to direct the pension funds to bear any part of the administration costs. Those who deal with companies must be deemed to know that they are likely to have pension schemes.

2.2 – Employer powers and duties

General

[2.2.1]

Air Jamaica v Charlton (Privy Council) [1999] 1 WLR 1399, [1999] OPLR 11 at 20A, [1999] PLR 247 at para 42

Employers' powers

Principle

The employer's ability to wind up its pension scheme was not a power (if it was, it would be void for perpetuity), but a liberty.

[2.2.2]

Attorney-General of Canada v Confederation Life (Ontario Court of Justice, unreported, 4 July 1995)

Employers' powers – unfunded schemes – constructive trusts – unjust enrichment

Facts and Decision

Confederation Life, a large insurer, became insolvent. It had never entered into a formal trust agreement in relation to its pension obligations, but the Board had approved a document providing that the trustees should ensure that the pension schemes were funded in a manner that would enable them to meet all their obligations. They were, however, pay-as-you-go schemes. Scheme members were supplied with a booklet summarising the benefits but which stated that it did not create or confer any contractual rights, and that all rights with respect to the benefits of a member would be governed by the group policy. Confederation Life also provided supplementary pensions for senior officers. Those pensions were paid in accordance with Board resolutions. Neither the resolutions nor the letters to senior officers required a fund to be established, and the supplementary scheme was not funded. The employees, former employees and their dependants, argued that the assets of Confederation Life were subject to a constructive trust in respect of the amount required to satisfy all pension liabilities, as did members of the supplementary scheme. The Court held that the evidence did not support a finding that there was a mutual understanding that the benefits would be pre-funded or secured, and there was nothing upon which to base a finding that the employees had any reasonable expectation that Confederation Life had undertaken to subordinate its own interests, and those of its policyholders, to those of the employees and retirees with respect to the establishment of such benefits. As Confederation Life did not stand in a fiduciary relationship towards the claimants in relation to the benefits, there could be no constructive trust imposed as a remedy for breach of such obligations. Nor would a constructive trust be imposed on the grounds of unjust enrichment, since any enrichment Confederation Life received as a result of the employees' services was unrelated to the detriment, the loss of pension, which they would now suffer. In any case, there were three juristic reasons why a constructive trust should not be imposed on the grounds of unjust enrichment:

(a) The 'enrichment' had been granted pursuant to a contract.
(b) The 'enrichment' was caused by the winding-up proceedings themselves, and the claimants were not entitled to jump the queue.
(c) The cessation of benefits was simply the result of the insolvency, and did not result from some morally questionable conduct on the part of Confederation Life.

[2.2.3]

Bairstow v Queens Moat Houses (High Court, unreported, 23 July 1999)

Employer's duties

Facts and Decision

The power of amendment of a pension scheme provided that amendments could be made by company resolution. However, the membership had to be consulted about rule amendments which could prejudicially affect their past or future rights, and notice of any such amendment had to be given by the administrator to all members of the scheme. The company passed a resolution changing the definition of pensionable salary, but did so by approving a resolution of its remuneration committee, which had not been delegated the power to amend the scheme rules. The Court held that the Board had not appreciated that it was exercising a rule amendment power. The executive directors had a clear duty to bring the relevant rules to the attention of the non-executives. No consultation of or notice to the members ever took place, and the Inland Revenue was not notified of the change. No employer could properly be said to be have acted consistently with its obligation of good faith in exercising an amendment power in this inefficient manner. The employer had an obligation of good faith in exercising its power with a view to the efficient running of the scheme, and there had been such a fundamental breach of this obligation that the purported exercise of the power of amendment was invalid.

[2.2.4]

British Coal Corporation v British Coal Staff Superannuation Scheme Trustees (High Court) [1995] 1 All ER 912, [1994] ICR 537, [1994] OPLR 51, [1993] PLR 303 at paras 54–67

Employers' powers – conflict of interest

Principle

The general trust law requirement that trustees do not profit from the exercise of their own discretions applies in a pensions context on a winding-up where the employer is the trustee, but there is no parallel requirement when the employer exercises the power of amendment in an ongoing scheme. The employer is entitled to exercise the power of amendment (if it has it) in any way which will further the purposes of the scheme to ensure that the legitimate expectations of the members and pensioners are met, without (so far as possible) imposing any undue burden on the employer or building up an unnecessarily large surplus. The employer itself has an interest in seeing that the scheme is effectively managed. If the assets of the scheme are so large that all legitimate expectations of the members and pensioners can be met without continued contribution by the employer at the rate originally provided, the employer can by amendment reduce or suspend contributions for a period. What it cannot do is set limits to the benefits for a collateral purpose, without regard to the beneficiaries' expectations. The *Imperial* duty of good faith applies equally to the power of amendment conferred on the employer in this case.

Clark v Nomura (High Court) [2000] IRLR 766

Employers' powers – reviewability

Principle

When an employer exercises its discretion under a discretionary bonus scheme which was not guaranteed in any way, and was dependent upon individual performance, the Court reviews that exercise of the discretion by reference to a test of irrationality or perversity (of which caprice would be a good example), i.e. that no reasonable employer would have exercised its discretion in this way. Of course, if and when the Court concludes that the employer was in breach of contract, then it will be necessary to reach a conclusion, on the balance of probabilities, as to what would have occurred had the employer complied with its contractual obligations; or assess, without unrealistic assumptions, what position the employee would have been in had the employer performed its obligation. That will involve the Court putting itself in the position of the employer, but it will only do so if it is first satisfied, on the higher test, not that the employer acted unreasonably, but that no reasonable employer would have reached the conclusion it did acting in accordance with its contractual obligations, and the assessment of the bonus then of course is by way of an award for damages.

[2.2.6]

Davis v Richards & Wallington Industries Ltd (High Court) [1991] 2 All ER 563, [1990] 1 WLR 1511, [1990] PLR 141 at paras 119, 120

Employers' duties

Principle

When considering whether to execute definitive rules, an employer is not subject to a fiduciary duty. There are, though, implied obligations to give the rules due consideration and not unreasonably to withhold approval.

[2.2.7]

Egan v Minister for Defence, Ireland (Ireland, High Court, 24 November 1988) [1999] 33 PBLR 10

Employers' powers

Facts and Decision

Mr Egan was an officer in the Air Corps. He sought permission from the Air Corps to retire, in accordance with the requirements of Irish statute. In practice, for many years all officers with Mr Egan's length of service had been allowed to retire. The Air Corps refused to allow him to retire, and Mr Egan applied for judicial review. The Court held that the decision was fair and reasonable in all the circumstances. Mr Egan had no legitimate expectation of being given permission to retire, given that at the time he applied the Corps had received numerous applications for retirements. The Corps was being neither unfair nor unjust in departing from its previous practice.

[2.2.8]

Hillsdown v Pensions Ombudsman (High Court) [1997] 1 All ER 862, [1996] OPLR 291 at 315E–317C, 318A-F, [1996] PLR 427 at paras 91–97, 101–102

Employers' duties

Principle

The implied obligation of trust and confidence prevents employers from using a power to suspend or determine their liability to contribute to a pension scheme, while at the same time using the power to adhere further employers for the purpose of running down a surplus certified to have arisen in relation to the service of the employees of other employers. It is one thing for an employer to take a contributions holiday in favour of its existing members, and quite another to introduce a large class of new members and take a contributions holiday in relation to them. Where the mode of application of surplus was given to the trustee alone in consultation with the actuary, the trustee should not cut itself off from the employer's concerns; but the employer was in breach of its implied obligation of good faith if it sought to enter into negotiations with the trustee when the trustee needed to consider the matter alone. It was also a breach of the employer's duty of good faith for it to induce the trustee to act in breach of trust by committing a fraud on a power.

[2.2.9]

Imperial Group Pension Trust v Imperial Tobacco (High Court) [1991] 1 WLR 589, [1991] ICR 524, [1991] IRLR 66, [1991] 2 All ER 597, [1990] PLR 263

Employers' duties

Facts and Decision

On the takeover of the principal employer, the Imperial Tobacco Pension Fund became a closed scheme and automatic annual pension increases were introduced in line with the lower of 5% and the rate of inflation. Inflation in due course increased above 5% and the principal employer announced that in no circumstances would it agree to any further increase in pension above that guaranteed level. Any such increase would have needed to have been made by amendment to the scheme rules, which required company consent. The Court held that there was no implied limitation of reasonableness on the company's right to refuse consent to amendments, but the pension benefits were part of the consideration which an employee receives in return for the rendering of his or her services. In every contract of employment there is an implied term that the employers will not, without reasonable and proper cause, conduct themselves in a manner calculated or likely to destroy or seriously damage the relationship of confidence and trust between employer and employee. That obligation applies as much to the exercise of the employer's rights and powers under a pension scheme as they do to the other rights and powers of an employer. The trust deed and rules themselves are to be taken as being impliedly subject to this duty, and the members can enforce this right in trust law as well as in contract. The employer must exercise its rights with a view to the efficient running of the scheme as a whole, and not for the purpose of forcing the members to give up their accrued rights in the existing fund for rights in a new scheme. *Woods v WM Car Services (Peterborough) [1981] IRLR 347* was applied.

Comment

When this case was first issued, as other commentators have noted, it was not invested with particular significance. After all, it was a decision made on an emergency application without full investigation of the facts, where the judge was asked to give, much against his own inclination, such indication as he could on hypothetical and unproved facts. However, with time this decision has come to be recognised as one of the bedrock decisions of pension law. The decision has been referred to in House of Lords judgments and in countless other cases.

The implied mutual duty of trust and confidence between employer and employee has been applied in many areas, and it has had a major impact on the scope of employer obligations under pension schemes. It has been used to restrict employers' actions in relation to withholding consent to pension increases, use of surplus and the power of amendment.

The biggest drawback with the use of the implied duty of trust and confidence in a pensions context is that there is inevitable uncertainty about the extent to which the employer can take into account its own interests. As acknowledged in this decision, there is no implied limitation of reasonableness on the employer's actions. However, many employer decisions under a pension scheme involve a weighing of the employer's interests directly against the members' interests. There is always a danger that the Court will take action whenever it disapproves of the employer's actions, making it difficult for employers or members to judge their chances of success in advance of litigation. With the House of Lords decision in *Malik & Mahmud v BCCI [1998] AC 20* which set out the duty in considerable detail, this risk may have lessened, but the doctrine will need to be developed considerably before employers can act with complete confidence in all circumstances.

[2.2.10]

Independent Pension Trustee v LAW Construction (Scottish Court of Session, Outer House) [1996] OPLR 259

Employers' duties – insolvency

Principle

The implied obligation of good faith is owed by an employer towards its employees, and not by the employer to a creditor of the employer, whether before or after the appointment of a receiver.

[2.2.11]

International Power v Healy (House of Lords) [2001] PLR 121

Employers' duties

Facts and Decision

The principal employer in each group of the Electricity Supply Pension Scheme was given the power under the scheme to make arrangements, certified by the actuary as reasonable, for dealing with an ongoing surplus. When a surplus emerged, some employers set two-thirds of the surplus against the employers' obligation to contribute. The Court held that this did not breach the employer's implied obligation of good faith.

[2.2.12]

Larsen's Executrix v Henderson (Outer House, Scotland) [1991] PLR 153

Employers' duties – insolvency

Principle

A receiver owed a duty of care to the employees of the company in receivership, and must act reasonably in all the circumstances, even though he may need to take decisions which have an adverse effect on the employees. A receiver would be acting unreasonably if he or she simply terminated a pension scheme without giving any warning to the employees concerned that there was a possibility that this might occur.

[2.2.13]

LRT v Hatt (High Court) [1993] OPLR 225 at 271C–272B, [1993] PLR 227, para 186, 188–189

Employers' duties

Facts and Decision

The Court found that there had been no breach of the implied obligation of good faith by the employer in this case. The employer had disclosed a minimum of information about changes being made to its pension schemes, but not so as to constitute non-disclosure.

The following principles were also upheld:

(a) An interim deed operates as an executory trust, and there was an obligation on the employer to prepare a definitive deed in accordance with its obligations. To the extent that those obligations remained undischarged, they remained to be satisfied.

(b) The fact that the employer was in financial difficulties was not a matter to which the Court attached any significance: impecuniosity is not a recognised ground for escaping legal obligations.

(c) It was at least arguable that the retrospective operation of a definitive deed, executed pursuant to an interim deed, would be effective not only as against the principal employer but also with regard to the subsidiaries that adhered to the scheme.

[2.2.14]

Mettoy Pension Trustees v Evans (High Court) [1991] 2 All ER 513, [1990] 1 WLR 1587, [1990] PLR 9 (paras 161–169, 176–179)

Employers' powers – employers' duties – interpretation

Facts and Decision

Whether a particular power given to an employer of a pension scheme is or is not a power which the employer must exercise as a trustee is, the Court held, a question of construction of the trust deed and rules in the light of the surrounding circumstances. If a power given to the employer to distribute surplus on a winding-up (which would otherwise return to the employer) is not a fiduciary power in the full sense, it is illusory from the beneficiaries' point of view. It would not, however, be pointless, given the tax advantages which the employer would receive. The beneficiaries' rights are derived from the contracts of employment of the members, as well as from the trust instrument. Surplus is derived in a balance of cost scheme from past employer overfunding, but it does not follow that surplus belongs in principle to the employer, and one does not start from an assumption that any surplus belongs morally to the employer. The separation of powers between the trustees and the employer in this case did not lead the Court to conclude that the power was inevitably intended not to be fiduciary.

[2.2.15]

Mihlenstedt v Barclays Bank (Court of Appeal) [1989] PLR 91, [1989] Ch 91, [1989] IRLR 522

Employers' powers

See [1.15.5].

[2.2.16]

Outram v Academy Plastics (Court of Appeal) [2000] PLR 283

Employers' duties – communication

Principle

The Court did not need to look beyond the terms of a contract of employment, express or implied, in order to determine whether employers owed a duty of a duty of care in tort to advise former members of a pension scheme whether to rejoin that pension scheme. If it was not inherent in the contractual relationship, it was not possible to see how it could be derived from the tort of negligence: *Scally v Southern Health and Social Services Board [1992] 1 AC 294* was applied.

[2.2.17]

Packwood v APS (Pensions Ombudsman) [1995] OPLR 369 at 380B–382F, [1995] PLR 183 at paras 40–58

Employers' powers

Facts and Decision

Where an employer considered the interests of its pension scheme's pensioners and decided to prefer its own interests, concluding that the industrial and public relations consequences were worth the cost savings, the Pensions Ombudsman held that it had not breached its duty of good faith.

[2.2.18]

Tek Corporation Provident Fund v Lorentz (Supreme Court of Appeal of South Africa) [1999] OPLR 137 at para 15

Employers' duties

Principle

The employer owes at least a duty of good faith to its pension scheme and its members and beneficiaries: *Imperial Group Pension Trust v Imperial Tobacco [1991] 1 WLR 589* was followed.

[2.2.19]

Re William Makin (High Court) [1993] OPLR 171, [1992] PLR 177

Employers' powers – conflict of interest

See [2.1.33].

Communicating with members

[2.2.20]

Brown v Royal Veterinary College (Industrial Tribunal) [1989] PLR 43

Employers' duties – communication

Facts and Decision

Mr Brown obtained from his pensions officer details of his early retirement entitlement. On the strength of these details, he resigned from employment to take early retirement. It subsequently transpired that his pension entitlement was in fact 30% less than the details he had been given by the pensions officer. His employer did not offer him his job back. The Court held that Mr Brown's resignation was made through a fundamental mistake, and his employer's failure to offer him his job back at a time when he had not left employment, and the post was not filled, was constructive unfair dismissal.

[2.2.21]

Gorham v British Telecommunications (High Court, unreported 29 January 1999)

Employers' duties – communication

Principle

Where an employer provides information to an employee in connection with pension matters, and the information is relied upon by the employee to the ultimate detriment of his or her dependants on his or her death, the law recognises a duty to the dependants: *White v Jones [1995] 2 AC 207* was applied.

[2.2.22]

McGrath v British Rail Board (Court of Session, Scotland) [1991] PLR 17

Employers' duties – communication

Facts and Decision

Mr McGrath was a railwayman who died in 1981 from a terminal illness. His widow sued his employer for negligence on the grounds that he had been wrongly advised shortly before his death by his employer that it was too late for him to opt to take out a widow's pension, with the consequence that she was not entitled to such a pension. The Court held that there was insufficient evidence that the employer had given incorrect advice.

[2.2.23]

Meinhardt v Unisys (United States Court of Appeals, 3rd Circuit) [1998] PLR 253 at paras 74–78

Employers' duties – communication

Principle

Fiduciaries who are under a duty to convey complete and accurate information when they speak to beneficiaries regarding plan benefits, remain under that duty even where they are absolved from liability for breaches of fiduciary duty which result from the beneficiary's exercise of control. So where members complained that fiduciaries had failed to give them adequate advice as to the risks of investments in a money purchase scheme, there was a triable issue.

[2.2.24]

Outram v Academy Plastics (Court of Appeal) [2000] PLR 283

Employers' duties – communication

Principle

Employers did not owe a duty of care in tort to advise former members of a pension scheme whether to rejoin that pension scheme: *Scally v Southern Health and Social Services Board [1992] 1 AC 294, Spring v Guardian*

Assurance plc [1995] 2 AC 296 and *University of Nottingham v Eyett [1991] 1 WLR 594* were applied. The Court did not need to look beyond the terms of the contract of employment, express or implied.

[2.2.25]

Scally v Southern Health and Social Services Board (House of Lords) [1992] I AC 294, [1991] PLR 195

Employers' duties – communication

Facts and Decision

Northern Irish medical staff had the right under statutory instrument to purchase additional years of pensionable service in the NHS Pension Scheme within 12 months from 10 February 1975, or (in the case of new joiners) within 12 months of joining the health service. This right was not made known to some employees, and as a consequence they did not exercise it. These employees brought claims against the Health Board in 1988, since they would have exercised the right had they known of it. The Court held that since there was only economic loss, there was no duty of care in tort, and there had been no breach of statutory duty such as would entitle the employees to damages. The terms of the contract of employment had not been negotiated with the individual employees, but resulted from negotiation with a representative body or were incorporated by reference. The term made available to the employee a valuable right contingent upon action being taken by him or her to avail himself or herself of its benefit, and the employee could not in all the circumstances reasonably be expected to be aware of the term unless it was drawn to his or her attention. In these circumstances, it was necessary to imply an obligation on the employer to take reasonable steps to bring the term of the contract to the employee's attention so that he or she might be in a position to enjoy its benefit.

[2.2.26]

Re Unisys Corp Retiree Medical Benefit 'ERISA' Litigation (United States Courts of Appeal, 3rd Cir, 1995) 57 F. 3d 1255

Employers' duties – communication

Facts and Decision

Senior executives of Unisys repeatedly told employees and pensioners over many years that their medical benefits could not be terminated after the employees had retired. The Court held that the employer owed a duty to its employees not to misinform employees through material misrepresentations and incomplete, inconsistent or contradictory disclosures, which had in fact been breached in this case.

[2.2.27]

University of Nottingham v Eyett (High Court) [1999] 1 WLR 594, [1999] OPLR 55, [1998] PLR 27

Employers' duties – communication

Facts and Decision

An employee took early retirement in accordance with his scheme entitlement. His employer did not draw to his attention that if he had waited another month, his pensionable salary would have included his most recent pay rise, and so his pension would have been higher. The Court held that it is not a breach of the employer's implied obligation of good faith if it fails to warn an employee, who is proposing to exercise important rights in connection with his contract of employment, that the way in which he is proposing to exercise them may not be financially the most advantageous way in the particular circumstances.

[2.2.28]

Varity Corp v Howe (United States Supreme Court) [1996] 516 US 489, 116 S Ct 1065

Employer's duties – communication

Facts and Decision

An employer persuaded many of its employees to transfer their welfare benefits to a new subsidiary, which it knew was unprofitable and never solvent. It did so as a deliberate deception. In doing so, the Court held, it was acting as a fiduciary, and had therefore violated the fiduciary obligations imposed upon it.

Amendments

[2.2.29]

Re Courage Group's Pension Schemes, Ryan v Imperial Brewing (High Court) [1987] 1 All ER 528, [1987] 1 WLR 495

Employers' powers – power of amendment

Principle

It did not matter, the Court held, that an employer could achieve the same, or nearly the same, result as it wanted to achieve by amendment of its pension scheme, through commercial transactions without any amendments to the schemes. If the purpose of the amendments was inconsistent with the purpose of the scheme, the amendments could not be made.

[2.2.30]

Wheeler v NBC Pension Trustee (Pensions Ombudsman) [1996] OPLR 337 at 345B–349E, [1997] PLR 1 at paras 24–49

Employers' powers – power of amendment

Facts and Decision

The National Bus Company scheme was shortly to be wound up following privatisation. The pension scheme power of amendment was subject to a restriction that no alteration or addition shall be made as would affect prejudicially any benefits then already accrued to or in respect of any member or pensioner, without his or her consent in writing. Pensions in payment under the scheme increased in line with national average earnings. Without obtaining the consent of the membership, the trustees agreed to an amendment to the rules which permitted them to secure benefits on a winding-up with annuities, under which the accrued benefits would be secured in line with the Retail Prices Index (RPI) plus 2¼% if they could be purchased more cheaply. There was already provision that the trustees could secure benefits with annuities on terms as similar as possible to the benefit entitlements, if they were unable to obtain annuities on the basis set out in the rules. In the absence of any definition, the Ombudsman held, accrued rights must not be given a technical and narrow meaning, since the proviso is an important protection of members' rights. There was no guarantee that national average earnings would exceed RPI plus 2¼%, but it would be too limited to interpret the proviso as meaning that alterations would be permitted unless they necessarily prejudiced a member's benefits: the test was whether the consent of any reasonable member could be taken for granted. This was not so on this occasion, and the restriction on the power of amendment had been breached.

Distribution of surplus

[2.2.31]

Hillsdown v Pensions Ombudsman (High Court) [1997] 1 All ER 862, [1996] OPLR 291 at 315E–317C, [1996] PLR 427 at paras 91–97

Employers' powers – surplus

Facts and Decision

In a scheme where the power to deal with surplus was vested solely in the hands of the trustee, the Court held that the implied obligation of trust and confidence prevented employers from using a power to suspend or determine their liability to contribute, while at the same time using the power to adhere further employers for the purpose of running down a surplus certified to have arisen in relation to the service of the employees of other employers. The employer was in breach of its implied obligation of good faith if it sought to enter into negotiations with the trustee, when the trustee needed to consider the matter alone.

[2.2.32]

International Power v Healy (House of Lords) [2001] PLR 121 at para 16

Employers' powers – surplus

Facts and Decision

Once it was accepted that an employer can act in its own interests and that the extent to which it is so doing could not be criticised, the Court held that the way in which pension scheme surplus was funded is not relevant.

A duty to make arrangements with surplus was held to include a power to discharge that duty, and thus the power of amendment need not be used to implement the arrangements made. However, the general wording of the power to discharge the duty to make arrangements were unlikely to have been intended to give the employer the power to do something which would contradict the express provisions of the scheme.

Power to wind up

[2.2.33]

Air Jamaica v Charlton (Privy Council) [1999] 1 WLR 1399, [1999] OPLR 11 at 19H–20A, [1999] PLR 247 at paras 39–42

Employers' powers – winding-up

Principle

A pension scheme is a continuing scheme, under which new members are continually joining and existing members leaving or taking their benefits. In order to wind up such a scheme three steps must be taken, though the first two may be taken simultaneously. First, the scheme must be closed to new entrants. If no further steps are taken, the scheme continues as a closed scheme, contributions continuing to be paid in respect of existing members but no new members being admitted. Secondly, contributions must cease to be paid in respect of existing members, who will either have been made redundant or have been transferred to a new scheme. At this stage the scheme is discontinued, since it ceases to be a continuing one. But pensions in payment continue to be payable until the third stage is reached and the scheme is finally wound up. The company's ability to wind up the scheme was not a power (if it was, it would be void for perpetuity), but a liberty. Where no formal requirements were set out for the discontinuance of the plan, it was necessary only for the company to cease deducting employee contributions and cease paying its own matching contributions.

[2.2.34]

Hillsdown v Pensions Ombudsman (High Court) [1997] 1 All ER 862, [1996] OPLR 291, [1996] PLR 427

Employers' powers – winding-up

Principle

Where an employer had been given the power to suspend or determine its contributions to a pension scheme for its own benefits, the Court held that there could be no question of a fiduciary duty being owed in relation to its exercise.

2.3 – Actuary's duties and powers

General

[2.3.1]

Fisons v Stannard (Court of Appeal) [1991] PLR 227 at paras 37, 42–44, [1992] IRLR 27

Actuaries' duties – transfers – certification

Principle

When trustees were considering a discretion to make a transfer out, it was the actuaries' duty to put trustees in a position, so far as the actuaries could, to make a properly informed decision. This included giving the trustees information on the relevance of the value of the pension scheme to the problem in hand in relation to actuarial principles, and the implications of their decision on future contributions. *Re Imperial Foods Ltd Pension Scheme [1986] 2 All ER 802* was considered: the function of the actuary in that case was to achieve a result which was fair as between all the persons interested. It was not for the courts to interfere with the certificate of an actuary, who clearly had all relevant factors well in mind, on a problem on which the views of actuaries as to the best practice differed.

[2.3.2]

Re George Newnes Group Pension Fund (High Court, unreported, 3 July 1969)

Actuaries' duties – transfers – reviewability

Facts and Decision

IPC took over the George Newnes group of companies in 1959 and closed its pension scheme in 1965, giving notice of dissolution. It made its own pension scheme available to the employees of the George Newnes group, offering them the option of annuities or taking a transfer. The dissolution rule of the George Newnes scheme provided that the terms and conditions of any such transfer were to be approved by the actuary, provided that the actuary should not approve terms and conditions which:

- together or separately, in his or her opinion, directly or substantially prejudiced the rights or interests of any member of the scheme at the dissolution date; or
- failed to make adequate provision to secure the future payment, to such persons as were at the dissolution date in receipt of pensions under the scheme, of the full amount of such pensions.

The actuary of the IPC scheme challenged the appropriateness of the valuation basis and assumptions used by the actuary to the George Newnes scheme for this purpose, since he had made no allowance for future service after the date of discontinuance. On a proper construction, the Court held that the dissolution rule did not require that future service had to be allowed for in ascertaining serving members' dissolution benefits. The function of an actuary in advising how a pension scheme of this kind should be dealt with, on the determination of the scheme, was to achieve the greatest practicable degree of fairness between various persons interested under the scheme, consistent with the rules governing that scheme. In performing this function an actuary must employ an expertise of great refinement, which involved assessing the weight to be given to many and various contingencies and near imponderables. The Court should be very slow to criticise or seek to control the exercise of any discretion or judgement reposed in or required of an expert of this kind in the exercise of a function of this character. The Court was unable to reach the conclusion that the method of calculation chosen produced such unreasonable or unfair results as to induce it to say that the method must be wrong.

The method of calculation rested in the actuary. Where a discretion of this kind was reposed in an expert, the burden rested on any party who criticised the decision of the expert to show that the expert had acted fraudulently or with some improper motive, or that he or she had been guilty of a mistake of a substantial character or had materially misdirected himself or herself.

Comment

This remains the leading case on the role of an actuary under a pension scheme. The key point is that the actuary is an expert, and so his or her decision may only be challenged in very limited circumstances. Provided that the actuary acts honestly and does not make an identifiable objective mistake, the decision is not open to challenge. This approach was followed in *Re Imperial Foods Ltd Pension Scheme [1986] 2 All ER 802.*

The consequence of this is that the Court will not normally involve itself in matters of actuarial principles except where the principles used are demonstrably not in accordance with standard actuarial practice. While *International Power v Healy [2001] PLR 121* does not directly address the point, the House of Lords' statement that the employer does not need to be sceptical about an actuarial certificate is implicit support for this approach. This is of course highly desirable, given that the courts do not have and do not pretend to have the expertise necessary to understand actuarial principles.

The main qualification to this is where the actuary has used an approach which is inconsistent with the terms of the rules. In *Hillsdown v Pensions Ombudsman [1997] 1 All ER 862* and *Stevens & others v Bell & others [2001] PLR 99*, where the actuary had been given a discretion under the scheme rules, the Court concluded that the rules were inconsistent with one particular basis of valuation. As always, the scheme rules are paramount.

[2.3.3]

Hillsdown v Pensions Ombudsman (High Court) [1997] 1 All ER 862, [1996] OPLR 291 at 314C–315E, [1996] PLR 427 at para 85–90

Actuaries' duties – surplus

Facts and Decision

Under the rules of a pension scheme, the actuary was obliged to certify any surplus not required to cover the immediate and prospective liabilities of the scheme, which would then be applied at the trustee's discretion in a number of different ways, which could include the suspension or reduction of the employer's contribution rate. The Court held that the aggregate method (which values the liabilities of a scheme for the past and future service of members against the assets actually held, together with the discounted value of future contributions) was not appropriate for this purpose. Since this method was directed at finding the appropriate contribution rate given an existing surplus or deficiency, and before surplus would emerge on this basis, the employer's contribution rate would necessarily be certified as zero. Such a contribution rate was inconsistent with the trustee's power to use surplus to reduce employer contribution rates. However, the appropriate actuarial techniques for the purpose of this obligation were a matter for the actuary's professional judgement, and might even be a subject upon which different techniques would be preferred by different experts.

[2.3.4]

Re Imperial Foods Ltd Pension Scheme (High Court) [1986] 2 All ER 802, [1986] 1 WLR 717

Actuaries' duties – transfers – certification

Facts and Decision

Imperial Foods' pension scheme was in surplus. Following a sale of a subsidiary, the employees of that company transferred to the new owners' scheme. The trustees of the Imperial Foods scheme made a transfer payment, calculated on a past service reserve basis in accordance with its actuary's certificate, as required by the scheme rules. The purchaser argued that transfer should have been made on a share of fund basis. The Court held that it was only where there was a cardinal error in principle that any successful challenge could be mounted to an actuarial certificate. It was not the Court's function to decide which of the two methods would be, in abstract terms, the more applicable. The Court must accept the certificate unless the actuary did not take into account all the circumstances he or she ought to have taken into account, or there was a mathematical error. The only mistake that the scheme actuary was alleged to have made was a matter of opinion, and it was conceded that his was a view which could have been held by a competent actuary. There was, therefore, no ground for overturning the certificate.

[2.3.5]

International Power v Healy (sub nom) (House of Lords) [2001] PLR 121 at para 17

Actuaries' duties – surplus – certification

Principle

Caution is a matter for the actuary in certifying pension scheme surplus. The scheme employer is not required to be sceptical about the actuarial certificate. (See also [2.3.7].)

[2.3.6]

Merchant Navy Ratings Pension Fund Trustees v Chambers (High Court) [2001] PLR 137

Actuaries' duties – section 67 of the Pensions Act 1995

Principles

Where a scheme actuary is asked to give a certificate under the *Pensions Act 1995, s 67*, to a change which would allow the trustees to effect the transfer of individuals from the scheme to another scheme, the test is whether the members would be adversely affected. The impact on the entitlement under the scheme in which the amendment is being made is not directly relevant. It is for the actuary to assess the impact on each member of the change.

[2.3.7]

National Grid Co plc v Laws (High Court) [1997] OPLR 207 at 214H–215C, 228C-H, [1997] PLR 174 at paras 19–23, 93–95

Actuaries' duties – surplus – certification

Facts and Decision

The Court observed that the National Grid pension scheme was not an ordinary balance of cost scheme, and the only duties under the rules were to deal with a past service deficit or surplus. The machinery for monitoring and adjusting the funding process was a clumsy one, and it was no criticism of the actuaries that they thought it necessary to give advice about future funding as well.

The actuary was obliged in this case to certify the arrangements for disposing of surplus. There was much, the Court held, to commend the interpretation that the actuary's certificate was a warrant of fairness, and not merely a certificate of technical correctness. (See also [2.3.5].)

[2.3.8]

Stevens & others v Bell & others (High Court) [2001] PLR 99 at paras 33 and 56

Actuaries' duties – surplus – certification – arbitration

Facts and Decision

The definition of disposable surplus in a pension scheme valued assets against the value of the accrued benefits. In determining whether there was a disposable surplus in the scheme, the Court held, the actuary could not therefore use the aggregate method of valuation, since it gave the employer the benefit of past service surplus against what would otherwise be its future service obligations.

When the actuary was required under the scheme rules to certify the amount of any disposable surplus, the actuary had to exercise professional judgement in deciding whether any, and if so how much of a surplus was a disposable surplus. No further restrictions were to be imputed into the actuary's duties on certification. Any actuarial forecast carried a more than just material risk of being wrong either way. It will be wrong, and may well be wrong to a material extent, and it is impossible to tell which way it will be wrong. The actuary was not bound to make an additional allowance, before he certified the amount of disposable surplus, to cover the risk of his being wrong one way. In deciding both on his actuarial assumptions and methods, he would decide on those that he thought appropriate, and apply them with the benefit of his professional skill and experience.

Where the actuary is to arbitrate between the employer and the trustees, the actuary must consider the proposals by the trustees and those put forward by the employer, and either side's objections to the other's proposals. He has to ensure that he is properly informed as to the circumstances of the scheme. He must then decide whether, and if so how, the trustees' proposed scheme ought to be modified so as to be the appropriate scheme to be put into effect in the circumstances, being fair and reasonable, and having regard to the interests of all concerned; members, pensioners and others, such as dependants, as well as the employer.

Role on interpretation of scheme documentation

[2.3.9]

Mettoy Pension Trustees v Evans (High Court) [1991] 2 All ER 513, [1990] 1 WLR 1587, [1990] PLR 9 (paras 127 and 137)

Actuaries' duties – interpretation of scheme documents

Principle

The relevant background facts or surrounding circumstances when interpreting the provisions of a pension scheme include common practice from time to time in the field of pension schemes generally, as evinced in particular by the evidence of the actuaries and by textbooks written by practitioners in the field. It was manifestly right that the rights of beneficiaries under a pension scheme depended first and foremost on the correct construction of the scheme documents, which was a legal matter, and not one on which actuaries were competent to testify.

2.4 – Solicitors

[2.4.1]

Esterhuizen v Allied Dunbar (High Court) 1 ITELR 211, [1998] 2 FLR 668

Solicitors' duties – execution of documents

Facts and Decision

Mr Dibden made arrangements with Allied Dunbar to make a will. Allied Dunbar prepared the will and sent it to him with instructions for execution. Mr Dibden did not follow them out properly, and as a result, the will was invalid. Mr Dibden died before the error was corrected. Mrs Esterhuizen, a potential beneficiary, sued Allied Dunbar. The Court held that Allied Dunbar owed a duty of care to Mrs Esterhuizen: *White v Jones [1995] 2 AC 207* was applied. A prudent solicitor regards it as his or her duty to take reasonable steps to assist his or her client in and about the execution of a will, rather than merely to inform the client how it is to be signed and attested. It is a curiosity of English law that the requirements of signature and attestation are, if not complex, comparatively strict. It was not enough for a solicitor or professional will provider to leave instructions with the will. To do no more would not only be contrary to good practice, but would also be negligent.

[2.4.2]

Griffiths v Dawson (High Court) [1993] OPLR 79, [1994] PLR 275, [1993] FLR 315

Solicitors' duties – pension rights on divorce

Facts and Decision

Lady Griffiths separated from her husband in 1979 after a 30 year marriage. In 1985, her husband initiated divorce proceedings after they had been separated for five years. Contrary to her specific instructions, Lady Griffiths' solicitor did not file a notice under *section 10* of the *Matrimonial Causes Act 1973*, by which a wife can apply for consideration of her financial provision. A decree absolute was accordingly granted on the divorce. As a consequence, Lady Griffiths lost her prospective entitlement to a share of her former husband's pension rights. The Court held that even if there had not been specific instructions, it would have been negligent for the solicitor not to file a notice under the *Matrimonial Causes Act 1973, s 10*, unless he or she had specific instructions not to do so.

[2.4.3]

HF Pension Trustees v Ellison (High Court) [1999] OPLR 67

Solicitors' duties – negligence – merger of firms

Facts and Decision

A solicitor advised a trustee, which was one of the trustees involved in the events under consideration in the case of *Hillsdown v Pensions Ombudsman [1997] 1 All ER 862*. In the decision in that case, the advice which the solicitor had given was disapproved. As a result, the transaction which was undertaken in that case was unwound. Legal costs, and a potential tax liability (which ultimately did not materialise) had been incurred as a result. The trustee sued the solicitor, and the firm of solicitors which subsequently merged with his firm, for negligence. The Court held that the successor firm was not liable in negligence for the earlier negligent acts of a co-partner, and could not be since such acts, by definition, could not have been done on its behalf.

[2.4.4]

Hinckley and Bosworth Borough Council v Shaw (High Court, 21 December 1998) 22 PBLR 39

Solicitors' duties – negligence

Facts and Decision

Mr Shaw was to be made redundant by his local-authority employer. The local authority increased his salary in advance of his redundancy so that his pension would be substantially higher. The council took advice from an external solicitor at the time, but did not explain to him the purpose of the increase. The council's discretion was exercised in breach of its duties to council tax payers, since this purpose was unlawful. The payment itself was therefore unlawful and void, and Mr Shaw was obliged to refund the money he had received as additional wages and pension. The Court held that the solicitor had not acted in a manner that the reasonably competent solicitor would have acted, in that he had not researched the law, he had not thought it necessary to take counsel's advice and it did not occur to him why the salary increase was being granted. If he had done so, he would have appreciated that the proposal was unlawful and void. He was, therefore, liable in negligence.

[2.4.5]

Securities and Investments Board v Pantell (No. 2) (Court of Appeal) [1993] Ch 256 at 271 and 284

Solicitors – Financial Services Act 1986 considerations

Principle

The Court held that it could make orders for compensation under the *Financial Services Act 1986*, s 6(2), against solicitors who had acted for a client carrying on unauthorised investment business, on the basis that they had been knowingly concerned in the contravention, despite the fact that they had not participated in, and had received no money from, the transactions.

Part 3 – Constitution of Trusts

3 – Introduction

This chapter deals with most of the provisions of a pension scheme which do not concern the calculation of benefits. The provisions relating to contributions, investment, winding–up and amendments each raise a sufficient number of issues to justify a chapter to themselves. This chapter gathers together other miscellaneous constitutional provisions relating to a pension scheme.

The single most important objective of any pension scheme founded under trust is to ensure that the trust is effectively established. Perhaps unsurprisingly, there have been very few pension cases which question whether a trust has been validly established. Interestingly, however, on each occasion a challenge to the trust's validity has been brought, the challenge has been successful. The threefold test of certainty of intention, certainty of the subject matter and certainty of the beneficiaries may be straightforward, but the courts have applied it with some rigour.

Pension schemes do not always set out their main purpose, but all schemes have one, whether explicitly or implicitly. The main purpose cannot be altered by amendment either explicitly or implicitly, but as *Re Courage Group's Pension Schemes, Ryan v Imperial Brewing [1987] 1 All ER 528* noted, the main purpose can be altered by degrees. The courts have taken a fairly broadbrush view as to what constitutes the main purpose: a change from final salary to money purchase provision did not alter the main purpose according to *Barclays Bank v Holmes [2000] PLR 339*, and a refund of surplus to an employer was held in *Stevens & others v Bell & others [2001] PLR 99* not of itself to infringe the main purpose.

Repayments of funds to an employer are always controversial. Repayments to employers of surpluses on windings–up are considered separately in Parts 9 and 11 on surpluses and winding up. The lawfulness of repayments from ongoing schemes depends in large part on the terms of the trust. Applying for a refund of surplus is not intrinsically in conflict with the main purpose, as noted above. *Taylor v Lucas Pension Trust [1994] OPLR 29* shows that the courts will not automatically prevent trustees from using statutory powers to apply for their scheme to be modified so that the employer can take a refund of surplus. However, the courts are rightly highly critical of employers who attempt to subvert the system. *McConnell v Boyd [1997] OPLR 53* shows how the courts take a tough line on employers who try to play fast and loose with pension scheme duties.

There is a rule of trust law, known as the rule against perpetuities, which prevents assets being tied up in trusts indefinitely. Its rules are complex, and have been modified by the *Perpetuities and Accumulations Act 1964*. Tax approved retirement benefits schemes are not subject to the rule against perpetuities. This exemption was introduced, retrospectively, following the decision in *Lucas v Telegraph Construction [1925] LN 211*. However, this exemption does not apply to unapproved schemes or to schemes which lose their exempt approved status, and so the case law on the rule against perpetuities remains of relevance. Its operation in a pensions context is complicated, and the courts in recent years have gone out of their way to ensure that the rule causes as little damage to the terms of the trust as possible. The effect of the decision in *Air Jamaica v Charlton [1999] 1 WLR 1399* that the rule against perpetuities must be applied separately to each individual settlement, is to minimise its impact, so that only benefits on a winding-up will ordinarily be affected; an approach prefigured by the decision in *Re Thomas Meadows & Co Ltd and Subsidiary Companies (1960) Staff Pension Scheme Rules [1971] Ch 278*.

The courts were initially wary of the notion of a power of substitution of principal employer, and the decision in *Re Courage Group's Pension Schemes, Ryan v Imperial Brewing* spent much time determining whether such powers could ever be consistent with the main purpose of a pension scheme. Ultimately, it set out a detailed test for the appropriateness of such a power, which if taken literally is fairly restrictive. The test requires that the substituted company must be recognisably the successor to the business and workforce of the company for which it is to be substituted, and that it must have succeeded to all or most of the former company's employees. If this prevents the replacement of principal employer by a holding company, this is unfortunate. Similarly, in the case of some demergers, it may be in the interests of all concerned that the demerging company becomes the principal employer, but it will not always be the case that it will be recognisably the successor to the business and the workforce, or that it has succeeded to all or most of the former company's employees. Fortunately, when this type of problem arose in *Taylor, Petitioner, Re Ellis & McHardy Ltd Retirement Benefits Scheme [1999] OPLR 275*, the Court took a pragmatic approach.

The courts have yet to reach a settled view on the nature of the power to appoint and remove trustees. Two nineteenth-century private trust cases, one a Court of Appeal decision, held that the power was fiduciary. However, the judiciary in pension cases in recent years have been trying to circumvent these decisions. *Simpson Curtis Pension Trustees v Readson*

[1994] OPLR 231 and *Independent Pension Trustee v LAW Construction [1996] OPLR 259* were both decided on the basis that the employer's power to appoint and remove trustees transferred to receivers as an asset of the employer. This is inconsistent with the concept of the power being fiduciary in the full sense of the word, since if it were, the employer would not be permitted to exercise it for its own benefit. One way of reconciling these conflicting lines of case law is to treat the power as fiduciary in a more limited sense, as canvassed in *Simpson Curtis Pension Trustees v Readson*. This has yet to be worked out, however, and it is unclear how, if at all, this differs from the employer's implied obligation of good faith where the power is vested in the employer.

3.1 – Establishment of trust

[3.1.1]

Attorney-General of Canada v Confederation Life (Ontario Court of Justice, unreported, 4 July 1995)

Certainty of trusts – unfunded schemes

Facts and Decision

Confederation Life, a large insurer, became insolvent. It had never entered into a formal trust agreement in relation to its pension obligations, but the Board had approved a document providing that the trustees should ensure that the pension schemes were funded in a manner that would enable them to meet all their obligations. They were, however, pay-as-you-go schemes. Scheme members were supplied with a booklet summarising the benefits but which stated that it did not create or confer any contractual rights, and that all rights with respect to the benefits of a member would be governed by the group policy. Confederation Life also provided supplementary pensions for senior officers. Those pensions were paid in accordance with Board resolutions. Neither the resolutions nor the letters to senior officers required a fund to be established, and the supplementary scheme was not funded. The employees, former employees and their dependants, argued that the assets of Confederation Life were subject to a trust in respect of the amount required to satisfy all pension liabilities, as did members of the supplementary scheme. The Court observed that in order for it to hold that a trust exists, there needed to be established certainty of intention on the part of the settlor to create a trust, certainty of the subject matter of the trust, and certainty of the object or persons intended to be the beneficiaries of the trust. In cases such as this one, where what was argued was that the alleged settlor and the proposed trustee were in effect one and the same, particular difficulties arose. All categories of claimants failed to sustain their claims, since there was neither certainty of subject matter nor of intention.

[3.1.2]

Re Flavel's Will Trusts (High Court) [1969] I WLR 444

Certainty of trusts

Facts and Decision

Mr Flavel specified in his will that the trustees were to use one third of his estate for the formation of a superannuation and bonus fund for the employees of his family company, the fund to be established and constituted in such manner as the trustees should in their absolute discretion think fit. Although the beneficiaries were specified, and that they were to take benefits on superannuation, the rest was left in obscurity. The Court held that while it would be possible to draw up a superannuation and bonus fund, no one could say with any certainty that it gave effect to Mr Flavel's intention.

[3.1.3]

Pappadakis v Pappadakis (High Court) The Times, 19 January 2000

Certainty of trusts

Facts and Decision

Mr Pappadakis purported to assign a life assurance policy under a declaration of trust. He did not name trustees, and the deed was executed by Mr Pappadakis only. The Court held that the declaration of trust was invalid, and the policy remained in the absolute ownership of Mr Pappadakis. The document could not take effect as an assignment of a policy, since it was impossible to assign anything to nobody. A voluntary and gratuitous assignment could not be saved from invalidity by equity holding it to be a declaration of trust by the unsuccessful assignor. The deed could not be construed to be a declaration of trust. It was not intended to be a declaration of trust, and equity will not hold a transaction to have been something which it was not intended to be. Rectification was also unavailable.

3.2 – Main purpose of the fund

[3.2.1]

Barclays Bank v Holmes (High Court) [2000] PLR 339 at paras 113, 115

Main purpose – money purchase benefits

Facts and Decision

The introduction of a money purchase section into a defined benefits scheme did not, the Court held, infringe a restriction on the power of amendment preventing amendments which caused the main purpose of the scheme to cease to be that of provision of retirement pensions. Nor was the introduction of such a section outside the general powers of the employer and trustees under the general law. The introduction of a new section was not for an extraneous or ulterior purpose such as was canvassed in *Re Courage Group's Pension Schemes [1987] 1 All ER 528*. Chadwick LJ's comments in *Edge v Pensions Ombudsman [2000] 3 WLR 79* about the nature of a defined benefits scheme were recording the fact that the scheme in that case was a defined benefits scheme and the consequences that followed as a result, and were not to be taken as laying down any general rules about amending such schemes.

[3.2.2]

Re Courage Group's Pension Schemes, Ryan v Imperial Brewing (High Court) [1987] 1 All ER 528, [1987] 1 WLR 495

Main purpose – power of amendment – effect of time

Principle

It is implicit in a power of amendment that it cannot be used to alter the main purpose of a pension scheme. A power can be exercised only for the purpose for which it has been conferred, and not for an extraneous or ulterior purpose. However, even the main purpose of a pension scheme may be changed by degrees: *Thellusson v Viscount Valentia [1907] 2 Ch 1* was considered. The main purpose may be enlarged by appropriate amendments to the rules, and once it becomes too late to challenge the amendments, the enlarged purposes become the new basis by reference to which any further proposed changes must be considered. Where on a reconstruction substantially the same persons continue to be employed in an undertaking, the substitution of the reconstructed company for the original principal employer for the purpose of a pension scheme is not only necessary and desirable, but can properly be said to promote the main purpose of the scheme and not to alter it.

[3.2.3]

Edge v Pensions Ombudsman (Court of Appeal) [2000] 3 WLR 79, [1999] OPLR 179 at 193C-G, 196C, [1999] PLR 215 at paras 34, 49

Main purpose – final salary scheme

Principle

The main purpose rule of the pension scheme under consideration embodied three concepts fundamental to a defined benefits pension scheme:

- First, the purpose of the scheme was to provide the retirement and other benefits to which the members, pensioners and dependants were entitled under the rules.
- Second, the fund out of which the benefits were to be provided was constituted and maintained by means of periodic payments. The amount of those payments depended not only on the rate of contributions but also on the number of members in service from time to time who were contributors, and on the number of employers who continue to participate.
- Third, the task of the trustees was to maintain a balance between assets, and liabilities valued on an actuarial basis.

The main purpose of the scheme is not served by putting an employer out of business, nor by setting contributions and benefits at levels which deter employees from joining or which cause resentment.

[3.2.4]

International Power v Healy (House of Lords) [2001] PLR 121 at para 16

Main purpose – refunds of surplus

Principle

It was not inconsistent with the main purpose of a pension scheme to make a payment to the employer. A surplus is (by definition) money in excess of what is needed to effect the main purpose of the scheme.

[3.2.5]

Lock v Westpac (Supreme Court of New South Wales) [1991] PLR 167 at 50

Main purpose – interpretation

Principle

The substratum of a pension scheme is to be determined as a matter of construction of the deed and having regard to the relevant circumstances.

[3.2.6]

LRT v Hatt (High Court) [1993] OPLR 225 at 264F, [1993] PLR 227 at para 155

Main purpose – scheme formed by merger

Principle

In the context of a new pension scheme established as an amalgamation of two existing pension schemes, the factual matrix was highly significant in assessing the purposes of this scheme. The purposes of the scheme included that amalgamation.

[3.2.7]

Stevens & others v Bell & others (High Court) [2001] PLR 99 at paras 52 and 53

Main purpose – refunds of surplus

Principle

A clause in a pension scheme allowing a repayment to the employer may be consistent with the main objects clause, if a negotiation between the trustees and the employer over the use of surplus which is intrinsic to the process is inherent within it.

[3.2.8]

UEB Industries v Brabant (Court of Appeal of New Zealand) [1991] PLR 109, [1992] 1 NZLR 294

Main purpose – refunds of surplus

Facts and Decision

UEB gave notice on 1 December 1988 that it was ceasing to contribute to the pension scheme which it sponsored for its employees, and the scheme was wound up. The scheme had a substantial surplus. The trustees proposed to use 70% of the surplus for the employer and 30% for the beneficiaries. In 1980, the scheme winding-up rule had been amended to authorise a refund of any unexpended balance to the company (previously there had been a permanent alienation clause), and the validity of this amendment was challenged. The Court held that the terms of the original permanent alienation clause made it perfectly clear that allowing the company to participate in the surplus would be to depart from the terms of the trusts. It was not possible to remove a restriction which prevented an amendment which would authorise a repayment of funds to the employer (Richardson J not relying upon this ground).

3.3 – Repayments to employers

[3.3.1]

Hillsdown v Commissioners of Inland Revenue (High Court) [1999] OPLR 173, [1999] STC 561

Refunds of surplus – tax treatment

Facts and Decision

Hillsdown obtained a refund of surplus from one of its occupational pension schemes. Following the decision in *Hillsdown v Pensions Ombudsman* [1997] 1 All ER 862, Hillsdown was obliged to repay the sum refunded. The Inland Revenue refused to reimburse the tax paid on the refund. The Court held that on a proper construction of the *Income and Corporation Taxes Act 1988, s 601*, a purported repayment of surplus in which no beneficial interest passed was not a payment for the purposes of this section.

[3.3.2]

McConnell v Boyd (High Court) [1997] OPLR 53

Breach of trust – calculation of loss

Facts and Decision

An employer was advised to make additional contributions of £5,000 for twelve consecutive months to restore its pension scheme to balance. These payments were made, but unknown to the other trustees, two trustees (who were also company directors) wrote cheques in ten of these months for £5,000 from the trustees to the company to counteract the effect of the standing order. The Pensions Ombudsman ordered that the trustees responsible pay £50,000 to the scheme plus interest. The trustees argued that only £5,000 loss was suffered, since the same £5,000 was moving back and forth between the scheme and the company. This submission was rejected by the Court as fanciful: the company was paying a liability by instalments, it was not paying a single sum repeatedly.

[3.3.3]

Merrett v Pensions Ombudsman (High Court) [1998] OPLR 161

Repayment to employer – provisional contributions

Facts and Decision

An employer contributed to its pension scheme for six months. When an actuarial valuation disclosed a surplus, it took a refund from the scheme. The employer was obliged under the scheme rules to contribute the amounts required to provide the benefits of the scheme. The Court held that the employer had been paying on account, as in previous years, and that nothing prevented it taking a refund. No one had intended that it was irrevocably committing itself to increasing the surplus.

[3.3.4]

Stevens & others v Bell & others (High Court) [2001] PLR 99 at paras 51–53

Main purpose – refunds of surplus

Principle

A clause in a pension scheme allowing a repayment to the employer may be consistent with the main objects clause, if a negotiation between the trustees and the employer over the use of surplus which is intrinsic to the process is inherent within it. The employer must comply with the duty of good faith recognised in *Imperial Group Pension Trust v Imperial Tobacco [1991] 2 All ER 597*.

[3.3.5]

Taylor v Lucas Pension Trust (High Court) [1994] OPLR 29, [1994] PLR 9

Refunds of surplus – statutory power of modification – trustees' duties

Facts and Decision

The Lucas Staff Pension Scheme was in very substantial surplus. Its provisions did not permit repayments from surplus to any employer, and the power of amendment was subject to a restriction that no amendment was authorised which would permit a repayment to any employer. There was no power to improve scheme benefits without the consent of the principal employer. Following negotiations between the employers and the trustees, a division of surplus was agreed, which included £121 million of benefit improvements and a repayment of £90 million of surplus to the employers. In order to achieve this, the trustee applied to the Occupational Pensions Board (OPB) for a modification order. Two members complained that it was a breach of duty for the trustee to apply for a modification order, since it was only entitled to have regard to the interests of the members and pensioners, who were the beneficiaries. If, however, the surplus was not eliminated, a substantial tax liability would fall due. The Court observed that the employer had an interest insofar as surplus could be used to relieve it of its obligation to contribute. On the facts, and having regard to the advice the trustee received, it could not be said that the decision to accept the proposals and apply to the OPB for a modification order was a decision which no reasonable body of trustees mindful of the interests of their beneficiaries could have reached, or that they were influenced by improper motives.

Comment

The decision in this case is interesting because of the way in which the Court construed the statutory power to apply for a modification order with the trustee's general duty to act in the interests of the beneficiaries. If the members had been successful in this case, the statutory power to apply for a modification order would have been unusable, since on the members' argument no trustee could ever apply for a modification order to alter the priorities on winding-up without committing a breach of trust. It was always unlikely that the Court would have construed the law in this way.

Also of interest is the Court's observation that the employer had an interest in the pension scheme surplus even where it did not have a beneficial interest, because of its liability to contribute to the scheme. This judicial recognition of the employer's additional interest as a contributor to the trust is apparently so far unique to pensions, but may be applicable in other trusts where third parties enter into a contractual liability to contribute to the trust.

3.4 – Perpetuity periods

[3.4.1]

*Air Jamaica v Charlton (Privy Council) [1999] 1 WLR 1399,
[1999] OPLR 11, [1999] PLR 247*

Perpetuity periods – winding-up

Facts and Decision

Air Jamaica operated a defined benefit pension scheme with a substantial surplus. The company was loss-making, and its assets were disposed to the private sector. As a result, all of the employees were made redundant. Some employees applied to Court for a declaration that the scheme had been discontinued and for an order that the surplus should be applied for the benefit of members and dependants. The scheme made no provision for repayment of surplus on a winding-up to the employer. The employer and the trustees purported to amend the scheme to remove a restriction on employer contributions being refunded to it, and to alter the winding-up rule to give the employer an interest in the distribution on winding-up. The Privy Council observed that on the facts, the scheme was in winding-up. The purported amendments were of no effect since the employer could not achieve in two steps what it could not achieve in one. Unlike English law, Jamaican law had no statutory provision disapplying the rule against perpetuities. A defined benefit scheme is properly regarded as a series of separate settlements. Every time an employee joins the scheme, a new settlement is created. The rule against perpetuities must be applied separately to each individual settlement, and each employee must be treated as a life in being in relation to his or her own settlement. All benefits paid on death or retirement were therefore valid. The only provisions struck down in this case were a widow's power to designate a beneficiary to receive benefits, and the distribution of surplus on a winding-up. On the proper construction of the trust deed, a resulting trust arose in favour of both employer and employees.

Comment

At first blush, the application of a Jamaican case on the rule against perpetuities, a rule which does not apply to British exempt approved retirement benefits schemes, would seem very limited. It is certainly true that the main ground of the decision will rarely need to be considered by British pension schemes, but the Privy Council made numerous observations about the nature of pension schemes which will be pored over by pension lawyers for years to come. These observations appear in many places through this book, and this is not the place to comment on all the relevant points in the judgment, there simply not being enough space to do so.

Two points in particular, however, are worthy of special note. The first is the Privy Council's confirmation that a power of amendment cannot be used to make an amendment in order to empower an amendment which was not previously permissible. This is a simple but important restriction on the use of powers of amendment.

The second point to note is more theoretical, concerning the nature of pension scheme trusts. The Privy Council analysed each member's interest as a separate settlement for the purpose of the rule against perpetuities. This is a very similar approach to that used in *Re Thomas Meadows & Co Ltd and Subsidiary Companies (1960) Staff Pension Scheme Rules [1971] Ch 278*. Neuberger J argued in *Barclays Bank v Holmes [2000] PLR 339* that this approach should be confined to the analysis of the rule against perpetuities. However, the Privy Council's analysis bears some similarities to the approach taken by the Court of Appeal in *Jones v Patel* (unreported), where the Court identified the member's pension scheme interest which transfers on bankruptcy as relating to the member's past and future entitlement under the pension scheme. The theoretical foundations of a pension scheme trust are still being worked through.

[3.4.2]

Re Flavel's Will Trusts (High Court) [1969] 1 WLR 444

Perpetuity periods – interpretation

Facts and Decision

Mr Flavel specified in his will that the trustees were to use one third of his estate for the formation of a superannuation and bonus fund for the employees of his family company, the fund to be established and constituted in such manner as the trustees should in their absolute discretion think fit. The Court held that the bequest was void for remoteness, breaking the rule against perpetuities (none of the statutory exemptions applying). The Court could not construe the class as being limited to the employees for the time being.

[3.4.3]

Lucas v Telegraph Construction (High Court) [1925] LN 211

Perpetuity periods – application to pension trusts

Principle

A private company pension scheme is not a charity, and thus is not exempt from perpetuity periods on that footing. Since the trusts in this case undoubtedly constituted a perpetuity, they were void.

[3.4.4]

Re Thomas Meadows & Co Ltd and Subsidiary Companies (1960) Staff Pension Scheme Rules (High Court) [1971] Ch 278

Perpetuity period – application to pension trusts

Facts and Decision

Under the rules of an insured pension scheme, which came into effect in 1960, the employer was obliged to keep a register of members, made up on 1 September each year. Each person on the register became entitled in certain events to a pension. The insurance company paid to the company the pensions which had to be provided under the scheme. The scheme gave powers which might be exercised outside the perpetuity period, and a dissolution might take place outside the perpetuity period. The Court held that this was void at common law, for breaking the rule against perpetuities. *Section 3* of the *Perpetuities and Accumulations Act 1964* has the capacity to save dispositions made otherwise than under instruments taking effect before that *Act* came into force. There was no warrant, though, for saying that the members' interests arose under the rules, which merely set out terms to affect the policy when it arose. The group policy created nothing until persons were brought within its ambit. It was wrong to suggest each annual premium was a disposition, because that drew a distinction between the policy and its fruits. The disposition was plainly the entry of each name on the register as regards the pension to be granted to that person. There was, however, a fresh disposition with regard to any higher benefits, in any case where a member had been promoted to a higher grade. Accordingly, the *Act* must be applied in regard to each payment coming into the scheme according to the date when the person insured was first entered on the register, or promoted to a higher grade. The perpetuity period ran separately for each individual from the date when they were entered on the register.

3.5 – Power of substitution of principal employer

[3.5.1]

Re Courage Group's Pension Schemes, Ryan v Imperial Brewing (High Court) [1987] 1 All ER 528, [1987] 1 WLR 495

Substitution of principal employer – proper use of power – main purpose

Facts and Decision

Following a hostile takeover, the principal employer of three pension schemes was sold to another company. Each of the pension schemes was in surplus, and the parent company sought to retain the benefit of the surpluses within the group. It therefore proposed amending each of the scheme rules to introduce a power of substitution of principal employer, so that it could be appointed as principal employer in the place of the existing principal employer. The Court observed that it was a novel and startling proposition that a company could be sold and continue to employ substantially the whole of the workforce for whose benefit the scheme was established, and yet the scheme itself could be excluded from the sale. It was obviously desirable that some provision for substitution should be included in a group pension scheme. It would be unfortunate if the whole scheme had to be wound up merely because on some reorganisation of the group the principal employer was put into liquidation. A pension scheme was established not for the benefit of a particular company but for the benefit of those employed in a commercial undertaking. Where on a reconstruction substantially the same persons continue to be employed in the undertaking, then the substitution of the reconstructed company for the original principal employer for the purpose of a pension scheme was not only necessary and desirable, but could properly be said to promote the main purpose of the scheme and not to alter it. However, in this case, the parent company did not employ and had never employed any of the employees for whose benefit the scheme had been established. Any such substitution would manifestly alter the main purpose of the scheme and be *ultra vires*. The validity of a power of substitution depended on the circumstances in which it was capable of being exercised, and the characteristics which must be possessed by the company capable of being substituted. The validity of any exercise depends on the purpose for which the substitution was made. Substitution must be necessary or at least expedient in order to preserve the scheme for whose benefit it was established. The substituted company must be recognisably the successor to the business and workforce of the company for which it was to be substituted. It must have succeeded to all or most of the former company's employees.

Comment

Re Courage is in many ways the foundation for modern pension case law. It was far from the first pension case to reach the courts, and the courts had already been obliged to consider the way in which general principles of trust law applied to pension schemes (for example in *Cowan v Scargill [1984] 2 All ER 750*). However, *Re Courage* was the first case to take a comprehensive look at how commercial considerations interrelated with the trust law duties of the pension scheme trustees.

The decision has in general stood the test of time well. The decision is founded on the Court's view of the purpose of the pension scheme power of amendment, and its conclusion that it was not intended to facilitate trafficking in surplus between employers where scheme members were not transferring from one employer to another. The Court's observations on the nature of the main purpose of a pension scheme remain required reading today.

The decision is slightly less helpful when exploring the circumstances in which a power of substitution of principal employer can be exercised. The Court put forward a test under which the substituted company must be recognisably the successor to the business and workforce of the company for which it was to be substituted, and must have succeeded to all or most of the former company's employees. However, in real life, company reorganisations are often not that simple. Sometimes the business and workforce are divided between several new companies. Sometimes there is no single recognisable successor to the former employer. If read literally, this decision would not permit the substitution of principal employer in such circumstances, even when it was in the interests of the beneficiaries as a whole. A better reading of the judgment is perhaps to treat it as illustrative of the circumstances in which a substitution will promote the purpose of the pension scheme, and not as an exhaustive list.

[3.5.2]

Hillsdown v Pensions Ombudsman (High Court) [1997] I All ER 862, [1996] OPLR 291 at 312G–313D, [1996] PLR 427 at paras 78–80

Substitution of principal employer – proper use of power

Principle

It is not possible to draw a hard and fast line between the creation of a power of substitution and its exercise. The whole transaction would need to be investigated before a proper view could be formed regarding the validity both of the Deed creating the power of substitution, and the Deed exercising that power.

[3.5.3]

Independent Pension Trustee v LAW Construction (Scottish Court of Session, Outer House) [1996] OPLR 259

Substitution of principal employer – insolvency – proper use of power

Facts and Decision

Law Construction Co. Ltd was principal employer of a pension scheme with other participating employers. It went into receivership in 1992, whereupon the other participating employers purported to appoint Law Holdings Limited as principal employer in its place, Law Construction acting by its directors. Law Holdings then purported to appoint Hymans Robertson Trustees as the scheme trustee. The receivers did not consent to this change of principal employer and purported to appoint Independent Pension Trustee as the scheme trustee. The Court held that during the currency of a receivership, the Board of directors of the employer had no power over assets in the possession or control of the receiver. These assets included rights and powers insofar as these had commercial value or significance. The manner of exercise of rights, powers and obligations under the pension scheme could bear on the value of exploitable assets such as goodwill, and as such had commercial value or significance. The directors therefore had no power to enter into a substitution of principal employer and appoint and remove trustees. The receivers' appointed trustee was, therefore, the proper scheme trustee. The power of substitution of principal employer was, though, a power which could be legitimately exercised by an employer to secure an advantage for itself.

Taylor, Petitioner, Re Ellis & McHardy Ltd Retirement Benefits Scheme (Court of Session, Inner House, Scotland) [1999] OPLR 275

Substitution of principal employer – informal use of power

Facts and Decision

Ellis & McHardy Ltd, which at the time carried on the business of coal distributors, established a pension scheme for its employees in 1971. By 1991, a company called North Eastern Farmers Ltd executed deeds in relation to the scheme as its principal company. Some scheme documentation had been lost, but there was no evidence that replacement of the principal employer had ever been formally documented. The principal company was defined in the definitive trust deed as including: 'any company which shall hereafter carry on substantially the same business as that now carried on by Ellis & McHardy Ltd and in succession hereto'. North Eastern Farmers Ltd did not carry on the coal distribution business (which had rapidly diminished in significance), but had acquired the bulk of the business of Ellis & McHardy Ltd as it then operated in 1985. For the purposes of assessing whether North Eastern Farmers Ltd carried on the same business as Ellis & McHardy Ltd, the Court held that what was required to be considered was the underlying undertaking as a matter of commercial reality: *Re Courage Group's Pension Schemes [1987] 1 All ER 528* was applied. Business was not synonymous with trade. On the evidence, North Eastern Farmers Ltd had succeeded to the undertaking in 1985 and was therefore the principal company. Mr Taylor, the sole trustee, who had been appointed by North Eastern Farmers Ltd had, therefore, been validly appointed.

3.6 – Appointment and removal of trustees

[3.6.1]

Clark v Hicks (High Court) [1992] OPLR 185, [1992] PLR 213

Appointment of trustee – independent trustee

Facts and Decision

Mr Clark, who was a partner in a firm of solicitors, was appointed as independent trustee of a pension scheme pursuant to *s 57C* of the *Social Security Pensions Act 1975* on 31 January 1992. He instructed his own firm to give legal advice in relation to the scheme. *Regulation 2* of the *Occupational Pension Schemes (Independent Trustees) Regulations 1990 (SI 1990 No 2075)* required that in order to qualify as an independent trustee, a person must not have provided services to the employer, trustees or managers of the scheme. This requirement was, however, satisfied if the last occasion on which the person provided services was more than three years before *s 57C* of the *Social Security Pensions Act 1975* started to apply in relation to the scheme. The trustee would also not qualify as an independent trustee if he or she was connected with or an associate of someone who had provided services. The obligation on insolvency practitioners under *s 57C* was in order to satisfy themselves that there was an independent trustee if and so long as the *section* applied. Accordingly, the Court held, Mr Clark ceased to be an independent trustee when he used his own firm.

[3.6.2]

Davis v Richards & Wallington Industries Ltd (High Court) [1991] 2 All ER 563, [1990] 1 WLR 1511, [1990] PLR 141 at paras 84–95

Resignation of trustee

Principle

Properly construed, where a power of appointment and removal of trustees permits the principal company to appoint a new trustee in the place of a trustee who has resigned from office, a trustee may resign office without further documentary evidence being required.

[3.6.3]

Denny v Yeldon (High Court) [1995] 3 All ER 624, [1995] OPLR 115, [1995] PLR 37

Appointment of trustee – removal of trustee – independent trustee

Facts and Decision

The administrator of an insolvent company appointed an independent trustee for its pension scheme as required by statute. The administrators and independent trustee then entered into a deed of amendment, conferring the power of appointment and removal of trustees on the trustees. The independent trustee resolved to wind up the scheme at a time when there were no more employees of the company. Subsequently, the administrator purported to replace its appointee with another independent trustee, exercising its statutory power. The Court held that as a matter of statutory construction, the administrator no longer had the power to appoint and remove independent trustees once the scheme had no further members in pensionable service. Accordingly, the purported replacement of the independent trustee was ineffective.

[3.6.4]

Hardman v Mineworkers' Pension Scheme Trustees (Pensions Ombudsman 16 May 1997) Case E00530

Appointment of trustee – election

Facts and Decision

The Mineworkers' Pension Scheme selected ten trustees from the pensioners by election. Mr Hardman stood for election. Each candidate had the right, under the articles of association of the trustee company, to provide brief biographical details and a personal statement amounting in total to not more than three hundred words. If so provided, the Committee was then required (unless it considered the contents to be misleading or defamatory) to circulate such details and statement with the ballot form. The pension scheme manager edited Mr Hardman's statement on the basis that it would mislead the electorate. Mr Hardman lost the election and complained to the Pensions Ombudsman. The Ombudsman held that the articles of association plainly imposed a duty to circulate the complete statement, subject to a discretion according to the words in parenthesis not to do so. The circulation of an edited or incomplete statement was not empowered. The pension scheme manager did not have the authority to edit the statement; this was vested in the Committee. The offending parts of the statement were not defamatory or misleading. The Ombudsman, therefore, directed that the election be re-run.

[3.6.5]

Independent Pension Trustee v LAW Construction (Scottish Court of Session, Outer House) [1996] OPLR 259

Appointment of trustee – insolvency

Principle

During the currency of a receivership, the Board of the employers has no power over assets in the possession or control of the receiver. These assets include rights and powers insofar as these have commercial value or significance. The manner of exercise of rights, powers and obligations under the pension scheme could bear on the value of exploitable assets such as goodwill, and as such had commercial value or significance. The directors, therefore, had no power to appoint and remove trustees.

[3.6.6]

LRT v Hatt (High Court) [1993] OPLR 225 at 259H–262G, [1993] PLR 227 at paras 135–148

Appointment of trustee – corporate trustee

Facts and Decision

Individual pension scheme trustees were replaced by a corporate trustee which was not a trustee corporation. *Section 37(1)(c)* of the *Trustee Act 1925* provides that a trustee shall not be discharged from his trust unless there will be either a trust corporation or at least two individuals to act as trustees to perform the trust. The Court held that where there was a very wide power of amendment, and none of the limitations on it had any bearing on the issue, it was permissible to treat as an exercise of that power the execution of any deed by the employer and the trustees which evinced an intention to achieve a result achievable by the exercise of that power, so long as there was not shown to be an intention not to exercise the power of amendment. It was not conclusive that the parties had no exercise of the power of amendment in mind. On a proper consideration of its context, *s 37(1)(c)* of the *Trustee Act 1925* was not a prohibition, but a warning that nothing in the *Act* should be taken as authorising the appointment of a sole trustee. The appointment was, therefore, effective.

[3.6.7]

Polly Peck International v Henry (High Court) [1998] OPLR 323, [1999] PLR 135

Appointment of trustee – Court discretion

Facts and Decision

Polly Peck was the principal employer and trustee of a pension scheme. The company went into administration, and the administrators applied to have the company replaced by an independent trustee. The Court held that it would not substitute an independent trustee for an insolvent employer acting as trustee, where the insolvent employer could not charge for its services and the independent trustee would not accept office unless the Court authorised it to charge for its services. The company administrator had power to act as trustee and it was part of his duties. It would not be more cost effective to replace it as trustee, and the evidence did not support a finding that the independent trustee had any necessary expertise which the administrator did not have.

[3.6.8]

Re Shortridge (Court of Appeal) [1895] I Ch 278

Appointment of trustee – nature of the power

Principle

The power of appointing new trustees is a power vested in that person in the character of a trustee, and is a fiduciary power: *Re Skeats' Settlement [1889] 42 Ch D 522* was followed.

[3.6.9]

Simpson Curtis Pension Trustees v Readson (High Court) [1994] OPLR 231, [1994] PLR 289

Appointment of trustee – removal of trustee – independent trustee – insolvency

Facts and Decision

A pension scheme's power of appointment and removal of trustees was vested in the principal employer. In 1989, the principal employer went into administrative receivership. In 1992, the administrative receiver purported to exercise the power of appointment and removal of trustees. The trustees who were replaced claimed that the administrative receiver did not have this power, and that it was a power for exercise by the Board of directors. The replacement trustees applied to Court for guidance. The Court held that the power of appointment of a new trustee was not an asset of the company in the true sense. Neither was the power of appointment nor of removal of a trustee a fiduciary power in the full sense. It was one thing to say that a power was a fiduciary power, and another to decide what it meant in the context of any particular power. Since the prime purpose of appointing the trustee was to enable the trustee to take proper steps to administer the scheme, and to ascertain what liability the company as principal employer might still owe to the pension scheme, this was a necessary step in the process of ascertaining the final value of the assets of the company. The appointment was therefore within the powers of the administrative receiver, both under the terms of the debenture and the terms of *Schedule 1* of the *Insolvency Act 1986*. ·

[3.6.10]

Re Skeats' Settlement (High Court) [1889] 42 Ch D 522

Appointment of trustee – nature of the power

Principle

The power of appointment of trustees is fiduciary. It followed from this that the person in whom the power was vested could not appoint himself or herself as trustee.

[3.6.11]

Taylor, Petitioner, Re Ellis & McHardy Ltd Retirement Benefits Scheme (Court of Session, Inner House, Scotland) [1999] OPLR 275

Resignation of trustee – trustees inquorate – powers of remaining trustees

Facts and Decision

The definitive trust deed of a pension scheme provided that upon the death or retirement of any trustee the principal company shall as soon as possible appoint a new trustee in his or her place, it being the intention that unless a trust corporation shall for the time being be acting as trustee, the number of trustees shall never be less than three. The scheme had only one trustee, his co-trustees having resigned. The Court held that nothing in the power of appointment and removal of trustees prevented a trustee who had become the sole trustee, by reason of the resignation of the other trustees, from acting as a trustee pending the appointment of new trustees.

3.7 – Expenses of beneficiaries

[3.7.1]

Independent Pension Trustee v Stevens (High Court, unreported, 13 November 2000)

Expenses of beneficiaries – Court discretion

Facts and Decision

A final salary pension scheme went into winding-up with a surplus on the insolvency of its employer. The employer's receivers made representations to the trustees, which the trustees found of assistance in finalising their proposals for the use of the surplus. The trustees asked for the Court's authority to pay the receiver's expenses in preparing their submissions, having no power to do so under the trust deed and rules. The Court declined to do so: while it had power to authorise remuneration for a trustee (see *Re Duke of Norfolk Settlement Trusts [1982] Ch 61*), and had authorised the expenses of a liquidator of a trustee company from the assets of a trust, it would have no jurisdiction to do so when the expenses had been incurred by a beneficiary and had been of no benefit to the trust property as a whole. Even if it had jurisdiction, it would have declined to exercise it in this case. The receivers were in a position to get legal advice as to the recovery of their expenses, and they neither sought nor obtained any assurance from the trustees that their expenses would be paid. They incurred costs because they thought it was in their own interests to do so.

Part 4 – Contributions

4 – Introduction

The contribution provisions of a pension scheme differ between money purchase schemes and defined benefits schemes. In a money purchase scheme, the employer and the members each undertake to contribute a fixed amount. Generally, the duty for both employers and members is straightforward to understand, although there may be questions about the circumstances in which the employer can meet its obligation to contribute from any surplus in the scheme, as may occur where a money purchase section has been established in a defined benefits scheme: *Barclays Bank v Holmes [2000] PLR 339* and *Kemble v Hicks (No. 2) [1999] OPLR 1* are examples of this problem. Whether such an offset is possible is a matter of construction of the scheme's provisions, which explains the contrasting results in these cases.

The position is more complex with defined benefits schemes. Ordinarily the member contributes a fixed amount (if members are required to contribute at all), and the employer undertakes to meet the balance of cost. However, the nature of the employer's obligation can vary substantially. The employer may be under an obligation to pay a minimum contribution. The employer may have control of determining the level of contributions, or control may be given to the trustees. Alternatively, the contributions may be set by agreement between the trustees and the employer. Occasionally, schemes place the responsibility in the hands of the scheme actuary. More commonly, the person setting the employer contribution rate is obliged to consult or act upon the advice of the actuary.

The precise wording of the employer's contribution liability is key to determining the employer's obligations in various circumstances: this is perhaps most sharply illustrated by *Re Canadian Union of Public Employees – CLC, Ontario Hydro Employees, Local [1000] and Ontario Hydro [1989] 68 OR (2d) 620*, where the employer had no right to take a contribution holiday merely because the scheme was in surplus. The general rule stated in *Tek Corporation Provident Fund v Lorentz [1999] OPLR 137* amounts to no more than that, and it can be displaced by clear words.

Members and employers may differ about the extent of the employer's obligation to contribute when the scheme is in deficit. Perhaps because in recent years most schemes have been in surplus, this has only been considered once by the courts, in *Thompson v Ritec (Employment Appeal Tribunal, unreported, 10 December 1996)*. With declines in scheme solvency over the last few years, however, I expect such disputes to reach the courts increasingly frequently.

Problems about member contributions are uncommon. There are two major reasons for this. First, the employer and trustees have much more effective control over member contributions than trustees have over employer contributions, since the sums are deducted from the members' wages in advance by the employer. Secondly, the basis of contribution is usually a fixed percentage, which leads to much less debate about the proper basis of calculation. It is notable that *Gissing v Liverpool Corporation [1935] 1 Ch 1*, the only case concerning ordinary member contributions, was about mistakes made by the employer about the deduction of member contributions.

One problem which affects all types of contribution is that they may not be paid on time. This is relatively unimportant in a defined benefits scheme, since cost of any opportunities lost falls upon the employer, which is usually responsible for paying across contributions, and employers are more likely than members to be tolerant of any delays by trustees in investing the contributions. However, late payment of contributions is critical in a money purchase scheme. Investing on the wrong day may result in a substantial difference in the amount of pension received in relation to that instalment. Because the widespread use of money purchase schemes is fairly recent in the United Kingdom, there is relatively little case law to date on the subject, but the guidance given in decisions about additional voluntary contributions shows how the Pensions Ombudsman takes such delays seriously, although he has not established a consistent benchmark against which trustees and employers can judge their conduct.

4.1 – Employer contributions

[4.1.1]

Air Products Canada v Schmidt (Supreme Court, Canada) [1995] OPLR 283, [1995] PLR 75 at paras 82–94

Employer contributions – employer's powers

Principle

Whether or not a contribution holiday is permissible must be decided on the applicable plan provisions. There is no objection in principle to employers taking contribution holidays when they are permitted to do so by the terms of the plan. When permission is not explicitly given in the plan, it may be implied from the wording of the employer's contribution obligation.

[4.1.2]

Barclays Bank v Holmes [2000] PLR 339 at paras 90–98

Employer contributions – employer's powers – interpretation – money purchase benefits

Principle

The Court held that where a money purchase section has been added to a final salary scheme, the employer may refuse to make contributions to the surplus on the basis that these contributions will effectively be met from the final salary surplus, if on a proper construction the scheme rules allow this to be done: *Kemble v Hicks (No. 2) [1999] OPLR 1* was considered. In this case, the contribution rule for the money purchase section allowed contributions to be credited to the members' accounts, and the two sections were part of one scheme. The Court held, therefore, that on a proper construction, surplus derived from the final salary section could be used to meet the employer's contribution liabilities under the money purchase section.

[4.1.3]

British Coal Corporation v British Coal Staff Superannuation Scheme Trustees (High Court) [1995] 1 All ER 912, [1994] ICR 537, [1994] OPLR 51, [1993] PLR 303

Employer contributions – waiving of outstanding liability

Facts and Decision

An employer had agreed with the trustees of the British Coal Staff Superannuation Scheme in 1983 that it would pay the cost of providing enhanced benefits on redundancies, in instalments with interest over a ten-year period. An actuarial valuation as at 5 April 1992 disclosed that the scheme was heavily in surplus. The employer sought to set off its outstanding liability to contribute, under the agreement about redundancy benefits, against the surplus. The scheme contained a prohibition against payments to the employer. The Court held that the release of the liability to pay an instalment under the 1983 agreement would constitute a payment out of the fund equivalent to a payment to an employer, and was therefore prohibited. The outstanding instalments were a real not actuarial asset. The employer's liability to pay future standard contributions and its liability to meet the costs of administration were future liabilities, and the value of those liabilities could be set against surplus without involving any transfer to the employer, because the set-off was made before any present liability had arisen.

[4.1.4]

Re Canadian Union of Public Employees – CLC, Ontario Hydro Employees, Local [1000] and Ontario Hydro (Supreme Court of Ontario, Court of Appeal) [1989] 68 OR (2d) 620

Employer contributions – calculation – interpretation of rules – surplus

Facts and Decision

Ontario Hydro operated a defined benefit pension scheme which was substantially in surplus. The scheme was established under statute, and imposed an obligation on the employer to contribute towards the cost of benefits the difference between the amount of the contributions of the employees and the amount of the cost of the benefits as determined by actuarial valuations. The employer proposed to set off the value of the surplus against its obligation to contribute. An actuarial valuation was required under the provision only for the purpose of ascertaining the cost of the benefits. The actuary was not empowered to set the overall level of employer contributions on such basis as he may determine, notwithstanding that his determination might be by reference to generally accepted actuarial principles. The Court held, therefore, that the existence of a surplus did not in and of itself permit the employer to take a contribution holiday. Before the surplus could be credited to or withdrawn by the employer for this purpose, it had to establish its entitlement to use the surplus either by way of a provision within the scheme, or by implication of law. On a proper construction, the employer was forbidden from using any of the surplus in any manner for its own benefit.

[4.1.5]

Cullen v Pension Holdings (High Court of New Zealand) [1992] PLR 134

Employer contributions – amendment – interpretation – surplus

Facts and Decision

The New Zealand Farmers' Co-operative Association of Canterbury operated a pension scheme which was substantially in surplus. It originally had an employer contribution rule which required the employer to contribute 9% of members' salaries, plus any further sum the employer may from time to time in its discretion determine. This was replaced in 1983 by a provision requiring the employer to make such annual contribution, after considering the advice of the actuary and the trustee, as was necessary to provide benefits payable under the scheme. The power of amendment was subject to a proviso that no amendment which would reduce or adversely affect a member's interest in the scheme could be made without that member's consent. No consent was obtained for the change to the contribution rule. On a proper construction of the trust deed, the Court held that the members were entitled to the entire fund including surplus, since there was no hint of credit, benefit or return to the Association in the original trust deed, which provided for the scheme to be actuarially divided among members on a winding-up. The consent of the members was, therefore, required to the 1983 amendment since it effectively removed prospects of future surplus in which they would have been entitled to a share. While it was possible that the 9% figure was insufficient to fund mandatory arrangements, and substitution of 'as necessary' obligations represented an actual improvement, the contrary was inferred in the light of the past accumulation of surplus, and the intrinsic unlikelihood that a significant commercial organisation would allow a pension scheme to drift into an insufficient position.

[4.1.6]

Harding and others (Trustees of Joy Manufacturing Holdings Ltd Pension and Life Assurance Scheme), petitioners (Court of Session, Inner House, Scotland) [1999] OPLR 235

Employer contributions – trustees' duties

Facts and Decision

The employer of a pension scheme which was substantially in surplus put forward proposals for merging it with other pension schemes which were not as well-funded. The trustees asked for guidance on their proper policy in relation to setting the contribution rate. The Court held that that policy must not relate to the level of benefits or increases, but must involve consideration of the appropriate level of security to be provided for members' benefits. They must also have an investment policy (though whether that differed from a policy on the appropriate level of security was open to debate).

[4.1.7]

Hospitals of Ontario v Ontario Hospital Association (Court of Appeal for Ontario) [1991] PLR 125

Employer contributions – employer's powers – surplus

Facts and Decision

An employer reduced its contributions to its pension scheme, which was in surplus. Members complained that by doing so, they were eroding the surplus in the scheme. The employer contribution rule required the employer to make contributions to the scheme on a basis determined by the actuary from time to time. The rules also provided that the contributions would be used to fund benefits provided by the scheme, to meet any unfunded liability or deficiency, and to meet the scheme's administrative expenses. This latter provision dealt only with the application of the contributions, and not with their calculation. The scheme also provided that no part of the scheme should be used for or diverted to purposes other than for the exclusive benefit of the employees or former employees of the employers. The Court held that this did not prevent the employer from reducing its contributions on the basis determined by the actuary: *Re Canadian Union of Public Employees – CLC, Ontario Hydro Employees, Local [1000] and Ontario Hydro [1989] 68 OR (2d) 620* was distinguished.

Nothing in the scheme required the actuary to use the net current service costs to determine the amount of annual employer contributions.

[4.1.8]

Re HSBC Staff Superannuation Fund (High Court of New Zealand, unreported, 9 April 2001)

Employer contributions – money purchase scheme – calculation

Facts and Decision

A money purchase pension scheme provided that the trustees had discretion to apply funds in a reserve account in payment of all or part of the employer's contributions to the scheme, which were payable at a level fixed under an appendix to the scheme rules. Employer contributions were subject to withholding tax under New Zealand law. The members argued that employer contributions made in this way were made before tax (since the payment by the trustees did not attract tax), which effectively would have increased the value of the employer contribution to them. The employer argued that the contributions made from the reserve account were made net of tax. The Court held that the employer contribution rule provided that the employer was obliged to contribute in accordance with the appendix after deducting tax (if any). The liability of the employer was therefore the net amount. Members and the employer needed a degree of certainty about the operation of the scheme, and no one would expect variables in contributions from the employer on behalf of members depending on how the contribution was paid.

[4.1.9]

International Power v Healy (House of Lords) [2001] PLR 121 at paras 18–26

Employer contributions – power to dispose of surplus

Facts and Decision

The principal employer in each group of the Electricity Supply Pension Scheme were given the power under the scheme to make arrangements, certified by the actuary as reasonable, to deal with ongoing surplus. The power of amendment prohibited any amendment which would make any of the monies of the scheme payable to any of the employers. When a surplus emerged, some employers set two-thirds of the surplus against the employers' obligation to contribute. The Court held that the release of a debt owed by the employer to the scheme was not a payment, although it had the same economic effect. Viewed against the fiscal background, the purpose of the restriction on the power of amendment was to prevent the employer from resorting to assets which had enjoyed the fiscal privileges accorded to the scheme. Since debts from the employer to the scheme which had not yet fallen due for payment had enjoyed no fiscal privileges, the restriction on the power of amendment did not prevent an amendment which allowed for the employer to set surplus against its obligation to contribute.

The case of *British Coal Corporation v British Coal Staff Superannuation Scheme Trustees [1995] 1 All ER 912* had, therefore, been wrongly decided to the extent that it held that the waiving of employer contributions was a payment out of the monies of the fund. Payments out of the fund are conceptually different from a reduction of the fund's assets; *Re BCCI (No 8) [1998] AC 214* was followed.

Company payments may be made in instalments rather than in one lump sum. A lump sum can be translated into an appropriate stream of periodic payments from an actuarial point of view.

[4.1.10]

Kemble v Hicks (No. 2) (High Court) [1999] OPLR 1 at 5G–7H

Employer contributions – employer's powers – interpretation – money purchase benefits

Facts and Decision

An employer established a money purchase section in its final salary scheme. The money purchase section was documented by booklet, and no amending deed was ever executed. The booklet provided that the employer would contribute at the rate of 8% of each member's basic annual salary, and these contributions, together with the member's own contribution of 4% of basic annual salary, would be allocated to the member's investment account. All employer contributions were paid from the surplus in the final salary section. The Court held that where a money purchase scheme was established under the same trust as a final salary scheme, it may be correct to regard them as part of the same overall scheme. However, within this overall scheme, the establishment of a money purchase scheme involved the setting up of what was a scheme quite separate from the final salary scheme, and to which different considerations applied. It was, therefore, improper in this case for the employer contributions to be met from surplus.

LRT v Hatt (High Court) [1993] OPLR 225 at 265A–268G, [1993] PLR 227 at paras 162–169

Employer contributions – minimum contribution rate – surplus

Facts and Decision

Both pension schemes under consideration in this case had a provision requiring the employer to make a minimum contribution of a multiple of the employees' contributions. Neither provided for proportional contributions alone. In so far as the minimum was inadequate, it was the employer that would have to provide the balance. The Court held that the general argument that surplus results from past overfunding was plainly not applicable to schemes of this type. The combination of a mandatory minimum contribution together with the employer's inability unilaterally to determine the schemes elevated members' rights on these points to private rights, of sufficient weight for them to be protected from removal on amalgamation.

Merrett v Pensions Ombudsman (High Court) [1998] OPLR 161

Employer contributions – overpayment

Facts and Decision

An employer contributed to its pension scheme for six months. When an actuarial valuation disclosed a surplus, it took a refund from the scheme. The employer was obliged under the scheme rules to contribute the amounts required to provide the benefits of the scheme. The Court held that the employer had been paying on account, as in previous years, and that nothing prevented it from taking a refund. No one had intended that it was irrevocably committing itself to increasing the surplus.

[4.1.13]

Mettoy Pension Trustees v Evans (High Court) [1991] 2 All ER 513, [1990] 1 WLR 1587, [1990] PLR 9 at para 178

Employer contributions – practice

Principle

While the power to set the employer contribution rate, if vested in the trustees, is more than a minor or administrative power, in practice employers' contributions are set by agreement between the employers and trustees, after consultation with the actuaries.

[4.1.14]

Providence Capitol Trustees v Ayres (High Court) [1996] 4 All ER 760, [1996] OPLR 215 at 220H–221A, [1996] PLR 395 at paras 15–16

Employer contributions – money purchase benefits

Principle

Where a pension scheme is established on a money purchase basis, a clause requiring the company to pay to the trustees such contributions as may be necessary to provide the benefits of the scheme does not explain the basis upon which the company is to contribute.

[4.1.15]

Tek Corporation Provident Fund v Lorentz (Supreme Court of South Africa) [1999] OPLR 137 at paras 23, 24

Employer contributions – defined benefits scheme

Principle

In a balance of cost scheme, the employer need only contribute when the need for contributions arises. As the Court observed: 'Present a surplus, absent a need and absent a liability.' It was, however, doubtful whether the employer could direct the trustees to preserve the surplus, even if only to allow it to take or prolong a contribution holiday, where the trustees had a separate power to increase pensions.

[4.1.16]

Thompson v Ritec Ltd (Employment Appeal Tribunal, unreported, 10 December 1996)

Employer contributions – constructive dismissal – implied obligation of good faith

Facts and Decision

Ritec was under an obligation to make pension contributions to Mr Thompson's fund in its pension scheme, but failed to do so from 1989 to March 1994, despite Mr Thompson's complaints from 1992 onwards. It was open about its failure, and the sum at stake was £6,000. Mr Thompson resigned, alleging constructive dismissal. The Appeal Tribunal observed that the key questions were whether Ritec had committed a fundamental breach of contract, whether Mr Thompson had affirmed the breach and whether Mr Thompson had acted reasonably in resigning: *Western Excavating (EEC) v Sharpe [1978] QB 761, [1978] 1 All ER 713* was applied. The Employment Tribunal had asked the right questions, but had not answered them separately. The Tribunal had considered that the consistent failure to make payments to a pension scheme was not a fundamental breach of contract, being less important than payment of salary, which having regard *Imperial Group Pensions Trust v Imperial Tobacco Ltd [1991] 1 WLR 589* was *prima facie* an incorrect approach. Because the Tribunal had misdirected itself, the matter was remitted for a rehearing.

[4.1.17]

UEB Industries v Brabant (Court of Appeal of New Zealand) [1991] PLR 109, [1992] 1 NZLR 294

Employer contributions – overpayment

Principle

It was not possible to characterise all contributions by an employer to its pension scheme, in excess of its minimum obligations, as prepayments of its contributions such as would take them outside the remit of the permanent alienation clause, where no appropriate accounting measures had been taken.

[4.1.18]

Wheeler v NBC Pension Trustee (Pensions Ombudsman) [1996] OPLR 337 at 354G–357A, [1997] PLR 1 at paras 83–97

Employer contributions – employer's duties

Principles

The Pensions Ombudsman held that it would be an improper use of an employer's power to suspend contributions to its pension scheme, when the threat was used to persuade a trustee to surrender powers which it held under the winding-up rule. It was also a breach of the employer's duty of good faith. The contribution rule provided in this case that the employers should pay such periodical contributions to the fund 'as the trustee with the advice of the actuary shall determine and agree with the employers' were appropriate, together with the members' contributions and the assets of the fund, to enable the fund to provide benefits. The winding-up rule and the contribution rule could not, the Ombudsman held, be understood in isolation from each other. The benefits to be provided under the winding-up rule were the standard benefits, except where amended by the winding-up rule. Since the trustee was under a duty to secure these benefits with an annuity, the company could not insist that the contribution rate be calculated on the basis that the scheme was ongoing, when it was not expected to be so, nor insist on a contribution rate which would make it unlikely that the trustee would be able to secure benefits on winding-up through the purchase of annuities.

4.2 – Power to waive debts

[4.2.1]

Barclays Bank v Holmes (High Court) [2000] PLR 339 at paras 106–111

Employer contributions – money purchase benefits – waiver of contribution obligation

Facts and Decision

A deed of amendment provided that an employer could apply surplus arising from the final salary section of a pension scheme to meet its obligation to contribute to the money purchase section of the same pension scheme. The Court held that that deed did not infringe a prohibition on alterations which purported to result in the return of any portion of the scheme to the employers. The dicta in *British Coal Corporation v British Coal Staff Superannuation Scheme Trustees [1995] 1 All ER 912* and *Edge v Pensions Ombudsman [2000] 3 WLR 79* were considered and applied.

[4.2.2]

British Coal Corporation v British Coal Staff Superannuation Scheme Trustees (High Court) [1995] 1 All ER 912, [1994] ICR 537, [1994] OPLR 51, [1993] PLR 303

Employer contribution – waiver of contribution obligation

See [4.1.3].

[4.2.3]

International Power v Healy (House of Lords) [2001] PLR 121 at paras 18–26, 27–33

Employer contributions – waiver of contribution obligation

Principle

The case of *British Coal Corporation v British Coal Staff Superannuation Scheme Trustees [1995] 1 All ER 912* was wrongly decided to the extent that it held that the waiving of employer contributions was a payment out of the monies of the fund. Payments out of the fund are conceptually different from a reduction of the fund's assets: *Re BCCI (No 8) [1998] AC 214* was followed.

Similarly, the *Pensions Act 1995, s 37*, did not prohibit the adjustment of funding rates in this way. It was not to be interpreted in the light of the wording of *s 40* of the *Pensions Act 1995*.

4.3 – Member contributions

[4.3.1]

Gissing v Liverpool Corporation (Court of Appeal) [1935] 1 Ch 1

Member contributions – interpretation of scheme

Facts and Decision

Miss Gissing was a cleaner and was subject to the provisions of the *Poor Law Officers' Superannuation Act 1896*, which established a contributory pension scheme. Owing to her employers' mistakes, contributions were not deducted from her salary for many years, but eventually in 1929 they started to make deductions, including an additional amount agreed with Miss Gissing for the arrears. Following a transfer of responsibilities, her new employer eventually ceased making deductions from her salary on the grounds that she was not within the scope of the *Act*, since she had not made the whole of her contributions as required by *s 124* of the *Local Government Act 1929*, which was a new provision. The Court held that Miss Gissing had made all the contributions she had been required to make, and the *Local Government Act 1929* was not to be interpreted as excluding private agreements on the timing of contributions between authorities and their employees, or circumstances where there had been an effort to comply with the *1896 Act* where the proper contributions had been made so far as possible in view of the mistake which had been made.

4.4 – Additional voluntary contributions

[4.4.1]

Coloroll Pension Trustees v Russell (European Court of Justice) [1995] All ER (EC) 23, [1994] ECR I–4389, [1994] IRLR 586, [1994] OPLR 179, [1994] PLR 211

Member contributions – additional voluntary contributions

Principles

The principle of equal treatment applies to all pension benefits paid by occupational schemes, without any need to distinguish according to the kind of contributions to which those benefits are attributed, namely employers' contributions or employees' contributions. However, in so far as an occupational pension scheme does no more than provide the membership with the necessary arrangements for management, additional benefits stemming from contributions paid by employees on a purely voluntary basis are not covered by *Article 119* (now *Article 141*) of the *Treaty of Rome*.

[4.4.2]

Cretchley v Abbey National (Pensions Ombudsman, 16 March 2000) Case J00355

Member contributions – additional voluntary contributions – maladministration

Facts and Decision

Mrs Cretchley was provided with an illustration in 1988 indicating that she could pay 14% of her salary in additional voluntary contributions without exceeding Inland Revenue limits, and therefore she decided to do so. When she made enquiries in 1998 about retiring early, she discovered that if she continued to pay additional voluntary contributions at 14% her benefits would exceed Inland Revenue limits, not only for early retirement but also for normal retirement. It transpired that the illustration was wrong in several respects. If Mrs Cretchley had been given the correct information, she argued that she would have been able to invest in the employer's share scheme, which would have been a very profitable investment. The Pensions Ombudsman agreed that the misquotation was maladministration, but did not accept that Mrs Cretchley would have invested in the share scheme. However, she could have invested elsewhere. Although there was no quantifiable financial loss, she had also suffered some distress and frustration. The Ombudsman awarded £250 as compensation for that distress and frustration.

[4.4.3]

Lavender v Trustees of the Motorola Additional Voluntary Contributions Plan (Pensions Ombudsman, 29 September 1999) Case J00119

Member contributions – additional voluntary contributions – maladministration

Facts and Decision

Mr Lavender complained that his additional voluntary contributions, which were being deducted on the 25th of each month, were taking up to 75 days to be credited to his account, owing to delays by the employer in paying them across. The Pensions Ombudsman held that this was excessive delay, and the trustees were directed to calculate the loss he had experienced on the basis that his additional voluntary contributions should have been paid on the 5th of each month following that to which his contributions related. The employer was directed to fund the loss so calculated.

[4.4.4]

Nuthall v Merrill Lynch (UK) Final Salary Plan trustees (Pensions Ombudsman, 25 March 1999) Case G00543

Member contributions – additional voluntary contributions – maladministration

Principles

There were excessive delays in paying over a member's additional voluntary contributions, where the delay extended from the 25th of one month to the 5th of the next month. The Pensions Ombudsman observed that the provisions of the *Pensions Act 1995* specify maximum periods within which payments must be transferred, but these were specified in order to avoid criminal liability, not maladministration. The existence of such long-stop sanctions does not absolve trustees or managers of their responsibility to ensure that good practices are established for all areas of pension scheme administration. The behaviour in this case constituted maladministration causing injustice on the part of the trustees, who had failed to ensure that the monies were transferred promptly, and on the part of the insurer in that it had not requested payment of the contributions via its direct debit mandate at the beginning of each month.

Part 5 – Pension Benefits

5 – Introduction

If the person in the street is ever asked to consider what sort of disputes may arise involving pensions, he or she will normally assume that most disputes will arise over eligibility for and calculation of benefits. As the length of this part shows, there are a substantial number of complaints about these subjects, but this Part by no means overwhelms other areas of complaint. Why is this? First, pension schemes are designed to provide benefits, and a great deal of attention is given to ensuring that the benefits documented reflect the parties' intentions. When direct attention is given to a problem, draftsmen generally succeed in resolving it.

Secondly, in most circumstances (but with three large exceptions) the terms of eligibility for benefits are not capable of serious dispute. The three exceptions comprise the bulk of this Part: incapacity benefits, the various other types of early retirement benefits and lump sum death benefits.

Eligibility for incapacity pension is almost bound to prove controversial in any pension scheme from time to time. Most eligibility questions are not likely to have nuanced gradations: either a member has been made redundant or the member has not been made redundant, and eligibility for a redundancy pension will be determined accordingly. Incapacity is a much more fluid concept. At one end is the member who is obviously completely incapacitated within the terms of the pension scheme provisions. At the other end of the spectrum is the member who is obviously not incapacitated. But in between it may not be obvious whether a member qualifies or not. Different doctors may take different views, and the trustees or employer will need to weigh the evidence. Where the member is refused a pension in such circumstances, he or she will probably feel aggrieved, and may well complain to the Pensions Ombudsman. *Key v Courtaulds [1999] OPLR 27* is an example of this.

A more substantial problem with incapacity pensions is that the wording of the provisions governing incapacity pensions differ significantly, and trustees and employers often fall into the trap of applying a test which they think should apply as opposed to the test which actually should be applied. This need not be the fault of the trustees: the wording itself may be complicated and the interpretation of the provision may be very difficult, as in *Harris v Shuttleworth [1995] OPLR 79* and *Derby Daily Telegraph v Pensions Ombudsman [1999] OPLR 125.*

Investigations into incapacity pensions are also by their very nature highly personal, and there is a fine dividing line between information being essential for the trustees or employers to consider whether the member is eligible and information being irrelevant. In unusual circumstances, where a condition could be feigned, trustees and employers may feel it necessary to obtain evidence from covert surveillance, despite the serious intrusion into the member's private life which this will necessarily entail. The Court has been more sympathetic to the quandary of the trustees and employer in such cases than the Pensions Ombudsman was at first inclined to be, as shown in *Law Debenture v Malley [1999] OPLR 167*. The Pensions Ombudsman has taken heed of the Court's guidance, as shown in the more recent Ombudsman determination of *Whight v Co-operative Insurance Society, Case H00487*. A third Pensions Ombudsman case involving covert surveillance, *Robinson v Atco-Qualcast, Case H00422*, is included for interest. Given the flagrant nature of the breaches in this case, there is no reason to assume that the Court would have reacted any differently from the Ombudsman.

Similar but lesser problems arise in relation to other early retirement pensions. There is occasionally doubt as to whether a member has genuinely been made redundant or has left service in circumstances which entitle the member to a pension, as *Wyn Jones v Home Secretary [1995] PLR 1* and *Teachers' Pension Agency v Hill [1998] OPLR 167* show.

Lump sum death benefits raise different problems. In such cases, trustees normally have a discretion as to whom they pay the benefits, and the nature of any challenge to their actions will normally be on the grounds that they have taken into account irrelevant considerations, or not taken into account relevant considerations. A Pensions Ombudsman case, *Elson v BT Supplementary Benefits Plan Trustees, Case F00859*, illustrates this. Trustees may also misapply the terms of the death benefit trust, as in *Wild v Smith [1996] [1996] PLR 275*, where the trustees did not check to make sure that the proposed beneficiary of the lump sum death benefit was eligible to receive it.

A further problem with lump sum death benefits arises in relation to the nomination form which members are usually asked to fill out. Such a form is evidently connected with the member's death, and *Danish Bacon Co Ltd Staff Pension Fund Trusts [1971] 1 WLR 248* had to consider the extent to which the requirements for making a will applied to such a nomination form. Its conclusion that a nomination form was not a testamentary disposition was pragmatic, and adopted by the Privy Council in *Baird v Baird [1990] PLR 87*. However, *Gold v Hill [1999] 1 FLR 54* recognised that such a nomination could form the basis of a trust. The precise nature of a nomination form is still being worked out.

5.1 – Eligibility

Cullen v Pension Holdings (High Court of New Zealand) [1992] PLR 134

Eligibility for benefits

Facts and Decision

The New Zealand Farmers' Co-operative Association of Canterbury operated a pension scheme which was substantially in surplus. The employer became a subsidiary of another company, which transferred employees and pensioners from the pension scheme of another of its subsidiaries into the Association's scheme in 1988. The transfer-in rule provided that if a member was entitled to benefit under another scheme, the trustee might accept a transfer value and grant additional benefits. The election of members to the scheme was made by the Association by written notice to the trustee, and the Association could elect as members such persons as it determined were entitled to contribute to and share in the scheme. This notice was, however, given only in 1990. 'Member' was defined by the scheme rules as any employee or retired employee permitted by the Association to contribute to and/or share in the benefits of the scheme. 'Employee' was defined as including any employee of the Association, and the Association was defined as the Association and any subsidiary or associate thereof or successor thereto. The fellow subsidiary was an associate of the Association, and the Court held that its employees were therefore eligible for membership of the scheme. However, its pensioners were not, since in the scheme rules contribution was a requirement for eligibility. The transferees were not validly elected as members in 1988 since the Association's resolution to agree to the transfer was not intended to operate as a notice of election to membership, and should not 'by some side wind' be treated as having done so. The 1990 notice was effective, but only from the date on which it was given.

[5.1.2]

Harding and others (Trustees of Joy Manufacturing Holdings Ltd Pension and Life Assurance Scheme), petitioners (Court of Session, Inner House, Scotland) [1999] OPLR 235

Eligibility for benefits

Facts and Decision

The employer of a pension scheme which was substantially in surplus put forward proposals for merging it with other pension schemes which were not as well-funded. The Court held that under the terms of the eligibility rule, the trustees could not refuse to admit any person as a contributing member if he or she met the requirements prescribed by the rules.

[5.1.3]

LRT v Hatt (High Court) [1993] OPLR 225 at 269C-H, [1993] PLR 227 at para 171

Eligibility for benefits – future employees

Principles

In a single continuously operating pension scheme there is no doubt that future employees are entitled to be admitted on the terms of the scheme unless the rules are altered in due form. However, where two schemes with different rules are being amalgamated into one, it is not the same situation. The fundamental issue on this aspect is whether on amalgamation an employer can make different rules for those who become employees after amalgamation. Future employees of the employer have no property rights at the date of the amalgamation which the employer cannot legitimately reserve the right to alter as a term of employing them at a later date. These future employees cannot object to being offered different terms.

5.2 – Preservation of leaving service benefits

[5.2.1]

Royal Masonic Hospital v Pensions Ombudsman (High Court) [2001] PLR 31

Preservation – unfunded schemes

Facts and Decision

The Royal Masonic Hospital operated an unfunded pension scheme. This scheme did not comply with the statutory requirements relating to the preservation of leaving service benefits. Following a complaint by a member, the Pensions Ombudsman held that the scheme was in breach of those requirements. On appeal, the Court held that the requirements did not apply to unfunded schemes.

[5.2.2]

Shucksmith v OPB (High Court) [1989] PLR 63

Preservation

Principles

In order to comply with the preservation requirements, the question in each case was to discover according to the ordinary rule of construction what rights are the rights of members of the pension scheme with long service benefits, and then see if those benefits are properly reflected in the short service benefits provided by the scheme. One should look at the sum of the pension benefits and see if the whole or any part of those benefits are to be taken as accruing by reference to an unequal formula which does not attribute a share in the pension on the basis of year by year accrual. Any such part must be dealt with on the base of uniform accrual. When it is impossible to know which of two bases will in the event be payable, one must apply the statute to each basis separately and satisfy oneself that the two bases taken together satisfy the statutory requirements. It would be wrong to ignore the limit put on each basis by the other.

5.3 – Distribution of lump sum death benefit

Re Baden's Deed Trusts, McPhail v Doulton (House of Lords) [1971] AC 424

Trustees' powers

Principles

Where a trust deed gave the trustees the obligation to distribute assets to a class of beneficiaries, this constituted a trust. The trust would be void only if it were void for uncertainty, and the test was whether it could be said with certainty whether a given individual was or was not a member of that class. The trustees would examine the field by class and category and might make diligent and careful inquiries, depending on how much money was at stake. This could be carried out without a complete list of names. If the trust is administratively unworkable, this may render the trust invalid.

[5.3.2]

Baird v Baird (Privy Council) [1990] PLR 87

Death benefits – nomination form

Facts and Decision

Mr Baird, who was the member of a pension scheme, died in 1972. He had nominated his brother to receive his lump sum death benefit some years before he married, and did not change his nomination form after his marriage. Under the scheme rules, the member could change his nomination before his death, but the consent of the management committee was required and it needed to be in a form provided by the company. Once the member died, the benefit was paid to the nominated beneficiary as of right. Both Mr Baird's brother and widow claimed the lump sum death benefit. The widow argued that the nomination form was a testamentary disposition and thus voided by the marriage. The Privy Council rejected this argument and awarded the lump sum to Mr Baird's brother.

[5.3.3]

Collins v Jones (High Court, unreported, 6 October 1999)

Death benefits – nomination

Facts and Decision

Mr Jones was a member of his employer's pension scheme. He executed a trust of the lump sum benefits payable on his death in service, with the benefits to be paid, in default of the trustees' exercising their discretion among members of a discretionary class, to his brother and sister-in-law. The discretionary class could be extended by Mr Jones by notice in writing to the trustees. Mr Jones died in 1997, but before he died he fell out with his brother. He wished to replace his brother and sister-in-law as residual beneficiaries with Ms Collins. He took legal advice, and his solicitors drew up a document, which he executed. This purported to revoke the nomination of his brother and sister-in-law as the residual beneficiaries to receive the death-in-service benefits and to replace them with Ms Collins. However, Ms Collins did not qualify as a member of the discretionary class for consideration, and the Court held that the discretionary class was not altered by the purported revocation. The revocation came to the attention of the trustees, but was not specifically addressed to them. In order to be effective to extend the class, the revocation and new nomination should have been addressed to or intended to go to the trustees. Since that did not happen, it was ineffective to extend the class of potential recipients of the lump sum death benefit. Since Mr Jones's intention was to replace the residual nominees and not to extend the class of potential beneficiaries, Ms Collins could not be granted rectification of the purported revocation. She was therefore ineligible for consideration for the lump sum death benefit.

[5.3.4]

Danish Bacon Co Ltd Staff Pension Fund Trusts (High Court) [1971] 1 WLR 248

Death benefits – nomination form

Facts and Decision

Under the terms of an employer's pension scheme, a member could nominate a person to receive a lump sum benefit on the member's death, and the trustees were obliged to follow that nomination. The member could change his or her nomination. The nomination form made provision for the member's signature to be witnessed. A member was invited to review his nomination and informed a trustee by letter that he wished to change his nomination, giving details of the new nominee. The trustee amended the nomination form without sending it to the member for signature. The member then died. The Court held that the nomination was a form of disposition, which had a somewhat special operation. It was very doubtful whether the nomination was a disposition under *s 53(1)(c)* of the *Law of Property Act 1925*, and therefore had to be in writing. However, even if it was there was no reason why the disposition in writing could not be satisfied by two or more documents. Since the alterations conformed to the authority given, the change in nomination was validly given. The nomination form did not need to satisfy the requirements of a will: it operated by force of the provisions of the trust deed and rules, and not as a testamentary disposition of the deceased. Although the nomination had certain testamentary characteristics, these did not suffice to make the paper on which it was written a testamentary paper. The nomination was not an assignment, since like a will, there was no contingent or revocable disposition until death. *Re Barnes [1940] Ch 267, Eccles Provident Industrial Co-operative Society v Griffiths [1912] AC 483* and *Bennett v Slater [1899] 1 QB 45* were considered. As a matter of general principle, an alteration in an instrument under hand made with the consent of all parties does not avoid the instrument, and it takes effect as altered. Turning to this specific case, while the nomination form required a witness, this was not a requirement of the trust deed and rules. Equity would not be astute to seize upon such a debatable matter as the absence of a witness's signature on the member's letter to the trustee, in order to invalidate the nomination. The change of nomination was therefore effective. There was substantial compliance with the rules to constitute a new nomination.

[5.3.5]

Elson v BT Supplementary Benefits Plan trustees (Pensions Ombudsman, 19 May 1998) Case F00859

Death benefits – nomination form

Facts and Decision

Ms Henderson was a member of the BT main pension scheme and the supplementary pension scheme. She had completed a death benefit nomination form in favour of her mother, father and brother for the supplementary scheme, and did not fill one out for the main scheme. She then moved in with Mr Elson who became partially dependent on her. She completed a nomination form for the main scheme in his favour, and wrote on it 'this expression of wish cancels any previous expression of wish I have completed relating to the benefit payable under the scheme on my death'. Ms Henderson was then diagnosed as having a terminal illness, with only months to live. She spoke to a welfare officer, who believed that the nomination form for the main scheme was all-encompassing. Shortly afterwards, she died. After her death, a copy of the first nomination form was found among her papers, with the words 'superseded by form signed 23/4/92' written in her handwriting. The main scheme paid its lump sum to Mr Elson, but the trustees of the supplementary scheme paid its lump sum in accordance with the nomination form for that scheme, to Ms Henderson's mother, father and brother. The Pensions Ombudsman held that the trustees had acted out of a misconceived view of the weight to be attached to the form. By treating the form as overriding, the trustees were distorting and hence not acting in accordance with the terms of the discretion conferred upon them. They had fettered their discretion out of existence. The trustees had therefore been guilty of maladministration, and the purported exercise of their discretion had to be set aside and treated as ineffective. Since the lump sum had not been paid within two years, it was payable to Ms Henderson's estate with interest from the second anniversary of Ms Henderson's death.

[5.3.6]

Gold v Hill (High Court) [1999] I FLR 54

Death benefits – nomination form

Principles

Mr Gilbert nominated Mr Gold to be his beneficiary for benefits under his employer's life insurance and accident benefit scheme, describing him as his executor on the nomination form in the box requiring a description of their relationship. In fact, his executor was his solicitor, Mr Hill. Mr Gold understood that he was to use the benefits as trustee for Mr Gilbert's common law wife and their children. Mr Gilbert then died. The Court held that the nomination in favour of Mr Gold was effective. Mr Gold was acting on behalf of Mr Gilbert's common law wife, and to the layman the word 'executor' might seem to express adequately the role he had in mind. The nomination took effect as a trust, and the terms of the trust were sufficiently precise. The nomination could be regarded as analogous to a secret trust. The nomination was not a disposition of an equitable interest within the meaning of s 53 of the *Law of Property Act 1925*: *Re Danish Bacon Co. Ltd Pension Fund Trusts [1971] 1 WLR 248* was considered and applied.

[5.3.7]

Re Gulbenkian's Settlements (Whishaw v Stephens) (House of Lords) [1970] AC 508

Trustees' powers

Principles

If a settlor directs trustees to make specified provision for an individual, then to give legal effect to that provision, it must be possible to identify that individual. If the settlor directs that a fund should be equally divided between members of a class, that class must be defined as the individual; the Court cannot guess at it. But where mere or bare powers are conferred upon donees of the power, whether trustees or others, the matter is quite different. Trustees have no duty to exercise it in the sense that they cannot be controlled in any way. If they fail to exercise it then those entitled in default of its exercise are entitled to the fund. Those entitled to the fund in default must clearly be entitled to restrain the trustees from exercising it save among those within the power. So the trustees or the Court must be able to say with certainty who is within and who is without the power.

[5.3.8]

Libby v Kennedy (High Court) [1998] OPLR 213, [1999] PLR 143

Death benefits – trustees' procedures – exercise of trustees' discretion

Facts and Decision

A pension scheme member died, and the pensions manager recommended that the trustees should pay the lump sum death benefit, in accordance with the member's nomination form, to his widow from his second marriage, the member having made provision for the children of his first marriage in his will in the light of the nomination form. One trustee signed the recommendation form without expressly stating whether he approved the recommendation form, while another expressly approved the recommendation form. The trustees of the scheme had previously minuted that 'where there were no difficulties in establishing the rightful beneficiary [for a death in service lump sum benefit], payment might be made with the consent of one employee trustee and one member trustee'. The payment was made and noted in the minutes of the next trustee meeting. Family members disputed the decision, and the Pensions Ombudsman agreed with them. On the trustees' appeal, the Court held that the minute really meant that two trustees could act in a fairly plain case. The minute was, therefore, an effective delegation of the power. Even if later on it turned out that the case was more complicated, this did not mean that the trustees did not have the authority. Nor was there a problem if the trustees did not consider whether the case might or might not be difficult, if it was highly improbable that the case was one which would cause them any difficulty. If a trustee signed and returned a form sent with a recommendation by the pensions manager, without entering any comment in the decision box, it could only be construed as agreement with the recommendation. The form must be construed as a matter of law and against the factual matrix by which it was sent, signed and returned. Even if the decision had not been validly delegated, when trustees noted the decision at the following meeting, on the facts the trustees knew exactly what had been done and why it had been done, and they therefore effectively ratified the decision.

[5.3.9]

Re Manisty's Settlement (High Court) [1974] 1 Ch 17

Trustees' duties

Principles

Trustees of a discretionary trust had unlimited power under the trust deed, for exercise of a power to distribute the trust funds, to add additional potential beneficiaries to the class under consideration. The Court held that the mere width of a power cannot make it impossible for trustees to perform their duty nor prevent the Court from determining whether the trustees are in breach. A person within the ambit of the power can require the trustees to consider exercising the power, and in particular to consider a request on his or her part for the power to be exercised in his or her favour. The trustees must consider this request, and if they decline to do so, or can be proved to have omitted to do so, then the aggrieved person may apply to the Court, which may remove the trustees and appoint others in their place. This was the only right and only remedy. The Court may also be persuaded to intervene if the trustees act capriciously, that is to say, act for reasons which could be said to be irrational, perverse or irrelevant to any sensible expectation of the settlor. There was no logical or legal objection to intermediate powers of this type.

[5.3.10]

Richardson v Merchant Navy Pensions Administration (Pensions Ombudsman, 12 May 1998) Case H00094

Death benefits – interpretation of rules

Facts and Decision

Mr Richardson was a merchant navy crew rating and member of the Merchant Navy Ratings Pension Fund. He went on sick pay in 1994, but returned to work in February 1995, when he was given a medical examination and passed unfit for sea service. He was dismissed without notice on 2 March 1995, and he lodged an appeal on 8 March 1995 against this decision. He was entitled to three months' notice. He died on 30 March 1995. His widow claimed a widow's pension on death in service and argued that a lump sum death benefit was payable on death in service. Service was defined under the scheme rules as all periods in respect of which contributions were paid to the scheme, and a lump sum was payable so long as contributions were being received up to the time of his death. The pension scheme administrators maintained that no contributions had been paid for the period after he had been dismissed, although contributions remained outstanding at his death for the period of service after 12 February 1995. The Pensions Ombudsman held that Mr Richardson's contract of employment was wrongfully terminated. Contributions were still being received up to the date of death, and any lack of clarity should be interpreted in favour of Mr Richardson's point of view and against the point of view of the party responsible for the drafting of the rule. Mr Richardson should therefore be treated as still being in service for the purpose of the rules, and his widow was entitled to the higher pension payable on death in service. The trustees were also ordered to consider to whom the lump sum death benefit should be paid.

[5.3.11]

Wild v Smith (High Court) [1996] OPLR 129, [1996] PLR 275

Death benefits – exercise of trustees' discretion

Facts and Decision

A pension scheme member died, leaving a live-in girlfriend and two children from a former marriage. The trustees were obliged to pay a lump sum death benefit, and had a discretion to pay it to a dependant or relative, or to divide it up between more than one person qualifying for consideration. The trustees determined that the live-in girlfriend was a dependant on the basis that the deceased and she were living together at the time of death. The Pensions Ombudsman found that they had no proper evidence of dependency and so there had been no valid exercise of the trustees' discretion. The Court held that the Ombudsman was perfectly entitled to conclude that the trustees had not investigated the matter as they should have done, and that this constituted maladministration.

5.4 – Payment of incapacity benefit

[5.4.1]

Derby Daily Telegraph v Pensions Ombudsman (High Court) [1999] OPLR 125

Incapacity pensions – interpretation of rules

Facts and Decision

The rules of Derby Daily Telegraph's pension scheme gave the employer the power to consent to a member's retirement on the grounds of serious ill health. The trustees had the power to vary or suspend the pension if the member recovered. Serious ill health was not defined under the pension scheme rules. The employer refused to grant a pension to one retiring employee since its doctor was of the opinion that she would be able to work again before her normal retirement date. Accordingly, on its view, she was not retiring on the grounds of serious ill health. The Court held that the employer's construction of the rules, while coherent, tended too much towards a detached and literal approach rather than a purposive and practical one. On a proper construction, the employer had only to assess whether or not the ill health from which the member was suffering was such that she could not continue performing her current job with the employer. If the answer was that she could not and so would have to leave service, then she would in principle be entitled on such retirement to the payment of an ill health pension. The employer was therefore directed to reconsider its decision.

[5.4.2]

Fernance v Wreckair (Industrial Court of New South Wales) [1993] PLR 191

Incapacity pensions – interpretation of rules

Facts and Decision

Mr Fernance was an apprentice plant mechanic who had left school at 16. He was involved in a car accident, following which it slowly became apparent that he was unable to continue in his job. He was a member of his employer's superannuation scheme, and he claimed a pension on the ground that he suffered total and permanent disablement, as required by the rules if he were to receive a pension. That definition made a person eligible for a pension if he or she had been absent from employment for six consecutive months and in the opinion of the insurer, after consideration of the medical evidence, he or she had become incapacitated to such an extent as to render him or her unlikely ever to engage in or work for reward in any occupation or work for which he or she was reasonably qualified by education, training or experience. The insurer, National Mutual, refused the application without any explanation. Mr Fernance sued his employer for the pension. The Court used a statutory power to correct the unfairness caused by National Mutual's failure to give reasons, and apparent excessive reliance on its own medical adviser. The definition in the rules required an assessment of the work for which the applicant was reasonably qualified at the date of assessment, and not at some future time as a result of retraining. On the facts, Mr Fernance was suffering total and permanent disablement within the terms of this definition, and was therefore entitled to his pension.

[5.4.3]

Garvin v Police Authority for City of London (Divisional Court) [1944] I KB 358, [1944] I All ER 378

Incapacity pensions – causation

Facts and Decision

Mr Garvin was a police officer who during the war worked twelve hours a day with irregular meals and constant wettings. He developed tuberculosis and retired, claiming a pension under the *Police Pensions Act 1921* on the basis that he was incapacitated by an injury suffered by him in the execution of his duty. The quarter sessions upheld his appeal, and the Police Authority appealed from this decision. The Court held that tuberculosis was an injury for the purposes of the provision. The words 'in the execution of his duty' were to receive a benevolent interpretation. There must be some degree of causal relation between the injury and the duty, but there was sufficient evidence for the Tribunal to conclude that there was such evidence. Mr Garvin was, therefore, entitled to his pension.

[5.4.4]

Haghiran v Allied Dunbar (Court of Appeal, unreported, 20 October 2000)

Incapacity benefits – interpretation of rules

Facts and Decision

Mr Haghiran ran an import/export business in Iranian goods, including antiquities and carpets. This involved 30–40 hours' work a week, with a considerable amount of heavy lifting. He had the benefit of a disability insurance policy taken out by the business, which paid out benefits if he was able to prove to Allied Dunbar's reasonable satisfaction that as a result of an accident or an illness he 'was able to perform no part' of the occupation he was engaged in immediately before the accident or the start of the illness. If he had more than one occupation he would not be able to claim if he was still able to perform any part of any of his occupations. Mr Hagirhan had pre-existing back problems. He then developed further back problems, and claimed under the policy. Allied Dunbar rejected Mr Haghiran's claim, and Mr Haghiran sued. The Court held that he had developed an illness in the form of pain perpetuation or pain syndrome, and minor depressive symptoms. These developments had heightened his pain awareness, and, in turn, had fed and exacerbated the pain syndrome. The Court held that his complaints of pain and disability were not entirely due to his pain syndrome, but to a very considerable degree stemmed from his own attitude to his condition. The Court accepted that Mr Haghiran believed himself to be far more disabled than in truth he was, but even so refused his claim. Mr Haghiran appealed on the basis that the Court had recognised that in reality he could not carry out his work because of his mental state and attitude consequent upon his illness, but nevertheless then ignored that reality and wrongly decided the case on the basis of what he could do if only he did not have this attitude. The Court of Appeal held that it was plain that, were Mr Haghiran unable to work solely because of his pain syndrome, exacerbated by his minor depressive symptoms, then his claim would be covered by the policy. Psychological overlay can aggravate an organic condition. But there came a point at which, however genuinely a claimant may regard himself as unable to work, he was in fact able to work and any non-return to work could not properly be said to be 'a result of an accident or an illness' but was rather a result of his erroneous, albeit genuine, belief that he cannot work. The judge's task was to decide not how disabled Mr Haghiran thought he was, but how disabled he actually was as a result of his illness. The mere fact that his attitude was genuine could not allow him to succeed in his claim under the policy.

[5.4.5]

Harris v Shuttleworth (Court of Appeal) [1995] OPLR 79, [1994] PLR 47, [1994] ICR 991

Incapacity pensions – interpretation of rules

Facts and Decision

Mrs Harris was employed by the National & Provincial Building Society. She developed cervical spondylosis and agoraphobia, and went absent from work. She was eventually dismissed, and she claimed an incapacity pension, which was payable on retirement of a member from service by reason of incapacity. The Court held that, on a proper construction of the rules, the words 'retirement' and 'incapacity' qualified each other. Where an employee was suffering from some condition which rendered him or her incapable of working in his or her job for a temporary period, but he or she was likely to be able to work again in that or a similar job at some time in the future, it was straining language to describe the termination of employment as 'retirement from the service by reason of incapacity'. However, dismissal did not preclude retirement in this case.

[5.4.6]

Kerr v British Leyland (Staff) Trustees (Court of Appeal, unreported, 26 March 1986)

Incapacity pensions – interpretation of rules – medical evidence

Facts and Decision

Mr Kerr was a member of a pension scheme established by interim trust deed, which provided that the definitive deed and rules should conform to the scheme booklet which had been circulated to employees. The booklet stated that if a member became incapacitated by illness or accident so that no further employment of any kind was possible, and it had been accepted that the incapacity was permanent, there would be payable a benefit of 4 times pensionable salary. Mr Kerr suffered a heart attack, and claimed the incapacity benefit. The trustees initially forwarded his claim to the insurers. They refused to pay out, since it was difficult to state that he was permanently unfit for any occupation; with a degree of weight loss and correction of anaemia, his symptoms might recede. When Mr Kerr's doctor challenged this, the trustees commissioned their own oral report, which supported the insurers. The Court held that the medical evidence was not properly put before the trustees by the doctors, and the trustees were ordered to reconsider their decision, giving Mr Kerr the opportunity to put in further medical evidence.

[5.4.7]

Key v Courtaulds (High Court) [1999] OPLR 27

Incapacity pensions – disputes of fact

Facts and Decision

Mrs Key suffered from pains in her neck and arms. She had to cease work because of the severity of the pain in April 1992, and was therefore dismissed. She applied for an incapacity pension from her employer's pension scheme, to which she would be entitled under the scheme rules if she retired owing in her employer's opinion to permanent incapacity in mind or body. The employer's doctor concluded that she would be able to return to work within two years, and would not be permanently incapacitated. The employer therefore did not agree to the incapacity pension being put into payment. Mrs Key challenged this decision before the Pensions Ombudsman, who concluded that the decision was not perverse, and that once the decision was made, subsequent medical evidence was of no relevance. Accordingly, the Court held that the employer's decision was properly made. The Ombudsman had material in front of him on which he could reach that conclusion, and the Court did not disturb his decision.

[5.4.8]

Law Debenture v Malley (High Court) [1999] OPLR 167

Incapacity pensions – covert surveillance

Facts and Decision

Law Debenture was one of the trustees of a pension scheme. In considering an application for incapacity pension, the trustees instructed a private investigator to carry out covert surveillance, and ultimately rejected the application. The member complained to the Pensions Ombudsman, who ordered the trustees to reconsider their decision and would have awarded £2,000 for non-pecuniary loss in respect of the covert surveillance. Law Debenture appealed to the High Court. The Court held that the Ombudsman could only overturn a trustee decision where the trustee had asked itself the wrong question, misdirected itself in law or its decision was perverse (no reasonable body of trustees could have arrived at that decision). There was no evidence of any of these things in this case. Covert surveillance was not unlawful and was a legitimate course to pursue on appropriate occasions. On this occasion, the covert surveillance could not be said to be of no material relevance.

[5.4.9]

Mihlenstedt v Barclays Bank (Court of Appeal) [1989] PLR 91, [1989] Ch 91, [1989] IRLR 522

Incapacity pensions – employer's duties

Facts and Decision

Mrs Mihlenstedt fell down stairs in 1976 and injured her back. In 1979 she divorced her husband, and she was caused much emotional distress. She was continuously absent from work from April 1982 until she was dismissed with notice in April 1983. She applied for an incapacity pension, which was payable when the employer was of the opinion that the member was unable by reason of physical or mental incapacity or infirmity to undertake any duties, or had thereby suffered a substantial loss of earning capacity and was likely permanently to remain so unable. The employer refused to grant Mrs Mihlenstedt an incapacity pension. The Court held that the reference in the scheme rules to undertaking any duties was a reference to duties in the bank's employment, while the reference to a substantial loss of earning capacity was a reference to earning capacity whether with the bank or otherwise. It was an implied term of the employment contract that the employer would discharge its functions in good faith. In this case, this meant that the bank would properly consider her claim. The bank had asked itself the right questions, and it had formed an opinion which it could tenably hold. Accordingly, it had fulfilled that duty.

[5.4.10]

Police Authority for Huddersfield v Watson (Divisional Court) [1947] 1 KB 842

Incapacity pensions – causation

Facts and Decision

Mr Watson, a police constable, was called upon to resign on account of ill-health. He was suffering from a duodenal ulcer which he claimed was the result of the conditions he experienced in the police service. The quarter sessions allowed his claim to a pension under the *Police Pensions Act 1921* on the basis that he was incapacitated for the performance of his duty by an injury received in the execution of his duty without his own default. Following *Garvin v Police Authority for City of London [1944] 1 KB 358*, the Court held that a police officer suffering from a bodily condition, including a duodenal ulcer, directly and causally connected with his service as a police officer has received an injury in the execution of his duty. Infection was not a necessary concept for the decision in *Garvin v Police Authority for City of London*. Mr Watson was, therefore, entitled to his pension.

[5.4.11]

R v Court ex parte Derbyshire (Divisional Court, unreported, 11 October 1994)

Incapacity pensions – causation

Facts and Decision

Miss Court retired from the police force and claimed an injury pension on the grounds that her condition amounted to an injury received without her own default in the execution of her duty. She had previously brought a claim against the constabulary on the grounds of sexual discrimination and sexual harassment, which were compromised with an apology to her and a payment of £2,000. The doctor assigned to assess her, Dr Wells, certified that she was suffering from stress, that she was disabled from performing the ordinary duties of a member of the police force and that the disability was likely to be permanent, and that the degree of disablement was 30%. However, the doctor certified that the condition was not a result of any injury received in the execution of duty as a member of the police force. Miss Court appealed, and on review, medical referee, Dr Bronks, certified that the psychiatric condition was largely if not entirely the result of events which occurred in the course of her work as a police officer. Dr Bronks was subsequently asked to complete a certificate of permanent disablement, which he completed believing he was a selected medical practitioner, certifying the disablement at 100%. The Court held that 'injury' was, for the purpose of assessing eligibility for an injury pension, not restricted to physical injury. Miss Court's stress was intimately connected with her public duty. It was impossible to say that no reasonable medical referee could have arrived at the conclusion that the injury was received in the execution of her duty. There was strictly no need for Dr Wells to assess the degree of disablement, having concluded that Miss Court had not developed her condition as a result of any injury received in the execution of duty as a member of the police force.

However, Dr Bronks was *functus officio* when he considered the question of degree of the disablement, and his certificate of permanent disablement was not part of the appeals process. As a matter of natural justice, the question of degree of disablement was to be referred to a new medical referee.

[5.4.12]

R v Merseyside Police Authority ex parte Yates (High Court, unreported, 19 February 1999)

Incapacity pensions – causation

Facts and Decision

Mr Yates was a police sergeant who retired on the basis of anxiety neurosis and depression. The condition was occasioned by the process of being accused (though ultimately cleared) of failing to carry out properly his duties as a custody sergeant because he had not taken any action against two other officers for allegedly assaulting a prisoner. The condition was certified by a doctor as a disablement, and one that was likely to be permanent. He claimed an injury pension on the grounds that his condition amounted to an injury received without his own default in the execution of his duty. The relevant regulation in the scheme regulations provided that the medical officer's opinion was final as to whether the person was disabled, whether the condition was likely to permanent, whether the disablement was the result of an injury received in the execution of his duty and the degree of the person's disablement. The Court decided that it could not apply anything other than a literal meaning to the regulation, however unsatisfactory it might be that a doctor should be deciding mixed questions of fact and law. No alternative was possible without rewriting the provisions. Mr Yates was obliged to subject himself to the disciplinary proceedings as part of his duties as an officer, and was therefore entitled to his pension.

[5.4.13]

R v Secretary of State for the Environment ex parte McClorry (High Court, unreported, 27 March 1998; decision upheld in Court of Appeal application for leave to appeal, unreported, 3 September 1998)

Incapacity pensions – interpretation of rules – permanence

Principles

Where an incapacity pension was payable where the member ceases to be in employment and was incapable of discharging efficiently the duties of that employment by reason of permanent ill-health or infirmity of mind or body, the incapacity must be present at the time of his or her ceasing to hold office. When assessing permanence, the test is 'until the date' at which the member would become entitled to a pension of his or her own volition. An application for a different type of incapacity pension was possible if further medical evidence arose of incapacity, so the Secretary of State had not erred in taking his decision on the evidence available rather than waiting for further evidence. On the facts, the Secretary of State was entitled to reach the conclusions he had reached, and these were not open to challenge by way of judicial review.

[5.4.14]

R v Sussex Police Authority ex parte Stewart (Court of Appeal) [2000] ICR 1122

Incapacity pensions – interpretation of rules

Facts and Decision

Ms Stewart was a police officer. She was certified as permanently disabled from performing the ordinary duties of a member of the police force by reason of scarring of ligaments and tendons of the left ankle, and she was retired from the force on the ground of permanent disability. She then started office work. In February 1998 she was recalled to see the force medical adviser, Dr O'Donnell, for further examination. Dr O'Donnell issued a certificate to the effect that she was not disabled from performing the ordinary duties of a member of the police force. The applicant exercised her right of appeal to a medical referee, arguing that she was still disabled because she was 'unable because of infirmity to perform all, or the overwhelming majority of, the ordinary duties of a police officer.' The medical referee examined Ms Stewart and reported that she was capable of carrying out regular sedentary work in an office, and of driving to and from that office for some distance, but that it was unlikely that she would function very well in extreme circumstances, i.e., where she may be needed to run or apprehend or tackle an individual. Under these circumstances she might have difficulty; she would be vulnerable and her reliability would be in question. The police authority issued a notice to stop the pension. Ms Stewart applied to Court to have that decision reviewed. The Court held that 'the ordinary duties' to which the relevant scheme regulation referred were the duties of her office, which officers had to be fitted both physically and mentally to perform. Given that several police jobs did not require physical fitness and in that respect were just like jobs in ordinary civilian life, the very concept of 'ordinary duties of a . . . member of the force' would otherwise be meaningless: the regulation could as well speak of unfitness for any ordinary job. The force was not obliged to retire Ms Stewart in the first place, and so eligibility for the pension was under the control of the police force. Ms Stewart's application was, therefore, successful.

[5.4.15]

R v West Yorkshire Fire and Civil Defence Authority ex parte McCalman and Lockwood (Court of Appeal, unreported, 30 June 2000)

Incapacity pensions – interpretation of rules – act of retirement

Facts and Decision

Mr McCalman and Mr Lockwood were firemen. Both suffered from back problems in the course of their work. Both were permanently unfit to act as operational firefighters, but fit to carry out non-operational duties. The authority instructed them to report for non-operational duties. Their contracts of employment, however, did not allow the authority to change their duties. Both claimed a pension under the Firemen's Pension Scheme by reason of their permanent disablement as firefighters. The pension was payable if a regular firefighter was required to retire on the grounds that he was permanently disabled. The authority refused to pay them such a pension, and the firemen applied for judicial review. The Court held that non-operational duties could not be described as firefighting. The scheme differentiated between those who were or may be required to engage in fire-fighting and those who were not. Under the structure of the scheme, the firemen were no longer able to perform their duty as firefighters and were therefore permanently disabled for the purpose of eligibility for the incapacity pension. Although the authority needed to take an action before the firemen could argue that they had been required to retire, that had happened here, since the instruction to report for non-operational duties was no offer, but an order. It was doubtful whether it was necessary for the authority's act to amount to a dismissal, but it probably did. The firemen were, therefore, entitled to their incapacity pensions.

[5.4.16]

Robinson v Atco-Qualcast (Pensions Ombudsman, 26 March 1999) Case H00422

Incapacity pensions – covert surveillance – employers' duties – trustees' duties

Facts and Decision

Mr Robinson applied for an ill-health pension under his employer's pension scheme following an accident at work. He would be entitled to a pension if he were no longer capable of following his normal employment. The responsibility for assessing eligibility for an ill-health pension was given to the trustees under the pension scheme, but the employer did not pass the claim to the trustees. When it received medical evidence broadly supporting Mr Robinson's claim, the employer instructed private investigators to carry out covert surveillance, following which the trustees rejected Mr Robinson's claim on the employer's instruction. The employer had given the private investigators copies of the medical evidence. The covert surveillance included an interview under false pretences and video surveillance of Mr Robinson's wife and daughter. Since it was for the trustees to make the decision, the Pensions Ombudsman held that the repeated failure of the employer to pass the case to the trustees was maladministration. The covert surveillance was an unwarranted intrusion into Mr Robinson's private life and that of his family and much of the evidence gathered was of no bearing on the claim. The commissioning of the covert surveillance was maladministration, as was the passing of medical evidence to a third party charged with the express duty of undermining Mr Robinson's case. Since the trustees had abrogated their responsibilities to scheme members, they were also guilty of maladministration.

[5.4.17]

Telstra v Flegeltaub (Supreme Court of Victoria, Court of Appeal) [2001] PLR 7

Incapacity pensions – interpretation of rules – refusal to submit to treatment

Facts and Decision

Ms Flegeltaub left employment, claiming a pension on the ground of total and permanent invalidity. Under the terms of the pension scheme's invalidity clause, the trustee could withhold such a pension if the condition was attributable to a material extent to deliberate action or inaction by any person for the purpose of causing a benefit to become or to continue to be payable from the scheme, including without limitation what the trustee considered to be an unreasonable refusal to submit to treatment. Her claim was rejected by a committee of the trustee, and by its Board of directors. On a proper construction, the trustee did not need to be of the opinion that an unreasonable refusal to submit to treatment was for the purpose of causing a benefit to become or continue to be payable from the scheme.

[5.4.18]

Whight v Co-operative Insurance Society (Pensions Ombudsman, 20 August 1999) Case H00487

Incapacity pensions – covert surveillance

Facts and Decision

Mr Whight became ill, receiving medical advice that it was unlikely that he would ever be able to work again. He applied for an ill-health pension, which was payable if the committee was satisfied that he was permanently incapable of continuing to work on medical grounds, either in his current role or in a suitable alternative form of employment. His application was refused because the committee was not satisfied of this. He was at no point offered alternative employment by his employer. The committee had used covert video surveillance by private investigators, which they did only very rarely, in situations where it was thought absolutely necessary to get at the truth behind a doubtful case, and where the alleged medical condition was such that investigation could reasonably be expected to produce an answer one way or another. The Pensions Ombudsman observed that covert surveillance was not unlawful, and this was an appropriate case for its use. The employer was, moreover, not under an obligation to offer Mr Whight alternative employment.

[5.4.19]

Young v NNC (Pensions Ombudsman, 29 September 1998) Case F00414

Incapacity pensions – interpretation of rules – medical evidence

Facts and Decision

Mr Young was employed as a draughtsman and went absent from work on medical grounds from January 1992. He applied for an ill-health pension from his employer's pension scheme, to which he was entitled if the trustees and his employer were satisfied that his cessation of service was due to serious ill-health or disablement such that it was not likely that he would ever again be capable of carrying out the duties of his normal employment with the employer, or any other employment offered to him prior to his cessation of service. His employer did not offer him alternative employment. The trustees turned his application down. The trustees took into account the possibility of further treatment or occupational therapy involving alternative employment possibilities, and formed the opinion that an otherwise fit man of Mr Young's age should be capable of gainful employment. The Pensions Ombudsman held that neither of these were matters which should have been taken into account. The Ombudsman treated the case as a dispute of fact, obtained independent medical evidence and concluded that Mr Young was not capable, and it was not likely at the time when he left work that he would ever again be capable, of carrying out his normal duties. Since no alternative work was made available to Mr Young, the trustees should not have been considering alternative work, but only whether he was capable or ever likely to be capable of resuming his duties as a draughtsman. The Pensions Ombudsman therefore awarded Mr Young an ill-health pension.

5.5 – Early retirement pension

[5.5.1]

Mock v Pensions Ombudsman (High Court, 31 March 2000) The Times, 7 April 2000, 36 PBLR 8

Early retirement pensions – interpretation of statute

Facts and Decision

Mr Mock was a civil servant between 1949 and 1962. In 1996, when he was 74, he wrote seeking a civil service pension. His claim was rejected by the Ministry of Defence and the Pensions Ombudsman. His claim was governed by the *Superannuation Acts 1834–1957*. The Court held that while nothing in those *Acts* expressly indicated that a person who left service before age 60 was not entitled to a pension, there were indications that a person should not be entitled to a pension unless he was still working as a civil servant when he was 60 or he was suffering from infirmity. The *Acts* did not give a civil servant a legal right to a pension, but merely set out where it would be lawful to pay a pension. Mr Mock's claim therefore failed.

[5.5.2]

Thomas v Pensions Ombudsman (High Court) [1996] OPLR 161

Early retirement pensions – retirement

Facts and Decision

A dentist, who was a member of the NHS pension scheme, was struck off the register in 1983. In 1992 he applied to be reinstated to the register, but was refused. He applied for an early retirement pension in 1995, on the grounds that he was forced to retire early, but was refused. The Court observed that *regulation 3* of the *National Health Service (Superannuation) Amendment Regulations 1981 (SI 1981 No 1205)* permitted early retirement in specified circumstances, the only one of which that was potentially relevant was where the Secretary of State had certified that the retirement was by reason of redundancy, or was in the interests of the efficiency of the service in which the member was employed. Neither of these criteria were satisfied, and the dentist was not able to take an early retirement pension.

[5.5.3]

Wyn Jones v Home Secretary (Crown Court with justices, sitting as an appeal court) [1995] PLR 1

Early retirement pensions – retirement

Facts and Decision

Mr Jones was an assistant police commissioner, and his royal warrant was withdrawn when he had completed 31 years' service and he was aged 50. He applied for an immediate pension. He would have been entitled to an immediate pension if he retired with at least 25 years' pensionable service and:

(a) he had been required to retire on account of age; or
(b) on the ground that his retention in the force would not be in the general interests of efficiency; or
(c) as an alternative to dismissal.

In having his royal warrant withdrawn, the Court held that Mr Jones could not be said to have retired within the meaning of the rules at all. In any case, even if he had retired, he had not done so on account of one of the three requirements listed above.

5.6 – Redundancy pension

[5.6.1]

Engineering Training Authority v Pensions Ombudsman (High Court) [1996] OPLR 167, [1996] PLR 409

Redundancy pensions – contract of employment – interpretation

Facts and Decision

An employee was to be made redundant shortly before his 50th birthday, at which point he would have been entitled to substantially improved pension benefits. He negotiated a deal by which he stayed in service until his 50th birthday, but accepted that he would not receive part of the improvement in his pension rights which would arise if he were made redundant aged 50 or over, and he also accepted a reduction in his lump sum redundancy payments. The Pensions Ombudsman found that the scheme rules provided that the employee was entitled to the enhanced pension benefits, even though the uplift was conditional upon payment of the necessary additional contributions to the scheme trustees, which had not happened. On a proper construction of the agreement negotiated between the employer and the employee, the employee's redundancy pension was fixed and the employer could not be compelled to make a payment of additional contributions.

[5.6.2]

Teachers' Pension Agency v Hill (High Court) [1998] OPLR 167

Redundancy pensions

Facts and Decision

Mrs Hill was employed on a succession of fixed term contracts as a teacher, and was a member of the Teachers' Superannuation Scheme, a statutory scheme. She was made redundant by her employers and her last fixed term contract was not renewed. Under the relevant pension scheme regulation, Mrs Hill was entitled to a preferential redundancy pension if her employer had notified the Secretary of State in writing that her employment was terminated by reason of her redundancy or in the interests of the efficient discharge of the employer's functions. Mrs Hill's employers wrote confirming that she was retiring on premature grounds and that her employment in pensionable service had been terminated before the contract of employment expired by reason of redundancy. The administrator refused to pay the pension, because her employment was not terminated by reason of her redundancy. The Court held that it was not enough that the employment had come to an end because a fixed term contract had run its natural course. Since no action was required by her employer, Mrs Hill's employment could not be said to have been terminated by her employer. Accordingly, the administrator had acted properly. To find the contrary would be to put employees on fixed term contracts in a better position than employees on indefinite contracts.

5.7 – Pension increases

Buckley v Hudson Forge (High Court) [1999] OPLR 249, [1999] PLR 151

Pension increases – trustee duties

Facts and Decision

Mr Buckley joined a new employer as an executive director in 1980. He was offered transfer terms to the new employer's scheme, which was on interim approval. These terms stated that pension increases would be at the trustees' discretion. Mr Buckley took the transfer. When definitive documentation was executed, discretionary pension increases put forward by the employer were made subject to employer consent. In practice, the principal employer was also the trustee. The scheme went into winding-up following the appointment of an administrative receiver to the principal employer. The terms of the winding-up rule made no provision for augmentation of benefits or for discretionary pension increases, and required the trustees to secure the liabilities and return any unexpended balance to the employers. On a proper construction, the Court held that the liabilities to be secured included any discretionary increases to pensions. The receiver had not considered exercising the power to increase Mr Buckley's pension, and in any case it was not within his powers as a receiver to act as scheme trustee: he would have been under a conflict of interest, such that he could not have validly or effectually have exercised the discretion. If the power had been properly considered for exercise, the trustee should have granted an augmentation.

[5.7.2]

Express Newspapers Pension Trustees v Express Newspapers plc (High Court) [1998] OPLR 261, [1999] PLR 9

Pension increases – merger – interpretation of rules

Facts and Decision

Trustees of one pension scheme made a bulk transfer to trustees of another scheme. One category of pensioners in the transferring scheme were not entitled to pension increases in that scheme. Following the transfer, these pensioners claimed that they were entitled to increases in accordance with the receiving scheme's pension increase rule. On a proper construction, the Court held that the receiving scheme's pension increase rule did not apply to the transferred pensioners. The rules as a whole applied only to members who had accrued their entitlement in the scheme, and the pension increase rule was no exception.

5.8 – Money purchase benefits

[5.8.1]

Bank of New Zealand Officers' Provident Association v Bank of New Zealand (High Court of New Zealand) [1999] PLR 117

Money purchase schemes – trustees' duties

Facts and Decision

Before 1990, the Bank of New Zealand's pension scheme was a defined benefits scheme. In 1990, members were given the opportunity to convert to a money purchase benefit structure, and many took this opportunity. The scheme developed a substantial surplus. The scheme's Board had a power to declare a distributed earnings rate for increasing the funds set aside for members. The scheme's Board put forward a proposal under which the provision for pensioners was disregarded when calculating the earnings for distribution, with the result that the cash account of each money purchase member was increased pro rata at a rate in excess of the calculated fund earnings. The notional fund set aside for defined benefits members was increased by the same rate, resulting in a contribution holiday for the employer. Taking the contribution holiday into account, the Bank obtained twice as much benefit from the proposal as the members. The Bank objected that the effect of this use of surplus was to favour disproportionately defined benefits members who withdrew before becoming entitled to the pension, and money purchase members. It applied to Court for a declaration that the trustees had misapplied the rule. The Court held that, on a proper construction, the purpose of the rule permitting the Board to distribute earnings was to allow the Board to distribute or allocate a proportion of the fund earnings each year, and the Board had a discretion to fix those earnings each year. Once these earnings were fixed, the rate for distribution could not exceed the fund earnings rate. The Bank accordingly succeeded in its application.

[5.8.2]

Barclays Bank v Holmes (High Court) [2000] PLR 339 at paras 78–80, 109, 116–118

Money purchase schemes – nature of benefits – main purpose

Principles

A member of a money purchase scheme should not be analysed as having a separate trust fund for his own benefit effectively embodied in his account. A dictum of Lord Millett in *Air Jamaica v Charlton [1999] 1 WLR 1399* was considered, but was held to be confined to identifying the impact of the rule against perpetuities. The case law determining that the use of surplus in a final salary scheme for meeting employer contributions was not a payment out of the scheme assets to an employer was equally applicable to the use of surplus to fund benefits in a money purchase section of a scheme. The observations of Chadwick LJ in *Edge v Pensions Ombudsman [2000] 3 WLR 79* on the nature of a defined benefits scheme were observations rather than an attempt to lay down the purpose of such a scheme. Establishing a money purchase section for a final salary scheme was not, therefore, in conflict with the main purpose of the scheme.

Part 6 – Loss of Pension Rights

6 – Introduction

Since the introduction of the preservation legislation, pension rights have been well-protected. Nevertheless, in limited circumstances pension benefits are subject to forfeiture. The Inland Revenue insists that pension benefits are not assignable, and the interrelationship of this requirement with other areas of the law has been considered by the courts.

The law relating to the treatment of pension rights on bankruptcy has changed repeatedly over the years. Parliament and the courts have agonised over the proper public policy boundary between individuals retaining pension rights and creditors receiving payment for debts incurred by bankrupts. Changes in the law in 1986 and 2000 mean that bankruptcies from different periods are treated in different ways. Further statutory changes are likely shortly. The court's analysis of bankruptcy is a three-stage process. First, the court must establish whether the pension rights form part of the estate. Secondly, the court must decide whether any protective trust in the pension scheme is effective to prevent transmission of the bankrupt's rights to the trustee in bankruptcy. Thirdly, the court must decide whether the trustee in bankruptcy has other rights to claim against the bankrupt's pension rights. The answers to these questions differ according to when the bankruptcy took place.

It is currently anticipated that Parliament will shortly bring into force *section 14* of the *Welfare Reform and Pensions Act 1999*, which will make protective trusts ineffective to the extent that they would otherwise prevent trustees in bankruptcy from claiming a member's pension assets. However, protective trusts will remain effective to the extent that they do not concern members' interests on bankruptcy (for example, if the member purports to assign part or all of his or her interest), and thus the case law on the interpretation of such clauses will remain important. *Ramsay v Caboche [1994] 119 ALR 215* and *Re Scientific Investment Pension Plan, Kemble v Hicks (No. 1) [1998] OPLR 41* will continue to be consulted.

Pension schemes are entitled to forfeit members' benefits on specific public policy grounds set out in the *Pensions Act 1995*. In practice, the mechanics of doing so are complicated, and *Haque v Bevis Trustees [1996] OPLR 271* shows the nature of the difficulties faced by pension scheme trustees. It is easy to overlook the operation of pension law in relation to contractual pension promises, but when these comprise occupational pension schemes, the employer is also constrained by the requirements of the *Pensions Act 1995*.

A mercifully rarely seen area of the law is the operation of forfeiture of pension benefits, which would otherwise be payable, as the result of a crime. The common law prevented criminals from profiting from heinous crimes on the ground of public policy. This had the capacity to cause injustice to the criminal, especially in cases of manslaughter through diminished responsibility or provocation, and Parliament enacted the *Forfeiture Act 1982* to give courts additional flexibility in dealing with such cases. The law on this *Act* is still developing, and the Court of Appeal decision in *Dunbar v Plant [1997] 4 All ER 289* appears to point to a new direction in this area of the law, shunning the approach tentatively favoured by the Court of Appeal in *Gray v Barr [1971] 2 All ER 949*. The courts are going to be readier to call into play this public policy rule, but after some hesitation, appear to have concluded that they can use their discretion under the *Forfeiture Act 1982* to mitigate its effects entirely. However, the law is still evolving, and further developments are awaited with interest.

6.1 – Anti-assignment clauses

[6.1.1]

Edmonds v Edmonds (High Court) [1965] 1 All ER 379

Assignment – protective trusts – divorce

Facts and Decision

Mr and Mrs Edmonds got divorced. Mrs Edmonds obtained an order for maintenance, which she attempted to enforce by an attachment of earnings against her husband's pension. The pension scheme included a clause that if a member suffered anything whereby the pension would but for that clause become vested in or payable to some other person, then the member's interest in the pension ceased, although the trustees could apply it for the benefit of the member. The trustees applied to Court for guidance. The Court held that the attachment of earnings order brought the forfeiture clause into operation. The pension therefore ceased and determined. The trustees still had the option to apply it for the benefit of the member. If the pension was not paid to Mr Edmonds but instead payments were made for his benefit, the pension would not count towards the earnings which fell to be paid. However, any discretionary payments paid to the husband fell within the terms of the attachment of earnings order.

[6.1.2]

Norman v Pensions Ombudsman (High Court) [1997] OPLR 85

Assignment – protective trusts

Facts and Decision

Mr Norman was the majority shareholder of Julsarben Limited and nominally an employee of that company. He was an active member of his employer's pension scheme. He entered into an agreement purporting to charge his interest in the scheme to that company and another company. The scheme had a rule providing that if an individual entitled to or in receipt of benefit under the scheme shall or shall purport to assign, mortgage or otherwise to deal with his beneficial interest under the scheme, or any part thereof, then he shall forfeit all such interest. He claimed that he had been tricked into entering into the agreement, and that it was a sham. The Pensions Ombudsman held that whether or not the charge was effective, the forfeiture rule took effect, and Mr Norman forfeited his pension. The Court held that a provision which contained a condition for forfeiture was not to be construed as including any matter which it did not on its true construction fairly include. Mr Norman was 'entitled' to benefit for the purpose of the forfeiture rule: in other places, the rules referred to members being entitled to benefits in circumstances where they were not in receipt of a pension and where the pension had not yet vested. The agreement purporting to charge the benefits was not part of the scheme for the purposes of *s 79(1)* of the *Pension Schemes Act 1993* because it was not an amendment which complied with the amendment rule. It was not contrary to public policy for the forfeiture rule to be given effect.

6.2 – Forfeiting pension

Haque v Bevis Trustees (High Court) [1996] OPLR 271

Forfeiture clause – transfers out

Facts and Decision

Mr Haque was employed by BCCI. When BCCI was placed in liquidation, Mr Haque left the United Kingdom for Pakistan. A warrant was issued for his arrest on charges of conspiracy to defraud and false accounting, but no steps were taken to extradite him. The liquidators notified the trustee of Mr Haque's occupational pension scheme that they were asserting claims against him for a sum in excess of the value of his pension. The scheme had a rule which gave the employer the right to recover from the scheme an amount equal to the value of any debt which had arisen due to any negligent, fraudulent or criminal act or omission of the member. However, in the event of dispute, no such right of recovery could be exercised until a court order or the award of an arbitrator had been made. Mr Haque disputed the claim, but the trustee still suspended the claim before court action was taken. The Court held that a distinction needed to be drawn between the right to recover and the exercise of the right to recover. The employer's right to recover might be prejudiced if the member's entitlement was not frozen pending the resolution of the issue through the courts. The trustee had, therefore, acted properly.

[6.2.2]

Whitchelo v Home Secretary (High Court) [1996] PLR 255

Forfeiture clause

Facts and Decision

Detective Sergeant Whitchelo retired on a disability pension from the police. Shortly after leaving the police force, he embarked on a series of blackmails. On conviction, the Secretary of State decided to forfeit 75% of his disability pension since he had committed an offence in connection with his service as a member of a police force which was either gravely injurious to the interests of the State or liable to lead to serious loss of confidence in the public service. The Court held that the essential requirement was that there was a link between the committing of the offence and the service as a police officer. It was not necessary for the officer still to be a police officer. On the facts, there was ample evidence to find a connection between Mr Whitchelo's service and the offences, since the knowledge for the *modus operandi* was gained during his police service. The Secretary of State's decision was therefore upheld.

6.3 – Setting off pension

[6.3.1]

Parlett v Guppy's (Bridport) Ltd (No. 2) (Court of Appeal) [1999] OPLR 309, [2000] PLR 195

Set-off of pension – occupational pension scheme

Facts and Decision

A company resolved at its annual general meeting to pay Mr Parlett, the managing director, a pension on his retirement calculated at 10% on £250,000, indexed from 1 August 1988 to the Retail Prices Index. Such an arrangement was, the Court held, an occupational pension scheme within the meaning of *s 1* of the *Pension Schemes Act 1993*. It was therefore not possible to set off against it claims which the company had against Mr Parlett.

6.4 – Effect of bankruptcy

[6.4.1]

Carman v Barron (County Court) [1996] PLR 229

Bankruptcy – anti-assignment

Facts and Decision

Mr Barron was made bankrupt in 1992, and among his assets were two retirement annuity contracts. The trustee in bankruptcy laid claim to them. The Court held that the policies vested in the trustee in bankruptcy in accordance with the *Insolvency Act 1986, s 306*, and the anti-assignment clause was of no effect.

[6.4.2]

Ex parte Huggins, In re Huggins (Court of Appeal) (1882) 21 Ch D 85

Bankruptcy

Facts and Decision

Mr Huggins held office as chief justice of Sierra Leone for two years, and was as a result given a pension. He then went into business, which failed, and he became bankrupt. The trustee in bankruptcy applied for an order declaring that the pension vested in him as part of the property of the bankruptcy. The Court held that the interaction of *ss 15, 17* and *90* of the *Bankruptcy Act 1869* had the effect that the pension vested in the trustee in bankruptcy, but that the Court could order that only a part of it should be set aside for the benefit of creditors.

Jones v Patel (Court of Appeal, unreported, 24 May 2001)

Bankruptcy – anti-assignment – mistake

Facts and Decision

Mr Patel was a member of the local government pension scheme, under which he was entitled to a pension and was granted discretionary benefits. He went bankrupt. The statutory instrument governing the scheme provided that every benefit was non-assignable and not chargeable with that person's debts or liabilities. As a matter of construction, the Court held that this did not deal with transmissions on bankruptcy. The entitlement under the statutory scheme was a chose in action, such as fell within the definition of 'property' and vested in the trustee in bankruptcy. The discretionary benefits were an interest incidental to property and also therefore fell within the definition of 'property'. While pension schemes provide benefits which are a form of deferred pay in some contexts, the scheme itself was not an unexecuted contract for personal services, and therefore the trustee in bankruptcy had the right to enforce payment even though the entitlement might arise from the term of a contract for service. Mr Patel had, however, continued to contribute following the commencement of bankruptcy, and it would be contrary to just dealings to allow the trustee in bankruptcy to take the benefit of the increase in value of the pension benefits caused by Mr Patel's mistaken belief that the pension benefits remained vested in him. *Krasner v Dennison [2001] Ch 76* was considered.

Kilvert v Flackett (High Court) [1998] OPLR 237, [1998] PLR 289, [1998] 2 FLR 806

Bankruptcy – anti-assignment

Facts and Decision

Mr Flackett was a dentist who was a member of the National Health Service Pension Scheme, a statutory scheme. He went bankrupt in October 1996 and attained his normal retirement date in April 1997. His trustee in bankruptcy claimed his lump sum and pension entitlement under s 310 of the *Insolvency Act 1986*. The Court held that its discretion must be exercised by reference to the general purpose of the legislation. The legislation's purpose was to vest in the trustee in bankruptcy all property belonging to the bankrupt at the commencement of the bankruptcy and after-acquired property in limited circumstances, and to provide that payments in the nature of income received between the bankruptcy and the discharge should also benefit the estate unless there were reasons to the contrary. The Court will seek to achieve proportionality between the creditors and the bankrupt, whilst not creating a situation in which the bankrupt is the slave of the creditors. Although the timing would determine, perhaps by chance, whether a payment came within *s 310* of the *Insolvency Act 1986*, Parliament must have appreciated this. There was no reason to give the bankrupt all of the benefit of the lump sum apart from that which was attributable to the period of bankruptcy: the legislation was more widely drawn than this. Plain justification would be needed for giving the bankrupt most of the lump sum, where this would enhance the bankrupt's income level above that required for his and his family's reasonable domestic needs during his bankruptcy.

[6.4.5]

Re Landau (High Court) [1998] Ch 223, [1996] OPLR 371, [1997] PLR 25

Bankruptcy – anti-assignment

Facts and Decision

Mr Landau was a solicitor who was made bankrupt. The trustee in bankruptcy sought to obtain control of the assets in his retirement annuity contract. The Court held that the bundle of rights comprising the policy was 'property' for the purpose of *s 436* of the *Insolvency Act 1986* and that it therefore formed part of the bankrupt's estate, and vested automatically in its entirety in the trustee in bankruptcy under *s 306* of the *Insolvency Act 1986*. The anti-assignment clause was not directed at transmissions on bankruptcy and so had no effect in this case. *S 310* of the *Insolvency Act 1986* dealt exclusively with property acquired after the bankruptcy had taken effect, and was therefore not relevant. *Ex parte Huggins, In re Huggins [1882] Ch D 85* was distinguished.

[6.4.6]

Lesser v Lawrence, Dennison v Krasner (Court of Appeal) [2001] Ch 76, [2000] PLR 213

Bankruptcy – anti-assignment

Facts and Decision

Two discharged bankrupts sought to resist the attempts by their trustees in bankruptcy from claiming all the proceeds of their retirement annuity contracts and personal pension schemes. The Court held that these pension arrangements formed part of the bankrupts' estates, and were the property of the trustees in bankruptcy: *Re Landau [1998] Ch 223* was approved. Any attempt to provide by contract that benefits will be inalienable on a bankruptcy must fail on grounds of public policy. *Section 310* of the *Insolvency Act 1986* had no application, since it applied to property only acquired by the bankrupt after the date of bankruptcy: *Ex parte Huggins, In re Huggins [1882] 21 ChD 85* had been superseded, following a change in the bankruptcy legislation.

Comment

This case has effectively settled the treatment of pension rights on bankruptcy under the *Insolvency Act 1986*. The Court of Appeal upheld the analysis of *Re Landau [1998] Ch 223* that the pension rights formed part of the bankrupt's estate. Accordingly, the pension would transfer to the trustee in bankruptcy unless the pension arrangement had an effective protective trust which operated to forfeit the benefits if the individual went bankrupt. The bankrupts appealed to the House of Lords, but the case was settled before it was heard.

Parliament has changed the law on the treatment of pension rights on bankruptcy since the date on which these bankruptcies took place, by the enactment of the *Welfare Reform and Pensions Act 1999*. Pension rights no longer form part of the bankrupt's estate, and protective trusts will cease to have effect when *section 14* of that *Act* is brought into force. This decision will remain of interest for some time, however, since anyone who went bankrupt between 29 December 1986 and 29 May 2000 will have their pension rights determined in accordance with the principles set out in this decision.

[6.4.7]

Re Lupton (Court of Appeal) [1912] 1 KB 107

Bankruptcy

Facts and Decision

An undischarged bankrupt who was in the civil service was granted a pension under the *Superannuation Act 1909* and a lump sum in cash. The Court held that this did not vest in the trustee in bankruptcy, but was compensation granted by the Treasury within the meaning of *s 53(2)* of the *Bankruptcy Act 1883*. Consequently, it fell to be dealt with in accordance with that provision, even though there was no legal obligation on the Treasury to pay the pension and lump sum.

[6.4.8]

Readman, Noter (Scottish Sheriff's Court, unreported, 23 July 1992)

Bankruptcy – powers of the trustee-in-bankruptcy

Facts and Decision

Mr Shand went bankrupt. One of his assets was a retirement annuity contract. The trustee of his sequestrated estate laid claim to the proceeds of the contract as an asset of the estate. The Court held that the retirement annuity contract was part of the bankrupt's estate: *Re Landau [1998] Ch 223* was followed. The trustee could also exercise the rights of the contract in such manner as he thought most appropriate for maximising the estate for the benefit of the creditors.

[6.4.9]

Trustee Corporation v Nadir (High Court, 12 December 2000) [2001] 21 PBLR 7

Bankruptcy – protective trusts

Facts and Decision

Mr Nadir was a well-known businessman who went bankrupt. The trustees in bankruptcy laid claim to his interest under his occupational pension scheme, but Mr Nadir disputed this. The scheme trustees applied to Court for guidance as to whether Mr Nadir's benefits remained payable to him, were vested in the trustee in bankruptcy or were held on protective trusts. Mr Nadir applied for a pre-emptive costs order. The Court was of the opinion that Mr Nadir's case faced formidable difficulties. The definitive deed post-dated the creation of the interest, and it would be very surprising if rules adopted in 1999 could remove rights vested in the trustees in bankruptcy many years previously. Secondly, the rules were adopted by deed in 1999 'with effect from the date of this Deed', and it was very difficult to read that as involving an 11-year retrospective effect.

6.5 – Protective trusts

[6.5.1]

Aitchison v NZI Life Superannuation Nominees (High Court, New Zealand) [1995] PLR 7

Bankruptcy – protective trusts – public policy

Facts and Decision

A New Zealand personal pension scheme had as one of its provisions a clause which provided for the forfeiture of a member's benefits in the event that a member became bankrupt. At the time that the clause was drafted, a New Zealand statutory instrument permitted the use of such forfeiture clauses. The provision in the statutory instrument was later repealed. Two members subsequently went bankrupt. Despite the revocation of the statutory instrument, the Court held that the clause forfeiting benefits in the event of bankruptcy remained effective.

Subject to any enactment to the contrary for the time being in force, a settlement is ineffective in so far as it purports to divest a settlor of an interest reserved in a trust fund in the event of bankruptcy. *Higinbotham v Holme (1811) 19 Ves Jun 88; 34 ER 451, Wilson v Greenwood (1818) 1 Swans 471, 481; 36 ER 469, 475, Re Robert Margrie (1876) 2 NZ Jur (NS) SC 121, Mackintosh v Pogose [1895] 1 Ch 505, Re Johnson Johnson [1904] 1 KB 905, Re Burroughs-Fowler [1916] 2 Ch 251, Caboche v Ramsay [1993] 19 ALR 215, Re Detmold (1889) 40 Ch D 585, Re Balfour's Settlement [1938] 1 Ch 928, Re Pots, ex parte Taylor [1893] 1 QB 648, Slater v Pinder (1871) LR 6 Exch 228* were all considered.

[6.5.2]

Re Coram (Federal Court of Australia, 12 June 1992) 109 ALR 353

Bankruptcy – protective trusts

Facts and Decision

Mr Coram resigned from his employment, thereby becoming entitled to a deferred pension benefit under his employer's pension scheme. He then went bankrupt. His trustee in bankruptcy obtained a Mareva injunction over Mr Coram's assets. The pension scheme contained a clause which stated that if any member became bankrupt or committed any act of bankruptcy, or did or suffered anything by which his rights or interests if absolutely vested in the member may or would become vested in or payable to any other person, the rights or interests affected 'shall thereupon determine'. The Court held that Mr Coram's benefit had already vested, and so the protective trust in the pension scheme was ineffective. The Mareva injunction in any case did not amount to a deprivation of the bankrupt's personal enjoyment of his rights or interests in the scheme; it merely regulated his mode of enjoyment of those rights or interests.

[6.5.3]

Lucas v Harris (Court of Appeal) (1886) 18 QBD 127

Bankruptcy – inalienability

Facts and Decision

Two retired officers of the Indian army were in receipt of pensions which were expressed by *s 141* of the *Army Act 1881* to be inalienable by the voluntary act of those entitled to them. A creditor sought to take their pensions in execution of a debt. On a proper construction of the *section*, the Court held that they were inalienable not only by the persons to whom they were granted but also absolutely inalienable, except in the manner provided in that *section*. Therefore it was not possible for a creditor to take the pension in execution of the debt: *Dent v Dent Law Rep 1 P & M 366* was distinguished, while *Birch v Birch SPD 163* and *Gathercole v Smith 17 Ch D 1* were followed.

[6.5.4]

Ramsay v Caboche (Federal Court of Australia) [1994] 119 ALR 215

Bankruptcy – protective trusts

Facts and Decision

Mr Alan Bond, a well-known entrepreneur, went bankrupt. He was the sole member of an employer-sponsored pension scheme, and his trustee in bankruptcy laid claim to his pension benefits. The rules of the scheme provided that on his retirement he would become entitled to specified benefits, subject to the deed and the rules. The rules contained a protective trust which provided, among other things, that if a person entitled to benefit went bankrupt his benefit would be immediately forfeited. The Court held that the protective trust was of no effect, because it was purporting to terminate an absolute interest.

[6.5.5]

Re Saunders (Court of Appeal) [1895] 2 QB 424

Bankruptcy – protective trusts – public policy

Facts and Decision

Mr Saunders was a retired major-general of the Indian army and was in receipt of a pension under the *Indian Pensions Act 1871*, an Indian Act of Parliament. He went bankrupt, and his trustee in bankruptcy sought payment of his pension by use of the judicial discretion under s 53(2) of the *Bankruptcy Act 1883*. The Indian legislature intended that officers should not be subject to any interference in the enjoyment of their pensions but s 27 of the *Insolvent Debtors (India) Act 1848*, a British Act, empowered a court to make an order interfering with the enjoyment of the pension in the case of an insolvency in India. The Court held that it had jurisdiction to order the payment of the pension to the trustee in bankruptcy, but it ought not to do so in this and similar cases. However, this was not an inflexible rule, and an order might be appropriate in other cases. Per Smith LJ, if the officer had other sources of income which would justify the making of the order, it should be made.

[6.5.6]

Re Scientific Investment Pension Plan, Kemble v Hicks (No. 1) (High Court) [1998] OPLR 41, [1998] PLR 141

Bankruptcy – protective trusts

Facts and Decision

A pension scheme member went bankrupt, and the trustee in bankruptcy laid claim to his pension entitlement. The pension scheme trustee claimed that the benefits had been effectively forfeited on bankruptcy. The Court held that a forfeiture clause purporting to forfeit an absolute interest in possession is void. A clause purporting to forfeit a limited interest in possession is void if on a true construction of the deed, the interest is not made determinable on the same events as those in which the forfeiture is expressed to operate. However, there is nothing objectionable about a forfeiture clause which purports to defeat a future interest before it falls into possession, or to create a gift over in the event in which an income interest in possession is on the true construction of the trust instrument made determinable. Where a forfeiture clause includes the wording 'if belonging absolutely to the member', the only meaning attributable to that wording is that in fact the benefits concerned do not belong absolutely to the member. The forfeiture clause was therefore effective in this case: *Re Smith [1916] 1 Ch 369* was distinguished. In that case, the interest was an absolute capital legacy to take effect immediately upon the testator's death, making it difficult if not impossible to give meaning to the words 'if belonging absolutely to the member'. *Caboche v Ramsay [1993] 19 ALR 215* was approved and distinguished.

[6.5.7]

Re Smith (High Court) [1916] 1 Ch 369

Bankruptcy – protective trusts – public policy

Facts and Decision

A testator died leaving a will under which his widow received the income from the residue of his estate during her lifetime with an absolute reversionary gift over to his children on her death. The will contained a clause providing that if by reason of bankruptcy of any beneficiary any part of the property, if his or her own absolute property, would become vested in or payable to or for the benefit of any assignees or creditors of the beneficiary, then the trust declared in favour of the beneficiary thenceforth ceased and determined. One of the testator's children went bankrupt during the lifetime of the widow. The Court held that the protective trust was void for repugnancy even as against contingent interests: it was drafted in general terms with regard to bankruptcy occurring at any time.

6.6 – Forfeiture of benefits for public policy reasons

[6.6.1]

Dunbar v Plant (Court of Appeal) [1997] 4 All ER 289

Forfeiture – public policy

Facts and Decision

Ms Plant and Mr Dunbar formed a suicide pact when Ms Plant was accused of theft. Mr Dunbar died, but Ms Plant lived. Ms Plant was guilty of aiding and abetting suicide, which was an offence to which the forfeiture rule applied. The Court held that it was sufficient that a serious crime had been committed deliberately and intentionally. The presence of acts or threats of violence was not necessary for the application of the forfeiture rule: the approach of *Gray v Barr [1971] 2 All ER 949, [1971] 2 QB 554* was not followed, and *Re H dec'd [1990] 1 FLR 441* and *Re S (deceased) [1996] 1 WLR 235* were disapproved. The *Forfeiture Act 1982* had forestalled any judicial modification of the forfeiture rule and there was no reason for the Court now to attempt to modify it. Where the public interest required no penal sanction, there were likely to be strong grounds for relieving the person who had committed the offence from all effect of the forfeiture rule. The discretion to relieve the effect of the forfeiture rule was a broad one, and it was legitimate to have regard to all the consequences of the order, but it was not right to approach the exercise of the discretion as if dealing simply with an *inter partes* dispute. The first and paramount consideration was whether the culpability attending the bene-ficiary's criminal conduct was such as to justify the application of the forfeiture rule at all. Each case must be assessed on its own facts. Had Ms Plant's decision to take her own life been an understandable reaction to the pending consequence of her theft, a case could well have been made out for saying that this gave to her participation in the suicide pact a culpability that should properly be reflected by the application, at least to a degree, of the forfeiture rule. However, this was not such a case: Ms Plant's reaction was an irrational and tragic one. The assets with which the case was concerned were in no way derived from Mr Dunbar's family. Accordingly, full relief against forfeiture was given.

[6.6.2]

Re H dec'd (High Court) [1990] 1 FLR 441

Forfeiture – public policy

Facts and Decision

Mr H killed his wife while suffering from hallucinations caused by anti-depressants. He was convicted of manslaughter on the ground of diminished responsibility. The recorder sentenced him by making an order under *s 37* of the *Mental Health Act 1983*, and told him he bore no responsibility. He did not order that Mr H's discharge from hospital be restricted. Mr H was the sole beneficiary under Mrs H's will, and had been nominated by her to receive benefits under the Principal Civil Service Pension Scheme. The public policy rule preventing a person convicted of an offence involving unlawful killing from benefiting from his crime was held not to apply. Mr H was not guilty of deliberate, intentional and unlawful violence or threats of violence: *Gray v Barr [1971] 2 All ER 949, [1971] 2 QB 554* was applied. If the rule had applied, the Court would have exercised its power under *s 2(1)* of the *Forfeiture Act 1981* to modify the effect of the rule in relation to Mrs H's estate and the pension entitlement.

[6.6.3]

Social Security Commissioner's Decision RG 3/90 (Social Security Commissioner, Scotland, 30 March 1990)

Forfeiture – public policy

Facts and Decision

A wife killed her husband and pleaded guilty to culpable homicide. She applied for modification under the *Forfeiture Act 1982* of the public policy rule preventing a person convicted of an offence involving unlawful killing from benefiting from her crime, so that she could receive the state widow's pension and the state widowed mother's pension. The Commissioner held that the public policy rule could not be waived completely: *Cross, Petitioner [1987] SLT 384* was followed, and *Re K, deceased [1985] 1 Ch 85* was not followed.

Social Security Commissioner's Decision CG 14509/96 (Social Security Commissioner) [1999] PLR 1

Forfeiture – public policy

Facts and Decision

A wife stabbed her husband to death and was subsequently convicted of manslaughter. The trial had heard evidence that the husband had a history of physical abuse of his wife. In common law, the wife would have been deprived of her widow's pension under the state earnings related pension scheme (SERPS). *Section 4* of the *Forfeiture Act 1982* gave the Social Security Commissioner a complete discretion as to whether to modify the effect of the common law rule. The Commissioner held that he must be guided by the findings of the jury, having regard to the evidence before them as set out in the judge's summing up and the issues in the case. The Commissioner also took account of the fact that the judge gave the wife a moderate sentence of imprisonment which resulted in her immediate release, and drew the implication that the judge had taken the view that she had suffered enough and that no further punishment was called for or was appropriate. However, it did not follow that the operation of the common law rule should be removed altogether. The Commissioner was obliged to take into account the very considerable extra burden on the national insurance fund which would be the direct result of her own unlawful act. Even though the purpose of the rule was not to impose additional punishment, a total lifting of all forfeiture was not appropriate in such circumstances. The Commissioner examined the wife's conduct since the trial, and the present need of the wife to re-establish herself and provide a stable home base for the children. He took account of the fact that the wife had not sought substantial provision for herself out of the husband's estate, but what was done about private property rights in consequence of a forfeiture was not and could not be a major determining factor in relation to social security benefits. The Commissioner lifted the operation of the forfeiture rule completely for the remaining period while the wife was still of working age, and restricted the operation of the rule to her personal benefits in later life dependent on her husband's contributions. The SERPS pension payable from age 60 was halved. The discretion under the *Forfeiture Act 1982* was held to depend very much on the individual facts in each case.

[6.6.5]

Szrabjer v United Kingdom (European Commission of Human Rights) [1998] PLR 281

Forfeiture – human rights

Facts and Decision

The Commission held that it is not a violation of a pensioner's right to the peaceful enjoyment of his or her possessions within the meaning of *Article 1* of *Protocol No. 1* of the *European Convention on Human Rights* to suspend payment of a pension under the State earnings related pension scheme (SERPS) while the pensioner was in prison. Prisoners and non-prisoners were not relevantly similar, so there was no breach of the right to the enjoyment of Convention rights without discrimination. Nor were persons in receipt of a SERPS pension in a relevantly similar position to members of a contracted-out scheme.

Part 7 – Amendment and Augmentation

7 – Introduction

With very limited exceptions, the terms of a trust cannot be changed except in accordance with any power of amendment which it contains. This makes the power of amendment perhaps the most important of any power in the constitution of a pension scheme set up under trust.

One way of visualising this is to imagine such a pension scheme as a box of fixed dimensions. All of its provisions are contained inside the box. The power of amendment, which itself is part of the structure of the box, allows you to change the terms of any of the provisions within the limits of the box. It may conceivably at some stage become desirable to change one or more of the provisions so that they no longer are confined by the limits of the box. It may conceivably, in the view of the trustees and the sponsoring employer, become more or less essential to change one or more of the provisions in this way. However, unless some free-standing legal principle (such as a statutory power of modification) permits you to do so, then no matter how desirable it may be, it is not possible to change those provisions in that way. You cannot go outside the defined boundaries.

This chapter is littered with examples of trustees and sponsoring employers who tried to go outside the terms of the boundaries, from *Re ABC Television Pension Scheme* (unreported) to *Wilson v Metro Goldwyn Mayer [1980] 18 NSWLR 730*. The courts have struck down such attempts time after time.

Of course, the next obvious question is to determine what are the boundaries of the power of amendment. The boundaries imposed may be explicit or implicit, but both types may require some interpretation. A good illustrative case is *Harwood-Smart v Caws [2000] PLR 101*. In that case, the trustees and the employer repeatedly amended the winding-up power with apparently complete disregard for the express restrictions on the power of amendment. The Court had to pick its way between those amendments which were unhappily expressed but lawful, and those which breached the restriction on the power of amendment and which were therefore struck down.

There is a more fundamental restriction on the power of amendment, which is discussed in *Re Courage Group's Pension Schemes, Ryan v Imperial*

Brewing [1987] 1 All ER 528. No amendment can change the scheme's main purpose, although the main purpose can be changed by degrees. In practice, this is less of a restriction than it might sound. It does not, for example, prevent an amendment adding a money purchase section to a defined benefits scheme, as noted by *Barclays Bank v Holmes [2000] PLR 339*.

One problem which comes up repeatedly is the extent to which the power of amendment can continue to be used when the scheme is in or near winding-up. The way in which the case law has developed has resulted in some fine distinctions resulting in radically different answers. Of course, this is a matter of the interpretation of the power of amendment in each case, but some general principles can be drawn.

First, it is difficult to see how a scheme could lawfully be amended in any significant respect once it has actually been discontinued (*Air Jamaica v Charlton [1999] 1 WLR 1399*). Secondly, where the clear words of the winding-up rule show that the scheme should be wound up and the trusts cease and determine, the power of amendment no longer continues to subsist (*Re ABC Television Pension Scheme, Jones v Williams [1989] PLR 17*). However, where there is an obligation to exercise the power of amendment which remains unfulfilled at the date of winding-up, the power of amendment has not been brought to an end (*Davis v Richards & Wallington [1991] 2 All ER 563*). Where the scheme is closed but not wound-up, the power of amendment continues to subsist (*Re Edward Jones Benevolent Trust, Spink v Samuel Jones* (unreported)), and even when the notice period for triggering the winding-up has been given, the power of amendment does not fall away until the winding up commence (*Municipal Mutual Insurance v Harrop [1998] OPLR 199*).

The courts approach the interpretation of the power of amendment in much the same way as they approach the interpretation of any other pension scheme power. Hopeful attempts to persuade the courts to take an extremely flexible view of the wordings of restrictions on powers of amendment have failed in cases as varied as *Lloyds Bank Pension Trust Corporation Limited v Lloyds Bank PLC [1996] OPLR 181*, *Re Alfred Herbert Ltd Pension and Life Assurance Scheme Trusts, Alfred Herbert v Hancocks [1960] 1 WLR 271*, *Ritchie v Blakeley [1985] 1 NZLR 630* and *Re Courage Group's Pension Schemes, Ryan v Imperial Brewing*. On the other hand, the courts have been equally cautious about implying restrictions into powers of amendment which are not explicitly stated. *Re Courage Group's Pension Schemes, Ryan v Imperial Brewing* struck the most cautious note, but still concluded that a power to substitute a principal employer could be properly incorporated in given circumstances. *Kearns v Hill [1991] PLR 161*, although not a pensions case, is perhaps more characteristic of the courts' approach to powers of amendment. *Aitken v Christy Hunt [1991] PLR 1* is another example of the courts' refusal to infer restrictions on the power of amendment when they are not necessary.

The courts have taken a pragmatic approach to procedural issues. In *LRT v Hatt [1993] OPLR 225* the Court was willing to treat a deed of appointment and removal of trustee as an exercise of the power of amendment when it was necessary, given that there was no apparent intention not to exercise that power. In *International Power v Healy [2001] PLR 121*, both Lord Hoffman and Lord Scott were relaxed about the necessity for documenting arrangements under the power of amendment, where there was a free-standing power to make arrangements for surplus. Lord Scott's observations about the circumstances in which an amendment was required are likely to be referred to on future occasions when there is doubt whether a change to a pension scheme has been properly incorporated.

The interrelationship between amendments and augmentations is only just starting to be explored. The decision in *Harding and others (Trustees of Joy Manufacturing Holdings Ltd Pension and Life Assurance Scheme), petitioners [1999] OPLR 235* was a little surprising, given that in most other cases the courts have been slow to imply restrictions into apparently unlimited powers, as illustrated by, for example, *Aitken v Christy Hunt*. In the past, this relationship between amendments and augmentations was of theoretical interest only, in most cases. However, s 67 of the *Pensions Act 1995* is now in force. This section prevents any exercise of a power to modify a scheme which would or might affect members' and pensioners' accrued rights and entitlements without their consent, unless an actuary certifies that in his or her opinion the exercise would not adversely affect their accrued rights or entitlements. If a power of augmentation is a power to modify the scheme, then an actuarial certificate is apparently necessary before the power can be exercised. If it is not, then can it be exercised on a class-wide basis without obtaining a certificate, thus circumventing the requirements of s 67 as it applies to powers of amendment? Lord Scott's test for the necessity of a deed of amendment is apposite here also.

The courts have barely begun to consider the impact of s 67. There have been three cases directly on this point so far: *Barclays Bank v Holmes [2000] PLR 339, Merchant Navy Ratings Pension Fund Trustees v Chambers [2001] PLR 137* and *South West Trains v Wightman [1997] OPLR 249*. The last of these decided a technical question about the enactment of s 67, which is likely to be of transitional interest only. *Barclays Bank v Holmes* answered a more substantive question: it confirmed that the restriction imposed by s 67 did not protect an interest in having surplus preserved for the member's benefit, thus allaying the gravest fears as to the extent of the members' interests which this *section* protected. This approach mirrors the approach of the United States Supreme Court in *Hughes Aircraft v Jacobson 105 F3d 1288 and 128 F3d 1305, reversed. Merchant Navy Ratings Pension Fund Trustees v Chambers* showed that the courts would look to the substance not to the form. In that case, the trustees proposed to amend the rules to provide for a transfer of pensioners to a new arrangement without their consent. Despite this apparently drastic step, the Court was not prepared to hold that this was automatically a breach of *s 67*, determining that this was a matter for the actuary's certificate. This echoed the approach of the New Zealand court in *Ritchie v Blakeley [1985] 1 NZLR 630* to a similar restriction on a power of amendment under consideration in that case. It is early days yet, but it appears that the courts are approaching *s 67* with a will to ensure that pension schemes are not too encumbered by inflexibility.

7.1 – Power of amendment

[7.1.1]

Re ABC Television Pension Scheme (High Court, unreported, 22 May 1973)

Amendment – winding-up

Facts and Decision

The pension scheme went into winding-up. The employer wished to alter the winding-up rule. Winding-up had commenced, however, and the Court held that clear words of the winding-up rule, that the scheme should then be wound up, the trusts ceased and determined and the scheme dissolved, excluded the possibility that the power of amendment continued to subsist.

[7.1.2]

Air Jamaica v Charlton (Privy Council) [1999] 1 WLR 1399, [1999] OPLR 11, [1999] PLR 247 at paras 45–46

Amendment – perpetuity – employer's obligations – multiple amendments

Principles

The exercise of a power of amendment which is void for perpetuity as against existing members is effective as against a member who joins the plan after the date of the amendment, if the member joins on the terms of the trusts of the plan as amended.

The company's power to amend the plan was subject to an obligation to exercise it in good faith. The company was not entitled simply to disregard or override the interests of the members. Once it became likely that the plan would need to be wound up, the company would be required to take that fact into account. It was difficult to see how the plan could lawfully be amended in any significant respect once it had actually been discontinued.

The power of amendment could not be used to achieve in two steps what could not be achieved in one. So it was not possible for a prohibition on the refund of money to the employer to be removed in one step, and then as a second step to insert a power to confer an interest on the employer in the trust fund.

[7.1.3]

Air Products Canada v Schmidt (Supreme Court, Canada) [1995] OPLR 283, [1995] PLR 75 at paras 60–72

Amendment – revocation of trust

Principles

The settlor of a trust can reserve any power to itself that it wishes, provided the reservation is made at the time the trust is created. The reservation by the settlor of an unlimited power of amendment does not include a power to revoke the trust. Such a power must be explicitly reserved in order to be valid.

[7.1.4]

Aitken v Christy Hunt (High Court) [1991] PLR I

Amendment – construction – implication of restrictions

Facts and Decision

A scheme was substantially in surplus. The power of amendment set out in the trust deed provided that the rules could be amended in such matter as 'the trustees shall in their absolute and uncontrolled discretion think fit'. This was so, provided that no amendment 'shall be made so as to make the main purpose for which the Pensions Fund was to be applied other than the provision of pensions to employees or their dependants, nor so as to enable any part of the Pensions Fund to be payable to the company'. The trustees purported to remove the requirements in the augmentation powers for employer consent to augmentations. They also closed the scheme to employees who joined after 1 August 1989. The employer challenged these actions. The Court held that there was no basis on which it could imply a further proviso into the power of amendment, that no amendment should be made to the rules which deleted a requirement for the employer's consent. Further, since the augmentation powers had not been in the initial version of the rules, it was not possible to imply such a restriction into the power of amendment which concerned those powers.

Such an amendment could not have been under consideration at the time when the power of amendment was drawn up. The trustees were also held to have the power to redefine who was an employee for the purpose of scheme membership.

[7.1.5]

Re Alfred Herbert Ltd Pension and Life Assurance Scheme Trusts, Alfred Herbert v Hancocks (High Court) [1960] 1 WLR 271

Amendment – construction of restrictions – benefits secured by contributions

Facts and Decision

A pension scheme had a power of amendment under which the right was reserved to amend the scheme from time to time in the event of unforeseen circumstances, on any anniversary of the starting date without prejudice to the pension benefits already secured by contributions already paid. An amendment was made in 1955 by which it was provided that, if a member died while in the service of the company at or after normal pension age, and before going on pension, the life assurance benefit applicable immediately prior to normal pension age would be paid: also payable was a cash sum equivalent in value to five years' payments of the pension, which would have been payable had the employee retired on the date of death. A later amendment provided that the employee could nominate the recipient of the death benefit from a class of potential beneficiaries, but without a nomination the benefit would be paid to the member's widow. Prior to this second amendment, only a refund of contributions would have been paid to members' estates. Mr Hancocks worked from 1897 to 1958 for the employer, when he died. He was married but estranged from his wife. He made no nomination and neither assented or dissented from either amendment. The company as scheme trustee applied to Court for guidance whether the amendments were valid, and if not, whether the benefits were payable to the widow or to the executors.

The Court held that these were not unforeseen circumstances of the type envisaged by the power of amendment, which was drafted to protect the employer's interest. The wording in the power of amendment 'without prejudice to the pension benefits secured by contributions already paid' suggested that the scope of the proposed change was limited to the company's part of the contract, and it was not intended that the company be enabled to change the beneficial interests, however much it might think that such changes would be in the interests of the beneficiaries. The amendment was not capable of binding the beneficiary without his consent, and it was not suggested in this case that Mr Hancocks had become so bound. The Court had, therefore, insufficient evidence to determine whether the estate could claim benefit at the 1955 level of benefits.

[7.1.6]

Austchem Nominees v AC Hatrick Chemicals (Supreme Court of New South Wales, unreported, 13 October 1988)

Amendment – trustees' duties

Facts and Decision

The principal employer operated a defined benefit pension scheme which was substantially in surplus. The principal employer wanted to amend the scheme rules so that the trustees could make transfer payments to another scheme on the basis of the members' actuarial interests, so that no element of surplus would be transferred. It also sought an amendment so that when a participating employer no longer employed any more employees, it would cease to participate. The members argued that the trustees could not agree to these changes since they would not be for the benefit of the beneficiaries as a whole, and the trustees would not be acting impartially. The Court held, however, that since there were arguments for and against the amendment, the trustees could properly agree to such an amendment. On the evidence before the Court, there was nothing to suggest the trustees had not considered their duties properly.

[7.1.7]

Bairstow v Queens Moat Houses (High Court, unreported, 23 July 1999)

Amendments – employer's duties

Facts and Decision

The power of amendment of a pension scheme provided that amendments could be made by company resolution. However, the membership had to be consulted about rule amendments which could prejudicially affect their past or future rights and notice of any such amendment had to be given by the administrator to all members of the scheme. The company passed a resolution changing the definition of pensionable salary, but did so by approving a resolution of its remuneration committee, which had not been delegated the power to amend the scheme rules. The Court held that the Board had not appreciated that it was exercising a rule amendment power. The executive directors had a clear duty to bring the relevant rules to the attention of the non-executives. No consultation of or notice to the members ever took place, and the Inland Revenue was not notified of the change. The employer had an obligation of good faith in exercising its power with a view to the efficient running of the scheme, and there had been such a fundamental breach of this obligation that the purported exercise of the power of amendment was invalid. Failure to consult or notify the membership rendered the amendment void, since the amendments might put the funding of the scheme at risk and the contracting-out certificate could be lost.

[7.1.8]

Barclays Bank v Holmes (High Court) [2000] PLR 339 at paras 112–130

Amendment – main purpose – new section – employers' duties – trustees' duties – section 67 of the Pensions Act 1995

Principles

The introduction of a money purchase section into a defined benefits scheme did not infringe a restriction on the power of amendment, preventing amendments which caused the main purpose of the scheme to cease to be that of provision of pensions on retirement. Nor was the introduction of such a section outside the general powers of the employer and trustees under general law. The introduction of a new section was not for an extraneous or ulterior purpose such as was canvassed in *Re Courage Group's Pension Schemes [1987] 1 All ER 528*. Chadwick LJ's comments in *Edge v Pensions Ombudsman [1998] OPLR 51* about the nature of a defined benefits scheme were recording the fact that the scheme in that case was a defined benefits scheme and the consequences that followed as a result from this, and were not to be taken as laying down any general rules about amending such schemes. The restriction imposed by *s 67* of the *Pensions Act 1995* did not protect an interest in having surplus preserved for the member's benefit. Accordingly, *s 67* did not prevent trustees and an employer from agreeing that a money purchase section could be established in a defined benefits scheme, with the employer's contributions being met from the surplus previously generated by the defined benefits scheme.

Baynham v Phillips Electronics (High Court) ['
253

Amendment – contract of employment – construction

Principle

A contract of employment contained a power of variation which allowed an employer to vary the contract from time to time with the employee's consent, which would not be unreasonably withheld. The Court held that this was power not apt to vary accrued rights, such as the right to private medical insurance cover, after the contract had come to an end.

[7.1.10]

Bestrustees v Stuart (High Court, unreported, 10 April 2001)

Amendment – sex discrimination – construction – retrospective exercise – effect of exercise of power which could not wholly be valid

Facts and Decision

The employer established a pension scheme with a normal retirement date of 65 for men and 60 for women, of which it was also trustee. The power of amendment provided that 'the employer may authorise the trustees in writing to alter the terms of the trust deed and rules', and that such alteration could have retrospective effect. It also provided that 'the trustees shall forthwith declare any such alteration to the rules in writing'. Following the decision in *Barber v GRE [1990] IRLR 240*, an announcement was issued on 26 April 1994 stating that the scheme rules were being amended to equalise normal retirement dates at age 65 for men and women. The rules were not in fact documented in legal format until 23 May 1996 (by which time individual trustees had been appointed), when new rules came into force, purportedly with effect from 6 April 1994. These rules equalised the normal retirement date at age 65, but while men who sought early retirement needed both employer and trustee consent, women who sought early retirement needed only the consent of the trustees. The scheme was wound up, and the independent trustee sought the Court's guidance on the proper calculation of members' benefits.

The Court held that benefits before 17 May 1990 accrued on the basis of a normal retirement date of 60 for women and 65 for men. Benefits from

May 1990 to 26 April 1994 accrued on the basis of a normal retirement date of 60 for both men and women; *Coloroll Pension Trustees v Russell [1995] All ER [EC] 23* was applied. The equalisation announcement could not take effect as an amendment for the purpose of the rules, since it was not a document under which the trustees declared the amendment: it referred to the rules being amended, the only natural interpretation of which was that this was being done separately. Benefits from 26 April 1994 to 23 May 1996, therefore, also accrued on the basis of a normal retirement date of 60 for both men and women. The 1996 amendments represented an attempt to comply with the ruling in *Barber,* but the attempt did not quite achieve its end. The Court gave as much effect as it could to the change, subject to the reasoning in *Barber* and *Coloroll,* and so the changes were effective, save to the extent that they unlawfully distinguished between men and women, and in so far as they did so distinguish, the Court then applied the principles in *Coloroll,* giving the people in the disadvantaged class the same advantages as those enjoyed by persons in the favoured class. The normal retirement date from 23 May 1996 was 65, therefore, but the early retirement terms were equalised on the basis available to female members.

Comment

This was a small case involving a small scheme, but the points at issue are of relevance to every pension scheme. Three points arose for determination:

(a) the extent to which compliance is required with formalities laid down for effecting amendments;

(b) the effect of a purported amendment made in excess of the trustees' powers; and

(c) the interaction of sex discrimination law derived from European law obligations and English trust law principles.

The reluctance to treat an announcement as an amendment is instructive. The Court laid considerable stress on the practical value of the formalities; in particular, the requirement that amendments be made in writing. It noted the difficulties which scheme members would have in determining whether an amendment had taken place if they were unable to find documentary proof. The judgment in this case details in a way rarely previously seen the reasons why the courts will not lightly waive procedural matters. It echoes the observations made by Staughton LJ in *Fisons v Stannard [1991] PLR 227* in very different circumstances that: 'In a matter as important as this . . ., I think it right to insist on a correct procedure in the decision making process.'

The decision examines in a very practical way how the courts will apply the rule in *Re Hastings-Bass [1974] 2 All ER 193* in relation to a power of amendment. That rule, which explains how courts will intervene when trustees exceed their powers, has the potential to wreck amendments. This would lead to great uncertainty. The Court strained in this case to salvage as much of the amendment as possible, given the honest and apparent intentions of the trustees. Such an approach will give great assurance to practitioners. The fusion of the rule in *Hastings-Bass* with European law principles represents a new step forward for pensions law.

[7.1.11]

British Coal Corporation v British Coal Staff Superannuation Scheme Trustees (High Court) [1995] 1 All ER 912, [1994] ICR 537, [1994] OPLR 51, [1993] PLR 303 at paras 54–67

Amendment – employer's duties

Principles

The general trust law requirement that trustees do not profit from the exercise of their own discretions applies in a pensions context on a winding-up where the employer is the trustee. There is, however, no parallel requirement when the employer exercises the power of amendment in an ongoing scheme. The employer, if it has a power of amendment, is entitled to exercise it in any way which will further the purposes of the scheme to ensure that the legitimate expectations of the members and pensioners are met: it must do so without, as far as possible, imposing any undue burden on the employer or building up an unnecessarily large surplus. What the employer cannot do is to set limits on the benefits provided for members or pensioners for a collateral purpose, without regard to their legitimate expectations. The *Imperial* duty of good faith applies equally to the power of amendment conferred on the employer in ongoing schemes and when winding up.

[7.1.12]

Canada Trust v Cantol (British Columbia Supreme Court, 24 July 1979) 103 DLR (3rd) 109

Amendment – restriction on power – refund of surplus

Facts and Decision

A pension scheme originally contained a provision that provided that the company had the right to amend or terminate the scheme, provided that no amendment or termination 'shall permit any part of the trust fund' to revert to, or be recoverable by the company, or to be used for or diverted to purposes other than the exclusive benefits of the scheme beneficiaries. The company purported to amend this provision to provide for surplus to be refunded to the employer after securing the benefits. Since the company had attempted an amendment in direct contradiction of its authority, the Court held that it was an ineffectual amendment.

[7.1.13]

Capital Cranfield v Sagar (High Court, unreported, 19 February 2001)

Amendment – scheme to be wound up – implication of restrictions

Facts and Decision

Systems Interfreight Limited set up a pension scheme in 1971. Its business was transferred in 1973 to its parent company, American Export Lines Incorporated, and again in 1974 to Worms Cargo Service UK Limited. All these businesses were merged in 1978 into Farrell Lines Incorporated. In October 1980, Farrell closed its European operations, making its employees redundant. Systems Interfreight was struck off the register of companies in February 1981 and was dissolved that same month. Under the scheme's winding-up rule, if the employer were dissolved, the trustees had the power to amend the scheme to provide for its continuance. The Court held that this power could still be exercised. Neither the fact that there had been a substantial delay, nor the fact that the amendment would be with a view to altering matters in connection with winding-up, were good arguments to the contrary. Given that there were express fetters, it would be wrong to imply additional fetters unless it was plainly necessary and obvious that they should be implied.

Capral Fiduciary v Ladd (New Zealand High Court, unreported, 12 July 1999)

Amendment – restriction on power – refund of surplus

Facts and Decision

The trustee and the employer came to an agreement over the use of surplus in a scheme, dividing it between the beneficiaries and the employer. Every member, pensioner and current spouse consented in writing to the proposal, and the trustee sought the Court's sanction. The power of amendment originally provided that no amendment could be made which made it possible for any part of the scheme to be used for any purpose other than the provision of pensions or related benefits. This had been subsequently amended to provide that there could be no reversion of any part of the scheme to the employer to any greater extent than permitted by the trust deed at the date of amendment, unless the trustee obtained the consent in writing of the beneficiary adversely affected. The subsequent amendment was held by the Court to be ineffective; *UEB Industries v Brabant [1991] PLR 109* was followed. *Re Philips New Zealand [1997] 1 NZLR 93* was therefore distinguished on the ground that the power of amendment in the scheme in this case was insufficiently wide to permit such an amendment. However, the rule in *Saunders v Vautier [1841] Cr & Ph 240* was applied, under which the beneficiaries could join together to change the terms of the trust if they unanimously agreed, and the proposal was therefore approved, the Court consenting on behalf of any future spouses.

[7.1.15]

Re Courage Group's Pension Schemes, Ryan v Imperial Brewing (High Court) [1987] I All ER 528, [1987] I WLR 495

Amendment – construction – testing validity – purpose of the power

Facts and Decision

A pension scheme's power of amendment provided that the company may by deed vary the provisions of the trust deed and rules, and the trustees 'shall concur in executing any such . . . deed'. The Court held that the wording was ambiguous, but on a proper construction was interpreted as meaning that unless the trustees concurred, the deed was invalid. The alternative, that the company had a unilateral power to amend, would give no effective protection to the interests of the beneficiaries. It would also make nonsense of the careful allocation of powers found elsewhere in the trust deed and rules. It is implicit in the power of amendment that it cannot be used to alter the main purpose of the pension scheme. However, each amendment must be tested by reference to the situation at the time of the proposed amendment, and not by reference to the original rules at the scheme's inception. Even the main purpose of a pension scheme may be changed by degrees; *Thellusson v Viscount Valentia [1907] 2 Ch 1* was considered. The main purpose may be enlarged by appropriate amendments to the rules, and once it becomes too late to challenge the amendments the enlarged purposes become the new basis by reference to which any further proposed changes must be considered. A power could be exercised only for the purpose for which it was conferred, and not for any extraneous or ulterior purpose. The rule-amending power is given for the purpose of promoting the purposes of the scheme, not for altering them. Accordingly, it could not be exercised for the purpose of replacing the principal employer with another company which had no connection with the previous principal employer. A purpose to retain within the control of a holding company a surplus which had been contributed by companies which the holding company had bought, and for which it had paid, was foreign to the purpose for which the power of amendment had been conferred, and invalidated any exercise of that power.

The power of amendment of another scheme in the group was subject to a proviso that the amendment must not vary or affect any benefits already secured by past contributions of any member, without his or her consent in writing. In the absence of express definition, the Court held that this did not exclude any benefit to which a member was prospectively entitled if he continued in the same employment and which had been acquired by past contributions. There was no reason to assume that he had retired from employment when he had not. The contrary argument placed a meaning on 'secured' which was not justified.

[7.1.16]

Davis v Richards & Wallington (High Court) [1991] 2 All ER 563, [1990] 1 WLR 1511, [1990] PLR 141 at paras 112–113

Amendment – winding-up – interim deed – construction – necessary party no longer in existence

Principles

The question of whether a particular power may be exercised is one of construction of the instrument creating that power. The power of amendment in this case conferred not merely a power to exercise the power of amendment – there was an obligation to do so, since definitive documentation had not yet been executed, and the rules contained a requirement for this to be done. Accordingly, the fact that the scheme had gone into winding-up did not have the effect of bringing the power of amendment to an end in this case. The power required the execution of several companies, one of which no longer existed, and it was a matter of common sense that execution of the deed would not be required of companies that had lost their legal existence.

[7.1.17]

Doyle v Manchester Evening News (High Court) [1989] PLR 47

Amendment – retrospective exercise – trustees' powers

Facts and Decision

The power of amendment in a pension scheme was exercised retrospectively to alter the definition of pensionable salary, to the detriment of some members. On the facts, the Court held that it was not an improper exercise of the trustees' powers. To the extent that it breached a restriction on the power of amendment, that no amendment could be made which would affect any pension being paid at the date of the amendment, because the pensions had fallen into payment, it was invalid. The effect of this was, however, simply to exclude from the amendment's effect pensions already being paid; the amendment was held to be valid in general.

[7.1.18]

Re Edward Jones Benevolent Trust, Spink v Samuel Jones (High Court, unreported, 8 March 1985)

Amendment – scheme to be wound up – purpose of the power

Facts and Decision

A non-contributory defined benefits pension scheme was closed in circumstances where dissolution would have normally followed, but the scheme continued for its existing members in accordance with a provision in the rules. The scheme was in surplus, and the trustees wished to augment the benefits of all categories of beneficiaries, including members who had transferred out from the scheme some time previously to another scheme of the employer. The Court held that the augmentation rule clearly was not wide enough to permit augmentation of benefits for those who had withdrawn from service. The power of amendment continued to subsist: *Re ABC Television Pension Scheme* (unreported) was distinguished. That case was understandable in the context of a winding-up, but had no application in a case where the rules, having given the trustees express power to continue the scheme rather than to wind it up, enabled the existing trusts and powers to be continued during the closed scheme period. Since the trustees would not distribute surplus at all if they could not distribute it equitably, they could properly exercise the power of amendment even though there was a restriction preventing any amendment operating so as to affect prejudicially the rights of any retired member, or any other person then entitled beneficially.

In addition, the Court upheld the principle that it would not be possible to introduce a new power to transfer out, in order to achieve an objective which could not have been achieved under the scheme's rules by amendment.

[7.1.19]

Gas & Fuel Corporation of Victoria v Fitzmaurice (Supreme Court of Victoria, Australia) [1991] PLR 137

Amendment – restriction on the power – construction

Facts and Decision

The Gas & Fuel Corporation established a statutory scheme in 1951. In 1990, public sector schemes in Australia were obliged to comply with the same prescribed operational standards as applied to private sector schemes if they wished to obtain the concessional tax treatment available to superannuation schemes. This required major changes to the scheme. The Corporation purported to amend the terms of the power of amendment (which specifically included a power to amend itself) to delete a proviso that no amendment could be made which would have the effect of reducing any benefit then provided under the scheme for or in respect of any contributor or pensioner, unless he or she consented in writing to the change. The Court was asked by the Corporation to rule on the interpretation of the scheme rules. The Court considered dicta in *Imperial Group Pension Trust Ltd v Imperial Tobacco Ltd [1991] 2 All ER 597*: that it was a relevant feature of the construction process that the corporation was not conferring a bounty, and that the members were not volunteers but paid their way. It followed that any construction of the power of amendment that involved an interpretation as admitting interference with the benefits given in respect of future service was one to be approached with caution. In the case of an institution of long duration and gradually changing membership, like a club or pension scheme, each alteration in the rules must be tested by reference to the situation at the time of the proposed alteration, and not by reference to the original rules at its inception; *Re Courage Group's Pension Schemes [1987] 1 All ER 528* was followed. It was clearly intended in this case that there be ample power and capacity to effect amendments to the scheme. However, the objective of the proviso was to protect the contributors and pensioners, and no reason was given why the intention was to limit the protection to benefits accrued up to the date of the limitation of amendment. It was more logical to suppose that the draftsman was intending to protect contributors against adverse changes made by any amendment. Moreover, the reference to the protection for contributors was more consistent with the protection of future benefits, since most of their benefits will not have vested at the date of the amendment.

[7.1.20]

Gra-Ham Australia v Perpetual Trustees (Supreme Court of Western Australia) [1992] PLR 193

Amendment – vested rights – retrospective exercise

Facts and Decision

The trustee and the manager of two unit trusts obtained the approval of a meeting of unit-holders to amend the terms on which it would repurchase units, and subsequently documented this by deed. The power of amendment gave them power to amend, but subject to the proviso that in the case of any amendment other than one required by statute, the trustee needed to be reasonably satisfied that the amendment did not adversely affect the interests of the unit-holders. If the trustee were not so satisfied, it needed first to obtain in a meeting the approval by ordinary resolution of the unit-holders. Some unit-holders claimed that the amendment was detrimental to them, retrospectively divested them of their rights and was not allowable by law. The power of amendment was sufficiently wide to be capable of defeating accrued rights, and the unit-holders would be taking up their units in the knowledge that there was a power in the trust deed to change the terms on which they held those units. In that context, the Court held, it was not helpful to speak in terms of interfering with vested rights. It was debatable whether the amendment was retrospective or not, but the authorities did not say that a retrospective amendment was beyond power or unlawful: that was a matter of construction of the trust deed.

[7.1.21]

Harwood-Smart v Caws (High Court) [2000] PLR 101

Amendment – restriction on power – refund of surplus – necessity – interim deed

Facts and Decision

A pension scheme's power of amendment was subject to a restriction that no amendment should cause all or any part of the scheme to revert to the company. This could not, the Court held, be interpreted as applying only while the scheme was ongoing; recourse to a practical and purposive interpretation of pension documentation was an approach only required when there was a difficulty in identifying with confidence the message which the documentation was conveying. A subsequent definitive deed gave the trustees a discretion to augment benefits to Inland Revenue limits 'in such manner and proportion as the Trustees in consultation with the Principal Employer shall decide', with any residue being repaid to the employer. On a proper construction, the Court held, this was a discretion only as to the direction of the augmentation of benefits, not as to whether to augment the benefits. The provision for repaying residue to the employer was validly made, despite the proviso to the power of amendment. It had been necessarily introduced for the purposes of obtaining Inland Revenue approval for the scheme, and so was introduced pursuant to a statutory provision which overrode those entrenched provisions. The next definitive deed made it plain that the trustees' discretion extended to the amount as well as to the direction of any augmentation; this amendment was, however, void since it breached the restriction on the power of amendment. This amendment could also not be saved for those members who joined after the date of the amendment, since the winding-up rule concerned the disposal of a single fund, making it impossible to reconcile the position of the two classes of members if the amendment were to be a valid for such members. Where an interim trust deed contained a requirement which was not replicated in a definitive deed, the members could compel its inclusion: *Davis v Richards & Wallington Industries Ltd [1991] 2 All ER 563* was followed.

[7.1.22]

Hillsdown v Pensions Ombudsman (High Court) [1997] I All ER 862, [1996] OPLR 291 at 310B–311C, [1996] PLR 427 at paras 67–70

Amendment – purpose of the power

Principle

Re Vauxhall Motor Pension Fund [1989] 1 PLR 31, 53 is an authority for the proposition that one cannot as a matter of construction find an implication restricting the ambit of the power to transfer by reference to the proviso in the power of amendment. But it is no authority on the question whether the power to transfer was proposed to be used for a collateral purpose in a way which would constitute a fraud on the power.

[7.1.23]

Hockin v Bank of British Columbia (British Columbia Court of Appeal) [1992] PLR 19

Amendment – refund of surplus – winding-up – construction

Facts and Decision

The Bank of British Columbia operated a balance of cost defined benefits scheme. The Bank had the right unilaterally to amend the scheme rules, but any amendment reducing the members' accrued benefits needed the approval in writing of a majority of the members. On a termination of the scheme, the entire fund was to be used for the benefit of the beneficiaries, and no part was to be returned to the Bank (subject to the provisions of any law of Canada governing the scheme). In 1986, an actuarial valuation disclosed a surplus. The Bank was taken over, and the active members' entitlements were transferred to a new scheme, leaving behind a very substantial surplus. The termination clause did not apply until termination, and the Court held that the Bank could therefore amend the scheme provisions so as to entitle it to remove any surplus prior to termination. The following cases were referred to, and were distinguished: *Heiliq v Dominion Securities Pitfield Ltd [1986] 55 OR (2d) 783 (Ont HC), Lear Siegler Industries Ltd and Canada Trust Company [1988] 6 OR (2d) 342 (Ont HC), Reevie v Montreal Trust Co of Canada [1984] 24 OR (2d) (Ont HC) 667; affirmed [1986] 25 DLR (4th) 312 (Ont CA), King Seagrave and Canada Permanent Trust Co [1985] 51 OR (2d) 667 (Ont HC); affirmed [1986], 130 OAC 305 (Ont CA); 16 OAC 240 (SCC), National Automobile, Aerospace and Agricultural Implement Workers Union of Canada v White Farm Manufacturing Canada Ltd [1988] unreported OSC, File #RE415/88, National Trust Co v Sulpetro Ltd [1989] 57 DLR (4th) 120 (Alta QB)* and *Little and Siefert v Kent-Maclean of Canada [1972] 72 DRS.* In none of these cases was the power of amendment sufficiently wide to permit such an amendment.

[7.1.24]

Re Imperial Foods Ltd Pension Scheme (High Court) [1986] 2 All ER 802, [1986] I WLR 717 (in an unreported passage discussed in LRT v Hatt)

Amendment – retrospective exercise

Principle

The retrospective operation of a definitive trust deed executed pursuant to an interim deed was upheld.

[7.1.25]

International Power v Healy (House of Lords) [2001] PLR 121

Amendment – power to make arrangements with surplus – construction – when amendments are required

Facts and Decision

The principal employers in each group of the Electricity Supply Pension Scheme were given the power under the scheme to make arrangements, certified by the actuary as reasonable, to deal with ongoing surplus. The power of amendment prohibited any amendment which would make any of the monies of the scheme payable to any of the employers. When a surplus emerged, some employers set around two-thirds of the surplus against the employers' obligation to contribute. The Court held that the release of a debt owed by the employer to the scheme was not a payment, although it had the same economic effect. Viewed against the fiscal background, the purpose of the restriction on the power of amendment was to prevent the employer from resorting to assets which had enjoyed the fiscal privileges accorded to the scheme. Since debts from the employer to the scheme which had not yet fallen due for payment had enjoyed no fiscal privileges, the restriction on the power of amendment did not prevent an amendment which allowed for the employer to set surplus against its obligation to contribute.

However, a duty to make arrangements with surplus was held to include a power to discharge that duty, and thus the power of amendment need not be used to implement the arrangements made. The general wording of that duty was unlikely to have been intended to give the employer power to do something which would contradict the express provisions of the scheme.

Per Lord Hoffman: it is essentially a practical question whether an amendment is needed. If arrangements are to endure for any length of time, an amendment is the most convenient and accessible way of recording them. It is a matter of pragmatic choice.

Per Lord Scott: the provisions of the scheme must be construed as a whole, and so construed, a power to make arrangements cannot be regarded as conferring on the employer a power of amendment free from the safeguards to which the normal power of amendment is subject. To the extent that arrangements are inconsistent with one or other of the provisions of the scheme, the implementation requires the amendment of the scheme pursuant to the power of amendment. Accordingly, arrangements which involve altering the contribution obligations of either the employer or the employees require an amendment of the scheme. An increase of the benefits payable under the rules, whether the increase takes the form of a lump sum one-off payment or any other form, requires amendment of the scheme. But the appropriation of surplus to meet accrued obligations of the employer does not require any such amendment.

Comment

It will seem off-beat to many to put a commentary on what most will regard as the leading case on surpluses in a Part on powers of amendment. I am unrepentant. This case was decided on the scope of the power of amendment, and both Lord Hoffman and Lord Scott made very useful general observations on powers of amendment. Its proper home is here. The very simplicity of the Court's analysis of powers of amendment defies further commentary, but this summary and the full judgment should be read and re-read carefully.

If I did not comment upon the role of surplus in this case, however, I would be remiss. The case took place against a backdrop of surplus to be distributed. Once it was accepted that the power to distribute surplus was vested in the employer and that the employer had exercised the power in good faith, the only question left was whether the arrangements had been lawfully adopted under the terms of the scheme. For the reasons given in this section, they had.

[7.1.26]

James Miller Holdings v Graham (Supreme Court, Victoria) [1992] PLR 165

Amendment – retrospective exercise – effect of exercise of power which could not be wholly valid

Facts and Decision

James Miller Holdings operated a pension scheme for its employees, of which it was also the trustee. The pension scheme was invested in a managed fund policy. The employer went into receivership on 8 December 1976. The receivers immediately determined that the employer would cease making contributions to the scheme. If the employer gave the three months' notice required to trigger the winding-up of the scheme, employees who had already retired by that date would get their pension in full, while those who had yet to retire would get only an equitable apportionment of what was left in the account, after all other members had received their entitlement in full. The receivers, therefore, purported to close the scheme retrospectively by deed of amendment. The power of amendment was subject to a restriction that no amendment shall detrimentally affect the benefits already secured in respect of a member at the date of amendment, without the consent in writing of that member. The consent of the members was not obtained. The receivers had power to exercise the power of amendment and power to discontinue the scheme, and the principles in *Edgar & Another and the Companies Act (1971–73) CCH Company Law Cases* was applied. The closure of the scheme by amendment would, though, detrimentally affect the benefits already secured, both by depriving the members of the right to receive a benefit if they left within three months of the effective date of the deed, and by enabling the employer to cease paying premiums three months earlier than otherwise. This was true whether the amendment was retrospective or immediate in effect. The Court held that the restriction on the power of amendment prevented the amendment being made at all, and did not operate so as to make the amendment take effect but without the detrimental effects.

[7.1.27]

Jones v Williams (High Court) [1989] PLR 17

Amendment – winding-up

Facts and Decision

Once the pension scheme concerned went into winding-up, it was not possible to alter the terms of the trust. A dictum of Geoff J in *Re West Sussex Constabulary's Widow's Children and Benevolent (1930) Fund Trusts [1971] Ch 1 at 9, [1970] 1 All ER 544* was applied.

[7.1.28]

Kearns v Hill (Court of Appeal, Australia) [1991] PLR 161

Amendment – beneficiaries

Facts and Decision

In a private trust, trustees by deed poll used the power of amendment to amend the definition of beneficiaries of a discretionary trust. This was held by the Court to be within the scope of the power of amendment. Nothing in the trust deed suggested that the list of beneficiaries was uniquely inviolable.

[7.1.29]

King Seagrave v Canada Permanent Trust (Ontario Court of Appeal, 20 February 1986) 13 OAC 305

Amendment – restriction on power – refund of surplus

Facts and Decision

An employer sought to amend its pension scheme to withdraw surplus funds. The funds were irrevocably committed to a trust fund and there was no power to revoke the trust. There was a procedure set out for distribution of surplus funds in the event that the scheme was discontinued. The Court held that tax considerations could not alter the structure of the trust so as to deprive the beneficiaries of their residual rights. *Re Reevie and Montreal Trust Co of Canada [1986] 25 DLR 312* was followed; there was no power to amend the scheme in the manner sought.

[7.1.30]

Lloyds Bank Pension Trust Corporation Limited v Lloyds Bank PLC (High Court) [1996] OPLR 181, [1996] PLR 263

Amendment – sex discrimination – restriction on power – construction

Facts and Decision

The Lloyds Bank Pension Scheme had a small class of female members with a normal retirement date of age 55. Comparable male members had a normal retirement date of age 60. The female members' accrual rate was also superior to that of male members. Following the series of European cases on sex inequality in pension schemes, the Bank and the trustee proposed to reduce the female members' benefits to the lower level that comparable male members received. The power of amendment, however, prohibited any amendment which would decrease the pecuniary benefits secured to or in respect of members, without the agreement of three-quarters of those members. On a proper construction of this prohibition, the Court held that no amendment could be made which would decrease the benefits payable to or in respect of a relevant member based on that member's:

- normal retirement date;
- completed pensionable service; and
- pensionable salary at that date (being after the date of a proposed alteration);

when the member leaves or dies while in pensionable service.

[7.1.31]

Lock v Westpac (Supreme Court of New South Wales) [1991] PLR 167

Amendment – restriction on power – refund of surplus – winding-up – employer's duties – trustees' duties

Facts and Decision

Westpac operated a pension scheme for its employees, the rules of which contained no express power to return surplus to the employer in any circumstances. The scheme was substantially in surplus. With the consent of the trustees, Westpac amended the scheme so that if the actuary advised that the scheme was in surplus, Westpac could either reduce its contributions or, with the consent of the trustees, could apply the surplus in one of a number of ways: these included a repayment of surplus to the employer. At the same time, benefit improvements were granted. A member challenged the validity of this amendment. The Court held that there was no express provision preventing an amendment of this type. On a proper construction of this scheme's provisions, a resulting trust could arise in favour of the employer on a winding-up. Even if this were incorrect, the fact that the scheme was established for the purpose of providing superannuation benefits for eligible employees did not mean that should there be a surplus, the whole of it should be held irrevocably on trust for the employees and awaiting the possibility of a scheme dissolution. There was therefore no implied qualification to the power of amendment. The employer was to exercise the power of amendment subject to an implied condition that it be exercised honestly and in good faith, but it was not a fiduciary power: *Imperial Group Pension Trust Ltd v Imperial Tobacco Ltd [1991] ICR 524* was followed. The trustees had a duty to act in the interests of the members, but were entitled to take into account the interests of Westpac. If satisfied that the overall package was fair to both Westpac and the members, the trustees were entitled to consent to an amendment enabling part of the surplus to be returned to Westpac.

[7.1.32]

LRT v Hatt (High Court) [1993] OPLR 225, [1993] PLR 227 at paras 139, 189

Amendment – informal exercise – retrospective exercise

Principles

It is permissible to treat any pension scheme deed as an exercise of the power of amendment which evinces a result achievable by the exercise of that power, so long as there is not shown to have been an intention not to exercise the power of amendment. It was not conclusive that the parties had no exercise of the power of amendment in mind.

It is likely that new employers, who adhered to a new fund following a merger, cannot legitimately avoid the correction of errors in the drawing up of the rules governing that fund. The retrospective operation of definitive documentation is arguably effective not only against long-standing employers from former schemes, but also against new employers who adhered to the new scheme.

[7.1.33]

Merchant Navy Ratings Pension Fund Trustees v Chambers (High Court) [2001] PLR 137

Amendment – trustees' duties – section 67 of the Pensions Act 1995

Facts and Decision

A pension scheme was in deficit. The trustee proposed (as an alternative to winding-up) that the scheme rules be amended to close the scheme to future accrual of benefit, and to allow the transfer of beneficiaries to a new scheme. The trustee applied to Court for approval of this proposal.

The Court held that it was not wrong in principle to amend the rules to provide for transfers to be made without consent, merely because an employer wished to cease to participate. Nor did the *Occupational Pension Schemes (Preservation of Benefits) Regulations 1991 (SI 1991 No 167)* prohibit such a transfer.

An amendment which allows a pensioner's benefits to be transferred without his or her consent was held not automatically to be prohibited by the *Pensions Act 1995, s 67*. This was a matter for the actuary to consider when deciding whether or not to issue a certificate.

[7.1.34]

Mettoy Pension Trustees v Evans (High Court) [1991] 2 All ER 513, [1990] 1 WLR 1587, [1990] PLR 9 at para 181

Amendment – trustees' powers – new section

Principles

Where an employer uses an existing trust structure to set up an entirely new benefit structure rather than establishing a new trust, the trustees must observe the fiduciary nature of the power of amendment: they do not have the same freedom as trustees joining in the execution of an entirely new trust.

[7.1.35]

Municipal Mutual Insurance v Harrop (High Court) [1998] PLR 149

Amendment – retrospective exercise – correction of error – winding-up

Facts and Decision

A pension scheme provided benefits calculated without reference to bonus. When a new edition of the rules was adopted, it included a reference to bonus as part of scheme salary for the purpose of calculating pension benefits. The employer's Board resolved to terminate the scheme on 18 June 1996, giving notice which expired on 30 September 1996. It also resolved to amend the definition of scheme salary retrospectively to remove the reference to bonus.

The power of amendment provided that 'The board [of Municipal Mutual Insurance] may at any time and from time to time by resolution and with the concurrence of the Trustees amend any of the provisions of these Rules', subject to certain provisos. It was conceded that the power could not in general be used retrospectively. Once that concession had been made, the Court held that there was nothing to justify an interpretation that it empowered the making of retrospective amendments for the purpose of correcting mistakes caused by an earlier rule change.

The Court in addition upheld the principle that the power of amendment may be exercised during the period of notice whose expiry will result in a winding-up event.

[7.1.36]

Packwood v APS (Pensions Ombudsman) [1995] OPLR 369 at 376H–377C, [1995] PLR 183 at para 22

Amendment – trustees' powers – maladministration

Principle

Where trustees failed to consider using a power of amendment under their sole control so as to enable the introduction of benefit increases for members (including pensioners), this was a breach of trust and maladministration.

[7.1.37]

Re Philips New Zealand (High Court, New Zealand) [1997] I NZLR 93

Amendment – restriction on power – construction – member consent – new section – refund of surplus

Facts and Decision

An employer established a defined benefit pension scheme, under which no money could be returned to the employer. The power of amendment was subject to a restriction that it would not affect in any way prejudicially the rights, interests or accrued benefits of any member without the written consent of the member, and no amendment should result in any part of the scheme becoming the property of the employer. Subsequently the scheme was converted so as to be run on a money purchase basis. The members and the employers agreed to divide the surplus between themselves on a 50:50 basis, and applied to Court for the exercise of their statutory power to amend the scheme. The Court held that it was very doubtful whether it in fact had a statutory power to amend, in the face of such a restriction in the scheme provisions. However, since all the members had given their informed consent, on a proper construction the power of amendment permitted such a change. Even if this were not the case, the unanimous consent of all interested parties permitted such a change; *Saunders v Vautier [1841] Cr & Ph 240* was applied.

[7.1.38]

Re Reevie and Montreal Trust Co of Canada (Ontario Court of Appeal) [1986] 25 DLR 312

Amendment – restriction on power – winding-up – refund of surplus

Facts and Decision

Canada Dry set up a defined benefit pension scheme in 1955. Its power of amendment, suspension and discontinuance contained a statement that all contributions made by the company were irrevocable, and together with all contributions made by members could only be used exclusively for the benefit of the scheme membership. It also contained a statement that if the company should discontinue the scheme, contributions made by the company could not be withdrawn and all funds would be used to secure benefits. In 1981, the scheme was amended. The power of amendment was purportedly rewritten to exclude both of these statements and provided for a refund of surplus to the company on the termination of the scheme. Canada Dry was sold in 1982. The scheme was then merged with another scheme. No current employees remained in the scheme, and the employer sought a refund of surplus after securing the other benefits. The power of amendment was held by the Court to be insufficiently wide to permit it to recover surplus funds, and the contrary argument was untenable: the relevant scheme section prior to 1981 specifically affirmed the irrevocability of the contributions and the fact that the members were the sole beneficiaries. The 1981 amendment was an attempted partial revocation of trust, and therefore wholly ineffective, since Canada Dry had no power to act in this way.

[7.1.39]

Ritchie v Blakeley (New Zealand Court of Appeal) [1985] 1 NZLR 630

Amendment – restriction on power – procedure

Facts and Decision

In order to retain tax advantages for a pension scheme, the trustees decided to amend its provisions so as to withdraw an option for members to take their benefits as a lump sum. The power of amendment was subject to two provisos:

(a) That no amendment shall be made which would reduce or adversely affect a member's interest in the scheme as established at the date of the amendment, without the written consent of that individual member; and

(b) That no amendment shall be made until the Government Actuary had notified the trustees in writing that the deed as proposed to be amended would retain his or her approval.

The trustees executed the deed of amendment in December 1983 without obtaining the consent of the members. The Government Actuary approved the amendment in March 1984. The amendment was held by the Court to be ineffective, because the Government Actuary's consent was needed in advance of execution, and conditionally executing the deed or delivery in escrow was not sufficient to comply with this formality. On a proper construction, the protection of the first proviso was to guarantee the financial interest of each member at the date on which the deed was executed. The change did not diminish the value of the benefits even though it limited the means of receiving that value, and the consent of the members was therefore not required.

[7.1.40]

Sulpetro Limited Retirement Plan Fund Trustee v Sulpetro (Alberta Court of Appeal, 23 February 1990) 66 DLR (4th) 120

Amendment – restriction on power – winding-up – refund of surplus

Facts and Decision

A pension scheme contained a restriction on the power of amendment preventing any amendment which 'shall vest in any Employer, directly or indirectly, any right, title or interest in the Fund'. The termination clause in the original trust deed provided that termination would not vest in any Employer, directly or indirectly, any right, title or interest in the fund. A subsequent deed provided that the scheme was exclusively for the benefit of the participating employees and their beneficiaries. The employer purported to change the scheme termination clause so that any surplus remaining after the distribution of assets to participants 'shall be returned to the Company'. The amendment was held by the Court to be contrary to law, since the employer had forever restricted itself from recovering any part of the scheme, either on amendment or on termination. Surplus from that scheme was vested in its employees as a class.

[7.1.41]

South West Trains v Wightman (High Court) [1997] OPLR 249, [1998] PLR 113 at paras 47–64, 75–79

Amendment – construction – section 67 of the Pensions Act 1995

Facts and Decision

When assessing whether proposed changes in specified pension rights were less favourable than the existing pension rights for the purposes of a statutory instrument, the Court held that it was proper to look outside the terms of the pension scheme, and examine the actual cash effect of the proposed changes. The legislature was more likely to be concerned with protecting practical rights sounding in money as opposed to more hypothetical legal or conceptual rights. Clear words would be required before the Court would conclude otherwise. In this case, the statutory instrument required the Court to look at both accrued and accruing pension rights, but one could not assume when identifying the rights that were protected that employees would receive pay increases; they had no right to this. Nevertheless, the right to have any pay increases treated as pensionable was a right which should be factored in. It was necessary to compare like with like, factoring in the effect of the passage of time and the effect of inflation.

Section 67 of the *Pensions Act 1995* did not prevent the implementation of an agreement entered into before the *section* came into effect which would otherwise be binding, even if its terms would have contravened the *section* had they been entered into after that date.

[7.1.42]

Taylor v Lucas Pension Trust (High Court) [1994] OPLR 29, [1994] PLR 9

Amendment – restriction on power – refund of surplus

Principle

Where a scheme has a restriction on a power of amendment prohibiting any change which will result in a refund to an employer, a modification order properly obtained authorised a change which would permit a payment of surplus to the employer.

[7.1.43]

Thrells v Lomas (High Court) [1993] 1 WLR 456, [1993] 2 All ER 546, [1992] OPLR 21, [1992] PLR 233

Amendment – winding-up

Facts and Decision

Thrells Limited went into insolvent liquidation in 1984. Its pension scheme's power of amendment was expressed in open-ended terms, with a prohibition on amendments which would impinge on accrued benefits, but the winding-up rule set out precisely how the benefits secured should be dealt with. The Court held that it was unthinkable that the power of amendment was intended to enable the employer to interfere with the operation of the winding-up rule once it had come into operation. This regime included the discretionary power to distribute surplus, which was therefore also not capable of amendment.

[7.1.44]

UEB Industries v Brabant (Court of Appeal of New Zealand) [1991] PLR 109, [1992] I NZLR 294

Amendment – winding-up – restriction on power – refund of surplus – effect of exercise of power which could not be wholly valid

Facts and Decision

In 1980, a pension scheme's winding-up rule had been amended to authorise a refund of any unexpended balance to the company (previously there had been a permanent alienation clause), and the validity of this amendment was challenged. The terms of the original permanent alienation clause made it perfectly clear that to allow the company to participate in the surplus would be to depart from the terms of the trusts. The Court held that it was not possible to remove a restriction which prevented an amendment which would authorise a repayment of funds to the employer (Richardson J not relying upon this ground). The company had argued that if the new restriction on the winding-up rule was invalid, the entire winding-up rule was bad and the purported winding-up was ineffective. There was, however, no evidence that the trustees had had such an all or nothing attitude when the restriction was introduced.

[7.1.45]

Re Vauxhall Motor Pension Fund, Bullard v Randall (High Court) [1989] PLR 31

Amendment – construction

Principle

A restriction on the power of amendment that prohibited amendments which would result in the payment to the employers of any part of the pension fund did not prevent the trustees making a transfer to a scheme from which the employer could receive a repayment of surplus. Such a restriction did not impose a general restriction on the assets of the fund.

[7.1.46]

Wheeler v NBC Pension Trustee (Pensions Ombudsman) [1996] OPLR 337 at 349A-B, [1997] PLR 1 at para 48

Amendment – restriction on power – trustees' duties

Principle

If the trustee wrongly, even if innocently, altered the members' benefits contrary to the power of amendment, its successor comes under an obligation to restore the original benefits.

[7.1.47]

Wilson v Metro Goldwyn Mayer (Supreme Court of New South Wales) [1980] 18 NSWLR 730

Amendment – winding-up – restriction on power – refund of surplus – employer's opinion

Facts and Decision

The Metro Goldwyn Mayer pension scheme provided that while the scheme continued, any surplus would be applied at the employer's discretion either towards the employer's contributions or in augmenting benefits. On a winding-up, however, all surplus would be used in augmenting benefits. The employer and the trustees had power to amend the scheme by deed in any respect which would, in the opinion of the employer, not prejudice any benefits secured by contributions made on behalf of any member prior to the date of amendment. The employer and trustees purported to amend the scheme so that any surplus on a winding-up would be made payable to the employer. The Court held that the employer was obliged to form its opinion as to whether the benefits were prejudiced on the basis of a correct understanding of the question to be considered, so that an opinion formed on an erroneous construction of the power of amendment could not constitute a relevant opinion for its purposes. On a proper construction, the benefits protected by the power of amendment included the benefits which members could receive under the winding-up provision. The amendment was, therefore, invalid.

7.2 – Augmentation of benefits

[7.2.1]

Buckley v Hudson Forge (High Court) [1999] OPLR 249 at 259B-G, [1999] PLR 151 at paras 54–57

Augmentation – winding-up – construction

Principles

The right to have pension scheme trustees consider whether to augment pensions creates a liability. Accordingly, when trustees have the obligation under a winding-up rule to secure 'other liabilities under the scheme', the trustees retain the power to grant augmentations.

[7.2.2]

Capital Cranfield v Sagar (High Court, unreported, 19 February 2001)

Augmentation – winding-up – necessary party no longer in existence

Facts and Decision

Systems Interfreight Limited set up a pension scheme in 1971. Its business was transferred in 1973 to its parent company, American Export Lines Incorporated, and again in 1974 to Worms Cargo Service UK Limited. All these businesses were merged in 1978 into Farrell Lines Incorporated. In October 1980, Farrell closed its European operations, making its employees redundant. Systems Interfreight was struck off the register of companies in February 1981 and was dissolved that same month. The scheme's augmentation power on winding-up required the trustee to consult with the principal employer and obtain its consent. Since the principal employer was dissolved and did not exist, the Court held that it was exercisable without the need for consent; *Davis v Richards & Wallington Industries Ltd [1991] 2 All ER 563* was followed.

[7.2.3]

Harding and others (Trustees of Joy Manufacturing Holdings Ltd Pension and Life Assurance Scheme), petitioners (Court of Session, Inner House, Scotland) [1999] OPLR 235

Augmentation – construction

Facts and Decision

The trustees of a pension scheme had power to give discretionary increases to pensions and deferred pensions after consultation with the principal employer, but the power of amendment was vested in the trustees and the employer jointly. The Court held that the power to give discretionary increases was not intended to confer on the trustees a general power (inconsistent with the balance of the power of amendment) unilaterally to increase the pension benefits under the scheme without the consent of the relevant employer.

Part 8 – Transfers and Mergers

8 – Introduction

Pension schemes, unlike most other trusts, are not hermetically sealed. Trustees can secure liabilities to provide benefits externally, and can be obliged to do so by a member who has a statutory right to request a transfer of the cash equivalent of his or her benefits to another pension arrangement. This has led to the courts being faced with unfamiliar questions, where the dispute between the parties has raised problems akin to those which arise on the termination of a trust, but which involve ongoing schemes.

Such transfers can take place by statutory right, by the use of a non-statutory provision for individual transfers, by the use of a provision for bulk transfers or by the use of the transfer provisions on partial winding-up (when one employer leaves a group scheme). These different, sometimes overlapping bases for transferring someone's benefits may come into play in different circumstances. However, the Court of Appeal in *Fisons v Stannard [1992] IRLR 27* was relatively relaxed about the fact that the wrong transfer power had been used in that case, preferring to concentrate on the need for the trustees to be satisfied that the amount transferred was fair each way. The Privy Council in *Wrightson v Fletcher Challenge Nominees [2001] All ER 89* went into more detail about this. Partial winding-up provisions should be treated quite differently from the winding-up provisions. The case concerned the wording of one scheme, but the points made are probably of wider application. Unless a scheme's partial winding-up provision specifically varied the trustee's duty, courts would normally follow the observation that it was the trustee's duty to identify the part of the scheme which was appropriate to the withdrawing company in the right of its members, and not in its own right. The Court's detailed analysis of the proper approach for trustees on such transfers will be referred to by lawyers for many years to come.

The courts have also had to contend with members' statutory right to take individual transfers. The courts have identified many problems with the legislation, which they have tried to repair as best they can. The statutory requirements can be deceptively demanding. In *Hamar v French [1997] OPLR 105* and *Miller v Stapleton [1996] OPLR 73*, it was held that a statutory transfer request could only be made to a scheme which was already in existence and tax-approved.

In this area, *Hamar v French* is the leading authority. The Court of Appeal analysed the nature of the legislative obligations. It noted that some of the obligations were to protect the State's interest – for example, the destination of the transfer payment. The State had a legitimate interest in ensuring that the recipient arrangement was an appropriate vehicle for providing pension provision. Such obligations could not be varied by the parties. However, some obligations were for the protection of the trustees, and the trustees were able to waive such requirements.

The effect of *Hamar v French* is that where a statutory request for a transfer value is in dispute, practitioners must first identify whether all the statutory requirements have been complied with. If they have not, the next step is to identify whether the requirements which have not been complied with are capable of being waived by the trustees. The final step is to determine whether the trustees have acted in such a way that they can be held to have waived their right to insist on a protection. This final step will be hard for members to demonstrate: in *Hamar v French* itself, the Court's decision was based on the fact that the trustees had not raised the argument that the transfer request had not been properly made before the Pensions Ombudsman had issued his determination.

There are other flaws in the legislation. *R v OPRA ex parte Littlewoods [1997] OPLR 375* shows that the circumstances in which a member can be prevented from taking a transfer can operate in an arbitrary way. Littlewoods must have been particularly frustrated given that the decision in *Haque v Bevis Trustees [1996] OPLR 271* had been issued the previous year. Those two decisions are hard to reconcile, with the decision in *Haque v Bevis Trustees* not dealing with the difficulties identified in *R v OPRA ex parte Littlewoods* in preventing such transfers.

Pension scheme liabilities can be secured outside the scheme by merger. In fact, this is merely another, ultimate, version of transferring out. Where two or more pension schemes merge, one scheme must receive all the assets and liabilities of the others (whether that receiving scheme is an existing scheme or a new scheme established for the purpose). From the viewpoint of the transferring schemes, they are transferring all the assets and liabilities to another arrangement. Because of the terminal nature of the transfer, trustees may be wary about releasing the assets from the terms of their trust without securing some form of advantage for the membership, and the Scottish decision of *Harding and others (Trustees of Joy Manufacturing Holdings Ltd Pension and Life Assurance Scheme), petitioners [1999] OPLR 235* concerned a set of trustees who sought guidance on the extent to which they should do so.

Transfers in generally seem to cause fewer problems than mergers and transfers out. One problem which has occurred arises when members have been promised benefits on transfers in, which the pension scheme does not in fact normally provide. The courts have found no reason not to apply the normal rules of contract, to the cost of the employer in both *Buckley v Hudson Forge [1999] OPLR 249* and *Nicol & Andrew v Brinkley [1996] OPLR 361.*

8.1 – Transfers in

[8.1.1]

Buckley v Hudson Forge (High Court) [1999] OPLR 249 at 269A–270F, [1999] PLR 151 at paras 104–111

Transfer in – communication – contract

Facts and Decision

A pension scheme member was offered benefits, which would be subject to pension increases at the trustees' discretion, should he transfer in his entitlement into a scheme on interim documentation from another scheme. The member subsequently agreed to transfer to the scheme. The Court held that he was contractually entitled to be considered for discretionary pension increases on those terms for such part of his benefits as were secured by the transfer value. The definitive documentation could not insert additional restrictions on the terms on which he received the discretionary pension increases.

[8.1.2]

Coloroll Pension Trustees v Russell (European Court of Justice) [1995] All ER (EC) 23, [1994] ECR I–4389, [1994] IRLR 586, [1994] OPLR 179 at 223C–G, [1994] PLR 211 at paras 94–99

Transfer in – sex discrimination

Principles

When a worker's pension rights are transferred from one occupational scheme to another owing to a change of job, the receiving scheme is obliged to increase the benefits it undertook to pay him or her when accepting the transfer so as to eliminate the effects, contrary to *Article 119* (now *Article 141*) of the *Treaty of Rome*, suffered by the worker in consequence of the inadequacy of the capital transferred – this being due, in turn, to the discriminatory treatment suffered under the first scheme. This applies only in relation to benefits payable in respect of periods of service subsequent to 17 May 1990. The rights accruing to the worker cannot be affected by the fact that he or she changes job. If need be, the receiving scheme should make a claim for necessary additional sums from the transferring scheme under national law.

[8.1.3]

Express Newspapers Pension Trustees v Express Newspapers plc (High Court) [1998] OPLR 261, [1999] PLR 9

Transfer in – construction of pension – increase rule – documentation of terms for transferring members

Facts and Decision

Trustees of one scheme made a bulk transfer to trustees of another scheme. One category of pensioners in the transferring scheme were not entitled to pension increases in that scheme. Following the transfer, these pensioners claimed that they were entitled to increases in accordance with the receiving scheme's pension-increase rule. On a proper construction, the Court held that the receiving scheme's pension-increase rule did not apply to the transferred pensioners. The rules as a whole applied only to members who had accrued their entitlement within the scheme, and the pension-increase rule was no exception. The benefits of the transferred pensioners were not set out at any point within the receiving scheme's documentation, although the company and the trustees had behaved as if they had complied with their obligation to document these benefits.

[8.1.4]

Hillsdown v Pensions Ombudsman (High Court) [1997] 1 All ER 862, [1996] OPLR 291 at 317D-H, [1996] PLR 427 at paras 99–100

Transfer in – duties of trustees

Principles

Where a receiving scheme trustee had not been party to an agreement entered into by a transferring scheme trustee regarding refund of surplus, it was not in breach of its duty to act in the best interests of its members when it failed to negotiate for some advantage for its members, before agreeing to an amendment of its scheme's rules. The transferring scheme trustee would have had a valid claim for restitution of the transfer payment if the receiving scheme trustee had refused to carry out the terms of an agreement of which it undoubtedly had clear notice.

[8.1.5]

Nicol & Andrew v Brinkley (High Court) [1996] OPLR 361

Transfer in – communication – contract

Facts and Decision

Following a business acquisition, Nicol & Andrew offered the employees transferring employment the opportunity to join a new pension scheme, which it established for them (of which Nicol & Andrew was also trustee). Subsequently it offered them the opportunity to transfer their past service entitlements from their old scheme into the new scheme, quoting specific credits which would be granted to them should they choose to do so. Many members agreed to transfer on these terms. These credits were incorrectly calculated, in the members' favour. Nicol & Andrew purported to withdraw these terms. The Court held, however, that the offer and acceptance clearly gave rise to a contract. It was absurd to suppose that the terms of that contract could now be altered.

8.2 – Transfers out

Aitken v Christy Hunt (High Court) [1991] PLR 1 at paras 45–53

Transfer out – construction of power of amendment

Facts and Decision

A provision of a pension scheme provided that the company could vary the trusts, may declare new trusts to the exclusion or addition of the existing trusts and may provide for the amalgamation of the scheme, provided that:

- no such variation shall be made so as to change the main purpose of the scheme; or to enable any part of the scheme to be paid to the company; and
- no such variation shall be effected unless all the trustees shall be parties to the instrument in writing.

On a true construction, the Court held that the provisos applied to all the different elements of the power given to the company under the clause. If this were not the case, the company could sidestep the restrictions on the power to vary the trusts by the simple expedient of revoking the existing trusts and inserting new trusts to such effect as it thought fit.

Austchem Nominees v AC Hatrick Chemicals (Supreme Court of New South Wales, unreported, 13 October 1988)

Transfer out – construction of power of amendment – trustees' duties

See [7.1.6].

[8.2.3]

Coloroll Pension Trustees v Russell (European Court of Justice) [1995] All ER (EC) 23, [1994] ECR I–4389, [1994] IRLR 586, [1994] OPLR 179 at 223E, [1994] PLR 211 at para 97

Transfer out – sex discrimination

Principles

Where a scheme has transferred unequalised liabilities to another scheme, it is the responsibility of the receiving scheme under *Article 119* (now *Article 141*) of the *Treaty of Rome* to do everything to bring about a situation of equality. Any claim for the necessary additional sums from the transferring scheme is to be made under national law.

[8.2.4]

Re Edward Jones Benevolent Trust, Spink v Samuel Jones (High Court, unreported, 8 March 1985)

Transfer out – exercise of power of amendment

Principle

It would not be possible for a pension scheme to introduce a new power to transfer out, in order to achieve an objective which could not have been achieved under the scheme's rules by amendment.

[8.2.5]

Fisons v Stannard (Court of Appeal) [1991] PLR 227, [1992] IRLR 27

Transfer out – surplus – trustee duties

Facts and Decision

Fisons agreed to sell part of its business to Norsk Hydro in April 1982. Fison's pension fund trustee, having considered the transfer basis at that time, eventually made a transfer on the total reserve basis in March 1983. The trustee reached this decision by 31 December 1982 on a basis put forward by the employers in April 1982. However, the trustee did so using the wrong transfer power, making a bulk transfer rather than using the power on a partial winding-up. In the meantime, the value of the fund had increased very substantially. The Court held that when trustees had more than one transfer power, they need to feel satisfied in each case that the amount to be transferred is fair 'each way'. From a practical viewpoint, therefore, there was no distinction of substance between the different transfer rules. The trustee owed duties to both the transferring and contributing members alike. The trustee should have given consideration to the current value of the trust fund and its implications, as this might materially have affected its decision. If the trustee had been told the current value of the fund at the date of the decision, and its implications, there were no doubt other matters which it would also have had to consider, such as how far a rise in stock market values could be regarded as a satisfactory basis for action.

Comment

This case is interesting as much for what the Court of Appeal was uninterested in as for the actual grounds of the decision. The majority of the Court of Appeal was unconcerned that the trustee had purported to use the wrong transfer rule, arguing that the trustee was under a generalised duty to make sure that the amounts being transferred were fair both ways. This common sense approach will take some pressure off trustees and their advisers.

The rationale for the central aspect of the decision is more difficult to follow, and it would have been of considerable assistance if the judges had expressed their thought processes on the key point in more detail. The Court of Appeal was being asked to determine whether the trustee had followed the correct approach for choosing the actuarial method for calculating the transfer value. This is not a question by itself of determining the size of the transfer value, but a question of determining what technique was to be used to determine the transfer value. This is the difference between ordering a meal and choosing the restaurant: the decision to choose a more upmarket restaurant does not automatically mean that you will pay more at the end of the night, since you may be extravagant in a downmarket restaurant or careful with your money in an upmarket restaurant.

The Court of Appeal effectively took the view that with the rise in the value of the scheme between the date of the original decision and the date when that decision came to be implemented, the scheme could have afforded to use a different transfer valuation basis (the equivalent of booking a table at a more upmarket restaurant), and that by not reconsidering its decision at the time, the trustee had been in breach of trust.

The decision is logical, but it depends on the Court making a value judgment about the significance of the rise in the stock market. No doubt in this case, the Court felt it apparent that the rise was sufficiently significant, but it gave no guidance about how trustees are to review these matters for themselves. Perhaps the single most useful lesson that can be drawn is that the case reaffirms the old trust law principle that trustees should not normally take decisions in advance of the time when the decision needs to be taken.

[8.2.6]

Hamar v French (Court of Appeal) [1997] OPLR 105, [1998] PLR 321 at paras 42–69

Transfer out – statutory right to a cash equivalent – waiving trustee protections

Principles

The Court held that where a transfer request is not made in the proper format, trustees are not bound to accept the request as having been properly made. The scheme of *s 95* of the *Pension Schemes Act 1993* is a hybrid. Some of its provisions clearly cannot be waived. Those which restrict the use to which a transfer value can be applied, for example, are imposed as a matter of policy. Other requirements, however, are purely formal. The requirement that the application be made in writing, for example, is clearly imposed for the benefit of the trustees; it might be unwise of them to waive the requirement, but it would be absurd to hold that they could not do so if they chose. Where a transfer request purports to exercise the statutory right to take a cash equivalent, trustees are not bound to treat the application as valid, but they can choose to do so if they wish (subject to having the necessary powers under the trust deed and the *Trustee Act 1925, s 15*). On the facts, the trustees had not claimed before the Pensions Ombudsman that the requests for a cash equivalent were not properly made. The trustees could not raise new issues which were closed to them on the pleadings below. (See also [8.2.7])

[8.2.7]

Hamar v Pensions Ombudsman (High Court) [1996] OPLR 55, [1996] PLR 1

Transfer out – statutory right to a cash equivalent – waiving trustee protections

Facts and Decision

Mr Hamar was a member and trustee of the Zengrange Limited Pension Fund, which was on interim documentation. He left the company (and was removed as a trustee) and applied for a transfer payment in October 1990. He did not specify the receiving scheme. He started his own business and established a new pension scheme, the Greplite Executive Pension Fund. He wrote again in August 1991 requesting a transfer payment to this scheme. Inland Revenue approval was eventually received for this scheme in April 1992. Inland Revenue approval for the Zengrange scheme was received in May 1992. *Section 95(1)* of the *Pension Schemes Act 1993* (which consolidated earlier legislation without material differences) required that any statutory application for a cash equivalent should specify a receiving scheme. The first request was, therefore, ineffective. Since the second request was made at a time when the Greplite scheme could not receive the transfer payment because it was not approved, the Court held that it was also ineffective. (See also [8.2.6].)

[8.2.8]

Hillsdown v Pensions Ombudsman (High Court) [1997] 1 All ER 862, [1996] OPLR 291, [1996] PLR 427

Transfer out – terms of transfer

See [8.1.4].

Law Debenture v Pensions Ombudsman (High Court) [1997] OPLR 31

Transfer out – statutory right to a cash equivalent – regulator's powers

Facts and Decision

Members of a scheme, having received transfer value quotations expressed to be guaranteed for three months, exercised their statutory rights to transfer a cash equivalent of their benefits to another scheme. Their scheme went into winding-up before the trustee paid the transfer values. In one case, the transfer value had been due for payment for more than 12 months before the date of winding-up. The scheme was in deficit on a winding-up basis. The Occupational Pensions Board (OPB) purported to extend retrospectively the time period for payment of transfer values. The Court held that the OPB had no power retrospectively to extend the time period for payment of transfer values. Members retained their statutory right to transfer their cash equivalent until the scheme had been fully wound up. On a proper interpretation of the rules, a member who had requested a transfer value fell in the second priority, and his transfer value had to be reassessed accordingly. This applied whether or not the 12 month time-limit for paying transfer values had expired, although in the latter case interest may well be payable. The purported guarantee was ineffective, since the provision of a cash equivalent quotation did not constitute a contractual offer, nor was the transfer application an acceptance of such an offer.

[8.2.10]

Merchant Navy Ratings Pension Fund Trustees v Chambers (High Court) [2001] PLR 137

Transfer out – trustees' duties – transfers without consent

Principles

It was not wrong in principle to provide for a pensioner to be compelled to transfer to another scheme merely because an employer wished to cease to participate in a scheme. The objective in this case was to protect, and so far as possible, ensure satisfaction of the pension benefits which it is the purpose of the scheme to provide. Since this was a wholly benign intention, it was not improper.

Even if a scheme member had no connection with any employer in a scheme, the provisions of *Reg 12, Occupational Pension Schemes (Preservation* of Benefits) Regulations 1991 (SI 1991 No 167) did not prevent the trustees from transferring the member's entitlement without consent to another scheme, provided that both the transferring scheme and the receiving scheme applied to employment with the same employer (whether or not the transferring beneficiary had ever been employed by that employer).

[8.2.11]

Miller v Stapleton (High Court) [1996] OPLR 73, [1996] PLR 67

Transfer out – winding-up – statutory right to a cash equivalent

Facts and Decision

Mr Stapleton was a member of the Rockwood Holdings PLC Group Pension Scheme. His employer was sold and he left service in 3 August 1990. The scheme went into winding-up on 10 August 1990, and at that stage, the scheme was thought to be 101% funded. Mr Stapleton requested a transfer to the scheme set up by the purchaser of his employer, following the receipt of a transfer value guaranteed for 3 months. The new scheme had not at that date been established. It was subsequently discovered that the Rockwood scheme could not pay out transfer values in full because of the illiquidity of the scheme investments, and the risk that annuity rates might move against the scheme. The trustees, therefore, refused to pay out Mr Stapleton's transfer value at the full amount, and were willing only to pay out 80% of his guaranteed entitlement. The Pensions Ombudsman held that this was maladministration, since the guarantee should have been paid in full. He ordered that the balance be paid, and that £750 be paid for non-pecuniary loss. The Court held, following *Hamar v Pensions Ombudsman [1996] OPLR 55*, that no valid application for a statutory transfer value had been made, and the Ombudsman's award must therefore be set aside.

[8.2.12]

R v OPRA ex parte Littlewoods (High Court) [1997] OPLR 375, [1998] PLR 63

Transfer out – statutory right to a cash equivalent – regulator's powers

Facts and Decision

A senior employee was dismissed, and it was alleged that he had engaged in fraud against his employer. The proceedings, if successful, would probably have bankrupted the employee. The employee made a statutory request for his cash equivalent of his pension rights. Because the employer's claim against the employee was not brought until more than 12 months after the employee had left service, the *Pension Schemes Act 1993, s 99(3)* (which would have obliged the scheme trustee not to pay the transfer value until 3 months after the proceedings had expired) did not apply. The trustee applied to the Occupational Pensions Board (OPB) for an extension of time on the ground that the interests of the members of the scheme generally would be prejudiced if the trustee was obliged to complete the transfer. The OPB refused to grant the extension. The Court held that, except perhaps in exceptional circumstances, which were not present in this case, the members' interests for this purpose must be only financial. Members' interests may be prejudiced by the loss of the chance that the employee would be bankrupted, thus forfeiting his pension and increasing the surplus, but this prejudice was too uncertain to permit the OPB to form the opinion that members' interests would be prejudiced. The OPB was, therefore, correct in refusing to grant the extension.

[8.2.13]

Reichhold v Wong (Superior Court of Justice, Ontario) [2000] PLR 277

Transfer out – trustees' duties

Principles

When the assets and liabilities in respect of members had been validly transferred to another scheme, they had no present benefit under the scheme, and the employer's duties and obligations ended with the completed transfer. There was no legal basis for a finding that a pension scheme administrator continued to owe a duty for the future to former members, where all the assets and liabilities relating to those persons had been transferred properly and legally.

[8.2.14]

Re Vauxhall Motor Pension Fund, Bullard v Randall (High Court) [1989] PLR 31

Transfer out – construction of transfer power

Principles

Where a transfer rule requires the transferring scheme trustees to obtain an undertaking from the receiving scheme trustees that it will maintain any restriction on the part of the assets transferred which are derived from contributions made by the members or other persons, the 'other persons' did not include the employer, but referred to those who had transferred in who may never have been members as defined. In the light of Inland Revenue practice, and the restrictions in the scheme rules on refunds of contributions, the restrictions referred to in the transfer rule clearly referred only to refunds to members and other persons who had transferred in.

[8.2.15]

Wrightson Ltd v Fletcher Challenge Nominees Ltd (Privy Council) [2001] All ER 89

Transfer out – partial winding-up – trustees' duties

Facts and Decision

A subsidiary participating in a group pension scheme was floated off. As a result, the former subsidiary ceased to participate in the group scheme and established a new scheme. The key clause in the group scheme provided that:

(a) upon any such cessation of participation there should be deemed to be a dissolution of such part of the scheme as the trustee determined to be appropriate to the participating company; and

(b) the provisions of the winding-up rule, so far as it related to the application of the scheme, should (*mutatis mutandis*) apply to the partial dissolution.

The scheme was in surplus, but the trustee did not transfer any surplus to the former subsidiary. The Privy Council held that while the question was finely balanced, the trustee was right to approach the determination with an open mind and without the presumption that either a share of fund basis or a benefits-based approach should be adopted. Not all the provisions of the winding-up rule were necessarily applicable on a partial winding-up; the words '*mutatis mutandis*' should be read as also meaning 'so far as appropriate'. The trustee had the power to include surplus in the transfer payment, but the power to do this came not from the order of priorities on winding-up, but from the overriding obligation on a winding-up not to pay but rather to secure the members' benefits. The winding-up priorities were thus of no assistance. It was correct to describe the scheme as cellular, each cell consisting of a participating company and its members, but that did not take the matter very far. The trustee's duty was to identify the part of the scheme which was appropriate to the withdrawing company in the right of its members, and not in its own right. The trustee's task was to identify a part of the scheme and not just to value accrued benefits, but this was a semantic point: there must be some valuation of members' entitlements even on a share of fund basis, to determine the proportions in which the scheme is divisible. On the facts, the trustee had exercised its discretion properly. There was only a relatively small surplus, and it might well disappear in a short period of time were market conditions to deteriorate.

8.3 – Merger

[8.3.1]

Re Blackwood Hodge (High Court) [1997] OPLR 179, [1997] PLR 67

Merger – construction of transfer power

Facts and Decision

Blackwood Hodge plc was taken over by BM Group plc in 1990, but minority shareholders retained a shareholding. Blackwood Hodge's pension schemes were in surplus. Its Board agreed to merge them with the BM Group's pension scheme, but without holding a Board meeting to decide this. The schemes were then run together, and eventually a merger deed was drafted. The transferring trustee purported to exercise its power under the rules on termination to transfer members' entitlements with their consent. The Court held that on a proper construction, this power applied only in relation to the making of transfer payments where the members had requested in writing that the trustees made such a payment, and did not confer a power of merger. The merger had, therefore, not effectively taken place. Without such a full-scale merger, it was difficult to see how surplus could pass from one scheme to another.

[8.3.2]

Brillinger v General Electric Company (United States, Court of Appeals, 2nd Circuit) [1998] PLR 169

Merger – surplus – construction of US statute

Facts and Decision

General Electric took over RCA, and as a result, two defined benefit plans were merged. The *Employee Retirement Income Security Act 29, USC s 1058* provided that a pension plan may not merge or consolidate with any other plan unless each participant in the plan would (if the plan then terminated) then receive a benefit immediately after the merger which was equal to or greater than the benefit he or she would have been entitled to receive immediately before the merger (if the plan had then terminated). Since in this case the transferring scheme was in surplus, transferring members maintained that this required that all benefits be augmented as if on a winding-up. The Court held that a distinction was drawn in statute between benefits and distribution of assets. The point at issue concerned excess assets, while *s 1058* was directed to benefits. The *section* did not have the effect, therefore, that the members maintained it had. Participants in a defined benefit plan are not entitled to increases in benefits because successful investment causes assets to grow so as to be greater than liabilities.

[8.3.3]

Harding and others (Trustees of Joy Manufacturing Holdings Ltd Pension and Life Assurance Scheme), petitioners (Court of Session, Inner House, Scotland) [1999] OPLR 235

Merger – trustees' duties

Facts and Decision

The employer of a pension scheme which was substantially in surplus put forward proposals for merging it with other pension schemes which were not so well funded. The employer proposed closing the scheme and making one third of the ongoing surplus available to the trustees for benefit improvements, which the trustees had provisionally decided to allocate as a 12% increase in benefits across the board. The trustees applied to Court for guidance on their duties in various areas. Under the terms of the scheme's eligibility rule, the trustees could not refuse to admit any person as a contributing member if he or she met the requirements prescribed by the rules. The trustees had power to give discretionary increases to pensions and deferred pensions after consultation with the principal employer, but the power of amendment was vested in the trustees and the employer jointly. The Court held that the power to give discretionary increases was not intended to confer on the trustees a general power (inconsistent with the balance of the power of amendment) unilaterally to increase the pension benefits under the scheme without the consent of the relevant employer. The trustees' policy, in relation to setting the employer's contribution rate, must not relate to the level of benefits or increases, but must involve consideration of the appropriate level of security to be provided for members' benefits. The trustees must also have an investment policy (though whether that differed from a policy on the appropriate level of security was open to debate). Unlike in England, in Scotland trustees may not surrender the exercise of their discretion to the Court. The trustees could properly agree to the merger on the basis of the benefit improvements they were proposing: the first instance decision in *Edge v Pensions Ombudsman [1998] OPLR 51* was considered.

[8.3.4]

LRT v Hatt (High Court) [1993] OPLR 225, [1993] PLR 227

Merger – procedure – members' rights

Facts and Decision

LRT operated two final salary schemes. It decided to merge the schemes, and after consultation with the unions, executed an interim deed. It sponsored the *London Regional Transport Act 1989*, which made provision for amalgamating the schemes in *s 16*, following which the merger was carried out. Disputes about the detail of the merger process arose, and the Court was asked whether the merger had been effective, and whether it was lawful for LRT to introduce the new scheme to the extent to which its provisions were detrimental to the transferring members' interests, and were not reasonably incidental to the process of merger.

The Court was also asked about the validity of parts of the merger process, having regard to technical defects within it. The only resolution of the Board of LRT to agree to the merger was passed before Royal Assent was given to the *London Regional Transport Act 1989*, and that delegated the responsibility of fixing the precise merger date to one officer. The Court held that the resolution was proleptic; that is, it was passed on the assumption that the terms of the *section* would not alter before the *Act* received Royal Assent. It could properly be described as having been made under *s 16* since the provisions of the *section* had not altered between the date the resolution was passed and the date the *Act* received Royal Assent, and all actions taken under the resolution took place after the date of Royal Assent.

The notices specified in *s 16* were issued after more than 28 days; the notice period specified in that *section*. Since the notice period for the notices was intended to give an opportunity for protest and investigation, there was not any significantly less effective opportunity for a potential objector to object.

Section 16 provided statutory authorisation for effecting amalgamation. LRT were, therefore, constrained in the merger process by the terms of the interim deed and *s 16* as properly interpreted. There is a well-established presumption that a private Act does not remove private property rights. The Court would, therefore, imply into the statutory process of amalgamation of pension schemes, a term that the performance of the employer's and trustees' duties under the interim trust deed was to be carried out so far as practicable, in a manner that would not remove the established private rights of members of the two schemes. The combination of a mandatory minimum employer contribution, together with the employer's inability unilaterally to determine the schemes, elevated members' rights on these points to the status of private rights, of sufficient weight for them to be protected from removal on amalgamation. No other rights were held to be subject to this protection.

Comment

Nothing is quite so instructive as a succession of mistakes, and in that light this case is an object lesson. The procedure adopted to secure the merger sanctioned by Parliament overlooked formalities at almost every turn. Fortunately for the merger's promoters, the Court took a flexible approach. In retrospect, this decision marks the high point of the courts' treating formalities as having been complied with. The Court paid due lip service to the limits to which even merest formalities can be dispensed with, but then found that these limits had not been reached. It is open to speculation whether the Court which decided *Buckley v Hudson Forge [1999] OPLR 249* or that which decided *Bestrustees v Stuart* (unreported) would have been as accommodating. However, in general the formalities which had been overlooked in this case were less serious than those overlooked in those cases.

There is a sharp contrast between the Court's liberal attitude towards mistakes of procedure and the failure to document member protections. The Court applied carefully the presumption that private Acts of Parliament do not remove private property rights, and the decision shows how seriously the courts will look at the substance of a merger where there is real doubt whether members have in fact been disadvantaged. It also shows how slow the courts are to treat such matters as interest in surplus as a private property right.

The Court had many opportunities to show off its practical skills in sorting out unfortunate oversights, commentaries on which are scattered throughout this book. To single out one, the Court had to consider a problem which had troubled successive generations of trust lawyers: whether a group of trustees could be replaced with a single corporate trustee which was not a trust corporation. The Court's imaginative approach to the provisions of *s 37(1)(c)* of the *Trustee Act 1925* may be argued about as a matter of legal theory, but in practice trust lawyers will be grateful for a sensible solution to a problem which was doubtless created by accident.

Part 9 – Use of Surplus

9 – Introduction

Surplus is a subject which inspires a lot of interest in pensions magazines, perhaps more than any other pensions issue. This interest is contagious, perhaps because surplus seems as if it is up for grabs for anyone who lobbies hard enough. When Paul Myners was asked to report on investment issues, he could not resist making a recommendation that the issue of ownership of surplus be revisited. It is hard to see how the subjects of investment and surplus are related.

Interest in surplus is all the more surprising, because when all is said and done, there is no law to speak of which is specific to pension scheme surplus. The English courts have been amazingly consistent on the subject, with very few exceptions. The key to understanding English cases about surplus is to realise that all of them turn on the rules of the pension scheme under consideration. There is no general principle that surplus is owned by the employer or the membership.

This is illustrated by the recent authoritative statement of Lord Hoffman in *International Power v Healy [2001] PLR 121*: a surplus is (by definition) money in excess of what is needed to effect the main purpose of the scheme, and the fact that part of the surplus was funded by contributions from the employees cannot displace the fact that a scheme confers the power to make arrangements with surplus upon the employer and no one else. Once it is accepted that the employer can act in its own interests and that the extent to which it is doing so cannot be criticised, the way in which the surplus was funded is not relevant.

However, these observations are only the logical conclusion to the line of thought that was first trailed in *Mettoy Pension Trustees v Evans [1991] 2 All ER 513*: while surplus is derived in a balance of cost scheme from past employer overfunding it does not follow that surplus belongs in principle to the employer, and one does not start from an assumption that any surplus belongs morally to the employer.

What has led some commentators astray is that surplus issues arise in two very different types of case. Cases of the first type, typified by *International Power v Healy* and *Mettoy Pension Trustees v Evans*, involve the Court applying provisions of a pension scheme, which may not be clear but which fully cater for the surplus problem with which the Court is faced. These cases are solved by a straightforward application of the provisions, once they have been identified.

The second type of case, typified by *Air Jamaica v Charlton [1999] 1 WLR 1399* and *Davis v Richards & Wallington Industries Ltd [1991] 2 All ER 563*, involves the Court applying rules of law to pension schemes which do not have provisions which adequately cater for the surplus problem with which the Court is faced. In this second category, the Court's judgment can be mistaken for an expression of moral views about the ownership of surplus. However, this is not so. For example, as the courts are frequently at great pains to point out, the implication of a resulting trust, a device commonly used to resolve such cases, may have nothing to do with the intentions of the parties (and indeed may even directly cut across their intentions). It is simply a rule for solving a problem which needs solving.

The only occasions on which the courts may need to take into account the moral issues arising from surplus are when they are considering the exercise of discretionary powers. These may occur in varied circumstances. The scheme may be winding up, and the trustees may have a discretion whether to distribute surplus to the members. A bulk transfer may be taking place, and the trustees may need to decide on the size of the transfer value. The scheme may have a rule to cater for surplus, under which the trustees have a discretion over the distribution of surplus. And so on.

Even in these circumstances, the courts have been notably averse to drawing moral conclusions. *International Power v Healy* epitomises the court's approach: identify the rules and then apply ordinary trust law principles. While that approach was stated with particular clarity by Lord Hoffman in that case, it did not differ in any material respect from the approach of Warner J in *Mettoy Pension Trustees v Evans*. The courts apply the same principles as are applied when considering any discretionary dispository power of appointment. This gives trustees and employers very wide latitude, provided they correctly apply the scheme provisions. *Edge v Pensions Ombudsman* shows how wide this latitude is, whereas *Hillsdown v Pensions Ombudsman [1997] 1 All ER 862* shows the limits of this latitude. To complete the picture, *Re Reevie and Montreal Trust Co of Canada [1984] 24 OR (2d) (Ont HC 667), [1986] 25 DLR (4th) 312 (Ont CA)* shows how the courts will apply the wording of the scheme provisions with rigour. Discretions will not be implied where they do not exist.

There are exceptions which prove every rule. *Thrells v Lomas [1993] 1 WLR 456* is a case where the Court held forth in great detail on the appropriate distribution of surplus. However, it is important to recognise the very special nature of that case. It was a case where the trustee surrendered its discretion to the Court to distribute surplus on a winding-up, and so the Court was considering how to distribute surplus not as a reviewing body but as a decision-maker. The Court could not set wide limits within which the trustees could operate; it was obliged to make an allocation itself. These circumstances arise very rarely indeed and the Court's comments in that case should not be interpreted as indicating a wider judicial approach to the competing claims on pension scheme surplus. Accordingly, *Thrells v Lomas* is summarised in Part 11 (Winding-up Powers) rather than in this Part.

9.1 – Use of Surplus

[9.1.1]

Air Jamaica v Charlton (Privy Council) [1999] I WLR 1399, [1999] OPLR 11, [1999] PLR 247 at paras 51–55

Surplus – winding-up – resulting trust

Principles

A restriction in a pension scheme, prohibiting the return of contributions to the employer, does not preclude the operation of a resulting trust in the employer's favour: *Re ABC Television Pension Scheme (1973)* was disapproved. Similarly, a resulting trust may be established in relation to member contributions. In this case, the winding-up rule provided that surplus would be used to improve members' benefits, but was invalid. It could not therefore be said that members had received all that they had bargained for. *Davis v Richards & Wallington Industries Ltd [1991] 2 All ER 563* was disapproved in part.

Because the pension scheme was a mutual insurance scheme, with each member entering into a separate settlement, the members' share of the surplus should be divided *pro rata*.

[9.1.2]

Air Products Canada v Schmidt (Supreme Court, Canada) [1995] OPLR 283, [1995] PLR 75

Surplus – winding-up – ongoing surplus – resulting trust

Facts and Decision

Two schemes in winding-up were in surplus, and employers and employees each laid claim to the surplus. The employers had previously enjoyed contribution holidays, and the employees challenged the validity of these holidays. In one scheme, the employer had purported to amend the rules so that on a winding-up, any surplus remaining once a maximum level of benefit improvements had been reached reverted to the employer (previously there had been a prohibition on refunds to the employer). The Court held that surplus exists only on paper during the continuation of a plan. Employees cannot claim a right to surplus in an ongoing plan because it is not definite. While a plan set up under trust is in operation, any surplus is an actuarial surplus. When the plan is terminated, however, the actuarial surplus becomes an actual surplus and vests. Surplus funds remaining on termination can revert on a resulting trust to both employers and employees in proportion to their respective contributions. *Davis v Richards & Wallington Industries Ltd [1991] 2 All ER 563* was disapproved. On the facts, both employers were entitled to take contribution holidays, but the employer which had purported to amend its scheme to allow for a refund of surplus was not entitled to participate in the surplus.

[9.1.3]

Bank of New Zealand Officers' Provident Association v Bank of New Zealand (High Court of New Zealand) [1999] PLR 117

Surplus – ongoing surplus – members' interests

Facts and Decision

In a pension scheme which provided both defined benefit and money purchase benefits, where the only provision dealing with the distribution of the whole fund was the winding-up rule, the Court held that members and the employer both had the right to be considered when entitlement to the corpus of the surplus on an ongoing basis was in question. The surplus (and that included surplus income) could only be dealt with in accordance with the rules. On the evidence, it was impossible to assess who was equitably entitled to the surplus in the fund based on past contributions. It was easy to see that both defined benefit and money purchase members were entitled to the income on the funds notionally to their credit, but it was hard for the Court to see any equitable claim to earnings on other funds.

[9.1.4]

Barclays Bank v Holmes (High Court) [2000] PLR 339 at paras 99–103, 106–111

Surplus – establishment of money purchase section – construction

Facts and Decision

On a proper construction, the Court held that the employer in a particular scheme could establish a money purchase section of a final salary scheme, and use the surplus generated by the final salary section for making its credits to the money purchase section. That conclusion was reinforced by considerations of commercial common sense and policy. Under the terms of this scheme, the employer had the right not to pay any contributions so long as there was sufficient surplus in the scheme. It did not seem very likely to the Court that in introducing the money purchase section the employer intended to lose the right which it previously had to debit surplus from its contributions. The surplus was not beneficially owned by any of the employees or pensioners. Furthermore, an employer was not obliged to provide a pension scheme, and it was in the public interest that employers should be encouraged to provide such schemes, and indeed relatively generous pension schemes. A dictum of Walker J in *National Grid Co plc v Laws [1997] PLR 157* was considered.

[9.1.5]

British Coal Corporation v British Coal Staff Superannuation Scheme Trustees (High Court) [1995] I All ER 912, [1994] ICR 537, [1994] OPLR 51, [1993] PLR 303

Surplus – employer obligation to contribute

Principles

The employer's liability to pay future standard contributions in a pension scheme, and its liability to meet the costs of administration, were future liabilities. The value of those liabilities may be set against surplus without involving any transfer to the employer (which would have been prohibited under this scheme), because the set-off was made before any present liability had arisen.

[9.1.6]

Brooks v Brooks (House of Lords) [1996] AC 375, [1995] 3 All ER 257, [1995] OPLR 125 at paras 132D–133A, [1995] PLR 173 at paras 30–37

Surplus – post-nuptial settlement

Facts and Decision

The Court held that, as regards the relationship between a company and an employee, a pension scheme represents deferred remuneration. Under the defined benefit scheme in this case the surplus belonged to the company, but the settlor was the employee, not the company. The company was not the settlor because the provision it made for the member by the scheme was in the member's capacity as an employee. As between an employee and his spouse, the position is different. The benefits which the employee acquired under the scheme formed the property of the marriage settlement. But those benefits do not include any entitlement to surplus. Accordingly, the Court's jurisdiction on a divorce when considering a pension scheme as a post-nuptial settlement does not extend to surplus.

[9.1.7]

Re Canadian Union of Public Employees – CLC, Ontario Hydro Employees, Local [1000] and Ontario Hydro (Supreme Court of Ontario, Court of Appeal) (1989) 68 OR (2d) 620

Surplus – employer's obligation to contribute

Facts and Decision

Ontario Hydro operated a defined benefit pension scheme which was substantially in surplus. The scheme was established under statute, and imposed an obligation on the employer to contribute towards the cost of benefits the difference between the amount of the contributions of the employees, and the amount of the cost of the benefits (as determined by actuarial valuations). The employer proposed to set off the value of the surplus against its obligation to contribute. An actuarial valuation was required under the provision only for the purpose of ascertaining the cost of the benefits. The Court held that the actuary was not empowered to set the overall level of employer contributions on such basis as he may determine, notwithstanding that his determination might be by reference to generally accepted actuarial principles. The existence of a surplus did not in and of itself permit the employer to take a contribution holiday. Before the surplus could be credited to or withdrawn by the employer for this purpose, it had to establish its entitlement to use the surplus either by way of a provision within the scheme or by implication of law. On a proper construction, the employer was forbidden from using any of the surplus in any manner for its own benefit.

[9.1.8]

Collins & Batchelor v Pension Commission (Ontario) & Dominion Stores (Ontario Divisional Court, 18 August 1986) 16 OAC 24

Surplus – refund to employer – regulator's duties

Facts and Decision

Dominion Stores applied for and obtained consent from the Pension Commission to take a refund of surplus. The Pension Commission did not consult the scheme membership. The members had been repeatedly told by Dominion that the funds in the scheme could not be used in any way by Dominion except for the provision of pensions, and believed that Dominion had no right to take such a refund. The Court held that the Pension Commission's duties were akin to those of a fiduciary. It was not bound to consent to the proposal, and therefore owed a duty of fairness to those whose interests may be affected by its decision. Members should have been given notice so that they could have had the opportunity to defend their interest. The amount of surplus which was capable of being refunded was a matter of actuarial opinion. The opinions of experts were known to vary, and the members should have had the opportunity to comment on the opinion provided by the employer. The members should have had the opportunity to put their point that Dominion had no right under the scheme documentation to remove any assets. The Pension Commission had failed in its duty of fairness, its decision was set aside and Dominion was ordered to repay the sums refunded to the pension scheme.

[9.1.9]

Re Courage Group's Pension Schemes, Ryan v Imperial Brewing (High Court) [1987] 1 All ER 528, [1987] 1 WLR 495

Surplus – origin of surplus – trustees' duties

Principles

Surpluses arise from what with hindsight can be recognised as past overfunding. Prima facie, if returnable and not used to increase benefits, they ought to be returned to those who contributed to them. In a scheme where the employer is obliged only to make such contributions (if any) as may be required to meet the liabilities of the scheme, any surplus arises from past overfunding by the employer alone to the full extent of its past contributions, 'and only subject thereto by the employees'. Employees have no legal right to a contributions holiday. However, it will only be in rare cases that the employer will have any legal right to repayment of any part of the surplus. Repayment will normally require amendment to the scheme, and thus co-operation between the employer and trustees. Where the employer seeks repayment, the trustees can be expected to press for generous treatment of employees and pensioners, and the employer to be influenced by a desire to maintain good industrial relations with its workforce.

[9.1.10]

Cullen v Pension Holdings (High Court of New Zealand) [1992] PLR 134

Surplus – employer's obligation to contribute – ownership of surplus

Facts and Decision

The New Zealand Farmers' Co-operative Association of Canterbury operated a pension scheme which was substantially in surplus. It originally had an employer contribution rule which required the employer to contribute 9% of members' salaries, plus any further sum the employer may from time to time in its discretion determine. This rule was replaced in 1983 by a provision requiring the employer to make such annual contribution (after considering the advice of the actuary and the trustee) as was necessary to provide benefits payable under the scheme. The power of amendment was subject to a proviso that no amendment which would reduce or adversely affect a member's interest in the scheme could be made without that member's consent. No consent was, however, obtained for the change to the contribution rule. The employer became a subsidiary of another company, which transferred employees and pensioners from the pension scheme of another of its subsidiaries into the Association's scheme in 1988. The transfer-in rule provided that if a member was entitled to benefit under another scheme, the trustee might accept a transfer value and grant additional benefits. The election of members was made by the Association by written notice to the trustee, and the Association could elect as members such persons as it determined were entitled to contribute to and share in the scheme. This notice was given only in 1990.

The Court held that the transferees were validly elected as members, but only from the date of the 1990 notice. On a proper construction of the trust deed, the members were entitled to the entire fund including surplus, since there was no hint of credit, benefit or return to the Association in the original trust deed, which provided for the scheme to be actuarially divided among members on a winding–up. The consent of the members was therefore required to the 1983 amendment since it effectively removed prospects of future surplus in which they would have been entitled to share. Since that consent had not been obtained, that amendment was of no effect.

[9.1.11]

Cunnack v Edwards (Court of Appeal) [1896] 2 Ch 679

Surplus – winding-up – resulting trust

Facts and Decision

A group of individuals associated themselves, and founded a subscription society for providing their widows with annuities. All the members eventually died, and the last widow died in 1892. The society had a surplus of £1,210. The society was not a charity, and there was no resulting trust. Accordingly, the surplus was payable to the Crown as *bona vacantia*.

[9.1.12]

Davis v Richards & Wallington Industries Ltd (High Court) [1991] 2 All ER 563, [1990] 1 WLR 1511, [1990] PLR 141

Surplus – winding-up – resulting trust – origin of surplus

Facts and Decision

A group of companies set up a final salary pension scheme as a successor to an earlier pension scheme by interim deed. A definitive deed was executed in circumstances where doubt arose as to its validity. If the definitive deed was ineffective, a resulting trust in favour of the employer arose. *Re ABC Television Pension Scheme (1973)* and *Jones v Williams [1989] PLR 17* were not followed. The employees contributed a fixed percentage and the employers contracted to pay the balance of costs in order to fund the employees' benefits. The surplus was therefore primarily funded by the employers' contributions, and only secondarily by the employees' contributions and transferred funds. The Court held that a resulting trust in favour of the employees was excluded since the employees had received the benefits for which they had contracted, and a resulting trust would have breached the statutory and Inland Revenue requirements under which the scheme was established. Any surplus referable to employee contributions devolved, therefore, as *bona vacantia*.

[9.1.13]

Edge v Pensions Ombudsman (Court of Appeal) [2000] 3 WLR 79, [1999] PLR 215 at paras 45–50, 66–69

Surplus – trustees' duties – ongoing surplus

Facts and Decision

When an actuary's report disclosed a surplus and recommended that consideration be given to benefit improvements, the Court held that the trustees of the pension scheme could not ignore this recommendation. They were obliged to consider whether to increase benefits, but could have decided not to do so. The beneficiary's right was to have the matter properly considered. If there was an actuarial surplus, the trustees must, in deciding whether to increase benefits, act in a way which appears to them fair and equitable in all the circumstances. In deciding what is fair and equitable in all the circumstances, the trustees may be expected to give weight to the claims of those whose contributions are or will be the effective source of the surplus. This does not, however, lead to the conclusion that trustees are bound to take any particular course as a result of that consideration. They may, and in most cases probably must, take other matters into consideration. Properly understood, the duty for trustees to act impartially is no more than the ordinary duty which the law imposes on a person who is entrusted with the exercise of a discretionary power: that he exercises the power for the purpose for which it is given, giving proper consideration to the matters which are relevant and excluding from consideration matters which are irrelevant. If pension fund trustees do that, they cannot be criticised if they reach a decision which appears to prefer the claims of one interest over others. The preference will be the result of a proper exercise of the discretionary power.

When negotiating with the employers over use of surplus, the Court also held that trustees are not obliged to put forward proposals that they do not think are fair to the employers. In this case, the trustees were in no real position to bargain with the employers, and they were entitled to conclude that 'half a loaf was better than no bread', and put forward a proposal which the employers would be likely to find attractive.

Fisons v Stannard (Court of Appeal) [1991] PLR 227 at paras 44, 47–50, [1992] IRLR 27

Surplus – ongoing surplus

Principle

Per Dillon LJ: the observation of Walton J in *Re Imperial Foods Ltd Pension Scheme [1986] 2 All ER 802* on the possibly ephemeral rise in the market value of pension funds was not a ruling of law, but a indication of matters which can properly be taken into account, in some cases at any rate, in considering what is just and equitable.

Per Staughton LJ: Walton J's view that surplus might be of a temporary nature, and there was no certainty that any of the existing employees would ever benefit from it, was questioned. The surplus in this case had arisen because the investments had performed better than was anticipated when the rate of Fisons' contributions was calculated. No doubt the value of the investments might fall again. Pension fund trustees must always be alive to that possibility. But there was no ground for regarding that as probable; the value of a marketable commodity today is what general opinion regards as likely to be its value tomorrow. The surplus might also disappear if Fisons decreased its rate of contribution, but one should assess the likelihood of this, given the discontent and industrial unrest this would cause. So where there was some degree of likelihood that the scheme would continue to be in surplus for the foreseeable future, and that the existing employees and pensioners would receive some benefit from that surplus in the future, trustees ought to have borne those points in mind in considering what was just and equitable for the purposes of exercising their discretionary power to make a transfer out.

[9.1.15]

Hillsdown v Pensions Ombudsman (High Court) [1997] 1 All ER 862, [1996] OPLR 291, [1996] PLR 427

Surplus – refund to employer – transfer of surplus to another scheme – ongoing surplus – trustee's duties – employer's obligations

Facts and Decision

A pension scheme was heavily in surplus. It had no provision under which surplus could be repaid to the employers, and a restriction on the power of amendment prohibiting any amendment which would result in the transfer of scheme assets to any employer. The trustee had the obligation to apply surplus at its unilateral discretion according to various specified methods. The employer threatened to use its powers to suspend contributions and adhere new employers and their employees to the scheme, in order to eliminate the surplus, unless the trustee agreed to an amendment of the scheme rules to permit transfer of all the assets and liabilities to another scheme from which a repayment of surplus could be made. The trustee agreed to such a transfer in return for benefit improvements. The Court held that the purpose of the amendment and transfer was the repayment of surplus to the employer, and this was an improper purpose for the exercise of the power of amendment, rendering its exercise a fraud on the power by the trustee. Where surplus was to be calculated by reference to immediate and prospective liabilities, the liabilities were limited to those ascertainable as either immediate or prospective on the date as at which the valuation was made. So liabilities attributable to an employer which had not yet adhered to the scheme were not immediate or prospective.

The implied obligation of trust and confidence prevents employers from using a power to suspend or determine their liability to contribute, while at the same time using the power to adhere further employers for the purpose of running down a surplus certified to have arisen in relation to the service of the employees of other employers. The employer was in breach of its implied obligation of good faith when it sought to enter into negotiations with the trustee, when the trustee needed to consider the matter alone. It was also a breach of its duty of good faith for it to induce the trustee to act in breach of trust by committing a fraud on a power. Hillsdown was therefore liable to refund the money received as a constructive trustee.

[9.1.16]

Hockin v Bank of British Columbia (British Columbia Court of Appeal) [1992] PLR 19 at paras 24–26

Surplus – winding-up – resulting trust

Principles

A pension scheme is fundamentally a trust, not of property, but for a purpose. The Bank of British Columbia's contributions to such a trust were not by the direction of the Bank or trustee, but were calculated from time to time by the actuary. The Bank was not alone as settlor. Strange as it might seem, it was to be observed that the beneficiary employees themselves also effected settlement of the trust with their own contributions. The Bank as settlor had no control in this case over excessive contributions which, after providing for all pension benefits and administration, resulted in the surplus in question. These were determined by the independent actuary.

The members and others claiming through them had their pension benefits provided without reduction in this case. When the purpose of the trust had been fulfilled, the Court rhetorically inquired, how could revocation of that part of the trust relating exclusively to surplus be contrary to or inconsistent with the settlement of the trust? When the whole reason for that part of the settlement monies which were in excess of the purpose to provide to pension benefits was not essential to the purpose of the trust, then to that extent the trust became unfounded, and it was necessarily implicit that the settlement ought to be partially revoked to restore the excess to the settlor.

[9.1.17]

Icarus v Driscoll (High Court) [1990] PLR 1

Surplus – winding-up – origin of surplus

Facts and Decision

A surplus arose on the winding-up of a scheme (which had been triggered by the employer's insolvency) which had been for many years non-contributory. That surplus had to a large extent arisen due to the success of the investments, and if the scheme had not terminated the employer could have reduced its contributions. In that sense, the Court held, the surplus was due to past over-funding by the employer.

[9.1.18]

Independent Pension Trustee v Stevens (High Court, unreported, 13 November 2000)

Surplus – winding-up – trustee's duties

Facts and Decision

A final salary pension scheme went into winding-up with a surplus on the insolvency of its employer. The trustees proposed to pay the employer a fixed sum with notional interest from the date that they had taken their decision to wind up, and apply the balance for the beneficiaries. It sought the Court's sanction for doing this. The Court held that what the trustees proposed was within their powers (although the decision was necessarily open to review until the decision was implemented), but the review that had taken place had been one-sided. The trustees had considered only the effect on the insolvency practitioners of not receiving the capital sum which the trustees would have paid to them, if they had implemented the decision immediately. They had not considered the present capital value of the scheme, which was less than at the time when the trustees had made their decision. The trustees should also have considered this before finalising their decision.

[9.1.19]

International Power v Healy (sub nom) (House of Lords) [2001] PLR 121, paras 7, 16, 17

Surplus – ongoing surplus – public policy – members' interests – uses for surplus – actuary's role – ownership of surplus

Principles

Per Lord Hoffman: 'There are only two ways of dealing with an actuarial surplus. You can pay more money out of the scheme or you can reduce the amount of money coming in.'

A surplus is (by definition) money in excess of what is needed to effect the main purpose of the scheme.

The fact that part of a surplus was funded by contributions from the employees cannot displace the fact that a scheme confers the power to make arrangements with surplus upon the employer, and no one else. Once it is accepted that the employer can act in its own interests, and that the extent to which it is doing so cannot be criticised, the way in which the surplus was funded is not relevant.

Where an actuary is required to certify and has certified that there is a surplus, the employer is not required to be sceptical about the durability of the surplus. Caution is a matter for the actuary in certifying the surplus. (See also [9.1.24] and [9.1.25])

[9.1.20]

Irish Pensions Trust v First National Bank of Chicago (Irish High Court, 15 February 1989) 37 PBLR 9

Surplus – winding-up – construction of winding-up rule

Facts and Decision

An employer's pension scheme wound up in surplus. The scheme winding-up rule provided that residual surplus was to be repaid to the employer 'in accordance with section 11'. Section 11 of the scheme prohibited any repayment to the employer except to the extent the employer had made contributions because of an 'erroneous actuarial computation', or where the employer had made a contribution as a result of a mistake of fact. On a proper construction, the Court held that the employer was entitled to receive the refund of surplus on a winding-up. The direction to repay was emphatic, and 'erroneous actuarial computation' was to be interpreted as including errors of actuarial assumption as well as errors of actuarial calculation.

[9.1.21]

Jones v Williams (High Court) [1989] PLR 17

Surplus – winding-up – resulting trust – construction of winding-up rule

Principles

A clause which expressly rules out a resulting trust in any circumstances can mean what it says. Where a trust deed is silent as to the destination of surplus, the law will supply a resulting trust in favour of the provider. This arises outside the trust deed as an implication of law. It is only where it is absolutely clear that in no circumstances is a resulting trust to arise that it will be excluded.

[9.1.22]

LRT v Hatt (High Court) [1993] OPLR 225 at 265A–268G, [1993] PLR 227 at paras 158–169

Surplus – winding-up – members' interests

Principles

Members of a pension fund have various rights and interests. At the top of the scale comes the right to receive a pension or other benefit in accordance with the rules as they stand from time to time (including the right to restrain improper exercises of fiduciary powers). Next comes the right (correlative to the duty of the employer to observe the implied term in contracts of employment) that the employer will not act in breach of the implied obligation of good faith. Thirdly, there are the expectations which members might quite legitimately harbour that discretions will be exercised in their favour where no breach of any duty is involved in the non-exercise of the discretion. Typically, this situation arises where there is a surplus discerned by the actuary of the fund. No doubt the larger the surplus the livelier the expectation, but in the great majority of pension funds it remains an expectation rather than a right. That is not to say that it is either without value or that the law will not protect it in appropriate circumstances: *Fisons v Stannard [1992] IRLR 27* and *Thrells v Lomas [1993] 2 All ER 546* were considered. Where, as here, the schemes provided for a minimum contribution by employers based on a multiple of the employees' contributions, it was quite impossible as well as simplistic to identify the owners of the surplus. *Mettoy Pension Trustees v Evans [1991] 2 All ER 513, Re Courage Group's Pension Schemes [1987] 1 All ER 528, UEB v Brabant [1991] PLR 109, Hockin v Bank of British Columbia [1992] PLR 19* and *Lock v Westpac [1991] PLR 167* were considered.

[9.1.23]

Mettoy Pension Trustees v Evans (High Court) [1991] 2 All ER 513, [1990] 1 WLR 1587, [1990] PLR 9 at para 177

Surplus – winding-up – ownership of surplus

Principle

Surplus is derived in a balance of cost scheme from past employer overfunding, but it did not follow that surplus belongs in principle to the employer and one does not start from an assumption that any surplus belongs morally to the employer.

[9.1.24]

National Grid Co plc v Laws (High Court) [1997] OPLR 207, [1997] PLR 157 at para 111

Surplus – ongoing surplus – public policy – members' interests – uses for surplus – actuary's role – ownership of surplus

Principle

It is a matter of real concern that the destination of surplus should depend, as it often seems to depend, on subtle and complex arguments about the meaning of the scheme documents. Any general exclusion of employers from surplus would tend, however, to make employers very reluctant to contribute to their pension schemes more than the bare minimum that they could get away with: that would be unfortunate. (See also [9.1.19] and [9.1.25])

[9.1.25]

National Grid Co plc v Laws (Court of Appeal) [1999] OPLR 95, [1999] PLR 37 at paras 43–46, 49, 54

Surplus – ongoing surplus – public policy – members' interests – uses for surplus – actuary's role – ownership of surplus

Principles

Members of a pension scheme have no rights in a surplus revealed by an actuarial valuation, but they have a reasonable expectation that any dealings with that surplus will pay a fair regard to their interests: *Re Courage Group's Pension Schemes [1987] 1 All ER 528 was* approved. Where trustees have a power to increase benefits, members have a reasonable expectation that if scheme funds permit, the power will be exercised to the extent that is fair and equitable in all the circumstances, having regard to the purpose for which the power was conferred: *Thrells v Lomas [1993] 2 All ER 546* was approved. There is no general proposition that members of a contributory pension scheme have interests in the application of surplus equivalent to rights of property. It would be wholly divorced from commercial reality if employers were obliged to contribute hundreds of millions of pounds which were not needed to fund the benefits: however, if the employers and their advisers wished to avoid such a result they must be careful to travel by a route which was permitted by the terms of the trust deed and not by one which was not. The solution to the problem lay within the terms of the scheme itself, and did not lie within a world populated by competing philosophies as to the true nature and ownership of an actuarial surplus. (See also [9.1.19] and [9.1.24])

[9.1.26]

Packwood v APS Trustees (Pensions Ombudsman) [1995] OPLR 369, [1995] PLR 189

Surplus – ongoing surplus – trustees' duties – employer's duties

Facts and Decision

The trustees of a funded occupational pension scheme had sole control of the power of amendment. The scheme was very substantially in surplus. The trustees had a duty from time to time to consider using the power of amendment to grant benefit increases to all members, and on the facts, the Pensions Ombudsman held that they had failed to do so for pensioners.

While the trustees did not have a formal power to defer collecting contributions in advance of the formal results of an actuarial valuation, in circumstances where the scheme was known to be very heavily in surplus the Ombudsman held that it would be unreasonable to hold the trustees liable for breach of trust, or maladministration causing injustice, through their failure to insist on further contributions. The company had not breached its implied obligation of good faith by considering the interests of the pensioners but then preferring its own interests.

[9.1.27]

Plamer v Abney Park Cemetery Co. Ltd (High Court, unreported, 4 July 1985)

Surplus – winding-up – resulting trust

Facts and Decision

The employer ran a contributory pension scheme for its employees. It ceased business in 1970, but the pension scheme continued to provide pensions for two members. One pensioner died, and the other agreed to have her pension secured with an annuity, leaving £20,000 in the scheme. The members' and employer's contributions were paid irrevocably into a common pool on a contractual basis. The employer was entitled to no return and the members were only entitled to their benefits. The balance therefore passed to the Crown as *bona vacantia*. *Cunnack v Edwards [1896] 2 Ch 679* was considered.

[9.1.28]

Re Reevie and Montreal Trust Co of Canada (Ontario Court of Appeal 20 February 1986) 25 DLR 312

Surplus – winding-up – resulting trust – construction of winding-up rule

Facts and Decision

Canada Dry set up a defined benefit pension scheme in 1955. By 1985, no current employees remained in the scheme, and the employer sought a refund of surplus after securing the other benefits. The company put considerable emphasis on the fact that the scheme was a defined benefit scheme. It was argued that once those defined benefits were paid, the members had no further rights and, therefore, there must be a power for the employer to deal with surplus funds. The Court held that this argument did not accord with the facts. While the scheme continued to operate, a surplus would simply afford a cushion against years during which a fund performs poorly, or it may lead to the reduction of future contributions. When the scheme was discontinued, other considerations arose. In this case, the scheme itself provided that on discontinuance the surplus be distributed to the members. The defined benefits did not prevent the members from benefiting from these specific additional rights.

[9.1.29]

Reichhold v Wong (Superior Court of Justice, Ontario) [2000] PLR 277

Surplus – winding-up – interests of transferred beneficiaries

Facts and Decision

An employer and the members of its pension scheme entered into an agreement to wind up the scheme, and to share the surplus between them. Application was made for court approval, but a representative of former members who had transferred to another pension scheme several years previously, following a sale of business, applied for the Court to determine whether such members had an interest in the surplus. Since the assets and liabilities in respect of such members had been validly transferred, the Court held that they had no present benefit under the scheme, and the employer's duties and obligations ended with the completed transfer.

[9.1.30]

Stevens & others v Bell & others (High Court) [2001] All ER 193, [2001] PLR 99

Surplus – ongoing surplus – actuary's role – uses of surplus

Facts and Decision

The Airways Pension Scheme had a substantial surplus of assets over liabilities. A question arose as to the meaning of Clause 11, which set out the actuary's duties. Clause 11(b) required the actuary to make a valuation of the assets and liabilities of the fund. If the actuary certified that a disposable surplus was attributable to an employer, the trustees were obliged within 3 months to make a scheme for disposing of the disposable surplus with the employer's agreement, or in default of agreement the matter would be referred to an outside actuary. Clause 11(d) set out how the disposable surplus was to be dealt with, and provided for it to be applied so far as possible against the employer's past and future contribution liabilities, but made no explicit provision as to how any further surplus should be dealt with.

The Court held that disposable surplus was not the same as surplus. It was a matter for the actuary to assess what additional reserves to make. On a proper construction of the scheme's rules, it was not correct to suggest that disposable surplus could not include residual surplus of this type. Clause 11 created a free-standing power for the trustees on a proper construction of the scheme's rules. The trustees could, but were not obliged, to make a scheme which disposed of the whole of the disposable surplus.

[9.1.31]

Taylor v Lucas Pension Trust (High Court) [1994] OPLR 29, [1994] PLR 9

Surplus – ownership of surplus

Principle

To the extent that a pension fund is in surplus, it does not in any intelligible sense belong to anyone.

[9.1.32]

Tek Corporation Provident Fund v Lorentz (Supreme Court of Appeal of South Africa) [1999] OPLR 137

Surplus – establishment of money purchase section – employer's obligation to contribute

Facts and Decision

An employer established a defined benefit scheme in 1991, and in due course this generated a surplus. In 1993, the employer established a money purchase scheme, and the overwhelming majority of members of the defined benefit scheme elected to transfer to the money purchase scheme. They took the actuarial value of their interest, but a substantial surplus remained in the defined benefit scheme. The employer took a contribution holiday in the money purchase scheme on the assumption that it could transfer surplus from the defined benefit scheme to the money purchase scheme for this purpose. In fact, the surplus was not transferred. Subsequently, two-thirds of the members of the money purchase scheme transferred to another scheme, and sought a share of the surplus in the defined benefit scheme. The Court held that defined benefit pension schemes do not exist to generate surpluses, but they may arise when reality and actuarial expectation do not coincide. Once a surplus arises it is ipso facto an integral component of the scheme: *Mettoy Pension Trustees v Evans*

[1991] 2 All ER 513 was followed. Only the rules of the scheme could form the basis for the employer laying claim to the surplus, there being no principle of common law or statute permitting it to do so. The rules of this scheme contemplated the possibility of surplus arising, but made no explicit provision for the employer to lay claim to surplus in any circumstances. The employer had power to determine how a substantial actuarial surplus was to be used after the trustees had made recommendations, within the limitations imposed by the *Pension Funds Act 1956* and the Registrar's practice. This did not give the employer an unfettered discretion, but the employer could derive benefit from the surplus. In a balance of cost scheme, the employer need only contribute when the need for contributions arises. In the words of the Court: 'present a surplus, absent a need and absent a liability'. It was, however, doubtful whether the employer could direct the trustees to preserve the surplus. The employees had no right to any increases in benefits under the defined benefits scheme, and so the employer and the trustees of the defined benefit scheme could not be required to transfer surplus to the money purchase scheme. Trustees have no inherent and unlimited power to deal with surplus as they see fit.

[9.1.33]

UEB Industries v Brabant (Court of Appeal of New Zealand) [1991] PLR 109, [1992] 1 NZLR 294

Surplus – winding-up – refund to employer – construction of winding-up rule

Facts and Decision

UEB gave notice on 1 December 1988 that it was ceasing to contribute to the pension scheme which it sponsored for its employees, and the scheme was wound up. The scheme had a substantial surplus. The trustees proposed to use 70% of the surplus for the employer and 30% for the beneficiaries. In 1980, the scheme winding-up rule had been amended to authorise a refund of any unexpended balance to the company (previously there had been a permanent alienation clause), and the validity of this amendment was challenged. The Court held that there was nothing at all incongruous in the view that on the termination of a scheme, any ultimate surplus should belong to the members and their dependants: *Mettoy Pension Trustees v Evans [1991] 2 All ER 513* and *Imperial Group Pension Trust v Imperial Tobacco Ltd [1991] 2 All ER 597* were considered. What must, however, be decisive were the terms of the trust constituted by the particular scheme. The terms of the original permanent alienation clause made it perfectly clear that to allow the company to participate in the surplus would be to depart from the terms of the trusts. It was not possible to remove a restriction which prevented an amendment which would authorise a repayment of funds to the employer (Richardson J not relying upon this ground). Nor was it possible to characterise all contributions by the employer in excess of its minimum obligations as pre-payments of its contributions such as would not be caught by the terms of the permanent alienation clause; no appropriate accounting measures had been taken.

[9.1.34]

Re Vauxhall Motor Pension Fund, Bullard v Randall (High Court) [1989] PLR 31

Surplus – construction of power to transfer out members' benefits

Facts and Decision

Trustees of a pension scheme, which did not permit refunds of surplus, proposed making a bulk transfer to another scheme where refunds of surplus were not prohibited. A restriction on the power of amendment, prohibiting amendments which would result in the payment to the employers of any part of the pension fund, did not prevent the trustees making a transfer to a scheme from which the employer could receive a repayment of surplus. The transfer power required the transferring trustees to obtain undertakings from the receiving scheme trustees of any restrictions applicable to such part of the assets transferred as derived from the members' or other persons' contributions. On a true construction, the Court held that the transfer power did not require the transferring scheme trustees to obtain undertakings from the receiving scheme trustees regarding restrictions on refunds of surplus. Even if this conclusion were incorrect, the restriction required would be a restriction on the power of amendment in the transferring scheme, which would have no meaning in the receiving scheme.

[9.1.35]

Wheeler v NBC Pension Trustee (Pensions Ombudsman) [1996] OPLR 337, [1997] PLR 1

Surplus – employer's duties – trustees' duties

Facts and Decision

The National Bus Company scheme was shortly to be wound up following privatisation, with a very substantial surplus. The employers entered negotiations with the trustees over the use of the surplus. In the course of those negotiations, the employers threatened to suspend their contributions until the scheme was in balance on a continuing fund basis, unless the trustees accepted the employers' proposals. The trustees duly accepted the employers' proposals, under which the employers waived their right to terminate, reduce or suspend their contributions. The trustees agreed for their part that any residual surplus would be repaid to the employers unless they agreed that some or all of it could be used in increasing the members' benefits. At the same time, adjustments were made to the winding-up rule. Pensions in payment under the terms of the scheme increased in line with national average earnings. Without obtaining the consent of the membership, the trustees agreed to an amendment to the rules which permitted them to secure benefits on a winding-up with annuities, under which the accrued benefits would be secured in line with the Retail Prices Index plus 2¼% if they could be purchased more cheaply than pensions secured in line with national average earnings. The Pensions Ombudsman held that this amendment breached a restriction on the power of amendment. The trustees would not have agreed to the package if they had believed that the employers had no power to suspend contributions in the manner they were threatening. The employers would have breached their implied obligation of good faith had they so acted, and it would have been an improper use of the power. The trustees agreed to the amendments on an erroneous assumption and the changes to the winding-up rule were set aside: *Re Hastings-Bass [1974] 2 All ER 193* was applied.

[9.1.36]

Wilson v Metro Goldwyn Mayer (Supreme Court of New South Wales) [1980] 18 NSWLR 730

Surplus – construction of winding-up rule – construction of power of amendment

Facts and Decision

The Metro Goldwyn Mayer pension scheme provided that while the scheme continued, any surplus should be applied at the employer's discretion either towards the employer's contributions or in augmenting benefits, but that all surplus would be used in augmenting benefits on a winding-up. The employer and the trustees had power to amend the scheme by deed in any respect which would, in the opinion of the employer, not prejudice any benefits secured by contributions made on behalf of any member prior to the date of amendment. The employer and trustees purported to amend the scheme so that any surplus on a winding-up would be made payable to the employer. On a proper construction, the Court held that the benefits protected by the power of amendment included the benefits which members could receive under the winding-up provision. The amendment was, therefore, invalid.

[9.1.37]

Wrightson Ltd v Fletcher Challenge Nominees Ltd (Privy Council) [2001] All ER 89

Surplus – ongoing surplus – origin of surplus – trustee duties

Principles

In a balance of cost scheme, any surplus arising on a final dissolution is generally regarded as the consequence of past overfunding by the employer: *Re Courage Group's Pension Schemes [1987] 1 All ER 528* and *Davis v Richards & Wallington Industries Ltd [1991] 2 All ER 563* were approved on this point.

There were two relevant features when considering the exercise of trustee discretion in relation to surplus which were present in every defined benefits scheme:

(a) The members had no proprietary rights in the scheme funds, which were just security for the payment of benefits to them.
(b) While the scheme was a continuing one, the surplus was merely an actuarial valuation which may be falsified by events.

One consequence of this was that the trustee should focus on the spreading of risk, and equality of treatment, between departing and continuing members.

Part 10 – Investment of Pension Schemes

10 – Introduction

Until the *Pensions Act 1995*, the investment duties of trustees were subject primarily to trust law constraints, with a limited amount of statutory regulation. Following the enactment of the *Pensions Act 1995*, however, trustees' investment powers are derived primarily from that *Act*. At present, it is unclear whether that change has fundamentally altered trustees' duties in this area, although the consensus is that it has not. The general view is that the *Pensions Act 1995* sets out the parameters within which trustees can exercise their investment functions, but that the considerations which they must bear in mind have been subject to only minor modification by the statutory regime. This remains to be tested.

None of the limited English case law to date is entirely satisfactory. *Cowan v Scargill [1984] 2 All ER 750* provides a comprehensive analysis of the operation of trustees' duties of investment so far as they relate to pension schemes, but Mr Scargill represented himself in that case. While Mr Scargill is famously articulate, he is not a trained lawyer (still less a trained pension lawyer). Inevitably the suspicion lingers that had his case been argued by a professional, the judge may have reached different conclusions either on the general principles to be applied or on the application of those principles to that case. Megarry J, who heard this case, has hinted at this concern in lectures since the case was decided.

There are very few English pension cases relating to investment issues. In the United States, there have been many more such cases, and I have broken my general rule of not including American cases. I have done so on three grounds. First, the new statutory basis for English pension scheme trustees' powers of investment is more closely analogous to the American structure than is the position in most areas of pension law. Secondly, it is better to have weakly persuasive authority to consider than to have no authority at all. Thirdly, when the English courts finally come to consider pension scheme investment problems, they will probably consider the American case law for themselves.

The Government has recently focussed on the issue of socially responsible investment. The case law in the area (on both sides of the Atlantic) is interesting. The courts seem to accept that trustees can take into account matters other than those which relate exclusively to investment concerns. However, the boundaries remain unclear. The *Bishop of Oxford v*

Commissioners for the Church of England [1993] 2 All ER 300 case, which is at least partly a pensions case (the Church Commissioners provide pensions to retired ministers), is perhaps special, given the nature of the trust. *Buttle v Saunders [1950] 2 All ER 193* is included to remind practitioners that there is potentially a difference between the duties on investing in ethically acceptable investments and on managing investments in an ethically acceptable manner. Paradoxically, trustees may properly determine that they can within limits insist on given ethical standards from the companies in which they invest, but must in certain circumstances behave in a manner which many would regard as dishonourable.

10.1 – Investment of Pension Schemes

[10.1.1]

American Communications Association v Retirement Plan for Employees of RCA Corporation and Subsidiary Companies (United States District Court, Southern District of New York) [1980] 488 F Supp 479

Investment – trustees' duties

Facts and Decision

Employees and unions complained about the poor investment perform-ance of the pension scheme operated by an employer. They alleged that the trustees had invested imprudently, but did not detail the facts complained of. The Court held that the mere fact that there may have been a decline in the value of the scheme's portfolio or a diminution of income in a given year did not by itself establish imprudent management. The standard to be applied was that of conduct, tested at the time of the investment decision, rather than performance, judged from the vantage point of hindsight. The claim was therefore dismissed.

[10.1.2]

Bishop of Oxford v Commissioners for the Church of England (High Court) [1993] 2 All ER 300, [1992] 1 WLR 1241, [1991] PLR 185

Investment – considerations unrelated to investment matters – trustees' duties

Facts and Decision

The Bishop of Oxford challenged the Church Commissioners' investment policy on the ground that it gave insufficient weight to ethical considera-tions. The Court held that *prima facie* the purposes of a trust will be best serviced by the trustees seeking to obtain the maximum return, whether from income or capital growth, which is consistent with commercial prudence. In a minority of cases, the position will not be so straightforward. There will be some cases when the objects of the charity are such that investments of a particular type would conflict with the aims of the charity: if so, the trustees should not so invest. There will also be some cases when trustees' holdings of particular investments might hamper a charity's work either by making potential recipients of aid unwilling to be helped because of the source of the charity's money, or by alienating some of those who support the charity financially: in these cases, the trustees will need to balance the difficulties they would encounter against the risk of financial detriment. Trustees would also need to take non-financial criteria into consideration where the trust deed so required. On the facts, the Church Commissioners had taken sufficient account of ethical considerations such that the Court would not make any directions.

[10.1.3]

Re Blackwood Hodge (High Court) [1997] OPLR 179 at 202H–203D, [1997] PLR 67 at paras 152–155

Investment – employer-related investment

Facts and Decision

Following a scheme merger, a scheme invested in assets connected with the receiving scheme's sponsoring employer. This self-investment was held by the Court not to be an advantage the receiving scheme's sponsoring employer derived from the merger, but an advantage derived from the willingness of the receiving scheme's trustees to invest in this manner.

[10.1.4]

Blankenship v Boyle (United States District Court, District of Columbia) [1971] 329 F Supp 1089

Investment – trustees' duties

Facts and Decision

The trustees of the mineworkers' union pension scheme accumulated large quantities of cash, which they put on deposit with a bank owned and controlled by the union. The account did not bear interest. The trustees were the Bank's largest customers. Income could have been earned by investing in Government securities without sacrificing liquidity. The trustees justified their conduct because they had a general concern about the future course of labour relations and other developments in the coal industry which might make it necessary to have money readily at hand, because of tax factors and because of inadvertence. The Court held that there was no inadvertence about the accumulation of cash: there was proof that the trustees knew at all times about it. The tax concerns were not real. While the labour relations concerns could justify the trustees in maintaining a substantial highly liquid reserve, it afforded no justification for the failure of the trustees to put the large accumulations of excess cash to work for the beneficiaries. The trustees owed a fundamental duty of undivided loyalty to the beneficiaries, and this duty had been breached by preferring the interests of the union.

[10.1.5]

Board of Trustees of the Employees' Retirement System of the City of Baltimore v Mayor and City Council of Baltimore City (Maryland, Court of Appeals) [1989] 317 Md. 72, 562 A. 2d 720

Investment – considerations unrelated to investment matters – trustees' duties

Facts and Decision

The City of Baltimore enacted two ordinances requiring that its pension schemes divest their holdings in companies doing business in South Africa or Namibia. The scheme trustees challenged the validity of those ordinances on various grounds, including the ground that the ordinances unlawfully altered the pension contracts of the beneficiaries with the City. The ordinance would exclude 40% of companies listed on the Standard & Poor 500 index, forcing the trustees to invest in companies with a lower market capitalisation. On the facts, the Court held that the evidence of the performance of South Africa-free equity funds was too short to be statistically significant. No witness expressed the opinion that the return would be reduced because of the ordinances. The initial cost of divestiture was found to be one-sixteenth of 1% of the schemes' total value, and the ongoing cost was one-tenth of 1% of the schemes' total value each year. The trustees were not in precisely the same position as the trustees of a conventional private trust. They were charged with fiduciary duties of loyalty and care towards the beneficiaries, but they had obligations to the City as well, since the City was paid half of all investment returns above 10%, and it was therefore a co-beneficiary. The ordinances did not impair the obligations of the beneficiaries' pension contracts with the City: this was a defined benefits scheme, and nothing in the evidence suggested that the ordinances would in any way jeopardise the amount of payment. The trustees owed duties of prudence and loyalty to the beneficiaries, and these were incorporated into the pension contracts, but the trustees' duty was not necessarily to maximise the investment return but rather to secure a just or reasonable return while avoiding undue risk. If social investment yielded economically competitive returns at a comparable level of risk, the investment should not be deemed imprudent. If the cost of investing in accordance with social considerations was *de minimis*, the duty of prudence was not violated. The duty of loyalty did not prevent trustees from considering the social consequences of investment decisions. If the costs of considering such consequences were *de minimis*, trustees ordinarily would not have transgressed that duty. The ordinances did not therefore change the terms of the pension contracts, since the trustees could have acted in the manner in which they were to be compelled to act even before the ordinances were passed.

[10.1.6]

Buttle v Saunders (High Court) [1950] 2 All ER 193

Investment – trustees' duties

Facts and Decision

Trustees of a private trust were in the final stages of negotiation for the sale of a property which they held, when a higher offer came in. They felt honour bound to proceed with the original offer. One of the beneficiaries applied for an injunction to prevent them from selling the property below the higher price offered. The Court held that trustees had an overriding duty to obtain the best price which they could for beneficiaries. It would, however, be an unfortunate simplification of the problem if one were to take the view that the mere production of an increased offer at any stage, however late in the negotiations, should throw on the trustees a duty to accept the higher offer and resile from the existing offer. Trustees have such a discretion in the matter as will allow them to act with proper prudence. Trustees may pray in aid the common-sense rule underlying the old proverb: 'A bird in the hand is worth two in the bush.' Each case must turn on its own facts. On the facts of this case, there was little risk of losing the existing buyer, and the new potential buyer had demonstrated that he was a very anxious buyer and would have submitted to stringent terms for the purchase. The trustees should not have resiled from the existing offer on the ground of commercial morality.

Cowan v Scargill (High Court) [1984] 2 All ER 750, [1985] Ch 270, [1990] PLR 169

Investment – considerations unrelated to investment matters – trustees' duties

Facts and Decision

Five trustees of the Mineworkers' Pension Scheme objected to an investment plan unless it was amended to prohibit an increase in overseas investment, and to prohibit an increase in investment in energies which were in direct competition with coal. The other trustees applied to Court for directions. The Court held that a power of investment must be exercised so as to yield the best returns for the beneficiaries, judged in relation to the risks of the investments in question. Trustees must put on one side their personal interests and views in considering what investments to make. They may even have to act dishonourably. The benefit which trustees must make paramount is not inevitably and solely financial benefit. However, the exceptions are likely to be very rare. The standard required is that the trustee must take such care as an ordinary prudent man would take if he were minded to make an investment for the benefit of other people for whom he felt morally bound to provide. *Re Whiteley [1886] 33 Ch D 347* was followed. Trustees have a duty to consider the need for the diversification of investments. These rules apply to pension schemes as much as to other trusts, subject to any contrary provision of the rules. The connection between a policy designed to ensure the general prosperity of coal mining and the best interests of the beneficiaries of the scheme was too remote and insubstantial. Further, the assets even of such a large scheme would not have any perceptible impact from the adoption of the policies. The Court made declarations to be implemented by the trustees.

Comment

Given that investment duties form a major part of the duties of a pension scheme trustee, it is astonishing how little case law there is on the subject. *Cowan v Scargill* sets out the framework of investment principles for pension scheme trustees, and only a very few cases add glosses to these principles, and these glosses are mostly around the periphery of the structure.

Cowan v Scargill confirms that there are no special investment duties of pension scheme trustees that do not apply to trustees of other types of trust.

However, it confirms the duty to consider the need for diversification of investments, which plays a much greater part in a multi-million pound pension scheme than in even a reasonably large private trust. The scale of a pension scheme and the nature of the liabilities gives new dimensions to the application of standard investment duties.

This case takes an unusually austere line towards the intrusion of trustees' own moral concerns on their trustee duties. While it is acknowledged that the benefit to members which trustees should make paramount need not only be financial, it held that the exceptions were likely to be very rare. As can be seen from the rest of this Part, the United States courts have been more receptive to trustees considering the social consequences of investment decisions. The decision in *Withers v Teachers' Retirement System of the City of New York [1978] 447 F Supp 1248* was considered in *Cowan v Scargill*, but was distinguished. The subsequent decision in *Board of Trustees of the Employees' Retirement System of the City of Baltimore v Mayor and City Council of Baltimore City [1989] 317 Md 72, 562 A 2d 720* is in itself hard to reconcile with *Cowan v Scargill*. With the shift in emphasis shown in *Bishop of Oxford v Commissioners for the Church of England [1993] 2 All ER 300* and *Martin v City of Edinburgh District Council [1989] PLR 9*, it is likely that when the courts come to consider *Cowan v Scargill* in future cases it will receive a more liberal interpretation than some commentators have suggested.

[10.1.8]

Donovan v Cunningham (United States Court of Appeals, 5th Circuit) [1983] 716 F 2d 1455

Investment – trustees' duties

Facts and Decision

The Secretary of State for Labor claimed that fiduciaries of an employee stock ownership plan had breached their fiduciary duties by buying stock above the market price from one of the members of the committee responsible for the plan. The fiduciaries had reached their decision on the basis of a report which was two years old. The Court held that prudent fiduciaries would have sought to analyse the effect of obvious changes in facts and assumptions in a report from advisers, either by their own efforts or with the help of advisers. An independent appraisal is not a magic wand that fiduciaries may simply wave over a transaction to ensure that their responsibilities are fulfilled. It is a tool, and like all tools, is useful only if used properly. Fiduciaries are responsible for ensuring that the information on which experts' opinions are based is complete and up-to-date.

[10.1.9]

Donovan v Walton (United States District Court, Southern District of Florida, Northern Division) [1985] 609 F Supp 1221

Investment – trustees' duties – collateral benefits for third parties

Facts and Decision

The Secretary of State for Labor brought a claim against pension scheme trustees for making an imprudent investment decision. The pension scheme was established under a collective agreement between an employer and a trade union. The trustees had decided to finance, construct and lease to the union a building. The Secretary of State argued that the construction costs were too high, that the union was undercharged on the lease and that the rate of return was too low. However, the trustees had taken continual advice from legal advisers, and had employed professional engineers and obtained two expert appraisals before buying the property. The designer and contractor were chosen after competitive bidding and before construction the trustees had obtained an updated cost estimate, independent review and feasibility study. An independent investment manager negotiated the terms of the lease with the union. The trustees met regularly to discuss the building's progress, and the trustees took cost-saving measures when the project went over budget. The trustees' behaviour was, therefore, held by the Court to be reasonable in the circumstances. On examination, the Secretary of State's evidence as to costs and rates of return was insubstantial. The issue to be resolved was not whether the construction and financing of the lease arrangement were prudent based on what one now knew, but rather whether, knowing what the trustees knew at the project's inception based on their investigation, it was reasonable for them to proceed as they did. The trustees had discharged their duty of prudence. The following precedents were considered: *Donovan v Cunningham [1983] 716 F.2d 1455, Katsaros v Cody 744 F.2d 270, Donovan v Mazzola 716 F.2d 1226, Davidson v Cook 567 F Supp 225, Donovan v Bierwirth 680 F.2d 263, Marshall v Glass/Metal Association and Glaziers and Glassworkers Pension Plan* and *Freund v Marshall & Illsley Bank 485 F Supp 629.* The union derived some benefit from its lease of office space from the scheme. However, this did not conflict with the duty on the trustees to discharge their duties solely in the interest of the participants and beneficiaries. It was no violation of a trustees' fiduciary duties to take a course of action which reasonably best promoted the interests of scheme participants simply because it incidentally also benefited another party: *Morse v Stanley 566 F Supp 1455* was followed.

Evans v London Co-operative Society (High Court) The Times, 6 July 1976

Investment – trustees' duties

Facts and Decision

Trustees of a pension scheme had the power to lend money to the employer, with any such loan to carry interest at the rate of 4½% or such other rate as might be agreed between the employer and the pensions committee. At all relevant times, the employer was the trustee. The employer notified the pensions committee that until further notice it was only prepared to pay interest at the rate of 3¾%. The Court held that the rule did not prevent the pensions committee from agreeing to this. The rules were then changed to provide that the loan would carry interest at such rate as may be agreed, providing that it was not less than 3¾%. The rate continued for many years at 3¾%, long after it was an appropriate rate, and without any consideration by the employer or the pensions committee. While the previous version of the rules did not require any consensus, because in default, a rate of 4½% operated, the new version of the rules required the pensions committee and the employer to reach agreement. The Court held that the pensions committee were therefore in breach of trust, and the employer was a full participant in that breach of trust because its Board knew exactly what it was doing. The correct principle for making the breach of trust good was that of compensation. The Court set a rate of interest for calculating the loss by reference to Government stocks.

Fouche v Superannuation Fund Board (High Court of Australia) (1952) 88 CLR 609

Investment – trustees' duties

Principle

The standard to be applied is the standard of the reasonably prudent man of business, and it was nothing to the point that the defendants in this case were not men of business at all.

Jones v AMP (High Court, New Zealand) [1995] PLR 53

Investment – trustees' duties

Facts and Decision

The bulk of the assets of the AMP pension scheme comprised an office building, and the surplus was invested in a unitised investment linked fund managed by AMP. The scheme power of investment allowed the trustees to invest in policies for life or endowment assurance, among other things. This fund was heavily weighted to investment in shares, and following the sharemarket crash in October 1987, the performance of the fund deteriorated sharply. Members claimed that they had suffered loss as a result of the trustee's actions. The Court held that the managed fund was on a true construction a policy for life assurance, and therefore a proper investment for the scheme. It possessed the essential features of a life assurance policy, providing benefits in the event of the death or the total and permanent disability of the insured person in return for the payment of premiums. The fact that the fund was managed by AMP did not prevent it being a contract of insurance. Investment in a managed fund did not mean that the investment power had been delegated. Allowing the premiums to be intermingled with premiums from other schemes did not constitute improper intermingling. *Cowan v Scargill [1984] 2 All ER 750* was followed on trustees' general investment duties. The trustee, although a trustee company, was not experienced in fund management and it would have been inappropriate for it not to have sought expert advice in respect of the investment of the scheme in equities. On the facts, the decision to choose AMP for the investment was above criticism, and the trustees reviewed the investment sufficiently regularly. Although the scheme did not have a formal investment strategy at this time, when it eventually adopted one it did not do much more than record what had always been the latent or tacit investment strategy.

[10.1.13]

Lewis v Inland Revenue Commissioners (Special Commissioners, 18 October 1999) [2000] 1 PBLR 16

Investment – trustees' duties

Facts and Decision

The trustees of the Redrow staff pension scheme sold 1.9 million shares in Redrow Group plc for just over £2.5 million to the company, in advance of its flotation on the stock exchange. As trustees it would have been very difficult for them to participate in the flotation when a cheaper and simpler alternative was available. The trustees simply did what any prudent investor would have done in the circumstances.

[10.1.14]

Marshall v Glass/Metal Association and Glaziers and Glassworkers Pension Plan (United States District Court, Hawaii) [1980] 507 F Supp 378

Investment – considerations unrelated to investment matters – trustees' duties

Facts and Decision

The Secretary of State for Labor complained to the courts about a pension scheme proposing to lend 23% of its assets for a speculative property venture. Under US law, trustees had a duty to diversify the investment of the scheme so as to minimise the risk of large losses, unless under the circumstances it was clearly prudent not to do so. The trustees made their decision without investment advice and they had little or no personal experience of lending or of finance. On the face of it and according to the standards of experienced lenders, the Court was of the opinion that a commitment of 23% of the scheme's total assets to a single loan subjected a disproportionate amount of the trust assets to the risk of a large loss. The trustees therefore had to show not only that the investment was prudent, but that there was no risk of large loss resulting from the non-diversification. The trustees argued that the project might be highly successful and profitable which would provide a high rate of interest to the scheme, as well as job opportunities for construction workers and recreational facilities. However, the job of the trustees when lending money was not to adopt the borrower's enthusiasm for his project, but to evaluate the prospective risks and returns to the scheme. While this development could well turn out to be a worthwhile, profitable project for another lender to finance, it was not as currently structured a prudent investment for this pension scheme.

[10.1.15]

Martin v City of Edinburgh District Council (Court of Session, Scotland) [1989] PLR 9

Investment – considerations unrelated to investment matters – trustees' duties

Facts and Decision

Edinburgh Council introduced an anti-apartheid policy, and decided that Council trust fund holdings with investments in companies contained in the United Nations list of transnational corporations with major investments in South Africa should eliminate their holdings in such investments. The Council did not seek the advice of professional advisers as to whether it was in the interests of the trusts and their beneficiaries to invest in South Africa. On the application of the leader of the Council opposition, the Court set aside the decision on the ground that the trustees did not apply their minds to this separate and major issue, which was their prime duty as trustees to take into account. The investment duty of the trustees is not merely to rubber-stamp the professional advice of financial advisers, and there is not an unqualified duty to invest trust funds in the most profitable investment available, although it is one of the matters trustees have a duty to consider. It is not reasonable or practicable to expect trustees to set aside all personal preferences, all political beliefs and all moral, religious or other conscientiously-held principles. Trustees must recognise that they have such principles or preferences, but nonetheless do their best to exercise fair and impartial judgement on the merits of the issue before them. If they cannot do this, they should abstain or resign. *Cowan v Scargill [1984] 2 All ER 750* was considered.

[10.1.16]

Meinhardt v Unisys (United States Court of Appeals, 3rd Circuit) [1998] PLR 253

Investment – money purchase schemes – trustees' duties

Facts and Decision

The Unisys Savings Plan was a money purchase scheme which gave its members the right to choose the investment vehicles in which they invested. It offered investment vehicles with substantial portfolios in

Executive Life, a company with liquidity problems. Members were not told of the exposure to risk. Executive Life became insolvent and as a result, many members lost substantial sums of money. The members sued Unisys, which applied to have the action struck out. The Court observed that there was a statutory duty to conduct an independent investigation into the merits of a particular investment. This required fiduciaries to review the data a consultant gathered, to assess its significance and to supplement it where necessary. There was a statutory duty to diversify the investments of a plan so as to minimise the risk of large losses. Where plan-wide investments were not available to offset losses, the proper test of this duty was to look at the concentration in the funds where the losses were incurred. There was also a statutory duty to convey complete and accurate information when speaking to beneficiaries regarding plan benefits, and the fiduciaries remained under that duty even though they were absolved from liability for breaches of fiduciary duty which resulted from the beneficiary's exercise of control. So members could bring an action on the basis that trustees had failed to give them adequate advice as to the risks of investments in a money purchase scheme, even where the members chose their own investment vehicle.

[10.1.17]

Nestle v National Westminster Bank (Court of Appeal) [1992] OPLR 85

Investment – trustees' duties – demonstrating loss

Facts and Decision

National Westminster Bank was the trustee of a private trust from 1922 to 1986, during which time the trust increased in value from £50,000 to £269,000. If the trust had matched the returns on shares in that period, it would have increased to £2.6 million, while to match the increase in cost of living in that period it would have needed to increase to £1 million. The trustee had invested in considerable part in investments which were exempt from income tax for overseas investors, some of the beneficiaries being resident overseas. The beneficiary who inherited the trust in 1986 sued for breach of trust. The trustee had misunderstood the extent of the investment power and failed to conduct a regular and periodic review of the investments. The trustee was not, however, shown to have committed a breach of trust by not holding a higher proportion of shares. The trustee's performance was not to be judged with hindsight. It was important to bear in mind that investment philosophy was very different in the early years of this trust 'from what became later'. It was not a breach of trust for the trustee to have some regard to the relationship between the trust's beneficiaries, or to the overseas status of some of the trust's beneficiaries. It was for the beneficiary to prove on a balance of probabilities that there was, or must have been, a loss, and that a prudent trustee knowing the scope of the trustee's investment power and conducting regular reviews would so have invested the trust funds as to make it worth more than it was worth when the beneficiary inherited it. The beneficiary had not done so in this instance.

[10.1.18]

Providence Capitol Trustees v Ayres (High Court) [1996] 4 All ER 760, [1996] OPLR 215 at 219C-D, [1996] PLR 395 at para 6

Investment – members' decisions

Facts and Decision

A pension scheme member agreed with other scheme members in giving an indemnity to the trustees against all losses associated with a loan of scheme assets to the sponsoring employer. Subsequently the member complained that the investment had been entered into in breach of trust. The Court held that investment in a loan to the sponsoring employer carried obvious risks, but those were risks which a member of the scheme might choose to take in order that the company might continue to trade. If the member made that choice, he could not complain if the investment was lost by reason of the failure of the company.

[10.1.19]

R v London Borough of Lewisham ex parte Shell UK Ltd (High Court) [1988] 1 All ER 938, [1990] PLR 241

Investment – statutory schemes – considerations unrelated to investment matters

Facts and Decision

During the period when apartheid was still operating in South Africa, Lewisham council decided to boycott Shell products and to stop its pension scheme investing in Shell because of its trading links in South Africa. Other oil companies also had extensive trading links in South Africa, but were not boycotted. The council was the creation of statute. Its only possible power for acting in the manner it had was s 71 of the *Race Relations Act 1976*. The Court held that the council could not use this statutory power to punish a person who had done nothing contrary to English law. Shell was not acting in any way unlawfully. The wish to change Shell policy towards South Africa was not merely to satisfy public opinion in the borough or to promote good racial relations, but was in order to put pressure on Shell to procure a withdrawal from South Africa. The council's purpose vitiated the decision as a whole. *Wheeler v Leicester City Council [1985] AC 241* was followed.

[10.1.20]

Swift v Dairywise Farms (High Court, 17 November 1999) [2000] 1 All ER 320

Investment – trustees' duties

Facts and Decision

Dairywise Ltd lent money to farmers who gave milk quotas as security, held by Dairywise Farms. Its pension scheme owned the freehold land to which the milk quotas were attached. Dairywise Ltd went into liquidation. The Court held that milk quotas could form the subject matter of a trust. Dairywise Farms held the milk quotas on trust for Dairywise Ltd. The scheme trustees knew at all times that Dairywise Farms was acquiring the milk quotas and 'the basis of it', and knew that the whole lending system depended on their acquiescence and co-operation. They were sufficiently 'mixed up' in the transactions that equity would compel them to do all such acts as were necessary to enable farmers to redeem their loans and Dairywise Ltd to enforce its security in the case of defaulting farmers. They were likewise under a duty to refrain from doing any act which put it out of their power to do those positive acts. This duty could be analysed in terms of knowing receipt of trust property, or in terms of estoppel.

[10.1.21]

Re Whiteley (Court of Appeal) [1886] 33 Ch D 347 (per Lindley LJ)

Investment – trustees' duties

Principle

'The duty of a trustee is to take such care as an ordinary prudent man would take if he were minded to make an investment for the benefit of other people for whom he felt bound to provide.'

[10.1.22]

Withers v Teachers' Retirement System of the City of New York (United States District Court for the Southern District of New York) [1978] 447 F Supp 1248

Investment – considerations unrelated to investment matters – trustees' duties

Facts and Decision

The Teachers' Retirement System of the City of New York agreed to buy New York City bonds as part of a financial plan to stave off the city's potential bankruptcy. The city's bankruptcy would result in the depletion of the scheme's resources in 8 to 10 years. Under normal circumstances the trustees would certainly not have bought the bonds in the same quantity, since they did not fit the scheme's normal investment criteria. The spectre of the city's bankruptcy was what determined the issue for the trustees. Some retired teachers sought an injunction on the basis this was a breach of the trustees' fiduciary duties. The Court held that the extension of aid to the city was simply a means to the legitimate end of preventing the exhaustion of the scheme assets in the interest of all the beneficiaries. The importance of the city's solvency lay not only in its role as the major contributor but also as the ultimate guarantor of the payment of pension benefits to scheme participants. The trustees had firm ground for believing that the alternative to purchasing the highly speculative city bonds would be the bankruptcy of their own scheme. The decision to invest was therefore a prudent one, and the trustees had fulfilled their fiduciary obligations.

[10.1.23]

Wright v Ginn (High Court) [1994] OPLR 83, [1995] PLR 33

Investment – employer-related investments – trustees' duties

Facts and Decision

A pension scheme held investments in land occupied by the employer, and had also made a substantial loan to the employer. These investments were in excess of the levels authorised under the *Occupational Pension Schemes (Investment of Scheme's Resources) Regulations 1992 (SI 1992 No 246)*. Time limits were set out in the *regulations* as to the extent to which such levels of investment could be maintained. These time limits did not, however, exclude the operation of *s 4* of the *Trustee Act 1925*, and so the Court held that the trustees would not be liable for breach of trust by reason only of continuing to hold an investment which had ceased to be authorised. The trustees could retain the loan as an authorised investment until the time when its value exceeded the prescribed limit, and thereafter were under an obligation to consider its disposal. They could retain the loan if and only if its continued retention could be justified by exclusively investment criteria.

Part 11 – Winding-up Powers

11 – Introduction

Eventually, all pension schemes come to an end. Although the rule against perpetuities does not apply to exempt approved retirement benefits schemes, social and economic changes make it more or less inevitable that any given pension scheme will wind up in due course. Employers become insolvent, or merge with other employers which have their own pension arrangements, or it becomes uneconomic for the employers to operate the pension scheme, or the employers simply change their remuneration strategy. For this reason, the overwhelming majority of pension schemes make specific provision for the scheme to be wound up on the occurrence of specified events, and then to apply the scheme's assets and liabilities in a given manner.

The winding-up provisions are not obviously any more complex to operate than any other constitutional provision of a scheme. However, a disproportionate number of cases arise which concern the proper way to wind up a scheme. Why is this so?

The first reason why so many cases involving winding-up provisions come to Court is that by definition the provisions are only used once. Trustees and advisers have no practice to fall back upon when considering what to do.

The second reason is that often windings-up take place when employers have become insolvent. Where employer powers are to be exercised, the insolvency practitioner may be faced with a conflict between his or her duties to the employer's creditors and the interests of the membership. This conflict may not be capable of resolution without court action. Typical of such cases are *Icarus v Driscoll [1990] PLR 1*, *Mettoy Pension Trustees v Evans [1991] 2 All ER 513*, *Thrells v Lomas [1993] 1 WLR 456* and *Re William Makin [1993] OPLR 171*. The courts have frequently had to consider the nature of the insolvency practitioner's duties in such cases: these are considered in Part 14 (Pensions and the Company's Business).

The third reason is that when the scheme is being wound up, there is no hiding place for difficult problems which are often swept under the carpet while the scheme is still ongoing: such problems must be resolved before the scheme is wound up. This means that the trustees will often take the opportunity to ask the Court for guidance on problems which they might otherwise have taken a view on. *Kemble v Hicks (No. 2) [1999] OPLR 1* is an example of such a case.

The fourth reason is that the winding-up provisions may date from the foundation of the scheme many years previously, and may therefore be in a format which is inappropriate for the structure of the scheme at the date of winding-up. This is perhaps the most common serious problem for pension schemes in winding-up, and is illustrated by *Re ABC Television Pension Scheme* (unreported), *Re Edward Jones Benevolent Trust, Spink v Samuel Jones* (unreported) and *Air Jamaica v Charlton [1999] 1 WLR 1399*.

The fifth reason is the converse of the fourth reason: the winding-up provisions may have been updated frequently, but in a manner which paid no heed to the rights previously enjoyed by categories of members and to restrictions on repayments to employers, resulting in confusion about the current status of the winding-up provisions. *Harwood-Smart v Caws [2000] PLR 101* shows the very complex problems that can arise in such circumstances.

The sixth reason applies only to defined benefits schemes. Such schemes are almost certain either to have a surplus or a deficit: it is most unlikely that they will be exactly in balance on a buy-out basis. This means either that there are sufficient funds to increase benefits or that benefits will need to be reduced. Both of these permutations inflame the interest of beneficiaries in the scheme, and in the case of a surplus, the employer will also take a keen interest. This is one of the relatively rare occasions in the life of a pension scheme where the interests of the members and the employer are in direct conflict. Any ambiguity may well reach Court. *Haig v Lord Advocate 1976 SLT (Notes) 16, Independent Pension Trustee v Stevens* (unreported) and *Jones v Williams [1989] PLR 17* all demonstrate this phenomenon.

The final reason is that ordinarily it is not possible to put right any problems with the winding-up provisions once they have come into play. Once a scheme enters winding-up, it will normally not be capable of alteration, for the reasons given in *Re ABC Television Pension Scheme*. The effect of that decision is to make the winding-up provisions self-contained, except to the extent that they explicitly or by necessary implication incorporate other provisions of the pension scheme. If there is a problem, the only way to resolve it is by getting the guidance of the Court. The courts on occasion have sought to soften the rigour of this rule, as demonstrated by *Davis v Richards & Wallington Industries Ltd [1991] 2 All ER 563* and *Re Edward Jones Benevolent Trust*. However, the judgment in *Air Jamaica v Charlton* included an observation that it was difficult to see how a pension scheme could lawfully be amended in any significant respect once it had actually been discontinued, and so the decision in *Re ABC Television Pension Scheme* has been given the backing of the Privy Council on this point, at least in so far as the power of amendment is concerned.

The single most common problem on the winding-up of a defined benefits scheme occurs where the winding-up provisions apparently do not provide for all the scheme assets to be distributed. The courts then need to decide:

(a)   whether the provisions are to be interpreted as covering a distribution of all the scheme assets in one way or another;

(b)   whether the sums not dealt with by the winding-up provisions are to be returned to the employer or members on a resulting trust basis; or

(c)   whether those sums are to be paid to the Crown as *bona vacantia*, since no one else has a valid claim on those sums.

The cases where this problem is considered can be viewed as cases about the use of surplus or cases about winding-up, but it is important to recognise that the rules being applied are mechanical rules of interpretation, and not statements of principle about ownership of surplus.

In such cases, the courts are becoming increasingly reluctant to find that the surplus passes to the Crown. With the decision in *Air Jamaica v Charlton* that a restriction in a pension scheme prohibiting the return of contributions to the employer does not preclude the operation of a resulting trust in the employer's favour, in future a Court will find that a resulting trust has been excluded only in the most unambiguous circumstances.

11.1 – Winding-up Powers

Re ABC Television Pension Scheme (High Court, unreported, 22 May 1973)

Winding-up – surplus – interpretation – power of amendment – resulting trust

Facts and Decision

A pension scheme went into winding-up. The winding-up rule provided that any surplus must be used to augment members' benefits, to limits based upon whichever was the greatest of:

(a) remuneration at the date of attainment of normal pension age (which was 65);
(b) remuneration five years prior to normal pension age; and
(c) the yearly average of remuneration in any three of the last ten years prior to normal pension age.

Unless the members were aged 58 or over, their entitlement did not qualify for augmentation, because they were unable to bring themselves within any of the three bases for calculating remuneration by reference to which their pensions could be augmented. The employer then wished to alter the winding-up rule. However, winding-up had commenced, and the Court held that the clear wording of the winding-up rule, that the scheme should then be wound up, the trusts ceased and determined, and the scheme dissolved, excluded the possibility that the power of amendment continued to subsist. Clause 3 of the scheme provided that 'no monies which at any time had been contributed by the employer shall in any circumstances be repayable to the employer'. This clause negatived the possibility of implying a resulting trust. Accordingly, any surplus was payable to the Crown as *bona vacantia*.

Comment

At the time this case was decided, it broke new ground. The courts by this stage were experienced in dealing with distributing the assets of private trusts which were being dissolved, but this was the first occasion on which the courts had to consider how a pension scheme winding-up provision worked. *Cunnack v Edwards [1896] 2 Ch 679* was a nineteenth-century case which looked at the treatment of surplus assets when a pension scheme terminated, but this involved no consideration of the terms of a winding-up provision since the scheme in that case had none.

The Court's conclusion that once winding-up has commenced the terms of the trust cannot be amended (unless specific provision is made to do so) can cause severe practical problems, as indeed it did in this case. However, while the Court's decision is austere, it is hard to see how else the Court could normally operate, at least in so far as the use of scheme assets is concerned. Once the scheme enters winding-up, any amendments to the way in which the assets are to be distributed will change the amounts in hard cash that the various interested parties receive. Such a provision would give so much power to those controlling it that it would need very explicit wording before a Court would force trust beneficiaries to submit to such a broad power.

[11.1.2]

Air Jamaica v Charlton (Privy Council) [1999] 1 WLR 1399, [1999] OPLR 11, [1999] PLR 247 at paras 39–42 and 46

Winding-up – employer's rights – perpetuity periods – power of amendment

Principles

In order to wind up a pension scheme three steps must be taken, though the first two may be taken simultaneously. First, the scheme must be closed to new entrants. If no further steps are taken, the scheme continues as a closed scheme, contributions continuing to be paid in respect of existing members but no new members being admitted. Secondly, contributions must cease to be paid in respect of existing members, who will either have been made redundant or have been transferred to a new scheme. At this stage the scheme is discontinued, since it ceases to be a continuing one. But pensions in payment continue to be payable until the third stage is reached and the scheme is finally wound up. The company's ability to wind up the scheme was not a power (if it was, it would be void for perpetuity), but a liberty. Where no formal requirements were set out for the discontinuance of the plan, it was necessary only for the company to cease deducting employee contributions and cease paying its own matching contributions.

It was difficult to see how a plan could lawfully be amended in any significant respect once it had actually been discontinued.

[11.1.3]

Buckley v Hudson Forge (High Court) [1999] OPLR 249 at 259B-G, [1999] PLR 151 at paras 54–57

Winding-up – interpretation – power of augmentation

Facts and Decision

The winding-up rule in a pension scheme did not explicitly set out the entire regime to apply during a winding-up in place of all the other rules. The winding-up rule in particular included no express provision allowing the trustees to direct an augmentation: it did, however, require the trustees to secure 'other liabilities'. The Court held that by implication this phrase included liabilities which would be incurred should the trustees augment pensions, and so the trustees retained the power to grant augmentations even after the scheme entered winding-up.

[11.1.4]

Canada Trust v Cantol (British Columbia Supreme Court, 24 July 1979) 103 DLR (3rd) 109

Winding-up – surplus – interpretation – power of amendment – resulting trust

Facts and Decision

A pension scheme originally contained a provision that provided that the company had the right to amend or terminate the scheme, provided that no amendment or termination shall permit any part of the trust fund to revert to or be recoverable by the company or to be used for or diverted to purposes other than the exclusive benefits of the scheme beneficiaries. However, the winding-up rule made no provision for the distribution of surplus. The company purported to amend this rule to provide for surplus to be refunded to the employer after securing the benefits. The Court held that since the company had attempted an amendment in direct contradiction of its authority, it was an ineffectual amendment. Since the purposes of the trust did not exhaust the fund, a resulting trust arose by operation of law and the balance of the fund was refunded to the employer (the scheme was non-contributory for the members).

Capital Cranfield v Sagar (High Court, unreported, 19 February 2001)

Winding-up – interpretation – power of amendment

Facts and Decision

Systems Interfreight Limited set up a pension scheme in 1971. Its business was transferred in 1973 to its parent company, American Export Lines Incorporated, and again in 1974 to Worms Cargo Service UK Limited. All these businesses were merged in 1978 into Farrell Lines Incorporated. In October 1980, Farrell closed its European operations, making its employees redundant. Systems Interfreight was struck off the register of companies in February 1981 and was dissolved that same month. The pension scheme took some steps towards winding-up, but remained in existence until 1998, when the trustee belatedly realised that it had a substantial surplus. The winding-up provision stated that 'the principal employer may at any time terminate its liability to contribute to the scheme by notice in writing to the trustees'. Systems Interfreight never gave such a notice, although Farrell and the trustees corresponded about the winding-up. In these circumstances, the trustees also had the power to terminate the scheme if they so resolved. However, there was no evidence that they had ever done so. Systems Interfreight remained the principal employer, having never been replaced. The Court held that the scheme had not been terminated, since on the facts neither the principal employer nor the trustees had taken the necessary steps. The scheme still had not been terminated even at the date of judgment. Under the winding-up rule, if the employer was dissolved, the trustees had the power to amend the scheme for the continuance of the scheme. This power could still be exercised. Neither the fact that there had been a substantial delay nor the fact that the amendment would be with a view to altering matters in connection with winding-up were good arguments to the contrary. Given there were express fetters, it would be wrong to imply additional fetters unless it was plainly necessary and obvious that they should be implied.

[11.1.6]

Cunnack v Edwards (Court of Appeal) [1896] 2 Ch 679

Winding-up – surplus – resulting trust

Facts and Decision

A group of individuals associated themselves, and founded a subscription society for providing their widows with annuities. All the members eventually died, and the last widow died in 1892. The society had a surplus of £1,210. The Court held that the society was not a charity, and there was no resulting trust. Accordingly, the surplus was payable to the Crown as *bona vacantia*.

[11.1.7]

Davis v Richards & Wallington Industries Ltd (High Court) [1991] 2 All ER 563, [1990] 1 WLR 1511, [1990] PLR 141

Winding-up – power of amendment – resulting trust

Facts and Decision

A group of companies set up a pension scheme by interim deed as a successor to an earlier pension scheme. The definitive documentation was almost ready for execution when the scheme went into winding-up owing to the insolvency of the principal company. The scheme was in surplus and the provisions to apply on winding-up were not set out in the interim documentation. The definitive documentation was executed after the scheme went into winding-up. The Court held that this definitive documentation was validly executed, and that its provisions took effect. If it had not been validly executed, the employees could compel its execution as a matter of contract, and on the basis that equity deems done that which ought to be done, the failure for it to be validly executed did not detract from the efficacy of the rules. If the definitive deed was ineffective and inefficacious, a resulting trust arose. *Re ABC Television Pension Scheme (1973)* and *Jones v Williams [1989] PLR 17* were not followed.

[11.1.8]

Re Edward Jones Benevolent Trust, Spink v Samuel Jones (High Court, unreported, 8 March 1985)

Winding-up – surplus – interpretation – power of amendment

Facts and Decision

A non-contributory defined benefits pension scheme was closed in circumstances where dissolution would normally have followed, but the scheme continued for its existing members in accordance with a provision in the rules. The scheme was in surplus, and the trustees wished to augment the benefits of all categories of beneficiaries, including members who had transferred out from the scheme some time previously to another scheme of the employer. The Court held that the augmentation rule clearly was not wide enough to permit augmentation of benefits for those who had withdrawn from service. The power of amendment continued to subsist, and in this respect *Re ABC Television Pension Scheme (1973)* was distinguished. That case was understandable in the context of a winding-up, but had no application in a case where the rules, having given the trustees express power to continue the scheme rather than to wind it up, enabled the existing trusts and powers to be continued during the closed scheme period. Since the trustees would not distribute surplus at all if they could not distribute it equitably, they could properly exercise the power of amendment even though there was a restriction preventing any amendment operating so as to affect prejudicially the rights of any retired member, or any other person then entitled beneficially.

[11.1.9]

H Williams Staff Pension Scheme (High Court, Ireland, 17 July 1992) [1999] 32 PBLR 20

Winding-up – interpretation

Facts and Decision

A defined benefit pension scheme went into winding-up in deficit. Its winding-up clause provided that 'the scheme shall be wound up and the fund dissolved' on the occurrence of specified events. However, the scheme could not be wound up and the fund dissolved on a single day. The Court held that the meaning of the clause was that on the happening of the specified events, the scheme was to be wound up as from that date. The priorities also had to be identified at that date. Although one priority referred to annuities being secured for the persons then entitled to benefits, the word 'then' was to be treated as referring to the date of winding-up. On a proper construction, this excluded those entitled to deferred pensions or to a refund of contributions.

[11.1.10]

Haig v Lord Advocate (Outer House, Scotland) 1976 SLT (Notes) 16

Winding-up – surplus – interpretation

Facts and Decision

A pension scheme provided that if a company went into liquidation its participation should terminate, and that any such termination should operate only in respect of members in the service of the company terminating its participation, and in respect of the appropriate part of the fund applicable to such members. The trust deed contained a clause requiring that the deed should contain no provision whereby payment of any part of the fund should be made to the company, and the power of amendment was similarly restricted. Although provision was made for associated companies in the rules, there was in fact only one employer, which went into liquidation following an application to wind up the company. The scheme wound up with a surplus, and the liquidator claimed the surplus. The Court held that the effective date for triggering the scheme winding-up was the date of application to wind up the company, and not the date the Court granted that petition. The deeds did not provide that in no circumstances should the funds be repaid to the company, merely that there should be no provision which had that result. If circumstances arose in which the trustees held funds without there being any provision in the trust deed directing them as to the disposal of the funds, the disposal must be regulated by the application of the law. However, in interpreting the deeds, the Court approached the problem having in mind the obvious intention of the settlor not to benefit the company. The Court would, therefore, favour a construction of unclear provisions which did not have the result of the company taking a benefit from the funds. The employer's claim to the surplus was rejected.

[11.1.11]

Harwood-Smart v Caws (High Court) [2000] PLR 101

Winding-up – surplus – interpretation – power of amendment

Facts and Decision

The trustees of a pension scheme applied for guidance as to the correct interpretation of the winding-up rule, which had been repeatedly amended. The Court held that where the winding-up rule of a pension scheme provided for the balance of the fund (after costs) to be applied for providing the appropriate benefits for members and dependants, without specifically providing for benefits to be augmented, the trustees must first allocate the funds (including surplus) equitably between the beneficiaries, subject only to the limits established by the Inland Revenue. The trustees had no discretion to leave any part of the surplus undistributed. The company had subsequently purported to amend the winding-up rule so that all surplus would be returned to it on a winding-up. This was prohibited by the power of amendment, which provided that 'no amendment shall cause all or any part of the scheme to revert to the company'. The next definitive deed gave the trustees a discretion to augment benefits up to Inland Revenue limits 'in such manner and proportion as they shall decide', with any residue being repaid to the employer. On a proper construction, this was held to be a discretion only as to the direction of the augmentation of benefits, not as to whether to augment the benefits. The next definitive deed made it plain that the trustees' discretion extended to the amount as well as to the direction of any augmentation; however, this amendment was void since it breached the restriction on the power of amendment. Nor could it be saved for those members who joined after the date of the amendment, since the winding-up rule concerned the disposal of a single fund, making it impossible to reconcile the position of the two classes of members if it were to be a valid amendment for such members. *Section 77 of the Pensions Act 1995* applied to schemes already in winding-up at that date.

[11.1.12]

Heilig v Dominion Securities Pitfield (Ontario High Court) 29 DLR (4th) 762

Winding-up – surplus – interpretation

Facts and Decision

Following a series of mergers, the trustees of a pension scheme, in contravention of an express provision in the trust deed, paid the surplus to the employer in 1981 prior to merger with another scheme. They did not hold another trustee meeting before the date of trial in 1985. The trust deed provided that it 'may be terminated at any time by the Company, and upon such termination . . . the Trust Fund shall be paid out by the trustees as directed by the Company', subject to the prohibition on repayments to the employers. The Court held that the employer's act of amalgamating the pension schemes effectively terminated the scheme in accordance with the provision of the trust deed. The Court could not breathe fresh life into a trust already killed or terminated by the employer. The money had to be repaid by the employer, and distributed to the beneficiaries.

[11.1.13]

Icarus v Driscoll (High Court) [1990] PLR 1

Winding-up – surplus – interpretation – exercise of employer's discretionary power – insolvency

Facts and Decision

A surplus arose on the winding-up of a pension scheme (which had been triggered by the employer's insolvency) that had been for many years non-contributory. The employer was the trustee, and the liquidator applied to Court for guidance as to how to use the discretion, vested in the employer/trustee under the scheme rules, to allocate surplus. The Court held that the employer was only bound to act in a responsible manner. That required it firstly to reach a decision to exercise its discretion, secondly to ascertain the relevant facts to allow it to exercise the discretion, and thirdly to make its decision in good faith. It was not necessary to look at each individual member; it was sufficient to take a more general view of the membership by categories. If the liquidator decided not to exercise the discretion in favour of any category of members, the surplus would be used to satisfy the claims of the creditors. It would not be improper to take into account that the principal employer

367

was in liquidation and that there were creditors, and for the liquidator to decide that no augmentation of benefits should be made.

[11.1.14]

Independent Pension Trustee v Stevens (High Court, unreported, 13 November 2000)

Winding-up – interpretation – surplus – exercise of trustees' discretionary power

Facts and Decision

A final salary pension scheme went into winding-up with a surplus on the insolvency of its employer. The winding-up rule provided for any residual surplus at the absolute discretion of the trustees either to be:

(a)   applied to provide benefits for such one or more of the persons who were entitled or prospectively entitled, in such manner and on such terms and conditions as the trustees should in their absolute discretion decide; or
(b)   paid to the employer.

The Court held that it was fairly obvious that what one would want to achieve with a surplus was reasonable flexibility for the trustees, and it would be odd if they were faced with an all-or-nothing choice. Applying the principles set down in *Investors Compensation Scheme Ltd v West Bromwich Building Society [1998] 1 All ER 98*, the Court concluded that the trustees were within their powers applying surplus partly for the members and partly for the employer. The trustees proposed to pay the employer a fixed sum with notional interest from the date that they had taken their decision, and apply the balance for the beneficiaries, and sought the Court's sanction for doing this. What the trustees proposed was, the Court held, within their powers (although the decision was necessarily open to review until the decision was implemented), but the review that had taken place had been one-sided. The trustees had considered only the effect on the insolvency practitioners of not receiving the capital sum which the trustees would have paid to them if they had implemented the decision immediately. They had not considered the present capital value of the scheme, which was less than at the time when the trustees made their decision. The trustees should also consider this, before finalising their decision.

[11.1.15]

James Miller Holdings v Graham (Supreme Court, Victoria) [1992] PLR 165

Winding-up – interpretation – power of amendment

Facts and Decision

James Miller Holdings operated a pension scheme for its employees, of which it was also the trustee. The pension scheme was invested in a managed fund policy. The employer went into receivership on 8 December 1976. The receivers immediately determined that the employer would cease making contributions to the scheme. If the employer gave the three months' notice required to trigger the winding-up of the scheme, employees who had already retired by that date would get their pension in full, while those who had yet to retire would get only an equitable apportionment of what was left in the account after all other members had received their entitlement in full. The receivers, therefore, purported to close the scheme retrospectively by deed of amendment, and returned the deed to the insurers under cover of a letter dated 4 January 1977 which confirmed that the company had ceased to make contributions to the scheme. The Court held that the proviso to the power of amendment prevented the amendment being made. The letter of 4 January 1977, however, took effect as notice of discontinuance, and so the scheme went into discontinuance on 4 April 1977 on the expiry of three months from that date.

[11.1.16]

Jones v Williams (High Court) [1989] PLR 17

Winding-up – surplus – resulting trust

Facts and Decision

The sponsoring employer of a pension scheme transferred its business to a partnership in 1966. As a result, the scheme went into winding-up, although this was unappreciated at the time. The employer in 1968 entered into a deed transferring its rights and powers under the scheme to the partnership. The partnership contributed to the pension scheme on behalf of its employees, and four new employees were allowed to join as members. The partnership assigned its business to another company in 1974, but no deed was entered into transferring the obligations relating to the pension scheme. The new company went into liquidation in 1981. After the benefits had been secured, there remained a surplus of £45,000. The power of amendment contained a restriction that no amendment should permit the payment or transfer to the company of any part of the fund. Rule 16 stated that 'no person shall have any claim, right or interest to or in respect of the fund except under and in accordance with the provision of the rules'. The rule setting out members' entitlements provided a measure of, and limit to, the members' entitlements. This was strengthened by Rule 16. The Court held that members could not participate in the surplus. *Haig v Lord Advocate 1976 SLT (Notes) 16* was considered. There was a resulting trust in favour of the original sponsoring employer: this had not been ousted by the 1968 deed, which was void since it proceeded from a fundamental misapprehension. The difference between an ongoing scheme and one which was liable to be wound-up was close to that between existent and non-existent goods. *Bell v Lever Bros [1932] AC 161* was distinguished.

[11.1.17]

Kemble v Hicks (No. 2) (High Court) [1999] OPLR 1 at 3B–4G, 4H–5F

Winding-up – insurance

Principles

Costs of winding-up insurance cover cannot be described as expenses of the administration and of the determination of a pension scheme, and so were not authorised for payment from scheme assets under a clause authorising payment of such expenses. Nor were such costs authorised in this case under the *Trustee Act 1925, s 57(1)*, since they were not authorised by the trust deed and were exclusively for the trustees' benefit.

[11.1.18]

Law Debenture v Pensions Ombudsman (High Court) [1997] OPLR 31 at 43B–E

Winding-up – transfers out

Principle

Under the *Social Security Pensions Act 1975, Schedule 1A, para 15(3)(c)* (now *s 99(4)(a)* of the *Pension Schemes Act 1993*), a member loses the right to any cash equivalent if a pension scheme is wound up. That provision referred to the completion of the winding-up process, and the right to a member's cash equivalent survives the start of a scheme's winding-up: the Court's observation in *Miller v Stapleton [1996] OPLR 73* was followed.

Mettoy Pension Trustees v Evans (High Court) [1991] 2 All ER 513, [1990] 1 WLR 1587, [1990] PLR 9

Winding-up – surplus – exercise of employer's discretionary power – insolvency

Facts and Decision

A pension scheme went into winding-up with a surplus, owing to the insolvent liquidation of the employer. The power to distribute surplus on a winding-up was vested in the employer alone. However, there was doubt as to whether the winding-up rule in its current form had been validly introduced by amendment. The trustees applied to Court to ascertain whether among other things the rules had been properly executed and if so:

- what the employer's duties were in exercising this power;
- whether the liquidator could exercise such a power; and if not
- who should exercise the power.

On the facts, the Court held that the trustees had not considered all the relevant considerations when introducing the relevant amendments. However, since the Court found that the employer was obliged to exercise the power to distribute surplus in accordance with full fiduciary duties, if the trustees had considered all the relevant considerations, they would have agreed to the change as drafted. Because the liquidator owed separate fiduciary duties to the creditors, he was under a conflict of duties and could not exercise the power. Instead, the Court would hear evidence on the subject and exercise the power itself.

The Court also held that the winding-up of a scheme which is triggered on the principal company 'going into liquidation' starts from the date on which the company in fact goes into liquidation, and not the date on which the company is retrospectively deemed to have gone into liquidation.

Comment

This case is one of the canons of pension law. The decision contains many observations on the Court's approach to pensions matters which are now taken for granted. Perhaps of most general application, it held that the Court's approach to the construction of documents relating to a pension scheme should be practical and purposive, rather than detached and literal. This dictum has been applied by the courts over and over again, though inevitably courts may differ as to the extent to which practicality and purposiveness can be taken.

Also, although this case is concerned with the distribution of assets on a winding-up, it established a wider principle about the way in which trustees exercise their powers. The decision applied a positive version of what has become known as the rule in *Hastings-Bass*. In *Re Hastings-Bass [1974] 2 All ER 193*, the Court stated that where a trustee is given a discretion as to some matter under which he acts in good faith, the Court should not interfere with his action, notwithstanding that it does not have the full effect which he intended, unless:

(a)   what he has achieved is unauthorised by the power conferred upon him; or
(b)   it is clear that he would not have acted as he did had he not:
    (i)   taken into account considerations which he should not have taken into account; or
    (ii)   failed to take into account considerations which he ought to have taken into account.

Mettoy Pension Trustees v Evans applied the test in its positive converse, and was willing to interfere if it found that the trustees would have acted differently if they had considered all relevant considerations.

One aspect of this decision is out of step with more recent case law developments. The Court held that the employer's sole power to distribute surplus on a winding-up was a full fiduciary power. Simultaneously, in *Icarus v Driscoll [1990] PLR 1*, the Court held that the same power in a different scheme was subject only to a requirement that the employer exercised it responsibly. At the time, *Mettoy Pension Trustees v Evans* looked the more rigorously argued decision, but with the development over the last decade of the concept of the employer's implied duty of good faith to its employees, the approach of *Mettoy* now looks out of line. If the point comes up for decision by the courts again, it is likely that it will be overturned.

[11.1.20]

Miller v Stapleton (High Court) [1996] OPLR 73 at 84C, [1996] PLR 67

Winding-up – transfers out

Principles

Where a pension scheme member has been offered a guarantee on his transfer value, it was a difficult question whether it was overridden by *s 129* of the *Pension Schemes Act 1993*, which provides that the statutory right to a cash equivalent does not override any provision of a scheme to the extent that it conflicts with priorities on a winding-up. It was not easy to see how the mere fact that a cash equivalent had been fixed under the *Pension Schemes Act 1993* could give that beneficiary a higher priority, if in the event the figure proved to be more than was justified by the funding of the scheme and the priority rules.

[11.1.21]

Municipal Mutual Insurance v Harrop (High Court) [1998] PLR 149 at paras 54–55

Winding-up – power of amendment

Principle

The power of amendment may be exercised during a period of notice the expiry of which will result in a winding-up event.

[11.1.22]

Providence Capitol Trustees v Ayres (High Court) [1996] 4 All ER 760, [1996] OPLR 215, [1996] PLR 395

Winding-up – interpretation – exoneration clause – insolvency

Facts and Decision

Mr Ayres, a member of a small self-administered scheme complained that:

(a)   the trustees' actions had resulted in his pension being paid on a money purchase basis at a lower rate than a previously-agreed defined benefit basis;

(b)   scheme property should not have been sold at the value for which it was in fact sold; and

(c)   loans which had been made to the sponsoring employer should not have been made.

The trustees had the benefit of an exoneration clause. The Pensions Ombudsman dismissed the last complaint, but upheld the first two complaints. The Court held that no finding had been made such as would invalidate the exoneration clause, and so the criticism of the sale of the property could not stand. On a proper construction, Mr Ayres had the benefit of a final salary promise for which any shortfall in the scheme was to be funded by the employer. However, the employer was now insolvent, and there was no evidence that any attempt to enforce the obligation on the company before it became insolvent would have been productive. The trustees did not have access to other members' entitlements for funding Mr Ayres's pension. The trustees' appeal was therefore upheld.

[11.1.23]

Rees v Dominion Insurance Co. of Australia (Supreme Court of New South Wales, 7 September 1981) 6 ACLR 71

Winding-up – interpretation, surplus – resulting trust

Facts and Decision

The Dominion Insurance Co. of Australia wound up voluntarily on 12 December 1979, by which time all employees had left its service. The company operated a defined benefits pension scheme, which was in surplus. The winding-up rule provided that:

(a) 'the scheme shall be terminated at any time if a resolution be passed for the winding-up of the employer otherwise for the purpose of reconstruction or amalgamation'; and

(b) 'upon such termination, the trustees shall distribute among the members any assets not then standing to the credit of any particular member'.

The rules also provided that no moneies 'shall revert or become the property of the employer'. All but one employee had received a refund of contributions before 12 December 1979, and the final employee received a refund in March 1980. 'Member' was defined under the rules as an employee of the employer. The Court held that since none of the former employees had been employees on 12 December 1979, none of them had a claim on the surplus. The rules excluded the possibility of a resulting trust. Accordingly, the surplus passed to the Crown as *bona vacantia*.

[11.1.24]

Re Reevie and Montreal Trust Co of Canada (Ontario Court of Appeal, 20 February 1986) 25 DLR 312

Winding-up – interpretation

Facts and Decision

Canada Dry set up a defined benefit pension scheme in 1955. The company was sold in 1982, and the scheme was then merged with another scheme. No current employees remained in the scheme, and the employer unsuccessfully sought a refund of surplus after securing the other benefits. In order not to lose out on receiving any benefit from the surplus, the employer then argued that the scheme had not been discontinued. The Court observed that after the sale:

(a) Canada Dry had no employees;

(b) there were no further contributions to be paid by either the employer or the employees;

(c) the accumulated pension obligations were to be paid out in one form or another; and

(d) the employer sought to recover the surplus.

The scheme had, therefore, discontinued.

[11.1.25]

Reichhold v Wong (Superior Court of Justice, Ontario) [2000] PLR 277

Winding-up – surplus – transfers out

Facts and Decision

The employer and members of a pension scheme entered into an agreement to wind up the scheme, and share the surplus between them. Application was made for court approval, but a representative of former members who had transferred to another pension scheme several years previously, following a sale of business, applied for the Court to determine whether such members had an interest in the surplus. The Court held that since the assets and liabilities in respect of such members had been validly transferred, they had no present benefit under the scheme, and the employer's duties and obligations ended with the completed transfer. There was no legal basis for a finding that a pension scheme administrator continued to owe a duty for the future to former members, where all the assets and liabilities relating to those persons had been transferred properly and legally. The plans for distribution were, therefore, approved.

[11.1.26]

Sulpetro Limited Retirement Plan Fund Trustee v Sulpetro (Alberta Court of Appeal) 66 DLR (4th) 120

Winding-up – power of amendment – surplus

Facts and Decision

A pension scheme contained a restriction on the power of amendment, preventing any amendment which 'shall vest in any Employer . . . any right, title or interest in the Trust Fund'. The termination clause in the original trust deed provided that termination would not vest in the employer any right, title or interest in the fund. A subsequent deed provided that the scheme was exclusively for the benefit of the participating employees and their beneficiaries, with no right of reversion to the employer. The employer purported to amend the termination clause to provide for any surplus to be refunded to the employer. The scheme was then merged with two other pension schemes into one scheme, which then wound up. The Court held that the amendment to the original scheme was contrary to law. Surplus from that scheme was vested in its employees as a class. The termination clause of the merged scheme provided that the undistributed assets 'shall be paid to the employer if permitted by law and if not shall be used to provide additional benefits for members and beneficiaries as determined by the employer'. The repayment was only ineffective as against surplus derived from the original scheme, and repayment could be made so far as it was derived from the other merged schemes.

[11.1.27]

Thrells v Lomas (High Court) [1993] I WLR 456, [1993] 2 All ER 546, [1992] OPLR 21, [1992] PLR 233

Winding-up – power of amendment – surplus – exercise of trustees' discretionary power

Facts and Decision

Thrells Limited went into insolvent liquidation in 1984. Its pension scheme entered winding-up as a consequence, the company being the sole trustee. The scheme was in surplus, and the liquidator surrendered the company's discretion to the Court, it having proved impossible to find anyone willing to accept appointment as trustee in the place of the company. The power of amendment was expressed in open-ended terms with a prohibition on amendments which would impinge on accrued benefits, but the winding-up rule set out precisely how the benefits secured should be dealt with. The Court held that it was unthinkable that the power of amendment was intended to enable the employer to interfere with the operation of the winding-up rule, once it had come into operation. The winding–up regime included the discretionary power to distribute surplus, which was therefore also not capable of amendment. *Section 11(3)* of the *Social Security Act 1990* prohibited payments to employers from scheme assets until all benefits had been secured, with increases in line with the retail prices index each year, limited to 5%. It was not possible first to secure benefits outside the scheme without providing for such increases, and then make a repayment to the employer. The requirements of *s 11(3)* applied in such circumstances to benefits as at the date the winding–up was triggered, and were of effect as at the date any payment was made. Accordingly, all scheme benefits must be given the increases set out under *s 11(3)* before any repayment could be made to the employer.

The Court also held that in exercising the discretion surrendered by the employer/trustee, the Court must act in the manner a reasonable trustee could be expected to act having regard to all the material circumstances. It must do what was just and equitable. The power to increase benefits was limited in this case to increasing the benefits of prospective pensioners. The purpose of the power was to enable the trustee in its discretion to increase prospective pensioners' pensions, to compensate for the fact that early leavers' pensions were geared to salary levels at a date which was earlier than the date at which the pensions would actually be paid (thus being subject to erosion by inflation). The scheme's surplus was derived in part from unnecessary overpayments made by the employer at a substantially higher rate than recommended by the actuary, higher investment returns than anticipated and the release of reserves held for members who in fact left before normal retirement age. Much of the surplus, though, could not be attributed to any source. The overfunding could be said in one sense to be at the expense of the employer. No evidence was before the Court about the financial needs of the prospective pensioners. The Court implemented the requirements of *s 11(3)* in full, making provision for the increases not to be franked against the increases on the Guaranteed Minimum Pensions, but ordered the balance to be returned to the employer.

[11.1.28]

UEB Industries v Brabant (Court of Appeal of New Zealand) [1991] PLR 109, [1992] 1 NZLR 294

Winding-up – power of amendment

Facts and Decision

In 1980, a pension scheme's winding-up rule had been amended to authorise a refund of any unexpended balance to the company (previously there had been a permanent alienation clause), and the validity of this amendment was successfully challenged. The company then argued that if the new restriction on the winding-up rule was invalid, the entire winding-up rule was bad and the purported winding-up was ineffective. However, the Court held that there was no evidence that the trustees had had such an all or nothing attitude when the restriction was introduced.

[11.1.29]

Wheeler v NBC Pension Trustee (Pensions Ombudsman) [1996] OPLR 337 at 355B–356A, [1997] PLR 1 at paras 86–90

Winding-up – employer contributions

Facts and Decision

A pension scheme's contribution rule required the employers to 'pay such periodical contributions to the Fund as the Trustee with the advice of the Actuary shall determine and agree with the Employers are, together with the members' contributions . . . and the assets for the time being of the Fund, appropriate to enable the fund to provide benefits'. The Pensions Ombudsman observed that the contribution rule and the winding-up rule could not be understood in isolation from each other. The benefits to be provided under the winding-up rule were the standard benefits except where amended by the winding-up rule. Since the trustee was under a duty to secure these benefits with an annuity, the company could not insist that the contribution rate be calculated on the basis that the scheme was ongoing, when it was not expected to be so, nor insist on a contribution rate which would make it unlikely that the trustee would be able to secure benefits on winding-up through the purchase of annuities.

[11.1.30]

Re William Makin (High Court) [1993] OPLR 171, [1992] PLR 177

Winding-up – surplus – exercise of trustees' discretionary power – insolvency – conflict of interest

Facts and Decision

William Makin & Sons Limited went into receivership in 1984 and liquidation in 1985. Its pension scheme had a substantial surplus deriving wholly from overfunding by the company, and went into winding-up on the company ceasing to carry on business. The employer was the trustee, and the trust deed gave the trustees a discretion to use any surplus on a winding-up to increase benefits to members. Any part of the surplus not so used was to be refunded to the employer. The liquidator sought directions whether it could exercise this power. The Court held that the power was a fiduciary power: *Icarus v Driscoll [1990] PLR 1* and *Mettoy Pension Trustees v Evans [1991] 2 All ER 513* were followed. If the power had become exercisable while the company was a going concern, the company could have exercised the power despite its conflict of interest. What the company could not have done would have been to have decided not to exercise the power, or to refrain from exercising the power with the consequence that the surplus or part of it would become payable to the company. The power was not capable of exercise by the liquidator, because of the liquidator's conflicting duties. The power was also not exercisable by the receivers, since the power was not an asset that was caught by the floating charge. The Court was doubtful whether it was appropriate for it to exercise the power itself, given the difficulty of weighing the competing claims of the creditors and the pensioners, and would have preferred to have appointed new trustees to carry out the role. However, in the interest of avoiding delay, the Court assumed this duty. Representative beneficiaries were obliged to prepare a scheme for distributing the surplus, and they were obliged to accept that they were excluded from any benefit under this scheme of arrangements.

Part 12 – Employment and Pensions

12 – Introduction

In the majority of pension schemes, the role of the employer is key. Consideration has been given to the legal aspects of the employer's powers and duties under the trust deed and rules in Part 2. However, the employer's relationship with the employee extends more widely than the terms of the pension scheme, and the employment relationship may have a dramatic impact on the member's pension rights.

Regardless of the terms of the pension scheme, if the employee is promised greater pension rights under his contract of employment, he will have a free-standing claim for pension. Equally, if he enters into a new contract under which he agrees to restructure his pension promise, then he will not be able to enforce the old pension promise even under the pension scheme if he has accepted a benefit in return for the restructuring. The law of contract may well radically alter the basis on which pension rights operate.

A key question which follows on from this is how the contract of employment should be interpreted so far as it relates to pension matters. There are no special principles for construing the pension terms of a contract, but there is likely to be more evidence of the factual matrix in which the pension terms were adopted in the terms of the employer's pension scheme and the scheme booklet than is common for other terms of the contract of employment.

Where the employee is claiming unfair dismissal, the employment tribunal only has jurisdiction to hear the claim if the employee was dismissed before he or she had attained normal retiring age within the meaning of *s 109* of the *Employment Rights Act 1996*. This definition has been regularly considered by the tribunals and courts. It is important to differentiate this statutory definition of normal retiring age, which is used only for this purpose, from the age under the pension scheme at which the member can take his or her normal retirement pension.

The influence of employment law in relation to pensions has been distorted by the impact of anti-discrimination legislation. By volume, discrimination cases comprise more than half of the employment law cases with pensions aspects. I have therefore made discrimination and pensions the subject of a separate part, although such issues in the main operate in an employment law context.

This part deals with the remaining employment issues which have direct pension implications, although it should not be forgotten that many other employment issues have an indirect impact. For example, I have not addressed at all the question of who is an employee, even though the question is often vital for establishing whether a person is eligible for pension scheme membership. A much fuller understanding of employment law is required for a complete appreciation of pensions issues than is covered by the scope of this book.

12.1 – Implications of employment relationship for pensions issues

[12.1.1]

Air Jamaica v Charlton (Privy Council) [1999] 1 WLR 1399, [1999] OPLR 11 at 20E, [1999] PLR 247 at para 46

Employer's duty of good faith

Principles

The employer's power to amend its pension scheme was subject to an obligation to exercise it in good faith: *Imperial Group Pension Trust v Imperial Tobacco Ltd [1991] 1 WLR 589* was approved. The employer was not entitled simply to disregard or override the interests of the members. Once it became likely that the scheme would be wound up, the employer would have to take this fact into account, and it was difficult to see how the scheme could lawfully be amended in any significant respect once it had actually been discontinued.

[12.1.2]

Baynham v Phillips Electronics (High Court) [1995] OPLR 253

Contract of employment – post-termination benefits

Facts and Decision

Phillips offered its group employees private medical insurance, such insurance to continue after retirement. The employees' contracts of employment contained a clause allowing the employer to vary the contract with the employee's consent, such consent not to be withheld unreasonably. In 1987, Phillips purported to reserve the right to withdraw cover. The Court held that pensioners who had retired before the purported variation had a contractual entitlement to private medical insurance that extended for life. The contractual right of variation was not apt to cover a right to vary rights which had accrued when the contract had come to an end, and did not survive that date. On the facts, the promise was sufficiently certain to be enforceable. Phillips could not, therefore, withdraw private medical insurance cover from pensioners who left service before 1987.

Dayco (Canada) v CAW-Canada (Canada Supreme Court, 6 May 1993) [1999] 42 PBLR 42

Collective agreement – post-termination benefits

Facts and Decision

An employer provided group insurance benefits to its employees under the terms of a collective agreement with the trade union. These benefits included life assurance for retirees. The collective agreement was terminated, and the employer notified all retirees that their life assurance benefits would be terminated the same day as the benefits for current employees were to cease. The union took the complaints of retirees to an arbitrator, who found jurisdiction to hear the complaint and found that retirees' rights could vest on retirement. The employer argued that the decision was wrong. The Court held that a promise to pay benefits to retired employees could, depending on the wording of that promise, survive the expiration of the collective agreement in which the promise was made.

Dorrell v May & Baker (High Court) [1991] PLR 31 at paras 47–60

Interpretation of scheme booklet – contract of employment

Facts and Decision

A pension scheme booklet stated that the rights and obligations of members were set out in the trust deed and rules, and that these were legal documents using terms which the average reader would find difficult to understand. It also emphasised that the booklet was for information only and must not be taken as in any way interpreting or modifying the trust deed and rules of the scheme. It gave instructions as to how they could be inspected. The Court held that the rules, therefore, were the right documents to consult. The booklet never formed part of the employment contract, nor was it in any way unfair. It gave a perfectly straightforward direction as to where the full contract terms could be found.

[12.1.5]

Fairport (No 3) (High Court) [1966] 2 Lloyd's Rep 253

Employee contributions – pensions as wages

Facts and Decision

Sailors were given judgment for their unpaid wages against a group of ship-owners, and claimed for them out of the proceeds of the sale of the ship on which they served. They claimed that these wages included contributions which were due to be made to a Greek pension scheme, but which had not been made. These contributions would normally be deducted from gross wages and paid to the scheme. Other creditors resisted this claim, which would give the sailors higher priority over the proceeds of the ship than them. Looking at the history of the scheme and the method of collection of contributions, the Court held that in fact and in law the contributions formed part of their wages.

[12.1.6]

The Halcyon Skies (High Court) [1977] 1QB 14, 20–26

Employee contributions – pensions as wages

Facts and Decision

Mr Powell was entitled under his contract of employment to be a member of the Merchant Navy Officers' Pension Fund, and to have his employer contribute on his behalf and deduct his contributions and pay them to the fund. His employer went into liquidation, with employer and employee contributions outstanding. The Halcyon Skies, a tanker owned by Mr Powell's employer, was sold, and Mr Powell sought to recover the contributions from the proceeds of sale. The employer had deducted Mr Powell's contributions, but had not paid them across. The Court held that Mr Powell was therefore entitled to revoke the instruction to pay them across and have the contributions repaid to him instead. Employers' as well as employees' pension contributions were recoverable by a seaman as wages if unpaid. There was no implied term that if the contributions were not paid to the pension scheme they would be paid to the employee. The fact that the scheme would probably pay an *ex gratia* pension was irrelevant to the assessment of damages: *Parry v Cleaver [1970] AC 1* was applied.

Employers' contributions to pension schemes, as well as employees' contributions, could properly be regarded as part of an employee's total wages in the broad sense of the word. The contributions were therefore the subject of a maritime lien in the employee's favour.

[12.1.7]

Hillsdown v Pensions Ombudsman (High Court) [1997] 1 All ER 862, [1996] OPLR 291 at 315F–317C, 318A-F, [1996] PLR 427 at paras 91–97, 101–102

Implied obligation of good faith

Principles

The implied obligation of trust and confidence prevents employers from using a power to suspend or determine their liability to contribute to a pension scheme while at the same time using the power to adhere further employers for the purpose of running down a surplus certified to have arisen in relation to the service of the employees of other employers. The employer was in breach of its implied obligation of good faith if it sought to enter into negotiations with the trustee when the trustee needed to consider the matter alone. It was also a breach of its duty of good faith for it to induce the trustee to act in breach of trust by committing a fraud on a power.

[12.1.8]

Imperial Group Pension Trust v Imperial Tobacco (High Court) [1991] 1 WLR 589, [1991] ICR 524, [1991] IRLR 66, [1991] 2 All ER 597, [1990] PLR 263

Implied obligation of good faith

Principles

In every contract of employment there is an implied term that the employers will not without reasonable and proper cause conduct themselves in a manner calculated or likely to destroy or seriously damage the relationship of confidence and trust between employer and employee. That obligation applies as much to the exercise of the employee's rights and powers under a pension scheme as they do to the other rights and powers of an employer. The scheme's trust deed and rules themselves are to be taken as being impliedly subject to this duty, and the members can enforce this right in trust law as well as contract. The employer must exercise its rights with a view to the efficient running of the scheme as a whole, and not for the purpose of forcing the members to give up their accrued rights in the existing fund for rights in a new scheme.

[12.1.9]

International Power v Healy (House of Lords) [2001] PLR 121 at para 16

Implied obligation of good faith

Principles

The submission that the employer, as regards its pension scheme, must bear in mind that the whole of the funding may be said to be either their [i.e. the employee's] contributions or payment for their services, would lead to the conclusion that the employer cannot act in its own interests, but the implied term of mutual trust and confidence does not go so far. Once it is accepted that the employer can act in its own interests, and that the extent to which it has done so in any given case cannot be criticised, the way in which the surplus was funded is not relevant.

[12.1.10]

Lloyds Bank Pension Trust Corporation Limited v Lloyds Bank PLC (High Court) [1996] OPLR 181 at 187E-H, [1996] PLR 263 at paras 28–30

Employment relationship – interpretation of scheme rules

Principles

For the purposes of interpreting a power of amendment, considerations of the employment relationship did not justify approaching the interpretation on the basis that it was likely to have been intended to confer a wide power of amendment. The purpose of the rule was to convey a message as to the nature of the amending power, and the message meant what it said, no more, no less: 'the issue is as to what that is.'

[12.1.11]

Malik & Mahmud v BCCI (House of Lords) [1998] AC 20, [1997] IRLR 462

Implied obligation of good faith

Principles

The emergence of the implied mutual obligation between an employer and an employee of trust and confidence was a sound development in law. It was a useful tool, now well established in law. The conduct of the employer did not need to be targeted at the employees for a breach to occur. The motives of the employer cannot be determinative or even relevant in judging employees' claims for breach of the implied obligation. If conduct objectively considered is likely to cause serious damage to the relationship between the employer and the employee, a breach of the implied obligation may arise. The employee need not be aware of the conduct while he or she was an employee. A breach arises only when there is no reasonable and proper cause for the employers' conduct, and then only if the conduct is calculated to destroy or *seriously* damage the relationship of trust and confidence.

[12.1.12]

McDonald v Horn (Court of Appeal) [1994] OPLR 281, [1994] PLR 155

Employer's contributions

Principle

Even in a non-contributory scheme, the employer's payments are not bounty. They are part of the consideration for the services of the employee.

[12.1.13]

McLennan v Standard Life (Sheriff's Court, Scotland, 28 September 1998) [2000] 24 PBLR 18

Termination of contract of employment

Facts and Decision

Mr McLennan was the managing director of his employer. He was employed under a contract under which each party was required to give not less than twelve months' notice. He wrote to one of his fellow directors on 9 March 1994 stating that he wished to tender his resignation from 1 April 1994, but he would be prepared to work out his notice period if necessary. No further communication between the employer and Mr McLennan took place. Mr McLennan died on 14 April 1994. His widow sued for the death in service benefits payable under the pension scheme. The Court held that it was conceivable that there was an intention to terminate the contract early, but there was no consensus as to the terms of any variation of contract. If so, this would leave the existing contract subsisting at the date of the deceased's death. The widow's case could therefore proceed.

[12.1.14]

Mihlenstedt v Barclays Bank (Court of Appeal) [1989] PLR 91, [1989] Ch 91, [1989] IRLR 522

Implied obligation of good faith

Facts and Decision

It was, the Court observed, an implied term of an employment contract that the employer will discharge its functions in good faith. In this case, this meant that Barclays Bank would properly consider Ms Mihlenstedt's claim. The Court held that the Bank had asked itself the right questions, and that it had formed an opinion which it could tenably hold. Accordingly, it had fulfilled that duty.

[12.1.15]

Parry v Cleaver (House of Lords) [1970] AC 1

Pensions as wages

Principle

The products of the sums paid into a pension fund are in fact delayed remuneration for an employee's current work. That is why pensions are regarded as earned income.

[12.1.16]

Petch v Customs & Excise (Court of Appeal) [1993] ICR 789

Contract of employment – duty of care – communications with trustees

Facts and Decision

Mr Petch had a mental breakdown and had to leave employment as a civil servant. He sought payment of injury benefit under the pension scheme. The Treasury, who had responsibility for assessing eligibility, wrote to the DHSS seeking certain information in relation to Mr Petch. The Treasury sent copies of those letters to Customs & Excise, his former employers, thereby seeking their views on the same question. Mr Petch argued that Customs & Excise's replies were negligent. The Court held that there was no distinction in principle between giving a reference in relation to an ex-employee to an employer from whom the ex-employee is seeking a job, and giving answers to queries about the ex-employee's work record put to the employer by the pension scheme trustees from whom the ex-employee was seeking a financial benefit. There was no duty of care owed by Customs & Excise to Mr Petch: the Court of Appeal decision in *Spring v Guardian Assurance Plc [1993] ICR 412* was followed. [N.B. The Court of Appeal decision in *Spring v Guardian Assurance* was subsequently overturned by the House of Lords in *Spring v Guardian Assurance [1994] IRLR 460, [1995] 1 AC 1*, and therefore presumably such a duty of care does in fact exist in these circumstances.] On the facts of this case, the duty of care had not been breached and Mr Petch in any case had suffered no loss.

[12.1.17]

Scally v Southern Health and Social Services Board (House of Lords) [1992] 1 AC 294, [1991] PLR 195

Implied terms in contract of employment – communication with employees

Principle

A term of the contract of employment made available to the employee a valuable right contingent upon action being taken by him to avail himself of its benefit, and the employee could not in all the circumstances reasonably be expected to be aware of the term unless it was drawn to his attention. The Court implied an obligation on the employer to take reasonable steps to bring the term of the contract to the employee's attention, so that he might be in a position to enjoy its benefit.

[12.1.18]

Sita GB v Burton (Employment Appeal Tribunal) [1998] ICR 17

Implied obligation of good faith

Principle

The implied obligation of trust and confidence could only be breached by reason of the actions of third parties in the rarest cases, even as a matter of principle.

[12.1.19]

South West Trains v Wightman (High Court) [1997] OPLR 249 266D–268G, 268H–270E, [1998] PLR 113 at paras 81–92, 94–102

Collective agreement – implied terms in contract of employment – implied obligation of good faith

Principles

The Court held that an agreement between a trade union and an employer as to pension rights would be validly incorporated into an individual employee's contract of employment if the contract of employment contained a clause stating that it was subject to terms and conditions settled under agreed collective bargaining procedures. The renegotiated basis for fixing levels of pension and pensions contribution was just as apt as the renegotiated basis for the payment of salary to be agreed in collective bargaining, so as to bind the employer and the employee contractually on an individual basis. In this case, the clause referring to the contract being subject to terms agreed under collective bargaining procedures went on to state that in the event of a conflict between the contract of employment and the trade union agreement, the contract of employment would prevail. This statement had to be read as referring to trade union agreements at the date of the employment contract.

Where pension terms and conditions were agreed with the employees which were inconsistent with the terms of the pension scheme, it was implicit in the agreement that the employees would not claim pension at a higher rate than that agreed and that the employer could obtain an injunction preventing the employees from claiming a higher pension if the employees tried to do so. There was a powerful case for saying that the employer would be under an obligation to restrain these employees if they tried to claim a higher pension, out of its implied duty of good faith owed to other employees.

[12.1.20]

Spooner v British Telecommunications (High Court) [2000] PLR 65 at paras 117–123

Implied terms in contract of employment

Facts and Decision

Where employees had taken voluntary early redundancy on terms which provided inferior pension benefits to those to which they were entitled on a proper construction under the pension scheme rules, the Court held that there was no implied term in the employees' contracts of employment preventing them from enforcing their pension rights: *South West Trains v Wightman [1997] OPLR 249* was distinguished. The offers of redundancy were made on the basis that what was being offered was something better than the employee would receive if he were made compulsorily redundant. The notion that by accepting the terms of the voluntary redundancy scheme an employee could somehow find himself worse off in terms of his pension benefit entitlement was completely inconsistent with that concept.

[12.1.21]

University of Nottingham v Eyett (High Court) [1999] I WLR 594, [1999] OPLR 55, [1998] PLR 27

Implied obligation of good faith – employer communications – implied terms in contract of employment

Facts and Decision

An employee took early retirement in accordance with his scheme entitlement. His employer did not draw to his attention that if he had waited another month, his pensionable salary would have included his most recent pay rise, and so his pension would have been higher. The member would have been aware that if he had not retired, he would have received another month's pensionable service and another month's salary, but had still elected to retire. The employer did not know that the employee was making a decision under the influence of any mistake. The Court held that it was not a breach of the employer's implied obligation of good faith for the employer to fail to warn an employee who was proposing to exercise important rights in connection with his contract of employment that the way in which he was proposing to exercise them might not be financially the most advantageous way in the particular circumstances. However, the principle underlying the employer's implied obligation of good faith did not exclude the possibility of that obligation having positive as opposed to negative content in appropriate circumstances. *Scally v Southern Health and Social Services Board [1992] 1 AC 294* was applied where the employees had no knowledge of the existence of a valuable right and had no means of knowing of its existence unless told by their employers. In this case, a careful reader of the scheme booklet would have been able to deduce from it the consequences of choosing a particular retirement date, so *Scally* had no application here.

Comment

This case confirmed the limited duties to communicate owed by employers to employees about their pension rights. Where all relevant information was available to the employee to work out how different choices would affect his or her pension rights, the employer has fulfilled its duties. The employer is under no further obligation to assist the employee in understanding these rights. There is a limited exception set out in *Scally v Southern Health and Social Services Board [1992] 1 AC 294*: where employees have no way of knowing about their contractual pension rights, employers have a duty to bring them to the attention of their employees. However, in most circumstances, this exception is irrelevant.

University of Nottingham v Eyett also decided that no breach of the employer's implied obligation of good faith was committed merely by failing to inform the member of the effect of timing on taking his or her entitlement. It was noted that the decided cases in which breach of the implied term had been established had all involved deliberate conduct by the employer, and the terms in which the duty had been expressed had consistently been in the negative form of prohibiting conduct calculated or likely to produce destructive or damaging consequences, rather than positively enjoining conduct which will avoid such consequences. In fact, *South West Trains v Wightman [1997] OPLR 249* was partly founded on the possibility that it would be a breach of the employer's implied obligation of good faith if it failed to stop some of its employees from trying to claim both existing pension rights and pay increases. That case remains exceptional in finding that there may be a positive duty in certain circumstances to take particular steps, which arises out of the implied obligation of good faith on employers.

Interestingly, the courts take a similar view of the duties of trustees and administrators, although those duties arise from very different principles of law. *NHS Pensions v Beechinor [1997] OPLR 99* held that administrators do not owe a duty of care to members to advise or warn of the consequences of any action. *NGN Staff Pension Plan Trustees v Simmons [1994] OPLR 1* went further, suggesting that trustees could be in breach of trust in some circumstances in volunteering information to beneficiaries.

[12.1.22]

Westport (No 4) (High Court) [1968] 2 Lloyd's Rep 559

Employee contributions – pensions as wages

Facts and Decision

The master of a Greek ship claimed against the proceeds of the sale of the ship for compensation for various expenses, including for contributions which he had deducted to be made to a Greek pension scheme, for which he had personal liability. He was given compensation by the Court for those contributions, out of the proceeds of sale.

12.2 – Pension aspects of the contract of employment

[12.2.1]

Engineering Training Authority v Pensions Ombudsman (High Court) [1996] OPLR 167 at 175B-E, [1996] PLR 409 at paras 38–39

Interpretation of employment contract

Facts and Decision

The Court held that the construction of a letter setting out redundancy pension terms depends upon what a reasonable person receiving that letter would have thought that the writer was saying. However, the reasonable person must be assumed to be reading the letter against the background as known to the parties. *Roscoe v Barclays Bank* (unreported) was considered.

[12.2.2]

North Warwickshire College v Cooke (Employment Appeal Tribunal, unreported, 23 April 1997)

Termination of employment contract

Facts and Decision

Mr Cooke fell ill and went on sick leave from October 1994. In early 1995 it was agreed that he would go on ill-health pension from the Teachers' Superannuation Scheme. He applied to retire on this basis from 31 August 1995 with the support of his employer, and eventually went onto pension on 21 November 1995. His entitlement to sick pay expired on 31 October 1995, but the employer granted an additional month's sick pay, taking him to 30 November 1995. Mr Cooke claimed that he had been wrongfully dismissed. This was, the Tribunal observed, a plain case on the facts: Mr Cooke had opted of his own free will to apply for ill-health retirement, subject to obtaining his pension benefits. There was no unilateral termination of the contract by the employer. Mr Cooke wanted to leave employment and his employer agreed to that course. The case fell squarely within the concept of consensual termination: *Birch v University of Liverpool [1985] ICR 470, [1985] IRLR 165* was applied. There had therefore been no dismissal.

[12.2.3]

Richmond v Borough of Broxbourne (Employment Appeal Tribunal, unreported, 16 June 1997)

Termination of employment contract

Facts and Decision

Mrs Richmond took voluntary redundancy from her employer, which had a discretion to enhance her pension. It indicated that it would do so, but failed to carry this out. Mrs Richmond alleged breach of contract. The Court held that on the facts Mrs Richmond had an enforceable legal right. Where an employer gave an indication to an employee which she was entitled to rely upon, it was unlikely in principle as a matter of law that an employer would be entitled to renege on that indication.

[12.2.4]

Roscoe v Barclays Bank plc (Court of Appeal, unreported, 21 October 1994)

Interpretation of employment contract

Facts and Decision

Mr Roscoe joined Barclays Bank in 1965 from Martin Bank. During the course of negotiations, he asked what effect his service with Martin's would have upon his entitlement to a pension at Barclays. His negotiator made enquiries, and wrote to Mr Roscoe to tell him that:

> 'Since my letter of yesterday, I have heard from my Head Office to the effect that your years of service with Martin's Bank will in fact qualify for pension with Barclays. The only limitation is that you will have to do 10 years' service with us before you qualify for any pension.'

Mr Roscoe already knew details of the benefit structure of the Barclays pension scheme. In 1973, Barclays introduced an amendment which gave employees the right to retire at any age between 60 and 65. Mr Roscoe assumed that if he chose that option he would be entitled to treat the whole of his years of service with Martin's Bank as qualifying service. Barclays advised him that credited pensionable service would only be taken into account to the same extent as it would have been if he had actually worked until age 65. The Court held that the words of the letter had to be read in their ordinary and natural sense. The words could not be anything other than a statement about the Barclays scheme. Mr Roscoe was entitled to assume that there was an implied undertaking on the part of Barclays that the scheme would not be varied so as to prejudice such rights as it then gave him. He was not entitled to assume that any novel benefits which the scheme introduced by way of future amendment would necessarily treat his years of service with Martin's Bank in exactly the same way as years of service with Barclays.

[12.2.5]

Rutherford v Radio Rentals (Court of Session, Scotland) [1992] OPLR 65

Interpretation of employment contract

Facts and Decision

Mr Rutherford was dismissed on medical grounds caused, he alleged, by an accident on work business. His staff handbook, which formed part of his contract of employment, set out details of personal accident cover for all employees in respect of any accident that might occur to any employee whilst engaged on the business of the company. When no payment was made on this basis, Mr Rutherford brought an action for breach of contract against his employer. Although the action was more properly for payment for a sum due than for a breach of contract, the Court allowed the action to proceed to full trial. Any dispute over the terms of the insurance policy were for the employer and insurer to resolve. Any dispute over the terms of the contract of employment would need to be resolved after sight of both the full insurance policy and the full contract of employment.

[12.2.6]

St John of God (Care Services) Ltd v Brooks (Employment Appeal Tribunal) [1992] IRLR 546

Unfair dismissal – changing terms and conditions of employment

Facts and Decision

Mr Brooks and three other employees were dismissed because they refused to accept altered terms and conditions of employment. The altered terms reduced holidays, abolished overtime rates for Saturday, weekend and bank holiday work, and a generous sick pay scheme was replaced by statutory sick pay only. Additionally, the Whitley Council provisions as to salary were no longer to apply. The employer had proposed these changes on the ground that they were necessary if the hospital was not to close as a result of cuts in its NHS financing. The employees claimed unfair dismissal. The Industrial Tribunal found that the employer had shown some other substantial reason for dismissal, namely the need to rearrange terms and conditions of employees' contracts. The Tribunal identified the crucial question as whether the terms offered were those which a reasonable employer could offer, and concluded that they were not. The employer appealed. The Appeal Tribunal observed that there was a danger in promoting the nature of the offer made by the employer of new terms and conditions to the status of a sole or crucial test. It was in principle wrong to exclude from consideration everything that happened between the time when the offer was made and the employee was dismissed. It was a potentially significant fact that a very large percentage of employees did accept the offer. It was entirely possible that the employer's legitimate interests and the employee's legitimate interests were irreconcilable. If there was a sound good business reason for the particular reorganisation, the unreasonableness or reasonableness of the employer's conduct had to be looked at in the context of that reorganisation. To look at the offer as the crucial question was to blur that aspect of the matter. Since the Employment Appeal Tribunal was not satisfied that the only result was that the dismissals were fair, the matter was remitted to the same Tribunal for reconsideration.

12.3 – Establishing normal retiring age

[12.3.1]

Age Concern Scotland v Hines (Employment Appeal Tribunal) [1983] IRLR 477

Establishing normal retiring age – unfair dismissal

Facts and Decision

Ms Hines had no contractual retiring age in her contract of employment. A practice had developed of women employees retiring at 60 and men employees at 65, but some were retained beyond those ages. There was no evidence of any normal retiring age before 1981. In February 1981, the employer approved new conditions of employment setting out a contractual retiring age of 60 for women and 65 for men, but providing that 'exceptionally employment may be continued beyond the normal retirement age by special arrangement with the chairman's committee', and that men could opt to retire at 60. Ms Hines was given permission to stay until age 65 in early 1982, but was subsequently dismissed a year later. She claimed unfair dismissal. The question arose what her normal retiring age was for the purpose of determining whether the Industrial Tribunal had jurisdiction to hear the claim. If she had accepted the employer's terms, her contractual retirement age was 60 and there had been no time for a practice to develop establishing a different normal retiring age: *Waite v Government Communications Headquarters [1983] IRLR 341* was applied. If she had not accepted the new terms, the statutory normal retiring age applied, which at the date of the decision was 60 for women. She was therefore dismissed above her normal retiring age and the Tribunal had no jurisdiction to hear her claim.

Barber v Thames Television plc (Court of Appeal) [1992] OPLR 141

Establishing normal retiring age – unfair dismissal

Facts and Decision

In the 1970s, Thames Television had many groups of employees on varying contractual retirement ages, and unequal retirement ages for men and women. In 1978 it equalised retirement ages for men and women within each group of employees, and prepared a scheme for the progressive reduction of retirement ages for all those whose retirement age was over 60. For the year 1988–89, the contractual retirement age was 64 for all employees in Mr Barber's category of employment, senior supervisors, whose retirement age was not 60 before 1 November 1988. Mr Barber reached 64 in early 1989 and was compulsorily retired. He claimed that he had been unfairly dismissed, and the question arose what his normal retiring age was for the purpose of determining whether the Industrial Tribunal had jurisdiction to hear the claim. The Industrial Tribunal concluded that employees in his group had a retiring age of 64, and that accordingly it had no jurisdiction to hear Mr Barber's complaint. Senior supervisors who were taken into employment before 1978 could constitute a group for the purpose of establishing normal retiring age for the purposes of *s 64(1)(b)* of the *Employment Protection (Consolidation) Act 1978*. The Tribunal had substantial grounds for concluding that they in fact formed such a group and their finding was upheld.

[12.3.3]

Bratko v Beloit Walmsley Ltd (Employment Appeal Tribunal) [1995] IRLR 630

Establishing normal retiring age – unfair dismissal

Facts and Decision

Mr Bratko was employed until his 64th birthday, when he was dismissed. His normal retirement age was 65 when he started work, but after unsuccessful negotiations between the employers and the unions, the employers wrote unilaterally to reduce his retirement age to 64. Mr Bratko claimed that he had been unfairly dismissed. The Industrial Tribunal held that his employers had conceded that the contractual retirement age was 65, but that the normal retiring age was 64, and therefore the Tribunal had no jurisdiction to hear Mr Bratko's complaint. Mr Bratko appealed. The Appeal Tribunal held that it was not possible to have a lower normal retiring age than contractual retirement age: dicta in *Brooks v British Telecommunications [1992] PLR 45* were preferred over dicta in *Barber v Thames Television plc [1992] OPLR 141*. Since the employers had not in fact conceded that the contractual retirement age was 65, the matter was remitted to a newly constituted tribunal for rehearing.

[12.3.4]

Brooks v British Telecommunications (Court of Appeal) [1992] PLR 45

Establishing normal retiring age – unfair dismissal

Facts and Decision

British Telecommunications operated a policy under which an employee could be compulsorily retired at 60, but there were circumstances in which the employee might be retained in employment thereafter if he or she were fit, efficient and there was a business need for his or her retention. In 1986 BT issued an announcement which reaffirmed that the normal retiring age for all employees was 60, and that retention beyond age 60 would become increasingly unlikely in the future. Some employees claimed that for the purposes of *s 64(1)(b)* of the *Employment Protection (Consolidation) Act 1978* the contractual retiring age was regularly departed from in practice, and since it had not been superseded by a definite higher age the statutory alternative of age 65 applied. The Court held that the test was what at the effective date of termination of the applicants' employment, and on the basis of the facts then known, was the age at which employees of all age groups in the applicants' position could reasonably regard as the normal age of retirement applicable to that group. *Hughes v DHSS [1985] IRLR 263* was distinguished. BT were implementing their announced policy, and to hold otherwise would be to confuse 'usual' with 'normal', and policy with variations in application caused by special reasons such as a temporary shortage of employees with a particular skill, or a temporary glut of work.

[12.3.5]

Highlands & Islands Development Board v MacGillivray (Scotland, Court of Session) [1986] IRLR 210

Establishing normal retiring age – unfair dismissal

Facts and Decision

Mr MacGillivray joined the Highland & Island Development Board's employment in 1966, when he was told orally that the normal retiring age was 65 and that this was a condition of service. In 1974, the Board proposed a change to age 60, and canvassed the opinions of employees. 13 out of 35 who responded, including Mr MacGillivray, opposed the change. The Board in April 1975 proposed a change, and put a note on Mr MacGillivray's file (and 6 out of the 7 other employees aged 45 or over who had objected to the change in 1974) that his employment would be reviewed when he reached age 60. Unless there were special reasons to the contrary, he would be given the opportunity to continue in employment subject to physical fitness and efficiency. In 1981 the policy on normal retiring age was changed, so that staff would be normally retired at age 60 except in exceptional circumstances. Mr MacGillivray was compulsorily retired in October 1983 shortly after his 60th birthday. He claimed unfair dismissal, arguing that the appropriate group for assessing his normal retiring age was the group of employees in service before April 1975. The Court held that the group in question should consist of those holding the same position as the claimant, and once that had been identified, it was not necessary to know anything more of them. Accordingly, the relevant group was the group in his position of employment in October 1983, his normal retiring age was 60, and accordingly the Industrial Tribunal had no jurisdiction: *Hughes v DHSS [1985] IRLR 263* was applied.

[12.3.6]

Hughes v DHSS (House of Lords) [1985] IRLR 263, [1984] ICR 557

Establishing normal retiring age – unfair dismissal

Facts and Decision

When Mr Hughes entered service in the civil service from local government in 1948, he did so on the basis that he could be retired at any time after reaching the age of 60. Established service could not normally be prolonged after age 65, though employment in a temporary capacity could be permitted after that age. In view of the manpower shortage at that time, staff who joined the civil service from local government were allowed to continue for the present in an established capacity until age 65 if they wished, provided that they were fully fit and efficient in their grade. In 1981 the DHSS issued a circular setting out a new practice for retirement for those in Mr Hughes's grade, so that those who were age 61 or over on 31 March 1982 would have to retire on that date, those who reached age 61 between 1 April 1982 and 31 March 1983 would have to retire on their birthday. After 31 March 1983 officers would retire on their 60th birthday. Mr Hughes was forced to retire on 31 March 1982, being just over age 61 on that date. He complained that he had been unfairly dismissed. The question arose what Mr Hughes's normal retiring age was for the purpose of *s 64(1)(b)* of the *Employment Protection (Consolidation) Act 1978*, since if he was at or over his normal retiring age when dismissed the Tribunal had no jurisdiction for hearing claims for unfair dismissal. The test laid down in *Waite v Government Communications Headquarters [1983] IRLR 341* for assessing an employee's normal retiring age was considered. The Court held that the concept of a 'group' was a short way of referring to employees holding a similar position to the claimant, taking into account his status as an employee, the nature of his work, his terms and conidtions of employment and nothing more. Mr Hughes's contractual retiring age was 60, but his head of department had a discretion to postpone that date. Where a particular category of employees was permitted as a matter of administrative policy to remain in employment to some higher age, the employees in that category had a reasonable expectation that the higher age had replaced age 60 as the normal retiring age. However, this remained the case only so long as no change in the administrative policy had been notified to the employees. Since the change in administrative policy pre-dated Mr Hughes's enforced retirement, his normal retiring age had changed to 61. Accordingly, the Tribunal had no jurisdiction to hear his complaint of unfair dismissal.

[12.3.7]

Post Office v Otomewo (Employment Appeal Tribunal, unreported, 12 May 1997)

Establishing normal retiring age – unfair dismissal

Facts and Decision

Mr Otomewo alleged that he had been unfairly dismissed. He was aged over 60. His contractual retiring age was 60, but over 60% of workers in his group applied to be retained beyond age 60, and without exception those who so wished were retained. The Industrial Tribunal found as a fact that the presumption that the contractual retiring age was the normal retiring age had been rebutted, and that Mr Otomewo's claim could be heard in accordance with *s 109* of the *Employment Rights Act 1996* since he was not yet 65. The Appeal Tribunal held that the contractual retiring age did not conclusively fix the normal retiring age. Where there was a contractual retiring age applicable to all or nearly all the employees, there was a presumption that the contractual retiring age was the normal retiring age for the group. The test was an objective one and statistics alone could not be conclusive. The finding of fact was not perverse, and *Brooks v British Telecommunications [1992] PLR 45* did not require the Tribunal to fix his normal retiring age at 60. The Tribunal's decision was therefore upheld.

[12.3.8]

Site Services v Sandieson (Employment Appeal Tribunal) [1993] OPLR 63

Establishing normal retiring age – unfair dismissal

Facts and Decision

Mrs Sandieson was employed until her 60th birthday, when she was given the option of retiring or transferring to another location. She refused both options and her employment was terminated. She claimed that she had been unfairly dismissed and discriminated against on the grounds of sex. Her contract of employment was silent as to retiring age, but her pension was due to mature on her 60th birthday. Her position was unique and there were no other employees engaged in a similar position. The Appeal Tribunal held that there was no contractual retiring age, and no material from which the Industrial Tribunal could infer a normal retiring age. It had therefore correctly applied the alternative statutory retiring age of 65. Mrs Sandieson's claim was therefore within the Tribunal's jurisdiction.

[12.3.9]

Swaine v Health and Safety Executive (Employment Appeal Tribunal) [1986] IRLR 205

Establishing normal retiring age – unfair dismissal

Facts and Decision

Mr Swaine had a contractual retirement age of 60. However, for most of his working career, normal retiring age was 65. The Government changed its policy about retirement, and at an annual staff meeting in 1983 the employers notified employees that there was pressure all round for a retirement age of 60, but that district alkali inspectors might be allowed to stay to age 63. Mr Swaine was dismissed at age 63, and claimed unfair dismissal. The Tribunal found that the normal retiring age had been changed to some time between age 62 and 63. The Appeal Tribunal held that normal retiring age could only be one definite date, and in the absence of such a definite date, the statutory alternative of age 65 applied. Accordingly, the Tribunal had jurisdiction to hear Mr Swaine's claim.

[12.3.10]

Waite v GCHQ (House of Lords) [1983] IRLR 341, [1983] 2 AC 714

Establishing normal retiring age – unfair dismissal

Facts and Decision

Lieutenant Colonel Waite had a contractual retirement age of 60. The Court held that the contractual retiring age does not conclusively fix normal retiring age for the purposes of *s 64(1)(b)* of the *Employment Protection (Consolidation) Act 1978*. Where there was a contractual retiring age applicable to all, or nearly all, of the employees holding the position which the employee in question held, there was a presumption that the contractual retiring age was the normal retiring age for the group. But it was a presumption which could be rebutted by evidence that there was in practice some higher age at which employees holding the position were regularly retired and which they had reasonably come to regard as their normal retiring age. The expression 'normal retiring age' conveys the idea of an age at which employees in the group could reasonably expect to be compelled to retire, unless there was some special reason in a particular case for a different age to apply. 'Normal' in this context was not a mere synonym for 'usual'. The word 'usual' suggested a purely statistical approach by ascertaining the age at which the majority of employees actually retired, without regard to whether some of them might have been retained in office until a higher age for special reasons. The proper test was not merely statistical. It was to ascertain what would be the reasonable expectation or understanding of the employees holding that position at the relevant time. The contractual retirement age will *prima facie* be the 'normal', but it may be displaced by evidence that it was regularly departed from in practice. The evidence may show that it has been superseded by some definite higher age, and if so, that will have become the normal retiring age. Alternatively, it may have been abandoned, with employees retiring at a variety of higher ages. In that case there would be no normal retirement age, and the statutory alternative would apply. On the facts, there was no practice that employees were permitted to hold office after age 60, and accordingly, the normal retiring age was 60. *Nothman v Barnet London Borough Council [1979] IRLR 35* was disapproved.

12.4 – Transfer of undertakings

[12.4.1]

Adams v Lancashire CC and BET (Court of Appeal) [1997] ICR 834, [1997] IRLR 436, [1998] OPLR 119, [1997] PLR 145

Transfer of undertakings – pension rights

Facts and Decision

Until 1993 Lancashire County Council had its own school catering service, with 3000 employees, most of whom were part-time dinner ladies working for relatively low rates of pay. As such, they were entitled to join the Local Government Pension Scheme. In 1993, Lancashire County Council sold the service to BET, and on taking over the service BET did not offer future service pension benefits to the dinner ladies. A test case was brought by trade unions to establish whether this constituted a breach of either the *Transfer of Undertakings (Protection of Employment) Regulations 1981 (SI 1981 No 1794)* or the *Directive 77/187/EEC*, the *Acquired Rights Directive 1977* which the *Regulations* purported to implement. On a proper construction, the Court held that *Article 3* of the *Directive* did not require national governments to require employers to provide protection for future service pension benefits. The *Regulations* imposed no such requirement on employers.

Comment

The problem at the heart of this case is a simple one, but it still remains the subject of controversy. Under European law (implemented in the United Kingdom under the *Transfer of Undertakings (Protection of Employment) Regulations 1981 (SI 1981 No 1794)*), employers who buy a business from another employer must replicate the terms and conditions of the employees' contracts of employment. There is special provision in relation to pension benefits, but there is controversy as to whether this constitutes a complete exemption so far as future service benefits are concerned. This decision held that it did.

This decision was not the end of the story, however. There is an exception to the pensions exemption in relation to rights under an occupational pension scheme which do not concern old age, invalidity or survivors' benefits. This exception is currently being considered, with the European Court of Justice due to determine shortly in *Beckmann v Dynamco Whicheloe MacFarlane* whether rights to redundancy pensions transfer on the sale of a business. Meanwhile, the present Government has been considering over many years how to improve the operation of the *1981 Regulations*. Further changes in the law can be expected soon.

[12.4.2]

Beckmann v Dynamco Whicheloe MacFarlane (High Court) [2000] PLR 269

Transfer of undertakings – pension rights

Facts and Decision

A quantity surveyor employed by the North West Regional Health Authority in the NHS was transferred under the *Transfer of Undertakings (Protection of Employment) Regulations 1981 (SI 1981 No 1794)* to a private contractor, and was made redundant two years later. She claimed that her right to a redundancy pension under the NHS Superannuation Scheme transferred to her contract with her new employer. The Court held that although the decision in *Frankling v BPS Public Sector [1999] IRLR 212* was clear, there were contrary arguments involving European Community law. The case raised fundamental questions on the construction of *Directive 77/187/EEC*, the *Acquired Rights Directive* and *Regulations 5* and *7* of the *Transfer of Undertakings (Protection of Employment) Regulations 1981*. The case was therefore referred to the European Court of Justice.

[12.4.3]

Eidesund v Stavanger Catering (EFTA Court of Justice) [1996] IRLR 684

Transfer of undertakings – pension rights

Facts and Decision

Mr Eidesund was entitled to have his employer pay certain pension insurance premiums to an insurance scheme under a collective agreement. His employer sold his business, and his new employer, Stavanger Catering, refused to pay the premiums. Mr Eidesund brought a claim to enforce the obligations, and the Norwegian Court requested an advisory opinion from the EFTA Court of Justice on the interpretation of *Article 3* of *Directive 77/187/EEC*, the *Acquired Rights Directive* (Norway being bound by its provisions by virtue of the EEA Agreement). The Court held that all rights and obligations pertaining to old-age, invalidity and survivors' benefits had been excluded from the general transfer of rights and obligations to the transferee employer by *Article 3(3)* of the *Directive*. The provision was interpreted as exempting the transferee employer from all involvement in this specific area, and it was not obliged to provide for further accruals of rights to old-age, invalidity or survivors' benefits after the date of transfer. Accordingly, it was not under an obligation to continue payment of pension premiums in accordance with the pension scheme established by the original employer.

[12.4.4]

Frankling v BPS Public Sector (Employment Appeal Tribunal) *[1999] IRLR 212, [1999] OPLR 295*

Transfer of undertakings – pension rights

Facts and Decision

The Eastbourne NHS Trust contracted out its payroll department to BPS in 1996. BPS moved the payroll function to Glasgow and made staff redundant. The NHS Superannuation Scheme would have offered redundancy pensions, but BPS did not. The redundant staff claimed that the right to redundancy pensions transferred under the *Transfer of Undertakings (Protection of Employment) Regulations 1981 (SI 1981 No 1794)* and *Directive 77/187/ EEC*, the *Acquired Rights Directive*, as benefits not relating to old age, invalidity or survivors. The Appeal Tribunal held that provisions of a scheme did not cease to relate to old age merely because the employee had taken early retirement. Accordingly, although the provisions had been triggered by redundancy, the benefits retained their character as retirement benefits. There was nothing inconsistent between this interpretation of the *Regulations* and *Article 3(3)* of the *Directive*.

[12.4.5]

Perry v Intec (Industrial Tribunal) [1993] IRLR 56, [1993] OPLR 1

Transfer of undertakings – pension rights

Facts and Decision

Mr Perry was employed by Cheltenham YMCA, which provided him with pension scheme benefits. His employment was transferred under the *Transfer of Undertakings (Protection of Employment) Regulations 1981 (SI 1981*

No 1794) to Intec, which did not offer a pension scheme. He applied for a declaration that his contract of employment included rights to pension provision. On a proper construction, the Tribunal held that *Reg 7* of the *Transfer of Undertakings (Protection of Employment) Regulations 1981* was inconsistent with *Article 3(3)* of *Directive 77/187*, the *Acquired Rights Directive.* Applying *Litster v Forth Dry Dock and Engineering [1989] IRLR 161*, the Tribunal reinterpreted the *Regulations* to transfer the obligation to provide Mr Perry with pension provision to Intec.

[12.4.6]

Warrener v Walden Engineering (Employment Appeal Tribunal) [1993] IRLR 420, [1993] ICR 967, [1993] OPLR 277, [1993] PLR 295

Transfer of undertakings – pension rights

Facts and Decision

Walden Engineering acquired the business of Richard Sizer in 1991. Mr Warrener's employment was transferred under the *Transfer of Undertakings (Protection of Employment) Regulations 1981 (SI 1981 No 1794)*. He was not provided with a replacement pension scheme, although he had previously been a member of Sizer's pension scheme. Mr Walden claimed that the failure to provide him with a pension scheme was a breach of the employer's obligations under the *Regulations*, as they should be interpreted in the light of *Directive 77/187/EEC*, the *Acquired Rights Directive.* The Appeal Tribunal observed that a contracted-out contributory scheme was a supplementary scheme outside the statutory social security schemes of member states, and so was not caught by the *Directive.* The effect of the *Directive* was not to catch such arrangements, and the wording of the *Regulations* was clear: *Perry v Intec [1993] IRLR 56* was disapproved.

12.5 – Trade union issues

[12.5.1]

Davies v Neath Port Talbot CBC (Employment Appeal Tribunal, unreported, 15 September 1999)

Trade unions – pension training courses

Facts and Decision

Mrs Davies was a part-time employee. She took time off to attend full-time union training courses, and claimed payment pursuant to *s 168* of the *Trade Union and Labour Relations (Consolidation) Act 1992*. She claimed that the time in lieu should be paid on the basis of a standard working week rather than her part-time working week. The Appeal Tribunal held that the training amounted to work within the meaning of *Article 119* (now *Article 141*) of the *Treaty of Rome*. Part-time workers were predominantly female, and she was entitled to equal pay for equal work. The wording of *s 169(2)* of the *Trade Unions and Labour Relations (Consolidation) Act 1992* was in conflict with *Article 119* (now *Article 141*), and Mrs Davies was entitled to full-time pay for her time on the course, as she had argued.

[12.5.2]

Dayco (Canada) v CAW-Canada (Canada Supreme Court, 6 May 1993) [1999] 42 PBLR 42

Trade unions – collective agreements – interpretation

Facts and Decision

An employer provided group insurance benefits to its employees under the terms of a collective agreement with the trade union. These benefits included life assurance for retirees. The collective agreement was terminated, and the employer notified all retirees that their life assurance benefits would be terminated the same day as the benefits for current employees were to cease. The union took the complaints of retirees to an arbitrator, who found jurisdiction to hear the complaint and found that the retirees' rights could vest on retirement. The employer argued that the decision was wrong and that the arbitrator had no jurisdiction. The Court held that the arbitrator had jurisdiction to hear the complaint. A promise to pay benefits to retired employees could, depending on the wording of that promise, survive the expiration of the collective agreement in which the promise was made. A collective agreement was rather like a contract for a fixed term. At the end of the term, the contract was said to 'expire' by mutual agreement. But the contract was not thereby rendered a nullity. It ceased to have prospective application, but the rights that had accrued under it continued to subsist. It would take very clear words to demonstrate that the parties intended to rescind their agreement by agreeing to enter into a successive agreement. The new collective agreement displaced the old one, which was no longer in force. But this was with respect to the current employment relationship, and said nothing about the previously accrued rights of the parties. Nothing differentiated the promise to pay retirement benefits from promises to pay regular wages or holiday pay. Retirement benefits may vest at the time of retiring under a collective agreement, and this is determined by the contractual agreement between the parties, not by subsequent bargaining between them. The following cases were considered: *Canadian Paperworkers Union v Pulp and Paper Industrial Relations Bureau [1977] 77 CLLC 16 109, Cominco Pensioners Union, Sub-local of United Steelworkers of America, Local 651 Cominco [1979] 2 Can LRBR 322, Re Coulter Manufacturing Ltd and United Automobile Workers, local 222 [1972] 1 LAC (2d).*

[12.5.3]

Povey & Stephens v Secretary of State for Environment (Court of Appeal) [1992] PLR 59

Trade unions – interpretation of scheme rules

Facts and Decision

The Trades Union Congress organised a day of support for the strike action by National Health Service workers by means of a token withdrawal of labour. NALGO did not instruct its members to withdraw their labour but advised them to do so for one day, 23 June 1982, and many local authority NALGO members did so. They then sought to exercise a right under the local government superannuation scheme to retain the day lost as reckonable service by the payment of an additional sum of money over the normal rate of contribution. The Secretary of State concluded that since the absence from duty was not in consequence of a trade dispute, they had no right to do this. On the facts, the Court held that one cause of the absence from duty was the existence of the trade dispute.

The NALGO members stayed away from work to show support for one side in the trade dispute. They therefore had the right to retain the day lost as reckonable service by payment of an additional sum of money.

[12.5.4]

South West Trains v Wightman (High Court) [1997] OPLR 249, [1998] PLR 113

Trade unions – collective agreements

Facts and Decision

An employer and trade union agreed that various elements of remuneration of train drivers would be consolidated into basic pay. These elements had previously been non-pensionable, and it was therefore agreed that the definition of pay for pensions purposes would be modified to restrict the pension effect of the consolidation of benefits. This change was not documented before s 67 of the *Pensions Act 1995* came into force. Some of the employees claimed the right to accrue pension at the higher rate set out in the terms of the rules. The Court held that specific provisions relating to the privatisation of the rail industry had not been breached, and s 67 of the *Pensions Act 1995* did not prevent the implementation of an agreement validly entered into before that *section* had come into effect. The agreement between the employers and the trade union had been validly incorporated into the employees' contracts, since those contracts contained a clause stating that the contracts would be modified by terms and conditions settled under agreed collective bargaining procedures. Pension issues were apt to be agreed in collective bargaining. It was implicit that the agreement could be enforced, to stop employees claiming pension at a higher rate.

[12.5.5]

STC Submarine Systems v Piper (Employment Appeal Tribunal) [1994] OPLR 13, [1993] PLR 185

Trade unions – pension training courses

Facts and Decision

Mr Piper was a trustee of his employer's pension scheme. He was also a shop steward. He was given paid time off for pursuing his trade union duties as required by s 27 of the *Employment Protection (Consolidation) Act 1978*, but not for pensions training organised by his trade union. He complained to an industrial tribunal. The Appeal Tribunal observed that there may be functions which are part and parcel of carrying out trade union offices which may not strictly fall within the word 'duties'. Mr Piper carried out such special responsibilities, which included reporting regularly to shop stewards on pensions matters, representing members and advising members on pensions issues. Mr Piper was therefore entitled to take paid time off for the pensions course.

[12.5.6]

Young v Carr Fasteners (Employment Appeal Tribunal) [1979] ICR 844

Trade unions – pension training courses

Facts and Decision

Ms Young was a shop steward. She went on a course approved by her union on 'Pensions and Participation' at Woodstock College. Her employers failed to pay her for the period during which she was absent on that course. She complained to an industrial tribunal, under s 57 of the *Employment Protection Act 1975*, on the ground that it was a period during which she said she had undergone training in an aspect of industrial relations relevant to the carrying out of her duties as an official concerned with industrial relations between her employers and their employees. The Appeal Tribunal observed that negotiations about pension rights, and advising members about pension rights, are as much a part of industrial relations as negotiating and advising about wage levels. It was not conclusive that the scheme was administered in such a way that no further employee could at the time be made a trustee, or that the scheme was substantially administered in accordance with the advice of the insurance company. Employees may need advice as to their participation in the pension scheme. Moreover, employees may well wish to consider making representations to the employers as to changes in the structure or administration of the scheme. These are matters which union officials may expect to consider and discuss on behalf of their members. Accordingly, instruction on member participation in pension schemes as covered by this course constituted training in aspects of industrial relations relevant to the carrying out of the duties of a trade union official. Ms Young was not precluded from making a claim by reason of the fact that at the date of the course she had not herself conducted such negotiations on behalf of any members. The case was remitted to an industrial tribunal for reconsideration if the employers still sought to argue that to attend this course was not in all the circumstances reasonable.

Part 13 – Discrimination and Pensions

13 – Introduction

The benefit design of pension schemes has been transformed by the law relating to sex discrimination. Until 1990, most long-standing schemes offered differential benefits to men and women, the most obvious of which was that men would usually have a later normal retirement age than women. This meant in practice that women's pension benefits were more valuable than men's.

Well before the decision in *Barber v GRE [1991] 1 WLR 72*, there had been straws in the wind that the benefits provided by pension schemes were not to be treated as being outside the employment relationship for the purposes of the European sex discrimination provisions. In *Worringham v Lloyds Bank [1981] ICR 558*, the European Court of Justice had treated employer contributions to pension schemes as pay for this purpose. In *Bilka-Kaufhaus GmbH v Weber von Hartz [1986] IRLR 317*, the European Court of Justice had treated access to pension schemes as pay for the purpose of the European sex discrimination provisions. Although the decision in *Barber v GRE* caused a sensation when it came out, hitting the front page headlines of the national newspapers, its conclusions had been speculated about in pensions circles well in advance of the decision itself.

The European Court of Justice was not blind to the financial consequences of its decision in *Barber v GRE*. It imposed a temporal limitation on the effect of its decision, so that only those bringing claims by that date could claim in respect of pension pre-dating the date of the *Barber* judgment, 17 May 1990. Unfortunately, the European Court of Justice expressed itself in imprecise terms, and the extent to which pension pre-dated 17 May 1990 itself became the subject of considerable litigation. The European Court of Justice eventually clarified its position in *Moroni v Collo GmbH [1993] OPLR 289* and *Ten Oever v Stichting Bedrijfspensioenfonds voor het Glazenwassers [1993] IRLR 601*, making it clear that claims after 17 May 1990 could only be brought in relation to benefits payable in respect of periods of employment subsequent to 17 May 1990. The Court also had to clarify what constituted a claim which pre-dated 17 May 1990 in *Dimossia Epicheirissi Ilektrismou v Evrenopoulos [1997] All ER (EC) 543*.

The temporal limitation imposed in the *Barber* decision was not unique or unprecedented. On 8 April 1976, the European Court of Justice decided in *Defrenne v Sabena (No. 2) [1976] ICR 547* that *Article 119* of the *Treaty of Rome* (now *Article 141*), which provided that men and women should receive equal pay for equal work, had direct effect in member states. Recognising that this decision was unexpected, and that it would have a disproportionate impact on the founder members of the EEC as opposed to those who joined later, the Court limited its retrospective effect to those who had started claims before 8 April 1976.

All of the pension cases referred to above were based on an extension of the application of *Article 119* (now *Article 141*) of the *Treaty of Rome*. The effect of the new temporal limitation imposed in the decision in *Barber v GRE* was to develop a distinction between those cases which the European Court of Justice determined were predictable from *Defrenne v Sabena (No. 2)*, where claims could be brought back to 8 April 1976, and those which the European Court of Justice determined fell within the terms of the *Barber* temporal limitation, where claims could be brought back only to 17 May 1990. The former included those pension cases such as *Bilka-Kaufhaus GmbH v Weber von Hartz [1986] IRLR 317*, *Vroege v NCIV Instituut [1995] All ER (EC) 193* and *Fisscher v Voorhuis Hengelo [1994] OPLR 297*, which concerned sex discrimination in relation to access to pension schemes. The latter included pension cases such as *Barber v GRE* itself and *Coloroll Pension Trustees v Russell [1995] All ER (EC) 23*, which concerned sex discrimination in relation to the benefits provided by pension schemes. Such a distinction is superficially attractive. However, it breaks down when the boundaries are explored, as cases such as *Magorrian v Eastern Health & Social Services Board [1997] OPLR 353* demonstrated. Further cases like *Quirk v Burton Hospitals NHS Trust 5 PBLR 8* can be expected. The distinction is probably too deeply embedded into European law to be abandoned now, but it makes no sense in logic.

So far, I have referred only to *Article 119* (now *Article 141*) of the *Treaty of Rome*. In fact, laws prohibiting discrimination in pensions come from a variety of sources. Under domestic law, the *Equal Pay Act 1970*, the *Sex Discrimination Act 1975* and the *Pensions Act 1995* all have anti-discrimination provisions relevant to pension schemes, not to mention various sets of regulations made under each of these Acts. In European law, *Directive 75/117/EC* (the 'Equal Pay Directive'), *Directive 76/207* (the 'Equal Treatment Directive') and *Directive 79/7* ('Equal Treatment in Social Security') all also have relevance in differing circumstances. There is separate domestic and European legislation about discrimination against race, disability, part-time workers and fixed-term workers, with more to follow. There is a bewildering array of legislation of which the practitioner must be aware before definitive advice can be given.

Nevertheless, some general principles apply to most anti-discrimination legislation. The first is perhaps obvious, but nevertheless has been overlooked on more than one occasion: there must be discrimination before a wrong can be put right under anti-discrimination legislation. *Stevenson v Lord Advocate* (unreported) is a good illustration of how the Court is unable to correct palpable unfairnesses unless it is demonstrated that the unfairness is discriminatory. *Barry v Midland Bank [1999] IRLR 581* notes the same point.

The second principle is the distinction between direct and indirect discrimination. Direct discrimination is discrimination on prohibited grounds, whether or not overtly stated. *James v Eastleigh BC [1990] 2 AC 751* shows how an apparently non-discriminatory term can in fact be directly discriminatory. Since the unequal state pension ages were a major contributory factor in many pension schemes choosing a normal retirement date of 65 for men and 60 for women, one could view the decision in *Barber v GRE* as the European Court of Justice concurring with the House of Lords on its analysis in that case. Under European law, direct sex discrimination is always unlawful and can never be justified. This seems reasonable, until the facts of *Roberts v Birds Eye Walls [1993] OPLR 203* arise for decision. In that case, the scheme provided sex-discriminatory benefits, but the discrimination exactly mirrored in reverse the sex discrimination of the state scheme in the basic state pension. The European Court of Justice dodged the issue by determining there was no discrimination since the overall result was neutral. However, it forgot its own argument when it came to decide *Bestuur van het Algemeen Burgerlijk Pensioenfonds v Beune [1995] OPLR 1*, where it came to the opposite conclusion on what was essentially the same question. As the High Court noted in *Marsh & Maclennan v Pensions Ombudsman [2001] PLR 51*, these cases are hard to reconcile.

The High Court in *Marsh & Maclennan v Pensions Ombudsman [2001] PLR 51* itself dodged a similar problem, but by more procedural means. Guaranteed minimum pensions, which are the contracted-out substitute benefits for the State Earnings Related Pension Scheme, are sex-discriminatory. Although the calculation of these is set down by statute, a contracted-out pension scheme is nevertheless providing sex-discriminatory benefits. The High Court evaded answering whether these benefits must be equalised by finding that the route which the case had taken to reach it was an improper use of jurisdiction. This problem will not go away, and most pension lawyers, if asked privately, believe that guaranteed minimum pensions must be equalised. It is amazing, and perhaps shocking, that 11 years after *Barber v GRE* so few schemes have taken the plunge to equalise them and that the point remains unresolved in the courts.

As well as direct discrimination, it is also possible to discriminate indirectly. This occurs when a condition is imposed in order to qualify for benefits which, although not directly discriminatory, makes it more difficult for a member of one group to comply with than a member of another group. Unlike direct discrimination, indirect discrimination can be lawful if the condition is objectively justifiable. Two questions arise from this: first, does the condition affect one group more than another? Secondly, is the condition objectively justifiable?

The first of these questions has received rather more judicial consideration than the second. It has not helped that the European Court of Justice has been rather unfortunate in its use of words in successive cases. However, *R v Secretary of State ex parte Seymour-Smith and Perez [1999] 2 AC 554* set out in detail the Court's considered guidance on how to determine whether indirect discrimination has taken place, and this decision, together with the House of Lords' application of the decision, should help employers and trustees in most cases to identify whether indirect discrimination has taken place.

Objective justification has not really been considered in the context of a private occupational pension scheme. *Megner v Innungskrankenkasse Vorderpfalz [1996] PLR 133* and *Nolte v Landesversicherungsanstalt Hannover [1996] PLR 125* show the European Court of Justice's views in relation to such justification in social security arrangements, and Lord Nicholls' comments in *Barry v Midland Bank [1999] IRLR 581* provide some guidance, but the case law in this area is still embryonic.

13.1 – Sex discrimination

General

[13.1.1]

Allonby v Accrington & Rossendale College (Court of Appeal) [2001] IRLR 364

Indirect sex discrimination – termination of employment – compatibility of statute with European law – testing for indirect discrimination

Facts and Decision

Ms Allonby was employed as a part-time lecturer at Accrington & Rossendale College on successive fixed-term contracts. Because she was in part-time employment, her service was not eligible for pension rights. In common with other part-time lecturers, Ms Allonby was made redundant, and offered the opportunity to provide lecturing services to the College through a contract with an agency company which was not controlled by the College. 55 out of 105 full-time College lecturers were male, but of the part-time College lecturers, 110 out of 341 were male. 18,050 out of 37,969 lecturers on the agency company's books were male. Ms Allonby claimed unfair dismissal and indirect sex discrimination. She argued that the College had acted with the motive of depriving her from membership of the Teachers' Superannuation Scheme. She had made out a case that it was a requirement or condition for continuous employment with the College that an employee must have previously been employed either on a full-time basis or under a contract which conferred proportionate benefits to a full-time contract. In determining the pool of men and women subject to the requirement or condition the Court held, snapshot figures were precisely what were needed to gauge the impact of the requirement for the purposes of identifying indirect sex discrimination. Where 21% of the women in the pool were capable of complying with the requirement or condition, and 38% of men in the pool were capable of complying, the Court was tempted to hold that the Employment Tribunal could not have failed to conclude that the difference was considerable. To find justifiability of indirect discrimination, the Employment Tribunal must weigh the justification against its discriminatory effect and must examine critically the employer's reasons for the dismissals, including the consideration of whether other lesser measures would have achieved the same effect. *Section 1(6)* of the *Equal Pay Act 1970* would prevent Ms Allonby from pursuing a claim that her pay should be at the same level as that of an employee of the College, and the Court therefore referred a question to the European Court of Justice asking whether *s 1(6)* of the *Equal Pay Act* was consistent with *Article 141* (formerly *119*) of the *Treaty of Rome*. It also referred a question to the European Court of Justice asking whether a male employment comparator was necessary where the administrators of the sector-wide occupational pension scheme from which she was excluded were a single discriminator.

[13.1.2]

Barber v GRE (European Court of Justice) [1990] ECR I–1889, [1990] IRLR 240, [1991] 1 WLR 72, [1990] PLR 95

Sex discriminatory pension scheme benefits – time limits

Facts and Decision

Mr Barber was a member of a non-contributory contracted-out occupational pension scheme. The normal pensionable age was 62 for men in Mr Barber's category of employment and 57 for women in Mr Barber's category of employment. Mr Barber was made redundant at age 52, and as a result his deferred pension was substantially less than it would have been had he been a woman. Moreover, if he had been a woman he would have been entitled to an immediate redundancy pension, but since he was a man he was not. The Court held that pension benefits under such a scheme were pay since they derived from the employment relationship. The obligation to provide equal benefits for equal work applied to each element of pay and not on a comprehensive assessment of the consideration paid to workers. *Article 119* (now *Article 141*) of the *Treaty of Rome* could be relied upon by applicants before national courts. Because of the serious difficulties which this judgment might create without temporal limitations having regard to the previous reasonable understanding of parties, *Article 119* could only be relied upon by workers in order to claim entitlement to pension with effect from the date of this judgment (17 May 1990), unless the claim had already been initiated by that date.

Comment

The principle decided in this case was very simple, but the complexities arising from this principle raise many difficulties, and are still being worked through now. As a result, this decision launched a flood of supplementary questions in subsequent cases. By the end of 1994, the European Court of Justice had issued roughly a dozen further judgments on the subject of equalising pension scheme benefits. It is doubtful whether it appreciated the degree of complexity and detailed legal argument which this decision would provoke.

More than half of this Part is devoted to the consequences of this decision, and the courts' clarification of its impact. The judgment in this case is not the place to look for answers to the detailed questions which pension scheme practitioners are likely to face on the subject of equalisation. The answers are more likely to be found in the supplementary cases, which forced the courts to consider in detail the limits of this decision. *Coloroll Pension Trustees v Russell [1995] All ER (EC) 23* is much more likely to give you a practical answer to any given problem than *Barber v GRE*.

And yet despite its abstract nature, this case is a milestone. It symbolises the fusion of employment law, pensions law and European law. It achieved banner headlines in the daily newspapers, and represented a breakthrough of pensions into the popular consciousness. It represented the bold establishment of a new principle that pension schemes should not provide sex–discriminatory pension benefits. For these reasons, this case is probably the most important pensions case ever.

[13.1.3]

Bavin v NHS Trust Pensions Agency (Employment Appeal Tribunal) [1999] OPLR 285

Discriminatory pension scheme benefits – transsexuals – marital status

Facts and Decision

Ms Bavin, who held a senior post in the NHS, enjoyed a long-term relationship with a female-to-male post-operative transsexual. She was a member of the NHS pension scheme, which provided benefits for widows and widowers. No benefits were payable to unmarried partners of scheme members. Since her partner could not marry her (remaining in the eyes of the law female), Ms Bavin brought a claim against the scheme alleging unlawful sex discrimination and a breach of *Article 119* (now *Article 141*) of the *Treaty of Rome* and *Directive 75/117/EC*, the *Equal Pay Directive*. The

Appeal Tribunal held that the scheme discriminated between members who were married and members who were not. The words 'widow' and 'widower' meant and could only mean the surviving spouse. It was not unlawful to deprive transsexuals of the right to get married, and it would be odd if Ms Bavin's partner had a valid claim against the scheme based upon his inability to get married. *P v S [1996] ECR I–2143* was distinguished.

[13.1.4]

Bilka-Kaufhaus GmbH v Weber von Hartz (European Court of Justice) [1986] IRLR 317, [1986] ECR 1607, [1987] ICR 110

Indirect sex discrimination – access to pension schemes – testing for indirect discrimination

Facts and Decision

Bilka-Kaufhaus employed both full-time and part-time employees. Part-time employees were eligible for pensions only if they had worked full time for at least 15 years over a total period of 20 years. Mrs Weber, who was a part-time employee who did not qualify for a pension, brought a claim alleging breach of *Article 119* (now *Article 141*) of the *Treaty of Rome*, on the basis that the requirement of a minimum period of full-time employment for the payment of an occupational pension placed women workers at a disadvantage, since they were more likely than their male colleagues to take part-time work so as to be able to care for their family and children. The Court held that since the scheme was not a social security scheme governed directly by statute, benefits paid to employees under the scheme constituted consideration received by the worker from the employer in respect of his or her employment, and the question of access to the scheme therefore fell within the scope of *Article 119*. Where the exclusion of part-time employees from an occupational pension scheme affected a far greater number of women than men, *Article 119* was infringed unless the employer could show that the exclusion was based on objectively justified factors unrelated to any discrimination on grounds of sex: *Jenkins v Kingsgate (Clothing Productions) [1981] IRLR 228* was followed.

Comment

It is interesting to note that the first of the European pensions cases concerned German pension arrangements. Almost without exception, the cases which followed concerned British or Dutch pension schemes. At the time this case came out, it represented a small but significant extension of the general principle that men and women should receive equal pay for equal work. The ten years since the European Court of Justice decision in *Defrenne v Sabena (No. 2) [1976] ICR 547* that *Article 119* (now *Article 141*) of the *Treaty of Rome* was directly enforceable had been marked by a gradual extension of the concept of 'pay' for the purpose of this principle. This case represented one more step along this road. In the aftermath of this case, far-sighted lawyers realised that the European Court of Justice might well not stop at insisting that men and women were given equal access to pension schemes, and might well insist that the benefits offered by the pension schemes were made equal also.

Apart from the general point of principle, the decision is also of interest for the Court's comments about indirect discrimination. The Court expressed the test for indirect discrimination in rather unfortunate terms, and the confusion this caused was not finally clarified until the decision in *R v Secretary of State ex parte Seymour-Smith and Perez [1999] 2 AC 554.*

As a result of the intense interest in the consequences of the decision in *Barber v GRE [1990] IRLR 240* and the consequent focus on how pension scheme benefits were to be equalised, some of the implications of the requirement to provide equal access to pension schemes for men and women remain unexplored. In *Coloroll Pension Trustees v Russell [1995] All ER (EC) 23*, the Court concluded that while trustees of employers' schemes are not party to the employment relationship, they are required to pay benefits which do not lose their character as pay, and that the direct effect of *Article 119* (now *Article 141*) could therefore be relied upon against trustees. It remains unclear whether this direct effect can be relied upon against trustees where the discrimination complained of is that the trustees had not paid benefits. In circumstances where no direct discrimination was identifiable and there was no reason for the trustees to suspect indirect discrimination, it would be extending the principle which the European Court of Justice used in the *Coloroll* case beyond responsibility for acting as the employer's agency into responsibility for not acting as the employer's agent.

[13.1.5]

Boyle v Equal Opportunities Commission (European Court of Justice) [1998] OPLR 289, [1999] PLR 103

Sex discriminatory pension scheme benefits – maternity leave

Facts and Decision

The Equal Opportunities Commission operated a non-contributory pension scheme. The scheme did not treat unpaid maternity leave as pensionable service. The Court held that the accrual of pension rights in the context of an occupational scheme constituted one of the rights connected with the employment contracts of workers for the purposes of *Article 11(2)* of *Directive 92/85* (*Council Directive on Community Law on Pregnancy and Maternity*), and could not therefore be made conditional upon the woman's receiving the pay provided for by her employment contract. *Article 119* (now *Article 141*) of the *Treaty of Rome* did not arise for consideration.

[13.1.6]

Coloroll Pension Trustees v Russell (European Court of Justice) [1995] All ER (EC) 23, [1994] ECR I–4389, [1994] IRLR 586, [1994] OPLR 179, [1994] PLR 211

Sex discriminatory pension scheme benefits – direct effect of European law – trustees' duties – employers' duties – equalising benefits – time limits – actuarial factors – additional voluntary contributions – single sex schemes

Facts and Decision

The Coloroll group of companies became insolvent, leaving various pension schemes to be wound up. Following the *Barber* decision, the trustee sought guidance as to how it should carry out its duties. The Court held that the principles laid down in the *Barber* judgment apply to both contracted-out and non-contracted-out schemes. The direct effect of *Article 119* (now *Article 141*) of the *Treaty of Rome* may be relied upon by both employees and dependants as against the trustees of an occupational pension scheme. Employers and trustees must use all the means available under domestic law to eliminate all discrimination in the matter of pay. Until equalisation has taken place, disadvantaged employees must be given the same benefits as advantaged employees, but Article 119 does not preclude equalisation for future service by reducing the advantages which the advantaged employees used to enjoy. The *Barber* judgment was limited in effect to benefits payable in respect of periods of service after 17 May 1990, unless the benefits were not linked to length of service, in which case the test was whether the operative event was before 17 May 1990. The national court is bound to ensure correct implementation of *Article 119*. Any problems arising from insufficiency of funds must be resolved on the basis of national law in the light of the principle of equal pay. The use of sex-specific actuarial factors does not fall within the scope of *Article 119*. In so far as an occupational pension scheme does no more than provide the membership with the necessary arrangements for management, additional benefits stemming from contributions paid by employees on a purely voluntary basis are not covered by *Article 119*.

The Court also held that *Article 119* is not applicable to pension schemes which have at all times had members of only one sex.

[13.1.7]

Defrenne v Sabena (No. 2) (European Court of Justice) [1976] ICR 547, [1976] ECR 455

Sex discrimination – direct effect of European law

Principles

The principle that men and women should receive equal pay, which is laid down by *Article 119* (now *Article 141*) of the *Treaty of Rome*, may be relied upon before the national courts. These courts have a duty to ensure the protection of the rights which that provision vests in the individuals. Except as regards those workers who had already brought legal proceedings or made an equivalent claim, the direct effect of *Article 119* cannot be relied on in order to support claims concerning pay periods prior to 8 April 1976, the date of this judgment.

[13.1.8]

Grant v South West Trains (European Court of Justice) [1999] PLR 69

Discriminatory benefits – same-sex couples – marital status

Facts and Decision

South West Trains offered concessionary fares to legal spouses of staff and common law spouses (subject to a statutory declaration being made that a meaningful relationship had existed for a period of two years or more), but not to same-sex partners. The Court held that it was not contrary to *Article 119* (now *Article 141*) of the *Treaty of Rome* or *Council Directive 75/117* (the *Equal Pay Directive*) to refuse to grant travel concessions to a person of the same sex as the worker with whom the worker had a stable relationship, where it would grant such concessions to a worker's spouse or to a person of the opposite sex with whom the worker had a stable relationship.

Marshall v Southampton and South-West Hampshire Area Health Authority (European Court of Justice) [1986] IRLR 140, [1986] ECR 723

Sex discriminatory normal retirement age – state pension age – direct effect of European law

Facts and Decision

A health authority had a policy that normal retirement age would be the age at which social security pensions became payable, i.e. 65 for men and 60 for women. Mrs Marshall was allowed to work until she was 62 by mutual agreement, but was then dismissed on the ground that she had passed the normal retirement age applied by the health authority to women. The Court held that *Article 5(1)* of *Directive 76/207* (the *Equal Treatment Directive*) meant that a general policy concerning dismissal of a woman solely because she had passed the qualifying age for a state pension, which age was different for men and for women under national legislation, constituted sex discrimination contrary to the *Directive*. *Article 5(1)* could be relied upon as against a state authority acting in its capacity as employer, in order to avoid the application of any national provision which did not conform to *Article 5(1)*.

[13.1.10]

Newstead v Department of Transport (European Court of Justice) [1988] IRLR 66

Sex discriminatory pension scheme obligations – statutory schemes

Facts and Decision

Mr Newstead was a civil servant in the Principal Civil Service Pension Scheme, a statutory scheme. His salary was subject to a compulsory deduction of 1.5% of gross salary to contribute to a fund for widows' pensions. Female civil servants were not obliged to contribute towards widowers' pensions. Mr Newstead argued that the obligation imposed on him was unlawfully sex discriminatory. The Court held that *Article 119* (now *Article 141*) of the *Treaty of Rome*, read together with *Equal Pay Directive 75/117*, did not prevent an employer from paying men and women the same salary but making a deduction for men only, even those who were unmarried, as a contribution to a widows' pension fund provided for under an occupational pension scheme which was a substitute for a statutory social security scheme. *Equal Pay Directive 76/207* also did not impose such an obligation.

[13.1.11]

P v S (European Court of Justice) [1996] ECR I–2143

Sex discrimination – transsexuals

Facts and Decision

P worked for Cornwall County Council and was born a man. He informed his employer that he was to undergo gender reassignment. After minor surgery, P was given three months' notice. The final operation took place after notice had been given but before it had expired. P then claimed she had suffered sex discrimination. The Court held that the scope of *Directive 76/207* (*Equal Treatment*) could not be confined simply to discrimination based on the fact that a person was of one or other sex. In view of its purpose and the nature of the rights which it sought to safeguard, the scope of the directive was also such as to apply to discrimination arising from the gender reassignment of the person concerned.

[13.1.12]

Worringham v Lloyds Bank (European Court of Justice) [1981] ECR 767, [1981] ICR 558

Employer contributions – pay

Principle

Contributions paid by an employer to a retirement benefits scheme, the Court held, are pay within the meaning of *Article 119* (now *Article 141*) of the *Treaty of Rome*.

Sex discrimination and normal retiring age

[13.1.13]

Bullock v Alice Ottley School (Court of Appeal) [1992] OPLR 199, [1992] PLR 125

Sex discrimination – normal retiring age

Facts and Decision

Alice Ottley School operated a normal retiring age for men of 65 and for women of 60. Mrs Bullock, who was a member of domestic staff, was allowed to work until she was 61 but was then compelled to retire. She was told that the school now had a common retirement age for members of staff doing the same job regardless of sex. She brought proceedings alleging sex discrimination. The school argued that it had changed its policy before Mrs Bullock's retirement and now operated a retirement age of 60 for all teaching, administrative and domestic staff, and 65 for all maintenance and ground staff. The Court held that there was no evidence that the change in policy was a sham. An employer could have a variety of retirement ages provided that in the system which it used there was no direct or indirect discrimination based on gender. In assessing direct discrimination, a tribunal must compare like with like, and it was apparent that the Tribunal in this case was satisfied that gardeners and maintenance men required quite different skills from those of Mrs Bullock and there were difficulties of recruitment justifying the later retiring age for gardeners and maintenance men. The group had not therefore been selected by gender. There was no indirect discrimination either. To justify a later retirement age which in fact though not by design consists wholly or largely of men, it was necessary for the employer to show a real and genuine need for this later retirement age. That need could be on economic grounds or on grounds of administrative efficiency, and possibly other grounds as well.

Melrose v Reigate Housing Society for the Elderly (Employment Appeal Tribunal, unreported, 7 July 1997)

Sex discrimination – normal retiring age

Facts and Decision

Mrs Melrose was employed as a matron at a retirement home. She had a contractual and normal retiring age of 60. A male handyman had a contractual and normal retiring age of 65. When Mrs Melrose was dismissed at age 60, she claimed that she had suffered sex discrimination. The Industrial Tribunal found as facts that had a male matron been employed, he would also have had a contractual and normal retiring age of 60, and that the handyman was not a true comparator. There were no grounds for disturbing these findings of fact.

Less favourable terms for one sex in a pension scheme

[13.1.15]

Barber v GRE (European Court of Justice) [1990] ECR I–1889, [1990] IRLR 240, [1991] I WLR 72, [1990] PLR 95

Sex discriminatory pension scheme benefits – direct effect of European law

Facts and Decision

Mr Barber was a member of a non-contributory contracted-out occupational pension scheme. The normal pensionable age was 62 for men in Mr Barber's category of employment and 57 for women in Mr Barber's category of employment. Mr Barber was made redundant at age 52. As a result, his deferred pension was substantially less than it would have been had he been a woman, and if he had been a woman he would have been entitled to a redundancy pension, but since he was a man he was not. He sued his employer for breach of the *Sex Discrimination Act 1975*. The Court held that pension benefits under such a scheme were pay since they derived from the employment relationship. The obligation to provide equal benefits for equal work applied to each element of pay, and not on a comprehensive assessment of the consideration paid to workers. *Article 119* (now *Article 141*) of the *Treaty of Rome* could be relied upon by applicants before national courts.

[13.1.16]

Clarke v Cray Precision Engineering (Industrial Tribunal) [1989] PLR 1

Sex discriminatory pension scheme benefits

Principle

Pension scheme benefits constitute pay for the purposes of *Article 119* (now *Article 141*) of the *Treaty of Rome*.

[13.1.17]

Coloroll Pension Trustees v Russell (European Court of Justice) [1995] All ER (EC) 23, [1994] ECR I–4389, [1994] IRLR 586, [1994] OPLR 179 at 216G–218A, [1994] PLR 211 at paras 26–36

Sex discriminatory pension scheme benefits – equalising benefits – interaction of trust law – national law and European law

Principles

Where national law prohibits employers and trustees from acting beyond the scope of their powers or in disregard of the provisions of a trust deed, they must use all the means available under domestic law, including recourse to the national courts, to eliminate all discrimination in the matter of pay. In the meantime, disadvantaged employees must be granted the same advantages previously enjoyed by the other employees. As regards subsequent service, *Article 119* (now *Article 141*) of the *Treaty of Rome* does not preclude equal treatment from being achieved by reducing the advantages which the advantaged employees used to enjoy.

Mitchell v Tameside MBC (Industrial Tribunal) [1992] OPLR 179, [1992] PLR 13

Sex discriminatory pension scheme benefits

Facts and Decision

Mrs Mitchell was employed by Manchester City Council and retired in 1982, drawing a pension from the Local Government Superannuation Scheme. She died on 10 October 1990. No pension was payable to her widower, though widow's pensions were payable on the death of a male pensioner. Survivors' pensions, the Tribunal held, fell within the definition of pay for the purposes of *Article 119* (now *Article 141*) of the *Treaty of Rome*.

[13.1.19]

Neath v Hugh Steeper (European Court of Justice) [1993] OPLR 329, [1994] PLR 1

Sex discrimination in pension scheme – actuarial factors in defined benefits schemes

Facts and Decision

A pension scheme member complained that the actuarial factors used for converting pension into lump sum or into transfer values were sex-discriminatory. The Court held that different actuarial factors may be used according to sex in a final salary contracted-out pension scheme, because the variability and inequality are due to the use of actuarial factors in the mechanism for funding the scheme. Inequality in employers' contributions paid under funded defined benefit schemes was therefore not a matter which European law required to be corrected. This conclusion extended to calculation factors for the lump sum commutation and the factors for transfer values.

[13.1.20]

Shell v Van den Akker (European Court of Justice) [1994] OPLR 345 at 352F–353H, [1994] PLR 211 at 229, paras 117–128

Sex discriminatory pension scheme benefits – equalising benefits

Principle

Article 119 (now *Article 141*) of the *Treaty of Rome* does not allow an occupational pension scheme, which sets a uniform retirement age for all its members, to maintain in favour of women as regards benefits payable in respect of periods of service completed after the entry into force of the new rule, a retirement age lower than that for men, even if such a difference is due to an election made by women before the judgment in *Barber v GRE [1990] ECR I–1889.*

[13.1.21]

Ten Oever v Stichting Bedrijfspensioenfonds voor het Glazenwassers (European Court of Justice) [1993] ECR I–4879, [1995] 2 CMLR 357, [1993] IRLR 601, [1993] OPLR 89, [1993] PLR 317

Sex discriminatory pension scheme benefits

Principles

Entitlement to a survivor's pension was a consideration deriving from the survivor's spouse's membership of the pension scheme, the pension being vested in the survivor and being paid to him or her by reason of the employment relationship between the employer and the survivor's spouse. A survivor's pension provided by an occupational pension scheme therefore falls within the scope of *Article 119* (now *Article 141*) of the *Treaty of Rome.*

Obligations to dependants of employees

[13.1.22]

Coloroll Pension Trustees v Russell (European Court of Justice) [1995] All ER (EC) 23, [1994] ECR I–4389, [1994] IRLR 586, [1994] OPLR 179 at 216A, [1994] PLR 211 at para 19

Sex discriminatory pension scheme benefits – survivors' benefits

Principles

The Court held that since the right to payment of a survivor's pension arises at the time of the death of the employee, the survivor is the only person who can assert it. If the survivor were to be denied this possibility, this would deprive *Article 119* (now *Article 141*) of the *Treaty of Rome* of all its effectiveness as far as survivors' pensions are concerned. They may therefore rely on *Article 119* against trustees and employers.

Exclusion of one sex from a pension scheme

[13.1.23]

Fisscher v Voorhuis Hengelo (European Court of Justice) [1994] OPLR 297, [1994] PLR 211 at 243

Direct sex discrimination – access to pension scheme

Facts and Decision

Married women were historically excluded from membership of a pension scheme. The Court held that the right to join an occupational pension scheme falls within the scope of *Article 119* (now *Article 141*) of the *Treaty of Rome* and is therefore covered by the prohibition of discrimination. *Bilka-Kaufhaus GmbH v Weber von Hartz [1986] IRLR 317* was followed.

[13.1.24]

Vroege v NCIV Instituut (European Court of Justice) [1995] All ER (EC) 193, [1994] ECR I–4541, [1994] IRLR 651, [1994] OPLR 335, [1994] PLR 211 at 232

Direct sex discrimination – access to pension scheme

Facts and Decision

Married women who worked less than 80% of the full working day were excluded from membership of a pension scheme. The Court held that the right to join an occupational pension scheme falls within the scope of *Article 119* (now *Article 141*) of the *Treaty of Rome* and is therefore covered by the prohibition of discrimination. *Bilka-Kaufhaus GmbH v Weber von Hartz [1986] IRLR 317* was followed.

Identifying discrimination

Direct discrimination

[13.1.25]

James v Eastleigh BC (House of Lords) [1990] 2 AC 751

State benefits – direct discrimination

Facts and Decision

Eastleigh Borough Council offered free leisure facilities to people who had reached State pension age, which at that date was 65 for men and 60 for women. Mr James brought proceedings alleging unlawful sex discrimination contrary to *s 29* of the *Sex Discrimination Act 1975*. The Court held that the criterion for free leisure facilities, State pensionable age, was itself a criterion which directly discriminated between men and women in that it treated women more favourably than men 'on the ground of their sex'. It followed inevitably that any other differential treatment of men and women which adopted the same criterion must equally involve discrimination 'on the ground of sex'. Mr James had therefore suffered unlawful sex discrimination.

Lander Carlisle v Highfield (Employment Appeal Tribunal, unreported, 19 October 2000)

Direct discrimination – role of Employment Appeal Tribunal

Principles

The Appeal Tribunal held that if an employment tribunal makes a finding of direct discrimination, a failure to find an actual or hypothetical comparator to the claimant fatally undermines its conclusion. The Tribunal must also consider whether as a matter of fact and law a suggested comparator was a correct comparator for the purpose of establishing direct discrimination. The Employment Appeal Tribunal can only make the decision itself if the Tribunal's decision was plainly and unarguably right or plainly and unarguably wrong. Where there were respectable arguments on the facts by each sides, the matter had to be remitted to an employment tribunal for rehearing.

P v S (European Court of Justice) [1996] ECR I–2143

Direct discrimination

Facts and Decision

P worked for Cornwall County Council and was born a man. He informed his employer that he was to undergo gender reassignment. After minor surgery, P was given three months' notice. The final operation took place after notice had been given but before it had expired. P then claimed she had suffered sex discrimination. The Court held that in view of its purpose and the nature of the rights which it sought to safeguard, the scope of *Directive 76/207 (Equal Treatment)* applied to discrimination arising from the gender reassignment of the person concerned.

Roberts v Birds Eye Walls (European Court of Justice) [1993] OPLR 203, [1993] PLR 323

Sex discriminatory pension scheme benefits – direct discrimination

Facts and Decision

Birds Eye Walls operated a pension scheme which between the ages of 60 and 65 paid a lower pension to women on early retirement pensions than to men, to take account of the State retirement pension which women received during that period and which men did not receive. The Court held that the principle of equal treatment presupposed that men and women to whom it applied were in identical situations. This was not so where the deferred payment was regarded as a supplement to the financial resources of the man or woman so concerned. The assessment of the amount of the bridging pension necessarily varied with the changes in the financial position of the man or woman over time. This was not direct discrimination contrary to *Article 119* (now *Article 141*) of the *Treaty of Rome*, because the mechanism for calculating the bridging pension was neutral.

[13.1.29]

Stella James v Barclays (Industrial Tribunal) [1989] PLR 35

Sex discriminatory pension scheme benefits – direct discrimination

Principle

It was direct discrimination where a female employee who had joined before a given date was compelled to retire at age 60, when a man in her grade who had joined before that given date would have had a contractual normal retiring date of 65.

Indirect discrimination

[13.1.30]

Allonby v Accrington & Rossendale College (Court of Appeal) [2001] IRLR 364

Discriminatory access to pension scheme – indirect sex discrimination – testing for indirect discrimination

Facts and Decision

Ms Allonby was employed as a part-time lecturer at Accrington & Rossendale College on successive fixed-term contracts. In common with other part-time lecturers, Ms Allonby was made redundant, and offered the opportunity to provide lecturing services to the College through a contract with an agency company which was not controlled by the College. 55 out of 105 full-time College lecturers were male, but of the part-time College lecturers, 110 out of 341 were male. 18,050 out of 37,969 lecturers on the agency company's books were male. Ms Allonby claimed unfair dismissal and indirect sex discrimination. She had made out a case that it was a requirement or condition for continuous employment with the college that an employee must have previously been employed either on a full-time basis or under a contract which conferred proportionate benefits to a full-time contract. In determining the pool of men and women subject to the requirement or condition, the Court held, snapshot figures were precisely what were required to gauge the impact of the requirement for the purposes of identifying indirect sex discrimination. Where 21% of the women in the pool were capable of complying with the requirement or condition, and 38% of men in the pool were capable of complying, the Court was tempted to hold that the Employment Tribunal could not have failed to conclude that the difference was considerable.

[13.1.31]

Bilka-Kaufhaus GmbH v Weber von Hartz (European Court of Justice) [1986] IRLR 317, [1986] ECR 1607, [1987] ICR 110

Discriminatory access to pension scheme – indirect sex discrimination – testing for indirect discrimination – objective justification

Facts and Decision

Bilka-Kaufhaus employed both full-time and part-time employees. Part-time employees were eligible for pensions only if they had worked full time for at least 15 years over a total period of 20 years. Mrs Weber, who was a part-time employee who did not qualify for a pension, brought a claim alleging breach of *Article 119* (now *Article 141*) of the *Treaty of Rome*, on the basis that the requirement of a minimum period of full-time employment for the payment of an occupational pension placed women workers at a disadvantage, since they were more likely than their male colleagues to take part-time work so as to be able to care for their family and children. The Court held that since the scheme was not a social security scheme governed directly by statute, benefits paid to employees under the scheme constituted consideration received by the worker from the employer in respect of his or her employment, and the question of access to the scheme therefore fell within the scope of *Article 119*. Where the exclusion of part-time employees from an occupational pension scheme affected a far greater number of women than men, *Article 119* was infringed unless the employer could show that the exclusion was based on objectively justified factors unrelated to any discrimination on grounds of sex. A pay policy implemented by the employer on the ground that it seeks to employ as few part-time employees as possible may be justification under *Article 119*, where it was found that the means chosen for achieving that objective corresponded to a real need on the employer's part, were appropriate with a view to achieving the objective in question and were necessary to that end. An employer is not obliged by *Article 119* to organise its occupational pension scheme in such a manner as to take into account the particular difficulties faced by persons with family responsibilities in meeting the conditions for entitlement to such a pension.

[13.1.32]

Dietz v Stichtung Thuiszorg Rotterdam (European Court of Justice) [1996] OPLR 385

Discriminatory access to pension scheme – indirect sex discrimination – time limits

Facts and Decision

Mrs Dietz was employed part-time as a helper for the aged. Because she worked less than 40% of the full-time working week, she was excluded from pension scheme membership. She took voluntary early retirement in November 1990, unaware that her employer was already planning to admit part-time employees with effect from 1 January 1991. She alleged that she had been indirectly discriminated against. The Court held that the right to join an occupational pension scheme falls within the scope of *Article 119* (now *Article 141*) of the *Treaty of Rome*. Administrators of an occupational pension scheme must comply with *Article 119*, and workers who are discriminated against may assert their rights directly against the administrators. The fact that a worker can claim retroactive membership does not enable him or her to avoid paying contributions for the period of membership concerned. The limitation of the effects in time of the judgment in *Barber v GRE [1990] ECR I–1889* does not apply to the right to join an occupational pension scheme or the right to payment of a retirement pension where the worker was excluded from membership in breach of *Article 119*. *Protocol 2* introduced by the *Treaty of Maastricht* does not place a temporal limitation on these rights.

[13.1.33]

Lander Carlisle v Highfield (Employment Appeal Tribunal, unreported, 19 October 2000)

Indirect sex discrimination – testing for indirect discrimination

Principles

What is colloquially known as adverse or disproportionate impact is essentially a matter of fact. An employment appeal tribunal can only interfere with an employment tribunal's finding if it can be shown to be perverse in the *Wednesbury* sense. However, where a tribunal had focused solely on statistical evidence alone, and had failed on the face of its reasoning to consider additional relevant factors, this was such an error as would justify intervention by the Employment Appeal Tribunal.

[13.1.34]

Lea v Greater Manchester Police Authority (Employment Appeal Tribunal) [1991] PLR 81

Discrimination against pensioners – indirect sex discrimination – testing for indirect sex discrimination – objective justification

Facts and Decision

Greater Manchester Police Authority had a policy of not considering applicants in receipt of a pension for its vacancies. Mr Lea was such an applicant, and he claimed that he had been indirectly discriminated against contrary to the *Sex Discrimination Act 1975*, since 4.7% of men in the economically active population of the United Kingdom were in receipt of a pension, while only 0.6% of women in that population were in receipt of a pension. An industrial tribunal upheld that complaint. The Employment Appeal Tribunal refused to overturn that decision. Mr Lea had suffered a detriment since there was a condition with which he could not comply. The pool was not statistically perfect, but it was most undesirable that elaborate statistical evidence should be required before the case could be proved: *Perera v Civil Service Commission No. 2 [1982] ICR 350* was applied. The Police Authority had not put in rival statistics or attempted to show that the statistics had been distorted. It was not possible to say that no reasonable tribunal would have concluded that 95.3% was considerably smaller than 99.4%, and so the Tribunal could properly conclude that a considerably smaller number of men could comply with the condition that they were not in receipt of a pension than women. The Police Authority had not shown that such a condition was objectively justifiable: accordingly the indirect discrimination was made out.

[13.1.35]

Molenbroek v Bestuur van de Sociale Verzekeringsbank (European Court of Justice) [1992] I–5943

Discriminatory state scheme benefits – indirect sex discrimination – objective justification

Facts and Decision

The Dutch social security pension provided a supplement for pensioners with dependent spouses who had not yet reached retirement age. The amount of the supplement depended exclusively on the income earned by the spouse. The benefit was held by the Court to be indirectly discriminatory and therefore contrary to *Article 4(1)* of *Directive 79/7* (*Equal Treatment in Social Security*), unless the legislation was justified by objective factors unconnected with any discrimination on grounds of sex. The allowance was intended to guarantee those concerned an income equal to the social minimum, irrespective of any income which they receive from other sources. The allocation of a social minimum formed an integral part of the social policy of the member states, and they enjoyed a reasonable margin of discretion as regards both the nature of the protective measures in the social sphere and the detailed arrangements for their implementation. Such an allowance was therefore not precluded by *Article 4(1)* of *Directive 79/7* since it made the grant regardless of sex, even though far more men than women would receive the supplement.

[13.1.36]

R v Secretary of State ex parte Seymour-Smith and Perez (European Court of Justice) [1999] 2 AC 554

Indirect sex discrimination – testing for indirect discrimination – objective justification

Facts and Decision

Ms Seymour-Smith and Ms Perez were dismissed within two years of starting employment. They both alleged that they had been unfairly dismissed, but UK statute did not allow employees with less than two years' employment to bring such claims. They sought judicial review of the legality of this rule, since they alleged that it was indirectly sex discriminatory. To ascertain whether indirect discrimination had taken place, the Court held that it had to be ascertained whether the statistics available indicated that a considerably smaller percentage of women than men was able to satisfy the condition of two years' employment. It could, however, also be the case that apparent sex discrimination was displayed if the statistical evidence revealed a lesser but persistent and relatively constant disparity over a long period between men and women who satisfy the condition. It was for the national court to determine the conclusions to be drawn from the statistics. Where 77.4% of men and 68.9% of women fulfilled the condition, such statistics did not on the face of it show that a considerably smaller percentage of women than men were able to fulfil the condition (see also [13.1.37]).

[13.1.37]

R v Secretary of State ex parte Seymour-Smith and Perez (House of Lords [2000] I All ER 857, [2000] I WLR 435, [2000] ICR 244, [2000] IRLR 263)

Indirect sex discrimination – testing for indirect discrimination – objective justification

Facts and Decision

Applying the test laid down by the European Court of Justice (see [13.1.36]), the House of Lords held that there had been indirect discrimination in this case. There had been a persistent and constant disparity of 10:9 over a period of 7 years across the entire male and female labour forces of the country as to those who could satisfy the condition, and this could not be brushed aside and dismissed as insignificant or inconsiderable. These figures were sufficient to demonstrate that the two year qualifying period had had a considerably greater adverse impact on women than men. However, the Government had shown objective justification for this.

[13.1.38]

Roberts v Birds Eye Walls (European Court of Justice) [1993] OPLR 203, [1993] PLR 323

Pension scheme benefits – testing for indirect sex discrimination

See [13.1.28].

[13.1.39]

Rokeby v Lynn (Employment Appeal Tribunal, unreported, 2 July 2001)

Indirect sex discrimination

Facts and Decision

Dr Lynn was a part-time teacher dismissed by his employer. He claimed unfair dismissal, but the Employment Tribunal dismissed his claim. Among other things, he claimed that he had suffered wrongful exclusion from his pension scheme, since all full-time new entrants in his position were automatically admitted to the scheme unless they informed the scheme that they did not wish to join. Dr Lynn had not informed the scheme administrators that he did not wish to join, but was not admitted to the scheme because part-time employees were required actively to elect to join the scheme. The Appeal Tribunal held that he had not suffered direct discrimination because he was in the same position as a female part-time employee. There was no hint that any teacher of either sex found that the condition of completing a form to opt into the scheme was impossible or difficult or burdensome or that it conduced to material delays, still less that a difference emerged between female and male part-time teachers. There was therefore no indirect discrimination. Any indirect discrimination was probably justifiable. The *Equal Pay Act 1970* was not of application, since full-time teachers were not comparators, because they were not doing the same work.

[13.1.40]

Staffordshire v Black (Employment Appeal Tribunal) [1995] OPLR 43, [1995] PLR 45

Testing for indirect discrimination

Facts and Decision

Mrs Black claimed that she had been discriminated against indirectly since she was a part-time worker who had been given a lesser credit on redundancy under the statutory scheme than a full-time worker would have received. This approach was taken by the Council on cost grounds. 89.5% of women were full-time workers, and 97% of men were full-time workers. The Appeal Tribunal noted that what constituted a 'considerably smaller proportion' as required by the *Sex Discrimination Act 1975* for assessing whether indirect discrimination in fact took place was a matter for the Industrial Tribunal. A difference of 7.5% is very small. 'Considerably' does not, though, mean 'worthy of consideration'. Exactly the same approach should be used when considering the free-standing European law duties of employers: tribunals should identify the condition which was being applied, and ask themselves whether the proportion of women who could comply with it was considerably smaller than the proportion of men. The Council's desire in this case not to find extra money to fund the redundancy payment might realistically be described as necessary. It was not for the Tribunal to substitute its own discretion for that of the Council.

[13.1.41]

Turner v Labour Party (Court of Appeal) [1987] IRLR 101

Discriminatory pension scheme benefits – indirect sex discrimination – marital status

Facts and Decision

Mrs Turner, a divorcee with three children, was required to join the Labour Party pension scheme. She claimed that the scheme was sex discriminatory, because pensions were payable to spouses of members but single parents, who were mostly women, were not allowed to pass their pension rights to their children except as a matter of trustee discretion. In fact, members could nominate any person who was a nominated dependant to receive a pension, though if the person was a child, the pension would only continue so long as the child was under 18, or under 22 if the child were still in full-time education. The Court observed that the fact that more men than women left surviving spouses followed from the fact that women tended to live longer than men and that women tended to marry men slightly older than themselves. A single woman might not wish to marry and could not be compelled to marry, but she could marry, so it could not be said that she could not comply with a condition of being married at a later date. Accordingly, there was no question of indirect discrimination, since there was no condition with which Mrs Turner could not comply.

Objective justification

[13.1.42]

Allonby v Accrington & Rossendale College (Court of Appeal) [2001] IRLR 364

Discriminatory access to pension scheme – indirect sex discrimination – objective justification

Principles

An employment tribunal should seek to weigh a justification for indirect sex discrimination against its discriminatory effect. The employer's reasons should not be accepted uncritically, and the Tribunal must at the minimum perform a critical evaluation of whether the employer's reasons demonstrated a real need for the action taken. If the aim of the action was itself discriminatory, it could never afford justification.

[13.1.43]

Barry v Midland Bank (House of Lords) [1999] IRLR 581 (per Lord Nicholls)

Objective justification

Principles

The ground relied upon as justification for sex discrimination must be of sufficient importance for the national court to regard this as overriding the disparate impact of the difference in treatment, either in whole or in part. The more serious the disparate impact, the more cogent must be the objective justification. No particular criteria are to be used when assessing the weight of the justification relied upon.

[13.1.44]

Bullock v Alice Ottley School (Court of Appeal) [1992] OPLR 199, [1992] PLR 125

Objective justification

Principles

To justify a later retirement age for a group which in fact, though not by design, consists wholly or largely of men, it was necessary for the employer to show a real and genuine need for this later retirement age. That need could be made out on economic grounds or on grounds of administrative efficiency, and possibly other grounds as well.

[13.1.45]

Shillcock v Uppingham School (Pensions Ombudsman) [1997] PLR 207

Discriminatory access to pension scheme – indirect sex discrimination – objective justification

Facts and Decision

Ms Shillcock was a former part-time employee who, like other employees earning less than the lower earnings limit for national insurance purposes, had been excluded from membership of her employer's pension scheme. The decision to exclude employees earning less than the lower earnings limit excluded a far greater number of female than male employees. While the employees would not have benefited from pension benefits under the scheme, they would have received valuable death in service cover. The Pensions Ombudsman held that there were no objectively justifiable economic reasons for excluding the employee from the scheme for this benefit. Had the employee been in the scheme, the deduction from benefits of the lower earnings limit would have been indirectly discriminatory since it did not achieve real fairness between lower and higher paid workers. The lower earnings limit should therefore be treated as pro-rated.

[13.1.46]

Smith v Avdel (European Court of Justice) [1994] OPLR 251 at 276C-F, [1994] PLR 211 at 238 at paras 206–209

Equalising benefits – objective justification

Principles

Article 119 (now *Article 141*) of the *Treaty of Rome*, the Court held, precludes the raising of retirement age retrospectively in order to achieve equal treatment, even if such a step could be objectively justified. The scheme administrators could not reasonably plead as justification financial difficulties, since the period of time involved in this case was relatively short and attributable in any event to the conduct of the scheme administrators themselves.

[13.1.47]

Strathclyde v Wallace (Scottish House of Lords) [1998] 1 WLR 259

Indirect sex discrimination – objective justification

Facts and Decision

A group of unpromoted women teachers claimed that they were doing the same work as principal teachers, many of whom were men, but were being paid at a lower rate. It was agreed that the disparity in pay between the unpromoted teachers and the principal teachers had nothing to do with gender. The Court held that *s 1(1)* of the *Equal Pay Act 1970* deems an equality clause into every contract of employment if it is not already included. However, *s 1(3)* provides that the equality clause 'shall not operate in relation to a variation between the woman's contract of employment and the man's contract of employment if the employer proves that the variation is genuinely due to a material factor which is not the difference of sex', and where a woman was employed in like work with a man in the same employment, the factor must be a material difference between the woman's case and the man's case. If a difference in pay was explained by genuine factors not tainted by discrimination, that was sufficient to raise a valid defence under *s 1(3)* of the *Equal Pay Act 1970*. If the difference was tainted with sex discrimination, that would be fatal to such a defence unless such discrimination could be objectively justified in accordance with the tests laid out in *Bilka-Kaufhaus GmbH v Weber von Hartz [1986] IRLR 317* and *Rainey v Greater Glasgow Health Authority [1987] 1 AC 224*.

Identifying the correct comparators of the opposite sex

[13.1.48]

Allonby v Accrington & Rossendale College (Court of Appeal) [2001] IRLR 364

Indirect sex discrimination – identifying comparators

Facts and Decision

Ms Allonby was employed as a part-time lecturer at Accrington & Rossendale College on successive fixed-term contracts. In common with other part-time lecturers, Ms Allonby was made redundant, and offered the opportunity to provide lecturing services to the College through a contract with an agency company which was not controlled by the College. 55 out of 105 full-time College lecturers were male, but of the part-time College lecturers, 110 out of 341 were male. 18,050 out of 37,969 lecturers on the agency company's books were male. Ms Allonby claimed unfair dismissal and indirect sex discrimination. She had made out a case that it was a requirement or condition for continuous employment with the College that an employee must have previously been employed either on a full-time basis or under a contract which conferred proportionate benefits to a full-time contract. The Court held that the claim for indirect discrimination would, therefore, be considered in the light of guidance from the European Court of Justice on other points.

[13.1.49]

Coloroll Pension Trustees v Russell (European Court of Justice) [1995] All ER (EC) 23, [1994] ECR I–4389, [1994] IRLR 586, [1994] OPLR 179 at 223H–224B, [1994] PLR 211 at paras 100–104

Sex discrimination – identifying comparators

Facts and Decision

The Court held that comparisons in cases of actual discrimination falling within the scope of the direct application of *Article 119* (now *Article 141*) of the *Treaty of Rome* are confined to parallels which may be drawn on the basis of concrete appraisals of the work actually performed by employees of different sex within the same establishment or service. Such comparisons are also possible between workers of different sex performing the same work but at different periods. In such a case, however, it will be for the national court to decide whether any difference of treatment may be explained by factors which are unconnected to any discrimination on grounds of sex. Where there had never been any workers of the other sex in the undertaking concerned, the essential criterion for ascertaining that equal treatment exists in the matter of pay, namely the performance of the same work and receipt of the same pay, cannot be applied.

Interrelationship of pension scheme benefits with the State scheme

[13.1.50]

Bestuur van het Algemeen Burgerlijk Pensioenfonds v Beune (European Court of Justice) [1994] ECR I–4471, [1995] IRLR 103, [1995] OPLR 1, [1994] PLR 211 at 249

State scheme benefits – testing for sex discrimination – marital status

Facts and Decision

Mr Beune was in receipt of a pension from the Dutch statutory civil service pension scheme. Part of the pension which he received incorporated the Dutch State pension, which provided better benefits for married men than for married women for service before 1 April 1985, with the consequence that when Mr Beune reached age 65, his civil service pension was lower than a married woman with identical service would have received. The Court held that the civil service pension fell within the scope of *Article 119* (now *Article 141*) of the *Treaty of Rome*. The benefits provided by the civil service pension were directly discriminatory and therefore needed to be equalised. The fact that only married men and not single men were placed at a disadvantage did not alter this conclusion.

[13.1.51]

James v Eastleigh BC (House of Lords) [1990] 2 AC 751

State benefits – testing for sex discrimination

Facts and Decision

Eastleigh Borough Council offered free leisure facilities to people who had reached State pension age, which at that date was 65 for men and 60 for women. Mr James brought proceedings alleging unlawful sex discrimination contrary to *s 29* of the *Sex Discrimination Act 1975*. The Court held that the criterion for free leisure facilities, State pensionable age, was itself a criterion which directly discriminated between men and women in that it treated women more favourably than men 'on the ground of their sex'. It followed inevitably that any other differential treatment of men and women which adopted the same criterion must equally involve discrimination 'on the ground of sex'. Mr James had therefore suffered unlawful sex discrimination.

[13.1.52]

Marsh & Maclennan v Pensions Ombudsman (High Court) [2001] PLR 51

Guaranteed minimum pensions – pension scheme substitute for sex discriminatory State scheme benefits – extent of obligation to equalise

Facts and Decision

Mr Williamson was an actuary who was a member of his employer's pension scheme, which was contracted out of the State earnings related pension scheme. After leaving service, he complained to the Pensions Ombudsman that scheme pensions were being incorrectly calculated, since the trustees had not equalised the guaranteed minimum pension. It could not be known how this would affect him until he reached age 60. The Pensions Ombudsman upheld his complaint and ordered that the scheme equalise guaranteed minimum pension entitlements. The trustee and employer appealed. The Court held that the submission that *s 62* of the *Pensions Act 1995* did not require the equalisation of guaranteed minimum pensions was compelling, but was not finally decided. Guaranteed minimum pensions were in the nature of calculation factors rather than pensions themselves or discrete elements of the scheme pension. The scheme pension should not be regarded as comprising two elements made up of a guaranteed minimum pension and the excess above it. There was, however, no sound reason why a scheme member should not be allowed to complain of a scheme term that has at most the potential for resulting in future discrimination, even if it had not yet actually resulted in any discrimination. Whether *Article 141* (formerly *Article 119*) of the *Treaty of Rome* required guaranteed minimum pensions to be equalised depended on whether *Article 141* required any pension equalisation when the differences arose from a mandatory statutory provision for the calculation of a pension benefit.

[13.1.53]

Roberts v Birds Eye Walls (European Court of Justice) [1993] OPLR 203, [1993] PLR 323

Pension scheme offset for state scheme benefits – identifying sex discrimination

Facts and Decision

Birds Eye Walls operated a pension scheme which between the ages of 60 and 65 paid a lower pension to women on early retirement pensions than to men, to take account of the State retirement pension which women received during that period and which men did not receive. The Court held that there was no discrimination contrary to *Article 119* (now *Article 141*) of the *Treaty of Rome*, because the mechanism for calculating the bridging pension was neutral. The fact that married women had an option to pay State pension contributions at a reduced rate did not require the private pension scheme to adjust the bridging pension accordingly, since that would confer an unfair advantage on the women who had so opted.

[13.1.54]

Shillcock v Uppingham School (Pensions Ombudsman) [1997] PLR 207

Pension scheme offset for State scheme benefits – indirect sex discrimination – objective justification

Facts and Decision

Ms Shillcock was a former part-time employee who, like other employees earning less than the lower earnings limit for National Insurance purposes, had been excluded from membership of her employer's pension scheme. The decision to exclude employees earning less than the lower earnings limit excluded a far greater number of female than male employees. While the employees would not have benefited from pension benefits under the scheme, they would have received valuable death in service cover. The Pensions Ombudsman held that there were no objectively justifiable economic reasons for excluding the employee from the scheme for this benefit. Had the employee been in the scheme, the deduction from benefits of the lower earnings limit would have been indirectly discriminatory and should be treated as pro-rated. Membership on these terms was backdated three years.

What is not sex discrimination

[13.1.55]

Barry v Midland Bank (House of Lords) [1999] IRLR 581

Sex discrimination – general unfairness

Facts and Decision

Mrs Barry had been a full-time employee of Midland Bank for 11 years, and then converted to part-time status for a further 2½ years. She was then made redundant. Under the terms of her employer's redundancy scheme, her compensation was calculated on her final salary and the number of years' service. No adjustment was made for the fact that part of her service had been served as full-time service, resulting in a substantially lower payment than if such an adjustment had been made. Mrs Barry claimed that she had suffered unlawful discrimination in her pay on the ground of sex. The Court held that the question was not one of fairness but whether Mrs Barry had established a breach of *s 1* of the *Equal Pay Act 1970* or of *Article 119* (now *Article 141*) of the *Treaty of Rome*. The primary objective was to cushion employees against unemployment and job loss, and as a result the calculation by reference to final salary was entirely appropriate, and did not have a discriminatory effect.

[13.1.56]

Coloroll Pension Trustees v Russell (European Court of Justice) [1995] All ER (EC) 23, [1994] ECR I–4389, [1994] IRLR 586, [1994] OPLR 179 at 221B–222D, [1994] PLR 211 at paras 72–85

Sex discrimination – actuarial factors

Principle

The use of actuarial factors varying according to sex in funded defined-benefit occupational pension schemes does not fall within the scope of *Article 119* (now *Article 141*) of the *Treaty of Rome*. Consequently, inequalities in the amounts of capital benefits or substitute benefits whose value can be determined only on the basis for funding the scheme are not struck at by *Article 119*. This applies also to reversionary pensions to dependants paid after the surrender of part of the employee's pension, and to reduced pensions paid on early retirement.

[13.1.57]

Grant v South West Trains (European Court of Justice) [1999] PLR 69

Sex discrimination – same-sex relationship

Principle

It is not contrary to *Article 119* (now *Article 141*) of the *Treaty of Rome* or *Council Directive 75/117* (the *Equal Pay Directive*) to refuse to grant travel concessions to a person of the same sex as the worker, with whom the worker had a stable relationship, where it would grant such concessions to a worker's spouse or to a person of the opposite sex with whom the worker had a stable relationship.

[13.1.58]

Neath v Hugh Steeper (European Court of Justice) [1993] OPLR 329, [1994] PLR 1

Sex discrimination – actuarial factors

Principle

It is not sex discrimination to use actuarial factors differing according to sex in a final salary scheme for the purpose of calculating lump sum commutations and transfer values.

[13.1.59]

Nolte v Landesversicherungsanstalt Hannover (European Court of Justice) [1996] PLR 117

Sex discrimination – social policy

Principle

European Directive 79/7 (Equal Treatment in Social Security) precludes the application of a national measure which, although formulated in neutral terms, works to the disadvantage of far more women than men, unless that measure is based on objective factors unrelated to any discrimination on the grounds of sex. A legitimate social policy aim is such an objective factor. Member states have a broad margin of discretion. A national legislature is reasonably entitled to consider that the exclusion of low-paid part-time workers from State pension benefits was necessary in order not to stifle the demand for minor employment, or provoke an increase in the black economy.

[13.1.60]

Nuthall v Merrill Lynch (UK) Final Salary Plan trustees (Pensions Ombudsman, 25 March 1999) Case G00543 at para 21

Sex discrimination – marital status

Facts and Decision

Mr Nuthall complained that his pension should be higher, since a married man would earn dependants' benefits, which he would not be able to use. The Pensions Ombudsman held that there is no basis in authority for regarding discrimination turning on marital status as unlawful.

[13.1.61]

Stevenson v Lord Advocate (Scottish opinion, unreported, 24 July 1997)

Sex discrimination – general unfairness

Facts and Decision

Mr Stevenson was a sheriff and as such entitled to a pension under the *Sheriffs' Pensions (Scotland) Act 1961*. He received the same salary as an English circuit judge, but his pension was significantly less generous. Mr Stevenson claimed that he had been unlawfully discriminated against on the ground of sex within the meaning of *Article 119* (now *Article 141*) of the *Treaty of Rome*, since he received a less favourable pension entitlement than a female circuit judge would receive. At all relevant times, the sheriffs were predominantly male and the circuit court judges were predominantly male. The Court held that while there were two groups, as the majority of both groups were male, he could not point to any sexual imbalance between the two groups. Mr Stevenson had not shown that the discrimination in relation to pension provisions was based on sex, and on that ground the action failed.

Trustees' and administrators' duties in relation to sex discrimination

[13.1.62]

Coloroll Pension Trustees v Russell (European Court of Justice) [1995] All ER (EC) 23, [1994] ECR I–4389, [1994] IRLR 586, [1994] OPLR 179 at 216B–D, 216G–218A, [1994] PLR 211 at paras 20–23, 26–36

Sex discrimination – trustees' duties

Principles

The Court held that while trustees are not party to an employment relationship, they are required to pay benefits which do not lose their character as pay. They are therefore bound to do everything within the scope of their powers to ensure compliance with the principle of equal treatment. The direct effect of *Article 119* (now *Article 141*) of the *Treaty of Rome* may be relied upon by both employees and their dependants against the trustees of an occupational pension scheme who are bound, in the exercise of their powers and performance of their obligations as laid down in the trust deed, to observe the principle of equal treatment. Where national law prohibits employers and trustees from acting beyond the scope of their powers or in disregard of the provisions of the trust deed, they must use all the means available under domestic law, including recourse to the national courts, to eliminate all discrimination in the matter of pay. In the meantime, disadvantaged employees must be granted the same advantages previously enjoyed by the other employees. As regards subsequent service, *Article 119* does not preclude equal treatment from being achieved by reducing the advantages which the advantaged employees used to enjoy.

[13.1.63]

Dietz v Stichting Thuiszorg Rotterdam (European Court of Justice) [1996] OPLR 385

Sex discrimination – administrator's duties

Principle

Administrators of an occupational pension scheme must comply with *Article 119* (now *Article 141*) of the *Treaty of Rome* and workers who are discriminated against may assert their rights directly against the administrators.

[13.1.64]

Fisscher v Voorhuis Hengelo (European Court of Justice) [1994] OPLR 297 at 327B-E, [1994] PLR 211 at 243, paras 240–243

Sex discrimination – administrator's duties

Principle

Administrators of an occupational pension scheme must, like the employer, comply with the provisions of *Article 119* (now *Article 141*) of the *Treaty of Rome* and a worker who is discriminated against may assert his or her rights directly against the administrator.

Receiving scheme's duties in relation to sex discrimination

[13.1.65]

Coloroll Pension Trustees v Russell (European Court of Justice) [1995] All ER (EC) 23, [1994] ECR I–4389, [1994] IRLR 586, [1994] OPLR 179 at 223C-G, [1994] PLR 211 at paras 94–99

Sex discrimination – duties of a receiving scheme

Principles

When a worker's pension rights are transferred from one occupational scheme to another owing to a change of job, the receiving scheme is obliged to increase the benefits it undertook to pay the worker when accepting the transfer so as to eliminate the effects, contrary to *Article 119* (now *Article 141*) of the *Treaty of Rome*, suffered by the worker in consequence of the inadequacy of the capital transferred, this being due in turn to the discriminatory treatment suffered under the first scheme. This applies only in relation to benefits payable in respect of periods of service subsequent to 17 May 1990. The rights accruing to the worker cannot be affected by the fact that he or she changes his job. If need be, the receiving scheme should make a claim for necessary additional sums from the transferring scheme under national law.

Interrelationship of employer and trustee duties in relation to sex discrimination

[13.1.66]

Coloroll Pension Trustees v Russell (European Court of Justice) [1995] All ER (EC) 23, [1994] ECR I–4389, [1994] IRLR 586, [1994] OPLR 179 at 218B-D, [1994] PLR 211 at paras 37–40

Sex discrimination – interrelationship of trustees' and employer's obligations

Principles

A national court is to use all means available to it under domestic law to ensure correct implementation of *Article 119* (now *Article 141*) of the *Treaty of Rome*, taking into account the respective liabilities of the employer and the trustees. In particular, it may order:

(a)   the employer to pay additional sums into the scheme;
(b)   that any sum payable by virtue of *Article 119* must first be paid out of any surplus funds of the scheme; or
(c)   that the sums to which members are entitled must be paid by the trustees out of the scheme's assets

even if no claim has been made against the employer or the employer has not reacted to such a claim.

Retrospective extent of judgments

[13.1.67]

Barber v GRE (European Court of Justice) [1990] ECR I–1889, [1990] IRLR 240, [1991] I WLR 72, [1990] PLR 95

Sex discriminatory pension scheme benefits – time limits

Principle

Because of the serious difficulties which the *Barber* judgment might create without temporal limitations having regard to the previous reasonable understanding of parties, the Court held that *Article 119* (now *Article 141*) of the *Treaty of Rome* could only be relied upon by workers in order to claim entitlement to pension with effect from the date of judgment (17 May 1990) unless the claim had already been initiated by that date.

[13.1.68]

Coloroll Pension Trustees v Russell (European Court of Justice) [1995] All ER (EC) 23, [1994] ECR I–4389, [1994] IRLR 586, [1994] OPLR 179 at 218G–219B, [1994] PLR 211 at paras 44–49, 51–56, 57–60

Sex discriminatory pension scheme benefits – time limits

Principle

The direct effect of *Article 119* (now *Article 141*) of the *Treaty of Rome* may be relied upon only in relation to benefits payable in respect of service subsequent to 17 May 1990, with the exception for those who initiated legal proceedings before that date. This time limit applies equally to survivors' pensions. Lump sum death benefits must be equalised where paid on any date on or after 17 May 1990, as must all other benefits not linked to service.

[13.1.69]

Defreyn v Sabena (European Court of Justice) [2000] PLR 261

Sex discriminatory social security benefits – time limits

Facts and Decision

Ms Defreyn became an employee of Sabena in 1960. In 1984, she took voluntary redundancy and was granted a pre-retirement payment with two years' notice, under which Sabena undertook to pay a supplement agreed under a collective agreement until the end of the month in which she reached her 60th birthday, which fell in November 1991. In 1993, the European Court of Justice delivered its judgment in *EC Commission v Belgium [1993] ECR I-673*, in which it declared that it was a breach of *Article 119* (now *Article 141*) of the *Treaty of Rome* to exclude female workers over age 60 from eligibility for additional payments under a collective agreement. Ms Defreyn therefore claimed for additional payments until her 65th birthday. The Court held that the payments were pay within the meaning of *Article 119*. However, they were also a benefit under an occupational social security scheme for the purposes of *Protocol 2* to the *Maastricht Treaty*, and therefore Ms Defreyn's claim was time-barred. A benefit which constituted pay for the purposes of *Article 119* could not be covered by *Directive 76/207* (*Equal Treatment Directive*).

[13.1.70]

Dietz v Stichtung Thuiszorg Rotterdam (European Court of Justice) [1996] OPLR 385

Discriminatory access to pension scheme – time limits

See [13.1.32].

[13.1.71]

Fisscher v Voorhuis Hengelo (European Court of Justice) [1994] OPLR 297 at 325B–327A, 327E-G, [1994] PLR 211 at 243, paras 227–239, 244–248

Discriminatory access to pension scheme – time limits

Facts and Decision

Married women were historically excluded from membership of a particular pension scheme. The Court held that the right to join an occupational pension scheme falls within the scope of *Article 119* (now *Article 141*) of the *Treaty of Rome* and is therefore covered by the prohibition of discrimination. Since it had been clear since the decision in *Bilka-Kaufhaus GmbH v Weber von Hartz [1986] IRLR 317* that this was the case, the direct effect of *Article 119* could be relied upon in order retrospectively to claim equal treatment as from 8 April 1976, the date of the judgment in *Defrenne v Sabena (No. 2) [1976] ICR 547*. Neither the judgment in *Barber v GRE [1990] ECR I–1889* nor *Protocol 2* to the *Maastricht Treaty* affected this right retrospectively to claim equal treatment for the right to join a scheme. However, the worker cannot claim more favourable treatment than he or she would have had if he or she had been duly accepted as a member, so the worker must pay contributions relating to the period of membership concerned.

[13.1.72]

Griffin v London Pensions Fund Authority (Employment Appeal Tribunal) [1993] OPLR 49, [1993] PLR 67

Sex discriminatory pension scheme benefits – time limits

Facts and Decision

Mrs Griffin retired through ill-health in 1971, claiming an ill-health pension from the local government pension scheme. Her pension was reduced when she reached age 60 in 1987 to take account of her State benefits. This reduction would take effect at 65 for men. Mrs Griffin therefore claimed that her former employer had discriminated against her. The Appeal Tribunal held that the claim was out of time, since it would inevitably require the *European Communities Act 1972*, *Article 119* (now *Article 141*) of the *Treaty of Rome* and *Directive 75/117/EC*, the *Equal Pay Directive*, as requiring the *Local Government Superannuation Regulations (SI 1986 No 24)* so as to impose a plainly retrospective obligation to pay Mrs

Griffin a greater pension than the funding of the scheme anticipated throughout her pensionable employment, and in circumstances where there was no means of funding the alteration out of contributions from or in respect of Mrs Griffin, for which there was no statutory justification.

[13.1.73]

Jordan v Electricity Association Services Limited (Industrial Tribunal) [1993] PLR 33

Sex discriminatory pension scheme benefits – time limits

Facts and Decision

Mrs Jordan retired from the Electricity Supply Pension Scheme on the grounds of incapacity on 30 March 1990, the trustees' decision as to entitlement taking place after 17 May 1990. Her incapacity pension was calculated by reference to her notional pensionable service to normal pension age. Women's normal pension age was 60, while men's was 65. Mrs Jordan claimed for an additional five years' notional pensionable service, on the grounds that she had been discriminated against. The Tribunal held that this was direct discrimination. The temporal limitation in the case of *Barber v GRE [1990] ECR I–1889* did not apply, since the discrimination arose from the crediting of fictitious contribution years between the employee's retirement for ill-health and the normal pension age. Such an increase in benefit owed nothing to the employee's actual contribution years and the trustees' decision took place after the temporal limitation came into effect.

[13.1.74]

Moroni v Collo GmbH (European Court of Justice) [1993] OPLR 289, [1994] PLR 211 at page 259

Sex discriminatory pension scheme benefits – time limits

Facts and Decision

The Court held that the direct effect of *Article 119* (now *Article 141*) of the *Treaty of Rome* may be relied on in order to claim equal treatment in the matter of occupational pensions only in relation to benefits payable in respect of periods of service subsequent to 17 May 1990, subject to the exception in favour of workers or those claiming under them who have, before that date, initiated legal proceedings or raised an equivalent claim under the applicable national law.

[13.1.75]

Shell v Van den Akker (European Court of Justice) [1994] OPLR 345, [1994] PLR 211 at page 229

Sex discriminatory pension scheme benefits – equalising benefits – time limits

Facts and Decision

Shell operated a pension scheme with a normal retirement date of 60 for men and 55 for women. In 1985, they equalised normal retirement dates for men and women at 60 for new joiners. All current women members were given the opportunity to change their normal retirement date to age 60 at that time. Not all women members elected to change their normal retirement date. Following the judgment in *Barber v GRE [1990] ECR I–1889*, Shell abolished the possibility of women in the closed class retaining their normal retirement date of 55. The Court held that it is insufficient when equalising benefits to set a uniform retirement age for all members, but to retain for a closed class a different retirement age for men and for women. *Article 119* (now *Article 141*) of the *Treaty of Rome* does not allow a situation of equality to be achieved otherwise than by applying to male employees the same arrangements as those enjoyed by female employees. This applied even where the female members of the closed class had been given the option to change their retirement age.

[13.1.76]

Smith v Avdel (European Court of Justice) [1994] OPLR 251 at 274D–275G, [1994] PLR 211 at page 238, paras 188–200

Sex discriminatory pension scheme benefits – equalising benefits – time limits

Facts and Decision

Following the judgment in *Barber v GRE [1990] ECR I–1889*, Avdel equalised its scheme benefits in 1991 by equalising the retirement age at 65 for all periods of service. Previously, women had a retirement age of 60 and men of 65. The Court held that *Article 119* (now *Article 141*) of the *Treaty of Rome* precludes an employer from raising the retirement age of women to that for men in relation to periods of service completed between 17 May 1990 and the date on which the equalisation takes place. However, *Article 119* does not prevent an employer from taking that step for future periods of service. For periods of service before 17 May 1990,

Community law imposed no obligation which would justify retroactive reduction of the advantages which women had up until then enjoyed.

[13.1.77]

Ten Oever v Stichting Bedrijfspensioenfonds voor het Glazenwassers (European Court of Justice) [1993] ECR I–4879, [1995] 2 CMLR 357, [1993] IRLR 601, [1993] OPLR 89, [1993] PLR 317

Sex discriminatory pension scheme benefits – time limits

Facts and Decision

Mrs Ten Oever was a member of her pension scheme until her death in 1988. At that time, the scheme provided a survivor's pension for widows only. This was changed in 1989, but not retrospectively. Mr Ten Oever brought a claim that he had been unlawfully discriminated against, following the release of the judgment in *Barber v GRE [1990] ECR I–1889*. The Court held that *Article 119* (now *Article 141*) of the *Treaty of Rome* may be relied upon for the purpose of claiming equal treatment in the matter of occupational pensions only in relation to benefits payable in respect of periods of employment subsequent to 17 May 1990, subject to the exception in favour of workers or those claiming under them who have, before that date, initiated legal proceedings or raised an equivalent claim under the applicable national law.

[13.1.78]

Vroege v NCIV Instituut (European Court of Justice) [1995] All ER (EC) 193, [1994] ECR I–4541, [1994] IRLR 651, [1994] OPLR 335, [1994] PLR 211 at page 232

Discriminatory access to pension scheme – time limits

Facts and Decision

Married women who worked less than 80% of the full working day were excluded from membership of a pension scheme. The Court held that the right to join an occupational pension scheme falls within the scope of *Article 119* (now *Article 141*) of the *Treaty of Rome* and is therefore covered by the prohibition of discrimination. Since it had been clear since the decision in *Bilka-Kaufhaus GmbH v Weber von Hartz [1986] IRLR 317* that this was the case, the direct effect of *Article 119* could be relied upon in order retrospectively to claim equal treatment as from 8 April 1976, the date of the judgment in *Defrenne v Sabena (No. 2) [1976] ICR 547.* Neither the judgment in *Barber v GRE [1990] ECR I–1889* nor *Protocol 2* to the *Maastricht Treaty* affected this right retrospectively to claim equal treatment for the right to join a scheme.

Equalising benefits

[13.1.79]

Bestrustees v Stuart (High Court, unreported, 10 April 2001)

Sex discrimination – equalising benefits – interrelationship of trust law and European law

Facts and Decision

An employer established a pension scheme with a normal retirement date of 65 for men and 60 for women, of which it was also trustee. Following the decision in *Barber v GRE [1990] ECR I–1889*, an announcement was issued on 26 April 1994 stating that the scheme rules were being amended to equalise normal retirement dates at age 65 for men and women. The rules were not in fact amended until 23 May 1996 when new rules came into force, purportedly with effect from 6 April 1994. These rules equalised normal retirement date at age 65, but while men who sought early retirement needed both employer and trustee consent, women who sought early retirement needed only the consent of the trustees. The scheme wound up, and the independent trustee sought the Court's guidance on the proper calculation of members' benefits. The Court held that the benefits before 17 May 1990 accrued on the basis of a normal retirement date of 60 for women and 65 for men. Benefits from 17 May 1990 to 23 May 1996 accrued on the basis of a normal retirement date of 60 for both men and women: *Coloroll Pension Trustees v Russell [1995] All ER (EC) 23* was applied. The 1996 amendments represented an attempt to comply with the ruling in *Barber v GRE [1990] ECR I–1889*, but the attempt did not quite achieve its end. The Court gave as much effect as it could to the change, subject to the reasoning in *Barber* and *Coloroll*, and so the changes were effective, save to the extent that they unlawfully distinguished between men and women, and in so far as they did so distinguish, the Court then applied *Coloroll*, giving the people in the disadvantaged class the same advantages as those enjoyed by persons in the favoured class. The amendments could not, therefore, be retrospective. The normal retirement date from 23 May 1996 was therefore 65, but the early retirement terms were equalised on the basis available to female members.

[13.1.80]

Coloroll Pension Trustees v Russell (European Court of Justice) [1995] All ER (EC) 23, [1994] ECR I–4389, [1994] IRLR 586, [1994] OPLR 179 at 218E-F, [1994] PLR 211 at paras 41–43

Sex discrimination – equalising benefits – interrelationship of national law and European law

Principle

Any problems arising because the funds held by the pension scheme trustees are insufficient to equalise benefits must be resolved on the basis of national law in the light of the principle of equal pay.

[13.1.81]

Lloyds Bank Pension Trust Corporation Limited v Lloyds Bank PLC (High Court) [1996] OPLR 181, [1996] PLR 263

Sex discrimination – equalising benefits – interrelationship of trust law and European law

Facts and Decision

Where the power of amendment of a pension scheme prohibited amendments which would decrease the pecuniary benefits secured to or in respect of members without the agreement of three-quarters of those members, the Court held that it was not lawful for the scheme to equalise benefits on the basis that future benefits would be reduced to the benefit level of the disadvantaged sex without the agreement of those members.

[13.1.82]

Shell v Van den Akker (European Court of Justice) [1994] OPLR 345, [1994] PLR 211 at page 229

Sex discrimination – equalising benefits

Principles

It is insufficient when equalising benefits to set a uniform retirement age for all members, but to retain for a closed class a different retirement age for men and for women. *Article 119* (now *Article 141*) of the *Treaty of Rome* does not allow a situation of equality to be achieved otherwise than by applying to male employees the same arrangements as those enjoyed by female employees. This applied even where the female members of the closed class had been given the option to change their retirement age.

[13.1.83]

Smith v Avdel (European Court of Justice) [1994] OPLR 251 at 275H–276B, [1994] PLR 211 at page 238, paras 201–205

Sex discrimination – equalising benefits

Principles

The application of *Article 119* (now *Article 141*) of the *Treaty of Rome* by employers must be immediate and full. Achievement of equality cannot be made progressive on a basis that still maintains discrimination, even if only temporarily. Transitional measures designed to limit the adverse consequences of equalisation for women are therefore prohibited.

Sex discrimination in public sector benefits

Barber v GRE (European Court of Justice) [1990] ECR I–1889, [1990] IRLR 240, [1991] 1 WLR 72, [1990] PLR 95

Sex discriminatory social security benefits

Principle

Article 119 (now *Article 141*) of the *Treaty of Rome* does not apply to the benefits awarded by national social security schemes, unlike those paid out under contracted-out private sector schemes.

Bestuur van het Algemeen Burgerlijk Pensioenfonds v Beune (European Court of Justice) [1994] ECR I–4471, [1995] IRLR 103, [1995] OPLR 1, [1994] PLR 211 at page 249

Direct sex discrimination – integration with State scheme benefits

Facts and Decision

Mr Beune was in receipt of a pension from the Dutch statutory civil service pension scheme. Part of the pension which he received incorporated the Dutch State pension, which provided better benefits for married men than for married women for service before 1 April 1985, with the consequence that when Mr Beune reached age 65, his civil service pension was lower than a married woman with identical service would have received. The Court held that the civil service pension fell within the scope of *Article 119* (now *Article 141*) of the *Treaty of Rome*. The benefits provided by the civil service pension were directly discriminatory and therefore needed to be equalised.

[13.1.86]

De Vriendt v Rijksdienst vor Pensioenen (European Court of Justice) [1998] I–2105

Sex discrimination – social security benefits – early retirement – link with State pension age

Principle

If a member State has maintained a different State pensionable age for male and female workers, it is entitled under *Article 4(1)* of *Directive 79/7/EEC* (*Equal Treatment in Social Security*) to calculate the amount of State pension differently depending on the worker's sex. This remains the case even where pensions are put into payment early.

[13.1.87]

Defrenne v Belgian State (European Court of Justice) [1971] ECR 445

Direct sex discrimination – social security benefits

Facts and Decision

Mme. Defrenne worked in the airline industry. The pensions of Belgian civil aviation aircrew were dealt with by royal decree. The Court held that social security schemes or benefits, and in particular retirement pensions, directly governed by legislation without any element of agreement within the undertaking or occupational branch concerned, cannot be brought within the concept of pay, being determined less by the employment relationship than by considerations of social policy. It followed that a retirement pension established within the framework of a social security scheme laid down by legislation did not constitute consideration which the worker received indirectly in respect of his or her employment from his or her employer, within the meaning of *Article 119* of the *Treaty of Rome* (now *Article 141*).

[13.1.88]

Drake v Chief Adjudication Officer (European Court of Justice) [1986] ECR 1995, [1986] 3 CMLR 43

Direct sex discrimination – social security benefits – marital status

Facts and Decision

Mrs Drake was married and lived with her husband. She held a variety of full and part time jobs until 1984, when she gave up work to look after her severely disabled mother. Because she living with her husband, she was ineligible for an invalid care allowance. A man who had given up work in such circumstances would still have received the allowance. The Court held that the benefit was covered by *European Directive 79/7 (Equal Treatment in Social Security)*, which applied to statutory schemes for protection among other things against invalidity, since the benefit was one which protected against the risk of invalidity, albeit not her own. The United Kingdom legislation therefore discriminated against her as a woman in contravention of the *Directive*.

[13.1.89]

Griffin v London Pensions Fund Authority (Employment Appeal Tribunal) [1993] OPLR 49, [1993] PLR 67

Sex discriminatory pension scheme benefits – statutory schemes

Facts and Decision

Mrs Griffin retired through ill-health in 1971, claiming an ill-health pension from the local government pension scheme. Her pension was reduced when she reached age 60 in 1987 to take account of her State benefits. This reduction would take effect at 65 for men. Mrs Griffin therefore claimed that her former employer had discriminated against her. Because the local government pension scheme was a statutory scheme, the Court held that her pension was not pay within the meaning of *Article 119* (now *Article 141*) of the *Treaty of Rome*.

Hepple v Adjudication Officer (European Court of Justice) [2000] All ER (EC) 513, [2000] 45 PBLR 23

Sex discrimination – disability pensions

Facts and Decision

The United Kingdom paid Reduced Earnings Allowance as a benefit under the Industrial Injuries Scheme. It was calculated on the basis of a comparison between earnings which the claimant was prevented from drawing as a result of suffering an accident at work or an occupational disease, and earnings available in any alternative occupation still considered suitable despite the disablement. Reduced Earnings Allowance was restricted in 1986 to those of normal working age, so that no one over State pensionable age (65 for men, 60 for women) could receive it. The Court held that this was permissible under *Article 7(1)(a)* of *Directive 79/7/EEC* (*Equal Treatment in Social Security*) only if the link with State pension age, and the resultant differences in the amount of the invalidity benefits by reference to sex, were necessary to ensure coherence between the pension scheme and the invalidity pension scheme. The derogation from the equal treatment principle had to be proportionate to the result pursued. It was for the national court to carry out the relevant assessment. If the discrimination was not within the scope of the derogation, the persons discriminated against could apply to the national court for an additional invalidity benefit.

[13.1.91]

James v Eastleigh BC (House of Lords) [1990] 2 AC 751

Direct sex discrimination – State benefits – integration with State pension age

Facts and Decision

Eastleigh Borough Council offered free leisure facilities to people who had reached State pension age, which at that date was 65 for men and 60 for women. Mr James brought proceedings alleging unlawful sex discrimination contrary to *s 29* of the *Sex Discrimination Act 1975*. The Court held that the criterion for free leisure facilities, State pensionable age, was itself a criterion which directly discriminated between men and women in that it treated women more favourably than men 'on the ground of their sex'. It followed inevitably that any other differential treatment of men and women which adopted the same criterion must equally involve discrimination 'on the ground of sex'. Mr James had therefore suffered unlawful sex discrimination.

[13.1.92]

Johnson v Chief Adjudication Officer (European Court of Justice) [1992] PLR 87

Direct sex discrimination – social security benefits – replacement of social security benefits

Facts and Decision

Mrs Johnson ceased working in order to look after her daughter with whom she lived alone. Some years later she wished to resume working but was unable to do so because of a back condition, for which she was awarded a non-contributory State invalidity pension. Payment of this pension ceased when she began to cohabit with her present partner on the grounds that she was then unable to fulfil the additional condition imposed on cohabiting women that she was incapable of performing normal household duties. Following changes in national legislation, the pension was abolished and a new benefit was introduced, for which those previously eligible for the pension could automatically benefit. Ms Johnson claimed that such treatment was discriminatory in contravention of *European Directive 79/7 (Equal Treatment in Social Security)*. The Court held that after the date on which the period laid down by the *Directive* for bringing national legislation into conformity with the *Directive* expired, a member state could not maintain any inequalities of treatment. Accordingly, making eligibility for benefit conditional on entitlement to a previous benefit which was sex discriminatory was not lawful, and the legislation was set aside on this point.

[13.1.93]

Megner v Innungskrankenkasse Vorderpfalz (European Court of Justice) [1996] PLR 133

Indirect sex discrimination – social security benefits – objective justification

Facts and Decision

Mrs Megner was a cleaner who worked two hours a day, five days a week. As a result, she was excluded from paying compulsory social security insurance and as such being entitled to social security and old age benefits.

She sought a declaration that such an exclusion was contrary to *European Directive 79/7 (Equal Treatment in Social Security)*, which set out a prohibition on sex discrimination in State benefits, since this affected far more women than men. As in *Nolte v Landesversicherungsanstalt Hannover [1996] PLR 125*, the ECJ held that social security benefits must not be indirectly discriminatory, unless a national government had objective justification for the measure. In this case, the German Government wished to avoid making low-paid part-time jobs uneconomic and forcing people into the black economy. This aim was not held to be sex-discriminatory. The ECJ gave a wide margin of appreciation in areas of social policy and the national legislature was reasonably entitled to consider that the legislation was necessary in order to achieve this aim.

[13.1.94]

Molenbroek v Bestuur van de Sociale Verzekeringsbank (European Court of Justice) [1992] I–5943

Indirect sex discrimination – social security benefits – objective justification

See [13.1.35].

[13.1.95]

Newstead v Department of Transport (European Court of Justice) [1988] IRLR 66

Direct sex discrimination – social security benefits

See [13.1.10].

[13.1.96]

Nolte v Landesversicherungsanstalt Hannover (European Court of Justice) [1996] PLR 125

Indirect sex discrimination – social security benefits – objective justification

Facts and Decision

Mrs Nolte worked less than 15 hours a week and earned less than 1/7th of the average German monthly salary. As a result, she did not need to pay compulsory social security insurance and was excluded from receiving a

State invalidity pension. Mrs Nolte claimed that such an exclusion was contrary to *European Directive 79/7 (Equal Treatment in Social Security)*, which set out a prohibition on sex discrimination in State benefits, since this affected far more women than men. The ECJ held that social security benefits must not be indirectly discriminatory, unless the national government had objective justification for the measure. In this case, the German Government wished to avoid making low-paid part-time jobs uneconomic and forcing people into the black economy. This aim was not held to be sex-discriminatory. The ECJ gave a wide margin of appreciation in areas of social policy and the national legislature was reasonably entitled to consider that the legislation was necessary in order to achieve this aim.

[13.1.97]

R v Secretary of State for Social Security ex parte Equal Opportunities Commission (European Court of Justice) [1992] OPLR 105, [1992] PLR 219

Sex discrimination – social security benefits – contributions – link to State pension age

Facts and Decision

Article 7(1)(a) of *Directive 79/7/EEC (Equal Treatment on Social Security)*, the Court held, authorises the determination of a statutory pensionable age which differs according to sex for the purposes of granting old age and retirement pensions, and also forms of discrimination which are necessarily linked to that difference. Accordingly, the fact that men must make contributions for 44 years to the State scheme and women for 39 years for the same amount of pension was not a form of discrimination which was contrary to this *Directive*.

[13.1.98]

R v Secretary of State ex parte Seymour-Smith and Perez (European Court of Justice) [1999] 2 AC 554

Indirect sex discrimination – objective justification

Facts and Decision

Ms Seymour-Smith and Ms Perez were dismissed within two years of starting employment. They both alleged that they had been unfairly dismissed, but UK statute did not allow employees with less than two years' employment to bring such claims. They sought judicial review of the legality of this rule, since they alleged that it was indirectly sex discriminatory. The Court held that if a considerably smaller percentage of women than men was capable of fulfilling the requirement of two years' employment, it was for the member State to show that the rule reflected a legitimate aim of its social policy, that that aim was unrelated to any discrimination based on sex, and that it could reasonably consider that the means chosen were suitable for attaining that aim. (See also [13.1.99].)

[13.1.99]

R v Secretary of State ex parte Seymour-Smith and Perez (House of Lords) [2000] I All ER 857, [2000] I WLR 435, [2000] ICR 244, [2000] IRLR 263

Indirect sex discrimination – objective justification

Facts and Decision

Applying the test laid down by the European Court of Justice (see [13.1.98]), the House of Lords held that there had been indirect discrimination in this case, but that the Government had shown objective justification. The Secretary of State had shown that the view of his predecessor that a two-year qualifying period would help reduce the reluctance of employers to take on more people was reasonable when the test was introduced by regulations in 1985, and this had not become an unreasonable view by 1991, the last relevant date.

[13.1.100]

R v Secretary of State for Social Security ex parte Smithson (European Court of Justice) [1992] PLR 77

Sex discrimination – social security benefits – link with State pension age

Facts and Decision

Mrs Smithson was aged 67 and suffered from serious ill-health. She was in receipt of a State pension, an occupational pension and housing benefit. If she had been a man, she could have de-retired from the State scheme until age 70 and claimed an invalidity State pension. This in turn would have entitled her to a higher rate of housing benefit. However, this option was not available to women aged over 65. She claimed that the United Kingdom legislation discriminated against her as a woman in contravention of

European Directive 79/7 (Equal Treatment in Social Security), which applied to statutory schemes for protection against:

(a) sickness;
(b) invalidity;
(c) old age;
(d) accidents at work, occupational diseases and unemployment; and
(e) social assistance;

in so far as it was intended to supplement or replace such schemes. The Court noted, however, that *Article 7(1)(a)* of the *Directive* stated that the *Directive* was without prejudice to the right of member states to exclude from its scope the determination of pensionable age for the purpose of granting old age and retirement pensions, and the possible consequences thereof for other benefits. The *Directive* had therefore not been contravened.

[13.1.101]

R v Secretary of State for Social Security ex parte Taylor (European Court of Justice) [2000] All ER (EC) 80, [2000] ICR 843

Sex discrimination – social security benefits – link with State pension age

Facts and Decision

Winter fuel payments were made only to those who were in receipt of the State retirement pension, which was payable from age 60 for women and age 65 for men. Mr Taylor argued that this was sex discriminatory. The Court held that the benefit was payable under a statutory scheme and was directly and effectively connected to the risk of old age such as brought it within *Article 3* of *Directive 79/7/EEC (Equal Treatment on Social Security)*. Discriminatory treatment such as that at issue was not necessarily linked to the difference in the statutory retirement age for men and women, and the Government could not therefore rely upon the derogation in *Article 7(1)* of the *Directive*.

Secretary of State for Social Security v Thomas (European Court of Justice) [1994] OPLR 137

Sex discrimination – social security benefits – link with State pension age

Principle

Where pursuant to *Directive 79/7/EEC* (*Equal Treatment on Social Security*) a member State prescribes different retirement ages for men and women for the purposes of granting old age and retirement pensions, the scope of the permitted derogation is limited to the forms of discrimination existing under other benefit schemes which are necessarily and objectively linked to the difference in retirement age.

Bringing claims

[13.1.103]

Executors of Evans v Metropolitan Police Authority (Court of Appeal) [1993] OPLR 69

Sex discrimination – prosecuting claims

Facts and Decision

Mrs Evans worked for the Metropolitan Police Authority from 1964 until her death in 1983. Her husband was not entitled to an ill-health pension, though a widow of a man employed in her position would have been so entitled. The executors and her widower brought an industrial tribunal claim on the grounds of sex discrimination in 1984. The claim was stayed pending the outcome of *Marshall v Southampton and South-West Hampshire Area Health Authority [1986] IRLR 140*. Neither side applied to have the case restored after that decision was issued in 1986. Following the decision in *Barber v GRE [1990] ECR I–1889*, the executors and the widower sought to have the claim relisted. The Court held that the case would not be dismissed for want of prosecution, since the Police Authority had not suffered serious prejudice. Neither the inconvenience of altering administrative records nor the uncertainty caused by the delay were likely to result in serious prejudice.

[13.1.104]

Howard v Ministry of Defence (High Court) [1995] OPLR 275

Sex discrimination – bringing claims – time limits

Facts and Decision

Mr Howard was the widower of an army major who left the army in 1973. Widows received pensions, but widowers did not. Mr Howard complained about this after his wife's death in 1979 and subsequently, but did not bring legal proceedings. He eventually lodged industrial tribunal proceedings in 1994. The Court held that his complaints were not an equivalent claim in national law such as would entitle him to raise a complaint which would normally be excluded by the time limit set out in *Barber v GRE [1990] ECR I–1889.* That exception to the normal time limit envisaged a claim equivalent to legal proceedings. He had not brought such a claim until 1994, and his claim therefore was time-barred.

[13.1.105]

Jones v Foxboro International (Employment Appeal Tribunal, 31 March 2000) [2000] 41 PBLR 33

Sex discrimination – withdrawing proceedings – setting aside tribunal decision

Facts and Decision

Mr Jones brought a claim for sex discrimination in 1991, being a member of a scheme with a normal retirement date of 65 for men and 60 for women. The claim was determined by a tribunal on a basis more favourable than would have been awarded had it been decided in accordance with the principles in the later case of *Coloroll Pension Trustees v Russell [1995] All ER (EC) 23.* Both Mr Jones and Foxboro International appealed, with both of these appeals eventually being withdrawn by agreement in 1995, following the issue of the *Coloroll* decision. Mr Jones then tried to enforce the Tribunal decision, on the basis that the terms of agreement had not prevented him from asserting his rights in this regard. Foxboro International claimed that the terms of this decision had been varied by agreement. The Appeal Tribunal held that the Tribunal decision was not automatically overridden by the *Coloroll* decision, but the parties had impliedly agreed to drop their claims on the basis set out in the *Coloroll* decision. Mr Jones's attempt to enforce the Tribunal decision therefore failed.

Calculating compensation

[13.1.106]

Marshall v Southampton (No. 2) (European Court of Justice) [1994] OPLR 91

Sex discrimination – calculating compensation – statutory limits

Facts and Decision

Miss Marshall was dismissed by her employer at her normal retirement date, and she claimed damages for compensation on the grounds that her normal retirement date was lower than that of male employees. Damages for unlawful sex discrimination were limited to £6,250 at the relevant time. The Court held that *Article 6 of Directive 76/207/EEC (Equal Treatment Directive)* prohibited the imposition of such an upper limit. Where the employer was an authority of the State, the employee could rely on the *Directive's* provisions to set aside such an upper limit.

13.2 – Racial discrimination

Barclays Bank v Kapur (Court of Appeal) [1995] OPLR 173

Race discrimination – direct discrimination – indirect discrimination

Facts and Decision

Barclays operated a subsidiary in East Africa, and provided a pension fund for its staff. In 1967 Kenya introduced a law requiring all jobs to be held by Kenyan nationals. Many of the employees were East African Asians who did not wish to take Kenyan nationality. The subsidiary offered such employees a compensation package including *ex gratia* pension provision. It also arranged for the parent company to take on 180 such employees, which offered them the standard pension provision available in the United Kingdom, but excluded their right under the fund rules to pension on their past group-service in East Africa, to which they would otherwise have been entitled. Some of these employees alleged that this was racially discriminatory. The Court held that it was not directly discriminatory, since there was not sufficient evidence to justify the inference that the employees had been discriminated against on the ground of their race. The compensation package granted in East Africa was a substitute for the crediting of African service, and all of it should be taken into account in assessing the question of detriment. An appropriate measure of calculating the compensation package's value was to use the rate of return on an endowment policy. On this basis, the employees had suffered no detriment and so could not therefore have suffered indirect discrimination.

[13.2.2]

Borawitz v Landesversicherungsanstalt Westfalen (European Court of Justice) [2000] 59 PBLR 8

Racial discrimination – social security

Facts and Decision

Mr Borawitz was in receipt of a German State disability pension. Under German law, he was deprived of a retroactive payment of additional pension since for the relevant period he had been resident in the Netherlands. He challenged this under European law. *EC Regulation 1408/71* provided that, with certain limited exceptions, persons resident in the territory of one member State must be subject to the same obligations and enjoy the same benefits under that State's social security legislation as the nationals of that member State. The Court held that this principle of equal treatment precluded national legislation which fixed the minimum amount of cash benefit that could be paid to a community national residing in another member State at a higher level than that required where that payment was made within the same member State, in circumstances where the payment to be sent to another member State did not involve expenses higher than those incurred in respect of the payment of the same benefit within the first member State.

[13.2.3]

Vos v Stadt Bielefeld (European Court of Justice) [1996] PLR 389

Race discrimination – social security benefits – social policy

Facts and Decision

A Belgian national worked in Germany. He performed military service in the Belgian army, during which time the German State pension institution suspended his membership of the German State scheme, since his employer made no contributions on his behalf. Military service was compulsory for German nationals, and while an employee was performing military service with the German army, an employer was obliged to maintain contributions to the German State pension scheme. The employer would then be reimbursed by the German Government for the contributions. The Court held that since the obligation to contribute arose while the employment contract was suspended, the obligation was not linked to the employment contract: *Südmilch v Ugiola [1989] ECR I-363* was distinguished. The continued payment of contributions was therefore not made by virtue of a statutory or contractual obligation incumbent on the employer as conditions of employment and work within the meaning of *Article 7(1)* of *Regulation (EEC) 1612/68* on freedom of movement for workers within the Community, and since the social advantage of the rule was essentially linked to the performance of military service for the German Government, it was not a social advantage that needed to be extended to non-nationals.

Part 14 – Pensions and the Company's Business

14 – Introduction

Pension schemes are often thought of as self-contained, but of course for employers that is very far from the case. Employers offer pension schemes as part of their remuneration package to employees and do so in order to recruit and retain staff. The funding commitment required from the employer is a very substantial cost of the business, and the value of any surplus which can be set against the employer's contribution liability may be a very valuable asset. It is no surprise that such matters attract a lot of attention from the employer in dealing with other business matters.

The courts have unhesitatingly held that a pension scheme is an intimate part of a company's affairs, as in *Denny v Yeldon [1995] 3 All ER 624*. If that were not enough, the observation in *Polly Peck International v Henry [1998] OPLR 323* that those who deal with companies must be deemed to know that they are likely to have pension schemes is judicial confirmation that pension schemes do not exist in a vacuum when it comes to consideration of the employer's position.

On occasion, the cost or value of the pension scheme to the employer must be valued. One common occasions when this occurs is when an undertaking is being sold to another employer. Such sales can be made by sale of company or by sale of business. The case law relating to the pensions aspects of transfers of undertakings is set out at Part 12 (Employment and Pensions) Chapter 4.

Business or share sales will be made by agreement. The terms of such agreements are litigated surprisingly rarely, given the sums at stake and their complexity. *Rosedale (JW) Investments v British Steel [2001] PLR 1* was a case where the courts were asked to resolve a dispute over adjustments in the purchase price arising from surpluses and deficits in pension schemes, and while a case on a very narrow point, shows how the courts approach such disputes in exactly the same way as any other contractual dispute.

Of course, sale and purchase agreements have formed the backdrop to many other cases. *Fisons v Stannard [1991] PLR 227* and *Nicol & Andrew v Brinkley [1996] OPLR 361*, for example, both arose out of bulk transfers on the sale and purchase of an undertaking. The difference in those cases, of course, was that the dispute arose between the members and the trustees and employers, rather than between the buyer and seller.

When the employer is making decisions about pensions as part of a remuneration package, it must do so in accordance with its constitution. When directors are interested in the decision, questions may arise as to whether they acted with propriety when voting on such decisions. *Bairstow v Queens Moat Houses (High Court, unreported, 23 July 1999)* and *Ireland Alloys v Dingwall [1999] 47 PBLR 12*, where the courts took a strict line with the directors, demonstrate the risks.

When an employer becomes insolvent, the conflicts between the interests of the pension scheme members and the employer becomes particularly acute. The insolvency practitioner will be under a duty to maximise the returns for the creditors, and if this means minimising payments to the scheme or taking the largest possible refund of surplus, then so be it. However, the employer also often has powers and duties under the pension scheme, and the insolvency practitioner is subject to the same constraints in exercising those powers and duties as a solvent employer would have been. This may often leave the insolvency practitioner in a conflict which only the courts can resolve. The courts have developed a fairly clear line on when the insolvency practitioner can act and which scheme powers the insolvency practitioner can exercise, and this is summarised in *Buckley v Hudson Forge [1999] OPLR 249*.

14.1 – Sale and purchase agreements

[14.1.1]

Rosedale (JW) Investments v British Steel (Court of Appeal) [2001] PLR 1

Sale and purchase agreements – interpretation

Facts and Decision

The Walker family sold their steel business to British Steel. This business had several pension schemes. The sale and purchase agreement made provision for the purchasers being compensated with an adjustment in the purchase price for any net deficit in the defined benefit pension schemes. To this end, it provided that a surplus could only be offset against a deficit if and to the extent that the seller's actuary and the purchaser's actuary agreed that such an offset could be achieved by completion or within six months of completion. The sellers and purchasers also undertook to use their best endeavours to procure that their actuaries expedited the determination and agreement. The six month time period came and went without agreement between the actuaries. On a proper construction, the Court held that the timescale in which the parties clearly envisaged the offset to take place was decisive, and the time period for the process of agreeing set-offs could not be indefinitely extended. Offsetting could not now take place.

14.2 – Directors' duties to shareholders and procedural formalities

[14.2.1]

Bairstow v Queens Moat Houses (High Court, unreported, 23 July 1999)

Directors' duties

Facts and Decision

The directors of a listed company were dismissed following the suspension in March 1993 of the company's shares on the Stock Exchange, after its profit level was far lower than expected. The directors claimed for wrongful dismissal. The company justified their dismissal on the grounds that the directors had each committed serious breaches of their service agreements. Among other things, the company claimed that the directors had sought to confer pension benefits on themselves by Board resolution which were not *bona fide* and in the best interests of the company. In relation to the pension enhancement resolutions passed by the Board, the managing director had failed to put before the non-executive Board members a copy of counsel's opinion on the proposed resolution, which advised that the pension benefits should be funded rather than, as the Board resolved, unfunded. This was bad faith, the Court held, and he was therefore in serious breach of his contract. The pension enhancement resolutions either did not create subsisting legal rights or were void. Accordingly, the directors could not claim benefits by reference to them. The benefits were of an unusually generous level, and even if the resolution had been effective, it would not have been in the interests of the company. By taking personal benefits from the company, the directors had committed breaches of fiduciary duty which amounted to grave misconduct and justified their dismissal.

Comment

This was a case of enormous complexity. The trial took a year and the judgment runs to nearly 500 pages. Certain aspects of the decision were appealed to the Court of Appeal, but none of these affect the pensions points under consideration. Despite the exhaustive argument and the lengthy judgment, the reasoning behind the decision must be treated with a little caution since the executives represented themselves. However, the reasoning is in accordance with what had previously been understood to be directors' duties on remuneration, and the case can probably be treated as reliable.

The key question was whether the directors had been acting *bona fide* in the best interests of the company. This case shows how the courts will look at such problems in a practical manner. The courts will not allow directors to keep relevant information from their fellow directors, and they will not allow directors to vote themselves excessive pensions. The Court not only struck down the relevant resolutions, it also held that the attempt to gain wrongful personal benefit was grave misconduct justifying the directors' dismissal.

This case should be compared with *Ireland Alloys v Dingwall (Scottish Outer House, 9 December 1997) [1999] 47 PBLR 12*. The Court in that case was equally reluctant to sanction the payment of enhanced directors' pensions, though it found a different route to strike down the increases to benefits. Neither of these cases is ground-breaking, but they affirm that the normal principles relating to directors' duties apply equally to pensions matters.

[14.2.2]

Re Blackwood Hodge (High Court) [1997] OPLR 179 at 197F–199C, 203G–204F, [1997] PLR 67 paras 119–128, 159–164

Directors' duties

Principles

A proposed pension scheme merger needed proper consideration by the directors of a sponsoring employer as to whether it was in the interests of the company. Failure to do so was a breach of duty by the directors. However, the mere fact that the directors were in breach of duty did not establish unfair prejudice, nor did it give rise to a presumption of unfair prejudice. The best interests of the company first needed to be identified. Since, on the facts in this case, merger had not taken place and the position could be unscrambled, there was no unfair prejudice.

[14.2.3]

Hinckley and Bosworth Borough Council v Shaw (High Court, 21 December 1998) 22 PBLR 39

Duties of council

Facts and Decision

Mr Shaw was to be made redundant by his local authority employer. The local authority increased his salary in advance of his redundancy so that his pension would be substantially higher. The Court held that the council's discretion was exercised in breach of its duties to council tax payers, since this purpose was unlawful. The payment itself was therefore unlawful and void, and Mr Shaw was obliged to refund the money he had received as additional wages and pension.

[14.2.4]

Ireland Alloys v Dingwall (Scottish Outer House, 9 December 1997) [1999] 47 PBLR 12

Directors' duties – quorum

Facts and Decision

Three directors held a Board meeting at which they established a pension scheme providing executive benefits for themselves. The quorum at Board meetings was two, but those two had to be disinterested. The act of providing pension benefits for themselves was, the Court held, a single act in which all had an interest, and not three separate decisions to provide pension benefits for each of them. The decision was therefore voided.

[14.2.5]

Parlett v Guppy's (Bridport) Ltd (Court of Appeal) [1996] BCC 299

Directors' duties – company assisting purchase of own shares

Facts and Decision

At an annual general meeting, Guppy's (Bridport) resolved to pay its chairman a higher salary, a bonus and an indexed pension. In return, the chairman agreed to transfer his shares in a company, Estates, which owned shares in Guppy's (Bridport), into the joint names of his sons and himself. Mr Parlett retired shortly afterwards and signed blank transfers of shares in Estates to his sons in return for them reaffirming the resolutions on his pay. His sons claimed that Estates gave financial assistance for the acquisition of its own shares and the agreement was therefore unenforceable by reason of *s 151* of the *Companies Act 1985*. Mr Parlett sued for his benefits. The Court noted that the pension and bonus were not immediately payable on the conclusion of the agreement, and therefore ought not be taken into account for the purpose of determining enforceability under *s 151*. Irrespective of whether there was or was not an enforceable agreement for Mr Parlett to be employed, the salary, bonus and pension accrued over the ensuing period during which he was in fact employed, so it could not be said that the agreement to pay the benefits had caused any reduction in the net assets of Guppy's (Bridport) if the chairman's services were worth the sums agreed. On the facts, the chairman's services were not worth the salary paid, but since the liability could have been met not by Estates but by other shareholding companies in the group, and it would have been the most beneficial course to the group as a whole that the contract be performed in accordance with the criminal law, there was no reduction in the net assets of Estates and the question whether any reduction was to a material extent did not arise.

14.3 – Dealings with third parties

[14.3.1]

Polly Peck International v Henry (High Court) [1998] OPLR 323 at 328E, [1999] PLR 135 at para 32

Dealings with companies

Principle

Those who deal with companies must be deemed to know that they are likely to have pension schemes.

14.4 – Unfair prejudice to minority shareholders

[14.4.1]

Re Blackwood Hodge (High Court) [1997] OPLR 179 at 199D–200A, 201A, 201B–202B, [1997] PLR 67 paras 129–133, 139, 140–146

Unfair prejudice

Facts and Decision

In determining whether a merger had caused unfair prejudice to shareholders of the sponsoring employer of a pension scheme in surplus, the Court considered the use to which surplus would have been put and the use to which surplus was actually put. It was not enough that the company was deprived of benefits from the surplus (or that the trustees of the receiving scheme would have obtained an advantage) for which it should have sought a *quid pro quo* from the sponsoring employer of the receiving scheme: it must also be shown that it would have obtained the *quid pro quo* through negotiations. On the facts, this would have been refused in this case.

14.5 – Corporate insolvency

[14.5.1]

Buckley v Hudson Forge (High Court) [1999] OPLR 249, [1999] PLR 151

Corporate insolvency – receivership – trustee discretions – conflict of interest

Facts and Decision

A receiver of a company which was a trustee could not, the Court held, validly or effectually exercise a discretion unless the power was given to the receiver under the debenture. Where the duties owed in the exercise of a trustee discretion conflicted with the duties owed to the debenture holder, *Polly Peck International v Henry [1998] OPLR 323* and *Denny v Yeldon [1995] 3 All ER 624* were distinguished on the grounds that in both of those cases the person in the position of conflict was an administrator and therefore an officer of the court. *Simpson Curtis Pension Trustees v Readson [1994] OPLR 231* was distinguished on the ground that the case concerned a power to appoint a new trustee. The trustee was, therefore, obliged either to apply to the Court, or to appoint a separate trustee.

[14.5.2]

Capital Cranfield v Sagar (High Court, unreported, 19 February 2001)

Corporate insolvency – dissolution of company – trustees' duties

Facts and Decision

Where a company had been struck off the register, the trustees of a pension scheme in surplus which might otherwise be paid in part or whole to the company asked the Court for guidance. The Court held that they had no locus to apply for the restoration of that company. It was highly questionable whether they owed a duty to its former shareholder, although the Court would have been uneasy about this conclusion had the former shareholder not been made a party to proceedings. *NGN Staff Pension Plan Trustees Ltd v Simmons [1994] OPLR 1* was considered: it would not be appropriate for the trustees to take any further steps with regard to informing the former shareholder of its right to apply (and its interest in so doing) to restore the company to the register.

[14.5.3]

Denny v Yeldon (High Court) [1995] 3 All ER 624, [1995] OPLR 115, [1995] PLR 37

Corporate insolvency – administration – appointment and removal of trustee

Principles

A company's pension scheme was, the Court held, an intimate part of a company's affairs. The administrator of an insolvent company therefore had the power to amend the trust deed to give the trustees the power to appoint and remove trustees: *Simpson Curtis Pension Trustees v Readson [1994] OPLR 231* was applied. Once a scheme had no further members in pensionable service, an administrator of an insolvent company no longer had the statutory power to appoint and remove independent trustees unless it was the trustee, or the power of appointment and removal of trustees was vested in the employer.

[14.5.4]

Icarus v Driscoll (High Court) [1990] PLR 1

Corporate insolvency – liquidation – trustee duties – conflict of interest

Facts and Decision

A surplus arose in a pension scheme on winding-up which had been for many years non-contributory for members. The winding-up had been triggered by the employer's insolvency. The employer was the trustee, and the liquidator applied to Court for guidance as to how to use the discretion vested in the employer/trustee under the scheme rules to allocate surplus. If he decided not to exercise the discretion in favour of any category of members, the surplus would be used to satisfy the claims of the creditors. The Court held that it would not be improper to take into account that the principal employer was in liquidation and that there were creditors.

[14.5.5]

Independent Pension Trustee v LAW Construction (Scottish Court of Session, Outer House) [1996] OPLR 259

Corporate insolvency – receivership – appointment and removal of trustees

Facts and Decision

During the currency of a receivership, the Court observed, a company Board has no power over assets in the possession or control of the receiver. These assets include rights and powers insofar as these have commercial value or significance. The manner of exercise of rights, powers and obligations under the company pension scheme could bear on the value of exploitable assets such as goodwill, and as such had commercial value or significance. The directors therefore had no power to enter into a substitution of principal employer, and to appoint and remove trustees.

[14.5.6]

James Miller Holdings v Graham (Supreme Court, Victoria) [1992] PLR 165

Corporate insolvency – receivership – winding-up of scheme – power of amendment

Facts and Decision

James Miller Holdings operated a pension scheme for its employees of which it was also the trustee. The pension scheme was invested in a managed fund policy. The employer went into receivership on 8 December 1976. The receivers immediately determined that the employer would cease making contributions to the scheme. If the employer gave the three months' notice required to trigger the winding-up of the scheme, employees who had already retired by that date would get their pension in full, while those who had yet to retire would get only an equitable apportionment of what was left in the account after all other members had received their entitlement in full. The receivers, therefore, purported to close the scheme retrospectively by deed of amendment, and returned it to the insurer under cover of a letter dated 4 January 1977 which confirmed that the company had ceased to make contributions to the scheme. The power of amendment was subject to a restriction that no amendment should detrimentally affect the benefits already secured in respect of a member at the date of amendment, without the consent in writing of that member.

The consent of the members was not obtained. On the facts, the Court held that the employees' employment did not terminate on the appointment of the receivers. The decision to cease contributing was not a total failure of the purpose of the scheme. The only feasible way of undoing the contract between the employer and the insurer would be by application of the doctrine of frustration, but the decision to discontinue payment of premiums could not be treated as an event frustrating the contract in the light of express provision in the trust deed for discontinuing payment of contributions. The receivers had power to exercise the power of amendment and power to discontinue the scheme: *Edgar & Another and the Companies Act (1971–73) CCH Company Law Cases* was applied. The closure of the scheme by amendment would detrimentally affect the benefits already secured both by depriving the members of the right to receive a benefit if they left within three months of the effective date of the deed, and by enabling the employer to cease paying premiums three months earlier than otherwise. This was true whether the amendment was retrospective or immediate in effect. The proviso to the power of amendment prevented the amendment being made at all, and did not operate so as to make the amendment take effect but without the detrimental effects. The letter of 4 January 1977, however, took effect as notice of discontinuance, and so the scheme went into discontinuance on 4 April 1977 on the expiry of three months from that date.

[14.5.7]

Larsen's Executrix v Henderson (Outer House, Scotland) [1991] PLR 153

Corporate insolvency – receivership

Facts and Decision

Mr Larsen was managing director of Highland Universal Fabrications Limited. This company went into receivership in 1982, but Mr Larsen remained in its employment until his death from cancer on 12 March 1983. The company operated a pension scheme which provided death benefits in the event of death in service before normal retirement age. However, the receivers did not maintain the insurance for the death in service benefits. As a result, no death in service benefit was paid. His widow sued the receiver in her capacity as executrix. The Court held that the receiver owes a duty of care to the employees of the company, and must act reasonably in all the circumstances, even though he may need to take decisions which have an adverse effect on the employees. A receiver would be acting unreasonably if he or she simply terminated a pension scheme without giving any warning to the employees concerned that there was a possibility that this might occur. However, Mr Larsen had been given this information on 10 January 1983, so the receiver had fulfilled his duty.

[14.5.8]

Mettoy Pension Trustees v Evans (High Court) [1991] 2 All ER 513, [1990] 1 WLR 1587, [1990] PLR 9 (paras 169–171)

Corporate insolvency – receivership – liquidation – trustee duties – conflict of interest

Principles

A fiduciary power vested in the hands of an insolvent employer cannot be exercised by receivers or liquidators, since their duties are primarily if not exclusively to the interests of the creditors and contributories. Their duties as trustees would conflict with these duties. In these circumstances, the Court should step in and was not obliged to appoint a new person to exercise the power. *Re Manisty's Settlement [1974] 1 Ch 17* at *25* was not followed.

[14.5.9]

Polly Peck International v Henry (High Court) [1998] OPLR 323 at 327E–328B, [1999] PLR 135 at paras 19–24

Corporate insolvency – administration

Principles

The duties of an administrator of an insolvent company include managing the affairs of the company, and if a company has set up a pension scheme and has become trustee of that scheme, the scheme and the trusteeship are part of the company's affairs which the administrator must manage: *Denny v Yeldon [1995] 3 All ER 624* was followed.

[14.5.10]

Simpson Curtis Pension Trustees v Readson (High Court) [1994] OPLR 231, [1994] PLR 289

Corporate insolvency – receivership – power of appointment and removal of trustees

Facts and Decision

An administrative receiver purported to exercise the power of appointment and removal of a company's pension scheme trustees. The Court held that the power of appointment of a new trustee was not an asset of the company in the true sense. However, since the prime purpose of appointing the trustee was to enable the trustee to take proper steps to administer the scheme, and to ascertain what liability the company as principal employer might still owe to the pension scheme, this was a necessary step in the process of ascertaining the final value of the assets of the company and was therefore within the powers of the administrative receiver, both under the terms of the debenture and the terms of *Schedule 1* of the *Insolvency Act 1986*.

[14.5.11]

Re Thirty-Eight Building Limited (High Court) [1999] OPLR 319

Corporate insolvency – preferences

Facts and Decision

An employer bought land from its pension scheme in 1987, but paid only the deposit. The balance was left outstanding on loan accruing interest. In March 1995, the employer made a declaration of trust, declaring itself to be trustee for the scheme of land and antiques to the value of £530,000, the balance on the loan. In December 1996, the employer went into creditors' voluntary liquidation owing £4 million. Four of the trustees were connected with the employer, but the fifth was not. The liquidators applied to have the declaration of trust avoided as a preference. The beneficiaries were the first four trustees and so were all connected with the employer. However, the trustees were the creditor and viewed collectively, the Court held, they were not connected with the employer. Additionally, they were not associates of the employer since the exception for trustees of pension schemes in *s 435(5)(b)* of the *Insolvency Act 1986* applied even in circumstances where all the beneficiaries were connected with the employer. Accordingly, collectively they were not connected with the employer, and the loan was not susceptible to being set aside as a preference.

[14.5.12]

Thrells v Lomas (High Court) [1993] I WLR 456, [1993] 2 All ER 546, [1992] OPLR 21, [1992] PLR 233

Corporate insolvency – liquidation – trustee duties – conflict of interest

Facts and Decision

Thrells Limited went into insolvent liquidation in 1984. Its pension scheme entered winding–up as a consequence, the company being the sole trustee. The scheme was in surplus, and the liquidator surrendered the company's discretion to the Court, it having proved impossible to find anyone willing to accept appointment as trustee in the place of the company. In exercising the discretion surrendered by the employer/ trustee, the Court held that it must act in the manner a reasonable trustee could be expected to act having regard to all the material circumstances. It must do what was just and equitable. Overfunding of the scheme could be said in one sense to have been at the expense of creditors. The Court implemented the requirements of *s 11(3)* of the *Social Security Act 1990* in full, making provision for the increases not to be franked against the increases in guaranteed minimum pensions, but ordered the balance to be returned to the employer.

[14.5.13]

United Electrical Radio v 163 Pleasant Street (United States Court of Appeal, Massachusetts) [1994] PLR 61

Corporate insolvency – extra-territorial jurisdiction

Facts and Decision

The plaintiffs included retired and disabled employees in the United States, and the issue was whether the defendants were contractually bound under Massachusetts law to provide medical and life insurance to the plaintiffs. One defendant was incorporated in Scotland and was the parent company of another defendant, which had become insolvent. The Court held that Massachusetts extra-territorial law gave the local court jurisdiction over the Scottish defendant, since it had taken a significant role in the management of the subsidiary.

[14.5.14]

Re William Makin (High Court) [1993] OPLR 171, [1992] PLR 177

Corporate insolvency – liquidation – trustee duties – conflict of interest

Facts and Decision

William Makin & Sons Limited went into receivership in 1984 and liquidation in 1985. Its pension scheme had a substantial surplus deriving wholly from overfunding by the company, and went into winding-up on the company ceasing to carry on business. The employer was the trustee, and the trust deed gave the trustees a discretion to use any surplus on a winding-up to increase benefits to members. Any part of the surplus not so used was to be refunded to the employer. The liquidator sought directions as to whether it could exercise this power. The Court held that the power was a fiduciary power: *Icarus v Driscoll [1990] PLR 1* and *Mettoy Pension Trustees v Evans [1991] 2 All ER 513* were followed. If the power had become exercisable while the company was a going concern, the company could have exercised the power despite its conflict of interest. What the company could not have done would have been to have decided not to exercise the power or to refrain from exercising the power, with the consequence that the surplus or part of it would become payable to the company. The power was not capable of exercise by the liquidator because of the liquidator's conflicting duties. The power was also not exercisable by the receivers, since the power was not an asset that was caught by the floating charge.

Part 15 – Taxation of Pension Schemes

15 – Introduction

Because exempt approved retirement benefits schemes are exempt from tax on investment income and capital gains, it is easy to assume that pension schemes are unlikely to have tax problems. Not so. There are limits to the tax exemptions that pension schemes enjoy, and the Inland Revenue patrols those limits with some vigour. These limits fall into the following two categories:

(a) limits on the income which is exempted from tax; and
(b) limits on the extent to which the tax reliefs can be used to obtain tax advantages.

The tax exemptions also come with strings attached, since the Inland Revenue uses its discretion to regulate heavily the benefits which can be paid from an exempt approved scheme, and the funding of such schemes. It has the power to withdraw the tax approved status of discretionary exempt approved retirement benefits schemes.

In general, benefits paid to beneficiaries from exempt approved retirement benefits schemes are taxable, with two major exceptions. Discretionary death benefits are not subject to inheritance tax, and a lump sums paid on drawing pension, within limits, is not subject to income or capital gains tax. Income tax is payable if benefits are paid when not authorised by the rules. The Inland Revenue has in recent years become increasingly hostile to the idea of drawing benefits while remaining with the former employer in any capacity, and has therefore challenged the validity of such payments under pension scheme rules.

Quite apart from income and capital gains taxes, pension schemes may incur other tax liabilities. Stamp duty may be incurred on some transactions, and since pension schemes can incur substantial professional fees, the proper treatment of value added tax charges may be of considerable importance. Unfortunately, the VAT legislation is arbitrary in its operation in relation to pension schemes. Despite several calls from the courts and VAT tribunals to remedy this, the legislation remains substantially unchanged.

15.1 – Withdrawal of tax approval

[15.1.1]

R v IRC ex parte Roux Waterside Inn (High Court) [1997] OPLR 239, [1997] PLR 123, [1997] TC 545

Withdrawal of approval – Inland Revenue's discretion

Facts and Decision

The trustee of an exempt approved pension scheme transferred £900,000 to a new pension scheme on interim tax approval, which the same day took steps to ensure that it was no longer a scheme capable of tax approval. This resulted in a 40% tax charge on the new scheme's assets, but those were, it was argued, to be assessed on the value of the assets taken the day before approval was lost, so no tax charge would in fact arise. The Inland Revenue withdrew approval from the transferring scheme, and the trustee of the transferring scheme applied for judicial review of this decision. The Revenue was entitled to withdraw approval if the transfer was not permitted under the *Occupational Pension Schemes (Transfer Values) Regulations 1985 (SI 1985 No 1931)* and the Practice Notes. The Court held that the Inland Revenue was entitled to look at the broad facts concerning the scheme and the purpose for which it was to be used: *WT Ramsey v Inland Revenue Commissioners [1982] AC 300* was applied. The new scheme was not approved or seeking tax approval – in fact, it was to be an unapproved scheme, and the Inland Revenue was justified in imputing the prime mover's knowledge to the officers of the trustee company. The transfer accordingly did not come within the terms of the *Regulations*. However, equity did not impose a constructive trust requiring the return of the funds from the new scheme to the transferring scheme, since no injustice had occurred and the imposition of equitable relief was unrequired and inappropriate. The withdrawal of tax approval was justified whether or not the tax avoidance scheme in fact worked.

15.2 – Discretion of Inland Revenue

[15.2.1]

Kelsall v Investment Chartwork (High Court) [1994] OPLR 243, [1994] PLR 19

Inland Revenue's discretion

Facts and Decision

The General Commissioners agreed that an employer contribution was not an ordinary annual contribution, but refused to increase correspondingly the assessment of the company's liability in the year in which it contributed. On appeal, the Court held that the General Commissioners had no power to overrule the Inland Revenue's exercise of its discretion on this point.

[15.2.2]

National Power v Feldon (High Court, unreported, 30 July 1997)

Withdrawal of approval – Inland Revenue's discretion

Principle

Where no amendment to a pension scheme was needed so as to bring a matter within the Inland Revenue's remit under *s 591B(2)* of the *Income and Corporation Taxes Act 1988*, it might still be possible for the Inland Revenue to withdraw approval, having regard to the wide terms of *s 591B(1)* of that *Act*: *R v Inland Revenue Commissioners ex parte Roux Waterside Inn [1997] OPLR 239* was considered.

15.3 – Tax reliefs on contributions

[15.3.1]

Kelsall v Investment Chartwork (High Court) [1994] OPLR 243, [1994] PLR 19

Ordinary annual contributions

Facts and Decision

In one tax year, an employer contributed £186,200 to its pension scheme, which was only ever provisionally approved. In the following five tax years it made no contributions at all. The Inland Revenue refused to treat the payment of £186,200 as an ordinary annual contribution and exercised its discretion to spread those contributions over five years. The General Commissioners agreed that the contribution was not an ordinary annual contribution, but refused to increase correspondingly the assessment of the company's liability in the year in which it contributed. On appeal, the Court held that the General Commissioners had no power to overrule the Inland Revenue's exercise of its discretion on this point.

[15.3.2]

Koenigsberger v Mellor (Court of Appeal) [1996] PLR 153

Member's contributions – relevant earnings

Facts and Decision

Mr Koenigsberger was a Lloyd's name and a barrister. He claimed relief on his contributions made from his Lloyd's earnings to his retirement annuity contract. The Court held that his income as a Lloyd's name was not income immediately derived by him from the carrying on or exercise by him of his trade as an individual, since an external name does not carry out any trade at all. The trade out of which the income arises consists of the business of underwriting, which is the job of the managing agent. Accordingly, the earnings were not relevant earnings and did not qualify for relief.

[15.3.3]

Sports Club v HMIT (Special Commissioners, 8 June 2000) [2001] 04 PBLR 23

Classification as pension contributions

Facts and Decision

Payments were made to two professional sports stars under contracts with promoters for promotional rights. The classification of these payments was challenged by the Inland Revenue, which argued that among other things, the payments made to one of the stars were payments pursuant to a retirement benefits scheme with a view to the provision of pension benefits within the meaning of s 595 of the *Income and Corporation Taxes Act 1988*. The Special Commissioners held that these payments were not made pursuant to a retirement benefits scheme. They were paid pursuant to the promotional agreement, and in return for them the promoters received the rights under the agreement.

15.4 – Taxation of overseas pensions

[15.4.1]

Albon v Inland Revenue Commissioners (Extra Division of the Inner House of the Court of Session as the Court of Exchequer in Scotland) [1998] STC 1181, 71 Tax Cas 174

Overseas pensions

Facts and Decision

Dr Albon worked outside the United Kingdom from 1960–64 and 1978–84, during which period he earned French and American pension and social security benefits. The Inland Revenue assessed these benefits under *Schedule D Case V*. The Court held that a pension stemming from contributions paid by an employee under the federal social security tax scheme cannot be regarded as an emolument of employment provided by the employer. Moreover, the pension payments were not themselves an emolument. Nor did Dr Albon have a contractual right to the pension. That being so, in terms of *Case V*, the issue was whether the pension payments made by the United States and French authorities were to be regarded as 'income arising from possessions out of the United Kingdom'. That matter had been settled authoritatively by *Aspin v Estill (Inspector of Taxes) [1987] STC 723*. It made no difference if United States social security benefits were not taxable in the United States.

[15.4.2]

Aspin v Estill (Inspector of Taxes) (Court of Appeal) [1987] STC 723

Overseas pensions

Facts and Decision

Mr Aspin was a British subject who worked in the United States of America for 20 years, returning to the United Kingdom in 1978. While in the United States he made social security contributions and as a result he became entitled to a retirement benefit. The Inland Revenue sought to tax him on those benefits. The Court held that the American social security payments received were unquestionably 'income arising from possessions out of the United Kingdom, not being income consisting of emoluments of any office or employment', and so were taxable under Schedule D Case V: *Colquhoun (Surveyor of Taxes) v Brooks (1889) 14 AC 493* and *Oppenheimer v Cattermole (Inspector of Taxes) [1975] STC 91, [1976] AC 249* were applied.

15.5 – Obtaining of tax advantages

[15.5.1]

Lewis v Inland Revenue Commissioners (Special Commissioners, 18 October 1999) [2000] 1 PBLR 16

Tax advantages

Facts and Decision

The trustees of the Redrow staff pension scheme sold 1.9 million shares in Redrow Group plc for just over £2.5 million to the company in advance of its flotation on the stock exchange, and accordingly sought payment of a tax credit. The Inland Revenue resisted payment, arguing that the trustee had received a tax advantage within the meaning of *s 709* of the *Income and Corporation Taxes Act 1988*. The trustees' were aware of the tax advantage of structuring the disposal of shares in this way and had taken counsel's advice on the subject. Their dominant motive for disposing of the shares was that the employer-related investment exceeded 5% of the scheme value, and they needed to reduce their shareholding below that level. The Special Commissioners held that the obtaining of a tax advantage was not one of the main objects of the scheme trustees when deciding to adopt the option of selling its shares to the company, rather than participating in the flotation of the shares. As trustees it would have been very difficult for them to have participated in the flotation when a cheaper and simpler alternative was available. The trustees simply did what any prudent investor would have done in the circumstances.

[15.5.2]

MacNiven v Westmorland Investments (House of Lords, unreported, 8 February 2001)

Tax advantages

Facts and Decision

A pension scheme owned an investment management subsidiary. The subsidiary borrowed money from the pension scheme on an interest-bearing basis. The pension scheme later lent money to the subsidiary so that it could repay the loan, so that the subsidiary could claim tax reliefs. The House of Lords confirmed that the repayment by the subsidiary of the interest constituted a 'payment' for the purposes of the legislation: the approach taken to the interpretation of tax statutes in the *Ramsay v IRC [1982] AC 300* series of cases was a rule of construction for identifying the business purpose for which the tax rule was intended, and where the wording of the statute was clear, *Ramsay v IRC* had no application.

[15.5.3]

Universities Superannuation Scheme v Commissioners of Inland Revenue (High Court) [1997] OPLR 15

Tax advantages

Facts and Decision

The trustee of an exempt approved retirement benefits scheme loaned money to a company to acquire property for development. It made further loans and eventually in return for one of these loans was given the right:

(a)   to acquire part of the land when the development was complete;
(b)   to acquire shares in the developer company;
(c)   to require the developer company's parent company to buy those shares at a price fixed by a specified calculation; and
(d)   to acquire shares in the developer company's parent company.

The rate of interest on the loan was intentionally set at a figure below the market rate applicable at that time to a long term loan. The trustee duly acquired the shares in the parent company. The agreement was subsequently varied so that instead of the trustee exercising its right to acquire the shares in the developer company, it would sell them to the developer company's parent company, which paid the purchase price to the trustee as a dividend. The trustee then attempted to reclaim a tax credit on the dividend. The Court held that the trustee had obtained a tax advantage such as required the Inland Revenue to make adjustments for counteracting that tax advantage under *Chapter I of Part XVII* of the *Income and Corporation Taxes Act 1988* (*ICTA 1988*). A person who was exempt from tax could obtain 'relief' from tax such as would constitute a tax advantage for the purpose of *s 709(1)* of *ICTA 1988*: *Sheppard v Commissioners of Inland Revenue (No. 2) [1993] TC 724* was not followed.

15.6 – Taxation of repayments

[15.6.1]

Hillsdown v Commissioners of Inland Revenue (High Court) [1999] OPLR 79, [1999] PLR 173, [1999] STC 561

Refunds of surplus – taxation – constructive trusts

Facts and Decision

Hillsdown obtained a refund of surplus from one of its occupational pension schemes. Following the decision in *Hillsdown v Pensions Ombudsman [1997] 1 All ER 862, [1996] OPLR 291, [1996] PLR 427*, Hillsdown was obliged to repay the sum refunded. On a proper construction of *s 601* of the *Income and Corporation Taxes Act 1988*, the Court held that a purported repayment of surplus in which no beneficial interest passed was not a payment for the purposes of this *section*.

[15.6.2]

International Power v Healy (House of Lords) [2001] PLR 121 at para 31

Refunds of surplus – taxation

Principle

Section 601(1) of the *Income and Corporation Taxes Act 1988* was plainly not intended to tax an employer on money which had never come into its pension scheme.

[15.6.3]

National Power v Feldon (High Court, unreported, 30 July 1997)

Refunds of surplus – taxation

Principles

It was neither unthinkable nor unknown in practice for a return of surplus to be made to an employer without consulting the Inland Revenue, and this was recognised by the terms of *s 601* of the *Income and Corporation Taxes Act 1988*, which imposed a 40% flat rate charge on any return to an employer, whether pursuant to *schedule 22* to the *Act* or not. This alternative was not necessarily limited to a return of assets on winding-up. However, it might still be possible for the Inland Revenue to withdraw approval, having regard to the wide terms of *s 591B(1)* of the *Act*.

15.7 – Taxation of breaches of trust

[15.7.1]

Hillsdown v Commissioners of Inland Revenue (High Court) [1999] OPLR 79, [1999] PLR 173, [1999] STC 561

Taxation of breaches of trust

Facts and Decision

Hillsdown obtained a refund of surplus from one of its occupational pension schemes. Following the decision in *Hillsdown v Pensions Ombudsman [1997] 1 All ER 862, [1996] OPLR 291, [1996] PLR 427*, Hillsdown was obliged to repay the sum refunded. The Inland Revenue refused to reimburse the tax paid on the refund. On a proper construction of *s 601* of the *Income and Corporation Taxes Act 1988*, the Court held that a purported repayment of surplus in which no beneficial interest passed was not a payment for the purposes of this *section*. If this conclusion were wrong, Hillsdown's claim against the Inland Revenue for restitution would have failed, since the Inland Revenue would not have been unjustly enriched. Similarly, Hillsdown would not have been granted judicial review since the Inland Revenue had no part to play in the decision to make the payments: the Court would only intervene if it was satisfied that the unfairness of which the applicant complained rendered the insistence by the Commissioners on performing their duties or exercising their powers an abuse of such powers by the Commissioners: *Re Preston [1985] AC 835* was applied.

[15.7.2]

R v IRC ex parte Roux Waterside Inn (High Court) [1997] OPLR 239, [1997] PLR 123, [1997] TC 545

Taxation of breaches of trust

Facts and Decision

The trustee of an exempt approved pension scheme transferred £900,000 to a new pension scheme on interim tax approval, which the same day took steps to ensure that it was no longer a scheme capable of tax approval.

This resulted in a 40% tax charge on the new scheme's assets, but those were, it was argued, to be assessed on the value of the assets taken the day before approval was lost, so no tax charge would in fact arise. The Inland Revenue withdrew approval from the transferring scheme. The Court held that the withdrawal of tax approval from an exempt approved pension scheme was justified in these circumstances, whether or not the tax avoidance scheme in fact worked.

[15.7.3]

Venables v Hornby (High Court, unreported, 14 June 2001)

Taxation of breaches of trust

Facts and Decision

Since Mr Venables was a trustee of his pension scheme, the Court held that if he was not entitled to receive the pension which was in fact granted to him, the scheme could have recovered any instalments from him as a constructive trustee. All of the following conditions were fulfilled:

(a)   the payment was in breach of trust;
(b)   the recipient was accountable to the trustees as an actual or constructive trustee; and
(c)   the recipient was able and prepared to account to the trustees.

Accordingly, there was no payment to him within the meaning of *s 600* of the *Income and Corporation Taxes Act 1988*: *Hillsdown v Commissioners of Inland Revenue [1999] OPLR 79* was followed, while *R v Commissioners of Inland Revenue ex parte Roux Waterside Inn [1997] OPLR 239* was distinguished.

15.8 – Trading

British Telecom Pension Scheme Trustees v Clarke (Court of Appeal) [2000] OPLR 53, [2000] PLR 157

Trading – sub-underwriting

Facts and Decision

The British Telecom Pension Schemes regularly undertook sub-underwriting of new issues. They did so in a habitual and organised manner. The sub-underwriting was undertaken as an essential part of the investment process. The Inland Revenue argued that the profits were taxable as income from a trade in accordance with *Case I* of *Schedule D*. The trustees maintained that they were entitled to claim the exemption set out in *s 592(3)* of the *Income and Corporation Taxes Act 1988* (*ICTA 1988*), which exempts from income tax any receipts taxable under *Case VI* of *Schedule D*, since, the trustees argued, they were not trading. The Special Commissioners concluded that the trustees were not trading and therefore the profits were exempt from income tax. The question was one of fact, and the Court of Appeal would not interfere with the decision of the tribunal unless it was manifestly wrong or vitiated by a mistake of law. In this case, the evidence was ambiguous, and while the Special Commissioners had shown some tendency to error, it had not vitiated their finding of fact. The Special Commissioners' decision was therefore upheld. This was not a test case in the full sense, since the huge size of this scheme made it untypical of the generality of pension schemes. The exemption from income tax payable under *Case VI* (but not *Case I*) of *Schedule D* in *s 592(3)* of *ICTA 1988* was not to be construed in such a way as to provide a generous measure of relief for pension schemes. The case law on *Case I* of *Schedule D* was extensive, and it was that, rather than any supposedly purposive construction of the *section*, which must be the guide. If sub-underwriting in a pension scheme is not otherwise exempt from tax, income from it is chargeable at the rate applicable to trusts, because it is not 'other property' within the meaning of *s 686(2)(c)* of *ICTA 1988*.

[15.8.2]

Koenigsberger v Mellor (Court of Appeal) [1996] PLR 153

Member's contributions – relevant earnings

Facts and Decision

Mr Koenigsberger was a Lloyd's name and a barrister. He claimed relief on his contributions made from his Lloyd's earnings to his retirement annuity contract. The Court held that his income as a Lloyd's name was not income immediately derived by him from the carrying on or exercise by him of his trade as an individual, since an external name does not carry out any trade at all. The trade out of which the income arises consists of the business of underwriting, which is the job of the managing agent. Accordingly, the earnings were not relevant earnings and did not qualify for relief. Not much store could be set by the notion of 'personal exertion' as being required for carrying out a trade: *Fry (Inspector of Taxes) v Shiels' Trustees (1914) 6 TC 583* and *M'Dougall (Curator Bonis for M'Dougall) v Smith (Surveyor of Taxes) (1918) 7 TC 134* were distinguished.

15.9 – Taxation of discretionary benefits

[15.9.1]

Re J Bibby & Sons Ltd Pensions Trust Deed (High Court) [1952] WN 402, [1952] 2 TLR 297, [1952] 2 All ER 483

Inheritance tax – discretionary benefits

Facts and Decision

An employee was a member of his employer's non-contributory pension scheme, which when he died, provided his widow with a pension. The pension was payable at the trustees' discretion. Since the trustees had an absolute discretion to give or withhold the pension, the Court held that it did not constitute property such as constituted part of the member's estate for inheritance tax purposes.

15.10 – Value Added Tax

[15.10.1]

BOC International v Commissioners of Customs & Excise (Value Added Tax Tribunal) [1982] VATTR 84

Value added tax

Facts and Decision

BOC established a subsidiary to act as the trustee company of three of its pension schemes. The trustee company incurred commission charges to its brokers in respect of the purchase of shares of various companies. The parent company sought to recover the tax as input tax, but Customs & Excise opposed this. The trustee company was group registered with the parent company for value added tax. The Tribunal held that where the function of investment of a pension scheme was entrusted to a company which formed part of a registered group with its parent company, such function of investment formed part of the business activity of the parent company by virtue of the provisions of the *Finance Act 1972, s 21(1)(b)*. The effect of that *subsection* was as though the investment functions were being carried out by the parent company itself. The parent company was therefore allowed to treat the value added tax on the investment services as input tax. *Commissioners of Customs & Excise v British Railways Board [1976] 1 WLR 1036* and *Linotype and Machinery Ltd v Commissioners of Customs & Excise [1978] VATTR 123* were distinguished.

[15.10.2]

British Airways Board v Commissioners of Customs & Excise (VAT Tribunal, unreported, 17 October 1979)

Value added tax

Facts and Decision

British Airways applied for the trust company of its pension scheme to be brought within group registration for the purposes of value added tax. The trust company was not a subsidiary, being a company limited by guarantee without a share capital. British Airways had the right to nominate half the trustees of the pension scheme, and the chairman was appointed from its nominees and the chairman had a casting vote. The articles of association of the trust company provided that the trustees of the pension scheme *ipso facto* became members of the trust company. Customs & Excise resisted this application, and British Airways and the trust company appealed to the VAT Tribunal. The Tribunal held that British Airways had control of the trust company: *Noble v Commissioners of Inland Revenue (1925) 12 TC 911* was applied. It did not accept the argument that because the trustees could only act in the interests of the beneficiaries under the pension scheme, British Airways did not control the trustees or the trust company. A company can only act within its powers, and the directors of a company can only act *bona fide* in the interests of the company as a whole. But this does not prevent another body corporate or individual having control of it, though the extent to which that control can properly be exercised is so limited. However, since the control was not empowered by statute but by statutory instrument, *s 21(8)* of the *Finance Act 1972* did not permit the companies to be grouped, and the appeal failed. The treatment of trustees of pension schemes for tax purposes in relation to input tax and *s 21* of the *Finance Act 1972* was beset with anomalies depending on the constitution of the trustees. Consideration might be given to the desirability of achieving greater consistency of treatment and fairness.

[15.10.3]

Century Life v Commissioners of Customs & Excise (Court of Appeal, 19 December 2000) [2001] 12 PBLR 9

Value added tax

Facts and Decision

Century Life undertook the personal pensions misselling review for Lincoln. It acted in Lincoln's name and corresponded on its headed notepaper. It issued questionnaires to policyholders with requests for benefit statements where appropriate and requested scheme booklets from trustees, independent financial advisers and other insurance companies. Where charged for this information, Century Life invoiced Lincoln on a monthly basis. It chased up replies by telephone or by visits, and checked that the case was one requiring review, that all the relevant information had been provided, that the correct scheme information was available and that Lincoln's procedures had been followed. It then analysed the case, and advised on any offer to be made to policyholders. If the service was an insurance transaction (which included related services provided by insurance brokers and insurance agents), it would not attract value added tax by virtue of *para 4 group 2* of *schedule 9* to the *Value Added Tax Act 1994*. However, Customs & Excise opposed this classification of Century Life's activities. The Court held that the services provided by Century Life were not only incidental to the insurance transactions, and therefore Century Life's activities fell within the scope of the *Article 13B* of the *Value Added Tax 6th Directive 77/388*. They also fell within the scope of exemption in *para 4 group 2* of *schedule 9* to the *Value Added Tax Act 1994*.

[15.10.4]

Commissioners of Customs & Excise v British Railways Board (Court of Appeal) [1976] I WLR 1036, [1976] 3 All ER 100

Value added tax

Facts and Decision

British Railways Board was the sole trustee of its pension schemes. It sought to recover as input tax the value added tax paid on the fees for professional advice in relation to the pension schemes. The Court held that the Board's performance of its functions as the trustee of the schemes was simply a part of its railway business. It maintained, managed and accounted separately for these funds, not as a professional trustee, but as the employer of the beneficiaries. It acted as a trustee, not for fun or out of philanthropic motives, but because the provision of proper pension arrangements was an integral part of the management of a modern business. There was no fundamental principle of taxation law that a person who is operating in a fiduciary capacity should be regarded separately from the same person when operating in relation to his or her own personal affairs. There was no justification in the *Finance Act 1972* for saying that the Board had to be regarded as other than one body in respect of its general undertaking on the one hand, and its administration of the pension scheme on the other hand. On the facts of this case, the administration of the pension scheme was in fact all part of the conduct of the general undertaking.

[15.10.5]

Linotype and Machinery v Commissioners of Customs & Excise (Value Added Tax Tribunal) [1978] VATTR 123

Value added tax

Facts and Decision

An employer attempted to reclaim the value added tax on the accounting, insurance and consultancy expenses payable by its pension scheme, to which it was obliged to contribute and meet the expenses of management. The value added tax was in respect of services supplied to the trustees of the pension scheme, and the Tribunal held that accordingly the employer was not entitled to deduct the tax charged on those supplies as input tax. The employer's control of the identity of the trustees did not confer on the employer a power of control over their actions.

[15.10.6]

Manchester Ship Canal v Commissioners of Customs & Excise (High Court) [1982] STC 351

Value added tax

Facts and Decision

The Manchester Ship Canal established three pension schemes. It took actuarial advice on the funding of these matters, the trustees being little if anything more than custodians of the schemes. The powers and duties in relation to funding and management were divided between the company and committees of management which it had set up. In two of the schemes, the actuary reported to the committee, and in one, the actuary reported to the company. The company was charged for actuarial advice on solvency matters and relating to the cost of augmentations. It sought to treat the value added tax as input tax, but Customs & Excise opposed this in so far as it related to advice on solvency matters. The Court observed that the supply of advice about actuarial insolvency was plainly made to the company, it related to something which was part of the management concerns of the company and the mere fact that under the rules the reports had to go to the committee could not alter the fact, which was clear, that the advice was for the purposes of the business carried on by the company. The company was therefore allowed to treat the value added tax on the actuarial advice as input tax. *Commissioners of Customs & Excise v British Railways Board [1976] 1 WLR 1036* and *Linotype and Machinery Ltd v Commissioners of Customs & Excise [1978] VATTR 123* were considered.

[15.10.7]

National Coal Board v Commissioners of Customs & Excise (High Court) [1982] STC 863

Value added tax

Facts and Decision

Customs & Excise raised an assessment of value added tax for the administrative services which the National Coal Board had supplied to its pension schemes. A provision of the pension scheme, introduced by amendment in order to avoid the payment of tax, provided that the employer contributions 'shall be reduced by such sum as may from time to time be agreed between the trustees and the Board as being fair and reasonable', having regard to the costs of managing and administering the scheme and the costs to the Board of services rendered by the Board in connection with or for the purposes of the scheme. The Court held that the alterations were genuine, and motive should not be taken into account when determining liability to pay value added tax. Looked at as a whole, the scheme was one whereby the Board's contribution was to be calculated on a basis which took account of the cost of running the scheme. The Board's activities should not be categorised as a supply of services, and the amounts deducted under the provision for services could not be regarded as consideration. The Board's activities did not, therefore, give rise to a liability for value added tax.

[15.10.8]

Plessey v Commissioners of Customs & Excise (Value Added Tax Tribunal) [1996] PLR 89

Value added tax

Facts and Decision

Representative beneficiaries of a pension scheme instructed solicitors in relation to a merger of funds. The representative beneficiaries were indemnified in respect of costs by the trustees. Plessey argued that the supplies of legal advice were made to the scheme and through it to Plessey, which could therefore recover the value added tax. However, the Tribunal held that the legal supplies were not made to Plessey or the trustees, since the clients of the solicitors were the representative beneficiaries. The value added tax was therefore irrecoverable.

[15.10.9]

Ultimate Advisory Services v Commissioners of Customs & Excise (Value Added Tax Tribunal) [1993] PLR 273

Value added tax

Facts and Decision

Ultimate Advisory Services sought to recover input value added tax connected with its company pension scheme. This value added tax related to solicitors' bills in relation to the improper charges of a co-partner of the trustees on a property development scheme. The employer had the legal responsibility for paying the fees under the trust deed. The Tribunal held that events within a scheme as a total entity may properly be regarded as being within the business activities of an employer, but the deployment of the fund within a scheme is the responsibility of the trustees. The legal advice in this case related to a specific investment by the trustees. The fact that the employer may have been instrumental in issuing instructions did not change the situation. The commonality of interest did not mean that the separation of powers and duties should be ignored. On the facts, the services were supplied to the trustees of the pension scheme and not to the employer. The employer's payment was not part of the purpose of the employer's business, and so the input tax was not recoverable.

[15.10.10]

Wellcome Trust v Commissioners of Customs & Excise (European Court of Justice) [1996] PLR 419

Value added tax

Facts and Decision

The Wellcome Trust was a charitable trust which owned a substantial shareholding in the Wellcome Foundation Limited. It sold some shares in that company, and other shares were exchanged for shares in a new holding company, Wellcome plc, raising £200 million. A second tranche of shares were sold by the bookbuilding method, a form of auction by which potential investors submit tenders for shares. The proceeds of this sale were used to buy new investments. The Trust sought to recover value added tax on the expenditure incurred in the preparation of the second share sale, as an economic activity within the meaning of *Article 4(2)* of *Directive 77/388/EEC* on the harmonisation of laws of the Member States relating to turnover taxes. The Court held that the mere exercise of the right of ownership by its holder cannot in itself be regarded as constituting an economic activity. Transactions in shares may fall within the scope of value added tax, in particular where such transactions are effected as part of a commercial share-dealing activity, or in order to secure a direct or indirect involvement in the management of the company in which the holding has been acquired. However, the Trust was forbidden to engage in such activities, and must therefore be taken to be confining its activities to managing a portfolio in the same way as a private investor. The Trust was therefore unable to reclaim the value added tax.

[15.10.11]

Winterthur Life v Customs & Excise (Value Added Tax Tribunal, 29 May 1997) 08 PBLR 21

Value added tax

Facts and Decision

Winterthur operated self-invested personal pension schemes established under trust, which invested in insurance policies. Customs & Excise sought to charge value added tax on the administration and transaction charges which the Winterthur companies, which were not the insurer, deducted from the proceeds of the policies. Winterthur appealed on the basis that the supplies were exempt under provisions of *Item 1, Group 2, Schedule 9* of the *Value Added Tax Act 1994* (which implemented the *Sixth EU Value Added Tax Directive*), being the making of arrangements for the provision of insurance, or under *Group 5, Schedule 9*, being for the transfer or receipt of, or any dealing with, money. The Tribunal held that the trusts should not be analysed in terms of conventional beneficial interests. They were much closer to the trusts attaching to an unadministered estate which does not confer on the legatees beneficial interests properly so called, but only the right to have the estate administered according to the terms of the will and to have their annuities or legacies paid or provided for accordingly. Their substantial purpose and effect was securing the provision of annuity and lump sum benefits out of a fund specifically set aside for the purpose. Properly read, the schemes gave rise to a contract of insurance, and the services provided by the Winterthur companies were part of the making of arrangements for the provision of insurance, such as entitled the supply to be exempt from value added tax.

- The general charges which were not divided between specific functions would not, were it necessary to so find, be exempt under the heads of Schedule 5.

- The charges on contributions received and on the installation or variation of a direct debit were *prima facie* exempt under *Schedule 5*.
- Charges for asset action and transaction charges might be exempt under *Schedule 5*, depending on the precise nature of the services provided.
- Charges for the appointment of an investment manager would not be exempt under *Schedule 5*.

However, in view of the main conclusion that the relevant services were exempt under *Item 1 Group 2 Schedule 9* of the *Value Added Tax Act 1994*, further investigation was unnecessary.

Part 16 – Pension Rights on Divorce

16 – Introduction

The pension rights of divorcing parties can easily be their most valuable assets, but despite this, the courts have yet fully to work through the best way in which to apportion their value and to divide up those rights. Three problems arise in relation to pension rights on divorce:

(a) whether the loss of such rights could cause grave financial hardship such as to justify refusing to grant the divorce;
(b) how to value the pension rights; and
(c) whether the Court could or should rewrite the terms of the pension trust.

The first of these questions has been considered repeatedly by the courts, but will require reconsideration now that Parliament has made provision for pension sharing orders. The circumstances in which the loss of rights to spouses' benefits will cause grave financial hardship must now be very limited indeed.

The valuation of pension rights for the purposes of divorce is a subset of the problem of how to value pension rights generally. The courts, not having advanced mathematical skills, do not find this process easy, even when they have the assistance of actuaries. Scottish courts have long in general taken pensions into account on divorce, unlike English courts, and so the relevant case law is all Scottish. It remains to be seen now that English courts must also take pension rights into account whether they will follow the same approach.

In the past, the courts have occasionally found methods to exercise jurisdiction over pension arrangements, and now with earmarking orders and pension sharing orders, the courts will be able to exercise this jurisdiction generally. However, the courts have yet to consider how this jurisdiction should be exercised in relation to pension sharing orders, and even in relation to earmarking orders, the principles are still being worked out.

This is an area of law which is in flux. It is likely that in the next few years, vague principles will be turned into hard case law. However, while the recent pension sharing legislation takes its time to bed down, practitioners will be feeling their way for some time to come.

16.1 – Pension Rights on Divorce

[16.1.1]

Archer v Archer (Court of Appeal) [1999] 1 FLR 327, [1999] 2 FCR 158, [1999] Fam Law 141

Divorce – grave financial hardship

Facts and Decision

The parties were married in 1971 and separated in 1991, with two children over the age of 18. The husband was aged 55 and the wife was 53. Throughout the marriage, the wife had been a wife and mother. The wife opposed the divorce which her husband sought. She argued that the dissolution of the marriage would result in grave financial or other hardship to her since she would lose the surviving widow's pension, and that it would in all the circumstances be wrong to dissolve the marriage, relying on *s 5(1)* of the *Matrimonial Causes Act 1973*. The wife had considerable capital assets and was in receipt of a periodical payments order from her husband. The wife's capital assets were worth about £500,000. The pension was worth some £11,000 a year gross, £9000 a year net. The Court held that the question under *s 5* had to be seen in two stages:

(a)   'Is there grave financial or other hardship?'; and
(b)   'Would it in all the circumstances be wrong to dissolve the marriage?'

The wife could expect in the ordinary course of events to outlive her husband, but not by all that much. She had no dependants. A judge could properly conclude that the condition that the wife might suffer if her ex-spouse predeceased her was hardship, but not grave hardship.

[16.1.2]

Bosworthick v Bosworthick (High Court) [1927] P 64

Divorce – post-nuptial settlement

Facts and Decision

Mrs Bosworthick promised to pay an annuity to her husband of £300 a year. This was, the Court held, a post–nuptial settlement for the purposes of the *Matrimonial Causes Act 1859*. The courts were to construe the relevant section liberally and widely.

[16.1.3]

Brooks v Brooks (House of Lords) [1996] AC 375, [1995] 3 All ER 257, [1995] OPLR 125, [1995] PLR 173

Divorce – post-nuptial settlement – Court's powers

Facts and Decision

A husband and wife divorced after 12 years of marriage. When they divorced, the husband was 63 and the wife was 54. The husband was the sole member of a small self-administered pension scheme, which was in substantial surplus. He had joined the scheme after his marriage. The Court held that in considering the purpose of the husband when entering into the scheme, the scheme must be looked at in the round and in the context of the circumstances then subsisting. Viewed in this light, the husband was taken to have entered into the scheme with the intention of providing for the retirement of himself and his wife by the highly tax efficient means afforded by the scheme. His pension would provide financial support for both of them in his retirement. If his wife were still alive when he retired, he could direct that part of his pension benefit should be used to make separate provision for her after his death. Should he die prematurely, the death benefits would be available for her. A disposition of this character fell within the wide meaning given to marriage settlement, and so far as it constituted a settlement made by the husband, the Court had the power to vary the scheme. The key feature was the presence of the right to surrender pension in favour of his wife, and the lump sum death benefit payable to his family. It would not, however, be right to vary one scheme member's rights to the detriment of other members. Directing a variation which does not meet with Inland Revenue approval would normally be prejudicial to the rights of the other scheme members.

[16.1.4]

Burrow v Burrow (High Court) [1999] 1 FLR 508, [1999] 2 FCR 549

Divorce – earmarking orders

Facts and Decision

Mrs Burrow sought a divorce from her husband. She obtained an earmarking order against his pension before the district judge. Mr Burrow appealed. The Court observed that disadvantages can arise where an earmarking order is made well before any sums can be expected to become payable under it. The husband in this case might not retire for another 15 years or more. It was difficult to predict with any reliability what might be the quantum of periodical payments which it might be appropriate for the husband to pay to the wife at the end of such a period. It would always be open to either party to make further application to vary the periodical payments order, and the Court would then be in at least as effective a position as it then was to make the appropriate order with up to date information and detail before it. Also, as and when the husband received his pension, then if the wife had not remarried and still had an entitlement to periodical payments from him, the sum which the husband received by way of annuity would of course be taken into account as and when any assessment of the correct periodical payments order was made. The Court rejected the concept of an entitlement in the sense of some accrued right required by one spouse against the other spouse's pension scheme. *T v T [1998] OPLR 1* was followed.

[16.1.5]

Carpenter v Carpenter (Sheriff Court) [1990] SLT (Sh Ct) 68, [1990] SCLR 206

Divorce – valuation of pension rights

Facts and Decision

Mrs Carpenter sought a divorce from her husband. Mr Carpenter was a police sergeant aged 45 and intended to retire on pension from age 50. Mrs Carpenter sought an award of half the capital value of the pension. There were special circumstances, the Court held, which would justify some proportion other than 50% being used for calculating the amount of a capital sum to be awarded to the pursuer. The certainty of the award which Mrs Carpenter would receive, set against the lack of certainty that Mr

Carpenter would receive any money at all in that he was required to survive to 1994, was one factor. A court must also consider the nature of the asset. Mrs Carpenter would receive a liquid asset in the form of a capital sum; Mr Carpenter would be left with a deferred asset. Mrs Carpenter would, in obtaining her liquid asset, denude the defender of personal savings and this was a factor which must be considered, as the Court must have regard for what was 'reasonable having regard to the resources of the parties'. Taking into consideration all the factors in the case, the special circumstances were such as would justify a court in considering that the net value of this particular asset should be shared 'fairly' by making a capital award to the pursuer of three-eighths of its value. *Muir v Muir [1989] SCLR 445* was considered and applied. Interest was not awarded on this sum, since the sum was for a period prior to any right to the award arising.

[16.1.6]

Dible v Dible (Court of Session, Scotland) [1997] SLT 787, [1997] SCLR 726

Divorce – valuation of pension rights

Facts and Decision

Mr and Mrs Dible separated after 32 years of marriage. Divorce proceedings were started five years later. Mr Dible was entitled to a pension, which had a surviving widow's pension attached. The Court was asked to decide how this should be taken into account in the divorce settlement. There was a substantial difference, the Court held, between the widow's benefit element of an interest in a pension scheme, and other contingent interests such as the prospective pensioner's right to a pension. The difference was that the very contingency which was the only event upon which a spouse could be said to become entitled to claim a share of the current estimated or calculated value of the interest was the contingency which rendered that interest nugatory, namely divorce. The character of the supposed asset or interest was such that it could not really form part of the matrimonial property for the purposes of division on divorce at all. *Bannon v Bannon [1993] SLT 999*, *Brooks v Brooks [1993] SLT 184*, *Welsh v Welsh [1994] SLT 828* and *Crosbie v Crosbie [1996] SLT (Sh Ct) 86* were approved, while *Gribb v Gribb [1994] SLT (Sh Ct) 43*, *Holmes v Holmes* (17 June 1996, unreported) and *Murphy v Murphy [1996] SLT (Sh Ct) 91* were disapproved.

[16.1.7]

Gardner v Gardner (High Court) [1992] PLR 159, [1993] 2 FLR 315

Divorce – grave financial hardship

Facts and Decision

Mr Gardner sought a divorce on the ground that he and his wife had been separated for five years. Initially his wife opposed this on the ground that this would cause her grave financial hardship. On Mr Gardner's retirement, her state pension would be reduced because of the share of Mr Gardner's pension which she would be awarded. After negotiations, terms were reached and a *decree nisi* was pronounced.

[16.1.8]

Gulline v Gulline (Sheriff Court, Scotland) [1993] OPLR 25, [1992] PLR 187

Divorce – valuation of pension rights

Facts and Decision

Mr and Mrs Gulline divorced. The parties disagreed about the capital sum to be paid in relation to Mr Gulline's police pension entitlement. On actuarial evidence, the Court valued that part of the entitlement referable to the period during which the marriage was continuing at the date when it was due to fall into payment, and discounted the value back to the date of separation. Since the pension entitlement would not come into payment for some time, the Court awarded interest on the capital sum until it was paid.

[16.1.9]

Jackson v Jackson (Court of Appeal) [1993] 2 FLR 848

Divorce – grave financial hardship

Facts and Decision

Mr Jackson petitioned for divorce on the basis that he had been separated from his wife for five years, but his wife opposed on the ground that she would suffer serious financial hardship, in that she would lose her potential widow's pension under her husband's pension scheme. The loss of a chance of acquiring 20 to 25% of income was, the Court held, grave financial hardship which would result from the dissolution of the marriage. However, the Court should take account of the impact of social security benefits in assessing grave financial hardship. In this case, every pound of pension which Mrs Jackson received would result in a reduction of one pound of social security benefit. Accordingly, she would not suffer grave financial hardship if the divorce were granted: *Dorrell v Dorrell [1972] 1 WLR 1087* was considered.

[16.1.10]

Le Marchant v Le Marchant (Court of Appeal) [1977] 3 All ER 610, [1977] 1 WLR 559

Divorce – grave financial hardship

Facts and Decision

Mr Le Marchant petitioned for divorce on the basis that he had been separated from his wife for five years, but his wife opposed on the ground that she would suffer serious financial hardship, in that she would lose her potential widow's pension under her husband's pension scheme. The Court held that it would be quite wrong to approach this kind of case on the footing that a wife was entitled to be compensated pound for pound for what she would lose in consequence of the divorce. Mrs Le Marchant had to show, not that she would lose something by being divorced, but that she would suffer grave financial hardship, which was quite another matter altogether. If grave financial hardship were established, the right approach was that the petition should be dismissed unless the petitioner could meet that concern by putting forward a proposal which was acceptable to the Court as reasonable in all the circumstances, and which was sufficient to remove the element of grave financial hardship which otherwise would lead to the dismissal of the petition.

[16.1.11]

Lort-Williams v Lort-Williams (Court of Appeal) [1951] P 395

Divorce – post-nuptial settlement

Facts and Decision

Mr and Mrs Lort-Williams divorced. Mrs Lort-Williams sought variation of a policy of assurance taken out by her husband during the marriage as a post-nuptial settlement. Although, the Court held, the wife's interest under the policy was contingent and dependent on certain factors, the policy had been taken out during the married life with the object of creating a fund from which the wife might benefit, and was *prima facie* a nuptial settlement. It did not cease to be that because it also did something else.

[16.1.12]

Miller v Miller (Sheriff's Court, Scotland) [2000] Fam LR 19, 49 PBLR 4

Divorce – valuation of pension rights

Facts and Decision

Mr and Mrs Miller sought a divorce. Mrs Miller sought value for Mr Miller's pension rights based on an actuarial approach different from the standard cash equivalent basis. On a proper construction, the Court held that the *Divorce etc (Pensions) (Scotland) Regulations 1996 (SI 1996 No 1676)* did not permit any basis other than a cash equivalent transfer value to be used. It was not appropriate to use an entirely different basis for valuation. It might, though, be feasible in certain cases to state the amount of the cash equivalent and then set out why it did not provide a fair value.

[16.1.13]

Muir v Muir (Sheriff Court) [1989] SCLR 445, [1989] SLT (Sh Ct) 20

Divorce – valuation of pension rights

Facts and Decision

Mr Muir sought a divorce from his wife. He was entitled to pension benefits from his employer's scheme, which he had joined after marriage. It was a non-contributory scheme. The parties disagreed as to how the value of the pension should be split. The Court decided not to share the pension entitlement equally. The pension benefit was not a realisable asset. Mr Muir, by being obliged to share this piece of matrimonial property with his ex-wife, would end up with no immediate cash return from the division, but his ex-wife would. This circumstance justified an alternative basis for division. On the circumstances of the case, the Court awarded Mrs Muir two-fifths of the value of the pension scheme.

[16.1.14]

T v T (High Court) [1998] OPLR 1 at 7H–9G, 12D–17D, [1998] PLR 221 at paras 46–57, 72–115

Divorce – earmarking orders

Facts and Decision

A husband and wife divorced in their mid 40s. The wife had a deferred pension benefit from 17 years' service payable from age 60 worth £373 per month (subject to indexation). The husband had a final salary benefit which if he remained in service to normal retirement date it was agreed would be worth £88,000 a year, and life cover worth at least £336,000 should he die in service, as well as money purchase benefits worth £2,000. These values were, the Court observed, inevitably speculative. Earmarking orders do no more than expand the routes available to the Court whereby implementation of already-available orders for periodical payments and lump sums can be channelled. Earmarking orders are supplementary to other forms of pension provision and not a new or distinct species. They therefore continue in force until the death or remarriage of the recipient. Since the value of the pension entitlements remained unclear and an appropriate periodical payments order could be made when the husband retired, there was no advantage in making an earmarking order at this stage. However, the trustees of the husband's scheme were directed to pay from any death benefits an amount to the ex-wife based on the periodical payments order in force at the time of his death.

Part 17 – Insurance Policies

17 – Introduction

Pension schemes are not directly concerned with insurance, but indirectly insurance comes into pensions in a number of ways:

- There are a variety of insurance products which can be used for securing or underwriting pension liabilities.
- Insurance products can be used to match death benefit promises.
- Trustees may take liability insurance to protect them against claims.

In each of these instances, the terms of the insurance policy are going to be critical for establishing the rights and liabilities of the pension scheme and its members. Cases involving the terms of insurance policies very much turn on the wording of the specific insurance policy concerned, as can be seen from the cases in this chapter.

Insurance law is a specialist area of the law far removed in scope from pension law. While the pension context may have implications for the interpretation of insurance policies, as indicated in *Royal Heritage Life v Pensions Ombudsman [1997] OPLR 171*, the principles of insurance law are quite different from those in pension law. If pensions practitioners find that they have a problem involving insurance law, ordinarily they should take specialist advice.

17.1 – Surrender values

[17.1.1]

Legal & General v Pensions Ombudsman (High Court) [2000] OPLR 153

Maladministration – refusal to disclose details of calculation of surrender values

Principle

The Pensions Ombudsman's powers to investigate maladministration did not include power to investigate the fairness of surrender terms of an insurance policy in which the pension scheme was invested. However, the refusal of the insurer to provide details of the calculation of payment under that contract could constitute maladministration. In the absence of specific provision to the contrary, where a contract provides for a payment to be made, calculated in accordance with a formula known to one party alone, that party must disclose the formula to the other party so that it can check that the calculation is correct.

[17.1.2]

Royal Heritage Life v Pensions Ombudsman (High Court) [1997] OPLR 171

Interpretation of policy

Facts and Decision

Mr George was a member of an insured pension scheme. He requested a transfer value to his new employer's scheme, and the transfer value paid by the insurer was reduced by 17% to reflect the early surrender penalties under the insurance policy securing the benefits. Mr George complained to the Pensions Ombudsman, who upheld his complaint. Royal Heritage Life appealed. The Court held that the rights of the members were to be determined by reference to the rules, which reflected the insurance-based nature of the scheme. There was provision under the scheme to assign the policy, but no request to do this had been received. The policy was a contract between the trustee and the insurance company. One condition of the policy was that before normal retirement date the insurance company should if the trustee so requested use the surrender value of the member's fund to secure pensions to the member. It was clear that the rules and the policy had to be read together and in such a way as to make sense of each and as a whole. Neither contained a provision stating which was to prevail if there were a conflict. The condition about securing pensions before normal retirement date did not only apply to actual early retirement. It applied at any time before normal retirement date and could therefore apply before the member was even entitled to take early retirement. The surrender value was therefore the proper amount to be paid, and Royal Heritage Life's appeal was successful.

17.2 – Guarantees

[17.2.1]

Equitable Life v Hyman (House of Lords) [2000] OPLR 101, [2000] PLR 249

Guarantees on annuity rates – exercise of insurer's discretion over distribution of final bonuses

Facts and Decision

Equitable Life offered policyholders the option of buying with-profits policies with guaranteed annuity rates. When market rates dropped beneath those guaranteed rates, it purported to use a power under its articles of association to distribute surplus through final bonuses, in order to equalise so far as possible the total value to the policyholder, whether or not he or she chose to exercise the right to a guaranteed annuity rate. The Court held that an implied term may be derived from the language of a document read in its particular factual setting. Additionally, no legal discretion could be used for purposes contrary to those of the instrument by which it was conferred. Equitable Life could not, therefore, use the power in its articles of association in this way.

[17.2.2]

Sun Alliance v Pensions Ombudsman (High Court, unreported, 17 October 2000)

Guarantees on annuity rates – increase in insurance

Facts and Decision

Sun Alliance withdrew guaranteed annuity rates in respect of new entrants, and additional premiums paid to an employer's pension scheme which was invested in an insurance policy. The terms of the policy required the acceptance in writing of Sun Alliance of any increase in insurance. Policyholders complained to the Pensions Ombudsman about the withdrawal of the guaranteed annuity rates. The Court held that the ordinary meaning of insurance is an agreement, in consideration of one or more premiums to pay on an occurrence of a specified future event, sums or benefits calculated in accordance with the terms of the policy. Thus there were two elements: the premium payable by the insured and the benefit payable by the insurer. An increase in such insurance must in principle involve an increase in both those elements. Therefore Sun Alliance were entitled to act as they did. There was no importance in the fact that no attempt had been made to segregate the various notional cash funds. Mathematically it could have been done, but unless there was a change in the guaranteed annuity rate, there was no point in so doing.

17.3 – Life assurance

Fontana v Skandia and Molesworths (Court of Appeal, 14 December 2000)

Life assurance – contract

Facts and Decision

Mr Gosley took out a *section 226* policy with Skandia Life. He also took out life assurance to the value of £100,000. He failed to pay his premium for the life assurance in 1989, and Skandia sent him a standard form letter stating that the terms of his scheme allowed 30 days of grace from the due date for contributions to be paid. Mr Gosley was abroad at the time and on his return settled his contributions, outside the 30 day period. Before his life assurance could be reinstated, Skandia required him to complete a declaration of good health. He did not do this. In April 1990, Mr Gosley died in a road accident. Skandia denied liability to pay, since evidence of good health had not been provided, and returned the contributions after the administratrix had signed a form agreeing that the payment of the amount constituted a full discharge of the liability of Skandia Life. Mr Gosley's administratrix sued for the balance of the life assurance. The Court held that the requirement for Mr Gosley to return evidence of good health was not an offer to reinstate cover, and Mr Gosley's sending of the cheque was not an offer to re-enter into life assurance, merely an invitation to Skandia to consider reinstatement. The life cover was not, therefore, reinstated. In any case, the waiver signed for receipt of the refund of contributions was effective in releasing any claims.

Fuji Finance v Aetna Life Insurance Co Ltd (Court of Appeal) [1996] 4 All ER 608, [1996] 3 WLR 871, [1996] LRLR 365

Life assurance

Facts and Decision

Tyndall Assurance issued Fuji with what it described variously as a life assurance policy or as a capital investment bond for £50,000; the life assured was stated to be Mr Tait. The policy required Tyndall to maintain nine funds as subdivisions of its long-term business fund, and linked the benefits payable under it to the value at maturity of the units in the funds to which it was linked. By the terms of the policy the policyholder might switch from one fund to another by giving Tyndall notice to that effect. The funds were valued periodically to determine bid and offer prices for the units. The procedure adopted by Tyndall was to fix the bid and offer prices of the units between 9 am and 10 am on the valuation day, on the basis of data taken from the Stock Exchange data stream at 4 pm the previous day. The well–informed investor could himself estimate on the morning of the valuation day the approximate bid price which Tyndall would have fixed, even though it would not be published until the following day, and act accordingly before the bid and offer prices were set. Between 24 March 1986 and 24 April 1991 Fuji exercised the switch option in this way, so that the value of the benefits payable under the policy increased at an annual average return of 90%. Aetna, which by then was liable for Tyndall's obligations, changed the basis at which it fixed the prices for units so that Fuji could no longer predict the prices for units. Fuji sued for breach of contract. The suggested measure of damages was put at a sum equal to the average return of 90% per annum on the policy monies compounded annually, for the rest of the lifetime of Mr Tait. Such a sum would be equivalent to the gross national product of the United Kingdom for 460,000 years. The Court held that the fact that the measure of the benefit payable on surrender was the same as that payable on death was insufficient to prevent this contract being recognised as insurance made on the life of any person. The essence of life assurance was that the right to the benefits were related to life or death. In this case, the right to surrender was related to the continuance of life, for it could not be exercised by Fuji after the death of Mr Tait. It was therefore a policy for life assurance within the meaning of *s 1* of the *Life Assurance Act 1774*, and in accordance with *s 3* of that *Act*, Fuji had no greater interest in the policy than the surrender value since it had no insurable interest in Mr Tait's life.

17.4 – Personal pension misselling

[17.4.1]

Century Life v Commissioners of Customs & Excise (Court of Appeal, 19 December 2000) [2001] 12 PBLR 9

Personal pension misselling – insurance transactions

Facts and Decision

Century Life undertook the personal pensions misselling review for Lincoln. The Court held that the services provided by Century Life were not only incidental to the insurance transactions, and constituted an insurance transaction. Century Life's activities therefore fell within the scope of the exemption from value added tax set out in the *Article 13B of* the *Value Added Tax 6th Directive 77/388* and *para 4 group 2* of *schedule 9* to the *Value Added Tax Act 1994*.

[17.4.2]

J Rothschild Assurance v Collyear (High Court) [1999] PLR 77

Personal pension misselling – non-disclosure to insurers

Facts and Decision

J Rothschild Assurance sold personal pension schemes to investors. They were prompted to consider the pension arrangements of their investors in accordance with a review initiated at Lautro's instruction into personal pension misselling, and offered investors compensation for any loss caused. The Lautro report followed a study by KPMG Peat Marwick, which in a random sample had identified that there was no evidence of substantial compliance in 91% of cases. J Rothschild Assurance's indemnity insurers sought to avoid their cover, on the grounds that:

(a)   they had failed to notify them of the claims (despite its solicitors having written to the agents within 6 weeks of the issue of the

Lautro bulletin to notify them of the review, and that some of the 2,500 policies effected might give rise to a claim);

(b)   they had not disclosed Lautro's enforcement bulletin, which dealt generally with the question of investors who were opting out of their occupational pension scheme; and

(c)   the claims were not claims made by the personal pension investor.

The insurers argued that in the absence of any claims initiated by investors, J Rothschild Assurance could not reclaim its costs from them, and that even if they were liable to claim, the £50,000 excess applied to each claimant, not to all the claimants referable to each broker. The Court held that the notice was valid. The insured's duty was to notify of events which might give rise to a claim, and the price of cover on a claims-made basis was the requirement to notify. There was no fraudulent intent in any non-disclosure of the circumstances of those investors who had opted out of their occupational pension schemes, so on their proper construction the policies were not avoided on the grounds of non-disclosure. The investors did not need to be proactive in the process, in order to be taken to be making a claim: it was sufficient that they return the questionnaire. Since the investors had made claims, J Rothschild Assurance was insured for its costs. However, the excess clause applied to each personal pension investor separately, and not to each broker.

[17.4.3]

Lloyds TSB General Insurance Holdings v Lloyds Bank Group Insurance Co., Abbey National v Lee (High Court, unreported, 7 September 2000)

Personal pension misselling – deductibles

Facts and Decision

Insurers of LAUTRO members received claims concerning the misselling of personal pension schemes conducted by various employees within the organisation of the insured company. The insurers argued that these claims had not resulted from a single act or omission, or a related series of acts and omissions, and therefore the deductible on such claims applied to each such act of misselling. The Court held that the deductible clause required it to ask, as a matter of common sense, whether the series of claims in question was the result of an act or omission of the kinds described in the insuring clause. Each of the claims represented a liability attaching to the insured company for failing to ensure that the financial services consultants complied with the obligation to give best advice. The insured companies were therefore able to aggregate such claims before the deductible clause fell to be applied.

. **[17.4.4]**

Needler Financial Services v Taber (High Court, unreported, 31 July 2001)

Personal pension misselling – damages

Facts and Decision

Mr Taber was negligently advised to take out a personal pension with Norwich Union. He sued for damages. Norwich Union demutualised, resulting in a windfall bonus being paid to his personal pension scheme in shares to the value of £7,815.77. The independent financial advisers argued that he needed to give credit for that windfall in assessing damages. The Court held that the relevant question was whether the negligence which caused the loss also caused the profit, in the sense that the latter was part of a continuous transaction of which the former was the inception. That question was one of fact. The demutualisation was not caused by the negligence of the financial advisers, and so Mr Taber did not need to give credit for it in his claim for damages for negligence.

17.5 – Liability insurance

[17.5.1]

London Borough of Redbridge v Municipal Mutual Insurance (High Court, 9 November 2000) 67 PBLR 10

Liability insurance – maladministration

Facts and Decision

The London Borough of Redbridge was insured by Municipal Mutual under a liability insurance policy. The insurer was not liable to pay where the Borough's liability was directly or indirectly caused by or arising from a criminal offence on the part of employees. The Pensions Ombudsman made a series of determinations against the Borough which obliged it to pay compensation to fourteen former employees. The former employees had taken early retirement in reliance upon misleading information provided by the Borough. The Pensions Ombudsman upheld the complaints on the grounds of maladministration. The insurer sought to avoid paying under the policy on the ground that the maladministration necessarily entailed the chief executive of the Borough being guilty of the criminal offence of misconduct in a public office. An allegation of that nature was, the Court held, wholly irrelevant to anything which the Pensions Ombudsman had jurisdiction to decide. It did not avail the insurer to say that liability might have been established on a different basis, and it was not possible to regard the Borough as having been made liable in consequence of the commission of the offence of misconduct in public office by one of its employees.

Part 18 – Social Security Law

18 – Introduction

This book is a collection of pension cases, not of social security cases, which would be a case book in its own right. So far as possible, I have incorporated social security case law in the context of other chapters. Extensive social security case law can be found in the relevant areas of Part 13 on discrimination and pensions, and Part 19 on European law. The following cases are a miscellany which did not belong in any other part, but which were of sufficient relevance to pensions practitioners to demand inclusion.

18.1 – Calculation of benefits

Pearse v Secretary of State for Social Security (Court of Appeal) [1992] OPLR 77, [1992] PLR 117

State graduated pension – calculation of benefits

Facts and Decision

In 1980, Mrs Pearse became entitled to a graduated pension of £0.36 a week. She did not satisfy the contribution conditions for a Category A State retirement pension. In 1981 her husband reached age 65 but deferred retirement, so Mrs Pearse did not yet become entitled to a Category B State retirement pension. In 1985, Mr Pearse retired and became entitled to a Category A pension. At the same time, Mrs Pearse became entitled to a Category B pension. She claimed entitlement for the period between 1981 and 1985, to be treated as days of increment entitling her to an increased rate of Category B pension. The Secretary of State argued that her graduated pension was a benefit such as would preclude her from claiming the period as days of increment, since if she had received any benefit under *Chapters I* and *II* of *Part II* of the *Social Security Act 1975*, this would preclude the period as being treated as days of increment. On a proper construction of *ss 36* and *37* of the *Social Security Act 1975*, the Court held that the graduated pension was not incorporated by reference into those *Chapters*, and so Mrs Pearse was entitled to have the period between 1981 and 1985 treated as days of increment entitling her to an increased rate of pension.

18.2 – Extent of benefits

Cottingham v Chief Adjudication Officer (Court of Appeal) [1993] PLR 79

State retirement pension – implementation of statutory requirements

Principles

A previously impermissible regulation was not made effective by a new empowering statute, it needed to be repealed and reissued so that it was subject to the negative procedure by which Parliament scrutinises delegated legislation, even if it were in identical form. It followed that under the legislation as it stood in December 1992, male pensioners receiving a Category A State retirement pension who lived with their wives did not need to give credit for their wives' occupational pensions for the purpose of reducing or eliminating the increases to the Category A pension which they would otherwise receive.

Johnson v Chief Adjudication Officer (European Court of Justice) [1992] PLR 87

Invalidity pension – eligibility – sex discrimination – replacement of benefit

Facts and Decision

Mrs Johnson ceased working in order to look after her daughter with whom she lived alone. Some years later she wished to resume working but was unable to do so because of a back condition, for which she was awarded a non-contributory State invalidity pension. Payment of this pension ceased when she began to cohabit with her present partner, on the ground that she was then unable to fulfil the additional condition imposed on cohabiting women that she was incapable of performing normal household duties. Following changes in national legislation, the pension was abolished and a new benefit was introduced, for which those previously eligible for the pension could automatically benefit. Ms Johnson claimed that such treatment was discriminatory in contravention of *European Directive 79/7 (Equal Treatment in Social Security)*. The Court held that *Article 2* of the *Directive* was to be interpreted as meaning that the Directive did not apply to a person who had interrupted his or her occupational activity in order to attend to the upbringing of his or her children, and who was prevented by illness from returning to employment, unless that person had been seeking employment and his or her search had been interrupted by the materialisation of one of the risks specified in *Article 3(1)* (sickness, invalidity, old age, accidents at work, occupational diseases and unemployment).

18.3 – Interrelationship with child support

[18.3.1]

Wakefield v Secretary of State for Social Security (Court of Appeal) [2000] 1 FCR 761, [2000] 1 FLR 510, [2000] Fam Law 312

Child support – calculation of benefit – incapacity pension from occupational pension scheme

Facts and Decision

Compensation payments for injury are not taken into account for the purposes of assessing maintenance under the *Child Support Act 1991*. Mr Wakefield was in receipt of an ill-health pension and an injury pension from the fire service. The child support commissioner took the injury pension into account for assessing child support. The Court held that he was right to do so, since the injury pension was not compensation for personal injury but periodic payments payable consequential on the injury.

Part 19 – European Law

19 – Introduction

More than many areas of the law, European law has a major part to play in pensions law. This reflects the diverse nature of pensions, drawing as it does on many different areas of the law. Part 13 on Discrimination and Pensions is founded almost exclusively on European law principles, and that Part can be regarded either as an extension of Part 12 on Employment and Pensions, or of this Part, depending on the perspective of the reader.

While the European Commission has sporadically taken an interest in pensions matters, as yet there is no pensions directive in force. This means that the application of European law to pensions issues so far is piecemeal. Pensions professionals are most familiar with European law in the context of sex discrimination.

However, the impact of European law on pension practice is not restricted to anti-discrimination provisions. European law on taxation, social security, transfers of undertakings and freedom of movement has a bearing on the manner in which pensions matters are carried out. Relevant decisions founded upon European law are integrated into the main body of this book at the appropriate places. This chapter concentrates on the principles of European law themselves which affect pension schemes. Inevitably, a book on pension law cannot give a rounded picture of general principles of European law.

Often one needs to consider whether the Government has implemented European law obligations into domestic law. Has it attempted to do so, but its attempt was defective, or has it completely failed to do so? The answer will have great practical consequences. If the Government has completely failed to implement the European law obligation, then individuals may take direct action against the Government for loss caused in accordance with the principles set out in *Francovich v The Italian Republic [1992] IRLR 84*. On the other hand, if the Government has attempted to do so, the courts will interpret statutory instruments in line with the underlying European law obligations, regardless of the literal wording of the domestic statute, in accordance with the principles set out in *Litster v Forth Dry Dock and Engineering Co Limited [1990] AC 546*. In such circumstances, individuals have no right of action against the Government, and must proceed as if the legislation had been properly drafted.

This leads to a practical problem in some cases. There may be genuine uncertainty about what the Government was intending to do in relation to any given set of regulations. Individuals may find it difficult to identify the right person to sue. Where an employer is a public sector body or has public functions, employees can bring claims against their employer under unimplemented Directives, since the employer is an emanation of the state. *Foster v British Gas [1990] PLR 189* shows that this right is not to be construed narrowly.

European law, almost by the very definition of the phrase, establishes consistent principles across the whole of the European Union. This has raised the idea in the minds of some commentators that in time multi-national employers may be able to establish pan-European pension schemes. As with many European ideals, the concept is appealing. However, there remain many obstacles at present. If the aim of a pan-European pension scheme is not to harmonise benefit structures but merely to facilitate the pooling of investments, such an aim can be achieved by limited modifications to European investment law without making provision for single pension schemes across Europe. It is understood that those proposing pan-European pension schemes are proposing something more formidable.

While tax legislation is being harmonised, and such cases as *Safir v Skattemyndigheten I Dalarnas Län [1998] PLR 161* break down obstacles in national tax legislation, many other areas of the law will need to be changed first. The member states of the European Union have radically different social security systems. The difficulties which member states have faced in drawing up rules for migrant nationals are demonstrated in a string of cases including *Bestuur van de Sociale Verzekeringsbank v Cabanis-Issarte [1996] PLR 353*, *Kulzer v Bayern [1998] ECR I–895* and *Rodriguez v Landesversicherungsanstalt Rheinprovinz [1998] ECR I–2461*, in which the national governments and the European Court of Justice struggled to draw up coherent principles which were fair to the migrant nationals. Most national pension schemes are either explicitly or implicitly tied to the benefits provided by those national systems.

In the United Kingdom, for example, contracted-out schemes have a benefit structure directly linked to that of the state scheme. Even schemes that are not contracted-out will have been designed using actuarial and economic assumptions which make allowance for the value of the State Earnings Related Pension. Similar interlinking can be found in other member states of the European Union.

Supposing that social security schemes can either be harmonised (which would entail enormous political argument in many of the member states) or somehow side-stepped in benefit design, further problems would remain. Life expectancy, likelihood of illness before retirement age and even national attitudes to personal investment differ substantially across the member states. If a unified benefit design is to be adopted, then it will be on a one-size-fits-all basis rather than made-to-measure. It is hard to see how this would be more attractive to workers than existing arrangements, which have presumably been established with national characteristics in mind.

None of the above is intended to reject the notion of a pan-European pension scheme out of hand, but the remaining obstacles must be recognised. The next step should be to work towards the establishment of a Europe-wide personal pension scheme vehicle, which should be a little easier since the investment decisions are left to the individual rather than taken for them by the managers of a collective pension scheme.

19.1 – Government liability for failure to implement European Union law

[19.1.1]

Adams v Lancashire CC & BET (High Court) [1996] ICR 935, [1996] IRLR 154, [1996] OPLR 195 at 209G-H, [1996] PLR 49 at paragraph 67

European Directive – liability of State

Principle

Whether the type of liability in *Francovich v The Italian Republic [1992] IRLR 84* could be relied on in litigation against a mere emanation of the State in which there was no successful claim based on direct vertical effect was a difficult and important issue.

[19.1.2]

Francovich v The Italian Republic (European Court of Justice) [1992] IRLR 84, [1992] ECR I–5357

European Directive – liability of State

Facts and Decision

Mr Francovich was employed by an undertaking which became insolvent, owing him instalments of salary. Having obtained judgment against the undertaking, which was unable to meet those liabilities, Mr Francovich relied on his entitlement provided for by *Directive 80/987* (on the protection of employees on the insolvency of the employer) to obtain payment under guarantees from the Italian Government. However, Italy had not implemented the terms of the *Directive*. The Court held that Mr Francovich could not rely upon the rights granted by the *Directive* when the State had failed to take the necessary measures to implement the

Directive within the prescribed period. However, a member State was liable to make good the damage suffered by individuals as a result of its failure to implement the *Directive* within the prescribed period.

19.2 – Interpretation of Directives and implementing legislation

[19.2.1]

***Adams v Lancashire CC and BET (Court of Appeal) [1997]
ICR 834, [1997] IRLR 436, [1998] OPLR 119 at 126A-F,
[1997] PLR 145 at paras 23–26***

European Directive – interpretation

Principle

The construction of a *European Directive* should be purposive. The question
was not what was the purpose of the *Directive* as a whole but what was the
purpose of the specific *Article*. That must be ascertained from its wording
in the light of the overall purpose of the *Directive*.

19.3 – Interpretation of legislation in line with European law obligations

[19.3.1]

Finnegan v Clowney Youth Training Programme (House of Lords) [1990] IRLR 299

European Directive – interpretation of implementing regulations

Facts and Decision

Mrs Finnegan, who lived and worked in Northern Ireland, reached age 60 on 22 March 1986, and was therefore dismissed as having reached retiring age. Her employer's policy was that women retired at 60 and men at 65. She claimed that she had been sexually discriminated against on the ground of sex contrary to *Article 8* of the *Sex Discrimination (Northern Ireland) Order 1976 (SI 1976 No 1043)*. This *Order* as originally enacted was in identical terms to *s 6(2)(b)* of the *Sex Discrimination Act 1975* as it was originally enacted (which had not applied to Northern Ireland). Between the enactment of the *Sex Discrimination Act 1975* and the *Sex Discrimination (Northern Ireland) Order 1976*, *Directive 76/207/EEC* (the *Equal Treatment Directive*) took effect. The *1975 Act* as originally enacted permitted unequal retirement ages, but the European Court of Justice held in *Marshall v Southampton and South West Hampshire Area Health Authority [1986] IRLR 140* that *Directive 76/207/EEC* did not. Both the *1975 Act* and the *1976 Order* were amended in 1986, but not with retrospective effect. The Court held that the *1976 Order* did not fall to be construed in line with the prior European law obligation imposed by *Directive 76/207/ EEC*; it was apparent that before the *Marshall* case Parliament perceived no conflict between the *Directive* and the provisions of the *1975 Act*. It would be wholly artificial to treat the *1976 Order* enacting identical provisions for Northern Ireland as having been made with the purpose of implementing the *Directive*, because it was made after the *Directive*. The interpretation of the *1976 Order* was for the United Kingdom courts, and therefore no reference would be made to the European Court of Justice.

[19.3.2]

Litster v Forth Dry Dock and Engineering Co Limited [1989] IRLR 161, [1990] AC 546

European Directive – interpretation of implementing regulations

Principle

Where regulations were expressly enacted for the purpose of complying with a *European Directive*, the courts of the United Kingdom were under a duty to give a purposive construction to the regulations in a manner which would accord with the decisions of the European Court of Justice on the *Directive*, and where necessary implying words which would achieve that effect.

[19.3.3]

Porter v Cannon Hygiene Limited (Northern Ireland Court of Appeal) [1994] OPLR 129

European Directive – interpretation of implementing regulations

Facts and Decision

Mrs Porter was employed as a van service person. Her employer retired her when she reached her normal retiring age of 60 in 1987. Men's normal retiring age was 65. Mrs Porter claimed unfair dismissal and sex discrimination. The *Industrial Relations (Northern Ireland) Order 1976* provided that it was unlawful for an employer to discriminate against a woman employed by it by dismissing her, but there was an exemption for provision in relation to death or retirement. The Court held that it could not reinterpret the *Order* in the light of the underlying European law obligation not to discriminate in cases where they were inconsistent, unless the employer was an emanation of the State. If in a given situation there were two possible interpretations of a provision in national law, and one of them accorded with the wording and purpose of a relevant *European Directive* while the other did not do so, the national court's duty was to prefer the interpretation which accorded with the *Directive*. However, if the wording was clear, that principle did not apply.

19.4 – Industry-wide schemes

[19.4.1]

Albany International BV v Stichting Bedrijfspensioenfonds Textielindustrie (European Court of Justice, 21 September 1999) [2000] 4 CMLR 446

Industry-wide schemes – monopoly

Principle

A pension fund charged with the management of a supplementary pension scheme set up by a collective agreement concluded between organisations representing employers and workers in a given sector, to which affiliation has been made compulsory by the public authorities for all workers in that sector, is an undertaking within the meaning of *Article 65* of the *EC Treaty*. However, *Articles 86* and *90* (now *82* and *86*) do not preclude the public authorities from conferring on a fund the exclusive right to manage a supplementary pension scheme in a given sector. It was incumbent on each member State to consider whether, in view of the particular features of its national pension system, laying down minimum requirements would still enable it to ensure the level of pension which it seeks to guarantee in a sector by compulsory affiliation to a pension fund.

[19.4.2]

Fédération Française des Sociétés D'Assurance v Ministère de l'Agriculture et de la Pêche (European Court of Justice) [1996] PLR 83

Industry-wide schemes – monopoly

Facts and Decision

The French voluntary supplementary pension scheme for self-employed farmers was managed exclusively by a central agricultural benevolent fund. A consortium of insurers challenged this monopoly on the grounds that it was contrary to *Article 85* of the *Treaty of Rome*. The ECJ was asked to rule whether the central agricultural benevolent fund was an undertaking within the meaning of *Article 85*. The Court held that the scheme was voluntary, and the benevolent fund's activity was therefore carried out in competition with the insurers. The scheme's social functions did not alter this conclusion. The benevolent fund was therefore an undertaking within the meaning of *Article 85*.

19.5 – Freedom of movement

[19.5.1]

Birchall v Secretary of State for Education (Employment Appeal Tribunal, unreported, 18 September 1996)

Freedom of movement – compulsory retirement age

Facts and Decision

Mr Birchall was employed as a teacher at the European School in Oxfordshire, having previously worked in Belgium. He was forced to retire at 60, and claimed that he had been unfairly dismissed. His normal retiring age was 60. He argued, among other things, that *Article 48* of the *Treaty of Rome*, which set out the protection of freedom of movement for workers, had been infringed by the operation of this normal retiring age. The Appeal Tribunal held that Mr Birchall had not shown a causal nexus between the denial of his right or benefit and the right of free movement. *Article 48* did not require a State to treat its own nationals no less favourably than another State treats its own nationals. The essence of Mr Birchall's complaint was not concerned with freedom of movement at all.

[19.5.2]

Munster v Rijksdienst vor Pensioenen (European Court of Justice) [1996] PLR 209

Freedom of movement – social security benefits

Facts and Decision

A Dutch national was employed in the Netherlands for 37 years and Belgium for 8 years. His wife was never in employment. In both the Netherlands and Belgium he obtained a retirement pension calculated solely in accordance with the rules of the State. His wife became entitled to a Dutch pension at age 65, and his pension was correspondingly reduced. When the Belgian authorities, which awarded the husband pension benefits on a household rate, became aware that the wife was in receipt of a pension, the husband's pension was reduced to the single person's rate on account of the fact that the wife was in receipt of a pension or an equivalent benefit. The Court held that substantive and procedural differences between the social security systems of individual States were unaffected by *Article 51* of the *EEC Treaty*. However, the application of national legislation in this case gave rise to unforeseen consequences which were incompatible with the aim of freedom of movement set out in *Articles 48* to *51* of the *EEC Treaty*, and the national court must so far as possible interpret domestic law in a way which accords with the requirements of Community law.

19.6 – Obligation on public bodies to introduce compliance with European law

[19.6.1]

Foster v British Gas (European Court of Justice) [1990] PLR 189

European Directive – liability of State

Facts and Decision

Two former female employees of British Gas complained about being forced to retire at age 60 (before privatisation) when male colleagues were allowed to work until age 65, in breach of *76/207/EEC* (the *Equal Treatment Directive*). The Court held that under European law, rights under *Directives* which had not been implemented by the State could be enforced directly against emanations of the State. Emanations of the State for this purpose included a body whatever its legal form which has been made responsible, pursuant to a measure adopted by the State, for providing a public service under the control of the State and has for that purpose special powers. (See also [19.6.2].)

[19.6.2]

Foster v British Gas (House of Lords) [1991] 2 AC 306, [1991] IRLR 268, [1991] PLR 73

European Directive – liability of State

Facts and Decision

There was no justification, the Court held, for giving the phrase 'under the control of the state' a narrow or strained construction. During the relevant periods in this case (see [19.6.1]), control was exercised by the Secretary of State who could give general and special directions to British Gas. Similarly, since British Gas had the express power to prevent anyone else from supplying gas in the United Kingdom, it had special powers such as brought it within the terms of the ECJ's ruling. The employees could therefore rely upon the terms of the *Directive* against British Gas.

19.7 – Tax

[19.7.1]

Bachmann v Belgium (European Court of Justice) [1992] ECR I–249, [1995] PLR 219

European law – social security contributions – tax

Principle

While legislation making the deductibility of sickness and invalidity insurance contributions conditional on those contributions being paid in that member State is contrary to *Articles 48* and *59* of the *EEC Treaty*, it may be justified by the need to preserve the cohesion of the tax system. Such legislation is not contrary to *Article 67* of the *EEC Treaty*.

[19.7.2]

European Commission v Belgium (European Court of Justice) [1995] PLR 245

European law – social security contributions – tax

Principle

It was not contrary to European law for a member State to make the deductibility from taxable income of supplementary pension or life assurance contributions conditional on those contributions being paid to an undertaking established in that member State, or a foreign insurance undertaking established in that member State.

[19.7.3]

Safir v Skattemyndigheten i Dalarnas Län (European Court of Justice) [1998] PLR 161

European law – tax – potential discrimination

Facts and Decision

An individual domiciled in Sweden paid capital life assurance premiums to a British insurance company operating on the Swedish market. In Sweden, premiums were not tax deductible, but the proceeds from policies were not subject to tax. Different tax treatments applied to Swedish life assurance companies and life assurance companies from other countries, with the aim of maintaining competitive tax neutrality between domestic and foreign savings companies. Foreign companies were obliged to register and declare premium payments, unlike Swedish companies. The surrender of policies early would be more expensive with a foreign company than with a Swedish company, and the regulatory burden fell more heavily on a policyholder with a foreign company. The Swedish tax authorities reached different decisions about the availability of exemptions with different companies from the same foreign country. The Court held that direct taxation is not within the purview of the European Union, but the powers retained by member States must be exercised consistently with Community law. *Article 59* of the *Treaty of Rome* precludes the application of any national legislation which without objective justification impedes a provider of services from actually exercising the freedom to provide them. It was difficult if not impossible to assess whether the tax regime in issue in this case was discriminatory. The legislation was therefore incompatible with *Article 59*.

[19.7.4]

Schumaker v Finanzamt Köln-Altstadt (European Court of Justice) [1995] PLR 209

European law – tax

Principle

Article 48 of the *Treaty of Rome* limits the right of a member State to set conditions about the tax liability of a national of another member State, and the manner in which tax is to be levied on such a person. It precludes a member State from taxing someone who is resident and a national of another member State more heavily than a worker resident in the first member State, and this includes giving residents alone the benefit of procedures such as annual adjustment of deductions at source, and assessment by the administration of tax payable on remuneration from employment.

[19.7.5]

Wielockx v Inspecteur der Directe Belastingen (European Court of Justice) [1995] PLR 203

European law – tax

Principle

A member State is not permitted to set out a rule, which allows its residents to deduct from their taxable income business profits which they allocate to form a pension reserve, but denies that benefit to other community nationals liable to pay tax. Such a rule cannot be justified even if under a double taxation convention the community national would pay tax on the pension in the State of residence.

19.8 – Social security

[19.8.1]

Arjona v Institutio Nacional de la Seguridad Social (European Court of Justice) [1997] ECR I–5501

European law – social security contributions – terms of accession

Facts and Decision

Mr Arjona, a Spanish national, was employed in Spain from 1952 until 1965, and then in Germany from 1966 until 1991, while continuing to contribute to the Spanish social security system until June 1968, after which date he made social security contributions in Germany. In 1994, the INSS (the Spanish social security office) awarded him, with effect from 1 April 1991, a pension calculated on the basis of contributions paid in Spain between 1962 and 1968 (the pension being calculated by reference to the last 96 months' contributions, which were salary-related). Mr Arjona disputed that amount on the ground that the reference period to be taken into account should be the period between 1982 and 1991, that is to say the end of his career in Germany. Before Spain joined the European Union, a social security convention was in force between Germany and Spain, which allowed the contribution basis level attained by workers at the end of their career in Germany to be taken into account, whilst referring to the contribution bases in force in Spain for the occupational category concerned. The Court held that *Article 47(1)(e)* of *Council Regulation 1408/71* (on the application of social security schemes to employed persons, to self-employed persons and to members of their families moving within the Community) as updated implied that the calculation of the average basis for contributions rests solely on the amount of contributions actually paid under the legislation concerned. The theoretical amount of the benefit thus obtained is to be duly increased as if the persons concerned had continued to work under the same conditions in the member State in question. However, where application of that provision so interpreted proved less advantageous than the application of a previous convention between those two states, for workers who were already employed in another member State before the *regulation* entered into force in the first member State, the competent Court should, by way of exception, apply the rules laid down by that convention.

[19.8.2]

Bestuur van de Sociale Verzekeringsbank v Cabanis-Issarte (European Court of Justice) [1996] PLR 353

European law – social security contributions – discriminatory state benefits

Facts and Decision

Mrs Cabanis-Issarte was a widow. Both her husband and she were French nationals who lived in the Netherlands from 1948 to 1960 and 1963 to 1969. When she was widowed, Mrs Cabanis-Issarte was able to claim a single person's pension under the Dutch State system. However, her pension was reduced to the amount corresponding to the years during which she was not insured under the scheme. The rules for making voluntary contributions to the State scheme were less favourable than they would have been for Dutch nationals. The Court held that a surviving spouse of a migrant worker could rely upon *Council Regulation 1408/71* for the purpose of determining the rate of contribution in relation to a period of voluntary insurance completed under a State pension scheme. The temporal effect of this judgment was limited so that it could not be relied upon in support of claims concerning benefits relating to periods predating the date of judgment (30 April 1996).

[19.8.3]

De Vriendt v Rijksdienst vor Pensioenen (European Court of Justice) [1998] ECR I–2105

European law – social security contributions – sex discrimination

Principle

If a member State has maintained a different State pensionable age for male and female workers, it is entitled under *Article 4(1)* of *Directive 79/7/EEC* (*Equal Treatment in Social Security*) to calculate the amount of State pension differently depending on the worker's sex. This remained the case even where pensions were put into payment early.

[19.8.4]

Kulzer v Bayern (European Court of Justice) [1998] ECR I–895

European law – social security benefits – freedom of movement

Facts and Decision

Mr Kulzer was a retired police officer. He was a German national with a child by a French national, whom he had divorced, and who had since died. After the death of the child's mother, the child went to live with her French grandparents, but visited her father regularly, and her father met the costs of her education and subsistence. He received no child allowance from the French authorities. He made a declaration of second residence on behalf of his daughter to the German authorities and applied for child allowance from the Bavarian state. The application was refused. The Court held that a person who was a retired civil servant and had worked only in the State of which that person was a national was covered by *Regulation 1408/71* (on the application of social security to employed persons, to self-employed persons and to members of their families moving within the Community) as updated, if that retired person was or had been subject to the legislation of a member State to which the *Regulation* applied. However, since German family allowances were only paid to workers compulsorily insured, and Mr Kulzer was a retired civil servant, *Article 73* of the *Regulation* did not apply to him. Nor did *Article 77(2)* of the *Regulation* apply to special schemes for civil servants, even if established by statute.

[19.8.5]

Megner v Innungskrankenkasse Vorderpfalz (European Court of Justice) [1996] PLR 133

European law – social security contributions – indirect discrimination – objective justification

Facts and Decision

Mrs Megner was a cleaner who worked two hours a day, five days a week. As a result, she was excluded from paying compulsory social security insurance and as such being entitled to social security and old age benefits. She sought a declaration that such an exclusion was contrary to *European Directive 79/7* (*Equal Treatment in Social Security*), which set out a prohibition on sex discrimination in State benefits, since this affected far more women than men. *Nolte v Landesversicherungsanstalt [1996] PLR 125* (see [19.8.7]) was followed.

[19.8.6]

Munster v Rijksdienst vor Pensioenen (European Court of Justice) [1996] PLR 209

Interaction of European law and national law – social security contributions

Principle

Substantive and procedural differences between the social security systems of individual States were unaffected by *Article 51* of the *EEC Treaty*. However, the national court must so far as possible interpret domestic law in a way which accords with the requirements of Community law.

[19.8.7]

Nolte v Landesversicherungsanstalt Hannover (European Court of Justice) [1996] PLR 125

European law – social security contributions – indirect discrimination – objective justification

Facts and Decision

Mrs Nolte worked less than 15 hours a week and earned less than 1/7th of the average German monthly salary. As a result, she did not need to pay compulsory social security insurance and was excluded from receiving a State invalidity pension. Mrs Nolte claimed that such an exclusion was contrary to *European Directive 79/7 (Equal Treatment in Social Security)*, which set out a prohibition on sex discrimination in State benefits, since this affected far more women than men. The ECJ held that social security benefits must not be indirectly discriminatory, unless the national Government had objective justification for the measure. In this case, the German Government wished to avoid making low-paid part-time jobs uneconomic and forcing people into the black economy. This aim was not sex-discriminatory. The ECJ gave a wide margin of appreciation in areas of social policy and the national legislature was reasonably entitled to consider that the legislation was necessary in order to achieve this aim.

[19.8.8]

Rodríguez v Landesversicherungsanstalt Rheinprovinz (European Court of Justice) [1998] ECR I–2461

European law – social security contributions – terms of accession

Facts and Decision

Mr and Miss Rodríguez lived in Spain. Their father was a Spanish national, who had been insured as an employed person for 56 months in Germany and 80 months in Spain. He died in Spain without having drawn a pension. The Landesversicherungsanstalt granted orphans' pensions until 31 December 1985 on the basis of the *Convention* between Germany and Spain on social security. It also informed them that as from 1 January 1986, the date on which Spain acceded to the European Communities, the Spanish pension insurance institution had sole competence to grant orphans' benefits. The Spanish pension insurance institution granted orphans' pensions to the claimants until they reached the age of 18, the age at which their entitlement to orphans' pension came to an end under Spanish law. The children then applied to the Landesversicherungsanstalt for orphans' pensions under German law, which provided that persons attending an educational establishment may continue to receive those benefits up to the age of 25. The Landesversicherungsanstalt refused that application on the ground that, once payment of the Spanish pensions had ceased, *Article 78(2)* of *Regulation 1408/71* (on the application of social security schemes to employed persons, to self-employed persons and to members of their families moving within the Community) as updated did not confer a right to the orphans' pension provided for by German law.

The Court held that the conditions relating thereto had not been satisfied in the circumstances of the case, as the deceased had not completed the required qualifying period of 60 months. *Article 78(2)(b)* of the *Regulation* did not become applicable in circumstances where a right to orphans' pension, which initially arose under *Article 78(2)(b)(i)* in the member State in which the recipient resided, had been lost by reason of the attainment of an age-limit, while in another member State, whose legislation was also applicable to the insured person, a right to orphans' pension would run beyond that date on application of the rule on aggregation laid down in *Article 79* of the *Regulation*. *Articles 48* and *51* of the *Treaty of Rome* precluded the loss of social security advantages which would result from the inapplicability of a bilateral social security convention, following the entry into force of *Regulation 1408/71*. However, that principle could not apply in so far as, when the benefits were set under *Regulation 1408/71* for the first time, a comparison had already been made of the advantages resulting from the *Regulation* and the *Convention* respectively, the outcome of which was that it was more advantageous to apply *Regulation 1408/71* than the *Convention*.

[19.8.9]

Sehrer v Bundesknappschaft & Landesversicherungsanstalt für das Saarland (European Court of Justice, 15 June 2000) [2000] 46 PBLR 8

European law – social security contributions

Principle

Article 48 of the *Treaty of Rome* (now *Article 39*) precludes a member State from calculating the sickness insurance contributions of a retired worker subject to its legislation on the basis of the gross amount of the supplementary retirement pension payable under an agreement which that worker draws in another member State, without taking account of the fact that a part of the gross amount of that pension has already been deducted by way of sickness insurance contributions in the latter State.

19.9 – Time limits

[19.9.1]

Johnson v Chief Medical Officer (Court of Appeal) [1993] OPLR 17; (European Court of Justice) [1995] OPLR 53

European law – time limits

Principle

Community law does not preclude the application of a national law limiting the period prior to bringing a claim, in relation to matters dealt with in *European Directive 79/7 (Equal Treatment in Social Security)*, in respect of which arrears of benefit are payable, even where that *Directive* has not been properly transposed into national law within the prescribed period.

19.10 – Remit of the Commission on pensions issues

[19.10.1]

France v European Commission (European Court of Justice)
[1998] PLR 55

European Commission

Facts and Decision

The European Commission issued a communication on an internal market for pension funds, worded in the language of a directive. The French Government applied for its annulment, as being beyond the scope of the Commission's powers. The Court held that the binding nature of the communication was not within the Commission's competence, and the communication was annulled.

Part 20 – Human Rights

20 – Introduction

With the enactment of the *Human Rights Act 1998*, human rights now permeate every aspect of law. In pensions, as in many other areas, the impact of that change is already beginning to be felt. Once again, space constraints have prevented the inclusion of directly relevant case law which did not directly concern pensions. The British courts have taken cautious first steps in relation to human rights considerations in the pensions arena. They have required compelling reasons to invoke human rights considerations, and even then have given the Government wide latitude in assessing the public interest.

The approach of the British courts very much parallels that of the European Court of Human Rights. Pension rights are not automatically treated as property rights protected by *Article 1* to *Protocol 1*, although benefits under SERPS appear to be so protected (as shown by the decision in *Szrabjer v United Kingdom [1998] PLR 281*). The European Court has been very ready to accept public policy reasons for apparent reductions in pension entitlements. It is notable that the only two pension cases where violations of human rights have been found both involved defects in the procedure for hearing appeals. It is likely that the biggest impact of human rights in pensions will be in the judicial process for determining pension rights and hearing pensions appeals.

20.1 – General

Venables v Hornby (Special Tax Commissioners) [2001] PLR 17 at paras 54–56, 57–58

Human rights – time limits – citation of cases

Principles

The issuing of an assessment is not a proceeding brought by or at the instigation of a public authority, such as would bring the case within the scope of the *Human Rights Act 1998*, where the events in question had otherwise occurred before that *Act* came into force.

The Special Tax Commissioners need considerable assistance in the way of citation of European Court of Human Rights decisions before being able to reach conclusions on Human Rights issues: *Barclays Bank v Ellis* (Court of Appeal, The Times, 24 October 2000) was considered.

20.2 – Right to a fair trial

[20.2.1]

Blake v Pensions Ombudsman (High Court) [2000] All ER 681

Human rights – right to fair trial

Principles

The requirements of *Article 6(1)* of the *European Convention on Human Rights* were encapsulated in the rules of natural justice long familiar in the English courts.

[20.2.2]

Deumeland v Germany (European Court of Human Rights) 9/1984/81/128

Human rights – right to fair trial

Facts and Decision

Mrs Deumeland claimed for a widow's pension under the State compulsory industrial accident insurance system. This claim, including the hearings of appeals, took 11 years to be determined, the delay partly being caused by the courts and partly by the conduct of Mrs Deumeland's son, who took over the claim after Mrs Deumeland's death. German law classified such a claim as a public law right. The Court held that for the purposes of *Article 6(1)* of the *European Convention on Human Rights*, Mrs Deumeland's claim was a private law claim, having regard to the personal and economic nature of the asserted right, the connection with Mr Deumeland's contract of employment and the affinities with insurance under ordinary law. That part of the delay attributable to the courts was a violation of the right to a fair trial.

[20.2.3]

Outram v Academy Plastics (Court of Appeal) [2000] PLR 283 at para 27

Human rights – right to fair trial

Principle

It was not a breach of a claimant's right to a fair trial to strike out a claim when the legal position was clear and an investigation of the facts would provide no assistance: *Osman v United Kingdom [1999] FLR 193* was distinguished, and *Kent v Griffiths* (Court of Appeal, unreported, 3 February 2000) was followed.

[20.2.4]

Schuler-Zgraggen v Switzerland (European Court of Human Rights) [1995] PLR 159

Human rights – right to fair trial

Facts and Decision

Mrs Schuler-Zgraggen was granted a full State incapacity pension after retiring from work with open pulmonary tuberculosis. She then gave birth to a baby boy. Following a further medical examination, her incapacity pension was cancelled on the grounds that her health had improved and she was 60–70% able to look after her home and child. She was not allowed to see the file at the Invalidity Insurance Board or take photocopies of medical reports, records of examinations and results of laboratory tests. She could have inspected the file previously at the Appeals Board, but failed to do so. Ultimately, the Federal Insurance Court ordered the Appeals Board to make the file available with copies. The Court held that if it had not done so, this would have been a breach of Mrs Schuler-Zgraggen's right to a fair trial because the Appeals Board had not let her have a complete, detailed picture of the particulars supplied to it. It was not a breach of Mrs Schuler-Zgraggen's right to a fair trial for no hearing to take place in the Federal Insurance Court, if as here she had the right to insist on such a hearing but failed to do so.

20.3 – Right not to be discriminated against

[20.3.1]

Schuler-Zgraggen v Switzerland (European Court of Human Rights) [1995] PLR 159

Human rights – right not to be discriminated against

Facts and Decision

Mrs Schuler-Zgraggen's State incapacity pension was reduced because the Federal Insurance Court made an assumption based on experience of everyday life that many married women give up work when their first child was born, and inferred from this that Mrs Schuler-Zgraggen would have given up work at this stage even had she not had health problems. The Court held that this was a difference of treatment arising out of Mrs Schuler-Zgraggen's sex which had no reasonable or objective justification, and was therefore a breach of Mrs Schuler-Zgraggen's right not to be discriminated against. Very weighty reasons would have to be put forward before such a treatment could be regarded as compatible with the *Convention*.

[20.3.2]

Szrabjer v United Kingdom (European Commission of Human Rights) [1998] PLR 281

Human rights – right not to be discriminated against

Facts and Decision

Mr Szrabjer contributed to the State earnings related pension scheme (SERPS) throughout his working life. He reached pensionable age and his SERPS pension was put into payment. He was then sent to prison on a criminal charge, and his SERPS pension was suspended during the period he was imprisoned. The Commission held that prisoners and non-prisoners were not in relevantly similar situations, and so no discrimination arose in the prisoners' entitlement to secure their *Convention* freedoms. Although members of contracted-out schemes could be treated differently, this also was not a relevantly similar situation.

[20.3.3]

Venables v Hornby (Special Tax Commissioner) [2001] PLR 17 at paras 51–53

Human rights – right not to be discriminated against

Facts and Decision

The Commission held that the evidence did not support the allegation that the Inland Revenue had been inconsistent in its treatment of taxpayers in the same essential position, to the extent that its conduct amounted to unlawful discrimination in terms of the taxpayer's right to peaceful enjoyment of his or her possessions contrary to *Article 14* of the *European Convention on Human Rights*. The best that could be said of the evidence was that it raised a *prima facie* case which might conceivably be sufficient to get leave for judicial review.

[20.3.4]

X v Netherlands (European Commission of Human Rights) No 4130/69, Dec 20.7.71, Yearbook 14, 224

Human rights – right not to be discriminated against

Facts and Decision

The Dutch social security system paid old age pensions to all at 65. However, a married woman was entitled to a pension even before attaining that age if her husband was 65 and had his pension. Some unmarried and divorced women complained that this was discriminatory and that their right to property had been violated. The Commission held that *Article 14* of the *European Convention on Human Rights* did not forbid every difference in treatment in the exercise of the rights and freedoms recognised. Before a distinction was to be accepted as being consistent with *Convention* rights, it had to be assessed in relation to the aim and effects of this justification to determine whether it was objective and reasonable. With regard to the contributions made to old-age and widows' and orphans' pension funds, such contributions were assessed on the basis of annual income up to a certain limit in excess of which no contribution was required. No distinction was made in this respect between married and unmarried or divorced women having an income, except in the case of a married couple where both spouses had an income of their own, in which case a joint assessment was possible. This difference was justified as being based on the legislator's appreciation of the general family pattern, while making allowances for the generally different situation of a married couple in comparison with that of a single person.

20.4 – Right to private property

Lesser v Lawrence, Dennison v Krasner (Court of Appeal) [2000] PLR 213 at paras 68–74

Human rights – right to private property

Principle

Article 1 of *Protocol 1* of the *European Convention on Human Rights* prohibited the deprivation of possessions except in the public interest and subject to the conditions provided for by law. In the case of the effect of statutory bankruptcy legislation, the relevant question was whether the vesting in the trustee in bankruptcy of the bankrupt's pension rights was in the public interest. Since Parliament had not been inactive over the last 25 years, it had been responding to a perception of what the public interest required in the field. It would be quite impossible to hold that Parliament did not take full account of what in its view the public interest required. It would in any case be impossible to construe:

(a) the wording of *s 436* of the *Insolvency Act 1986* to define property in such a way so as to exclude rights under retirement annuity contracts and personal pension schemes; or

(b) the definition of the bankrupt's estate in *s 283(1)* of the *Insolvency Act 1986* in such a way as to exclude such rights, where the contract contained a restriction on alienation; or

(c) *s 306* of the *Insolvency Act 1986* in such a way as to exclude such rights, where the contract contained a restriction on alienation; or

(d) *s 310* of the *Insolvency Act 1986* so as to apply to income from property which has vested in the trustee in bankruptcy under *s 306*.

The *Human Rights Act 1998* would not, therefore, assist the bankrupts.

[20.4.2]

Müller v Austria (European Commission of Human Rights) No 5849/72 Comm Report 1.10.75, DR 3, p31

Human rights – right to private property

Facts and Decision

Mr Müller was a locksmith and a member of the Austrian Workers' Old Age Insurance Scheme for 37 years, which was insufficient to entitle him to a full pension. He then went to work in Liechtenstein. He paid contributions to both the Liechtenstein social security scheme and the Austrian Workers' Old Age Insurance Scheme with the permission of the Austrian authorities. Six years later he was retrospectively removed from the Austrian scheme, following a bilateral social security convention between the Liechtenstein and Austrian Governments. This caused him to lose 3% of the value of his pension. The Commission held that the right to an old age pension is not included as such among the rights and freedoms guaranteed by the *Convention*. The operation of a social security system is essentially different from the management of a private life insurance company. Because of its public importance, the social security system must take account of political considerations, in particular those of financial policy. In some cases, a substantial reduction of the amount of the pension could be regarded as affecting the very substance of the right to retain the benefit of the old age insurance system. However, that did not arise in this case. *Article 1* of *Protocol 1* had therefore not been breached.

[20.4.3]

Szrabjer v United Kingdom (European Commission of Human Rights) [1998] PLR 281

Human rights – right to private property

Facts and Decision

Mr Szrabjer contributed to the State earnings related pension scheme (SERPS) throughout his working life. He reached pensionable age and his SERPS pension was put into payment. He was then sent to prison on a criminal charge, and his SERPS pension was suspended during the period he was imprisoned. The Commission held that this was not a breach of his right under *Article 1* of *Protocol 1* of the *European Convention on Human Rights*. Although SERPS was a State benefit, it was a pecuniary right. However, it could be considered as in the public interest for prisoners' pensions to be suspended, because otherwise they would be left in the advantageous position of accumulating a lump sum by receiving a regular pension, without having any outgoing living expenses.

[20.4.4]

X v Netherlands (European Commission of Human Rights) No 4130/69, Dec 20.7.71, Yearbook 14, 224

Human rights – right to private property

Facts and Decision

The Dutch social security system paid old age pensions to all at 65. However, a married woman was entitled to a pension even before attaining that age if her husband was 65 and had his pension. Some unmarried and divorced women complained that this was discriminatory and that their right to property had been violated. The Commission held that the benefits accruing under old-age and widows' and orphans' pension schemes did not constitute a property right which could be described as 'possessions' within the meaning of *Article 1* of *Protocol 1* of the *European Convention on Human Rights*.

[20.4.5]

X v Sweden (European Commission of Human Rights) 8 EHRR 252

Human rights – right to private property

Facts and Decision

The applicant was a pensioner who retired before State pension age and received a pension from both his employer and the State. When he reached State pension age, his State pension benefits were co-ordinated with his social insurance benefits with the result that his State pension was reduced. The Commission held that a right to a pension was not automatically a property right guaranteed by *Article 1* of *Protocol 1* of the *European Convention on Human Rights*. A payment of contributions to a pension scheme may in certain circumstances create a property right so guaranteed. However, even if payment of contributions created a right to derive benefit, *Article 1* of *Protocol 1* did not entitle the person to a pension of a particular amount: *Müller v Austria No 5849/72 Comm Report 1.10.75, DR 3, p31* was followed. The right to a pension based on employment can also in certain circumstances be assimilated to a property right. The applicant had not been deprived of a property right which he previously had, and it was without reproach that a co-ordination was made between the social benefits and the pension benefits.

Part 21 – The Systems of Safeguard

21 – Introduction

Pension schemes are subject to a wide range of different control mechanisms. I have brought them all together into one large chapter, so that the practitioner can more easily see how they fit together.

The traditional method for resolving disputes is through the courts, and there is now a substantial body of case law about the litigation process which is specific to pension schemes. The process under which trustees are to bring legal action has long been settled in private trusts. The procedure is set out in *Re Beddoe, Downes v Cottam [1893] 1 Ch 547*, and the different categories of litigation were set out in *Re Buckton [1907] 2 Ch 411*. No one has ever questioned the application of *Re Beddoe's* principles to pension schemes, since they are of such obvious relevance. The classification of categories of litigation used in *Re Buckton* was adopted for pension schemes in *McDonald v Horn [1994] OPLR 281*.

It is, incidentally, no coincidence that the case law on the appropriate course of action for trustees is set out in cases about legal costs. It is through the award or refusal of costs that the Court can express its approval or disapproval of the legal route which has been taken to pursue the claim.

The different categories of litigation can themselves be classified in different ways. For example, the first category of pensions litigation set out in *Re Buckton* concerns proceedings brought by trustees to have the guidance of the Court as to the construction of the trust instrument, or some question arising in the course of the administration. *Merchant Navy Ratings Pension Fund Trustees v Chambers [2001] PLR 137* adopted the private trusts classification of such proceedings used in *Public Trustee v Cooper* (unreported). This raises the obvious observation, therefore, as to just how similar pension scheme litigation is to private trust litigation at every level.

There are some areas of difference. The biggest difference is the ability of pension scheme beneficiaries in some circumstances to bring claims against the trustees at the expense of the scheme. This development, instigated in *McDonald v Horn* and followed repeatedly since, has given scheme members more leverage than most trust beneficiaries have to ensure that the pension scheme is being properly administered.

Pensions litigation can be founded in a number of different legal areas, with differing time limits before such claims lapse. No special principles apply to pensions litigation in any of these various legal areas, although as always, the application of special facts can modify the impact of the law relating to time limits. However, special time limits apply to bringing a complaint to one of the innovations of pensions law: the Pensions Ombudsman.

One problem with litigation through the courts is that it is expensive, and this can prohibit members with even a very strong case from pursuing their claims. The Government recognised this, and introduced the office of Pensions Ombudsman to hear such claims in 1990. The Pensions Ombudsman is in fact a misnomer. Unlike almost all other Ombudsmen, he (and all office-holders to date have been men) may issue binding determinations which have the force of county court judgments. He is in substance a one-man tribunal.

Neither the courts nor the Ombudsman have yet reached a settled practice about how this unique role should operate. Since he has the power to issue legally-binding determinations, the courts have insisted on him applying the law and not effectively administering palm-tree justice. On the other hand, the courts have struggled to set limits which allow him to operate with sufficient freedom to provide fair and low-cost justice for members.

Successive governments have not fully understood this tension in the Pensions Ombudsman's role. When the office was established, his jurisdiction made no provision for the Court protections given to beneficiaries in class actions, though nothing in his jurisdiction specifically barred him from hearing such complaints. The courts interpreted this omission as requiring the Ombudsman to refrain from hearing class actions where members could be disadvantaged, first in *Edge v Pensions Ombudsman [2000] 3 WLR 79*, then in *Marsh & McLennan v Pensions Ombudsman [2001] PLR 51*. The second of these cases is particularly striking. The potential prejudice to other members of the Ombudsman deciding the case was relatively minor, but the Court was not prepared to countenance it taking place without a full hearing of the arguments for and against.

The Government is therefore currently in the process of changing the Ombudsman's jurisdiction. It is specifically providing for him to hear such class actions, although there is no sign at present of the safeguards conventionally built into class actions. It has yet to identify the balance to be struck between convenience for complainants and litigation protections for all parties, and this is likely to prove a fertile source of dispute for some time to come.

Every aspect of the Pensions Ombudsman's jurisdiction is still evolving: how he is to apply his time limits; how he is to investigate cases; how he is to weigh the evidence; the appeal procedure; costs on his appeal; the orders he may make, and so on. There is now a considerable body of case law, and this strange creation – not quite judge, not quite tribunal – is beginning to be understood.

There are, of course, other ways of pursuing pension claims which may be more appropriate in different circumstances. Where the dispute is a contractual one with the employer, the Employment Tribunal will normally be a better route: *Gbadebo v Department of Environment* (unreported) and *Engineering Training Authority v Pensions Ombudsman [1996] OPLR 167* demonstrate this.

The principles about the treatment of pension when calculating loss vary according to the nature of the action. When damages are being sought in tort or for breach of contract, the principle applied is deceptively simple: pension rights are a form of insurance, and it is not open to the defendant to take advantage of the victim's good sense in taking out insurance. This means that pension benefits are taken out of account when calculating damages, even when the damages sought are for loss of wages, or when the defendant is the sponsor of the pension scheme (see *Parry v Cleaver [1970] AC 1*). This is true even when the victim is claiming for loss of pension rights, at least in so far as the pension being paid does not relate to the same period as the period when the victim is claiming for loss (see *Longden v British Coal [1998] OPLR 223*). Many lawyers feel that this looks suspiciously like double recovery; that the claimant is having his cake and eating it. However, the courts have stood firm on this principle despite repeated challenges.

The courts have traditionally been wary of actuarial evidence when calculating loss. This is not owing to a lack of respect for actuarial techniques: as will be deduced from Part 2, the courts recognise the actuary's role as an expert and will not interfere with actuarial decisions unless manifestly wrong or such that no reasonable actuary would have reached that decision. The courts' difficulty with using actuarial evidence when calculating loss goes to the fundamentally different principles for deciding a court case and for performing actuarial calculations. Actuarial calculations are based on the assumption that over a large body of people, life expectancy andhealth are fairly predictable, based on the law of averages. Court cases are determined not on the law of averages, but on what will happen in the case before the Court. It is not good enough to know what will happen in the long run in many hundreds of similar cases: what the Court needs to know is what will happen in the case immediately before it.

It is for this reason that the Court of Appeal in *Mitchell v Mulholland (No. 2) [1972] 1 QB 65* felt free to adjust the actuarial calculation downwards. This Court of Appeal decision has been criticised for misunderstanding the nature of actuarial calculations. In fact, it understands them better than most of its critics. As it correctly noted, the risks of overpayment in a given case were significantly greater than the risks of underpayment if the actuarial standard was used. When the Court is faced with an individual case, it must make adjustments accordingly to reach the par result.

Actuarial principles have also been argued upon in relation to other areas. In *Auty v National Coal Board [1985] 1 WLR 784*, the Court of Appeal conclusively rejected the idea that the courts should take any notice of actuarial principles about future economic trends. The Court's judgment in that case, which followed *Mitchell v Mulholland (No. 2) [1972] 1 QB 65*, ruled out the value of such evidence as largely speculative. As a matter of principle, this also must be correct. Actuarial assumptions as to future inflation, for example, are based entirely on the presumption that the future will be broadly the same as the past. That is a comforting notion, but one supported by neither logic nor past experience.

Because of the sums of money involved and because of financial scandals, the Government has seen fit to impose regulators for some pensions issues; first the Occupational Pensions Board, and then since 1997, the Occupational Pensions Regulatory Authority. At present, case law on the new regulatory authority's powers is very limited, but this is sure to grow in time. It should not be forgotten that pension schemes may involve other areas which are regulated: the Financial Services regulators and even, as *Australian Securities Commission v AS Nominees [1996] PLR 297* demonstrates, Companies House, can conceivably become involved in pension schemes. The structures of safeguard of pensions in the United Kingdom are complex indeed.

21.1 – Pension scheme litigation

Types of proceedings

[21.1.1]

Re Buckton [1907] 2 Ch 411

Types of proceedings

Principle

Trust litigation can be divided into three categories:

- First, proceedings brought by trustees to have the guidance of the Court as to the construction of the trust instrument or some question arising in the course of the administration. In such cases, the costs of all parties are usually treated as necessarily incurred and ordered to be paid out of the fund.
- Secondly, there are cases in which the application is made by someone other than the trustees, but which raise the same kind of point as in the first class and would have justified an application by the trustees. This second class is treated in the same way as the first.
- Thirdly, there are cases in which a beneficiary is making a hostile claim against the trustees or another beneficiary. This is treated in the same way as ordinary common law litigation and costs usually follow the event.

[21.1.2]

Harding and others (Trustees of Joy Manufacturing Holdings Ltd Pension and Life Assurance Scheme), petitioners (Court of Session, Inner House, Scotland) [1999] OPLR 235

Types of proceedings

Principle

Unlike in England, in Scotland trustees may not surrender the exercise of their discretion to the Court.

[21.1.3]

McDonald v Horn (Court of Appeal) [1994] OPLR 281, [1994] PLR 155

Types of proceedings – special nature of pension trusts

Principle

The classification used in *Re Buckton [1907] 2 Ch 411* was adopted. Additionally, however, where a pension scheme beneficiary is suing on behalf of himself or herself and many others, he or she may seek prior indemnity from the fund, on an analogous basis to minority shareholders in a company. *Wallersteiner v Moir [1975] QB 373* was applied. What distinguishes a pension fund member from the ordinary trust beneficiary is that the former has given consideration for his or her interest. The relationship between the parties is a commercial one and the pension fund members are entitled to be satisfied that the fund is being properly administered. Even in a non-contributory scheme, the employer's payments are not bounty. They are part of the consideration for the services of the employee.

[21.1.4]

Merchant Navy Ratings Pension Fund Trustees v Chambers (High Court) [2001] PLR 137

Types of proceedings

Principle

Following *Public Trustee v Cooper* (unreported, 20 December 1999), there are at least four distinct types of applications involving the exercise of trustee discretions:

(a)   To determine whether some proposed action is within the trustees' powers.

(b)   To determine whether the proposed course of action is a proper exercise of the trustees' powers where there is no real doubt as to the nature of the trustees' powers and the trustees have decided how to exercise them, but the decision is particularly momentous and the trustees wish to obtain the blessing of the Court.

(c)   To surrender their discretion to the Court.

(d)   Where the trustees have actually taken action, and that action is attacked as being either outside their powers or an improper exercise of their powers.

[21.1.5]

NGN Staff Pension Plan Trustees v Simmons (High Court) [1994] OPLR 1

Types of proceedings – trustees' duties

Facts and Decision

When the Advocate-General gave his opinion in the case of *Coloroll Pension Trustees v Russell [1995] All ER (EC) 23*, it was apparent that if it was followed by the European Court of Justice it would be to the advantage of male members in a pension scheme with unequalised actuarial factors to bring claims against the trustees as soon as possible. The NGN Staff Pension Plan trustees were trustees of such a plan, but it was in winding-up. They applied to Court to ask what they should do. The Court held that it was not for the trustees to initiate proceedings of any sort so as to improve the lot of one class of beneficiaries at the expense of another, unless there was an express power for the purpose or the proceedings could be justified as being in the interests of the trust as a whole. Neither was the case here. The trustees' obligation was to apply the law of the European Community as declared by the European Court of Justice, including any temporal limitation it saw fit to impose. It was no part of the trustees' duty to advise one class of their beneficiaries in connection with a proposed change or clarification of the law which might have some effect on that particular class of beneficiary's interest, let alone where the consequence would be to damage the other class of beneficiary.

[21.1.6]

Thrells v Lomas (High Court) [1993] 1 WLR 456, [1993] 2 All ER 546, [1992] OPLR 21, [1992] PLR 233

Types of proceedings – Court's duties

Issues

Thrells Limited went into insolvent liquidation in 1984. Its pension scheme entered winding–up as a consequence, the company being the sole trustee. The scheme was in surplus, and the liquidator surrendered the company's discretion to the Court, it having proved impossible to find anyone willing to accept appointment as trustee in the place of the company. In exercising the discretion surrendered by the employer/trustee, the Court held that it must act in the manner a reasonable trustee could be expected to act having regard to all the material circumstances. It must do what was just and equitable.

Appropriate forum

[21.1.7]

Edge v Pensions Ombudsman (Court of Appeal) [2000] 3 WLR 79, [1999] OPLR 179 at 207D-F, [1999] PLR 215 at para 87

Appropriate forum – class disputes

Principle

The Pensions Ombudsman is not the appropriate forum for hearing class disputes, and he should decline to entertain such complaints.

[21.1.8]

Gbadebo v Department of Environment (Employment Appeal Tribunal, unreported, 13 January 1997)

Appropriate forum – identifying pension entitlement

Facts and Decision

Mr Gbadebo was a civil servant until 1976, when he became an employee of Trinity House. He transferred back to the civil service in 1988. Trinity House employees received pension benefits which were similar to those applicable to civil servants under the Principal Civil Service Pension Scheme. Mr Gbadebo had transferred his pension entitlement under special public service terms from the civil service scheme to the Trinity House scheme, and on returning to the civil service, he transferred his entitlement back again under the same special terms. He applied to the Industrial Tribunal for a ruling under *s 11* of the *Employment Protection (Consolidation) Act 1978* whether special protections on redundancy continued to apply after transfer. The Tribunal was concerned that any declaration it might give might involve the scheme trustees, who were not before it, and that any declaration would be not so much a determination of matters which should have been included in Mr Gbadebo's contract of employment, as a declaration of the effect of those terms. It therefore dismissed Mr Gbadebo's application. Since Mr Gbadebo identified an implied term which he argued was one of the terms of his contract, the matter was remitted to the Tribunal for it to consider whether that term was indeed a term of his contract.

[21.1.9]

Hutchings v Islington (Court of Appeal) [1998] PLR 239

Appropriate forum – statutory scheme

Facts and Decision

Mr Hutchings was a member of the Local Government Superannuation Scheme. He claimed that his pension had been miscalculated. The Court held that although the pension rights which Mr Hutchings was entitled to under the scheme were statutory rights, they were private law rights which he enjoyed by virtue of his contract of employment. Accordingly, he could bring his claim through the County Court since it was an action founded on contract for the purposes of *s 15(1)* of the *County Courts Act 1984*. It was not an abuse of court for Mr Hutchings to bring court proceedings before exhausting the statutory appeal proceedings under the Local Government Superannuation Scheme: there was no provision in the scheme preventing Mr Hutchings following this course of action, and in any case, the point at issue was a point of law and not a point which vested a discretion in the Secretary of State, who would hear the appeal. In the absence of express provision to the contrary, the courts could make a declaration in an appropriate case.

[21.1.10]

Laws v National Grid Co plc, Machin v National Power (High Court, interlocutory) [1998] OPLR 187, [1998] PLR 295

Appropriate forum – pre-emptive costs

Facts and Decision

Pensioners who had lost an appeal from the Pensions Ombudsman wished to apply for a pre-emptive costs order for an appeal to the Court of Appeal. The question arose where that application should be heard. The High Court held that it had jurisdiction to hear such an application even where the matter was to be heard by the Court of Appeal.

[21.1.11]

Marsh & McLennan v Pensions Ombudsman (High Court) [2001] PLR 51

Appropriate forum – class disputes

Issues

Mr Williamson was an actuary who was a member of his employer's pension scheme, which was contracted out of the state earnings related pension scheme. After leaving service, he complained to the Pensions Ombudsman that scheme pensions were being incorrectly calculated, since the trustees had not equalised the guaranteed minimum pension. It could not be known how this would affect him until he reached age 60. The Court held that the Pensions Ombudsman should not have exercised his jurisdiction to hear Mr Williamson's complaint in generalised terms about the scheme, since other members comprised classes of interested persons one or more of which might well have had a very real interest in arguing against any general equalisation direction: *Edge v Pensions Ombudsman* [2000] 3 WLR 79 was applied. The Ombudsman should have declined jurisdiction, or should at most have decided the equalisation question simply as between Mr Williamson, the employer and the trustee.

[21.1.12]

Seifert v Pensions Ombudsman (Court of Appeal) [1997] OPLR 395 at 400E-H, [1999] PLR 29 at paras 19–22

Appropriate forum

Principle

In order to enforce an entitlement to a pension, a member could have made a brief foray to the county court. However, the matter could also fall to be heard by the Pensions Ombudsman. The exercise of the Pensions Ombudsman's powers is no doubt intended to be simple, swift and cheap. The Ombudsman and his staff must adopt a procedure which is fair to both parties in all the circumstances of the case.

Time limits

Breach of contract

[21.1.13]

Preston v Wolverhampton (House of Lords) [2001] PLR 39

Time limits – breach of contract – recurrent breaches

Principles

Limitation periods in breach of contract do not begin to run only from the date of the termination of employment where the breach is a recurrent breach rather than a continuing breach: the periods run in relation to each recurrent breach. This means that where the breach is a recurrent breach, only breaches in the last six years are in time.

Time begins to run for employees on fixed term contracts from the end of each fixed term contract, unless there was a stable employment relationship without breaks, in which case time runs from the end of the final fixed term contract.

[21.1.14]

Scally v Southern Health and Social Services Board (House of Lords) [1992] 1 AC 294, [1991] PLR 195

Time limits – breach of contract – continuing breaches – identification of breaches

Facts and Decision

Northern Irish medical staff had the right under statutory instrument to purchase additional years of pensionable service in the NHS Pension Scheme within 12 months from 10 February 1975, or (in the case of new joiners) within 12 months of joining the health service. This right was not made known to some employees, and so they did not exercise that right. The Secretary of State originally had a discretion to extend the 12 month time limit, but this was removed in August 1983. These employees brought claims against the Health Board in 1988 since they would have exercised the right had they known of it. The Court held that the claims were not time-barred, since the employer remained under a continuing duty to bring to the employees' attention the opportunity to seek the Secretary of State's discretion to make the purchase out of time, until the date when the discretion was removed.

Negligence

[21.1.15]

Bradstock v Nabarro Nathanson (High Court) [1996] OPLR 247

Time limits – negligence – identification of breaches

Principle

In determining time limits for actions for negligence, time runs from the date when damage occurred, not from the date when it was known that the advice was negligent.

[21.1.16]

Glaister v Greenwood (High Court, 26 February 2001) [2001] 14 PBLR 16

Time limits – negligence – imputed knowledge

Facts and Decision

Mr Glaister claimed that he was negligently advised by his cousin, an independent investment adviser, to transfer his early leaver benefits from his employer's pension scheme to a Norwich Union insurance policy, rather than transfer it to his new employer's occupational scheme following a takeover. The Norwich Union plan was purchased on 18 October 1991 and the proceedings were commenced on 10 November 1998. Mr Glaister's cousin denied negligence, and argued that the claim was statute barred, because the cause of action accrued in 1991. The Court observed that although Mr Glaister thought that Mr Greenwood had not advised him adequately by 1994, he did not have actual knowledge of the alleged loss before 11 November 1995, three years before the issue of proceedings. Nor did he have imputed knowledge. Mr Glaister's claim was therefore in time under *s 14A* of the *Limitation Act 1980*.

[21.1.17]

HF Trustees v Ellison (High Court) [1999] OPLR 67

Time limits – negligence

Facts and Decision

Mr Ellison advised one of the trustees involved in the events under consideration in *Hillsdown v Pensions Ombudsman [1997] 1 All ER 862*. His advice was given in May 1989, and the trustee completed the transaction in reliance on that advice in June 1990 at the latest. In the decision in that case, the advice which Mr Ellison had given was disapproved. As a result, the transaction which was undertaken in that case was unwound. Legal costs, and a potential tax liability (which ultimately did not materialise) had been incurred as a result. The trustee sued Mr Ellison and the firm of solicitors which subsequently merged with his firm for negligence, starting its claim in October 1997. The Court held that time limits began to run from the date of knowledge of the advice which led to the loss, not from the date when the advice was appreciated to be capable of forming the subject matter of a claim in law. Accordingly, the claim was time-barred: *Bradstock v Nabarro Nathanson [1996] OPLR 247* was followed.

Pensions Ombudsman

Legal & General v Pensions Ombudsman (High Court) [2000] OPLR 153

Time limits – Pensions Ombudsman – extensions of time

Principle

The Pensions Ombudsman's decision that a complaint made outside the normal three-year time limit was still within such further period as he considered reasonable was at the margins of rationality, when the complainant decided to postpone bringing any complaint until it knew whether another complainant's complaint had been accepted. The Ombudsman never inquired into the reasons for this policy. However, the Court could not say that no reasonable Ombudsman acting within due appreciation of his responsibilities would have held the period reasonable, and so the Court did not disturb the Ombudsman's decision. It was totally improper of the Ombudsman to reach this decision without giving the respondent any opportunity to make representations on this issue, and the Ombudsman should have acknowledged his error.

Shillcock v Uppingham School (Pensions Ombudsman) [1997] PLR 207

Time limits – Pensions Ombudsman – sex discrimination

Principle

Where a former part-time employee brought her claim for indirect sex discrimination to the Pensions Ombudsman, the earliest time of exclusion from the pension scheme about which she could complain was three years before she brought the complaint to the Ombudsman, and the Ombudsman therefore should not award membership backdated to a date before that date.

[21.1.20]

Westminster v Haywood (No. 2) (High Court) [2000] PLR 235

Time limits – Pensions Ombudsman – extensions of time

Facts and Decision

Following the Court of Appeal's decision in *Westminster v Haywood [1997] 2 All ER 84* regarding the extent of the Pensions Ombudsman's jurisdiction in relation to schemes which did not provide long service benefits, the Ombudsman's jurisdiction was widened. Mr Haywood then brought another complaint to the Pensions Ombudsman about the same facts. Westminster Council argued that the complaint was time-barred. The Court held that the Ombudsman's decision to hear the complaint out of time was reasonable, indeed the only decision he could rationally have reached in the circumstances.

Race discrimination

[21.1.21]

Barclays Bank v Kapur (House of Lords) [1991] PLR 45

Time limits – race discrimination – continuing breaches

Facts and Decision

Barclays operated a subsidiary in East Africa, and provided a pension fund for its staff. In 1967 Kenya introduced a law requiring all jobs to be held by Kenyan nationals. Many of the employees were East African Asians who did not wish to take Kenyan nationality. The subsidiary offered such employees a compensation package including *ex gratia* pension provision. It also arranged for the parent company to take on 180 such employees, which offered them the standard pension provision available in the United Kingdom, but excluded their right under the fund rules to pension on their past group-service in East Africa, to which they would otherwise have been entitled. Some of these employees alleged that this was racially discriminatory. Barclays claimed that these complaints were time-barred since this was a deliberate omission from the late 1960s and early 1970s, and if the employees were to bring Industrial Tribunal complaints, they should have done so within three months of that deliberate omission. The

Court held that the proper classification of the complaint was that the pension provisions were a continuing act lasting throughout the period of employment and so still in time. A suitable comparison was where employees of one race were paid less than employees of another race. If the employer continued to do this, this would be a continuing act lasting throughout the employment of the disadvantaged employee. A man works not only for his current wage but also for his pension, and to require him to work on less favourable terms as to pension is as much a continuing act as to require him to work for lower current wages.

Sex discrimination

[21.1.22]

Dietz v Stichting Thuiszorg Rotterdam (European Court of Justice) [1996] OPLR 385

Sex discrimination – time limits

Principle

National rules relating to time limits for bringing actions under national law may be relied upon against workers who assert their right to join an occupational pension scheme or to payment of a retirement pension, provided that they are not less favourable for such actions than for similar actions of a domestic nature, and that they do not render the exercise of rights conferred by Community law excessively difficult or impossible in practice.

[21.1.23]

Dimossia Epicheirissi Ilektrismou v Evrenopoulos (European Court of Justice) [1997] All ER (EC) 543, [1997] 2 CMLR 407, [1997] ECR I–2057

Sex discrimination – time limits

Facts and Decision

The DEI was a State body governed for most purposes, including employment purposes, by private law. Its pension and insurance scheme offered spouses' benefits, but only in the case of widowers where the widower was without means, totally unfit for work and had been maintained by the deceased spouse for the five years preceding her death.

Mr Evrenopoulos applied for a survivor's pension on 20 January 1989, and on receiving no reply, brought an action for annulment of the implied rejection of his claim. He had not followed the proper procedure, but the Court gave him an extension of time to correct that mistake in November 1990, and he was allowed to restart his action in 1991. The ECJ held that on a proper construction of *Protocol 2* to the *Maastricht Treaty, Article 119* (now *Article 141*) of the *Treaty of Rome* may be relied upon in proceedings initiated before 17 May 1990 in order to obtain benefits under an occupational social security scheme, even if the action was declared inadmissible on the ground that the applicant had not lodged a prior objection, where the national court has granted an extension of the period prescribed for lodging such an objection. Mr Evrenopoulos had suffered sex discrimination, and was entitled to receive the benefits that would have been paid to the favoured sex on the same terms: *Coloroll Pension Trustees v Russell [1995] All ER (EC) 23* followed.

[21.1.24]

Fisscher v Voorhuis Hengelo (European Court of Justice) [1994] OPLR 297 at 327H–328B, [1994] PLR 211 at 243, paras 249–251

Sex discrimination – time limits

Principle

National rules relating to time limits for bringing actions under national law may be relied upon against workers who assert their right to join an occupational pension scheme, provided that they are not less favourable for that type of action than for similar actions of a domestic nature and that they do not render the exercise of rights conferred by Community law impossible in practice.

[21.1.25]

Gillespie v Mothercare UK Limited (Industrial Tribunal) [1995] OPLR 157, [1995] PLR 183

Sex discrimination – time limits

Facts and Decision

Mrs Gillespie worked part-time from 1975 to 1992, during which period she was excluded from membership of her employer's pension scheme. She left service in 1992, and brought a claim in 1995 that she had been indirectly discriminated against when she was excluded from the scheme. The Industrial Tribunal held that it had no jurisdiction to hear the case, since it was time-barred, having been presented well outside the statutory six-month time limit.

[21.1.26]

Howard v Ministry of Defence (Employment Appeal Tribunal) [1995] OPLR 275

Sex discrimination – bringing claims – time limits

Facts and Decision

Mr Howard was the widower of an army major who left the army in 1973. Widows received pensions, but widowers did not. Mr Howard complained about this after his wife's death in 1979 and subsequently, and eventually lodged Industrial Tribunal proceedings in 1994. The Court held that his complaints were not an equivalent claim in national law such as would entitle him to raise a complaint which would normally be excluded by the *Barber* time limit, since that exception envisaged a claim equivalent to legal proceedings. In any case, Mrs Howard's service predated the judgment in *Defrenne v Sabena (No. 2) [1976] ICR 547*, and was therefore time-barred by virtue of that case also.

[21.1.27]

Levez v Jennings (European Court of Justice, 1 December 1998) Case C-326/96

Sex discrimination – time limits

Principle

A national rule under which entitlement to arrears of remuneration was restricted to the two years preceding the date on which the proceedings were instituted was not in itself open to criticism under the principle of equivalence (which requires procedural rules for infringements of community law and national law to be applied without distinction). However, it would deprive the employee of the means to enforce the principle of equal pay before the courts if it were to allow an employer to rely on a rule such as that where the employer had provided inaccurate or deliberately misleading information. To determine whether the principle of equivalence had been breached, the national court would have to consider both the purpose and the essential characteristics of allegedly similar domestic actions.

[21.1.28]

Magorrian v Eastern Health & Social Services Board (European Court of Justice) [1997] OPLR 353, [1998] PLR 1

Sex discrimination – time limits – access to pension scheme

Facts and Decision

Mrs Magorrian was a part-time worker. Access to a higher accrual rate for pension was dependent on completing 20 years' full-time service at a higher grade from which part-time workers were excluded (she had completed 20 years' part-time service). She claimed for indirect discrimi-nation for the full period of her employment, although the *Occupational Pension Schemes (Equal Access to Membership) Regulations (Northern Ireland) 1976 (SI 1976 No 238)* provided that in proceedings concerning access to membership of an occupational pension scheme, the right to be admitted to the scheme was to have effect from a day no earlier than two years before the proceedings were instituted. The Court held that such a rule rendered any action by individuals in Mrs Magorrian's position impossible in practice, and was therefore not lawful under European law. The claim was for recognition of entitlement to full membership through acquisition of the long-server status, and not for a retroactive award of additional benefits.

[21.1.29]

Preston v Wolverhampton (European Court of Justice) [2000] PLR 171

Sex discrimination – time limits – access to pension scheme

Facts and Decision

Following the decisions of the European Court of Justice in *Vroege v NCIV Instituut [1995] All ER (EC) 193* and *Fisscher v Voorhuis Hengelo [1994] OPLR 297*, many former part-time employees brought claims to employment tribunals alleging that they had been indirectly discriminated against by having been excluded from a pension scheme. The Government introduced regulations imposing time limits which purported to restrict these claims. The ECJ held that a statutory time limit which limited such claims to the pension which the claimant would have earned in the last two years before the claim was brought breached the principle of effectiveness and was to be struck down. However, a statutory time limit which prevented claims being made for indirect discrimination by reason of being excluded from membership of a pension scheme, unless brought within 6 months of the claimant leaving employment, was valid under European law. It satisfied the principle of effectiveness. It was for the national court to assess whether the time limit satisfied the principle of equivalence. (See also [21.1.30].)

[21.1.30]

Preston v Wolverhampton (House of Lords) [2001] PLR 39

Sex discrimination – time limits – access to pension scheme

Principle

The 6 month time limit for bringing claims (see [21.1.29]) satisfied the principle of equivalence, since even if breach of contract was a valid comparator action, which was doubtful, the rules of procedure for bringing the sex discrimination claim were not less favourable than those for bringing a claim for breach of contract. Limitation periods in breach of contract do not begin to run only from the date of the termination of employment: where the breach was (as in this case) a recurrent breach rather than a continuing breach, the periods run in relation to each recurrent breach. Employment tribunals (which hear sex discrimination claims) result in lower costs, a quicker decision and less formal proceedings. Time begins to run for employees on fixed term contracts from the end of each fixed term contract unless there was a stable employment relationship without breaks, in which case time runs from the end of the final fixed term contract.

Comment

This case is interesting, not so much for the point which it decided (which while important, is merely a matter on which certainty is required one way or another), but for the Court's more general observations about the nature of time limits. The House of Lords reached the conclusion that a failure to admit an employee to a pension scheme had the character of a recurrent breach rather than a continuing breach, and that accordingly time limits begin to run from the date of each breach. They reached exactly the opposite conclusion in *Barclays Bank v Kapur [1991] PLR 45*, in a case which concerned racial discrimination. Admittedly that case concerned the failure to grant past service pension rights rather than the failure to admit an employee to a pension scheme, but if anything that makes the different results in the cases still more surprising. These two cases are not easily reconciled.

[21.1.31]

Quirk v Burton Hospitals NHS Trust (Employment Appeal Tribunal, 12 January 2001) 5 PBLR 8

Sex discrimination – time limits – distinguishing issues of access to benefits from unequal benefits

Facts and Decision

Mr Quirk worked as a nurse in the NHS from 1963, and was a member of the NHS statutory pension scheme. Originally, the NHS scheme offered comparable female employees the right to draw pension from age 55, while male employees such as Mr Quirk had the right to draw pension from their normal retirement age of 60. Following the judgment in *Barber v GRE [1990] ECR I-1889*, all nurses were entitled to retire at age 55, but while all of a female nurse's pensionable service counted for the purpose of calculating her pension, only service after 17 May 1990 counted for the purpose of calculating a male nurse's pension. Mr Quirk complained that he had been wrongfully discriminated against. The Appeal Tribunal held that Mr Quirk's claim failed because of the temporal limitation set down in the *Barber* judgment: *Bilka-Kaufhaus GmbH v Weber von Hartz* and *Magorrian v Eastern Health & Social Services Board [1998] All ER (EC) 38* were distinguished.

[21.1.32]

Shillcock v Uppingham School (Pensions Ombudsman) [1997] PLR 207

Sex discrimination – time limits

Principle

Where a former part-time employee brought her claim for indirect sex discrimination to the Pensions Ombudsman, the earliest time of exclusion from the scheme about which she could complain was three years before she brought the complaint to the Ombudsman, and the Ombudsman therefore should not award membership backdated to before that date.

Conduct of litigation

[21.1.33]

Bestrustees v Stuart (High Court, unreported, 10 April 2001)

Representation of parties

Principle

It could be argued in this case that there were more than three different interests. However, one had to invoke a degree of practicality and common sense in a case like this. The amount in the pension scheme was less than £4 million and the scheme was almost certainly in deficit, possibly significantly so. The number of potential beneficiaries was less than 100. In these circumstances, it would be quite inappropriate to require every conceivable different interest to be represented by separate solicitors and counsel. All the possibilities had been fully canvassed before the Court and although limiting the parties to three could in a perfect world be said to be over-simplifying, to take it beyond three would have been quite inappropriate.

[21.1.34]

Bradstock v Nabarro Nathanson (High Court) [1996] OPLR 247

Replacement of parties

Principle

The Court had no jurisdiction to allow members of a pension scheme to take over proceedings against third parties originally brought by the trustees.

Representation orders

[21.1.35]

Aitken v Christy Hunt (High Court) [1991] PLR 1 (in argument after judgment)

Representation orders

Principle

Where a beneficiary acting on behalf of all the beneficiaries has wholly succeeded in his arguments, the Court will not make a representation order, it being theoretically possible that some oddly-minded beneficiary might wish to argue the contrary.

Actuarial evidence

[21.1.36]

Auty v National Coal Board (Court of Appeal) [1985] 1 WLR 784

Actuarial evidence – evidence on future economic performance

Principle

The Court of Appeal held that the Hight Court had correctly rejected actuarial evidence about the lost value of increases on pension by reference to inflation, on the grounds that such evidence was based on hearsay and speculative in its nature: the dicta in *Mitchell v Mulholland (No. 2) [1972] 1 QB 65* were affirmed.

In the judgment of Oliver LJ:

'Actuarial evidence is no doubt of the greatest assistance where one is seeking to value interests in a fund of ascertained amount for the purposes of purchase, sale or exchange. Indeed, such valuations are the foundation of virtually all schemes propounded under the *Variation of Trusts Act 1958*. But as a method of providing a reliable guide to individual behaviour patterns, or to future economic and political events, the predictions of an actuary can be only a little more likely to be accurate (and will certainly be less entertaining) than those of an astrologer.'

Comment

The quotation given above in this case is often used to poke fun at actuaries. Despite its withering tone, it expresses precisely the Courts' reservations about accepting actuarial evidence. Actuarial principles work reasonably well in practice in predicting what will happen to a large body of people, but are almost entirely useless when it comes to predicting what will happen in the future life of one individual. Since most cases turn upon what is going to happen in the case in question, and not upon what will happen in the long run over many thousands of cases, actuarial evidence is of very limited use in most court cases.

Actuarial evidence has limitations in other ways as well. Inevitably it is based on historical data, and operates on the presumption that the future will be roughly similar to the past. As common experience will show, this is not necessarily so at all. In fact, the actuarial evidence which the courts were being asked to admit in this case almost certainly would not have withstood the test of time. The courts were being asked to make findings about future levels of inflation. Since 1984 the rates of inflation have in the main been significantly below the rates over the decade preceding 1984. Doubtless the actuarial evidence reflected the past experience rather than what happened in practice. The case is a good example of the limitations of actuarial work.

[21.1.37]

Re AXA Equity & Law Life Assurance Society PLC (High Court, 11 January 2001) [2001] 08 PBLR 29

Actuarial evidence – weighing evidence

Principle

The Court had no actuarial skills and was in no better position (in fact in a much worse position) to forecast future relevant events and market movements than were the parties in this case. Accordingly, its approach was to accept the views of the independent actuary and the Financial Services Authority as advised by the Government Actuary's Department in preference to those of the proposers where they were in conflict, except if there were a compelling reason, based on proven fact or demonstrable mistake in calculation or forecast, which pointed to a contrary view.

[21.1.38]

M'Donald v M'Donald (House of Lords, Scottish decision, 12 March 1880) V HLSe 519

Actuarial evidence – evidence on future life expectancy

Principle

When valuing residual interests in a trust, the Court should not just use average life expectancy as set out in life tables, but should also hear any facts relevant to the probable duration of the individual's life. His or her state of health and the ailments from which he or she has suffered, if calculated to shorten life, must be relevant to such an issue. The onus of proof is on a party seeking to prove that the individual's life is not an average life. The Court should also place a value on the chance of other beneficiaries inheriting.

[21.1.39]

Mitchell v Mulholland (No. 2) (Court of Appeal) [1972] I QB 65

Actuarial evidence – evidence on future economic performance

Principle

Evidence on the change in the cost of particular goods and services and on the probable beneficial use of damages awarded in personal injury cases in general should be inadmissible. Where sound and precise evidence can be given as to the probable rate of increase in the cost of some specific item becoming greater than the probable rate of benefit by the use of the capital sums to be awarded, the matter may possibly be different, though such a possibility seemed remote: the dicta from *O'Brien v McKean 42 ALJR 223* and *Watson v Powles [1968] 1 QB 596* were adopted. Life expectancy tables deal merely with the average case, and the Court has still to allow for the chance of the plaintiff departing, in either direction, from the average. The chances were equal either way, but as a matter of calculation it could be shown that the chance of shorter life was of greater significance than that of longer life.

[21.1.40]

O'Brien's Curator Bonis v British Steel (Scottish First Division, unreported, 26 April 1991)

Actuarial evidence – use of actuarial tables

Facts and Decision

Mr O'Brien suffered very severe injuries at work. He sued his employer through a *curator bonis*. The valuation of his future earnings fell to be assessed. The Court observed that it would take judicial notice of the tables set out in the publication 'Actuarial Tables with Explanatory Notes for Use in Personal Injury and Fatal Accident Cases (1984)' which were prepared under the chairmanship of Michael Ogden QC on the following points:

- It was of general interest for the insight which it provided into the importance of selecting an appropriate multiplier, and of the effect of lengthening or shortening the period over which the loss is assumed to run.
- The tables provided computations which could be used to arrive at an appropriate mulitplier.

It would not, however, be right to use the tables as a starting point to determine the multiplier appropriate for use in this case, although they could be used as a check.

[21.1.41]

Rowley v London and North Western Railway (Court of Exchequer) [1873] VIII LR Ch 221

Actuarial evidence – evidence on future life expectancy – use of actuarial tables – actuarial evidence given by non-actuary

Facts and Decision

Mr Rowley was an attorney who was killed, and his widow sued for negligence. He had covenanted to pay an annuity on the joint lives of himself and his mother. He was 40 at the date of death, and his mother was 61. Mrs Rowley called an accountant as an expert witness on life expectancy, and he had given evidence on the average duration of human lives by reference to tables known as the Carlisle Tables. The Court held that the average and probable duration of a life was material, and though the witness was not an actuary, but only an accountant, as he had given evidence that he was experienced in the business of life insurance, his evidence was admissible, though subject to remarks on its weight. The jury might be properly directed to consider the lives in question as average lives, unless there was some evidence to the contrary.

[21.1.42]

S v Distillers (High Court) [1970] I WLR 114, 124

Actuarial evidence – weight of evidence

Principle

When assessing the present value of future income needs, a preoccupation with actuarial figures could lead judges to a lop-sided view of the case, with the result that they failed in their overriding duty to be fair to both parties: *Arthur Robinson (Grafton) v Carter 41 ALJ 327* was followed. What the Court would do was to look at the actuarial tables, use them as a guide, exercising great caution, and would do everything it could to avoid any overlapping of heads of loss.

[21.1.43]

Spiers v Halliday (High Court) The Times, 30 June 1984

Actuarial evidence – use of actuarial tables

Principle

The Court decided, with regret, that it could not have regard to the report and actuarial calculations which had been produced by the working party chaired by Michael Ogden QC. The Court was bound by existing authority and principle not to do so.

[21.1.44]

Sullivan v West Yorkshire Passenger Transport Executive (Court of Appeal) [1985] 2 All ER 134

Actuarial evidence

Facts and Decision

In an action under the *Fatal Accidents Act 1976*, the plaintiff wanted to call actuarial evidence. The Court held that such evidence was genuinely expert evidence, and it did not have the power to prevent such expert evidence being called.

Watson v Powles (Court of Appeal) [1968] 1 QB 596

Actuarial evidence – weight of evidence

Principle

The Court remained quite unconvinced that at that stage the actuarial approach to valuing future loss afforded the Court such a precise tool as it would desire to have in its hand. The traditional approach of the courts would continue to be used. The actuarial approach may sometimes be helpful, but it should not be the general practice.

[21.1.46]

Wrightson v Fletcher Challenge Nominees (High Court of New Zealand) [1999] PLR 317 at paras 47–49

Actuarial evidence – weight of evidence

Principle

Experts do not enter the witness box in order to present a case. The experts are there to draw upon their skill and experience with professional objectivity, oblivious to the litigation consequences. Their integrity is usually obvious within a few minutes of entering the witness box. Nothing destroys an expert's credibility quicker than:

- the spontaneous volunteering of evidence thought to score points for their 'side';
- a uniformity of arguments all pointing in the same direction;
- an unwillingness to consider anything which might point the other way;
- a readiness to advance matters which fall outside the expert's strict area of expertise;
- the volunteering of arguments which are not directly responsive to questions; and
- a tendentious style of delivery.

Right to see scheme documentation

[21.1.47]

Boram v Mirror Group pension scheme trustees (Pensions Ombudsman, 14 January 1998) Case F00814

Trust documentation – beneficiaries' rights

Facts and Decision

A pension scheme altered commutation and early retirement actuarial factors on actuarial advice. Under the scheme rules, commutation factors were set by the company but had to be certified by the actuary as reasonable. Early retirement benefits had to be calculated using a basis of calculation adopted by the trustee and certified by the actuary as reasonable. Mr Boram entered into correspondence regarding these changes and asked to see a copy of the advice. The actuarial advice was paid for at least in part from the scheme assets. The trustee refused to release the advice and Mr Boram complained to the Pensions Ombudsman. The Pensions Ombudsman observed that the documents containing the actuarial advice were trust documents, including those that related to the company's decision, since the trustee had jointly paid for the advice. The advice contained information required by the trustee in order to reach a decision, but did not disclose the details of the deliberations of the trustee or the reasons why it came to the decision it did. If the trustee's submission that the documents were not subject to disclosure were correct then a trustee could seek to argue that every document generated by or for it was in some way 'relating to' its deliberations. The Ombudsman therefore ordered that the documents be disclosed. *Re Londonderry's Settlement [1965] Ch 918* was applied.

[21.1.48]

Fernance v Wreckair (Industrial Court of New South Wales) [1993] PLR 191

Trust documentation – beneficiaries' rights

Facts and Decision

Mr Fernance was an apprentice plant mechanic who had left school at 16. He was involved in a car accident, following which it slowly became apparent that he was unable to continue in his job. He was a member of his employer's superannuation scheme, and he claimed a pension on the ground that he suffered total and permanent disablement. The insurer National Mutual refused the application without any explanation. Mr Fernance sued his employer for the pension. The Court used a statutory power to correct the unfairness caused by National Mutual's failure to give reasons, and apparent excessive reliance on its own medical adviser.

[21.1.49]

Hartigan v Rydge (Australian Court of Appeal, 18 December 1992) [1999] 43 PBLR (40)

Trust documentation – beneficiaries' rights

Facts and Decision

Sir Norman Rydge instigated the establishment of a discretionary trust. He left a memorandum of wishes as to how the trust should be applied and the trustees stated that they were paying regard to that memorandum in performing their obligations. Potential beneficiaries sought access to the memorandum of wishes. The Court held that the beneficiaries were not entitled to have access to the memorandum of wishes of Sir Norman Rydge: *Re Londonderry's Settlement [1965] Ch 918* was followed, and *Chaine-Nickson v Bank of Ireland [1976] IR 393* (Irish High Court) was considered. The law has chosen with some firmness to preserve the confidentiality of communications between beneficiaries and their trustee, to allow those communications to be taken into account in the exercise of powers without being revealed, and to ensure that, unless the trustees make them public, their reasons for the exercise of their power remain with them. It has done this for some two centuries. There is wisdom in what it has done. The law allows trustees to act without detailing their reasons, not to encourage secrecy, but to avoid litigation.

[21.1.50]

Re Londonderry's Settlement (Court of Appeal) [1965] Ch 918

Trust documentation – benficiaries' rights

Facts and Decision

The trustees of a private trust had discretionary powers to distribute the income and capital of the trust. One beneficiary was dissatisfied with the share allocated to her, and sought disclosure of the relevant correspondence and minutes. The trustees resisted. The Court held that the beneficiary had no right to inspect minutes of meetings and agenda prepared for those meetings in the absence of an action impugning the trustees' good faith. Any document which relates to the trustees' deliberations on a discretionary matter is protected from disclosure in the absence of an action impugning the trustees' good faith, whether or not it is a trust document. Very different considerations apply when it comes to discovery in an action where a beneficiary is impeaching the validity of the trustees' actions.

[21.1.51]

Wheeler v NBC Pension Trustee (Pensions Ombudsman) [1996] OPLR 337 at 357F–358B, [1997] PLR 1 at paras 102–106

Trust documentation – beneficiaries' rights

Principle

Where circumstances had arisen where a trustee, if it were not to have committed a breach of trust, must have had quite extraordinary reasons for exercising its discretion in the manner in which it did, the presumption that a trustee had acted correctly fell away, and so it could be required to give reasons for the exercise of its discretion: *Wilson v Law Debenture [1995] 2 All ER 337* was distinguished.

[21.1.52]

Wilson v Law Debenture (High Court) [1995] 2 All ER 337, [1995] OPLR 103, [1994] PLR 141

Trust documentation – beneficiaries' rights

Facts and Decision

Law Debenture was the trustee of the Chloride (UK) Pension Scheme. It made a bulk transfer to another scheme which included no allowance for the surplus in the scheme. Two transferring members objected to the terms of transfer and sought disclosure of the trustee papers. The Court held that in the absence of evidence to the contrary, the presumption is that a trustee has exercised his or her discretion properly and the Court will not compel the trustee to disclose the reasons for the exercise of a discretion by that trustee. *Re Londonderry's Settlement [1965] Ch 918* was followed. It was wrong to suggest that in the absence of express provision to the contrary pension scheme trustees were bound to give reasons for the exercise of their discretions. Pension scheme trustees were not under more onerous obligations than those imposed by the general trust law on this point.

Comment

Some pension cases are markedly different in feel from private trusts cases, while others feel as if the pensions aspects of the case are almost irrelevant. This case belongs firmly in the latter category. This is slightly unfair, in that the Court went out of its way to consider whether the pensions nature of the trust altered the nature of the trustees' obligations to disclose documentation, but the Court emphatically concluded that it did not.

This decision has come in for considerable criticism from some pension practitioners, but in truth there was no outcome to this case which would have been entirely satisfactory. On the basis of this decision, pension scheme beneficiaries who have paid for their benefits by the sweat of their brow are unable to check whether the trustees in whom they are obliged to place so much faith are performing their duties satisfactorily. On the other hand, if the trustee in this case had been obliged to disclose the reasons for its actions, pension scheme trustees would be exposed to a much higher risk of litigation, and members fishing for information could become a major administrative burden for schemes with a large membership and a vociferous pensioner action group. In the circumstances, the Court chose the easiest path and elected to follow the existing precedents.

Costs of proceedings

[21.1.53]

Aitken v Christy Hunt (High Court) [1991] PLR 1 (in argument after judgment)

Costs – proceedings brought by trustees – hostile litigation

Principle

Where the trustees had confidence in the correctness of their own views and acted accordingly, but the employer disputed the validity of their actions, the only prudent course of action was to go to Court to test the matter. The employer could have taken proceedings itself, in which case the matter would have been self-evidently hostile litigation, where the employer would have been at risk certainly as to its own costs and probably also in relation to the costs of other parties. However, in the circumstances of this case, one of the questions before the Court was both difficult and less hostile, so the Court ordered that the costs of the trustees and the representative beneficiary be met from the fund on the indemnity basis, and no order for costs was made in relation to the employer.

[21.1.54]

Re Beddoe, Downes v Cottam (Court of Appeal) [1893] 1 Ch 547

Costs – protection for trustees

Facts and Decision

A trustee of a private trust defended a claim against him, acting on legal advice. The defence was unsuccessful, and the trustee sought an order to recover his costs from the trust. The legal costs amounted to nearly a quarter of the trust fund. The Court held that a trustee can only be indemnified out of the trust against costs, charges and expenses properly incurred for the benefit of the trust. A trustee who brings or defends an action unsuccessfully and without leave from the Court had to show that the costs so incurred were properly incurred. The fact that the trustee acted on counsel's opinion is in all cases a circumstance which ought to weigh with the Court in favour of the trustee, but counsel's opinion is no indemnity to the trustee even on the question of costs. The point of law was not difficult, the defence to the litigation was idle and fruitless and the Court would not have authorised the trustee to defend the action at the expense of the trust if the trustee had applied for leave to do so. The trustee ought therefore only to have had such costs as he would have incurred had he applied for leave to defend at the expense of the estate.

[21.1.55]

Bradstock v Nabarro Nathanson (High Court) [1996] OPLR 247

Negligence – transfer of proceedings – costs

Facts and Decision

Trustees of a pension scheme sued their solicitors in relation to advice about use of surplus. However, they were advised that the scheme was now so depleted that there was a real risk that there would be insufficient assets in the scheme to meet the costs of both sides, should the trustees lose, and the trustees would be at personal risk as to costs. The trustees therefore decided to drop the proceedings. Two pensioners applied to take over the proceedings. The Court held that it had no jurisdiction to allow the pensioners to take over the proceedings. A claim for the tort of negligence does not form part of the trust property, although any damages recovered would be. In any case, the application would not protect the trust property from having to meet the solicitors' costs if the action was unsuccessful.

[21.1.56]

Re British Airways Pension Schemes (High Court, interlocutory) [2000] PLR 311

Costs – proceedings brought by trustees – representative beneficiaries – pre-emptive costs orders

Facts and Decision

British Airways had proposed a merger of its two pension schemes. Active members and pensioners of one scheme were hostile to the proposal, but were also suspicious of each other. The trustees applied to Court for guidance as to whether they could proceed with the merger, and joined representative beneficiaries to an originating summons. The trustees and employer sought to require the representative active member and the representative pensioner to use the same legal team, there being no conflict of interest between the two classes. The representative active member applied for a pre-emptive costs order that his legal expenses be met from the scheme on the indemnity basis, on the ground that he instructed a separate legal team. The Court held that *Re Buckton [1907] 2 Ch 411* and *McDonald v Horn [1994] OPLR 281* were not to be interpreted as preventing it from making such an order. It would be a remarkable result if a member joined as a representative for an extensive class would not be entitled to his or her costs out of the scheme. There must be many cases where the trustees consider it desirable to join a particular beneficiary as a representative even if it might not be necessary to do so. A beneficiary who is so joined in normal circumstances should have his or her costs paid out of the scheme, as that is the necessary and automatic consequence. *Re Buckton* should be interpreted accordingly. The trustees, moreover, named the active member as a defendant. The Court did not identify a conflict, but it was conceivable that conflicts could arise, and the beneficiaries had deeply held views that there was such a conflict. It would be a major step for the Court to override the deeply held views of beneficiaries. While costs would be increased, they would not be increased by much. Once the merits or otherwise of the merger had been decided at trial, it was to be hoped that everyone would accept the decision with as good grace as possible, but there would be little chance of that if the active members were denied separate representation. A pre-emptive costs order was therefore granted.

[21.1.57]

British Coal Corporation v British Coal Staff Superannuation Scheme Trustees (High Court) [1995] 1 All ER 912, [1994] ICR 537, [1994] OPLR 51, [1993] PLR 303

Costs – proceedings brought by trustees – hostile litigation

Principle

Since the trustees could properly have brought proceedings on the matter under consideration in this case, and the employer had brought proceedings in effect as beneficiary, the costs of all parties were ordered to be paid from the pension scheme on the indemnity basis.

[21.1.58]

Re Buckton [1907] 2 Ch 411

Costs – categories of litigation

Principle

Trust litigation can be divided into three categories:

- First, proceedings brought by trustees to have the guidance of the Court as to the construction of the trust instrument or some question arising in the course of the administration. In such cases, the costs of all parties are usually treated as necessarily incurred and ordered to be paid out of the fund.
- Secondly, there are cases in which the application is made by someone other than the trustees, but which raise the same kind of point as in the first class and would have justified an application by the trustees. This second class is treated in the same way as the first.
- Thirdly, there are cases in which a beneficiary is making a hostile claim against the trustees or another beneficiary. This is treated in the same way as ordinary common law litigation and costs usually follow the event.

[21.1.59]

Elliott v Pensions Ombudsman (High Court) [1998] OPLR 21

Appeals from Pensions Ombudsman – costs

Principle

Where the Pensions Ombudsman appeared in a successful appeal against his determination, he was ordered to pay the costs of the appellants only to the extent that those costs had been increased as a result of his participation at the hearing. Other than that, the appellants and the Ombudsman should each bear their own costs. The fact that an appeal from the Ombudsman was necessary and that it resulted in the setting aside of the relevant part of his determination was not a sufficient ground for ordering him to pay the costs. Some of the costs of appeal were inevitably incurred by the appellants whether or not the Ombudsman took any part at the appeal hearing.

[21.1.60]

Evans v London Co-operative Society (High Court) The Times, 6 July 1976

Costs – hostile litigation

Principle

Where a pension scheme member brought an action personally doing a very great service indeed to the pension scheme and to all existing and future beneficiaries, with some courage in the circumstances and possibly some financial hardship if he was not indemnified, he would be entitled to his costs on the common fund basis, even though the action was an action of a normal litigious nature.

Independent Trustee Services v Rowe (High Court) [1998] OPLR 77

Costs – proceedings brought by trustees – benefit substantially for one beneficiary

Facts and Decision

A small-self administered scheme wound up on the insolvency of its employer. The scheme provided benefits for and in respect of only one member, who was also one of the trustees. The scheme had made a doubtful investment, apparently at the initiative of a former trustee. The trustees took advice from their solicitors, who in turn instructed counsel. Counsel was of the opinion that there had been a breach of trust, but that the chances of a claim succeeding were speculative, given that the member-trustee's own state of knowledge would be important. The solicitors did not communicate counsel's doubts to the trustees, and did not suggest that the professional trustee should receive an indemnity from the member-beneficiary. Legal proceedings were brought. The solicitors perceived themselves as acting primarily for the member-trustee. A counterclaim was brought against another former trustee, and the professional trustee attended meetings with that trustee's solicitors. The professional trustee became doubtful about the advice it had received and took separate legal advice. Its own solicitors were much more doubtful about the strength of the claim. The professional trustee obtained the Court's permission to resign from the trusteeship, and sought its costs and professional fees from the scheme. The Court held that the costs of instructing its own solicitors were expenses incurred in or about the execution of the trusts for the purpose of *s 30(2)* of the *Trustee Act 1925*, and the trustee was therefore entitled to those expenses. The suggestion that the costs were incurred in the professional trustee's personal interests and not *qua* trustee was a distinction without a difference. It could recover its own fees and expenses, including those incurred in attending meetings with the former trustee's solicitors, which it did for the benefit of the scheme. The trustee was also entitled to an indemnity from the member-trustee directly, since the litigation was for the benefit of the member-trustee: *Hardoon v Bellios [1901] AC 118* was applied and considered.

[21.1.62]

Law Debenture v Malley (High Court, interlocutory) [1999] OPLR 153 at 163, [1999] PLR 367 at paras 46–50

Appeals from Pensions Ombudsman – costs

Principle

The Court had the jurisdiction to make an order at an interlocutory hearing that the Pensions Ombudsman would not have to bear the appellants' costs, irrespective of the result. However, the Court would require special or unusual circumstances before it would do so.

[21.1.63]

Laws v National Grid Co plc, Machin v National Power (High Court, interlocutory) [1998] OPLR 187, [1998] PLR 295

Costs – pre-emptive costs orders

Facts and Decision

Two pensioners successfully complained to the Pensions Ombudsman about the use of surplus in a pension scheme. When the company appealed, they applied to be given pre-emptive costs orders for their defence of the Pensions Ombudsman's determination. The Court held that since the pensioners could have started their action through the Court, the circumstances of the case would have been akin to that in *McDonald v Horn [1994] OPLR 281*. While the pensioners did not follow this course, this did not rule out their application, since winning before the Ombudsman could effectively be regarded as akin to a successful court claim which they were defending. If they could have obtained pre-emptive costs to pursue an action for the benefit of the pension fund, in principle they should be able to apply for a like order to resist an appeal. *McDonald v Horn [1994] OPLR 281* and *Re Buckton [1907] 2 Ch 411* were considered. Where:

(a)   the Ombudsman had found in the members' favour and the trustees accepted that the applicants had at least an arguable case;
(b)   the case was akin to *McDonald v Horn*;
(c)   the appeals involved difficult questions and substantial sums of money, and it was desirable that the applicants should have the opportunity to be properly represented before the Court;
(d)   the Ombudsman might appear but would not necessarily advance all the arguments that the applicants would wish to advance; and

(e)   there were no other special circumstances;

a pre-emptive costs order was given.

On losing in the High Court, the representative beneficiaries named in two linked proceedings at first instance applied for a pre-emptive costs order to allow their appeal to be heard in the Court of Appeal. The Court held that this was a case which, as had been decided before the hearing at first instance, justified a *McDonald v Horn* order, and once that was decided, it was not right for the jurisdiction of the Court to depend on who won and who lost. The case was truly exceptional in terms of the amounts of money involved and the numbers of beneficiaries potentially affected. The points of law involved were of sufficient difficulty and importance for the judge to decide that leave to appeal should be granted. The beneficiaries could claim a respectable degree of support for their position. The two cases involved were procedurally different, one being an appeal from the Pensions Ombudsman and the other being an originating summons, but they raised exactly the same issues so they should stand or fall together. The application was granted, but costs were limited to £100,000 excluding VAT for the two groups of appellants.

[21.1.64]

McDonald v Horn (Court of Appeal) [1994] OPLR 281, [1994] PLR 155

Costs – hostile litigation – pre-emptive costs orders

Facts and Decision

Pension scheme members brought proceedings alleging that the trustees had committed dishonest breaches of trust. The members sought a prospective order that their costs should be met from the scheme assets. The Court adopted the classification in *Re Buckton [1907] 2 Ch 411*, but held that where a pension scheme beneficiary is suing on behalf of himself and many others, he may seek prior indemnity from the fund, on an analogous basis to minority shareholders in a company: *Wallersteiner v Moir [1975] QB 373* was applied. What distinguishes a pension fund member from the ordinary trust beneficiary is that the former has given consideration for his interest. The relationship between the parties is a commercial one and the pension fund members are entitled to be satisfied that the fund is being properly administered. Pre-emptive costs orders should, though, be made with caution. The Court should not authorise any legal process until it has explored the possibility of independent investigation by a person acceptable to both parties. A pre-emptive costs order was granted.

Comment

Many cases have referred to the differences between pensions trusts and private trusts. This case was one of the first to be decided explicitly on the basis of such differences. The history of the principles underlying this decision are complicated. Trustees of all trusts are able to bring proceedings at the expense of the fund, subject to obtaining the prior sanction of the Court to do so. In the 1970s, the courts noted that company shareholders were singularly disadvantaged in challenging the actions of the company management. The company courts therefore imported this trust law concept, determining that shareholders could with prior court approval in appropriate cases bring an action against the company's management, with costs being met from the company's assets. Such an action is known as a derivative action.

While trustees could bring actions at the expense of the trust, beneficiaries did not have this right, which could be a real disadvantage where they had lost confidence in the trustees. The Court in this case therefore reimported the concept of the derivative action, so that pension scheme beneficiaries in appropriate cases could obtain court approval to sue. Its logic is restricted to trusts where the beneficiary has given value for his or her interest in a commercial relationship, which entitle the beneficiary to be satisfied that the fund is being properly administered. This case is one of the few trust cases which hinges on the pension character of the trust.

Although the Court of Appeal stressed that the jurisdiction to award members their costs pre-emptively should be used in exceptional circumstances only, the jurisdiction has now been used on several occasions in a range of circumstances, including *Laws v National Grid [1998] OPLR 187* and *Re British Airways Pension Schemes [2000] PLR 311*. This practical and effective means of keeping delinquent trustees in check is performing a valuable role.

[21.1.65]

Miller v Stapleton (High Court) [1996] OPLR 73, [1996] PLR 67

Appeals from Pensions Ombudsman – costs

Principle

Costs were awarded against the Pensions Ombudsman on an appeal against one of his decisions at which he was represented.

Miller v Stapleton (Court of Appeal) [1996] OPLR 281

Appeals from Pensions Ombudsman – costs

Principle

The observations in *Providence Capitol Trustees v Ayres [1996] 4 All ER 760* about the role of the Pensions Ombudsman on appeals were approved.

[21.1.67]

NHS Pensions Agency v Pensions Ombudsman (High Court) [1996] OPLR 119

Appeals from Pensions Ombudsman – costs

Principle

Where the Pensions Ombudsman had been equivocal in advance of an appeal about what his stance was on the legal position, so that a hearing was required which could otherwise have been avoided, the Court ordered him to pay half of the costs of the successful appellants.

[21.1.68]

Nicol & Andrew v Brinkley (High Court) [1996] OPLR 361 at 365H–366A

Costs – Pensions Ombudsman's powers

Principle

The Pensions Ombudsman's power to give directions clearly imports power to direct in an appropriate case that compensation should be paid, including compensation for inconvenience and distress. That power must include power to award compensation for expenses reasonably incurred in taking advice and preparing a complaint.

[21.1.69]

Norman v Pensions Ombudsman (High Court) [1997] OPLR 85 at 95B-G

Costs – appeals from Pensions Ombudsman – awards against appellant beneficiary

Principle

When a pension scheme member appealed against a determination of the Pensions Ombudsman but was unsuccessful, the trustees were entitled to their costs from the scheme on the indemnity basis. The Court gave the trustees leave to take those costs from the part of the scheme which represented the appellant's entitlement. Such an order held the balance between the beneficiaries. It did not matter whether the assets were kept in separate funds or whether they were pooled: all that would happen was that there would be an accounting exercise to attribute this particular liability to benefits which would otherwise come to the appellant.

[21.1.70]

Providence Capitol Trustees v Ayres (High Court) [1996] 4 All ER 760, [1996] OPLR 215, [1996] PLR 395

Appeals from Pensions Ombudsman – costs

Principle

Only in exceptional cases where the Tribunal does not appear and does not take part in appeals will an order for costs be made against it. It would therefore be oppressive to make an order for costs against the Pensions Ombudsman in circumstances where his determination has been over-turned on appeal but where he has not made himself a party to the *lis* by appearing at the appeal: *R v Newcastle-under-Lyme Justices ex parte Massey [1994] 1 WLR 1684* at *1691H* was applied. In suitable cases it may be appropriate for the Pensions Ombudsman to appear in order to argue questions of law for the assistance of the Court. But if he does so on his own initiative, he must risk the possibility that an order for costs will be made against him if his arguments are unsuccessful. To avoid that risk he may think it appropriate either to refer the question of law to the Court under *s 150(7)* of the *Pension Schemes Act 1993* or to apply to the Court at an interlocutory stage of the appeal for a direction whether the Court would be assisted by his arguments. If such application is made, the Court will then be in a position to give such comfort as it thinks fit to the Pensions Ombudsman in relation to the risk that a costs order might be made against him.

[21.1.71]

Seifert v Pensions Ombudsman (High Court) [1997] 1 All ER 214, [1996] OPLR 231 at 243D–244F, [1996] PLR 479 at paras 44–55

Appeals from Pensions Ombudsman – costs

Principle

The Court should be very slow in categorising, as an act of resistance to an appeal, the Pensions Ombudsman writing letters to the Court with the aim of assisting the Court by setting out his understanding of the matters raised by the appellant. One should only categorise his participation as an effort to resist the challenge to his determination if he can be seen to be seeking to influence rather than inform the Court, or to make a partisan rather than a balanced presentation. If the Ombudsman has not taken part in or resisted the appeal, it should only be in the most exceptional circumstances that the Ombudsman should be held liable for costs: *Providence Capitol v Ayres [1996] 4 All ER 760* was followed. The question was whether the Ombudsman's decision and conduct in this case were so glaringly wrong as to require the expression of the Court's disapproval in this matter: the dicta from *R v Liverpool Justices ex parte Roberts [1960] 1 WLR 585* at 586–7, *R v Willesden Justices ex parte Utley [1948] 1 KB 397* at 400 and *R v Newcastle-under-Lyme Justices ex parte Massey [1994] 1 WLR 1684* were applied. (See also [21.1.72].)

[21.1.72]

Seifert v Pensions Ombudsman (Court of Appeal) [1997] OPLR 395 at 404B, [1999] PLR 29 at para 47

Appeals from Pensions Ombudsman – costs

Principle

Having had the benefit of full argument of the case before it (see [21.1.71]), the Court of Appeal concluded that this was not a case where the Pensions Ombudsman should be required to pay the costs of the appeal from his decision.

640

[21.1.73]

Sun Alliance v Pensions Ombudsman (High Court, unreported, 17 October 2000)

Appeals from Pensions Ombudsman – costs

Principle

The practice with respect to costs established in *University of Nottingham v Eyett [1999] 2 All ER 445* was followed, although the Court was by no means happy with the practice, since it was not invited to depart from it.

[21.1.74]

Taylor v Lucas Pension Trust (High Court) [1994] OPLR 29, [1994] PLR 9

Costs – hostile litigation

Principle

The usual rule, where an application is made by trustees to determine or to seek the determination by the Court of a question of doubt or difficulty which arises in the administration of their trust, is that the costs of all the parties including representative beneficiaries are paid out of the trust fund. That rule is applied also where the application is made by a beneficiary and the Court is satisfied that the question raised is one which ought to have been raised by the trustees. None of this applies to a hostile application in which the beneficiaries challenge the good faith of the conduct of the trustees.

[21.1.75]

Trustee Corporation v Nadir (High Court, 12 December 2000) [2001] 21 PBLR 7

Costs – hostile litigation – pre-emptive costs orders

Facts and Decision

Mr Nadir was a well-known businessman who went bankrupt. The trustees in bankruptcy laid claim to his interest under his occupational pension scheme, but Mr Nadir disputed this. The scheme trustees applied to Court for guidance as to whether Mr Nadir's benefits remained payable to him, were vested in the trustee in bankruptcy or were held on protective trusts. Mr Nadir applied for a pre-emptive costs order. The Court held that Mr Nadir's position was hostile to that of the trustees in bankruptcy, being a contest over the beneficial interest, and there was no reasonable basis for extending the pre-emptive costs jurisdiction to this case. Even if the Court had jurisdiction, it would not have exercised it in this case, since Mr Nadir's case faced formidable difficulties and he had not shown that he was unable to fund legal representation.

[21.1.76]

University of Nottingham v Eyett (High Court) [1999] 2 All ER 445, [1999] 1 WLR 594, [1999] OPLR 55, [1999] PLR 25

Appeals from Pensions Ombudsman – costs

Principles

The Pensions Ombudsman was ordered to pay the appellant's costs only to the extent that they were increased by the Ombudsman's appearance: *Elliott v Pensions Ombudsman [1998] OPLR 21* was followed, and *Providence Capitol Trustees v Ayres [1996] 4 All ER 760* was not followed. The Ombudsman's determination raised questions of law on which it was desirable for the Court to have the assistance of argument on both sides. The fact that the Ombudsman in the event offered no argument on two points illustrated that assistance.

Neither a non-appearing respondent complainant nor a non-appearing respondent Ombudsman are at risk as to costs, but the reasons why this is so are different. If complainants were at risk as to costs, it would discourage them from complaining to the Pensions Ombudsman in the first place. It does not follow that a complainant who seeks to uphold a determination should not be at risk as to costs in the normal way.

Settlement

[21.1.77]

Gibbs v Ebbetts (Court of Appeal, unreported, 20 October 1997)

Construction of agreement to settle litigation

Facts and Decision

Mr Ebbetts had been in litigation with his former employer and the trustees of its pension scheme about whether a bonus of £200,000 should have been included in the calculation of his pension, but this dispute was settled on terms that payments made to Mr Ebbetts were in full and final settlement of the trustees' claims against him, the trustees accepting the terms of settlement 'with respect to the proceedings'. New trustees later discovered that his pension also erroneously included other non-pensionable bonuses, and brought new proceedings to recover these overpayments. The Court observed that the totality of the claims arose in relation to claims against Mr Ebbetts in the context of the accurate and appropriate calculation of his pension entitlement. The trustees' settlement 'with respect to the proceedings' was nothing more than a means to identify the proceedings in relation to which the settlement was being made, and was not a counter-offer. The trustees' new proceedings were therefore doomed to fail.

[21.1.78]

Jones v Foxboro International (Employment Appeal Tribunal, 31 March 2000) [2000] 41 PBLR 33

Construction of agreement to settle litigation

Facts and Decision

Mr Jones brought a claim for sex discrimination in 1991, being a member of a scheme with a normal retirement date of 65 for men and 60 for women. The claim was determined by a tribunal on a basis more favourable than would have been awarded had it been decided in accordance with the principles in *Coloroll Pension Trustees v Russell [1995] All ER (EC) 23*. Both Mr Jones and Foxboro International appealed, with both of these appeals eventually withdrawn by agreement in 1995, following the issue of the *Coloroll* decision. Mr Jones then tried to enforce the Tribunal decision, on the basis that the terms of agreement had not prevented him from asserting his rights in this regard. Foxboro International claimed that the terms of this decision had been varied by agreement. The Appeal Tribunal held that the Tribunal decision was not automatically overridden by the *Coloroll* decision, but the parties had impliedly agreed to drop their claim on the basis set out in the *Coloroll* decision. Mr Jones's attempt to enforce the Tribunal decision therefore failed.

Pursuing misselling of personal pension

[21.1.79]

Cocking v Prudential (High Court) [1996] OPLR 35, [1996] PLR 235

Interaction of financial services review and litigation – staying litigation

Facts and Decision

Individuals who had been sold personal pension schemes claimed that they had been wrongly advised by the relevant insurance companies to take out the personal pension. The financial services regulators had already required that the insurers conduct a full review of such claims with a view to compensating those who had been missold a personal pension. The insurers argued that the proceedings should be stayed on the ground that if the actions were allowed to proceed, there would be a flood of litigation which would disrupt and delay the orderly progress of the review of personal pension misselling to the general disadvantage of those within the review's ambit. The Court observed that its jurisdiction to stay actions is a wide one which is and should remain without definition. If it were not for the scale of the problem, the insurers would not have made their application. Having regard to the fact that the individuals would not be compensated for the costs of obtaining individual advice under the review, and the delays which had already occurred in the review, the Court declined to issue the stay. The Court was not satisfied that there was likely to be the flood of litigation suggested by the insurers. The support of a trade union for an individual bringing such a claim was also not grounds for a stay.

[21.1.80]

Glaister v Greenwood (High Court, 26 February 2001) [2001] 14 PBLR 16

Time limits – imputed knowledge

Facts and Decision

Mr Glaister claimed that he was negligently advised by his cousin, an independent investment adviser, to transfer his early leaver benefits from his employer's pension scheme to a Norwich Union insurance policy, rather than transfer it to his new employer's occupational scheme following a takeover. The Norwich Union plan was purchased on 18 October 1991 and the proceedings were commenced on 10 November 1998. Mr Glaister's cousin denied negligence, and argued that the claim was statute barred, because the cause of action accrued in 1991. Although Mr Glaister thought that Mr Greenwood had not advised him adequately by 1994, he did not have actual knowledge of the alleged loss before 11 November 1995, three years before the issue of proceedings. In the course of 1995 Mr Glaister was seeking to use the PIA investigation to determine whether he had a claim, and the Court held that there was no reason to doubt his evidence that he did not know whether the review would indicate that he had a claim. Nor did he have imputed knowledge. The Securities & Investment Board (SIB) factsheet which had been widely distributed and which Mr Greenwood received in April 1995 referred to the fact that 5 million personal pensions had been sold since 1988 and that regulators were requiring investment firms to review policies sold since 1988. Since pensions mis-selling had come to light in 1993 there must have been tens (if not hundreds) of thousands who had 'known or suspected for some time' that they had been badly advised. If the suggestion that they take legal advice had been intended to be acted upon it would have been expressed more clearly and more emphatically. If it had been, many thousands of individuals would have been put to the expense of seeking wholly unnecessary legal advice. The whole tenor of the leaflets was to calm fears and assure holders of personal pensions that the authorities had set up an automatic review procedure through which they would obtain redress. Mr Glaister's claim was therefore in time under *s 14A* of the *Limitation Act 1980*.

[21.1.81]

Gorham v British Telecommunications (Court of Appeal) [2000] 1 WLR 2129, [2000] PLR 293

Duty of care – causation

Principle

Where a life office had sold a personal pension to an occupational pension scheme member, it owed a duty of care to the member's dependants: *White v Jones [1995] 2 AC 207* was applied. There was force in the submission that the dependants should be in no better a position than the member would have been had he brought a claim based on a breach of duty to himself, and so arguably any claim should be reduced to reflect his contributory negligence. However, since the member had not taken action when he had been informed that the personal pension was inferior to the occupational pension scheme of which he had previously been a member, the chain of causation had been broken at that point, and the question of the position of the dependants in relation to the member's contributory negligence did not arise.

Court appointment of trustees

[21.1.82]

McDonald v Horn (High Court) [1993] OPLR 183, [1994] PLR 33 at paras 49, 50

Court-appointed trustees

Principle

The Court will not normally appoint a judicial trustee where no complaint has been made, and is always reluctant to appoint one where disputed charges are made against the trustee which are the subject of litigation (at least if the trust assets can otherwise be protected pending the resolution of such charges). However, in the context of a pension fund it is unjust that the administration of funds to which members have contributed and which require the continual exercise of discretions as to, for example, the grant of discretionary benefits, should be controlled by persons in whose fairness and probity the beneficiaries no longer have confidence. Delay of relevant court proceedings was also a relevant consideration. A judicial trustee was therefore appointed in this case.

21.2 – Liability

Apportioning liability

[21.2.1]

Friends Provident v Hillier Parker (Court of Appeal) [1995] 4 All ER 260

Apportioning liability

Principle

Liability for breach of trust is liability for the purposes of the *Civil Liability (Contribution) Act 1978.*

Exoneration clauses

[21.2.2]

Armitage v Nurse (Court of Appeal) [1997] PLR 51

Exoneration clauses – interpretation

Facts and Decision

A beneficiary under a private trust complained that the trustees had committed various breaches of trust. The trust provided that no trustee 'shall be liable for any loss or damage which may happen to [the fund] or any part thereof at any time or from any cause whatsoever unless such loss or damage shall be caused by his own actual fraud.' The Court held that this exclusion clause was valid. It did not exclude liability for equitable fraud (which included any unconscientious use of a power). It was not contrary to public policy to exclude liability for gross negligence, and this clause excluded liability in such circumstances. None of the claims of breach of trust before the Court concerned allegations of fraud.

Comment

This is not a pension case, but it is the leading case on exoneration clauses. It decided that there was no rule of public policy which prevented provisions of trusts which exempted trustees from liability for any breaches of trust, apart from those which constituted equitable fraud from taking effect. The most important consequence of this is that trustees can be exonerated even for the most scandalously negligent acts, provided they were not reckless.

This approach makes perfect sense when considering exonerations in contracts, where the parties have the opportunity to negotiate appropriate terms. It can also be justified in relation to private trusts, where the beneficiaries are being given unilateral benefits under the trust. It is much less justifiable in relation to commercial trusts such as pension schemes, where members have paid for their entitlements, but who are not involved in the drafting process.

[21.2.3]

Bogg v Raper (Court of Appeal) The Times, 22 April 1998

Exoneration clauses

Facts and Decision

Where a solicitor drafted a clause in a will which exonerated the executors and trustees from potential liabilities in the execution of the trusts of the will, the Court held that he was entitled to rely upon that clause if he subsequently became a trustee under the will.

[21.2.4]

Elliott v Pensions Ombudsman (High Court) [1998] OPLR 21 at 30D–31A, 33G–34B, 34C-D

Exoneration clauses – interpretation

Facts and Decision

Trustees had the benefit of an exoneration clause which provided that no trustee should as trustee of the scheme or in respect of the exercise of his rights or powers incur any personal responsibilities or be liable for anything whatever except for breach of trust knowingly and intentionally committed by him. The Court held that this required the trustee not only to act knowingly and intentionally, but also to know that the action was a breach of trust or intend to commit the breach of trust: *Armitage v Nurse [1997] PLR 51* was applied, and *Midland Bank Trust Co (Jersey) v Federated Pension Services [1996] PLR 179* was not followed. The Court would have been unwilling to construe the clause more narrowly unless driven to that by the wording used, given that trustee exoneration clauses of this kind had long been understood to provide protection to trustees in these circumstances. The same question arose when considering whether the trustees had breached their irreducible core of duties, since this required a finding of dishonesty or bad faith. It was unclear whether the Pensions Ombudsman had found that the trustees had acted consciously in breach of trust. The onus of proof that the exoneration clause applied may lie on the trustees, but this was not of assistance where it was unclear what the Ombudsman was finding. The matter was remitted to the Ombudsman for redetermination.

[21.2.5]

Midland Bank (Jersey) v Federated Pension Services (Court of Appeal, Jersey) [1996] PLR 179, paras 75–81, 82–113, 115–138

Exoneration clauses – interpretation

Principles

In relation to contracts, parties are free to contract on whatever terms they may choose, subject to the law relating to public policy. However, where a party seeks to exclude liability he or she will only be held to have achieved this if the exclusion is expressed in clear unequivocal and unambiguous terms. All exculpatory clauses are restrictively construed. The *contra proferentem* rule applies. This embraces two related rules: first, the party seeking to rely on the clause must show that the case falls within its provisions, and any doubt will be resolved against him; secondly, in situations of ambiguity the words of the document are to be construed more strongly against the party who made the document and who now seeks to rely on them.

In the case of a trust rather than a contract, the beneficiaries had no contact with the trustee and the trustee owed fiduciary duties which went far beyond the usual obligations under a commercial contract, so the courts will take as restrictive a view as is permissible and appropriate. There is no general principle preventing a trustee from protecting himself or herself against liability for breach of trust by clear words, save in the case of fraud. *Seton v Dawson (1841) 4 D 310, Knox v Mackinnon (1888) 13 App Case 753, Rae v Meek (1889) 14 App Cas 558 HL (Sc), Carruthers v Carruthers [1896] AC 659 HL (Sc), Wyman v Patterson [1900] AC 271 HL (Sc), Clarke v Clarke's Trustees [1925] SC 693, Wilkins v Hogg (1861) 5 LT (NS) 467; 31 LJ Ch 41, Pass v Dundas (1880) 43 LT 665, Robertson v Howden (1892) 10 NZLR 609, Re Poche (1984) 6 DLR (4th) 40* and *Baskerville v Thurgood [1992] 18 WAC 214* were all considered.

Where a trustee is exempted from liability for anything whatever other than a breach of trust knowingly and wilfully committed, the wording is capable of being construed as meaning that liability arises only if the act committed was known by the trustee at the time of commission to be a breach of trust, but on balance the proper construction was that such knowledge is not essential before liability is incurred, provided that the breach of trust was knowingly and wilfully committed. *Re City Equitable Fire Insurance [1925] 1 Ch 407, Re Young and Harston's Contract (1895) 31 Ch D 168 CA, Elliot v Turner (1843) 13 Sim 485, Re Mayor of London and Tubbs' Contract [1894] 2 Ch 524 CA, Lewis v Great Western Railway Co (1877) 3 QBD 195 CA, Leeds City Brewery v Platts [1925] 1 Ch 532, Re Chapman [1896] 2 Ch 796 CA, Re Munton [1927] Ch 262 CA*, and *Re Vickery [1931] 1 Ch 572* were considered.

[21.2.6]

Re the Minworth Limited Pension Scheme, Anderson v William M Mercer (Pensions Ombudsman, 22 April 1999) Cases F00265, F00463 and G00264

Exoneration clauses – interpretation

Facts and Decision

Pension scheme trustees had the benefit of an exoneration clause which exempted them from liability except where the loss was by reason of wilful and individual fraud or default on the part of the trustees. The Pensions Ombudsman held that where a professional trustee had failed to give proper thought to the risk of funding problems caused by investment mismatching over a period of two years, it was recklessly indifferent to the fact that it was in breach of its duties and therefore not entitled to the benefit of the exoneration.

[21.2.7]

Providence Capitol Trustees v Ayres (High Court) [1996] 4 All ER 760, [1996] OPLR 215 at 219H–220B, [1996] PLR 395 at paras 9–10

Exoneration clauses – interpretation

Principle

Where the trustees were exonerated for breaches of trust unless proven to have been made in conscious bad faith, if the Pensions Ombudsman did not make a finding of conscious bad faith, a determination that a trustee was in breach of duty could not stand: *Wild v Smith [1996] OPLR 129* was followed.

[21.2.8]

Seifert v Pensions Ombudsman (High Court) [1997] 1 All ER 214, [1996] OPLR 231 at 240F-H, [1996] PLR 479 at para 33

Exoneration clauses – interpretation

Principle

Former trustees are able to rely upon an exoneration clause. Such clauses constitute part of the terms on which a trustee accepts his appointment and provide protection in respect of his conduct as a trustee. If his acts whilst a trustee cannot give rise to liability because of an exoneration clause, they cannot subsequently do so merely because he ceases to be a trustee.

[21.2.9]

Wakelin v Read (Court of Appeal) [2000] PLR 319

Exoneration clauses – interpretation

Facts and Decision

Mr Read was the chairman of a pension scheme trustee and the chairman of the scheme's employer. The pension scheme trustee bought a property from the employer and rented it back to the employer. The employer was in financial difficulties and could not sell the property to any other buyer. The employer went insolvent, and when the trustee sold the property, it received one third of the price which it had paid the employer. The trustee sought to deduct this loss from the entitlement of Mr Read on the grounds that there had been a *prima facie* breach of trust, and the director had been in breach of his duties such that he was liable as a constructive trustee. He complained to the Pensions Ombudsman, who concluded that he could not find that Mr Read had been dishonest unless he also concluded that his fellow trustee directors had been dishonest. The trustee had argued that Mr Read's fellow trustee directors had not been dishonest. The Ombudsman therefore found that Mr Read had not been dishonest and therefore the trustee was not entitled to withhold payment of his pension, but refused to order the trustee to pay Mr Read his pension on the ground that he did not come with sufficiently clean hands. Mr Read appealed, but the High Court substituted a finding that Mr Read had been dishonest since the Ombudsman had proceeded on an erroneous understanding of the test for dishonesty. The matter was remitted by the Court of Appeal to the Ombudsman for redetermination. The Ombudsman had not finished his investigation as to whether Mr Read had been a dishonest accessory, and only he could complete that investigation. Mr Read had not been given the opportunity to answer some of the Ombudsman's criticisms, and the facts were not sufficient such that a properly instructed tribunal could only have come to one conclusion. The Ombudsman was limited to those courses of action which would be open to a court in litigation, and therefore could not refuse to order the trustee to pay Mr Read his pension if he was otherwise entitled to receive it.

[21.2.10]

Walker v Stones (Court of Appeal, The Times, 26 September 2000)

Exoneration clauses – interpretation

Facts and Decision

The trustees of a private trust, who were solicitors, entered into transactions, as a result of which the trust shareholdings were made less valuable. The beneficiaries sued for breach of trust. The trustees relied upon an exoneration clause which exempted them from liability for anything done in the professed execution of the trusts unless they were guilty of dishonesty. The Court held that one of the trustees was entitled to the benefit of the exoneration because he had not acted dishonestly, but that the other, although he actually held the belief that what he was doing was in the interests of the beneficiaries, could not rely on the exoneration because no reasonable solicitor trustee could have believed that what he was doing was for the benefit of the beneficiaries, and his belief could not be regarded as honest. The test of honesty was dependent among other things on the role and calling of the trustee.

Wight v Olswang (Court of Appeal) [1999] TLR 376

Exoneration clauses – interpretation – professional trustees

Facts and Decision

Two separate exonerations were given to the trustees of a private settlement, one of which was for all trustees and one of which specifically excluded from its scope trustees who charged remuneration for so acting. The Court held that they could only be reconciled, where the subject matter of the clauses overlapped, by reading both clauses as being subject to the same exclusion for trustees who charged remuneration for so acting. The Court expects a paid trustee to exercise a higher standard of diligence and knowledge than an unpaid trustee.

[21.2.12]

Wild v Smith (High Court) [1996] OPLR 129 at 137H, [1996] PLR 275 at para 37

Exoneration clauses – interpretation – Pensions Ombudsman

Facts and Decision

A pension scheme clearly provided that a trustee was not to be held personally liable in the absence of dishonesty or wilful breach. The Court observed that the draftsman did not have in mind the possibility of awards of compensation for distress and inconvenience by the Pensions Ombudsman. However, nothing justified imposing a personal liability on a trustee contrary to the terms upon which he or she took his or her trust.

Indemnities

[21.2.13]

Johnson v EBS Pensioner Trustees (High Court, unreported, 8 March 2001)

Indemnity

Facts and Decision

Mr Johnson was a solicitor and trustee of a pension scheme for a businessman. The pension scheme took over liability for the lease of a property in 1990, where the mortgagees on the property were being advised by Mr Johnson's firm. In 1994, the property ceased to be self-financing. Mr Johnson settled the arrears and claimed reimbursement from the scheme assets under the terms of the scheme indemnity and the indemnity set out in *s 30(2)* of the *Trustee Act 1925*. This was resisted by the businessman on the grounds that Mr Johnson had paid the arrears in the capacity of trustee for the mortgagees. On the facts, the Court held that Mr Johnson had paid the arrears in his capacity of pension scheme trustee and was therefore entitled to reimbursement.

Constructive trusteeship

[21.2.14]

Hillsdown v Pensions Ombudsman (High Court) [1997] 1 All ER 862, [1996] OPLR 291 at 323C–326D, [1996] PLR 427 at paras 121–136

Constructive trusteeship

Facts and Decision

Receipt of trust property by a third party does not, the Court held, without more, constitute the recipient a constructive trustee. The categories of constructive trust are usually referred to as 'knowing assistance' and 'knowing receipt'. In both categories, some form of knowledge is required. In considering whether a constructive trust arises in a case of knowing receipt of trust property, the basic question is whether the conscience of the recipient is sufficiently affected to justify the imposition of such a trust. In this case, the employer's honest belief that it was entitled to do and receive what it did was outweighed by the fact that the employer had taken a very active part in persuading the trustee to agree to a breach of trust, that its technique in the persuasion was to threaten to do something it was not entitled to do and that the employer was unjustly enriched by the wielding of a big but misguided stick. The employer was sufficiently guilty to justify the imposition of a constructive trust, subject to possible defences. These did not include change of position caused by the employer's agreement to benefit improvements and the tax charge paid (except to the extent that it was irrecoverable) – the employer had no right of veto over use of surplus in this case.

[21.2.15]

Hillsdown v Pensions Ombudsman (second judgment) (High Court) [1996] PLR 427 at para 141

Constructive trusteeship – accounting for interest and tax

Facts and Decision

It had been established that an employer was a constructive trustee of amounts which it had received as a repayment of surplus from its pension scheme (net of 40% tax) (see [21.2.14]). The Court held that the employer was liable to repay the net sums it had received. However, the employer was not liable to account for interest on tax unless it received such interest, since it was only accountable on actual receipt, and it was not liable to account for interest except at the statutory simple interest, since it had not been found to have committed a knowing and guilty breach of trust: *Wallersteiner v Moir (No. 2) [1975] QB 373* at *397–8* was distinguished. In this case, the assets were wrongly removed from the trusts of one scheme using a second scheme as a conduit. When they were returned, they were to be returned on the trusts of the first scheme, however awkward that might be in practice. But this was not a punitive jurisdiction, and the first scheme should not be assumed to be in winding-up, because this would probably confer far greater benefits on the beneficiaries than they would otherwise have received. Instead, the trustee should carry out the obligations imposed by the first scheme's surplus rule as at the successive valuation dates, starting with the date on which the assets had been transferred from the first scheme to the second scheme.

Claims against trustee directors and trust companies

[21.2.16]

Australian Securities Commission v AS Nominees (Federal Court of Australia) [1996] PLR 297 at paras 41–57, 73–81

Trustee directors' duties – professional trustees

Principle

A trustee company must take as much care for the beneficiaries as an ordinary trustee. These requirements have a flow-on effect into the duties and liabilities of the directors of such companies. When and to the extent that the directors of a trustee company are themselves concerned in the breaches of trust of their company, they are liable to the company according to the same standard of care and caution as is expected of the company itself. However, this rule is only operative when the trust business itself is involved. Trustee companies owe a higher standard of care than that of the ordinary prudent business person: *Bartlett v Barclays Trust Co. Ltd (No. 1) [1980] Ch 515* was followed. Whether directors owe fiduciary duties directly to the beneficiaries of trusts of which the company is a trustee was doubted.

[21.2.17]

Fouche v Superannuation Fund Board (High Court of Australia) (1952) 88 CLR 609

Trustee directors' duties

Facts and Decision

The Superannuation Fund Board was established by statute. It entered into a land transaction which involved serious breaches of trust, causing loss. The Court held that the individual corporators were personally liable to make good any loss sustained by the scheme.

HR v JAPT (High Court, interlocutory) [1997] OPLR 123, [1997] PLR 99

Trustee directors' duties

Facts and Decision

Beneficiaries of a pension scheme which had as its trustee a 30p trustee company brought claims against the trustee and its directors on various grounds. One of the trustee directors applied to have the claims against him struck out.

The Court upheld the following principles:

(a) Directors of trustee companies ordinarily stand in a fiduciary duty only to the company itself: *Bath v Standard Land Co [1911] 1 Ch 618* was followed, while *Re French Protestant Hospital [1951] Ch 567* and *Abbey and Malvern Wells Ltd v Ministry of Local Government [1951] Ch 728* were not followed. Whilst exceptional facts can be envisaged in which the implication of a direct fiduciary relationship between a beneficiary of a pension scheme and the directors of company acting as trustee of that scheme was justified, such an implication could not be drawn from directors of a trustee company acting as directors of a trustee company might be expected to act (alleged carelessness apart).

(b) Where it is alleged that a trustee director has been dishonest within the meaning of *Royal Brunei Airlines v Tan [1995] 2 AC 378* (meaning that he participated in a transaction where he knew that it involved a misapplication of trust assets to the detriment of the beneficiaries, or if he deliberately closed his eyes and ears or chose deliberately not to ask questions so as to avoid learning something he would rather not know and proceeded regardless), he could be liable for knowingly assisting a breach of trust where the breach of trust has been committed by the trustee company of which he is director.

(c) Directors of trustee companies do not owe a direct tortious duty of care to the beneficiaries unless the director assumed personal responsibility. This would not include activity of a kind which one might expect of a director of a trustee company: *Williams v Natural Life [1997] 1 BCLC 131* (Court of Appeal) was distinguished.

(d) It was arguable that a beneficiary of a trust could enforce the fiduciary duty owed by a director to a trustee company if the chose in action represented by a breach of that fiduciary duty was a trust asset.

(e)   The Court would only attribute the company's misdeeds to the directors where special circumstances exist indicating that the company's separate legal personality was a façade concealing the true facts: *Woolfson v Strathclyde Regional Council [1978] AC 159* was followed. In the case of a trustee company with no assets and no income, and no function other than the management and administration of a pension scheme, there was no concealment of any relevant fact, nor was the corporate form a 'device or sham or cloak'.

Comment

The differing legal status of trustees and the directors of trustee companies had been debated for many years before this decision. This case confirms the different effects of the different legal structures, the consequences of which may be alarming for pension scheme members and others seeking to impose liability on trustee directors.

This case concerned an application to strike out various bases of claim against a trustee director. Only one of these applications succeeded, but the Court expressed scepticism about many of the other bases of claim. The only arguments which the Court endorsed whole-heartedly were that a director could be held liable for knowingly assisting a breach of trust of the corporate trustee, and that members may be able to sue the director directly for breaches of fiduciary obligations owed to the corporate trustee if the right to sue the director was a trust asset. These are much more limited grounds for suing for breach of duty than members have against individual trustees. Where, as here, the corporate trustee is valueless, this potentially leaves members with no effective remedy where serious wrongs have been committed.

The Court evidently had sympathy with the idea that the trustee directors should be held to owe a direct fiduciary duty to the scheme members, but it held itself bound by Court of Appeal precedent. In one of the most unusual passages in any judgment, the Court effectively announced its advance support for any prospective challenge to that precedent – *Bath v Standard Land Co [1911] 1 Ch 618*. Whether the Court will ever be taken up on that remains to be seen.

[21.2.19]

Wakelin v Read (High Court) [1998] OPLR 147 at 155H–156D, [1998] PLR 337 at para 31–32

Trustee directors' duties

Principle

The Pensions Ombudsman could properly hold that directors of the same trustee company had differing levels of responsibilities for breaches of trust in relation to the same acts, such that two trustee directors could be honest but grossly negligent, while a third trustee director was dishonest.

Claims involving third parties

[21.2.20]

Fouche v Superannuation Fund Board (High Court of Australia) (1952) 88 CLR 609

Claims by third parties

Facts and Decision

A third party cannot, the Court held, enforce a contract entered into by a trustee of a pension scheme where the trustee would be in breach of trust in honouring it. In this case, the corporate trustee was established by statute, had no assets other than assets held on trust and could not make a contract except out of trust funds in its hands. If the contract was made in breach of trust, it could not be enforced against the corporation as trustee and could not be enforced against the trust fund. Moreover, it could not be enforced against the trustee personally, because it was a corporation which had no legal personality except in its capacity as trustee.

[21.2.21]

HR v JAPT (High Court, interlocutory) [1997] OPLR 123 at 136H–138B, [1997] PLR 99, paras 59–66

Claims against third parties

Principle

Where it is alleged that a trustee director has been dishonest within the meaning of *Royal Brunei Airlines v Tan [1995] 2 AC 378* (meaning that he participated in a transaction where he knew that it involved a misapplication of trust assets to the detriment of the beneficiaries, or if he deliberately closed his eyes and ears or chose deliberately not to ask questions so as to avoid learning something he would rather not know and proceeded regardless), he could be liable for knowingly assisting a breach of trust where the breach of trust has been committed by the trustee company of which he is director.

[21.2.22]

Re Johnson (High Court) (1880) XV Ch 548

Claims by third parties

Facts and Decision

Mr Johnson left a will establishing a trust. In breach of trust, his executor continued to carry on his business. He made loans to the business out of the interest of one beneficiary, and made profits out of the business for which he did not account to the trust. The creditors of the business sought to have recourse to the trust assets. The Court held that the right of the creditors was to put themselves in the place of the trustee. If the trustee is not entitled, except on terms to make good a loss to the trust estate, the creditors cannot have a better right. The creditors' petition was therefore dismissed.

[21.2.23]

Perring v Draper (High Court, unreported, 3 July 1997)

Claims by third parties – indemnities

Facts and Decision

Trustees of a private trust held a lease, on which £125,000 of liabilities had accrued. The trustees were entitled to an indemnity under the trust. The Court held that the trustees were entitled to be indemnified out of the trust fund to such extent as the trust fund was sufficient to provide such an indemnity. They were not relieved from personal liability from a contract into which they had entered by reference to any general proposition of law.

Tracing and claiming scheme assets

[21.2.24]

Bishopsgate Investment Management v Homan (Court of Appeal) [1994] PLR 179

Tracing assets – equitable charges

Facts and Decision

Following Robert Maxwell's death, it emerged that pension schemes managed by Bishopsgate Investment Management (BIM) had been improperly paid into the accounts of various companies within the Maxwell group, including Maxwell Communication Corporation (MCC), where the sums were paid into bank accounts which were either overdrawn at that time or subsequently became overdrawn. MCC was hopelessly insolvent and was placed into administration. The administrators recovered a substantial part of MCC's assets and sought to make an interim distribution among creditors. BIM opposed this on the ground that it had an equitable charge in priority to all other unsecured creditors. The Court held that it is not possible to trace through an overdrawn bank account, since the money previously impressed with the trust ceased to exist: *Re Goldcorp Exchange Limited [1994] 3 WLR 199* and *Re Diplock [1948] Ch 465* were followed. This remained so even when an account returned to balance. BIM's claim therefore failed.

Derby v Scottish Equitable (Court of Appeal) [2001] PLR 163

Tracing assets – estoppel – change of position

Facts and Decision

Mr Derby came to draw his personal pension. Scottish Equitable miscalculated his pension entitlement, and when Mr Derby queried this, Scottish Equitable confirmed their erroneous calculations. Mr Derby, therefore, took a tax-free cash lump sum, and used the rest to take out an annuity with Norwich Union. Scottish Equitable had overpaid Mr Derby by £172,000. He spent most of the lump sum on reducing his mortgage, and the remaining £9,600 he used to improve his lifestyle, though modestly and not irreversibly. Eventually, Scottish Equitable realised their mistake and asked for its money back. Norwich Union agreed that it would unwind the pension policy which it had granted. The Court held that carelessness did not automatically prevent Scottish Equitable from recovering the money: the recovery of money in restitution is not as a general rule a matter of discretion for the Court. Mr Derby had changed his position only in relation to the money used to improve his lifestyle. The payment of the mortgage did not count as a change of position, since he had suffered no detriment in paying off a debt which would have had to have been met sooner or later (although detriment was conceivable if the debt had been obtained on favourable terms). The defence of estoppel was not applicable, and Mr Derby could therefore only rely upon the defence of change of position. Mr Derby was therefore obliged to repay the overpayment in its entirety, except for the £9,600 in relation to which he had changed his position: *Lipkin Gorman v Karpnale [1991] 2 AC 548* was applied.

Hillsdown v Pensions Ombudsman (second judgment) (High Court) [1996] PLR 427 (in argument about stay)

Recovering scheme assets – stays of execution

Facts and Decision

The Court would not stay an order against an employer to repay a payment of surplus pending the outcome of an appeal on the grounds that it would result in overpayments being made to pensioners if the appeal was successful. Any overpayment of income to beneficiaries could be rectified over further payments. There might be cases where there would be a payment that could not be adjusted by a future adjustment of the accounts, but that was a relatively small risk. The beneficiaries who received this money would do so, if there was an appeal, in the knowledge that there was going to be an appeal, and that circumstances might change if the Court of Appeal saw matters differently.

21.3 – Calculation of loss

Breach of trust

[21.3.1]

Armstrong v East-West Airlines (Supreme Court of New South Wales) [1995] OPLR 239 at 248B-G

Calculation of loss to pension scheme – interest

Principle

Where assessing loss caused by a breach of trust by an employer/trustee resulting in delay in paying benefits, interest for late payment should be awarded at the trustee rate (based on the yield on 10-year Government bonds) and not the mercantile rate. The member was not obliged to produce evidence of what in fact he or she would have done with his or her benefit had it been paid when it should have been paid: one of the purposes of using the trustee rate was to absolve plaintiffs from that task.

[21.3.2]

Bartlett v Barclays Trust Co Ltd (No 1) [1980] Ch 515 at 538

Calculation of loss caused by breach of trust – set-off

Principle

The general rule as stated in the textbooks is that where a trustee is liable in respect of distinct breaches of trust, one of which has resulted in a loss and the other in a gain, he or she is not entitled to set off the gain against the loss, unless they arise in the same transaction. The relevant cases are, however, not altogether easy to reconcile. Accordingly, where a gain had resulted from a breach of trust committed from following exactly the same policy and exemplifying the same folly as a breach of trust which resulted in a loss, the Court would allow the trustee this element of salvage in the course of assessing the cost of the shipwreck.

[21.3.3]

Jones v AMP (High Court, New Zealand) [1995] PLR 53 at para 106

Calculation of loss to pension scheme – investment return

Facts and Decision

Scheme members had argued that investment losses caused by a breach of trust involving wrongful investment in shares should be calculated by reference to the actual return on a fixed interest investment. The Court did not agree. This procedure would mean that the beneficiaries would have obtained the benefit of the rise in share and property prices which took place prior to the stockmarket crash, but would have avoided the downward losses which followed. A fixed interest investment also may not have been the appropriate investment for most members of the scheme.

[21.3.4]

McConnell v Boyd (High Court) [1997] OPLR 53

Calculation of loss to pension scheme – identifying loss

Facts and Decision

An employer was advised to make additional contributions of £5,000 for twelve consecutive months to restore its pension scheme to balance. These payments were made, but unknown to the other trustees, two trustees (who were also company directors) wrote cheques in ten of these months for £5,000 from the trustees to the company to counteract the effect of the standing order. The Pensions Ombudsman ordered that the trustees responsible pay £50,000 to the scheme plus interest. The trustees argued that only £5,000 loss was suffered, since the same £5,000 was moving back and forth between the scheme and the company. This submission was rejected by the Court as fanciful: the company was paying a liability by instalments, it was not paying a single sum repeatedly. The trustees also argued that the winding-up of the scheme was deferred as a result of the breach of trust, and that the Ombudsman should be ordered to redetermine the loss accordingly. The Court held that the distinction referred to by Lord Browne-Wilkinson in *Target Holdings v Redfern [1995] 3 WLR 352* was a distinction between funds vested in trustees, and funds in which during the course of a commercial transaction money becomes held on a bare trust for a party to that transaction. On that analysis, a pension scheme was an example of a traditional trust, and the money wrongfully extracted was to be restored to the fund with interest.

Personal injuries and negligence

[21.3.5]

Auty v National Coal Board (Court of Appeal) [1985] I WLR 784

Personal injury – calculation of pension loss

Facts and Decision

Four coal miners suffered injuries at work in unrelated accidents. Three of them were forced to stop working, and the fourth died, leaving a widow. As a result of this, the miners' entitlements under the pension scheme were less than they would have been had they been able to continue working, and the widow received a death in service widow's pension rather than a death in retirement widow's pension. The miners and the widow brought claims of negligence against the National Coal Board, and claimed for pension loss, including the value of potential index-linking of the lost element of pension under the pension scheme rules. The Court held that where pension increases were not guaranteed but increased in accordance with the cost of living index, if funds were available from normal contributions at the date the decision fell to be taken or if the Board was prepared to make extra deficiency payments, the supposedly higher value of the index linking was essentially tenuous, and the Court was justified in making no allowance for inflation in assessing loss of future pension. The widow could not claim for loss of an opportunity to obtain a widow's pension at a later date, when she had not lost the opportunity of a widow's pension because she was already in receipt of a widow's pension. The two benefits were therefore mutually exclusive.

[21.3.6]

Barry v Ablerex Construction (Midlands) (Court of Appeal, unreported, 21 March 2001)

Personal injury – discount rates

Principle

The discount rate of 3% in *Wells v Wells [1998] 3 WLR 329* was binding on lower courts until the Lord Chancellor set a rate under the *Damages Act 1996*: *Warren v Northern General Hospital Trust [2000] 1 WLR 1404* was followed.

[21.3.7]

Cantwell v Criminal Injuries Compensation Board (Scotland) (Scottish House of Lords) The Times, 16 July 2001

Personal injury – calculation of pension loss

Facts and Decision

Mr Cantwell was a police officer assualted in the course of his duty. He was obliged to retire early on an ill-health pension, and lost his normal retirement pension which he would have received three years later. He sought to claim for loss of pension rights from the Criminal Injuries Compensation Board, arguing that his ill-health pension should not be taken into account. The Court held that on a proper construction of *s 10* of the *Administration of Justice Act 1982*, the ill-health pension fell to be set off against the normal retirement pension in years when the normal retirement pension would have been payable: *Parry v Cleaver [1970] AC 1* was considered and applied, *Auty v National Coal Board [1985] 1 WLR 784* was considered, and *Leebody v Liddle [2000] SCCR 495* was approved. The periods before and after normal retirement age require to be considered separately.

[21.3.8]

Dews v National Coal Board (House of Lords) [1988] AC 1

Personal injury – calculation of pension loss

Facts and Decision

Mr Dews was a miner. He was injured at work and was absent on sick leave for 31 weeks, during which time he received no pay and made no pension contributions to his employer's pension scheme, of which membership was compulsory for miners. He suffered little or no loss of pension rights. He sued for negligence, and claimed for the unpaid wages, without any offset for the unpaid contributions. The Court held that Mr Dews could not recover both the contributions and the pension that those contributions would have purchased, for that would be to allow double recovery. The Court applied separate considerations to that part of his earnings which was to be used for immediate expenditure and that part which was intended to provide a pension for his retirement, and offset the contributions from Mr Dews's damages award: *Parry v Cleaver [1970] AC 1* was considered. It was not a critical feature that this was a compulsory pension scheme.

[21.3.9]

London Ambulance Service National Health Trust v Swain (Court of Appeal, 12 March 1999) [1999] 46 PBLR 13

Personal injury – calculation of pension loss

Facts and Decision

Mr Swain was injured at work through his employer's negligence and forced to take early retirement at age 57 (his normal retirement date was 60). He claimed for damages, including pension loss. The Court held that payments of ill-health pension and lump sum did not fall to be taken into account until such time when Mr Swain would have retired, when the Court was comparing like with like: *Parry v Cleaver [1907] AC 1* and *Longden v British Coal [1998] OPLR 223* were applied. The lump sum had to be notionally reapportioned as payments of pension, to be allocated between the periods before and after the date when Mr Swain would have retired, and the updated Ogden tables were to be used for this purpose: *Longden v British Coal* was considered and applied. It was wrong when taking the ill-health benefits into account to adjust the lump sum received to the level that they would have been had Mr Swain taken early retirement: that was beside the point. The multiplier to be used to adjust Mr Swain's lump sum to age 60 was 3% a year: *Wells v Wells [1998] 3 WLR 329* was applied.

[21.3.10]

Longden v British Coal (House of Lords) [1998] OPLR 223, [1998] PLR 71

Personal injury – calculation of pension loss

Facts and Decision

Mr Longden was employed by British Coal and a member of the employer's pension scheme. He was badly injured in an accident which was British Coal's fault, and retired on an incapacity pension. In his negligence action against British Coal, he claimed for pension loss, since his pension benefits at normal retirement age would have been substantially higher if he had not been injured. British Coal sought to offset the value of the incapacity pension from the date it was put into payment against the value of the normal retirement pension Mr Longden would otherwise have received, being the net loss of his pension. The Court held that the receipts from pension before the date when they were subsumed into the general retirement pension were receipts which were not to be brought into account when assessing damages of any type, including damages referable to pension loss: *Parry v Cleaver [1970] AC 1, Smoker v London Fire and Civil Defence Authority [1991] PLR 63* and *Dews v National Coal Board [1988] AC 1, 15* were applied. The only reason why incapacity and disability pension payments received after the normal retirement age must be brought into account in computing the claim for loss of pension after that age is that the claim at this stage is for loss of pension, so one cannot properly calculate the loss of pension arising in this period without taking into account receipts of the same character arising in the same period. However, a lump sum representing a commutation of part of the annual pension must be set off against the loss claimed, to the extent that the lump sum is referable to the period after normal retirement age.

[21.3.11]

NHS Pensions v Beechinor (High Court) [1997] OPLR 99 at 101F, [1997] PLR 95 at para 8

Calculation of pension loss

Principle

In so far as the Pensions Ombudsman can give damages for tort, a single sum only could be awarded representing the damages suffered at the date of the commission of the tort.

[21.3.12]

Parry v Cleaver (House of Lords) [1970] AC 1

Personal injury – calculation of pension loss

Facts and Decision

Mr Parry was a police officer injured while directing traffic owing to the negligence of a driver. He retired on an ill-health pension. He sued for damages, and the question arose as to how his pension rights should be treated in the calculation of damages. The Court held that money paid under insurance is not to be taken into account because the plaintiff has bought the insurance, and it would be unjust and unreasonable to hold that the money which he had prudently spent on premiums, and the benefit from it, should benefit the wrongdoer. A contributory pension is a form of insurance. Like every other kind of insurance, what the member gets back depends on how things turn out. A pension is intrinsically of a different kind from wages. Wages are a reward for contemporaneous work but a pension is the fruit, through insurance, of all the money which was set aside in the past in respect of the employee's past work. The pension should therefore not be taken into account when calculating damages, except for the period after normal retirement age, when assessing the amount of pension loss, where the loss would be the difference between the full pension which he would have received if he had served his full time and his ill-health pension. *Payne v Railway Executive [1951] 2 All ER 910, Baker v Dalgeish [1922] 1 KB 361, Judd v Board of Governors of Hammersmith, West London and St Mark's Hospitals [1960] 1 All ER 607* were approved, and *Monmouthshire County Council v Smith [1956] 2 All ER 800, Browning v War Office [1962] 3 All ER 1089, Carroll v Hooper [1964] 1 All ER 845, Elstob v Robinson [1964] 1 All ER 848* were disapproved.

Comment

The treatment of pension in the calculation of damages has long been controversial, and this case was the culmination of one hundred years of conflicting judgments. It remains an area where many lawyers dislike the practical consequences because it apparently results in claimants being paid twice, and the Court's logic has been challenged repeatedly since, despite the fact that this is a House of Lords decision. The courts have stood firm, even when the principles have resulted in what its opponents would argue were absurd consequences. Defendants were disappointed in *Smoker v London Fire and Civil Defence Authority [1991] PLR 63, Longden v British Coal [1998] OPLR 223, Hopkins v Norcros [1994] OPLR 121* and *Clark v BET [1997] OPLR 1*, all of which firmly applied the same principles: the member's pension benefits are not to be taken into account for the purposes of calculating loss (even when the member is claiming for loss of damages, except when one is comparing equivalent periods of payment), since the member paid for those benefits with contributions and labour.

Despite its counter-intuitive results, the underlying principle of this case is highly appealing. Why should a defendant effectively take the benefit of an employee's pension scheme terms, when it would have had to pay more if the employee had not been pensioned? The results can seem unfair when an employer is the defendant, but as was noted in *Hopkins v Norcros*, it is open to employers to make provision in the contract of employment, at least in so far as claims for wrongful dismissal are concerned.

Pidduck v Eastern Scottish Omnibuses (Court of Appeal) [1990] PLR 59

Personal injury – calculation of pension loss

Facts and Decision

Mr Pidduck was killed in a coach accident. His widow (who was also his executrix) sued the coach operators under the *Fatal Accidents Act 1976* as amended. He was a pensioner under a non-contributory occupational pension scheme. The Court held that before any assessment of loss could take place, the plaintiff needed to show that she had suffered injury, which was described as loss of dependency based on financial support. The death benefits which Mrs Pidduck received were not to be taken into account in the calculation of loss of dependency, since this was paid under a separate section of the scheme and not connected with Mr Pidduck's pension. *Parry v Cleaver [1970] AC 1* was considered, and *Auty v National Coal Board [1985] 1 WLR 784* was distinguished.

[21.3.14]

Smoker v London Fire and Civil Defence Authority (House of Lords) [1991] PLR 63

Personal injury – calculation of pension loss

Facts and Decision

Mr Smoker, a fireman, successfully brought a claim for negligence against his former employer. His employers sought to set off the value of his pension rights earned in its employment against the damages to be paid. The House of Lords held that the case was indistinguishable from *Parry v Cleaver [1970] AC 1*, since the identity of the tortfeasor should not be relevant in assessing damages. The House of Lords declined the invitation not to follow that decision. *Guy v Police Authority for Northern Ireland* (unreported, 14 April 1989) was approved.

[21.3.15]

Van Oudenhoven v Griffin Inns (Court of Appeal) [2000] 1 WLR 1413

Personal injury – discount rates

Principle

The discount rate of 3% in *Wells v Wells [1998] 3 WLR 329* was binding on lower courts until the Lord Chancellor set a rate under the *Damages Act 1996*: *Warren v Northern General Hospital Trust* was followed.

[21.3.16]

Warren v Northern General Hospital Trust (Court of Appeal) [2000] 1 WLR 1404

Personal injury – discount rates

Principle

The discount rate of 3% in *Wells v Wells [1998] 3 WLR 329* was binding on lower courts until the Lord Chancellor set a rate under the *Damages Act 1996*, and it was not permissible to use the basis on which that rate was calculated to arrive at a different discount rate. The need for certainty to facilitate settlements, coupled with the undesirability of extensive evidence from accountants, actuaries or economists with a view to persuading the courts to change the discount rate, militated strongly against any court seeking to do so before the Lord Chancellor acted.

[21.3.17]

Wells v Wells (House of Lords) [1998] 3 WLR 329

Personal injury – discount rates

Facts and Decision

The Court was required to assess the lump sum damages to be awarded in personal injury cases in respect of loss of earnings for the future. The Court held that the ordinary investor could be presumed to have enough to live on to meet his or her day-to-day requirements. The plaintiffs in this case were not in that happy position, and could not afford to wait for long-term recovery in market prices: they needed the income and a portion of capital to meet their current cost of care. So it did not follow that a prudent investment for the ordinary investor would be prudent for the plaintiffs in this case. Until the Lord Chancellor exercised his powers under *s 1* of the *Damages Act 1996*, the discount rate for multipliers should be 3% per annum. This rate was based on the return on index-linked Government stock, which provided a relatively risk-free investment.

[21.3.18]

West v Versil (Court of Appeal, unreported, 2 July 1996)

Personal injury – calculation of pension loss

Facts and Decision

Mr West contracted asbestosis as a result of the negligence of his former employer. As a consequence, he chose to retire at age 60 instead of carrying on working until age 65, and drew his pension on a surviving spouse rather than a single life basis, thus reducing the size of his pension. He claimed damages for loss of his pension rights. The Court held that Mr West had no valid basis for claiming any shortfall in receipt of pension rights during his lifetime which was attributable to his own decision to opt for payments on a surviving spouse rather than a single life basis. The diminution of pension caused by the fact that Mr West would make no further contributions to the scheme, and by the fact that he was drawing a pension instead of allowing the income to continue to accumulate, should be disregarded also.

Wrongful/unfair dismissal

[21.3.19]

Benson v Dairy Crest (Employment Appeal Tribunal) [1991] PLR 59

Unfair dismissal – calculation of pension loss

Facts and Decision

Mr Benson successfully brought a claim to an Industrial Tribunal alleging that he had been unfairly selected for redundancy. The Industrial Tribunal needed to consider the calculation of pension loss, and concluded that there was no evidence of loss of pension rights. The Appeal Tribunal held that it was very difficult to identify why Mr Benson had been awarded no damages for loss of pension rights, and the matter was remitted to the same Industrial Tribunal for reconsideration in the light of the booklet 'Industrial Tribunals Compensation for Loss of Pension Rights', which was an excellent and careful study of the issues.

[21.3.20]

Bingham v Hobourn Engineering Limited (Employment Appeal Tribunal) [1992] OPLR 69, [1992] PLR 151

Unfair dismissal – calculation of pension loss

Facts and Decision

Mr Bingham was unfairly dismissed by his employer. For the purposes of assessing his pension loss, his employer sought details of the pension scheme offered by his new employer. Mr Bingham argued that this was irrelevant, and sought to rely upon the guidelines set out in the booklet 'Industrial Tribunals Compensation for Loss of Pension Rights'. No evidence was put in before the Industrial Tribunal, and it concluded that it could not make an award under the heading of loss of pension rights on the grounds that it was not satisfied that there would be some loss accruing to Mr Bingham. The Appeal Tribunal observed that while the booklet was a valuable guide, it was not a bible to be followed in every detail, as the booklet itself made plain. There was no duty on the Tribunal to apply the approach set out in the booklet. The conclusion the Tribunal reached that it would not make an award unless and until it was satisfied there was some loss was a conclusion of fact, and as such not appealable.

[21.3.21]

Bristow v Lenting (Employment Appeal Tribunal, unreported, 22 August 1996)

Unfair dismissal – calculation of pension loss

Principles

The value of pension benefits should not be deducted from an award for unfair dismissal: *Parry v Cleaver [1970] AC 1* and *Hopkins v Norcros [1994] OPLR 121* were applied.

[21.3.22]

Bold v Brough Nicholson & Hall (High Court) [1964] I WLR 201

Wrongful dismissal – calculation of pension loss

Facts and Decision

Mr Bold was the managing director of his employer. He was entitled to six months' notice if he was to be dismissed. He was a member of his employer's defined benefit pension scheme. If he retired with the consent of the employer, he was entitled to an immediate pension and life assurance benefits continuing until normal retirement age of 65. However, if he did not, he would be entitled only to a refund of his contributions with interest. Mr Bold was dismissed without notice at age 55 and he claimed damages for, among other things, loss of pension and life assurance under the scheme. The employer argued that it could give six months' notice to discontinue the whole scheme, in which case no pension would be payable, and therefore no damages should be paid. The Court did not find that argument impressive. This was a substantial company with subsidiaries and many employees. It was not in serious business difficulties, and there was nothing to suggest that the employer would wind up the scheme solely to defeat a claim by Mr Bold. However, Mr Bold was not entitled to the immediate pension, since he had not retired with employer consent. This implied initiative on the part of the employee, and it would be false to describe Mr Bold's departure as early retirement. He was therefore entitled only to a refund of contributions with interest.

[21.3.23]

Cannock Chase Technical College v Clancy (Employment Appeal Tribunal) [2001] PLR 175

Unfair dismissal – calculation of pension loss

Facts and Decision

Mr Clancy was employed as a senior lecturer, and was unfairly dismissed by his employer at age 48. He was a member of the Teachers' Pension Scheme. The Employment Tribunal concluded that he would have remained in employment until his normal retirement date of 60 had he not been dismissed. As a result of being dismissed, his pension from age 60 would be £3,407 a year lower and his lump sum at age 60 would be

£10,221 lower. The Tribunal assessed loss by reference to the employer contributions which would have been made, totalling just under £20,000. The Appeal Tribunal held that this decision was perverse, since this sum could not possibly replace the loss of pension which Mr Clancy had suffered, and the case was remitted for expert actuarial assessment. The guidelines in the booklet 'Industrial Tribunals Compensation for Loss of Pension Rights' might very well need revision, and careful consideration needed to be given as to whether it could still be relied on. The booklet was ten years old, and the actuarial tables upon which it was based were twenty years old. The limit for tribunal claims had now been raised to £50,000, making a full and accurate computation more likely to be needed in more cases.

[21.3.24]

Cawthorn & Sinclair v Hedger (National Industrial Relations Court) [1974] ICR 146, [1974] IRLR 49

Unfair dismissal – calculation of pension loss

Facts and Decision

Mr Hedger was unfairly dismissed. He claimed, among other things, for loss of pension rights. He had found a new job, which did not have a pension scheme, whereas his previous employer offered a final salary pension scheme. The Court held that the logical starting point in assessing loss was the previous employer's annual contribution to the employee's pension.

[21.3.25]

Chubb Fire v Miller (Employment Appeal Tribunal) [2000] All ER (D) 1374, [2000] 65 PBLR 4

Unfair dismissal – calculation of pension loss

Facts and Decision

Mr Miller was unfairly dismissed by his employer while he was looking around for new work. The Employment Tribunal awarded him damages for pension loss. The employer appealed on the ground that the loss would have occurred anyway when he changed jobs. On the facts as found by the Tribunal, the Appeal Tribunal observed that Mr Miller had not obtained new employment prior to dismissal and the dismissal therefore took away the option to continue in his existing employment. There was therefore a sufficient causal link between the dismissal and the loss of pension rights.

[21.3.26]

Clark v BET (High Court) [1997] OPLR 1

Wrongful dismissal – calculation of pension loss

Facts and Decision

Mr Clark was wrongfully dismissed as chief executive of BET after Rentokil's takeover of BET, and he brought proceedings to recover damages. His contract was jointly under English law and the law of the U.S. State of Georgia. Among the various heads of loss, he claimed pension loss. He had been a member of BET's funded unapproved retirement benefits scheme, under which he was entitled to an immediate pension. This would be payable unreduced in the event of an immediate pension becoming payable 'following' the acquisition by any party of control of BET. The Court held that whether 'following' meant to convey the notion that it was subsequent in time or whether it required a causative link between the acquisition and the immediate pension, on the facts Mr Clark was entitled to his unreduced pension. Although the law of Georgia required a discount rate of 5%, the promise was to benefits under a United Kingdom scheme, and therefore the British discount rate should be used in its entirety. On the facts, the appropriate discount rate was 3%. Mr Clark did not need to give credit for the pension received during his notice period: *Hopkins v Norcros [1994] OPLR 121* and *Longden v British Coal [1998] OPLR 223* were applied.

[21.3.27]

Cope v Carnaud Metal Box Aerosols plc (Employment Appeal Tribunal, unreported, 10 October 1995)

Unfair dismissal – calculation of pension loss

Facts and Decision

Mr Cope was unfairly dismissed, though he was held 50% to blame for what had happened. The Industrial Tribunal did not make any allowance in respect of his pension, and Mr Cope had not raised this before the Tribunal. The Appeal Tribunal held that it was the duty of Mr Cope to tell the Tribunal what he thought his losses were, but it was an error of law for the Tribunal to fail to consider it. It decided not to remit the matter to the

Industrial Tribunal, but used a rough and ready way of assessing pension loss, by basing the calculation on the employer and employee calculations that would have been made.

[21.3.28]

Gill v Harold Andrews Sheepbridge (National Industrial Relations Court) [1974] ICR 294, [1974] ITR 219, [1974] IRLR 109

Unfair dismissal – calculation of pension loss

Facts and Decision

Mr Gill was unfairly dismissed by his employer. The Industrial Tribunal made no award in respect of loss of pension rights. Under the employer's scheme, the employer and employee made equal weekly contributions. After Mr Gill was dismissed, he had his contributions refunded to him with 4% compound interest. The Court held that the Tribunal should have awarded damages for loss of the value of the employer's contributions up to the date of dismissal, and from the date of the dismissal until such time as Mr Gill would find future employment. Consideration needed to be given to the question as to whether or not in future employment Mr Gill would receive the benefit of an equivalent pension scheme. The matter was remitted to the Tribunal to evaluate the loss of pension rights, since they had indicated that they regarded Mr Gill as bearing contributory blame, but had not assessed the percentage.

[21.3.29]

Harris v Simpson (Alberta Court of Queen's Bench) 56 AR 201

Wrongful dismissal – calculation of pension loss

Facts and Decision

Mr Harris was wrongfully dismissed by his employer. He was then entitled to pension benefits, but if he had taken early retirement, the pension would have been substantially higher than if he left on termination. The Court held that the employer was not permitted to profit from its wrongful act (it did not matter that the employer did not have a direct interest in the scheme), and was accordingly estopped from denying Mr Harris the option of electing the early retirement option under the scheme. This could be justified on a wider basis. An employee who had been wrongfully dismissed was to be put in the same position as if the contract had been performed, and so if the employee could have properly sought his pension benefits under a more advantageous characterisation during the notice period to which he would have been entitled, he should be deemed to have done so: *McKie v City of Moncton and City of Moncton's Employees' Pension Board (1981) 34 NBR (2d) 5, 85 APR 5* was followed. Mr Harris was entitled to interest on his unpaid pension instalments from the date they were due.

[21.3.30]

Hill v Sabco Houseware (UK) (Employment Appeal Tribunal) [1977] ICR 888

Unfair dismissal – calculation of pension loss

Facts and Decision

Mr Hill was unfairly dismissed. He was awarded damages by the Industrial Tribunal based on a refund of his own contributions to the employer's pension scheme. The Appeal Tribunal observed that many contributory pension schemes start with a waiting period of service before the member qualifies for any pension at all. When a person leaves one employed position for another and is faced with that situation, that was a factor which should not be overlooked in assessing the amount of compensation. The Tribunal should have looked back and forward to assess the position as a whole. Furthermore, where the Tribunal was making an assessment of loss it could only be an estimate. It was awarding a capital sum and therefore ought never in these cases to deal with them purely as actuarial calculations or arithmetical sums.

[21.3.31]

Hopkins v Norcros (Court of Appeal) [1994] OPLR 121, [1994] PLR 27

Wrongful dismissal – calculation of pension loss

Facts and Decision

Mr Hopkins was the chief executive of Norcros, and was dismissed without notice. He received an immediate pension unreduced for early payment as a result of being dismissed. He claimed for wrongful dismissal, and Norcros attempted to set off against his damages the increase in the value of his pension. The Court applied *Parry v Cleaver [1970] AC 1*: the fact that this was a case of breach of contract rather than tortious liability was not a relevant distinction.

[21.3.32]

Kerrigan v Rover Group (Employment Appeal Tribunal, 26 October 1999) 34 PBLR 5

Unfair dismissal – calculation of pension loss

Facts and Decision

An employee was unfairly dismissed. The Employment Tribunal deducted pension payments from his payment for loss. The Appeal Tribunal held that the deduction was made in error, and it was disapplied: *Hopkins v Norcros [1994] OPLR 121* was applied.

[21.3.33]

Rubenstein and Roskin v McGloughlin (Employment Appeal Tribunal) [1997] ICR 318, [1997] IRLR 557

Unfair dismissal – calculation of pension loss

Facts and Decision

Miss McGloughlin was dismissed on suspicion of dishonesty. She then received an invalidity allowance. An Industrial Tribunal by majority found that she had been unfairly dismissed. The Appeal Tribunal held that the invalidity allowance was not a pure insurance payment, being only partly funded by the employee's contributions. Under *s 74(1)* of the *Employment Protection (Consolidation) Act 1978*, the Tribunal was to make an award of such amount as it considered just and equitable. This required either detailed evidence of the funding position or a broader approach. The latter was to be preferred, and having regard to the analogy of the statutory system and to general considerations of equity, half the invalidity benefit received was deducted.

[21.3.34]

Silvey v Pendragon plc (Court of Appeal, unreported, 9 May 2001)

Wrongful dismissal – calculation of pension loss

Facts and Decision

Mr Silvey had been employed by his employers for 38 years when his service was terminated by reason of redundancy two weeks before his 55th birthday. If he had been allowed to serve out his notice, his pension benefits would have been substantially higher because of a provision in his pension scheme. Mr Silvey sued for breach of contract. The Court held that the loss plainly resulted from the breach of contract and not the selection of the termination date. The loss of pension rights was not too remote to be recoverable in law. It was common knowledge that it was common for the amount of an employee's pension to increase with length of service, and indeed for that increase to occur in steps. The question to ask was whether it was within the reasonable contemplation of the parties when the contract was made that it was not unlikely that if the employer gave notice to the employee as he approached his 55th birthday and was a member of the pension scheme, he would lose pension rights on his 55th birthday. The answer was plainly yes. The pension loss was therefore recoverable.

[21.3.35]

Smith Kline & French v J I Coates (Employment Appeal Tribunal) [1977] IRLR 220

Unfair dismissal – calculation of pension loss

Facts and Decision

Dr Coates was unfairly dismissed. The Industrial Tribunal had found that Dr Coates had failed to mitigate his loss, but awarded pension loss on the basis of the employers' contributions for the unmitigated period for which he would be unemployed. The Appeal Tribunal held that four factors should be considered when considering pension loss:

(a) Where it was difficult or unreasonable to use the ultimate pension as a basis, the loss can be measured by looking at the contributions made by the employer in the past and an estimate of what the employer would have had to pay for the future.

(b)   In other cases, it may be appropriate to measure the loss by the cost of an annuity or sum equal to the lost pension, or representing the difference between it and a frozen pension.

(c)   If either of the above approaches is resorted to, there should be taken into account all mitigating factors such as accelerated payment, the likelihood of remaining in employment until retirement, a possible loss of tax allowance, a chance of obtaining similar benefit, and at what stage a similar benefit may first be obtained.

(d)   The employee must prove his or her loss, and in instances where an employee is not represented there is a duty upon the Industrial Tribunal to raise the question and, in particular, themselves to investigate the question in those three areas to which reference has just been made.

It was harsh on the employer if loss of pension rights was to be compensated in full when the Tribunal had assessed Dr Coates as responsible for 50% of the loss owing to his failure to mitigate. The Tribunal should have considered whether or not a figure should have been included based on the amount of contribution made before Dr Coates was dismissed. The thinking behind this was that a person who had been paying in, and for whom the employer had been paying in, was entitled to regard the employer's contribution as something made on his or her behalf: in other words, he or she had an equity in that sum.

[21.3.36]

Sturdy Finance v Bardsley (Employment Appeal Tribunal) [1979] IRLR 65

Unfair dismissal – calculation of pension loss

Facts and Decision

Mr Bardsley was unfairly dismissed after four years' service. He was a member of his employer's pension scheme, which was contributory. He did not take a deferred pension, and claimed for his employer's contributions. The Appeal Tribunal held that it was reasonable for it and the Employment Tribunal to take the contributions as the basis of loss, even though the employer would have paid contributions both to the scheme and to Mr Bardsley directly.

[21.3.37]

Sweetlove v Redbridge and Waltham Forest Area Health Authority (Employment Appeal Tribunal) [1979] ICR 477, [1979] IRLR 195

Unfair dismissal – calculation of pension loss

Facts and Decision

Mr Sweetlove was unfairly dismissed, but acted unreasonably in refusing reinstatement. The Industrial Tribunal did not make any assessment in relation to pension loss. The Appeal Tribunal held that since he had failed to mitigate his loss by accepting reinstatement, he was deprived of the right to claim any loss.

[21.3.38]

Tidman v Aveling Marshall (Employment Appeal Tribunal) [1977] ICR 506, [1977] IRLR 218

Unfair dismissal – calculation of pension loss

Facts and Decision

Mr Tidman was unfairly dismissed. The Industrial Tribunal did not consider whether the compensation award should include an element for loss of pension rights. The Appeal Tribunal held that this was an error. Loss of pension rights had begun to assume a far larger proportion of the different heads of compensation than used to be the case. In future cases, it was the duty of an Industrial Tribunal to raise pension loss as one of the five different categories of the compensation award. The Industrial Tribunal should hear evidence about this head of loss and then make up its own mind in accordance with its own experience and common sense.

Racial discrimination

[21.3.39]

Barclays Bank v Kapur (Court of Appeal) [1995] OPLR 173

Racial discrimination – calculation of pension loss

Facts and Decision

Where pension scheme members had been given compensation for the loss of pension rights, the roll-up rate of interest to be used when assessing whether such compensation had been indirectly discriminatory was, the Court held, the return on a long-term investment, which a high street bank deposit rate evidently was not. The members were entitled to apply the payments as they chose, but if they wanted to replace the lost years of service they could and should have invested them on a long-term basis. The return on an endowment policy would be appropriate.

[21.3.40]

Chan v Hackney LBC (Employment Appeal Tribunal) [1997] ICR 1014

Racial discrimination – calculation of pension loss

Facts and Decision

Mr Chan had been constructively dismissed on the grounds of racially discriminatory treatment, and unlawfully discriminated against on the ground of his race by his employers. The Employment Tribunal deducted his invalidity benefit from his compensation for injury to feelings and damages for loss of earnings. The Appeal Tribunal observed that a disablement pension, as in *Parry v Cleaver [1907] AC 1*, should not be confused with invalidity benefit. It was not an error of law to deduct such a benefit from the damages award, and the Employment Appeal Tribunal would not disturb the Tribunal's decision.

21.4 – Pensions Ombudsman

Jurisdiction

[21.4.1]

Bennett v Ferranti (Pensions Ombudsman, 8 July 1998) Case G00016

Pensions Ombudsman's jurisdiction

Facts and Decision

The Pensions Ombudsman investigated a complaint and made a determination against a group pension manager.

[21.4.2]

Century Life v Pensions Ombudsman (High Court) [1995] OPLR 351, [1995] PLR 135

Pensions Ombudsman's jurisdiction

Facts and Decision

The Pensions Ombudsman investigated complaints against insurance companies which had provided insurance policies for insured occupational pension schemes, which were funded and established under trust with separate trustees as 'managers' of the scheme. *Section 146(1)* of the *Pensions Scheme Act 1993* permits the Ombudsman to investigate complaints against 'trustees or managers'. The Court held that the phrase 'trustees or managers' does not bear the same meaning wherever it appears in the *Act*. On a true construction, the Ombudsman had jurisdiction to hear complaints against managers of schemes even when there were separate trustees. It was clear that Parliament did not want at the outset to give the Ombudsman jurisdiction to deal with maladministration by employers and others such as actuaries. On the facts, there was ample evidence for the Ombudsman to conclude that the insurance companies were 'managers'.

[21.4.3]

City & County of Swansea v Johnson (High Court) [1999] OPLR 39 at 50F-H, [1999] PLR 187 at para 48–49

Pensions Ombudsman's jurisdiction

Principle

The Pensions Ombudsman has the power to order that interest is payable on awards, even when the award has not yet been quantified.

[21.4.4]

Duffield v Pensions Ombudsman (High Court) [1996] OPLR 149 at 158D-G, [1996] PLR 285 at para 55

Pensions Ombudsman's jurisdiction

Principle

Although the Pensions Ombudsman's powers of investigation were specifically made retrospective, there were serious doubts as to whether this extended to his power to make compensatory awards, in relation to matters which did not give rise to a legal liability at the time they took place.

[21.4.5]

Edge v Pensions Ombudsman (High Court) [1998] 2 All ER 547, [1998] OPLR 51 at 57F-G, 74B, [1997] PLR 15 at paras 27, 138

Pensions Ombudsman's jurisdiction

Principles

In a case in which the maladministration complained of consists of an alleged breach of trust, the Pensions Ombudsman has no power to direct remedial steps to be taken that are not steps that a court of law could properly have directed to be taken: *Hillsdown v Pensions Ombudsman [1997] 1 All ER 862* was followed.

The Pensions Ombudsman was no more entitled to sit in judgment on the reasons given by trustees for the exercise of a discretionary power than a court would have been. (See also [21.4.6].)

[21.4.6]

Edge v Pensions Ombudsman (Court of Appeal) [2000] 3 WLR 79, [1999] OPLR 179 at 202H–207F, [1999] PLR 215 at paras 71–87

Pensions Ombudsman's jurisdiction

Principle

The regulations establishing the Pensions Ombudsman's jurisdiction make no general provision for the representation of class interests. The interests of natural justice require that a class must have its interests properly represented before findings are made which would have an adverse effect on those interests. Where an investigation would affect interests which were not represented before the Ombudsman, the Ombudsman has the formal legal power to entertain the complaint, but he should exercise his discretion not to do so. (See also [21.4.5].)

Comment

This case pinpoints an essential weakness in the Pensions Ombudsman's jurisdiction. When his jurisdiction was originally established, it was intended that he should investigate relatively small-scale pension problems. Yet the size of the problems with which he should deal was left undefined.

In due course, the Ombudsman started to be faced by problems which had an impact on more than one member. These could take several formats. The trustees may have committed misdeeds in relation to one member, but because the scheme was in winding-up, any additional money awarded to that member would result in other members' entitlements being reduced. Such was the case in *Seifert v Pensions Ombudsman [1997] 1 All ER 214*, for example. Or the employer may have committed a single misdeed that had a detrimental impact on the entitlement of every member, as in *Hillsdown v Pensions Ombudsman [1997] 1 All ER 862*. In these cases, the Ombudsman had no hesitation in asserting jurisdiction, and the courts did not query him in so doing.

Eventually, the Ombudsman received complaints in which a member was affected adversely, but where any decision by the Ombudsman in favour of that member could itself affect adversely other members. The Court held in this case that he should exercise his discretion not to hear such cases. Since the Ombudsman was entitled to issue legally binding determinations, he was judged by the standards of the courts in assessing which cases he should take on. It followed that he should not take on cases where he could adversely affect parties who could not be represented before him.

This gave the Ombudsman an apparently arbitrary jurisdiction. Two members of two different pension schemes could have apparently equally important problems, but one could be heard by the Ombudsman, and one could not, solely on the basis of how other members would be affected. This rule is hard to justify to members. The Government is therefore in the process of extending the Ombudsman's jurisdiction so that he can hear class actions.

However, in solving one problem, the Government is laying the foundations for another. The Government envisaged the Ombudsman as a low cost solution for hearing legal disputes which could not otherwise be heard by the courts. It is now giving the Ombudsman the power to hear the sorts of cases which the courts are fully capable of hearing, but without building into the Ombudsman's jurisdiction the same safeguards that exist in the courts. The courts' rules have evolved for good reason. Sooner or later parties will have cause to regret their absence.

Article 6 of the *European Convention on Human Rights* gives everyone a right to a fair trial. There is some doubt as to how the use of representative beneficiaries in large trusts cases fit with this right. It is at least arguable that where a case is investigated without an oral hearing, beneficiaries who have been represented by others have been deprived of their right to a fair trial. The Ombudsman may well find that his quick and flexible jurisdiction builds up rigid rules of its own to cater for the more complex cases. The blurring of the lines between the Ombudsman and the courts will accelerate.

[21.4.7]

Engineering Training Authority v Pensions Ombudsman (High Court) [1996] OPLR 167 at 176B–177A, [1996] PLR 409 at paras 44–48

Pensions Ombudsman's jurisdiction

Principle

The Pensions Ombudsman's jurisdiction in relation to employers is clearly directed to their functions under or in relation to the pension scheme in question. It does not give the Ombudsman jurisdiction to investigate complaints about the ordinary contractual relations between employer and employee. These are matters for the Employment Tribunal or an action in the Court for breach of contract.

[21.4.8]

Ewing v Stockham Valve trustees (Northern Ireland Court of Appeal, unreported, 4 February 2000)

Pensions Ombudsman's jurisdiction

Facts and Decision

Pension scheme trustees discovered that a former trustee had been receiving benefits from the scheme for five years, when she had previously transferred out the whole of her entitlement. They instructed their solicitors to write to her informing her of the mistake, informing her that the pension would be stopped immediately, and requesting payment in seven days or the trustees would institute legal proceedings to recover the overpaid sums. She complained to the Pensions Ombudsman who found that she had been aware that she was not entitled to the benefits, but the demand for the money to be repaid was maladministration. He also held that the scheme solicitors were administrators for the purpose of his jurisdiction, and made an award against them also. The trustees and the solicitors appealed. The Court held that it was a question of fact and degree whether a solicitor was an administrator for this purpose, depending on the terms of the retainer. Where the solicitor is simply instructed to write a letter of claim to the debtor, he or she is acting as the trustees' agent and could not be said to be concerned with the administration of the trustees.

[21.4.9]

Hillsdown v Pensions Ombudsman (High Court) [1997] 1 All ER 862, [1996] OPLR 291 at 320H–323B, [1996] PLR 427 at paras 112–120

Pensions Ombudsman's jurisdiction

Principle

The Pensions Ombudsman's jurisdiction is defined in *s 151(2)* of the *Pension Schemes Act 1993* in very wide terms. There is no express limitation on the steps which the Ombudsman can direct to be taken or refrained from. Where the remedy discerned is one which is equally applicable in relation to a large number of other authorised complaints on the same facts, and it is a remedy to which the particular claimant in question is entitled, then there is jurisdiction to grant that remedy.

In the context of a complaint of maladministration against an employer about its participation in a transaction involving improper payment out of sums which in large measure found their way (as they were from the outset intended to do) into the employer's hands, it would not be permissible for the Pensions Ombudsman to require the employer to refund the sums it received unless the Court would be in a position to make such an order. It would be wrong for the answer to the question 'are you legally liable to repay this sum?' to depend on the Tribunal to which resort is had. Since the two jurisdictions were mutually exclusive, there would not be differences on such fundamental matters as whether there was a liability to repay a capital sum.

[21.4.10]

London Borough of Redbridge v Municipal Mutual Insurance (High Court, 9 November 2000) 67 PBLR 10

Pensions Ombudsman's jurisdiction

Principle

An allegation that the chief executive of the London Borough of Redbridge had been guilty of the criminal offence of misconduct in a public office was wholly irrelevant to anything which the Pensions Ombudsman had jurisdiction to decide.

[21.4.11]

Marsh & Maclennan v Pensions Ombudsman (High Court) [2001] PLR 51

Pensions Ombudsman's jurisdiction

Facts and Decision

Mr Williamson was an actuary who was a member of his employer's pension scheme, which was contracted out of the State earnings related pension scheme. After leaving service, he complained to the Pensions Ombudsman that scheme pensions were being incorrectly calculated, since the trustees had not equalised the guaranteed minimum pension. It could not be known how this would affect him until he reached age 60. The Pensions Ombudsman upheld his complaint and ordered that the scheme equalise guaranteed minimum pension entitlements. The trustee and employer appealed. The Court held that the Pensions Ombudsman should not have exercised his jurisdiction to hear Mr Williamson's complaint in generalised terms about the scheme, since other members comprised classes of interested persons, one or more of which might well have had a very real interest in arguing against any general equalisation direction: *Edge v Pensions Ombudsman [1998] 2 All ER 547* was applied. The Ombudsman should have declined jurisdiction, or should at most have decided the equalisation question simply as between Mr Williamson, the employer and the trustee. His decision was therefore set aside, since the Ombudsman did not determine that he was deciding that Mr Williamson's guaranteed minimum pension had to be equalised with that of a woman with a like earnings history.

[21.4.12]

Re the Minworth Limited Pension Scheme, Anderson v William M Mercer (Pensions Ombudsman, 22 April 1999) Cases F00265, F00463 and G00264

Pensions Ombudsman's jurisdiction

Principle

An actuary to a pension scheme must by the very nature of his or her work be 'concerned with the administration' of the scheme, and the Pensions Ombudsman therefore had jurisdiction to hear complaints against the actuary.

[21.4.13]

NHS Pensions v Beechinor (High Court) [1997] OPLR 99 at 100C, [1997] PLR 95 at para 1

Pensions Ombudsman's jurisdiction

Principle

It was difficult to believe that Parliament intended the Pensions Ombudsman's jurisdiction to extend to commissions of tort by pension scheme administrators against a pension scheme member or to overriding defences of limitation, and that the respondent should be deprived of the substantive and procedural safeguards of trial before a judge.

[21.4.14]

Nicol & Andrew v Brinkley (High Court) [1996] OPLR 361 at 365E-G

Pensions Ombudsman's jurisdiction

Principle

The Pensions Ombudsman had jurisdiction to hear complaints about an employer's breach of contract in relation to a pension scheme where the employer was also the trustee, and the contract was formed as trustee so as to bind future trustees.

[21.4.15]

Nuthall v Merrill Lynch (UK) Final Salary Plan trustees (Pensions Ombudsman, 25 March 1999) Case G00543 at para 15

Pensions Ombudsman's jurisdiction

Principle

The Pensions Ombudsman's role is to ensure that matters relating to occupational pension schemes are properly dealt with, and the investment performance of the insurer is not within his remit.

[21.4.16]

Wakelin v Read (Court of Appeal) [2000] PLR 319 at paras 70–71, 73–76, 87

Pensions Ombudsman's jurisdiction

Principle

The observation of the High Court in *Westminster v Haywood [1996] 2 All ER 467* that the Pensions Ombudsman's task in delivering rapid, unlegalistic justice, without cutting too many corners, was a dauntingly difficult one was approved. The Pensions Ombudsman is limited to those courses of action which would be open to a court in litigation: the dictum of Knox J in *Hillsdown v Pensions Ombudsman [1997] 1 All ER 862* was approved. The Ombudsman therefore had no discretion to refuse relief on application by a pensions scheme member for payment of his benefits, if he made a determination that the member was not dishonest and so had not dishonestly assisted a breach of trust.

[21.4.17]

Westminster v Haywood (High Court) [1996] 2 All ER 467, [1996] OPLR 95 at 103A–C, 105F–106A, 106B–106H, [1996] PLR 161 at paras 28, 45–47, 49–52

Pensions Ombudsman's jurisdiction

Principles

A very important part of the legislative purpose behind the Pensions Ombudsman's jurisdiction was to provide a quick, inexpensive and informal means of settling complaints and disputes about occupational pensions. The Pensions Ombudsman's task in delivering rapid, unlegalistic justice, without cutting too many corners, is a dauntingly difficult one.

The classification of an approach to the Ombudsman, as a complaint of maladministration or a dispute of fact or law, to determine whether he has jurisdiction over public service pension schemes, is one which has to be made in practice by the Ombudsman himself. Most approaches will be properly classified as complaints even though they raise issues of fact or law.

The steps that the Ombudsman may take are not limited to exhortation or censure. The concept of injustice has been left undefined, but any remedy for injustice must be appropriate and proportional and not such as to risk causing some new injustice. (See also [21.4.18] and [21.4.19].)

[21.4.18]

Westminster v Haywood (Court of Appeal) [1998] Ch 377, [1997] OPLR 61 at 69E–G, [1997] PLR 39 at para 42

Pensions Ombudsman's jurisdiction

Principles

It is very difficult to accept the notion that by administering two schemes as one, Westminster City Council could confer on the Pensions Ombudsman a jurisdiction which he would not have if it administered them separately.

The jurisdiction of the Pensions Ombudsman is limited to the investigation and determination of complaints by persons entitled to long service benefits *as such*, i.e. in relation to their long service benefits. [NB. The Ombudsman's jurisdiction has since been changed by statute.] (See also [21.4.17] and [21.4.19].)

[21.4.19]

Westminster v Haywood (No. 2) (High Court) [2000] PLR 235

Pensions Ombudsman's jurisdiction

Facts and Decision

Following the Court of Appeal's decision in *Westminster v Haywood [1998] Ch 377* (see [21.4.18]) regarding the extent of the Pensions Ombudsman's jurisdiction in relation to schemes which did not provide long service benefits, the Ombudsman's jurisdiction was widened. Mr Haywood then brought another complaint to the Ombudsman about the same facts. The Ombudsman heard the complaint and found that there had been maladministration but no injustice. Westminster Council argued that:

(a)   the Ombudsman had no jurisdiction to hear a case predating a change in the law;

(b)   Mr Haywood's case had in any case already been determined by legal action and was closed under the legal doctrine of *res judicata*; and

(c)   the complaint was time-barred.

The Ombudsman argued that there was no right of appeal against a finding of maladministration alone. The Court held that the Council had the right to appeal against determinations even though no adverse direction had been made: *Law Debenture v Malley [1999] OPLR 153* was followed. While there was a presumption against the legislation having retrospective effect, it was of limited weight. The Pensions Ombudsman was established under legislation designed to improve the legal protection available to members. It did something less than create new private rights or duties, but provided a form of redress to members against maladministration. The provision of the Pensions Ombudsman as an alternative medium to the ordinary courts, for redress of maladministration involving breaches of pre-existing private rights or duties, could occasion no concern on grounds of retrospectivity. Any concern must be limited to complaints involving no such breach. Such concern carried limited weight, since standards have always been expected of those who manage schemes. The Pensions Ombudsman was expressly empowered to investigate complaints which arose before his office was constituted. Nothing in the language of the legislation justifies discrimination between the Ombudsman's original jurisdiction and his extended jurisdiction. The change in the law was retrospective. The doctrine of *res judicata* was applicable to the Ombudsman. Since the decision of the Court of Appeal in *Westminster v Haywood* was founded on the basis that the Ombudsman had no jurisdiction to hear the complaint, it did not operate to bar a rehearing of the merits of the claim. The Ombudsman's decision to hear the complaint out of time was reasonable, indeed the only decision he could rationally have reached in the circumstances. (See also [21.4.17].)

[21.4.20]

Wild v Smith (High Court) [1996] OPLR 129 at 136D–137B, [1996] PLR 275 at para 29–33

Pensions Ombudsman's jurisdiction

Principle

The Pensions Ombudsman has jurisdiction to make determinations against former trustees. The whole purpose of the power to investigate past misconduct would be negated if there were no power to make orders against those responsible at the time, or if they could avoid the Ombudsman's jurisdiction by retiring.

Pensions Ombudsman's duties

[21.4.21]

City & County of Swansea v Johnson (High Court) [1999] OPLR 39, [1999] PLR 187

Pensions Ombudsman's duties – fairness

Facts and Decision

The Pensions Ombudsman upheld a complaint from a member of a Council severance and compensation scheme that the Council had failed for many years to consider properly whether he was eligible under its pension scheme, and that when it had finally looked at the matter, it had offered him a derisory sum under the scheme. On appeal, the Court concluded that the scheme was within the Ombudsman's jurisdiction. However, the Ombudsman had failed to give the Council the opportunity to comment on evidence of health submitted on Mr Johnson's behalf. The least bad option in this case was to remit the matter to the Ombudsman for reconsideration. The Council had failed throughout to ask itself the right questions under the compensation scheme, so it had only itself to blame for the matter being an issue before the Ombudsman.

[21.4.22]

Hamar v French (Court of Appeal) [1997] OPLR 105 at 118C, 118G, [1998] PLR 31, at paras 70, 73

Pensions Ombudsman's duties

Principles

Investigations by the Pensions Ombudsman are informal. There are no pleadings. The issues are defined by the complaint and the response to it. The jurisdiction of the Ombudsman is limited to the investigation of the complaint actually made to him. He can invite the complainant to add to his or her complaint and may suggest new matters of defence to the other party, and so extend the scope of the enquiry. But he is not bound to do so, and he cannot be criticised if he does not.

The Pensions Ombudsman was the sole tribunal of fact. His function was to reach a conclusion on the facts found or undisputed.

[21.4.23]

Westminster v Haywood (High Court) [1996] 2 All ER 467, [1996] OPLR 95 at 108C–109A, [1996] PLR 161, paras 63–66

Pensions Ombudsman's duties – identifying injustice

Facts and Decision

The Court held that the Pensions Ombudsman erred in failing to identify the injustice which he considered the complainant had suffered in consequence of maladministration on the part of the respondent. The Ombudsman identified failures, and it could not be said that a finding of maladministration was perverse or unsupported by the facts. However, compensation for maladministration which was negligent misrepresentation should put the complainant in the same position as he would have been in had the respondent complied with its duty and provided him with correct information, and not put him in the position he would have been in had the incorrect information been correct. On the evidence in this case, there was no pecuniary loss.

Pensions Ombudsman's procedure

Blake v Pensions Ombudsman (High Court) [2000] All ER 681

Pensions Ombudsman's procedure – fairness – human rights

Facts and Decision

Mr Blake was made redundant by his local government employer, he worked part-time in private practice for a while, then considered a return to local government. He telephoned to find out whether re-employment with the local government employer would affect his pension. He claimed that he was told that earnings from local government would not affect his pension. In fact, this was incorrect. When he took the job and found his pension entitlement was reduced, he complained to the Pensions Ombudsman. The Ombudsman held an oral hearing and afterwards obtained a telephone note from a third party. The Ombudsman's office did not send Mr Blake a copy of this note, but informed him that they had received such a note. The Ombudsman then issued a final determination that a conversation had taken place between Mr Blake and the council as Mr Blake alleged, but that Mr Blake would have taken the job anyway. Mr Blake complained that the Ombudsman had breached natural justice and that he had acted perversely, having insufficient evidence for reaching such a finding of fact. The Court observed that it would have been better if the Ombudsman had sent Mr Blake a copy of the note for his comment, but he had alerted him to its existence, and Mr Blake had been given the opportunity to ask for a copy or comment, which he had not taken. The Ombudsman was under no obligation to give Mr Blake an opportunity to comment on a preliminary decision. Nor was the finding of fact that Mr Blake would have accepted the job anyway perverse – the indications were far from one way.

[21.4.25]

Brooks v Civil Aviation Authority (Scottish Court of Session, unreported, 30 June 2000)

Pensions Ombudsman's procedure – extent to which Ombudsman must be investigative

Facts and Decision

The Pensions Ombudsman received a complaint from a scheme member that he had been dismissed on the ground of ill-health, but had not been credited with the pension payable in such circumstances. The complaint had already been rejected by an Employment Tribunal, the Employment Appeal Tribunal and an arbitrator. The Ombudsman also rejected the complaint. The Court held that the Ombudsman was entitled to adjudicate on a complaint based on a review of existing material, and was not bound to carry out a fresh, independent investigation into the facts and circumstances of the complaint. He had a wide discretion to decide how best to conduct the investigation.

[21.4.26]

City & County of Swansea v Johnson (High Court) [1999] OPLR 39 at 47H–48E, [1999] PLR 187 at paras 32–37

Pensions Ombudsman's procedure – fairness

Principle

Fairness to respondents to complaints requires that they be given the opportunity by the Pensions Ombudsman to comment on evidence which is highly material to the substance of the complaint.

[21.4.27]

Duckitt v Pensions Ombudsman (High Court) [2000] OPLR 167

Pensions Ombudsman's procedure – findings of dishonesty

Facts and Decision

The Pensions Ombudsman investigated a complaint where the trustees had made loans to the employer which had subsequently become insolvent, so that the loans were irrecoverable. The trustees sought to rely upon their exoneration clause, which exempted them from liability unless they had committed a breach of trust which constituted a fraud, or was a deliberate and culpable disregard by them of the interests of the beneficiaries. The Ombudsman concluded that the loan had been maladministration and that the exoneration did not apply. The trustees appealed, and it was agreed before the appeal was heard that the matter needed to be reconsidered by the Ombudsman. The Ombudsman then held an oral hearing, at which he confirmed that there had been a serious breach of trust. He found that the trustees had acted throughout with an overriding concern for the survival of the company and with a deliberate, as well as culpable, disregard for the interests of the scheme. He gave no reasons for finding that the breach of duty was deliberate. The Court held that there was no finding of fact for justifying such an inference. The Ombudsman also found that the course of action that the trustees pursued in making the series of loans established that they were recklessly indifferent as to whether or not they were acting in the interests of the member of the scheme, so as to come within the meaning of fraud. The Court held that there was no logical connection between the fact that there was a sequence of breaches of trust and a finding that it was a dishonest breach of trust. Their behaviour was equally consistent with a misguided view as to their duties. These were very serious allegations and it was incumbent on the Ombudsman before he made findings to that effect to have substantive evidence to justify it, and to give full and sufficient reasons for doing so. The determination was set aside and the exoneration held to apply. (See also [21.4.27].)

[21.4.28]

Duckitt v Pensions Ombudsman (Court of Appeal) [2001] PLR 155

Pensions Ombudsman's procedure – findings of dishonesty

Principle

The duty to state reasons is a duty to tell the parties why they have won or lost. The decision-maker must have regard to every material consideration; but he does not have to state every material consideration to which he has had regard: *Re Poyser & Mills' Arbitration [1964] 2 QB 467* and *Meek v City of Birmingham District Council [1987] IRLR 250* were considered. It was obvious that this was a serious case in which allegations of fraud were being made. It was trite law that in those circumstances fraud must be as distinctly proved as it was alleged. The Court insists on a high standard of proof. (See also [21.4.26].)

Duffield v Pensions Ombudsman (High Court) [1996] OPLR 149 at 154A-B, 156B–157A, 157C-F, 157G–158C, [1996] PLR 285 at para 23, 39–43, 46–47, 49–53

Pensions Ombudsman's procedure – fairness – investigation of related complaints not specifically made – detailing criticisms

Facts and Decision

The Pensions Ombudsman investigated a complaint for maladministration arising out of events ten years previously. The complaint was originally against the insurers, but the Ombudsman issued a provisional determination (ultimately finalised in similar terms) finding that the trustees had been reckless and behaved throughout as if they did not know that or care whether they needed advice. No advance warning had been given to the trustees that they might be the subject of criticism.

The Court observed that the Ombudsman is given very wide powers. Parliament has given very little assistance in defining precisely what kind of orders it is intended that the Ombudsman should be allowed to make, and in particular how far he is entitled to impose financial penalties going beyond those which would otherwise be applicable under the general law. Given the potentially draconian nature of the jurisdiction, there is a paramount need for fairness to all concerned, including those who may ultimately be held liable. The Ombudsman should have particular regard to the practical and personal consequences for those involved.

Failure to give a trustee (whether past or present) the opportunity to comment on any allegations contained in a complaint or dispute before releasing a provisional determination was a breach of *s 149(1)* of the *Pension Schemes Act 1993*, such as would make the proceedings against that trustee void. It was also a serious breach of the ordinary principles of natural justice. It was no answer that the trustee was given a chance to comment after the provisional determination: fairness, as well as the statutory scheme, required that he or she should be given an opportunity to respond at the formative stage of the investigation.

The Ombudsman is entitled to reinterpret a complaint against an administrator as a complaint against the trustees.

Where serious criticisms are being made, it is incumbent on the Ombudsman to deal with them with sufficient particularity for those affected to understand the case.

Elliott v Pensions Ombudsman (High Court) [1998] OPLR 21 at 34E–35F

Pensions Ombudsman's procedure – fairness – oral hearing – findings of dishonesty

Principle

Where trustees, who had protested their innocence throughout, are being accused by the Pensions Ombudsman of dishonesty, they must be granted the opportunity to attend an oral hearing. Dishonesty is a most serious finding to make against any person, going against that person's integrity. The matter is not left simply to the unfettered discretion of the Ombudsman. The touchstone was to conduct the investigation with fairness. If the trustees had found themselves defendants to proceedings for breach of trust brought in a court of law, it would be unthinkable for a court to refuse the trustees an oral hearing on their defence to the claim, and instead proceed to find them guilty of dishonesty simply on the basis of written submissions. The trustees should not be in any worse position because the complaints happen to be made to the Ombudsman.

Comment

There has been much speculation about the impact of the *Human Rights Act 1998* on the Pensions Ombudsman's procedure. This case shows that domestic legal principles should not be overlooked. Before the *European Convention on Human Rights* had been incorporated into national law, the Court determined this case on the principles of natural justice.

This case may usefully be bookended with *Blake v Pensions Ombudsman [2000] All ER 681*. That case, decided after the enactment of the *Human Rights Act 1998*, dismissed the idea that the case law on *Article 6* of the *European Convention on Human Rights* could add much to the existing domestic case law. As that case noted, the *Convention* and domestic law were directed at the same end. Here at least the *Human Rights Act 1998* is likely to have relatively little impact.

[21.4.31]

Law Debenture v Malley (High Court, interlocutory) [1999] OPLR 153 at 160C-F, 161C–162H, [1999] PLR 367 at para 29–31, 40–44

Pensions Ombudsman's procedure – extent to which trustees must fulfil direction with no sanction ordered

Facts and Decision

The Pensions Ombudsman issued a direction against the trustees of a scheme which was wound up with no assets, where the trustees had the benefit of an exoneration clause and an indemnity policy. The Court held that the trustees were under an obligation to fulfil the direction, and the complainant may choose to compel the trustees to perform that obligation. It could not be said to be merely an academic question.

The task of the Ombudsman is to make investigations into complaints or disputes of a given type, whether of fact or law, and having done so to make a determination of the matter in dispute before him. An adverse determination against the respondent is appealable, whether or not there is a consequential order that compensation is to be paid to the complainant.

[21.4.32]

Legal & General v Pensions Ombudsman (High Court) [2000] OPLR 153

Pensions Ombudsman's procedure – fairness in extending time limits – maladministration in his office's practices

Principle

It was totally improper of the Pensions Ombudsman to reach a decision that a complaint made outside the normal three-year time limit was still within such further period as he considered reasonable without giving the respondent any opportunity to make representations on this issue, and the Ombudsman should have acknowledged his error. Where a person has been entrusted with the role of investigating maladministration by others, he must surely be ready to acknowledge maladministration on his own part in the course of his investigation.

[21.4.33]

Libby v Kennedy (High Court) [1998] OPLR 213 at 217E-F, [1999] PLR 143 at paras 20–21

Pensions Ombudsman's procedure – findings of fact without documentary evidence

Principle

The Pensions Ombudsman should not reject a claim that information had been made available to the trustees even if there is no documentary evidence, without first asking each of the trustees whether the claim was true.

[21.4.34]

Marsh & Maclennan v Pensions Ombudsman (High Court) [2001] PLR 51

Pensions Ombudsman's procedure – precision

Principle

The nature, effect and the requirements of a direction of the Pensions Ombudsman to equalise guaranteed minimum pensions were so imprecise and uncertain that he was in error in making it. He ought to have gone no further than, at most, making a determination that the trustee and employer must have regard to the potentially discriminatory effects of the guaranteed minimum pensions regulations in ensuring that pension payments to members were not discriminatory.

[21.4.35]

Seifert v Pensions Ombudsman (High Court) [1997] 1 All ER 214, [1996] OPLR 231 at 238D–239C, [1996] PLR 479 at paras 20–25

Pensions Ombudsman's procedure – fairness – formulating the complaint

Principle

A determination by the Pensions Ombudsman can damage or destroy reputations, as well as impose financial penalties. In these circumstances it is mandatory that the Ombudsman comply both with the statutory procedure contained in *s 149(1)* of the *Pension Schemes Act 1993* designed to ensure fairness and with the principles of natural justice. These require that he make clear to the respondents to a complaint the specific allegations made in the complaint and to be investigated, and of any amendment to the allegations. It is highly desirable that the Ombudsman expresses in his own words in plain and simple language what he perceives to be the substance of the allegation, to limit the risk of misunderstanding. The principles of natural justice also require that he disclose to the respondents all potentially relevant information obtained by him, so as to enable the respondents to have a fair opportunity to provide any answer which they may have. These are the minimum requirements for fairness and accordingly for a decision that can be allowed to stand. (See also [21.4.35].)

[21.4.36]

Seifert v Pensions Ombudsman (Court of Appeal) [1997] OPLR 395 at 400H, 402G, 403A, [1999] PLR 29 at paras 22, 36, 38

Pensions Ombudsman's procedure – fairness – formulating the complaint

Principle

The Pensions Ombudsman and his staff must adopt a procedure which is fair to both parties in all the circumstances of the case. The Court could not therefore give a ruling on how many letters the Ombudsman must refer back and forth between complainant and the accused before he calls a halt. When a letter had been relied upon by the Ombudsman in framing a provisional determination without giving the others concerned the opportunity to comment, the others concerned were then put on notice. The whole history of the dispute in this case was fraught with imprecision and misunderstanding. In the nature of things this was liable to happen when a person untrained in the law makes a complaint on a somewhat technical subject, unless the adjudicator insists on knowing precisely what the complaint is, even if he has to define it for himself. (See also [21.4.34].)

Comment

This case received much publicity at the time, not least because Lightman J at first instance made particularly stinging criticisms of the Pensions Ombudsman. The Court of Appeal moved to pour oil on troubled waters, but the remainder of Dr Farrand's tenure as Pensions Ombudsman was marked by open disputes with the judiciary. For this reason alone, this case was historically important.

However, the case also has legal significance. The Court of Appeal approved the Ombudsman's practice of issuing provisional determinations, and went out of its way to avoid being prescriptive as to how the Ombudsman should conduct investigations. This approach has been continued by more recent decisions, such as *Brooks v Civil Aviation Authority* (unreported).

The Court of Appeal appeared to endorse the recommendation of the High Court that the Ombudsman should ensure that a complaint to him is defined, if necessary in the Ombudsman's own terms. In practice, this recommendation has not always been followed, which has led to problems in other cases as well.

The High Court decision, although overturned, should not be ignored. The commentary on the principles of natural justice is of a piece with the approach in *Elliott v Pensions Ombudsman [1998] OPLR 21* and *Duckitt v Pensions Ombudsman [2000] OPLR 167.*

[21.4.37]

Wakelin v Read (High Court) [1998] OPLR 147, [1998] PLR 337 at para 37

Pensions Ombudsman's procedure – refusal to grant legal entitlement – failure to explain – oral hearings

Principle

It was doubtful whether the Pensions Ombudsman had the discretion to resolve a dispute in favour of a member, but to refuse to grant him any relief on the grounds that, by virtue of an unpleaded case which the Ombudsman had found to be proved, the member did not have sufficiently clean hands. The Ombudsman did not explain whether he was finding that the member had a legal right to which he was declining to lend his assistance to enforce, or whether he was declining to make a finding and leaving the member the option of bringing conventional legal proceedings. This failure to elucidate was probably a flawed exercise of his statutory discretion. (See also [21.4.38].)

[21.4.38]

Wakelin v Read (Court of Appeal) [2000] PLR 319 at para 96

Pensions Ombudsman's procedure – refusal to grant legal entitlement – failure to explain – oral hearings

Principle

It was surprising that neither side in this case had asked for an oral hearing. While the Pensions Ombudsman procedure was intended to be simple, swift and cheap, the dispute involved a large amount of money and an allegation of dishonesty. It was unlikely that the difficulties faced by the appellate courts would have occurred had there been oral evidence and oral submissions on conventional lines. (See also [21.4.37].)

[21.4.39]

Westminster v Haywood (High Court) [1996] 2 All ER 467, [1996] OPLR 95 at 105F–106A, [1996] PLR 161, paras 45–47

Pensions Ombudsman's procedure – classification as maladministration or dispute of facts and law

Principle

The classification of an approach to the Pensions Ombudsman as a complaint of maladministration or a dispute of fact or law is one which has to be made in practice by the Ombudsman himself. Most approaches will be properly classified as complaints even though they raise issues of fact or law.

Maladministration

[21.4.40]

Armstrong v East-West Airlines (Supreme Court of New South Wales) [1995] OPLR 239 at 246B

Maladministration – delegation to untrained staff – delay

Principle

Delegation of pension scheme matters to personnel unfamiliar with the terms of the trust, resulting in errors and delay, was a breach of trust. Delay in commencing work on the calculation of pension scheme benefits, resulting in delay in the payment of benefits, was also a breach of trust. However, delay caused by an unexpectedly high workload was not a matter for which the trustee ought to be criticised. The trustee should pay interest for the time lost by the delay apart from that caused by the unexpectedly high workload.

[21.4.41]

City & County of Swansea v Johnson (High Court) [1999] OPLR 39 at 49B-C, [1999] PLR 187 at paras 39–40

Maladministration – mistake of law – delay

Principle

A mistake of law is not *ipso facto* maladministration. If a council 'fences' with a complainant's claim over a period of years without seriously considering whether it had a duty to deal with it on its merits, this could constitute maladministration.

[21.4.42]

Edge v Pensions Ombudsman (Court of Appeal) [2000] 3 WLR 79, [1999] OPLR 179 at 206G–207A, [1999] PLR 215 at para 82–85

Maladministration – classification as dispute or maladministration

Facts and Decision

Where a pension scheme member complained about the exercise of a trustee discretion subsequently implemented by deed, the Pensions Ombudsman treated the matter as a complaint of maladministration. The Court held, however, that it would have been open to him to have treated the matter as a dispute as to the validity of the deed.

[21.4.43]

Ewing v Stockham Valve trustees (Northern Ireland Court of Appeal, unreported, 4 February 2000)

Maladministration – sending a letter before action

Facts and Decision

Pension scheme trustees discovered that a former trustee had been receiving benefits from the scheme for five years, when she had previously transferred out the whole of her entitlement. They instructed their solicitors to write to her informing her of the mistake, informing her that the pension would be stopped immediately, and requesting payment in seven days or the trustees would institute legal proceedings to recover the overpaid sums. She complained to the Pensions Ombudsman who found that she had been aware that she was not entitled to the benefits, but the demand for the money to be repaid was maladministration. The Court found it very difficult to agree with the Ombudsman's finding that sending the letter had been maladministration on the trustees' part, but was not prepared to go quite so far as to say that the Ombudsman had made an error of law in so holding (although it would have held that there was no maladministration if it was investigating the matter from scratch). No reasonable tribunal could say that the member had suffered any injustice. The award in the member's favour was therefore set aside.

[21.4.44]

Hillsdown v Pensions Ombudsman (High Court) [1997] 1 All ER 862, [1996] OPLR 291 at 311G–312A, [1996] PLR 427 at para 73

Maladministration – relationship with breach of trust

Principle

There can be a breach of trust without there being maladministration. Unauthorised but successful investments are a very common example of such breaches. It is not necessarily maladministration for a decision maker to take a wrong view of the law: *Westminster v Haywood [1996] 2 All ER 467* was considered.

[21.4.45]

Hogg Robinson v Pensions Ombudsman (High Court) [1998] OPLR 131

Maladministration – delay – mistakes in transfer values

Facts and Decision

The trustees of the Digital Pension Plan employed external administrators. Mr Bower, a member of the scheme, requested a transfer value. The administrators misquoted the amount, since they had failed to take proper account of the additional voluntary contributions and an augmentation which he had been granted. The time taken to resolve these mistakes resulted in his transfer quotation expiring, and the trustees declined to extend the period of validity of the quotation. As a result of market fluctuations during the period of delay, the value of the transfer amount declined by £40,000. Mr Bower complained to the Pensions Ombudsman, who found that both the trustees and the administrators had exhibited maladministration, and awarded them to pay £40,000 as compensation. Both the administrators and the trustees appealed. The Court held that the maladministration could be put as a failure to give clear and accurate information about what the correct transfer value was, or as a failure to comply with the requirements of the *Occupational Pension Schemes (Disclosure of Information) Regulations 1986 (SI 1986 No 1046)*. However, even if there had been no breach of the *regulations*, the poor performance of a duty which the administrators had assumed would be maladminstration. It was not maladministration by the trustees to refuse to extend the guarantee period, even though it was austere. Nor was it maladministration by the trustees to fail to consider individual problems where they had the power to delegate the regular administration of the scheme and they had selected a company with an excellent reputation. While the Ombudsman had material for concluding that the failure of the administrators to supply Mr Bower with a full and accurate statement of his transfer value caused him the loss, he had not done so. The Ombudsman also needed to consider, which he had not considered, whether the failure to supply Mr Bower with a revised statement in sufficient time to exercise his rights within the guarantee period was maladministration, and if so, whether Mr Bower's loss was suffered in consequence of that maladministration. The matter was remitted to the Ombudsman for redetermination on that basis.

Comment

This case is the most complete practical example of what the courts will and will not accept as maladministration. The determination of maladministration is for the Pensions Ombudsman, but he must do so within the parameters of his jurisdiction.

The Court's conclusion that it was not maladministration for the trustees to refuse to extend the guarantee period is important. It establishes the trustees' right to stick to statutory timetables in all but the most extreme circumstances, and trustees are not obliged to apply some vague concept of fairness in such matters.

The Court also confirmed that the Ombudsman must apply a causal approach to maladministration if he is to link the loss to the maladministration. Although the Court set aside the determination, it showed sympathy for the Ombudsman's instincts on this case and effectively guided the Ombudsman to a legally watertight route to achieve the same result. On redetermination, the Ombudsman took that guidance and once again found for Mr Bowers.

[21.4.46]

Law Debenture v Malley (High Court) [1999] OPLR 167

Maladministration – covert surveillance – relevancy of evidence used

Facts and Decision

Law Debenture was one of the trustees of a pension scheme. In considering an incapacity pension, the trustees instructed a private investigator to carry out covert surveillance, and ultimately rejected the application. The member complained to the Pensions Ombudsman, who ordered the trustees to reconsider their decision and would have awarded £2,000 for non-pecuniary loss in respect of the covert surveillance. Law Debenture appealed to the High Court. The Court held that the Ombudsman could only overturn a trustee decision where the trustee had asked itself the wrong question, misdirected itself in law or its decision was perverse (no reasonable body of trustees could have arrived at that decision). There was no evidence of any of these things in this case. Covert surveillance was not unlawful and was a legitimate course to pursue on appropriate occasions. On this occasion, the covert surveillance could not be said to be of no material relevance.

[21.4.47]

Law Debenture v Pensions Ombudsman (High Court) [1997] OPLR 31 at 42G

Maladministration – relationship with breach of trust

Principle

A breach of trust, even if excusable, need not technically amount to maladministration. Something rather more must be proved.

[21.4.48]

Legal & General v Pensions Ombudsman (High Court) [2000] OPLR 153

Maladministration – fairness of insurance policy – refusal to provide information

Principle

The Pensions Ombudsman's powers to investigate maladministration did not include power to investigate the fairness of terms of an insurance policy in which a pension scheme was invested. However, the refusal of the insurer to provide details of the calculation of payment under that contract could constitute maladministration. In the absence of specific provision to the contrary, where a contract provides for a payment to be made calculated in accordance with a formula known to one party alone, that party must disclose the formula to the other party so that it can check that the calculation is correct.

Miller v Stapleton (High Court) [1996] OPLR 73, [1996] PLR 67

Maladministration – provision of advice – non-pecuniary loss

Principles

Investigation of maladministration is not the normal function of a court: it does not as such give rise to a cause of action in law. The courts have not attempted a definition of maladministration. Parallels may be drawn from *R v Local Commissioner ex parte Eastleigh BC [1988] QB 855, 863*, where for local authorities maladministration is concerned with the manner in which decisions are reached, and the manner in which they are or are not implemented. It has nothing to do with the nature, quality or reasonableness of the decision itself. Further parallels may be drawn with the tests used by the Parliamentary Commissioner for Administration: bias, neglect, inattention, delay, incompetence, ineptitude, perversity, turpitude, arbitrariness, rudeness, refusing to answer reasonable questions, knowingly giving advice which is misleading or inadequate, faulty procedures and so on. However, both of these Ombudsmen are dealing with authorities operating in the public sphere. There are material differences of subject matter for the Pensions Ombudsman, who is investigating schemes established under private law. *Hamar v Pensions Ombudsman [1996] OPLR 55* was considered in relation to trustees' duties to give advice. Trustees acting on proper advice are entitled to assert their view of the law before the Ombudsman; that is a normal and proper part of good administration. Giving advice *bona fide* which is reasonably believed to be correct in law, but ultimately turns out not to be, would not normally amount to maladministration. Where trustees give advice, it should be as clear and accurate as possible. It may be maladministration to offer guaranteed cash equivalents before an up-to-date valuation had been completed. The Ombudsman should distinguish between findings of fact and law, and findings of maladministration.

It was doubtful whether the legislation establishing the Pensions Ombudsman empowered him to award compensation for non-pecuniary distress and disappointment. Such a power is the exception rather than the rule, and express words would have been expected. Further, where the trustees were entitled to an indemnity from the scheme assets, as here, any additional payment for compensation would be at the expense of other beneficiaries.

[21.4.50]

Re the Minworth Limited Pension Scheme, Anderson v William M Mercer (Pensions Ombudsman, 22 April 1999) Cases F00265, F00463 and G00264

Maladministration – investment mismatching – overpaid transfers – failure of administrators and trustees to consult each other

Facts and Decision

A pension scheme went into winding-up in 1991 following the insolvency of the principal employer. The scheme assets were held in a managed fund, and were transferred into the cash fund in 1991. This resulted in a mismatching of assets and liabilities, and through market movements, the scheme solvency suffered. The administrators continued to pay transfer values in full, despite the deteriorating funding position. The Pensions Ombudsman held that if the independent trustee did not know what investment matching was, it should have taken advice. Once it was aware of the concept, the trustee had an obligation to take appropriate advice: *Bartlett v Barclays Bank Trust [1980] 1 All ER 139* was applied. The trustee had failed to consider properly the scheme investments and had failed to make proper arrangements for the receipt of investment advice. This was maladministration. The administrators were also under a duty to inform the trustee of this responsibility, and this also was maladministration: however, it would be inconsistent with the Ombudsman's finding that the primary obligation lay with the trustee, to find that this maladministration of the administrators had caused injustice. The administrators' failure to alert the trustees to the worsening funding position because of the effect of the movements in gilt yields, and the large number of transfer values being paid, was maladministration causing injustice by the administrators.

[21.4.51]

NHS Pensions v Beechinor (High Court) [1997] OPLR 99, [1997] PLR 95

Maladministration – duty to advise

Principle

There was no maladministration by administrators where there was no general duty of care on the administrators to advise or warn the pension scheme member, or to provide a full explanation of the advantages and disadvantages of the member's alternative decisions in relation to the pension scheme benefits.

[21.4.52]

Nuthall v Merrill Lynch (UK) Final Salary Plan trustees (Pensions Ombudsman, 25 March 1999) Case G00543

Maladministration – payment of contributions – standards to be used – delays

Facts and Decision

The Pensions Ombudsman held that there had been excessive delays in paying over a member's additional voluntary contributions, where the delay extended from 25th of one month to the 5th of the next month. The provisions of the *Pensions Act 1995* specified maximum periods within which payments must be transferred, but these were specified in order to avoid criminal liability, not maladministration. The existence of such long stop sanctions does not absolve trustees or managers of their responsibility to ensure that good practices are established for all areas of pension scheme administration. The behaviour in this case constituted maladministration causing injustice on the part of the trustees, who had failed to ensure that the monies were transferred promptly, and on the part of the insurer in that it had not requested payment of the contributions via its direct debit mandate at the beginning of each month.

The Pensions Ombudsman also upheld the following principles:

(a)   There was no merit in the proposition that it was unreasonable to judge actions which occurred up to 10 years ago by the standards of today.

(b)   The fact that delays appear to be normal within the pensions industry does not render them necessary, reasonable or acceptable.

(c)   Good administrative practice requires that quotations of transfer values should be provided promptly. In this instance the trustees failed to provide the quotation within an acceptable time limit and their failure to do so constituted maladministration.

(d)   The time elapsing between the submission of the application for payment of the transfer values of both the complainant's scheme benefits and his AVC fund was 6 weeks and 7 weeks respectively. These were not excessive delays, and there was therefore no maladministration.

[21.4.53]

Robinson v Atco-Qualcast (Pensions Ombudsman, 26 March 1999) Case H00422

Maladministration – covert surveillance – relevancy of evidence used

Facts and Decision

The Pensions Ombudsman held that covert surveillance had been an unwarranted intrusion into Mr Robinson's private life and that of his family, and much of the evidence gathered was of no bearing on the claim. The commissioning of the covert surveillance was maladministration, as was the passing of medical evidence to a third party charged with the express duty of undermining Mr Robinson's case.

[21.4.54]

University of Nottingham v Eyett (High Court) [1999] 1 WLR 594, [1999] OPLR 55, [1998] PLR 27

Maladministration – relationship with employment and trust law

Principle

Where a complaint of maladministration is being considered, the parties' rights and obligations fall to be determined in accordance with established principles of trust and employment law.

[21.4.55]

Westminster v Haywood (High Court) [1996] 2 All ER 467, [1996] OPLR 95 at 106B-H, [1996] PLR 161, paras 49–52

Maladministration – nature of statutory duty – identifying the maladministration

Principle

Pension scheme trustees must now be regarded as being under a statutory duty not to cause injustice by maladministration. The notion that maladministration is concerned with the *manner* in which decisions are reached and the *manner* in which they are or are not implemented can quite readily be applied to the duties of trustees of pension schemes. The decisions which pension scheme trustees have to take and implement have at least as much in common with decisions of official administrators as they have with decisions of trustees of family settlements. It is not necessarily maladministration for a decision maker to take a wrong view of the law. Taking and acting on a wrong view of the law may be maladministration if the decision-maker knows or ought to know that the state of the law is uncertain, and that those who may be adversely affected by the uncertainty need to be warned about it. (See also [21.4.56].)

[21.4.56]

Westminster v Haywood (Court of Appeal) [1998] Ch 377, [1997] OPLR 61 at 70C-E, [1997] PLR 39 at para 48–49

Maladministration – nature of statutory duty – identifying the maladministration

Principle

It is essential in dealing with a claim of injustice by maladministration to identify the injustice, and the relevant maladministration which caused it. The maladministration in this case was the failure to warn the pension scheme member that there was some doubt as to the amount of his pension, or as to whether Westminster Council had promised to pay him more than he could lawfully be paid. Properly identified, the maladministration caused neither pecuniary loss nor anxiety or distress, but the reverse. The most that can be said is that this inevitably led to disappointed expectations. (See also [21.4.55].)

[21.4.57]

Westminster v Haywood (No. 2) (High Court) [2000] PLR 235

Maladministration – effect of finding

Principle

A finding of maladministration is a serious slur on the reputation of a person concerned in the management of a scheme and (in particular if he or she is a professional manager) may be highly damaging. The manager has accordingly a substantial and legitimate interest in clearing his or her name. (See also [21.4.58].)

[21.4.58]

Westminster v Haywood (No. 2) (Court of Appeal, interlocutory, unreported, 6 April 2000)

Maladministration – effect of finding

Principle

The observation of the High Court (see [21.4.57]) was approved.

[21.4.59]

Whight v Co-operative Insurance Society (Pensions Ombudsman, 20 August 1999) Case H00487

Maladministration – covert surveillance

Principle

Covert surveillance is not unlawful, and this was an appropriate case for its use. It was not, therefore, maladministration to have used it in this case.

Circumstances in which the Pensions Ombudsman may intervene in exercises of trustee discretions

[21.4.60]

Edge v Pensions Ombudsman (Court of Appeal) [2000] 3 WLR 79, [1999] OPLR 179, [1999] PLR 215

Pensions Ombudsman – trustees' discretions

Principle

Properly understood, the duty for trustees to act impartially is no more than the ordinary duty which the law imposes on a person who is entrusted with the exercise of a discretionary power: that he or she exercises the power for the purpose for which it is given, giving proper consideration to the matters which are relevant and excluding from consideration matters which are irrelevant. If pension fund trustees do that, they cannot be criticised if they reach a decision which appears to prefer the claims of one interest over others. The preference will be the result of a proper exercise of the discretionary power. The principles under consideration in a private pension scheme were analogous to those in the different context of public law cases (though the extent to which the analogy could be taken was not under consideration): *Harris v Shuttleworth [1995] OPLR 79*, *Wild v Smith [1996] OPLR 129* and *Associated Provincial Picture Houses v Wednesbury Corporation [1948] 1 KB 223* were considered.

[21.4.61]

Elson v BT Supplementary Benefits Plan trustees (Pensions Ombudsman, 19 May 1998) Case F00859

Pensions Ombudsman – trustees' discretions

Facts and Decision

When trustees had made a decision as to how to apply a lump sum death benefit on a misconceived view of the weight to be attached to the nomination form, the Pensions Ombudsman held that by treating the form as overriding, the trustees were distorting and hence not acting in accordance with the terms of the discretion conferred upon them. They had fettered their discretion out of existence. The trustees had therefore been guilty of maladministration, and the purported exercise of their discretion had to be set aside and treated as ineffective.

[21.4.62]

Harris v Shuttleworth (Court of Appeal) [1995] OPLR 79 at 86H–87A, [1994] PLR 47 at para 36, [1994] ICR 991

Pensions Ombudsman – trustees' discretions

Principle

Trustees must ask themselves the correct questions. They must direct themselves correctly in law; in particular they must adopt a correct construction of the pension fund rules. They must not arrive at a perverse decision, i.e. a decision to which no reasonable body of trustees could arrive, and they must take into account all relevant but no irrelevant factors. Only if the trustees fail on one of these grounds can the Court intervene.

[21.4.63]

Wild v Smith (High Court) [1996] OPLR 129 at 135B-D, [1996] PLR 275 at para 23

Pensions Ombudsman – trustees' discretions

Principle

Trustees are subject to review by the Court, not as a Court of Appeal, but with a limited role (following *Harris v Shuttleworth [1995] OPLR 79*; see [2.1.14]). The Pensions Ombudsman is put in the same position in reviewing the decisions within his jurisdiction as the Court. Even where a decision is given to the trustees, the Ombudsman can review it on the same grounds as could the Court.

Power to make compensation payments

[21.4.64]

Bennett v Ferranti (Pensions Ombudsman, 8 July 1998) Case G00016

Awards for non-pecuniary loss

Facts and Decision

The Pensions Ombudsman ordered a group pensions manager to pay compensation to a member whom he had misled into believing that her pension and lump sum would be higher than was actually the case.

[21.4.65]

City & County of Swansea v Johnson (High Court) [1999] OPLR 39 at 51A-D, [1999] PLR 187 at paras 50–51

Awards for non-pecuniary loss – quantum

Principle

The proper level of an award for compensation for distress is a matter of law. When assessing the proper level of compensation, the Pensions Ombudsman must only take into account relevant considerations. In the absence of very exceptional circumstances an award in excess of £1,000 ought not to be considered as appropriate by way of damages for distress.

[21.4.66]

Duckitt v Pensions Ombudsman (High Court) [2000] OPLR 167

Awards for non-pecuniary loss

Principle

If the Pensions Ombudsman is to make an award of compensation for distress or inconvenience, he must in each case consider whether the evidence justifies such an award, and if so what that award should be. He should set out both the evidence relied upon and the reasoning. The parties were entitled to know on what evidence and how the Ombudsman had reached the conclusion that distress or inconvenience had been occasioned, and how he reached the conclusion that the amount of any award was appropriate in the particular circumstances of the case.

[21.4.67]

ITN v Ward (High Court) [1997] OPLR 147 at 158A-G, [1997] PLR 131 at paras 41–45

Awards for non-pecuniary loss

Facts and Decision

Where the Pensions Ombudsman had awarded damages for distress and disappointment for trustees wrongly telling members that their benefits were guaranteed to increase at 4% per annum, the Court held that the past history of pension increases could be left out of account by the Ombudsman. No matter how generous the trustees may have been in the past by making *ad hoc* payments over that rate, the members had been denied the comfort and security of guaranteed future increases.

[21.4.68]

Law Debenture v Malley (High Court) [1999] OPLR 167

Awards for non-pecuniary loss – quantum

Facts and Decision

Law Debenture was one of the trustees of a pension scheme. In considering an incapacity pension, the trustees instructed a private investigator to carry out covert surveillance, and ultimately rejected the application. The member complained to the Pensions Ombudsman, who ordered the trustees to reconsider their decision and would have awarded £2,000 for non-pecuniary loss in respect of the covert surveillance. The decision was overturned, but the Court held that an award for £2,000 would in any case have been excessive. Very exceptional circumstances did not arise in this case, and the normal limit of £1,000 would have applied.

[21.4.69]

NHS Pensions Agency v Pensions Ombudsman (High Court) [1996] OPLR 119

Awards for non-pecuniary loss

Principle

Where the Pensions Ombudsman awards damages for distress and inconvenience, there must be something in the evidence or the facts found that justifies the award in a particular case. Mere evidence of maladministration is not sufficient, and the distress and inconvenience must be distress and inconvenience beyond that of being involved in a dispute.

[21.4.70]

Westminster v Haywood (High Court) [1996] 2 All ER 467, [1996] OPLR 95 at 109A to 110H, [1996] PLR 161, paras 67–76

Awards for non-pecuniary loss – quantum

Principle

The Pensions Ombudsman has power to award compensation for distress or inconvenience. With a solvent private-sector scheme and a solvent employer, the burden would be likely to fall ultimately on the employer, who would usually have covenanted to pay the balance of the overall cost of the scheme. That may involve rough justice in most cases. When setting the level of compensation, the Ombudsman will be anxious not to remedy one injustice by creating another, and the ultimate burden of any compensation directed must therefore be a relevant consideration. £1,000 to an ex-employee with 24 years' service who had sustained injustice was on the high side, but not so excessive as to be wrong in law. (See also [21.4.71].)

[21.4.71]

Westminster v Haywood (Court of Appeal) [1998] Ch 377, [1997] OPLR 61 at 70C-G, [1997] PLR 39, paras 47–49

Awards for non-pecuniary loss – quantum

Facts and Decision

Whether or not, the Court held, the Pensions Ombudsman has jurisdiction to award compensation payments, it was inappropriate to award £1,000 where a pension scheme member had suffered at most only disappointed expectations as a result of the maladministration. There were two objections. First, which could probably have been overcome without too much difficulty, was that the maladministration was not something of which the member complained. Secondly, the member had received £1,580 in excess of his entitlement, and was not being asked to repay them. The overpayments which the member received fully compensated him for any disappointment. (See also [21.4.70].)

Grounds of appeal

[21.4.72]

Hamar v French (Court of Appeal) [1997] OPLR 105 at 118H–119A, 119C-D, [1998] PLR 321 at para 75, 77

Appeal from the Pensions Ombudsman – points of law

Principle

Appeals from the Pensions Ombudsman are on a question of law only. Where it has not been a matter of dispute between the parties whether a transfer request had been validly made, and the ground of challenge on appeal is that the transfer request had not been validly made, this was a matter of fact. Appeals from the High Court are also on a matter of law only. However, the High Court has jurisdiction to disturb the determination of the Pensions Ombudsman only if it was not reached by a correct application of the law to the facts found by him or not in dispute before him. If the judge finds an error of law where there was none, the Court of Appeal is bound to correct him or her.

Key v Courtaulds (High Court) [1999] OPLR 27

Appeal from the Pensions Ombudsman – points of fact

Principle

The factual findings of the Pensions Ombudsman can be challenged if it can be shown that there really was no foundation at all for the factual conclusion. At that point the factual determination becomes and depends upon an error of law in approach. This requires an objection that the Ombudsman's conclusions were those that no tribunal properly approaching the available evidence could have reached. That is a very high hurdle to surmount.

[21.4.74]

Law Debenture v Malley (High Court, interlocutory) [1999] OPLR 153 at 162D-E, [1999] PLR 367 at para 41

Appeal from the Pensions Ombudsman – no directions made

Principle

Trustees found guilty of maladministration may appeal against a determination by the Pensions Ombudsman that they were guilty of maladministration, whether or not the Ombudsman went on to make directions to compensate the complainant.

[21.4.75]

Legal & General v Pensions Ombudsman (High Court) [2000] OPLR 153 at 158E–159H

Appeal from the Pensions Ombudsman – preliminary issues

Principle

There is no jurisdiction for the High Court to hear an appeal from decisions of the Pensions Ombudsman on preliminary issues.

[21.4.76]

Westminster v Haywood (No. 2) (High Court) [2000] PLR 235

Appeal from the Pensions Ombudsman – no directions made

Facts and Decision

Following the Court of Appeal's decision in *Westminster v Haywood [1998] Ch 377* regarding the extent of the Pensions Ombudsman's jurisdiction in relation to schemes which did not provide long-service benefits, the Ombudsman's jurisdiction was widened. Mr Haywood then brought another complaint to the Pensions Ombudsman about the same facts. The Ombudsman heard the complaint and found that there had been maladministration but no injustice. The Ombudsman argued that there was no right of appeal against a finding of maladministration only. The Court held that Westminster City Council had the right to appeal against determinations even though no adverse direction had been made: *Law Debenture v Malley [1999] OPLR 153* was followed. (See also [21.4.77].)

[21.4.77]

Westminster v Haywood (No. 2) (Court of Appeal, interlocutory, unreported, 6 April 2000)

Appeal from the Pensions Ombudsman – no directions made

Facts and Decision

The High Court decision on this point (see [21.4.76]) was approved.

[21.4.78]

Wild v Smith (High Court) [1996] OPLR 129 at 136B-C, [1996] PLR 275 at para 28

Appeal from the Pensions Ombudsman – maladministration

Principle

When dealing with the Pensions Ombudsman's decision on maladministration, the Court can only interfere if he has gone wrong in law, or reached a decision which is unreasonable in the *Wednesbury* sense.

Appeal mechanism

[21.4.79]

City of Edinburgh v Rapley (Court of Session, Inner House, Scotland) [2000] OPLR 67

Appeal from the Pensions Ombudsman – time limits for appeal

Facts and Decision

The Pensions Ombudsman made a determination in favour of Mrs Rapley. He issued guidance to complainants, but copied to respondents stating that as a general rule appeals from his determinations in Scotland had to be started within 42 days of receiving the determination. The City of Edinburgh appealed on the 42nd day after receiving the determination, relying on the Ombudsman's guidance. In fact, the time limit in Scotland for appeals from the Pensions Ombudsman was 14 days. In view of the circumstances and the importance of the case, the Court allowed the City of Edinburgh to bring their appeal out of time. It observed that appellants should keep in mind that the Court's rules made different provisions in relation to different tribunals constituted under different statutes. Those who are responsible for sending out guidance notes must also take care to avoid misleading or inaccurate wording.

[21.4.80]

Dolphin v Pensions Ombudsman (High Court) [1995] OPLR 331 and 345, [1996] PLR 95

Appeal from the Pensions Ombudsman – Pensions Ombudsman as party

Principle

The Pensions Ombudsman is, to the extent that he is able to do so, a proper party to an appeal from his own determinations, to assist the Court in arriving at the correct determination. There is no comparable appeals process or jurisdiction. If the Ombudsman could not appear on appeals, the benefit of the Ombudsman's jurisdiction would be taken away for complainants.

[21.4.81]

Hillsdown v Pensions Ombudsman (High Court) [1997] 1 All ER 862, [1996] OPLR 291 at 319A-D, [1996] PLR 427 at para 105

Appeal from the Pensions Ombudsman – new points of law

Principle

It may well be proper for a court to deal with points of law not raised before the Pensions Ombudsman or dealt with in his determination if, but only if, the resolution of the point of law does not involve an investigation of facts which have not previously been investigated.

[21.4.82]

ITN v Ward (High Court) [1997] OPLR 147 at 155G–157A, [1997] PLR 131, paras 33–35

Appeal from the Pensions Ombudsman – new points of law

Principle

The Pensions Ombudsman may point out alternative legal routes to the same conclusions as he has reached, as long as they were derivable from the findings of fact he has made: the dictum from *Hillsdown v Pensions Ombudsman [1997] 1 All ER 862* was approved. Public policy considerations make it desirable for the Court to consider all the consequences which flow from findings of fact made by the Ombudsman. However, he should notify the appellant of the existence of an alternative route sufficiently well in advance, so that there is no risk of the appellant being taken by surprise and the hearing of the appeal being adjourned at the last moment.

[21.4.83]

Law Debenture v Malley (High Court, interlocutory) [1999] OPLR 153, [1999] PLR 367

Appeal from the Pensions Ombudsman – abuse of process

Facts and Decision

The Pensions Ombudsman found trustees had been guilty of maladministration in considering an application for an ill-health pension, and directed them to pay the complainant £79.50 for the costs of a medical report he had obtained. He also directed the trustees to reconsider the application and made strong recommendations that the trustees consider paying the complainant £2,000 as compensation for non-pecuniary injustice. One trustee appealed against this determination, and the Ombudsman applied to Court to strike out the appeal. The Court observed that it has an inherent jurisdiction to strike out notices of appeal on the grounds of abuse of process. In this case, however, the outcome of the appeal was not of purely academic interest – while the scheme had been wound up and the trustees had the benefit of an exoneration, the trustees were under a continuing duty to carry out the Ombudsman's directions. Trustees had the right to appeal against determinations, even if no directions were made against them, on the basis of the determination on a given point. Since the trustee had good grounds for appeal on other directions made against it, there was no reason to deprive it of the right to appeal against the award of £79.50, even if it was trifling.

[21.4.84]

Marsh & Maclennan v Pensions Ombudsman (High Court) [2001] PLR 51

Appeal from the Pensions Ombudsman – new points of law

Principle

An appellant from the Pensions Ombudsman to the High Court may raise a new point of law not raised before the Pensions Ombudsman, subject to the appellate court's discretion to exclude it. The usual practice of the Court of Appeal, to allow a pure point of law not raised in the Court below, was to be adopted: *Pittalis v Grant [1989] 1 QB 605* was followed, and *Jones v Governing body of Burdett Coutts School [1999] ICR 38* was distinguished.

[21.4.85]

Miller v Stapleton (Court of Appeal) [1996] OPLR 281

Appeal from the Pensions Ombudsman – Pensions Ombudsman as party

Principle

The Pensions Ombudsman is a proper party to an appeal from his determination, and consequently also a proper party to further appeals to the Court of Appeal: *Dolphin v Pensions Ombudsman [1995] OPLR 331,*

345 and *Providence Capitol Trustees v Ayres [1996] 4 All ER 760* were considered. It was open to question whether he should play an active part in the appeal in defending his own determinations, and his role before the judge was a matter for the judge to consider.

Court's powers on appeal

[21.4.86]

British Telecom Pension Scheme Trustees v Clarke (Court of Appeal) [2000] OPLR 53, [2000] PLR 157

Appeal from the Pensions Ombudsman – Court's powers

Principle

Where the Court was unsure whether it would have reached the same conclusion as the original Tribunal, if the case fell within a no man's land, the decision was not one with which the appellate Court should interfere.

[21.4.87]

Duckitt v Pensions Ombudsman (High Court) [2000] OPLR 167

Appeal from the Pensions Ombudsman – Court's powers

Principle

Where the Pensions Ombudsman's determination displays a lack of logic and a lack in the evidence required to justify a finding, the Court will set aside the Ombudsman's determination. Allegations of dishonesty and deliberate wrongdoing are very serious allegations, and it is incumbent on the Ombudsman before he makes a finding to that effect to have substantive evidence to justify it, and to give full and sufficient reasons for doing so.

[21.4.88]

Elliott v Pensions Ombudsman (High Court) [1998] OPLR 21 at 32F–32H, 33F

Appeal from the Pensions Ombudsman – findings of fact

Facts and Decision

The Court had a real doubt in this case as to whether the Pensions Ombudsman had found that the respondents to a complaint had acted in conscious breach of trust, as he would have needed to find if they were to be deprived of the protection given by an exoneration clause. Since this was the foundation of a determination against them, the Court remitted the matter to the Ombudsman for rehearing on this critical issue.

[21.4.89]

Key v Courtaulds (High Court) [1999] OPLR 27

Appeal from the Pensions Ombudsman – Court's powers – findings of maladministration

Principle

A determination of the Pensions Ombudsman is final and binding, subject only to an appeal on a point of law: *Macaulay v Pensions Ombudsman [1998] OPLR 107* was followed. The factual findings can be challenged if it can be shown that there really was no foundation at all for the factual conclusion. At that point the factual determination becomes and depends upon an error of law in its approach.

[21.4.90]

Macaulay v Pensions Ombudsman (High Court) [1998] OPLR 107, [1998] PLR 211

Appeal from the Pensions Ombudsman – Court's powers

Principle

A determination of the Pensions Ombudsman is final and binding, subject only to an appeal on a point of law. The Court can only interfere with a decision as involving an error of law if:

- the Court is satisfied that there was no evidence to support it; or
- it could be said to be an inference drawn from other facts found by the Ombudsman which point inexorably to the opposite conclusion, as being the only one which a properly directed tribunal could reach.

[21.4.91]

Wakelin v Read (Court of Appeal) [2000] PLR 319

Appeal from the Pensions Ombudsman – Court's powers – findings of fact

Principle

The Court will be reluctant to order that a case be reheard, but there are some circumstances where it is unavoidable. It is for the first instance tribunal to evaluate the evidence and find the facts. That is not the function of the tribunal hearing the appeal on a point of law. There are of course cases in which it is possible to say with confidence that there is no more evidence to be heard, that the primary facts found by the tribunal are sufficient to entitle the appellate tribunal to conclude that a properly instructed tribunal could only come to one conclusion, and that there is no point in remitting the case for a further hearing. However, where the Pensions Ombudsman and the parties had not addressed their evidence or argument to the issue of whether there had been a dishonest breach of trust and the part played by the complainant, because the parties did not rely in terms on the complainant's role and the Ombudsman mistakenly thought he was inhibited in law, the investigation as to whether the complainant was dishonest was incomplete. Only the Ombudsman could complete the investigation.

[21.4.92]

Wirral BC v Evans (Court of Appeal) [2000] All ER (D) 1728

Appeal from the Pensions Ombudsman – findings of maladministration

Principle

The Pensions Ombudsman was, from his experience and training, much better suited than a court to conclude whether maladministration had actually occurred or not.

When the Pensions Ombudsman should appeal against Court decisions

[21.4.93]

Duckitt v Pensions Ombudsman (Court of Appeal) [2001] PLR 155

Pensions Ombudsman appeal from High Court

Facts and Decision

The Pensions Ombudsman sought permission to appeal against a decision of the High Court overturning one of his determinations. He did so for guidance on two points of principle: the scope of the Ombudsman's duty to give reasons, and the proper approach of the Court to the reasons given. The Court of Appeal held that on this matter the position in law was abundantly clear. This case required the Ombudsman to identify whether a breach of trust was deliberate or reckless, and the High Court's decision was entirely consistent with the numerous authorities. The Ombudsman also sought guidance on the evidence that was required before the Ombudsman may make a finding or draw an inference of dishonesty on the part of pension scheme trustees. The Court held that no issue of principle arose in the present case, and the application for permission to appeal was therefore dismissed.

[21.4.94]

Edge v Pensions Ombudsman (Court of Appeal) [2000] 3 WLR 79, [1999] OPLR 179 at 207G–208E, [1999] PLR 215 at paras 89–91

Pensions Ombudsman appeal from High Court

Principle

The Pensions Ombudsman is entitled to apply for permission to appeal from an adverse decision of the High Court. However, unless there is some point of principle in relation to which conflicting decisions of the High Court make it difficult for him to perform his proper functions without further guidance from the Court of Appeal, he should accept and act upon decisions of the High Court.

21.5 – Other regulatory bodies

Company law

[21.5.1]

Australian Securities Commission v AS Nominees (Federal Court of Australia) [1996] PLR 297

Company regulators – winding-up when just and equitable

Facts and Decision

The Australian Securities Commission, which regulated companies in Australia, with the support of the Insurance and Superannuation Commissioner, applied for the winding-up of ten companies or the appointment of receivers and managers, in order to secure a removal of trustees and managers of a number of superannuation and unit trusts. The trustee companies had been run largely at the direction of, and in some real measure for, the benefit of one director. The Court observed that the directors had shown little appreciation of their own responsibilities as directors and of the trusteeship obligations of their companies, with the consequence that repeated breaches of corporation law and breaches of trust had occurred. Trust funds had been invested recklessly and improvidently, often where blatant conflicts of interest were present. In one case fraud of some magnitude was perpetrated on the investor beneficiaries of the superannuation trusts. Two companies acted as a single entity, to the extent of sharing a single bank account. Both the companies and the trusts had deficient and defective record-keeping, concealing these misdeeds. The Court wound up the companies on the ground that it was just and equitable to do so. It observed that when the public regulator brought proceedings to wind up a company, it may not be supported by those interested in the company, but it was then that the public interest responsibility was most pronounced. The use of superannuation both as a means for making retirement provision and for increasing national savings was an accepted instrument of public policy. The protection of investors in the particular context of superannuation was a ground for holding that it was just and equitable to wind up a company.

Financial services

Melton Medes v Securities and Investments Board (High Court) [1994] PLR 167

Financial services regulators – statutory duties

Facts and Decision

The Securities & Investments Board (SIB) conducted an investigation into the affairs of a company's pension scheme, concentrating on a loan which the pension scheme made to the company. SIB passed on information gathered in the course of this investigation to members bringing a hostile action against the pension scheme trustees and the company. The company claimed that settlement negotiations failed as a result, and sued SIB for breach of its statutory duty under *s 179* of the *Financial Services Act 1986*. The Court held that *s 179* did not create a private law right, and the claim therefore failed. SIB was established in the interest of and for the protection of investors. *Section 179* was apt to control in the public interest the use and dissemination of information acquired, rather than to subject SIB in this respect to private law actions. There was not a 'scintilla' of evidence in this case to support an allegation that SIB had acted in bad faith, which would be necessary to establish liability on SIB's part. On the facts, there was also no disclosure in contravention of *s 179* since the facts disclosed did not relate to the company's business affairs, and expressions of opinion were not apt to be caught by the *section*.

R v Personal Investment Authority ex parte Lucas Fettes (High Court) [1995] OPLR 187

Financial services regulators – reasonableness of rules

Facts and Decision

The Personal Investment Authority (PIA) issued rules which required every member:

(a)   to embark on a review entailing an analysis of all personal pension sales in specified categories between 1988 and 1994;

(b)   to contact all relevant customers; and

(c)   to assess the extent to which loss has been caused to the investors.

Lucas Fettes, a member of the PIA, objected that there had been no consideration of the cost to each member company before the requirement had been imposed, and that it would unfairly handicap the member company in any dispute it may have with its clients. The Court held that the *Financial Services Act 1986* gives the PIA a wide discretion in deciding what it needs to do adequately in the interests of the industry. The requirement that its rules and practices relating to discipline must be fair and reasonable addressed the machinery for discipline, and not the grounds on which disciplinary action could be taken. The PIA was obliged to have satisfactory arrangements for taking account of, and framing rules for, the costs to those to whom the rules were going to apply. However, the PIA had consulted its members, who had the opportunity to complain of the cost, and this was entirely satisfactory. It could not possibly be said that it was irrational for the PIA not to approach each PIA member individually. The PIA was following the advice of the Securities and Investments Board, and this had already been held not to be irrational in *R v Securities and Investments Board ex parte Independent Financial Advisers Association [1995] OPLR 137*. Leave for judicial review was refused.

R v Securities and Investments Board ex parte Independent Financial Advisers Association (Divisional Court) [1995] OPLR 137, [1995] PLR 123

Financial services regulators – reasonableness of rules – relationship between rules and professional negligence insurance duties

Facts and Decision

The Securities & Investments Board (SIB) established guidance on how firms facing claims of personal pension misselling should handle such claims. The Independent Financial Advisers Association challenged its contents and its validity. The Court held that SIB had no power to enforce the provisions of its statement directly against independent financial advisers, with the possible exception of the few who were directly regulated by SIB. To the extent that the guidance required independent financial advisers to take any step which would invalidate its insurance cover, it was wholly irrational and required revision. It was, though, entirely reasonable for SIB to expect that advisers should complete urgently the review of the position of any investor whose time limit under the general law may be short or about to run out.

Pensions Regulators

Collins & Batchelor v Pension Commission (Ontario) & Dominion Stores (Ontario Divisional Court, 18 August 1986) 16 OAC 24

Pensions Commission – refunds of surplus

Facts and Decision

Dominion Stores applied for and obtained consent from the Pension Commission to take a refund of surplus. The Pension Commission did not consult the scheme membership. The members had been repeatedly told by Dominion that the funds in the scheme could not be used in any way by Dominion except for the provision of pensions, and believed that Dominion had no right to take such a refund. The Court held that the Pension Commission's duties were akin to those of a fiduciary. It was not bound to consent to the proposal, and therefore owed a duty of fairness to those whose interests may be affected by its decision. Members should have been given notice so that they had the opportunity to defend their interest. The amount of surplus which was capable of being refunded was a matter of actuarial opinion. The opinions of experts were known to vary, and the members should have had the opportunity to comment on the opinion provided by the employer. The members should have had the opportunity to put their point that Dominion had no right under the scheme documentation to remove any assets. The Pension Commission had failed in its duty of fairness and its decision was, therefore, set aside.

Law Debenture v Pensions Ombudsman (High Court) [1997] OPLR 31 at 43E–44D

Occupational Pensions Board – statutory rights to cash equivalents

Principle

The Occupational Pensions Board had no power to extend retrospectively the statutory period for payment of cash equivalents after that statutory period had expired.

[21.5.7]

R v Dixon (Court of Appeal) [2000] OPLR 47

Occupational Pensions Regulatory Authority – late payment of contributions

Facts and Decision

Mr Dixon was the finance director of Biltons Ltd. He failed to pay across member contributions to its pension scheme on time in nine consecutive months, and in three consecutive months he failed to pay across the member contributions at all. He had not appreciated that this was a criminal offence under the *Pensions Act 1995*. When he found out that he had been committing a criminal offence, he told the Occupational Pensions Regulatory Authority (OPRA). He was convicted of the criminal offence and sentenced to prison. He appealed on the sentence. The Court observed that he had been ignorant of the fact that he had been committing a criminal offence. He had contacted the authorities himself, and had pleaded guilty. He was of previous good character. He had been motivated by a desire to keep the company going and to continue to provide work for the employees, which while not an excuse, distinguished this from cases where employees' contributions had been siphoned off for some motive which had nothing at all to do with their well-being. The criminal offence was shortly to be abolished. In all the circumstances, a custodial sentence was not appropriate.

[21.5.8]

R v OPRA ex parte Littlewoods (High Court) [1997] OPLR 375 at 381E, [1998] PLR 63 at para 23

Occupational Pensions Regulatory Authority – trustee representations

Principle

Trustees have only themselves to blame if the Occupational Pensions Regulatory Authority (OPRA) fails to address arguments which would support the trustees' case, when they make an application to OPRA to grant an extension of the period for carrying out their duties in relation to a statutory right to a cash equivalent.

[21.5.9]

Shucksmith v Occupational Pensions Board (High Court) [1989] PLR 63

Occupational Pensions Board – preservation requirements

Facts and Decision

A trustee complained that the Occupational Pensions Board (OPB) had wrongly applied the preservation requirements to his pension scheme. The Court held that it was doubtful whether a trustee of a scheme which the OPB had confirmed satisfied the preservation requirements had the right to apply to Court. The OPB's function was to understand what were the long-service benefits that the scheme member enjoyed, and then discover whether the benefits secured by the rules in the event of premature leaving of employment complied with the statutory requirements. There was no requirement to classify any given scheme as being defined benefit or money purchase: pension schemes take a multitude of different forms. The OPB was right in seeking to construe the rules of the scheme. Where the rules provided for two alternative benefits, it would be wrong to ignore the limitations that each placed upon the other.

Glossary – Pension Scheme Definitions

Most pension scheme rules have extensive sections of definitions, and those of course govern the provisions under consideration. Equally, when considering statutory provisions, Acts of Parliament and statutory instruments have extensive sets of definitions, and where terms are left undefined, common terms are often defined in the *Interpretation Act 1978*. The Pensions Management Institute/Pensions Research Accountants Group publication 'Pensions Terminology: A Glossary for Pension Schemes' is a good general guide to the meaning of standard pension scheme terms. However, from time to time, key words and phrases of pension schemes and of statute have been left undefined. The courts have often been required to consider the definitions of individual words and phrases, and some of those which have come up in a pensions context or which are relevant to pension schemes are set out below.

Appropriate

Wrightson v Fletcher Challenge Nominees (Privy Council) [2001] All ER 89

Principle

When a trustee must consider in the exercise of a discretion what is **appropriate**, the matters to be considered are more limited than when it must exercise a discretion **as it thinks fit**.

Annuity

Attorney-General of Canada v Confederation Life (Court of Appeal for Ontario, unreported, 20 January 1997)

Facts and Decision

Confederation Life, a large insurer, became insolvent. It provided supplementary pensions for senior officers. Those pensions were paid in accordance with Board resolutions. Neither the resolutions nor the letters to senior officers required a fund to be established, and the supplementary scheme was not funded. The letter to officers informed them that if they were dismissed with cause, the pensions would not vest. Policyholders took priority over Confederation Life's general assets in the winding-up. The senior officers of the supplementary scheme argued that by virtue of their pension benefits they were policyholders in respect of the amount required to satisfy all pension liabilities. **Insurance** was defined by the Court as the undertaking by one person to:

- indemnify another person against loss, or liability for loss, in respect of a certain risk or peril to which the object of the insurance may be exposed; or
- pay a sum of money or other thing of value upon the happening of a certain event;

and included life insurance. The only way in which the senior officers could qualify as policyholders was if the pension benefits constituted an **annuity**. There was no intention that **annuities** be created, nor was there ever any intention that the necessary funding be provided. Most, if not all of the senior officers, would have been aware that there was no funding whatever. The context of this case involved the distribution of the assets of an insurance company, and the potential dilution of the rights of the owners of commercially purchased insurance policies who were protected from the time of purchase by reserves. The dilution would be effected by employment agreements whose only similarity to policies of insurance or **annuities** was the promise of periodic payments for a life or lives. Yet they were dependent on good behaviour, and to the knowledge of all, dependent upon the continued financial health of Confederation Life. It would be a distortion to convert an employer-employee contract into a policy of insurance.

Re British Union & National Insurance Company (Court of Appeal) [1914] 2 Ch 77

Facts and Decision

An insurance company granted an **annuity** to a former employee by deed in settlement of claims for breach of contract. It was the only **annuity** that the company had ever granted. The insurance company went into liquidation, and the employee claimed priority as an **annuity** holder over other creditors. The Court held that the **annuity** was a life **annuity** within the meaning of s 30 of the *Assurance Companies Act 1909*, and therefore the former employee took priority on the winding-up.

Ceylon Commissioner of Inland Revenue v Rajaratnam (Privy Council) [1971] TR 451

Principle

For the purposes of the English tax legislation, an **annuity** does not mean only a purchased **annuity**: *Foley v Fletcher (1858) 3 H & N 769* explained. So a deed of covenant made without consideration to pay an **annuity** also constituted an **annuity** for these purposes.

O'Connor v Minister of National Revenue (Exchequer Court of Canada) [1943] 4 DLR 160

Principle

The word **annuity** is a word that is often loosely and therefore ambiguously used. Judicial decisions have clarified its meaning for income tax purposes where the **annuity** is payable under the terms of a contract. But where it is used in respect of a payment under a will its meaning is not nearly as clearly settled. Ordinarily an **annuity** is thought of as a series of annual payments which a person has purchased or arranged for with a sum of money or other asset of a capital nature: the dictum of *Winter v Mouseley 2 B & Ald 802* was adopted, *Foley v Fletcher (1858) 3 H & N 769* was considered. The mere fact that a payment is described in a contract as an **annuity** does not necessarily make it such: *Secretary of State in Council of India v Scobie [1903] AC 299, Perrin v Dickson [1929] 2 KB 85, [1930] 1 KB 107*, and *Sothern-Smith v Clancy [1941] 1 All ER 111* were reviewed. In a contractual **annuity** the person who put up the capital, and transferred it to the person or company that is charged with the obligation to pay the **annuity**, is ordinarily himself the recipient of the **annuity** when it becomes payable. His capital has gone but his right to receive the annual payments takes its place. The **annuity** under a contract is in a sense the result of an inseparable blending of capital and interest. On the other hand, no such state of affairs exists in the case of an **annuity** received under the provisions of a will, and the tests that are applicable to contractual **annuities** are not applicable to testamentary ones. The recipient of the **annuity** is not the contributor of the capital that made the **annuity** possible.

As it thinks fit

Wrightson v Fletcher Challenge Nominees (Privy Council) [2001] All ER 89

Principle

When a trustee must consider in the exercise of a discretion what is **appropriate**, the matters to be considered are more limited than when it must exercise a discretion **as it thinks fit**.

Associate

Cullen v Pension Holdings (High Court of New Zealand) [1992] PLR 134

Facts and Decision

The New Zealand Farmers' Co-operative Association of Canterbury operated a pension scheme which was substantially in surplus. The employer became a subsidiary of another company, which transferred employees and pensioners from another of its subsidiaries' pension schemes into the Association's scheme in 1988. The transfer-in rule provided that if a member was entitled to benefit under another scheme, the trustee might accept a transfer value and grant additional benefits. The election of members was made by the Association by written notice to the trustee, and the Association could elect as members such persons it determined were entitled to contribute to and share in the scheme. **Member** was defined as any employee or retired employee permitted by the Association to contribute to and/or share in the benefits of the scheme. **Employee** was defined as including any employee of the Association, and the Association was defined as the Association and any subsidiary or **associate** thereof or successor thereto. The Court held that the fellow subsidiary was an **associate** of the Association, and its employees were therefore eligible for membership of the scheme. The usual connotation of **associate** was one of alliance. The Oxford Diction-ary's primary definition was: 'one who is united to another by community of interest, and shares with him any enterprise, business or action; a partner, comrade, companion.' In the general business community the commonplace meaning arises frequently enough.

Benefits already secured

James Miller Holdings v Graham (Supreme Court, Victoria) [1992] PLR 165

Facts and Decision

James Miller Holdings operated a pension scheme for its employees of which it was also the trustee. The pension scheme was invested in a managed fund policy. The power of amendment was subject to a restriction that no amendment shall detrimentally affect the **benefits already secured** in respect of a member at the date of amendment without the consent in writing of that member. The consent of the members was not obtained. The Court held that the **benefits already secured** referred in this case to **benefits already secured** in respect of a member under the managed fund policy, and was a benefit which under the terms of the contract of insurance the employer was contingently entitled to receive upon the happening of an event which would give it a present vested right to receive it.

Compensation

R v Secretary of State for Education and Employment ex parte NATFHE (High Court, unreported, 28 August 1997)

Facts and Decision

The Secretary of State submitted that payment to a teacher, whether by lump sum or periodic payment which was triggered by early retirement, was more aptly described as **compensation** rather than **superannuation**. The Court held that the reasoning behind the Secretary of State's submissions was sound.

Contributing service

Cowan v Charlesworth (High Court) [1989] PLR 79

Facts and Decision

Members of the Mineworkers Pension Scheme went on strike. The question arose as to whether their service while on strike was **contributing service**, which was defined as any period of service while in eligible employment in relation to which normal contributions were required to be paid by the member. In the context of this scheme, the Court held that **contributing service** was a period of eligible employment during which contributions are made by or on behalf of a member, or are deemed to have been so made. Members on sick pay would be in **contributing service**, but members on strike would not.

Deferred member

NBC Pension Trustees v Harrod (High Court) [1999] OPLR 113 at 121F-H, [2000] PLR 183 at paras 34–36

Principle

For the purposes of *s 124(2)* of the *Pensions Act 1995*, **deferred members** means the individuals who will at some point in the future, on retirement, on reaching a specified age, on death or whatever the event may be, become entitled to specified calculable pension rights. It does not include persons who are no more than beneficiaries under a discretionary trust, and who may or may not receive anything.

Dependant

Crowe Engineering v Lynch (Ireland, High Court, 24 July 1991) 36 PBLR 9

Facts and Decision

Mr Doyle, who was a member of his employer's pension scheme, died leaving a wife from whom he was separated, children and a girlfriend (who remained married though separated) with whom he was cohabiting. The pension scheme provided for payment of a lump sum death benefit to one or more dependants at the trustees' discretion. **Dependants** were defined under the rules as including any person who at the date of death was **dependent** on the member for all or any of the ordinary necessities of life. The trustees sought the Court's guidance as to whom they could consider for these benefits. The Court held that Mr Doyle's girlfriend qualified as a **dependant**. While her husband was still legally responsible for her, the definition of **dependant** referred to a factual situation as well as a situation where there was a legal obligation. A person may be **dependent** on another for the ordinary necessities of life without there being any legal obligation on that other person to pay.

Wild v Smith (High Court) [1996] OPLR 129, [1996] PLR 275

Principle

The concept of **dependence** is a very familiar one in the law generally, and requires that the person in question is **dependent** in the proper sense of that term. It is not sufficient if he or she was merely deriving benefit from the earnings of the person who it is suggested the person in question is dependent upon; he or she must be to some extent **dependent** upon the person for the ordinary necessaries of life, having regard to his or her class and position in life: *Simmonds v White Brothers [1899] 1 QB 1005* was followed.

Disposable surplus

Stevens & others v Bell & others (High Court) [2001] PLR 99

Principles

Disposable surplus, to be certified by the actuary for use for discharging the employer contribution obligation, is not the same as surplus. It is a matter for the actuary to assess what additional reserves to make. The actuary may legitimately be influenced by knowledge of how the **disposable surplus** might be applied for eliminating the employer's contribution obligation, depending on its amount. However, the actuary may not take into account how any residual part of the **disposable surplus** might be applied by the trustees. On the proper construction of the scheme's rules in this case, it was not correct to suggest that **disposable surplus** could not include residual surplus of this type.

Where residual **disposable surplus** may be disposed of by the trustees, the actuary was not obliged to make a reserve from the surplus to allow for a material risk that the **disposable surplus** allocated to the employer's contribution obligation would not in fact be sufficient. The actuary would be issuing his certificate using his professional skill and experience.

The aggregate method of actuarial valuation was not appropriate for identifying **disposable surplus**.

Entitled

Norman v Pensions Ombudsman (High Court) [1997] OPLR 85 at 92B-H

Facts and Decision

Mr Norman was the majority shareholder of Julsarben Limited and nominally an employee of that company. He was an active member of his employer's pension scheme. He entered into an agreement purporting to charge his interest in the scheme to that company and another company. The scheme had a rule providing that if an individual **entitled** to or in receipt of benefit under the scheme shall or shall purport to assign, mortgage or otherwise to deal with his beneficial interest under the scheme, or any part thereof, then he shall forfeit all such interest. The Court held that Mr Norman was **entitled** to benefit for the purpose of the forfeiture rule: in other places, the rules referred to members being **entitled** to benefits in circumstances where they were not in receipt of pension, and where the pension had not yet vested.

Incapacity

Harris v Shuttleworth (Court of Appeal) [1995] OPLR 79, [1994] PLR 47, [1994] ICR 991

Principle

In a scheme which has as its primary object the provision of benefits at normal pension age, in order to show entitlement to a pension which is triggered on retirement from service by reason of **incapacity**, the employee must show that on a balance of probability his or her **incapacity** was likely to last until at least normal pension age. The **incapacity** must be one which affects both his or her ability to work for this employer and any other similar employer.

Insurance

Attorney-General of Canada v Confederation Life (Ontario Court of Justice, unreported, 4 July 1995)

Facts and Decision

Confederation Life, a large insurer, became insolvent. It had never entered into a formal trust agreement in relation to its pension obligations, but the Board had approved a document providing that the trustees should ensure that the pension schemes were funded in a manner that would enable them to meet all their obligations. They were, however, pay-as-you-go schemes. Scheme members were supplied with a booklet summarising the benefits, but which stated that it did not create or confer any contractual rights, and that all rights with respect to the benefits of a member would be governed by the group policy. Policyholders took priority over Confederation Life's general assets in the winding-up. The employees, former employees and their dependants argued that by virtue of their pension benefits they were policyholders in respect of the amount required to satisfy all pension liabilities. The Court held that the members of the main scheme were policyholders for the purposes of Canadian legislation. **Insurance** was defined as the undertaking by one person to:

- indemnify another person against loss, or liability for loss, in respect of a certain risk or peril to which the object of the **insurance** may be exposed; or
- pay a sum of money or other thing of value upon the happening of a certain event;

and included life **insurance**. There was no concept of premium, but the consideration was found in the retirees' former contributions of labour, skill and knowledge.

Century Life v Commissioners of Customs & Excise (Court of Appeal, 19 December 2000) [2001] 12 PBLR 9

Facts and Decision

Century Life undertook the personal pensions misselling review for Lincoln. The Court held that the services provided by Century Life were not only incidental to the **insurance** transactions and constituted an **insurance** transaction. Century Life's activities therefore fell within the scope of the exemption from value added tax set out in the *Article 13B of the Value Added Tax 6th Directive 77/388* and *para 4 group 2* of *schedule 9* to the *Value Added Tax Act 1994*.

Fuji Finance v Aetna Life Insurance Co Ltd (Court of Appeal) [1996] 4 All ER 608, [1996] 3 WLR 871, [1996] LRLR 365

Facts and Decision

Tyndall Assurance issued Fuji with what it described variously as a life assurance policy or as a capital investment bond for £50,000; the life assured was stated to be that of Mr Tait. The policy required Tyndall to maintain nine funds as subdivisions of its long-term business fund, and linked the benefits payable under it to the value at maturity of the units in the funds to which it was linked. The Court held that the fact that the measure of the benefit payable on surrender was the same as that payable on death was insufficient to prevent this contract being recognised as **insurance** made on the life of any person. The essence of life assurance is that the right to the benefits is related to life or death. *Joseph v Law Integrity Insurance Co Ltd [1912] 2 Ch 581, Re National Standard Life Assurance Corp [1918] 1 Ch 427*, and *NM Superannuation Pty Ltd v Young (1993) 113 ALR 39* were considered. In this case, the right to surrender was related to the continuance of life, for it could not be exercised by Fuji after the death of Mr Tait. It was therefore a policy for life assurance within the meaning of *s 1* of the *Life Assurance Act 1774*.

Sun Alliance v Pensions Ombudsman (High Court, unreported, 17 October 2000)

Principle

The ordinary meaning of **insurance** is an agreement in consideration of one or more premiums to pay on the occurrence of a specified future event, sums or benefits calculated in accordance with the terms of the policy.

Interests

R v OPRA ex parte Littlewoods (High Court) [1997] OPLR 375 at 379G–380B, [1998] PLR 63 at paras 12–15

Principle

In the context of the Occupational Pensions Regulatory Authority's (OPRA) power under *s 99(4)* of the *Pension Schemes Act 1993* to grant an extension to trustees for the payment of transfer values if the **interests** of the members of the scheme generally will be prejudiced, the **interests** of the members will ordinarily only be financial, although there is a possibility that in some circumstances quite exceptionally the **interest** might be wider. Righteous indignation was not an interest of this type. A payment which materially affects the size of the fund or of any surplus in the fund could prejudice the financial **interest** of members.

Leaving the service

Harris v Shuttleworth (Court of Appeal) [1995] OPLR 79 at 88H, [1994] PLR 47 at para 53, [1994] ICR 991

Principle

Leaving the service is not synonymous with being dismissed. **Leaving the service** may include the employee leaving of his or her own volition, leaving because he or she has been given notice to terminate his or her employment, or the employee being dismissed for misconduct.

Managers

Century Life v Pensions Ombudsman (High Court) [1995] OPLR 351 at 355C, 361H–363C, [1995] PLR 135 at paras 15, 53–60

Principle

The phrase '**trustees or managers**' does not bear the same meaning wherever it appears in the *Pension Schemes Act 1993*. The word **managers** is an ordinary English word, and in a typical insured scheme the interested onlooker would be bemused if it were suggested that the insurance company was not managing, and not therefore the **manager** of the scheme. There is no obvious good reason why in a trust scheme, the trustees but not the **managers** should be amenable to the jurisdiction of the Pensions Ombudsman.

Member

LRT v Hatt (High Court) [1993] OPLR 225 at 258G–259G, [1993] PLR 227 at paras 130–134

Facts and Decision

Where the provisions of a company's articles provided that directors needed to be drawn from the **members**, but the pension scheme had no **members** because no rules were yet in force, the Court held that the references needed to be understood as referring to the rules if and when framed, otherwise the articles would be unworkable.

Negligence/Gross negligence

Armitage v Nurse (Court of Appeal) [1997] PLR 51 at para 31

Principle

English lawyers have always had a healthy disrespect for any distinction between **negligence** and **gross negligence**: it has been doubted whether any intelligible distinction exists. However, civilian systems such as the Scottish system draw the line in a different place: *Hinton v Dibber (1842) 2 QB 646* and *Grill v General Iron Screw Collier Co (1866) 35 LJCP 321* were considered.

Normal health

Venables v Hornby (High Court, unreported, 14 June 2001)

Facts and Decision

Mr Venables was the managing director of a company, working 50 hours a week. He decided to step down as managing director at age 53 since he had high blood pressure, mild diabetes and was seriously overweight, but remained as an unpaid non-executive director, giving advice on occasion. His pension scheme paid him his pension, but the Inland Revenue sought to charge him tax under *s 600* of the *Income and Corporation Taxes Act 1988* on the grounds that it was not a payment expressly authorised from the pension scheme. The scheme allowed for a pension before age 60 only if the member 'retires' in **normal health**. The Court held that the expression **normal health** in the context of a pension scheme could only mean 'fit to do the job'. Even in the abstract, Mr Venables was in **normal health**: high pressure and mild diabetes are common conditions in overweight middle-aged men.

Occupational pension scheme

City & County of Swansea v Johnson (High Court) [1999] OPLR 39, [1999] PLR 187

Facts and Decision

The Local Government Superannuation Scheme provided both a pension scheme and a severance and compensation scheme. The definition of occupational pension scheme in *s 1* of the *Pension Schemes Act 1993* had been modified since the decision in *Westminster v Haywood [1998] Ch 377*. This scheme provided compensation on a no–fault basis, on termination of employment as a result of injury sustained or disease contracted in the course of employment. The Court held that it therefore provided benefits in the form of pensions or otherwise, payable on termination of service. The requirement of the definition of the **occupational pension scheme** set out in *s 1* of the *Pension Schemes Act 1993* that the benefit be paid to an earner with qualifying service was a reference only to the service that qualified the earner for the benefit. The scheme was therefore an **occupational pension scheme** within the meaning of the *section*.

Hamar v Pensions Ombudsman (High Court) [1996] OPLR 55 at 60H–61C, [1996] PLR 1 at para 23

Principle

A pension scheme on interim documentation which has not yet received Inland Revenue approval is an **occupational pension scheme** for the purposes of *s 1* of the *Pension Schemes Act 1993* when it was capable of having the effect of providing benefits, since the whole purpose of the scheme that it should have effect as a pension scheme and approval should be obtained.

NBC Pension Trustees v Harrod (High Court) [1999] OPLR 113, [2000] PLR 183

Principle

Where all that is left of a wound–up pension scheme is a contested cause of action for breach of trust, there is for the time being at least nothing that 'is capable of having effect so as to provide benefits in the form of pensions', and so the scheme is no longer an **occupational pension scheme** within the meaning of *s 1* of the *Pension Schemes Act 1993*.

Parlett v Guppy's (Bridport) Ltd (No. 2) (Court of Appeal) [1999] OPLR 309, [2000] PLR 195

Facts and Decision

A company resolved at its annual general meeting to pay Mr Parlett, the managing director, a pension on his retirement calculated at 10% on £250,000, indexed from 1 August 1988 to the Retail Prices Index. Such an arrangement was held by the Court to be an **occupational pension scheme** within the meaning of *s 1* of the *Pension Schemes Act 1993*.

Westminster v Haywood (High Court) [1996] 2 All ER 467, [1996] OPLR 95 at 103H, [1996] PLR 161 at para 32

Principle

An **occupational pension scheme** could conceivably be found in a simple contract of employment.

Westminster v Haywood (Court of Appeal) [1998] Ch 377, [1997] OPLR 61 at 68A–69G, [1997] PLR 39 at paras 29–42

Facts and Decision

The Local Government Superannuation Scheme provided both a pension scheme and a severance and compensation scheme. The Court held that under *s 1* of the *Pension Schemes Act 1993* as it was then defined, the severance and compensation scheme could not by itself constitute an **occupational pension scheme**. It was very difficult to accept the notion that by administering two schemes as one, the Council could confer on the Pensions Ombudsman a jurisdiction which he would not have if it administered them separately. There was no evidence that the Council's two schemes were administered as one. The information provided to employees and pensioners differentiated where necessary, while the fact that the payments were being made together was purely a matter of administrative convenience.

Pay

Cole v Bryson (Privy Council) [1993] OPLR 149

Facts and Decision

Under the terms of a pension scheme, each member's pension was calculated by reference to the retirement rate of **pay** of the employee, which was the average weekly rate for the last year of employment or for the last three years prior to retirement, whichever was the greater. The Privy Council held that the retirement rate of **pay** was a weekly sum, but the calculation of that weekly sum could only be arrived at by taking a total figure for the period of one to three years, and dividing it by the appropriate number of weeks. Accordingly, it would be a wholly artificial interpretation to treat it as referring only to the hourly rate of **pay**. Elements of **pay** paid at a piece rate were therefore also included within this definition.

Neath v Hugh Steeper (European Court of Justice) [1993] OPLR 329 at 345C, [1994] PLR 1 at para 31

Principle

The contributions made by the employees to a contributory pension scheme are an element of **pay**, since they are deducted directly from the employee's salary. The employer's contributions in a final salary scheme are not **pay** since they ensure the adequacy of the funds necessary to cover the cost of the pensions promised, that being the substance of the employer's commitment.

Payment

Hillsdown v Commissioners of Inland Revenue (High Court) [1999] OPLR 79, [1999] PLR 173 at paras 12–37, [1999] STC 561

Principle

A repayment of surplus which subsequently has to be repaid to a pension scheme is not a **payment** for the purposes of *s 601* of the *Income and Corporation Taxes Act 1988*. Where no beneficial interest passed and the sums had to be returned, the purported **payments** were not really **payments** at all in the eyes of the law.

MacNiven v Westmorland Investments (House of Lords, unreported, 8 February 2001)

Facts and Decision

Where a pension scheme subsidiary was lent money by the pension scheme to pay back interest accrued to the pension scheme, in order that the subsidiary could benefit from tax relief, the Court held that the **payment** by the subsidiary was a **payment** within the terms of *s 338* of the *Income and Corporation Taxes Act 1988*.

Venables v Hornby (High Court, unreported, 14 June 2001)

Facts and Decision

The Court held that since Mr Venables was a trustee of his pension scheme, if he was not entitled to receive the pension which was in fact granted to him, the scheme could have recovered any instalments from him as a constructive trustee. All of the following conditions were fulfilled: the payment was in breach of trust, the recipient was accountable to the trustees as an actual or constructive trustee, and the recipient was able and prepared to account to the trustees. Accordingly, there was no **payment** to him within the meaning of *s 600* of the *Income and Corporation Taxes Act 1988: Hillsdown v Commissioners of Inland Revenue [1999] OPLR 79* was followed.

Pecuniary benefits secured

Lloyds Bank Pension Trust Corporation Limited v Lloyds Bank PLC (High Court) [1996] OPLR 181 at 190E, [1996] PLR 263 at para 46

Principle

Where rules refer to **pecuniary benefits secured**, the natural interpretation was that they refer both to benefits accrued to date and to all future benefits promised under the pension scheme.

Pension

Westminster v Haywood (Court of Appeal) [1998] Ch 377, [1997] OPLR 61, [1997] PLR 39

Principle

It is a perfectly accurate use of the word **pension** (the dictionary definition of which is 'periodical payment made esp. by government, company or employer, in consideration of past services or of relinquishment of rights etc.') to mean periodical payments as distinguished from lump sum benefits, whether paid out of a superannuation fund or otherwise.

Pensionable pay

HM Treasury v Lane (Court of Appeal) [1993] OPLR 155

Facts and Decision

Pensionable Pay was defined for the purposes of the Principal Civil Service Pension Scheme as salary and pensionable emoluments in whichever of the three years prior to leaving service gave the highest figure. Pensionable emoluments were listed, and included additional emoluments paid on a permanent basis and for extra responsibility. Where there were special circumstances, the Civil Service Department could agree to count as pensionable an emolument which was normally non-pensionable. Mr Lane was an ambassador, and claimed that his language allowances should be treated as pensionable. As a member of the diplomatic service, he was expected as far as possible to learn the languages of the country in which he was serving, and was therefore given an operational language allowance for the country in which he was serving. He also received a language continuation allowance for the languages he had learnt in a previous post and which he had maintained; this allowance was payable for five years after changing posts. The Court held that it was an extra responsibility since it was a requirement of the ambassador that he should have sufficiently good Italian to be able to transact business. An emolument is permanent if it will necessarily last as long as the holder occupies the post in question. It does not cease to be permanent because it will not be payable when he no longer holds that post. The operational language allowance was therefore pensionable, but the language continuation allowance was not.

Pensionable salary

Doyle v Manchester Evening News (High Court) [1989] PLR 47

Facts and Decision

Employees, who had previously been paid additional non-pensionable allowances, had these allowances consolidated into salary, which was ordinarily pensionable. The employer had the power to certify **pensionable salary**, and purported to certify that the consolidated allowances were not pensionable. The Court held that this certificate was invalid, since it purported to certify a salary which was not in fact the true salary received by the employees. The consolidated allowances were pensionable. However, this was subject to the power retrospectively to amend the rules to make these elements of salary non-pensionable.

Pensionable service

Jones v London County Council (High Court) [1936] 1 Ch 50

Facts and Decision

Ms Jones was employed by successive poor law authorities since 1904 without a break in service. She had contributed under the *Poor Law Officers' Superannuation Act 1896* for some of her service, but for later parts of her service she had contracted out of the scheme benefits in accordance with the *Poor Law Officers' Superannuation Act Amendment Act 1897*. Later, she asked to be readmitted to the scheme and was required to make good the unpaid contributions, which she did. On her transfer to London County Council in 1930, her new employer argued that she was not entitled to do this. The Court held that there was no express prohibition against such an agreement being entered into, and there was no reasonable ground on which the legislature should prohibit such an agreement. Consequently, there was no proper ground on which to infer such a prohibition by implication, and Ms Jones was entitled to pension on the full period of her service.

Pounder v London County Council (Court of Appeal) [1934] 1 KB 26

Facts and Decision

Mr Pounder was a porter for Gloucestershire County Council, and since it provided no pension scheme, he was entitled to pension under the *Poor Law Officers' Superannuation Act 1896*. He then became a male nurse for London County Council, and applied for a pension under the *Asylums Officers' Superannuation Act 1909*, which provided a more generous pension scheme. *Section 124(1)* of the *Local Government Act 1929* provided that where any officer by whom the annual contributions required by the *1896 Act* had been made was transferred to the service of any council, then if the council to whose service he was transferred had no superannuation scheme, the *1896 Act* applied to him and shall continue so to apply to him so long as he was in the service of the council of any county. It would continue to do so until under such statutory provisions as may be made for the superannuation of persons employed by the councils of all counties and county boroughs, there became available to him a superannuation scheme not less favourable than as was laid down in a statutory standard. The Court held that *s 124* of the *1929 Act* assumed that the officer could be serving in one capacity at one time and in another capacity at another time, but that it should still count as the service of an officer of a county council. The *section* contemplated that the service of the council of any county made the *1896 Act* continue to apply, and that the service need not be continuous. Accordingly, his pension was governed by the *1896 Act* and not the *1909 Act*. While this was a case of omission, the Court could not supply the omission.

Permanent

Harris v Shuttleworth (Court of Appeal) [1995] OPLR 79 at 91E, [1994] PLR 47 at para 71, [1994] ICR 991

Principle

There is no practical difference between incapacity which is likely to last until normal pension age, and incapacity which is described as **permanent**.

HM Treasury v Lane (Court of Appeal) [1993] OPLR 155

Principle

An emolument is **permanent** if it will necessarily last as long as the holder occupies the post in question. It does not cease to be **permanent** because it will not be payable when he or she no longer holds that post.

Mullett v BSC Pension Fund Trustees (Court of Appeal) [1992] PLR 71

Facts and Decision

British Steel provided some of its employees with company cars. The cars remained at all times the property of British Steel, and the employees could be required at any time to return them on request. Some employees argued that these were 'emoluments of a **permanent** character' and therefore to be included in the definition of salary for the purposes of calculating their pension. The Court observed that there would be a serious administrative difficulty in seeking to work this scheme if the word **permanent** had any other meaning than something coterminous with the employee's salary. Something could not be **permanent** if it could be withdrawn without notice, and at the behest of the employer, at any time during the still-continuing employment of the employee whose contributions and pensions one has to consider. The word **permanent** in the definition of salary in a pension scheme trust deed has to be construed in the context in which it is found, namely one relating to the contracts of employment of employees. It was in that context that the emoluments, contributions and pensions were referable and to be calculated. **Permanent** could not mean perpetual, but the inquiry has to concern whether under the relevant contract of employment the queried emolument would persist from when first granted until the end of that employment.

R v Secretary of State for the Environment ex parte McClorry (Court of Appeal, application for leave to appeal to the Court of Appeal approving unreported decision of 27 March 1998, unreported, 3 September 1998)

Principle

When assessing **permanence** for an incapacity pension payable where the member ceases to be in employment, and was incapable of discharging efficiently the duties of that employment by reason of **permanent** ill-health or infirmity of mind or body, the test for **permanence** was to look at the member's position up until the ordinary retirement age contemplated by the scheme regulations.

Permanent and total disablement

Fernance v Wreckair (Industrial Court of New South Wales) [1993] PLR 191

Facts and Decision

Mr Fernance was an apprentice plant mechanic who had left school at 16. He was involved in a car accident, following which it slowly became apparent that he was unable to continue in his job. He was a member of his employer's superannuation scheme, and he claimed a pension on the grounds that he suffered **total and permanent disablement**, as required by the scheme rules. That definition made a person eligible for the pension if:

(a) he had been absent from employment for six consecutive months; and
(b) the insurer after consideration of the medical evidence was satisfied that the member has become incapacitated to such an extent as to render him unlikely ever to engage in or work for reward in any occupation or work for which he was reasonably qualified by education, training or experience.

Mr Fernance sued his employer for the pension. The Court held that the definition in the rules required an assessment of the work for which the applicant was reasonably qualified at the date of assessment, and not at some future time as a result of retraining. On the facts, Mr Fernance was suffering **total and permanent disablement** within the terms of this definition.

Prejudice

R v OPRA ex parte Littlewoods (High Court) [1997] OPLR 375 at 380E-H, [1998] PLR 63 at paras 19–21

Principle

When considering whether the interests of the members of a pension scheme generally will be **prejudiced**, the interests of the members will ordinarily only be financial. There was a real possibility of financial **prejudice** to the interests of members generally if, on a future bankruptcy of a member with very substantial pension benefits, the possibility was lost of a forfeiture of that member's pension benefits. However, the members generally can only acquire any benefit from the extension of the period for payment if in the future eventuality that the member is bankrupted:

(a)   the trustee does not on grounds of hardship exercise the discretionary power to benefit the member and his family to the full extent of the entitlement; and

(b)   any accretion to the surplus is applied in the form of increased benefits to members.

Accordingly there is at best a real possibility of **prejudice**, and whether there will be **prejudice** is a matter of conjecture. It is not therefore possible in these circumstances for the Occupational Pensions Regulatory Authority (OPRA) to form the opinion that the interests of the members generally will be **prejudiced**.

Premiums payable

Bold v Brough Nicholson & Hall (High Court) [1964] 1 WLR 201

Facts and Decision

Mr Bold was the managing director of his employer. He was entitled to six months' notice if he was to be dismissed. He was a member of a discretionary pension and life assurance scheme, under which the employer committed to pay all premiums payable during the period of his services under two insurance policies, and the employer agreed that it would not perform any act, or neglect to perform any act, which might decrease or determine the benefits to which Mr Bold was entitled thereunder. Mr Bold was dismissed without notice, and claimed damages for the amount required to complete the premiums until the expiry of his contract of employment. The Court held that the employer had bound itself to pay all premiums payable during the period of Mr Bold's services thereunder, namely until the expiry of his contract of employment. Mr Bold was therefore entitled to the damages he claimed.

Regular employment

O'Neill v HSS Executive (Pensions Ombudsman, 8 June 1999) Case H00615

Facts and Decision

Mr O'Neill would qualify for an ill-health pension if he was permanently incapable of engaging in any **regular employment**. **Regular employment** was undefined. The Pensions Ombudsman held that before a decision could be reached on whether he qualified, the employer (which had responsibility for determining eligibility for such pensions) had to consider:

(a) what was a reasonable requirement for the number of hours to be worked over any specified period of time in order to qualify as **regular employment**;
(b) whether **regular employment** should involve being able to hold down employment with one employer, or a very small number of employers, on a medium or long term basis;
(c) whether **regular employment** implied a minimum level of earnings;
(d) whether due weight should be given to the fact that attempting to resume work might result in his medical condition worsening, perhaps irretrievably; and
(e) whether there were any other features of this case which merited particular consideration.

Retires

Venables v Hornby (High Court, unreported, 14 June 2001)

Facts and Decision

Mr Venables was the managing director of a company, working 50 hours a week. He decided to step down as managing director at age 53 since he had high blood pressure, mild diabetes and was seriously overweight, but remained as an unpaid non-executive director, giving advice on occasion. His pension scheme paid him his pension, but the Inland Revenue sought to charge him tax under *s 600* of the *Income and Corporation Taxes Act 1988* on the grounds that it was not a payment expressly authorised from the pension scheme. The scheme allowed for a pension before age 60 only if the member '**retires**' in normal health. The Court held that it was a matter of fact and degree whether a person had retired, which connoted withdrawing from active work. Mere reduction in workload was not retirement, but the fact that Mr Venables remained a director throughout did not prevent him from retiring. There was sufficient evidence for the Special Commissioner properly to conclude that Mr Venables had retired.

Retirement

Brooks v National Westminster Bank (Court of Appeal, unreported, 8 November 1983)

Facts and Decision

Mr Brooks was employed by the Royal Masonic Institution for Girls as an assistant engineer. In May 1978, after he had been employed for 18 years, he strained his back badly whilst going about his job. He was off work for many months and eventually his employer decided that he might not be able to do any more useful work for it. Accordingly it dismissed him. Mr Brooks claimed the incapacity pension benefits to which he would be entitled on **retirement** from his employer's pension scheme. The Court held that on a proper construction of the trust deed and rules, benefits on **retirement** were payable only when the employee left of his own volition. **Retirement** and dismissal are two separate concepts. A person may be induced to retire, put under pressure to retire or even compelled to retire, but the **retirement** remains his or her own act and not the employer's act. As Mr Brooks was beyond any doubt dismissed, albeit dismissed honourably and through no fault of his own, he did not retire. However, the Court expressly refrained from basing its decision on the observation that Mr Brooks had not given up work and taken further full-time employment.

Bold v Brough Nicholson & Hall (High Court) [1964] 1 WLR 201

Facts and Decision

Mr Bold was the managing director of his employer. He was entitled to six months' notice if he was to be dismissed. He was a member of his employer's defined benefit pension scheme. If he retired with the consent of the employer, he was entitled to an immediate pension and life assurance benefits continuing until normal **retirement** age of 65. However, if he did not, he would be entitled only to a refund of his contributions with interest. Mr Bold was dismissed without notice at age 55 and he claimed damages for, among other things, loss of pension and life assurance under the scheme. The Court held that Mr Bold was not entitled to the immediate pension, since he had not retired with employer consent. This implied initiative on the part of the employee, and it would be false to describe Mr Bold's departure as early **retirement**. He was therefore entitled only to a refund of contributions with interest.

Dorrell v May & Baker (High Court) [1991] PLR 31

Facts and Decision

Mr Dorrell was a fireman who developed vertigo, with the result that he could no longer work in his job. He was therefore dismissed. He claimed an incapacity pension, which was payable if a member **retired** from service at any time before normal retirement date on account of incapacity. The Court observed that there was no firm rule as to whether a reference in the rules to **retirement** excluded cases where the member had been dismissed: *Young v Associated Newspapers [1971] 11 KIR 413* and *Brooks v National Westminster Bank* (unreported) were considered. In this case, as in *Brooks v National Westminster Bank*, **retirement** meant the act of an employee choosing to retire from work — a contrast could be made with the standard leaving service benefits, which applied where the member's service terminated before normal retirement date.

Harris v Shuttleworth (Court of Appeal) [1995] OPLR 79, [1994] PLR 47, [1994] ICR 991

Principle

Retirement was capable in its context in this case of being understood in a transitive passive sense. *Brooks v National Westminster Bank* (unreported, 8 November 1983) was distinguished, since in that case the entitlement to pension was excluded if the member was dismissed.

Harris v Simpson (Alberta Court of Queen's Bench, 2 October 1984) 56 AR 201

Facts and Decision

Mr Harris was wrongfully dismissed by his employer. He was then entitled to pension benefits, but if he had taken early **retirement**, the pension would have been substantially higher than if he left on termination. The

Court held that the employer was not permitted to profit from its wrongful act (it did not matter that the employer did not have a direct interest in the scheme), and was accordingly estopped from denying Mr Harris the option of electing the early **retirement** option under the scheme. This could be justified on a wider basis. An employee who had been wrongfully dismissed was to be put in the same position as if the contract had been performed, and so if the employee could have properly sought his pension benefits under a more advantageous characterisation during the notice period to which he would have been entitled, he should be deemed to have done so: *McKie v City of Moncton and City of Moncton's Employees' Pension Board (1981) 34 NBR (2d) 5, 85 APR 5* was followed.

McKie v City of Moncton and City of Moncton's Employees' Pension Board (New Brunswick Court of Queen's Bench) (1981) 34 NBR (2d) 5, 85 APR 5

Facts and Decision

Mr McKie was employed in a fire department for 32 years until he was arrested and charged with the deliberate setting of a fire. He was duly convicted, and was diagnosed as suffering from Alzheimer's disease. The City Council, his employer, purported to resolve to dismiss him with effect from the date of his arrest. As a result, he received a refund of contributions with interest from the City's pension scheme. If he had retired, he would have been entitled to a pension. The Court held that the Council meeting was not held as a public meeting and the resolution to dismiss Mr McKie was therefore invalid and ineffectual under Canadian law. Even if he had been effectually discharged in a technical sense, such a discharge could only be considered a flagrant denial of natural justice insofar as it affected his pension rights. The only logical approach the Court could take was to deem Mr McKie to have applied for **retirement** on the date of the Council meeting, and pay him a pension including back-payment with effect from that date.

Spooner v British Telecommunications (High Court) [2000] PLR 65 at paras 107–113

Principle

Where '**retirement** in the public interest' is defined as **retirement** before the retiring age on grounds of redundancy, on structural grounds, or on grounds of limited efficiency, there was nothing in that definition to suggest that the meaning of the defined expression was to be restricted to dismissal on any of those grounds. Use of the verb 'to retire' in the passive mood reflected no more than the fact that someone who volunteered to become a willing victim was not to be regarded as a wholly free agent.

Stephenson v London Joint Stock Bank (Court of Appeal) [1903] 52 WR 183, [1902] 19 TLR 138

Facts and Decision

Mr Stephenson was employed by the London Joint Stock Bank and was entitled to an allowance if he retired with the consent of his employer. He was sent a letter informing him that he was required to resign his appointment in the Bank. The Court held that there could be no doubt that Mr Stephenson was dismissed. While the employer used polite instead of peremptory language, their doing so did not alter the fact that it was a dismissal. He was therefore not entitled to his pension.

Surrey Police Authority v Beckett (Court of Appeal, unreported, 31 July 2001)

Facts and Decision

Mr Beckett was a deputy chief constable appointed on a five year fixed-term contract from 1995, having been in the police force for 30 years. Each party was obliged to give 3 months' notice in writing to terminate the contract, other than by reasons of its expiry. In 1998 he was accused of sexual harassment and charged with indecent assault. He was acquitted of the criminal charge in 2000, and the Police Authority then brought disciplinary action against him. Before the action could be completed, the fixed term contract expired, and Mr Beckett purported to retire. The Court observed that under the *Police Regulations 1995 (SI 1995 No 215)*, a police officer could retire only if he or she had given to the Police Authority 3 months' written notice of his or her intention to retire. Mr Beckett had not done this, and the contract itself should not be regarded as a written notice of an intention to retire on the expiry of the fixed term. However, **retirement** in this context necessarily meant **retirement** on a date not otherwise prescribed by a fixed term appointment. Accordingly, Mr Beckett had retired and the disciplinary proceedings automatically lapsed.

Wyn Jones v Home Secretary (Crown Court with justices, sitting as an appeal court) [1995] PLR 1

Principle

Where an assistant police commissioner had his royal warrant withdrawn, he could not be said to have retired.

Young v Associated Newspapers (High Court) [1971] 11 KIR 413

Facts and Decision

Mr Young and two other journalists were dismissed by their employer, having completed more than ten years' pensionable service, and were all aged 55 or over. The provisions of their pension scheme provided that they were entitled to a pension if they retired with the consent of the company within ten years of pension age, which was defined as 65 for men and 60 for women. The journalists argued that they had retired with the consent of the employer. The Court held that an employee who is dismissed is not *prima facie* retiring with the consent of those who dismiss him or her. It would be a misuse of language to describe a journalist who was given notice as retiring with the consent of the company. The expression 'a person retiring', had it appeared on its own, would have *prima facie* excluded a case where the employee was dismissed. This was all the more so where it was coupled with the words 'with the consent of the company', because a person cannot, in any meaningful sense, be said to consent to his or her own act. On a construction of the remainder of the rules, the *prima facie* presumption was not displaced. The Court was therefore reluctantly compelled to decide against the journalists' claim. *Stephenson v London Joint Stock Bank [1903] 52 WR 183* and *Bold v Brough, Nicholson & Hall [1964] 1 WLR 201* were considered.

Scheme

Barclays Bank v Holmes (High Court) [2000] PLR 339

Facts and Decision

Barclays Bank operated a defined benefits pension scheme, which was substantially in surplus. It established a money purchase section, and applied surplus generated from the defined benefits section to set against its obligation to contribute to the members' accounts in the money purchase section. The Pensions Ombudsman held that the money purchase and final salary sections were separate **schemes**, following *Kemble v Hicks (No. 2) [1999] OPLR 1.* The Court held that there may be a presumption that two different types of pension provision set up by different sections under a single document were intended to be two trust funds. If there were such a presumption, however, it was not a particularly strong one, since the overall purpose of the two types of **scheme** was the same. The presence of two different sets of provisions on winding-up did not indicate that there were two **schemes**. The following factors weighed in favour of it being a single **scheme**:

(a)   until winding-up took place, the terms of the winding-up rule lay more happily with the concept of a single trust;

(b)   the contribution rule provided for the cross-subsidy between sections, and employers' contributions were referred to as 'credited' while employee contributions were referred to as 'paid', indicating a distinction between the two; and

(c)   the operation of the incapacity benefits rule was more consistent with one **scheme**.

The existence of members' accounts could be said to give rise to a separate trust for each member (though this was inconsistent with Inland Revenue approval), and if so, would be an argument in favour of there being two **schemes**. On balance, the Court concluded there was a single **scheme**.

Kemble v Hicks (No. 2) (High Court) [1999] OPLR 1 at 5G–7H

Principle

Where a money purchase **scheme** was established under the same trust as a final salary **scheme**, it may be correct to regard them as part of the same overall **scheme**. However, within that overall **scheme**, the establishment of a money purchase **scheme** involved the setting up of what was a **scheme** quite separate from the final salary **scheme** and to which different considerations applied.

Reichhold v Wong (Superior Court of Justice, Ontario) [2000] PLR 277

Facts and Decision

Where an employer had a single pension plan with six parts, the separate nature of which was recognised and where the Pension Commission of Ontario specifically recognised the separate nature of each of the six parts of the plan and precluded surplus from any one part being transferred to other parts, and there had always been separate accounting, the Court held that there were six legally distinct pension plans.

Secured

James Miller Holdings v Graham (Supreme Court, Victoria) [1992] PLR 165

Facts and Decision

James Miller Holdings operated a pension scheme for its employees of which it was also the trustee. The pension scheme was invested in a managed fund policy. The power of amendment was subject to a restriction that no amendment shall detrimentally affect the benefits already **secured** in respect of a member at the date of amendment, without the consent in writing of that member. The consent of the members was not obtained for changes to the scheme. The Court held that 'benefits already **secured**' referred in this case to benefits already **secured** in respect of a member under the managed fund policy, and was a benefit which under the terms of the contract of insurance the employer was contingently entitled to receive upon the happening of an event which would give it a present vested right to receive it. The word **secured** was not used in this contract in the sense of a right given against property as security for a debt, in the way that it is commonly used in relation, for example, to mortgages.

Lloyds Bank Pension Trust Corporation Limited v Lloyds Bank PLC (High Court) [1996] OPLR 181 at 189F–190E, [1996] PLR 263 at paras 42–45

Principle

It is a fair and natural use of language to describe the pension scheme under which the promised pension benefits are to be provided as **securing** the benefits, including both those benefits which at any particular moment can be regarded as earned by past service, and also those benefits which at the same moment are in the nature of promised future benefits. Not only was the word a natural one to use in that context, it was probably the most appropriate one. The ordinary reader would regard the **securing** of benefits to refer to all pension benefits under the scheme, including those to be earned by future service.

Service

Re Bedford (deceased), National Provincial Bank v Aulton (High Court) [1951] Ch 905, [1951] 1 All ER 1093, [1951] WN 310

Facts and Decision

A company director left gifts to all employees who at his death had at least five years' **service**. The Court held that this was a requirement for five years' aggregate **service**, and there was no reason to imply, or indeed that there was any indication of, an additional requirement that such **service** needed to be continuous. *Re Marryat [1948] 1 All ER 796, Re Lawson [1914] 1 Ch 682* and *Re Drake [1921] Ch 99* were considered. However, absence on war service was not **service** for this purpose: *Re Cole [1919] 1 Ch 218* was distinguished.

Re Drake (High Court) [1921] Ch 99

Facts and Decision

A testator left legacies to employees 'who should have been in his **service** for five years but less than ten years,' or 'who should have been in his **service** for ten years prior to his decease.' The Court held that absence on military service did not count towards the period of **service**. However, the period of **service** need not be continuous for the purpose of qualifying for the legacy.

Re Lawson (High Court) [1914] 1 Ch 682; 83 LJ Ch 519; 110 L.T. 573

Facts and Decision

A testator left a bequest to each of his domestic servants who had been in his **service** for two years prior to his decease who were not under notice to leave, whether given or received. The Court held that a continuous period of two years before the death of the testator was required in order to qualify. However, the **service** did not need to be from day to day.

Re Marryat (High Court) [1948] 1 All ER 796; [1948] Ch 298

Facts and Decision

A testator made a bequest to each employee 'who shall have been in the **service** of such company at my death for a period of five years and upwards and shall not then be under notice'. The Court held that a continuous period was required in order to qualify for the legacy. The phrase 'a period' reinforced that conclusion: *Tyler v London & India Docks Joint Committee (1892) 9 TLR 11* and *Re Lawson [1914] 1 Ch 682* were considered. Apprentices of the testator whose **service** was transferred to the company were also treated as being in **service** for the purposes of the bequest.

Tyler v London and India Docks Joint Committee (Court of Appeal) (1892) 9 TLR 11

Facts and Decision

Mr Tyler was employed by an employer which operated a pension scheme. He was entitled to a pension if he left service at a time when he had been in **service** for not less than ten years. The Court held that such a period must mean ten continuous years.

Spouse

Chief Adjudication Officer v Bath (Court of Appeal) The Times, 28 October 1999

Facts and Decision

Mr and Mrs Bath went through a Sikh marriage in 1956 in a service administered in accordance with Sikh custom and religion. They lived together until Mr Bath's death in 1994. There was some evidence that the temple was not registered for performing marriages in 1956. There was no suggestion in the evidence that either of the couple were aware of any defect. The Court held that the common law presumed from the fact of extended cohabitation as man and wife that the parties had each agreed to cohabit on that basis, and there was a rebuttable presumption that the statutory requirements for marriage, first introduced by the *Marriage Act 1753*, had been duly complied with. This presumption applied on this occasion, and any defects in the marriage ceremony were therefore disregarded.

Martin v Grey, re Stolliday (High Court, unreported, 13 May 1998)

Facts and Decision

A mother and son died in a road accident caused by Mr Grey's negligence. The mother's widower brought proceedings under the *Law Reform (Miscellaneous Provisions) Act 1934* and the *Fatal Accidents Act 1976*. They were in the process of divorcing, and a decree nisi had been pronounced, although the decree absolute had not been pronounced. The Court held that the fact of the decree nisi did not affect the statutory entitlement. It was a line drawn by Parliament. The husband was entitled to benefit just as much as he would have been debarred had the accident happened a day after the decree absolute.

Superannuation

R v Secretary of State for Education and Employment ex parte NATFHE (High Court, unreported, 28 August 1997)

Facts and Decision

The Secretary of State submitted that payment to a teacher, whether by lump sum or periodic payment which was triggered by early retirement, was more aptly described as **compensation** rather than **superannuation**. The Court held that the reasoning behind the Secretary of State's submissions was sound.

Trustees or managers

Century Life v Pensions Ombudsman (High Court) [1995] OPLR 351 at 355C, [1995] PLR 135 at para 15

Principle

The phrase '**trustees or managers**' does not bear the same meaning wherever it appears in the *Pension Schemes Act 1993*. On a true construction, the Pensions Ombudsman had jurisdiction to hear complaints against managers of schemes even when there were separate trustees.

Variation

Aitken v Christy Hunt (High Court) [1991] PLR 1 at 45–53

Principle

It would be quite accurate to refer to the declaration of new trusts to the exclusion of existing trusts, or the amalgamation of a pension scheme with another scheme, as a **variation**.

Widow/Widower

Bavin v NHS Trust Pensions Agency (Employment Appeal Tribunal) [1999] OPLR 285

Facts and Decision

Ms Bavin, who held a senior post in the NHS, enjoyed a long-term relationship with a female-to-male post-operative transsexual. She was a member of the NHS pension scheme, which provided benefits for widows and widowers. No benefits were payable to unmarried partners of scheme members. The Court held that the words **widow** and **widower** meant and could only mean the surviving spouse.

Ward v Secretary of State for Social Services (High Court) [1989] PLR 109

Facts and Decision

A widow remarried, and subsequently had the marriage annulled on the grounds of non-consummation. She applied to have her war **widow's** pension reinstated (it lapsed on remarriage). The Court held that since the remarriage was voidable rather than void, the marriage remained effective to prevent her from requalifying for a **widow's** pension since no provision was made for the restoration of the pension.

Wilful default

Armitage v Nurse (Court of Appeal) [1997] PLR 51 at paras 21–25

Principle

In the context of a trustee exclusion clause, **wilful default** means a deliberate breach of trust: *Re Vickery [1930] 1 Ch 572* was followed.

Midland Bank (Jersey) v Federated Pension Services (Court of Appeal, Jersey) [1996] PLR 179 at paras 115–138

Principle

There are two strands of case law on the meaning of the phrase **wilful default**. One line of authority holds that this requires only a want of ordinary prudence. The other line of authority holds that **wilful default** meant that the person knew what he was doing, intended to do what he was doing and had acted as a free agent. The Court did not try to resolve these conflicting lines of case law.

Re Vickery [1930] 1 Ch 572

Principle

In the context of *s 30(1)* of the *Trustee Act 1925*, a person is only guilty of **wilful default** if he is conscious that in doing the act which is complained of or in omitting to do the act which it is said he ought to have done, he is committing a breach of duty, or is recklessly careless whether it is a breach of his duty or not. A trustee in general is not excused merely because he honestly believed that he was justified in doing the act in question. *In re Trusts of Leeds City Brewery, Ld.'s Deeds [1925] Ch 532* and *In re City Equitable Fire Insurance Co. [1925] Ch 407* were considered.

Abbreviations

AC	Appeal Cases
ACLR	Australian Current Law Review
ALJ	Australian Law Journal
All ER	All England Law Reports
ALJR	Australian Law Journal Reports
ALR	Australian Law Reports
App Cas	Appeal Cases
APR	Atlantic Provinces Reports
AR	Alberta Reports
BCAC	British Columbia Appeal Court
BCLC	Butterworths Company Law Cases
Can LRBR	Canadian Labour Relations Boards Reports
Ch	Chancery
Ch D	Chancery Division
CLLC	Canadian Labour Law Reports
CMLR	Common Market Law Reports
Comm Report	European Commission of Human Rights Report
Cr &Ph	Craig & Phillip's Reports, temp. Cottenham
D	Digest
DLR	Dominion Law Reports
DRS	Dominion Report Service
ECR	European Court Reports
EHRR	European Human Rights Reports
Exch	Exchequer Division
F.2d	Federal Reporter, Second Series (USA)
F.3d	Federal Reporter, Third Series (USA)
F. Supp.	Federal Supplement (USA)
Fam Law	Family Law Reports
Fam LR	Family Law Reports
FCR	Family Court Reports
FLR	Family Law Reports
ICR	Industrial Cases Reports
IR	Irish Reports
IRLR	Industrial Relations Law Reports
ITELR	International Trust and Estate Law Reports
ITR	Industrial Tribunal Reports

KB	King's Bench
KIR	Knight's Industrial Reports
LAC	Labour Arbitration Cases
LJ Ch	Law Journal Reports, Chancery
Lloyd's Rep	Lloyd's Law Reports
LN	Law Notes
LR Ch	Law Reports, Chancery Division
LT	Law Times Reports
LT (NS)	Law Times (New Series)
NBR (2d)	New Brunswick Reports, Second Series
NSWLR	New South Wales Law Reports
NZ Jur (NS) SC	New Zealand Jurist Report (New Series)
NZLR	New Zealand Law Reports
OAC	Ontario Appeal Court
OPLR	Occupational Pension Law Reports
OR (2d)	Ontario Reports (Second Series)
P	Probate
P & CR	Property & Compensation Reports
PBLR	Pensions Benefit Law Reports
PLR	Pension Law Reports
QB	Queen's Bench
QBD	Queen's Bench Division
SC	Session Cases
S Ct	Supreme Court Reporter (USA)
SCCR	Scottish Criminal Case Reports
SCLR	Scottish Civil Law Reports
SLT	Scots Law Times
SLT (Notes)	Scot Law Times (Notes)
SLT (Sh Ct)	Scots Law Times (Sheriff Court Reports)
Tax Cas	Reports of Tax Cases
TC	Tax Cases
TLR	Times Law Reports
TR	Taxation Reports
US	United States Supreme Court
VATTR	Value Added Tax Tribunal Reports
WLR	Weekly Law Reports
WN	Weekly Notes

Table of Cases

Table of Statutes

Table of Statutory Instruments

Index